The Nature of the Intellectual Property Clause:
A Study in Historical Perspective

The Nature of the Intellectual Property Clause: A Study in Historical Perspective

Edward C. Walterscheid

William S. Hein & Co., Inc.
Buffalo, New York
2002

Library of Congress Cataloging-in-Publication Data
Walterscheid, Edward C.
The nature of the intellectual property clause : a study in historical
perspective / by Edward C. Walterscheid.
   p. cm.
Includes bibliographical references and index.
ISBN 1-57588-709-6 (cloth : acid-free paper)
  1. Intellectual property—United States—History—18th century.
2. Constitutional history—United States. I. Title.

KF2980 .W35 2002
346.7304'8'09—dc21   2001051905

Printed in the United States of America

This volume is printed on acid-free paper
by William S. Hein & Co., Inc.

TABLE OF CONTENTS

PREFACE

In researching my 1998 book *To Promote the Progress of Useful Arts: American Patent Law and Administration, 1787–1836,* I was surprised to discover that the Supreme Court had in fact created "revisionist" history or what Kenneth Burchfiel called "pseudohistory" in support of its interpretation of the intellectual property clause in *Graham v. John Deere Co.*[1] While I found that the historical record was in substantial agreement that the introductory or "to" language of the clause was intended as a limitation on the patent power of Congress, it did not support the particular view espoused by the Court. In particular, its reliance on the purported views of Thomas Jefferson to support its interpretation of the clause seemed entirely misplaced, in that Jefferson had nothing whatever to do with the drafting of the Constitution and never set forth any interpretation of the clause More to my dismay, I found that the Court had materially mischaracterized and misrepresented both the role and the views of Thomas Jefferson in the development of the nascent United States patent system.[2]

That was a decade ago, and I had only recently reinvented myself as a legal historian specializing in the history of intellectual property law in the United States. My naivete concerning the accuracy of judicial reliance on the historical record has long since disappeared, to be replaced with a healthy skepticism. But when I sought to ascertain what constitutional scholars and historians had to say about the origin and interpretation of the intellectual property clause, I was again surprised, this time by the dearth of relevant discussion. Most constitutional treatises mention the clause only in passing. What has been written about it has been almost entirely the product of practicing patent and copyright lawyers, created not infrequently as a form of advocacy for a particular perspective or position. There was no detailed book-length treatment of the clause in any historical context.

The most detailed discussion of the clause is found in *Nimmer on Copyright,* but that discussion is limited almost entirely to the copyright

---

1. K. J. Burchfiel, *Revising the "Original" Patent Clause: Pseudohistory in Constitutional Construction,* 2 HARV. J. L. & TECH. 155 (1989).
2. *See The Use and Abuse of History: The Supreme Court's Interpretation of Thomas Jefferson's Influence on the Patent Law,* 39 IDEA 195 (1999); *Patents and the Jeffersonian Mythology,* 29 J. MARSHALL L. REV. 269 (1995).

provision of the clause and it provides a less than complete historical perspective. As shown in the present work, I on occasion find myself in rather strong disagreement with the views expressed in this treatise. I have been unable to find any comparable treatment of the patent provision of the clause.

In the present work I have sought to analyze the clause as it has been viewed over time from its origins to the present day. Although I treat the modern interpretation of the clause, I wish to emphasize that this is primarily a work of history directed to the evolution in interpretation of the clause from its drafting to the present. The treatment and interpretation of the clause by both Congress and the judiciary has varied over time, more so than most patent and copyright practitioners suppose. Particularly in modern times, both Congress and the courts have tended to adopt a much more liberal view of the copyright provision of the clause than they have of the patent provision.

As the present work demonstrates, the grant of power to Congress in the clause is much broader than merely authority to issue patents and copyrights. Yet this is a point that is routinely ignored in almost all modern discussions of the clause. In addition, there has been a propensity through time to assume that a major—if not the primary—purpose of the clause is to reward the private interest of authors and inventors. Yet on its face the purpose of the clause is to promote the public interest through an increase of the public domain or commons of intellectual ideas and thought. Although the Supreme Court has sought to emphasize that the public interest must be balanced against the private interest of authors and inventors, it has provided no guidelines or parameters as to how this balance is to be achieved. This is an issue the courts increasingly will have to address—particularly in the copyright arena.

CHAPTER ONE
INTRODUCTION AND OVERVIEW

A. A Most Unusual Clause

The United States patent and copyright law derives from a constitutional grant of authority to Congress "to promote the Progress of Science and useful Arts, by securing for limited Times to Authors and Inventors the exclusive Right to their respective Writings and Discoveries."[1] But—and this is a point that is reiterated throughout this work—the clause provides broader authority than merely the power to create patents and copyrights. The clause is nowhere found in any of the early proposals for congressional authority presented to the federal convention.[2] Rather, it was in the nature

---

1. U.S. CONST. art 1, § 8, cl. 8. This clause is frequently referred to as either the patent clause, the copyright clause, or the intellectual property clause, depending on the context in which it is being discussed. Any of these descriptors is in a sense misleading in that, as Bugbee notes, the clause contains "no reference to 'property' itself (or to patents or copyrights as such)." *See* BRUCE W. BUGBEE, GENESIS OF AMERICAN PATENT AND COPYRIGHT LAW at 129 (Washington, D.C. 1967). A more correct description of the clause, at least in the context of the times, would be the "science and useful arts" clause, because the term "intellectual property" was unknown in the eighteenth century. Nonetheless, because intellectual property law is to a substantial extent derived from the grant of authority set forth in this clause, I will follow what is increasingly becoming standard usage and refer to it as the intellectual property clause. But "intellectual property" covers more genres than simply patents and copyrights. *See* note 42 *infra*. Moreover, in styling the clause "the intellectual property clause" I in no way wish to intimate or imply that the grant of authority set forth therein is limited to the power to create patents and copyrights or indeed other forms of intellectual property. See generally the discussion in Chapter Five, *infra*.

2. In modern times, the convention almost always is referred to as the constitutional convention, but in an historical sense this too is a misnomer, in that the convention was not called for the purpose of creating a constitution. Rather the convention came about because of a formal congressional resolution issued February 21, 1787 stating that "it is expedient that on the second Monday in May next, a convention of delegates, who shall have been appointed by the several states, be held in Philadelphia . . . for the sole and express purpose of

of a committee substitute for certain proposed powers that had been presented rather late in the game and had yet to be acted upon. It was first presented to the convention less than two weeks before it adjourned, and was unanimously approved without debate.[3]

The almost total lack of discussion in the federal convention was followed by an equal lack of discussion in the ratifying conventions.[4] It received only the briefest of mention and there was no opposition to it. The impression is left that it was one of those innocuous and straightforward clauses which failed to raise the passions or concerns of anyone in the debates on either the content of the Constitution or its ratification. Of all the commentary set forth in *The Federalist* concerning the content of the Constitution, that with respect to the intellectual property clause is among the briefest.[5] But it was neither as innocuous nor as straightforward as it at first glance appeared. Indeed, it was a most unusual clause.

What made it unusual was its format. Through the years that format has caused major interpretational difficulty. While there has been universal recognition that the clause grants authority to Congress to create the limited-term property rights known as patents and copyrights, there has

---

revising the Articles of Confederation and reporting to Congress and the several legislatures such alterations and provisions therein as shall when agreed to by Congress and confirmed by the states render the federal constitution adequate to the exigencies of Government and the preservation of the Union." *See* III THE RECORDS OF THE FEDERAL CONVENTION OF 1787, at 13–14 (Max Farrand ed., New Haven 1937). At the end of the eighteenth century and through most of the nineteenth century the convention almost always was called the federal convention, and I will follow this historically correct usage here.

3. *See infra* Chapter Three, Part G.
4. The substitution of "intellectual property clause" for "contract clause" renders Leonard Levy's pungent comments with respect to the contract clause highly apropos, namely:

> Original intent analysis of the [intellectual property clause] . . . does not quite resemble the empty page describing the sex life of a steer, but scarcity of evidence makes the inquiry hardly more productive. Almost no one cared about the [intellectual property] clause either at the Constitutional Convention or during the ratification controversy. Those advocating ratification and those opposed to it could not have been more apathetic than they were about the clause.

See LEONARD LEVY, ORIGINAL INTENT AND THE FRAMERS' CONSTITUTION at 124 (New York 1988).
5. *See infra* Chapter Four, note 77 and accompanying text.

been substantial disagreement as to what language of the clause constitutes a grant of power and which language serves as a limitation or restriction on the grant of power. Early on, the grant of power was argued to reside in the introductory language, i.e., "To promote the Progress of Science and useful Arts," and the remaining language, i.e., "by securing for limited Times to Authors and Inventors the exclusive Right to their respective Writings and Discoveries," was thought to be a restriction on the general grant of authority to only the power to issue the limited-term monopoly rights known as patents and copyrights. This had the clear advantage of treating the intellectual property clause in a manner consonant with the grammatical structure of each of the other enumerated powers granted to Congress.[6] It had the distinct disadvantage of restricting the authority of Congress "To promote the Progress of Science and useful Arts" *only* to the issuance of patents and copyrights, as Jefferson and Madison and various members of Congress would strenuously contend.[7]

In modern times, the language of the clause has tended to be interpreted quite differently. Thus, the grant of power has been interpreted to reside *only* in the "by" language, and the "to" language has been viewed as a statement merely of purpose. Whether this statement of purpose is also a restriction or limitation on congressional authority has been a matter of considerable dispute. The clause is thus literally treated as though the grant of power is: "To secure for limited Times to Authors and Inventors the exclusive Right to their respective Writings and Discoveries." The advantage of this approach is that it avoids any argument that Congress is expressly limited *only* to the issuance of patents and copyrights for the purpose of promoting "the Progress of Science and useful Arts."[8] A major disadvantage is that this is not literally the language of the clause, and such interpretation renders the grammatical construction of the clause quite different than that afforded to every other enumerated congressional power. As demonstrated in this work, there is nothing in the contemporaneous record to suggest that the Framers intended this to be the case. Nor is there any good rationale why the clause should be treated in isolation from the other enumerated powers.

---

6. Even a cursory look at article I, § 8 reveals that every other enumerated grant of power resides in the language beginning with "To."
7. *See infra* Chapter Five.
8. Thereby opening up the general welfare clause, the commerce clause, and the necessary and proper clause as avenues of authority to Congress to promote the progress of science and useful arts by means other than patents and copyrights.

While much of the present work is devoted to analyzing how the nature of the intellectual property clause has been historically interpreted to affect the patent and copyright power, a major thesis is that both the early and the modern construction and interpretations of the clause are incorrect and arise out of a tendency to view the clause in isolation rather than as one of a series of grammatically consistent enumerated powers. The unusual nature of the clause arises out of an inartful attempt by the Framers to ensure that as a part of a general power "To promote the Progress of Science and useful Arts" Congress would also have the specific power to create the limited-term monopolies known as patents and copyrights. In this view, the "by" language is not the sole grant of power nor is it a limitation on a more generic grant of power set forth in the "to" language. Rather, it is an attempt to ensure that the generic grant of power set forth in the "to" language would specifically *include* the authority to issue patents and copyrights, an authority that the Framers did not believe Congress would have unless it was expressly set forth. In this view, the proper construction of the clause is: "The Congress shall have Power . . . To promote the Progress of Science and useful Arts, [including] by securing for limited Times to Authors and Inventors the exclusive Right to their respective Writings and Discoveries."[9]

B. The Views of Thomas Jefferson

Jefferson didn't like the clause at all. Because he was serving as Minister to France, Jefferson was the founding father most conspicuous by his absence from the federal convention. One may only speculate as to what the style and content of the Constitution might have been had he been present to take active part, but there is good reason to believe that he would have opposed the intellectual property clause. While the convention was in progress, Jefferson wrote a letter to a French citizen who had invented a method of better preserving flour and had inquired as to whether the government of the United States might be interested in purchasing it. In his response, Jefferson stated:

> I am not authorized to avail my country of it by making any offer for its communication. Their policy is to leave their citizens free, neither restraining nor aiding them in their pursuits. *Though the interposition of*

---

9. *See infra* Chapter Five.

government, in matters of invention, has its use, yet it is in practice so inseparable from abuse, that they think it better not to meddle with it. . . .[10]

While ostensibly representing the views of government, the emphasized language was in reality Jefferson's personal view.[11] It is highly suggestive that Jefferson, had he been present at the federal convention, would have opposed granting to Congress a power to secure to inventors for limited times exclusive rights in their discoveries.

Exactly why Jefferson came to hold the view that the issuance of patents was "inseparable from abuse" is unclear, but hold it he did. He undoubtedly viewed patents as monopolies and his antipathy toward monopolies had become well developed through the activities of the French monopoly in the tobacco trade held by the deeply entrenched agricultural lobby known as the Farmers-General.[12] At a deeper level, however, patents to him represented a subversion of the personal freedom and liberty that was central to his political philosophy. Many years later he would write of them as "embarrassments" to the social fabric, and he meant that sincerely. To him, patents represented a clear governmental interference in the affairs of individuals. He truly believed that government should neither restrain nor aid its citizens in their individual pursuits.[13]

Thus he would have been surprised and more than a bit taken aback had he known that less than two weeks after he wrote this letter the federal

---

10. Letter from Thomas Jefferson to Jeudy de L'Hommande (Aug. 9, 1787), *in* 12 THE PAPERS OF THOMAS JEFFERSON at 11 (Julian P. Boyd et al. eds., 1956) (emphasis supplied).
11. The government Jefferson referred to was the second Continental Congress operating under the authority granted by the Articles of Confederation, and he was correct as to its lack of authority but wrong as to the reason for that lack of authority. There is nothing to indicate that the Congress had ever imparted to Jefferson any views that it might have held regarding the granting of rights to inventions. What the Congress did understand was that under the Articles it could only exercise that authority expressly delegated to it by the states which did not include authority to issue patents or to provide in any other fashion for exclusive rights with regard to inventions. Therefore, it made no attempt to do so. Moreover, since 1781 various state governments had indeed interposed in the matter through the issuance of state patents, although Jefferson may have been unaware of the scope of this practice. To a considerable extent Jefferson was speaking ex curia and assuming that his views were consonant with those of the U.S. government.
12. JOSEPH J. ELLIS, AMERICAN SPHINX at 80 (New York 1997).
13. For a discussion of his views during this period concerning government and the freedom of the individual, see ELLIS, *id.* at 97–115.

convention was being presented with proposals which ultimately resulted in an express grant of authority to Congress to interpose in the matter of invention in exactly the manner that he thought so inseparable from abuse. But he would shortly have the opportunity to voice his concerns. When Madison sent him a draft of the Constitution, he wrote back in December 1787 expressing his general satisfaction, but also noting his concern that it did not have a bill of rights. In setting forth his views on what should be in a bill of rights, he indicated that it should provide "clearly and without the aid of sophism . . . for the restriction of monopolies."[14] He made no specific mention of the express grant of authority to Congress "to promote the progress of science and useful arts, by securing for limited times to authors and inventors the exclusive right to their respective writings and discoveries," but neither did he make any attempt to distinguish desirable monopolies (which copyrights and patents presumably were).

When he found that the Constitution had been ratified, he expressed his pleasure to Madison in July 1788 and went on to amplify his views on monopolies, and specifically those authorized by the intellectual property clause, saying: "[I]t is better . . . to abolish . . . Monopolies, in all cases, than not to do it in any." He acknowledged that precluding patent and copyright monopolies "lessens the incitements to ingenuity, which is spurred by the hope of a monopoly for a limited time, as of fourteen years" but argued that "the benefit even of limited monopolies is too doubtful to be opposed to that of their general suppression."[15] In essence he wanted the intellectual property clause amended to remove any congressional authority to create or grant "exclusive rights" even of a limited term.[16]

Madison's response several months later gently but firmly disagreed:

> With regard to Monopolies they are justly classed among the greatest nusances [sic] in Government. But is it clear that as encouragements to literary works and ingenious discoveries, they are not too valuable to be wholly renounced? Would it not suffice to reserve in all cases a right to the public to abolish the privilege at a price to be specified in the grant of it? Is there not also infinitely less danger of this abuse in our Governments than in most others? Monopolies are sacrifices of the many to the few. Where the power is in the few it is natural for them to sacrifice the

---

14. Letter from Thomas Jefferson to James Madison (Dec. 20, 1787), *in* 1 THE REPUBLIC OF LETTERS at 512 (James Morton Smith ed., 1995).
15. Letter from Thomas Jefferson to James Madison (July 31, 1788), *id.* at 545.
16. It is an interesting question whether Jefferson would have opposed the clause, had it merely given Congress power "To promote the Progress of Science and useful Arts."

many to their own partialities and corruptions. Where the power, as with us, is in the many not the few, the danger can not be very great that the few will be thus favored. It is much more to be dreaded that the few will be unnecessarily sacrificed to the many.[17]

Madison's view that copyrights and patents were monopolies that should be tolerated because of the public good they could produce was in essence the common law justification for these limited-term monopolies.

Although he continued to be skeptical about the merits of Madison's argument about the need to protect the few from the dictates of the many,[18] Jefferson now resigned himself to the inevitability that Congress would have authority to legislate with respect to patents and copyrights. But he still would have preferred a change in the Constitution regarding that authority. In August 1789 he informed Madison that it would have pleased him if the proposed Bill of Rights had stated: "Monopolies may be allowed to persons for their own productions in literature, and their own inventions in the arts for a term not exceeding ___ years, but for no longer term, and for no other purpose."[19] He was no more successful now than he had been earlier, but this language does suggest a greater degree of knowledge and sophistication in Jefferson concerning the patent custom at this time than generally has been supposed.

First of all, it indicates an awareness—or at least an assumption—by Jefferson that the constitutional language did not preclude patents of importation, i.e., patents granted for imported technology from another country.[20] Had this language been adopted in the Bill of Rights, it would have avoided much later difficulty as to whether patents of importation were authorized under American law.[21] It also makes clear that he opposed any authority to grant such patents. His aversion to patents of importation

---

17. Letter from James Madison to Thomas Jefferson (Oct. 17, 1788), *in* THE REPUBLIC OF LETTERS, *supra* note 14, at 566.
18. He would never accept as valid Madison's concerns about the dangers posed by a tyranny of the majority.
19. Letter from Thomas Jefferson to James Madison (Aug. 28, 1789), *in* THE REPUBLIC OF LETTERS, *supra* note 14, at 630.
20. Madison had a contrary view, although there is no evidence that he ever discussed it with Jefferson. Indeed, Madison's view that patents of importation were unconstitutional would have a major impact on the development of the new American patent law. *See infra* Chapter Eight.
21. The first patent statutes were ambiguous in their wording and did not expressly preclude patents of importation which were routinely granted in both France and Great Britain. For a discussion on this point, see E. C. Walterscheid, *Novelty in Historical Perspective*, 75 J. PAT. & TRADEMARK OFF. SOC'Y 777 (1993).

at this time is perhaps not surprising, because he still strongly believed that the destiny of the United States resided primarily in its agricultural production rather than in any manufacturing base.

Jefferson's language also suggests a rather clear understanding of—and antagonism toward—the British parliamentary practice of extending the term of issued patents beyond the fourteen years authorized by the Statute of Monopolies.[22] He preferred to preclude Congress from having any right to change the term for issued patents or to extend the term or renew any issued patent.[23] In short, he wanted the constitutional equivalent of what you see is what you get, for as a practical matter, his language would have made it impossible to either renew a patent or extend its term, because to do so would have required a constitutional amendment. Madison, who was fully cognizant of the difficulties associated with getting Congress to accept the proposed Bill of Rights, was not about to add to those difficulties by throwing Jefferson's language into the hopper.[24] Unlike Jefferson, he was aware that putting such specific language into the Constitution was contrary to its whole philosophical framework.[25]

Jefferson would never again mention the constitutional language in any of his writings, although he certainly had the opportunity to do so. In 1804 and 1805, Oliver Evans, who had received the third federal patent issued, made several unsuccessful efforts to have the term of the patent extended by special act of Congress. He now took a different approach and on December 13, 1806, presented a more general petition seeking modification of the patent law to expressly allow for term extension.[26] A week later, he wrote to President Jefferson, enclosing the petition, because "one word from you would promote it more than all my feeble exertions."[27] Jefferson

---

22. For an extreme example of this practice, see G. E. Frost, *Watt's 31 Year Patent*, 73 J. PAT. & TRADEMARK OFF. SOC'Y 136 (1991).
23. For the trials and tribulations associated with the renewal and term extension of the third federal patent issued, see P. J. Federico, *The Patent Trials of Oliver Evans*, 27 J. PAT. OFF. SOC'Y 586, 657 (1945).
24. For an interesting discussion of those difficulties, see Paul Finkelman, *James Madison and the Bill of Rights: A Reluctant Paternity*, 9 SUP. CT. REV. 301 (1990).
25. He was also fully aware that the unusual detail set forth in the intellectual property clause was contrary to the general approach taken in the Constitution.
26. Although it was anonymous, there is clear evidence that it was written by Evans. It carried the resounding title of Address of the Advocate of Patentees, Inventors of Useful Improvements in the Arts and Sciences; Petitioners to Congress for Redress of Grievance . . . In Defense of Mental Property.
27. GRENVILLE BATHE & DOROTHY BATHE, OLIVER EVANS: A CHRONICLE OF EARLY AMERICAN ENGINEERING at 127 (Philadelphia 1935).

finally responded to Evans in May 1807, saying that while an inventor certainly should be allowed the benefit from his invention for some period of time, "[i]t is equally certain that it ought not be perpetual."[28] This response was fully in accord with—and indeed dictated by—the constitutional language, but Jefferson made no reference whatever to it.

Bedini's assertion that, following his exchange of correspondence with Madison concerning the intellectual property clause, Jefferson continued to have "serious reservations and doubts concerning the constitutionality of the [patent] practice"[29] finds no support in the contemporaneous record and is almost certainly incorrect. Indeed, it is belied by Jefferson's statement in his later years that "[s]ociety may give an exclusive right to the profits arising from them, as an encouragement to men to pursue ideas which may produce utility, but this may or may not be done, according to the will and convenience of society, without claim or complaint from anybody."[30] To his last days, Jefferson would doubt the utility or desirability of a patent system, but he never questioned the right of the country to have one.

C. Other Monopoly Concerns

Jefferson's aversion to monopolies was in no way unique. Among a variety of reasons why his fellow Virginian and delegate to the federal convention, George Mason, refused to sign the proposed Constitution was that "[u]nder their own construction of the general clause at the end of the enumerated powers, the congress may grant monopolies in trade and commerce."[31] In addition, the New York ratifying convention recommended that certain amendments be sought to it, among which were "[t]hat the congress do not grant monopolies, or erect any company with exclusive advantages of

---

28. Letter from Thomas Jefferson to Oliver Evans (May 2, 1807), *in* XI THE WRITINGS OF THOMAS JEFFERSON at 200–02 (Andrew A. Lipscomb et al. eds., 1904).
29. SILVIO O. BEDINI, THOMAS JEFFERSON, STATESMAN OF SCIENCE at 207 (1990).
30. Letter from Thomas Jefferson to Isaac McPherson (Aug. 13, 1813), *in* XIII THE WRITINGS OF THOMAS JEFFERSON, *supra* note 28, at 334.
31. 2 AMERICAN MUSEUM at 534–36 (1787). He was referring to the necessary and proper clause which read: "The Congress shall have Power . . . To make all Laws which shall be necessary and proper for carrying into Execution the foregoing Powers, and all other Powers vested by this Constitution in the Government of the United States, or in any Department or Officer thereof." U.S. CONST. art. I, § 8, cl. 18.

commerce."[32] Likewise, the ratifying conventions of Massachusetts, New Hampshire, and North Carolina all requested an amendment "that congress erect no company of merchants, with exclusive advantages of commerce."[33] Although they are not addressed to the patent monopoly per se, these views demonstrate why the delegates to the federal convention saw the need to expressly set forth the authority of Congress to secure "for limited times to authors and inventors, the exclusive right to their respective writings and discoveries."

It is in the context of a discussion of the above noted monopoly concerns by the ratifying conventions that the only contemporaneous comment by a member of the public with respect to the patent provision of the clause has been found. It was simple and to the point, i.e., "As to those monopolies, which, by way of premiums, are granted for certain years to ingenious discoveries in medicine, machines and useful arts; they are common in all countries, and more necessary in this, as the government has no resources to reward extraordinary merit."[34]

The clause was briefly mentioned during two of the state ratification contests, but apparently only in the context of its grant of authority to Congress to establish copyright. In Pennsylvania the point was made that:

> the power of securing to authors . . . the exclusive right to their writings . . . could only with effect be exercised by the Congress. For, sir, the laws of the respective states could only operate within their respective boundaries and therefore, a work which has cost the author his whole life to complete, when published in one state, however it might there be secured, could easily be carried into another state in which a republication would be accompanied with neither penalty nor punishment—a circumstance manifestly injurious to the author in particular. . . .[35]

In North Carolina in response to an argument concerning lack of mention of freedom of the press in the proposed Constitution, a fervid proponent, James Iredell, stated that "the future Congress will have . . . authority . . . to secure to authors for a limited time the exclusive privilege of publishing

---

32. 4 AMERICAN MUSEUM at 156 (1788).
33. See Remarks on the amendments to the federal constitution, proposed by the conventions of Massachusetts, New Hampshire, New York, Virginia, South and North Carolina, with the minorities of Pennsylvania and Maryland by the rev. Nicholas Cottin, D.D., 6 AMERICAN MUSEUM at 303 (1789).
34. Id.
35. Thomas McKean Speaking at the Pennsylvania Convention on the Ratification of the Federal Constitution, II THE DOCUMENTARY HISTORY OF THE RATIFICATION OF THE CONSTITUTION 415 (J. Kaminski et al. eds., 1984).

their works. This authority has long been exercised in England, . . . and . . . such encouragement may give birth to many excellent writings which would otherwise have never appeared.[36] Just as in the federal convention itself, the limited monopolies authorized by the clause were not a point of contention in the state ratifying conventions.

D. Unique Aspect

In the eighteenth century those who thought about such matters—and this certainly included the delegates to the federal convention—took for granted that it was the duty of enlightened government to aid in the development of learning and of new trades and industry in the country, or as they would put it, "to promote the progress of science and useful arts."[37] But there is a tendency to forget that the power granted to Congress "to promote the progress of science and useful arts" is unique among the congressional powers set forth in the Constitution in that it alone specifies a particular mode for exercising the general power, i.e., "by securing for limited times to authors and inventors the exclusive right to their respective writings and discoveries." No other constitutional grant of authority to Congress sets forth a specific means for exercising that authority.[38] Indeed, the committee of detail which was responsible for preparing a working draft from which the delegates ultimately crafted the

---

36. MARCUS IV, NORFOLK AND PORTSMOUTH JOURNAL, XVI THE DOCU-MENTARY HISTORY OF THE RATIFICATION OF THE CONSTITUTION 382 (J. Kaminski et al. eds., 1984).

37. As Chief Justice Marshall put it in 1832:

> To promote the progress of useful arts is the interest and policy of every enlightened government. It entered into the views of the framers of our Constitution, and the power "to promote the progress of science and useful arts, by securing for limited times to authors and inventors the exclusive right to their respective writings and discoveries" is among those expressly given to Congress.

Grant v. Raymond, 31 U.S. (6 Pet.) 218, 241 (1832).

38. *Cf.* the statement by Patterson & Lindberg that "the fact that the U.S. Constitution empowers Congress to enact copyright statutes" is "one of the few instances in which that document prescribes a subject of congressional legislation." *See* L. RAY PATTERSON & STANLEY W. LINDBERG, THE NATURE OF COPYRIGHT, A LAW OF USERS' RIGHTS at 4, 5 (Athens, Ga. 1991). The only other instance is that set forth in the same clause prescribing patents as a subject of congressional legislation.

Constitution in general deliberately avoided placing such details in the clauses being proposed. As Edmund Randolph explained it:

> In the draught of a fundamental constitution, two things deserve attention:
>
> 1. To insert essential principles only, lest the operations of government should be clogged by rendering those provisions permanent and unalterable, which ought to be accommodated by time and events, and
> 2. To use simple and precise language, and general propositions, according to the example of the constitutions of the several states.[39]

It is precisely because the delegates hewed to these first principles that the Constitution has been such an enduring framework of government for the United States.

Why then does the intellectual property clause not simply grant Congress power "to promote the progress of science and useful arts" and let it go at that? Why was the particular mode of action incorporated into the clause, and was this incorporation intended to restrict the authority of Congress to this particular mode? As is shown, the early federal Congresses certainly thought that this incorporation meant that they had no authority to fund scientific research. Constitutional scholars and legal historians have failed totally to address this issue,[40] although it has a great deal of relevance in light of the hundreds of billions of dollars that have been spent on federal research and development. I argue herein that the Framers[41] in incorporating a specific mode intended only to assure that Congress would have authority to legislate with respect to the limited term monopolies known as patents and copyrights, rather than intending that they be the exclusive means of promoting the progress of science and useful arts.

---

39. II THE RECORDS OF THE FEDERAL CONVENTION OF 1787, at 137 (Max Farrand ed., 1937).
40. Cf. Goldberg's statement that "[t]he origins of the patent clause, with emphasis on the key goal of spurring progress, have been exhaustively studied." *See* STEVEN GOLDBERG, CULTURE CLASH at 34 (New York 1994).
41. Richards notes that "it is significant that a trend exists in the originalism debate that strict originalists tend to capitalize terms like the "Framers" while looser originalists, modern historians, and anti-originalists use the lower case." *See* Neil M. Richards, *Clio and the Court: A Reassessment of the Supreme Court's Uses of History*, XIII J. L. & POLITICS 809, 845 (1997). Suffice it to say here that my decision to capitalize "Framers" is not intended to place me in any camp, nor is it in any way intended to reflect my views on originalism.

Because they are the short-hand terms used to describe particular authority granted by the intellectual property clause, it is useful at the onset of this discussion to set forth definitions of "patents," "copyrights," and "intellectual property" as used in modern parlance, recognizing at the same time that there are nuances not encompassed within these simplified definitions. Those set forth by Nance, and slightly modified here, are as good as any, namely: "Roughly speaking, patents are federal statutory rights over [or with respect to] novel inventions or designs. Copyrights are federal statutory rights over [or with respect to] original literary or artistic expressions." In turn, "intellectual property may be defined as embracing rights to novel ideas as contained in tangible products of cognitive effort."[42] There are other definitions to be discussed,[43] but these will do for starters.

E. Patent Custom and Copyright Practice

There is little question but that the Framers were cognizant of the extant English patent custom and copyright practice and desired to grant Congress authority to emulate them, at least in broad outline. The extent to which the Framers were aware of the nuances involved in the patent custom and copyright practice or of the differences in the way in which the two types of limited-term exclusive grants were treated under the common law is much less clear.

Much has been written about the debt which the United States patent system owes to its English antecedents, yet it is something of a misnomer

---

42. Dale A. Nance, *Foreword: Owning Ideas,* 13 HARV. J. L. & PUB. POL'Y, 757 (1990). As pointed out by Hughes, the various genres of intellectual property include patents, copyrights, trademarks, trade secrets, original semiconductor masks, and "gathered information." *See* Justin Hughes, *The Philosophy of Intellectual Property,* 77 GEO. L.J. 287, 292 (1988). According to Rosenberg: "A fundamental principle common to all genres of intellectual property is that they do not carry any exclusive right in mere abstract ideas. Rather, their exclusivity touches only the concrete, tangible, or physical embodiments of an abstraction." *See* P. D. ROSENBERG, 1 PATENT LAW FUNDAMENTALS § 1.03 (2d ed. 1985).
43. See, for example, the definition of "patent custom" given in the text following note 46 *infra,* and the definitions of "intellectual property" given in Chapter Two, *infra.*

to call the English patent practice prior to 1800 a patent system.[44] A major reason why that early patent practice fails to qualify as a proper patent system was the lack of an adequately established legal frame of reference for it.[45] What then exactly was the "patent custom" known to the Framers and apparently[46] authorized by the Constitution?

Simply put, it was the practice of the state giving some form of limited-term monopoly privilege to engage in a new trade or craft, sometimes denominated an industry, to that person or persons responsible for introducing it into the state. The privilege consisted of a temporary and exclusive right to exploit the subject matter, either invention or importation, covered by the grant, whether it be called a patent or something else.

It is important to recognize that the patent custom known to the Framers involved privileges rather than property rights as such. The distinction between a patent privilege and a patent property right is an important one, and one not always recognized in the early literature on the patent law. Nonetheless, inventors, who had the most practical interest in the matter, were increasingly aware of the distinction, and in the eighteenth century

---

44. In a seminal work, Christine MacLeod has sought to explain how a patent *system* developed in England. While her major emphasis may be said to be on the administrative aspects of that development, she makes abundantly clear that the creation of an effective patent system as such was dependent on the development in consonance of applicable legal principles under a rule of law. CHRISTINE MACLEOD, CREATING THE INDUSTRIAL REVOLUTION, THE ENGLISH PATENT SYSTEM, 1660–1800 (Cambridge 1988). She begins her work with an admission that "[b]etween 1660 and 1800 the 'patent system' was something of a misnomer." *Id.* at 1. *Cf.* D. Seaborne Davies, *Further Light on the Case of Monopolies,* 48 L. Q. REV. 394 (1932) ("the Patent System was introduced into England *as a system* in the second year of Elizabeth's reign). *Id.* at 396. *See also* W. H. PRICE, THE ENGLISH PATENTS OF MONOPOLY (Boston 1906), contending that in the closing years of the sixteenth century the English patent system already was well developed. *Id.* at 5.
45. As an early authority on the English patent law states in a work first published in 1846, "this branch of our law may therefore now be said to have *at last* assumed the form of *a regular system*" (emphasis supplied). WILLIAM M. HINDMARCH, A TREATISE ON THE LAW RELATIVE TO PATENT PRIVILEGES at 6 (London 1846).
46. The term "apparently" is used advisedly, because the interpretation given to the intellectual property clause by the first federal Congress, which precluded patents of importation, was actually a substantial restriction of the patent custom as understood by the Framers. For a discussion on this point, see Chapter Eight.

began to argue that they had a natural, inherent property right in their inventions which it was the obligation of the state to protect.

Patent law and patent systems developed out of a realization that there was indeed a societal need to both recognize and protect a property right with respect to invention (as opposed to a privilege), although for reasons having very little to do with any perceived "natural law" right.[47] This realization was only beginning to come into full flower in England at the time the United States moved to a federal form of government. Because Great Britain was the mother country and its laws were most familiar to the Framers, it is not surprising that in authorizing Congress to have authority to create what was essentially a new property right with regard to invention, they should look to the law pertaining to the patent privilege in England.[48]

What was true with respect to the patent custom was also true with respect to copyright. There was a long history of copyright practice in England, and the Framers also turned to it as the predicate for a grant of

---

47. In 1791 France became the first and only country to enact a patent law providing a property right in invention as of natural right. As enacted on January 7, 1791, this statute provided:

> The National Assembly, considering that any new idea, the manifestation or development of which may become useful to society, belongs basically to the one who has conceived it, and that it would be a violation of the Rights of Man, in their essence, not to regard an industrial discovery as the property of its author . . . decrees as follows: 1. Any discovery or new invention, in any kind of industry, is the property of its author.

See Frank D. Prager, *A History of Intellectual Property From 1545 to 1787*, 26 J. PAT. OFF. SOC'Y 711, 756–57 (1944). Four years later, France would back off from this view that the Rights of Man required an invention to be considered as the property of the inventor, and no other country would espouse the view that an inventor has a natural, inherent property right in his or her invention. *Cf.* MacLeod's statement that "in 1790–1791 . . . both France and the United States had established patent systems . . . embodying the concept of an inventor's natural right to his intellectual property." *See* Christine MacLeod, *The Paradoxes of Patenting: Invention and Its Diffusion in 18th- and 19th-Century Britain, France, and North America*, 32 TECH. & CULTURE 885, 888 (1991).

48. The term "property right" as used herein involves the limited-term exclusive right with regard to the invention as opposed to a property right in the invention itself. The distinction is an important one, for as Machlup has pointed out, "it is almost embarrassing how often the controversial idea of a property right in *invention* is confused with the noncontroversial idea of a property right in a *patent*." *See* FRITZ MACHLUP, AN ECONOMIC REVIEW OF THE PATENT SYSTEM, U.S. Senate, Comm. on Judiciary, 85th Cong., 2d Sess. (1958) at 53.

authority to Congress to create a property in copyright for authors. But by authorizing Congress to issue the limited-term exclusive grants known as patents and copyrights in the same clause and by using the term "securing" as the operative verb in each instance, the Framers failed to recognize, or ignored, the fact that they were creating an interpretational contretemps which would take decades to resolve and which is argued even to this day. Simply put, under the common law as understood in 1787 patents were a privilege whereas copyrights were exactly what the name suggested, namely an established legal right. Thus, by granting Congress the power of "securing" to authors and inventors the exclusive right to their respective writings and discovers, did the Framers intend merely to give Congress power to create a property right, be it designated a patent or a copyright, or did they obligate Congress to protect a property right already existing in inventors and authors? The answer was not at all obvious at the end of the eighteenth century.

F. Issues, General and Specific

It has been suggested that 1787 "marked the culmination of the provincial patent and copyright movements and a turning point in the law of intellectual property."[49] If this were indeed the case, then why were there no intellectual property proposals included in any of the systems of governance first proposed to the convention? If, as has been argued, the need for an intellectual property clause was deemed to be so important,[50] why were the proposals that finally resulted in this clause presented so late in the history of the convention? Indeed, why was there perceived to be any need for such a clause at all? (As I demonstrate, a plausible argument can be made that the power to issue patents and copyrights is found in the commerce clause, so that there is no need for a separate intellectual property clause.) Where did the words "science" and "useful arts" come from and why are they included in the clause? (They are not found in any of the proposals which are argued to have resulted in the clause.) Why is a balanced style of composition used which combines in one clause two separate and distinct grants of authority, i.e., the power to legislate with

---

49. BUGBEE, *supra* note 1, at 129.

50. Donner argues that in 1787 "the states felt a strong need for national copyright laws to secure to authors their property rights in their works" and that as a consequence there was a "strong desire of the Framers to include a copyright clause in the Constitution." *See infra* Chapter Three, note 5 and accompanying text.

respect to patents and the power to legislate with respect to copyrights? (Again, as is shown, this particular style would result in interpretational difficulties in the twentieth century.)

This combination of two separate and distinct grants of authority in one clause raises the question of whether the Framers contemplated any distinction between the rights granted to inventors and those granted to authors.[51] As late as 1760 an English Attorney General had ridiculed the notion of any such distinction,[52] but distinctions had clearly developed under the common law. These distinctions would be incorporated in the new United States patent and copyright law authorized by the constitutional language. While stating that "there are substantial differences between the patent and copyright law,"[53] the Supreme Court at the same time has recognized "the historic kinship between patent law and copyright law."[54] Modern commentators have referred to "a law of copyright pretending that every work of art is an invention distinctive enough to be patented."[55] One purpose of the present work is to explore what constitutional distinctions, if any, exist between the patent power and the copyright power authorized by the clause.

Although, on its face, the purpose of the clause appears to be to grant Congress authority "to promote the progress of science and useful arts," it was unclear what this meant. It would be argued in the early federal Congresses that the clause was in fact a grant of such authority but also a restriction or limitation of the manner in which such authority could be practiced. That is to say, on its face the clause appeared to restrict such authority to the granting of the limited term exclusive rights known as patents and copyrights. Moreover, it is important to recognize that the late eighteenth and early nineteenth centuries were a different era, with the patent system and patent law authorized by the clause being perceived to be primarily for the purpose of rewarding inventors with public benefits accruing only incidentally to this primary purpose. Indeed, as late as 1831

---

51. The literal wording of the clause, i.e., the use of the phrase "the exclusive right" to refer to both the patent right and copyright, is such as to suggest that they contemplated no particular distinction, but see Chapter Seven, Part A.
52. *See infra* Chapter Two, note 54.
53. Sony Corp. v. Universal City Studios, Inc., 464 U.S. 417, 442 (1984).
54. *Sony,* 464 U.S. at 439. While doctrine formulated in one area may be applied to the other, care should be taken in doing so. *Id.* at n.19.
55. *See* MARK ROSE, AUTHORS AND OWNERS, THE INVENTION OF COPYRIGHT at 2 (Cambridge 1993), quoting NORTHROP FRYE, ANATOMY OF CRITICISM at 96 (Princeton 1957).

a Supreme Court justice in his capacity as circuit judge would contend that "congress have declared the intention of the law to be to promote the progress of useful arts by the benefits granted to inventors; not by those accruing to the public."[56]

The modern view that "[t]he patent law is directed to the public purposes of fostering technological progress, investment in research and development, capital formation, entrepreneurship, innovation, national strength, and international competitiveness"[57] would have been almost completely foreign. Lip service would certainly have been given to the concept of fostering technological progress (it was called promoting the progress of useful arts[58]) if for no other reason than that it was a part of the constitutional language, but the remainder of these purposes would have been totally alien. In modern economic theory and practice, no attempt is made to justify the patent system on the rationale that it is intended to reward inventors. Yet this was presumed to be a primary purpose of the patent system at the beginning of the nineteenth century, and much judicial interpretation and administrative practice was predicated on this point of view.[59]

Although commentators and judicial opinions would rather quickly come to view the purpose of the patent system authorized by the clause as "to promote the progress of science and useful arts,"[60] this was not the way either the Framers or the early federal Congresses perceived the matter. Rather, to them the clause clearly encompassed two separate powers packaged together; one to promote the progress of science, i.e., knowledge, through the exclusive grant known as a copyright, and the other to promote the progress of useful arts through the exclusive grant known as a patent. Thus, the title to the first copyright act makes no reference to useful arts

---

56. Whitney v. Emmett, 29 F. Cas. 1074, 1082 (No. 17,585) (E.D. Pa. 1831) (Baldwin, J.).
57. Hilton Davis Chem. Co. v. Warner-Jenkinson Co., 62 F.3d 1512, 35 U.S.P.Q.2d 1641, 1660 (Fed. Cir. 1995) (quoting Newman, J., concurring).
58. The Patent Acts of 1790 and 1793 were both entitled "An Act to Promote the Progress of Useful Arts."
59. As shown in Chapter Four, William Thornton, the first Superintendent of Patents from 1802 to 1828, strongly believed that the patent system was intended primarily to reward and protect the interest of inventors.
60. Without ever recognizing or accepting the essential corollary to this view that if this was indeed the case then the system of copyrights also authorized by the clause must also be for this same purpose.

or, for that matter, to science,[61] and the titles to the first two patent acts refer only to useful arts and do not mention science.[62]

Another interpretational issue that would arise had to do with the nature of the limited term exclusive rights authorized by the clause. At least in the context of the patent provisions of the clause, a major question would arise during the nineteenth century as to whether these rights constituted monopolies. Those arguing that they were monopolies would contend that the patent grant must be narrowly construed, whereas those arguing that they were not literally monopolies would just as vigorously argue for a liberal construction of the patent grant. Issues of this type continue to be addressed in the modern literature on intellectual property.

Both Congress and the courts would raise other interpretational issues. Indeed, as is shown, the interpretation given to the clause by the House of Representatives in the first federal Congress materially influenced the American definition of patentable novelty and made it fundamentally different than that of any other country with a patent custom. Moreover, the question of the applicability of the common law to the interpretation of the clause would soon rear its head. As has been noted, without perhaps realizing it, the Framers had created a contretemps by their use of the term "securing" and making it applicable to both the rights of inventors and authors. The problem was that under the common law copyright and patents were treated quite differently. The Supreme Court would ultimately determine that there was no common law of patents and copyrights in the United States, but that would not occur for four decades.[63]

G. Federation

In looking at the origins of the clause it is essential to remember that the severe limitations on the power of the national government under the Articles of Confederation, including its absolute lack of any authority to protect intellectual property, had to do with the fact that the United States

---

61. It was titled "An Act for the Encouragement of Learning."
62. The term "science" does not appear at all in the Patent Act of 1790 and occurs only once in the Patent Act of 1793, which refers to a "person skilled in the art or science."
63. Meshbesher seeks to emphasize "as emphatically as possible that . . . the origins . . . of patent law" in the United States were not predicated on the common law way of thinking. *See* Thomas M. Meshbesher, *The Role of History in Comparative Patent Law*, 78 J. PAT. & TRADEMARK OFF. SOC'Y 594, 595 (1996).

came into being as a federation of thirteen existing states.[64] By and large, national governments today—as indeed was the case toward the end of the eighteenth century—are recognized as being vested with any and all powers necessary to govern, except as such power might be limited by a national constitution. It is assumed, in the natural course of things, that all political power resides in the national government and the political subdivisions are administrative units granted only such power as the national government is willing to delegate. With the notable exception of Great Britain, there were few nations in the eighteenth century with recognized constitutional limitations on the power of government. But it was precisely because of the British history of unwritten constitutional law and practice, that this principle was known and understood in the infant United States.

Indeed, one of the arguments used to support the right of the American colonies to revolt was that the government of Great Britain had violated the unwritten English constitution in the manner in which it had sought to govern the colonies. The need of the people to have constitutional limits on the governing authority was plainly recognized as the various states quickly adopted constitutions during and immediately after the American Revolution. But it was one thing to limit the rights of state government by a state constitution and quite another to limit those rights by what was in essence a delegation by the people of a major portion of those rights to a national government.[65]

---

64. The content of this and the next paragraph is taken in part from C. COLLIER & J. L. COLLIER, DECISION IN PHILADELPHIA, THE CONSTITUTIONAL CONVENTION OF 1787, at 184–85 (New York 1986).

65. In 1812 Chancellor Kent of New York clearly enunciated the differences in powers granted to a national government being created ab initio and those granted to a national government which is federal in nature, saying:

> When the people create a single, entire government, they grant at once all the rights of sovereignty. The powers granted are indefinite, and incapable of enumeration. Every thing is granted that is not expressly reserved in the constitutional charter, or necessarily retained as inherent in the people. But when a federal government is erected with only a portion of the sovereign power, the rule of construction is directly the reverse, and every power is reserved to the member that is not, either in express terms, or by necessary implication, taken away from them, and vested exclusively in the federal head. This rule has not only been acknowledged by the most intelligent friends of the constitution, but is plainly declared in the instrument itself.

Livingston v. Van Ingen, 9 Johns. R. 507, 574 (N.Y. 1812).

This then is a part of the unique nature of the Constitution. It was drafted and ratified not so much for the purpose of limiting the power of the national government but rather to enhance that power, albeit in a carefully controlled and balanced way. The Articles of Confederation had addressed the issue by a most limited and restrictive grant of powers from the states to the Congress acting as the national government. The authority to issue patents and copyrights was not a part of that limited grant. It was only with the ratification of the Constitution that Congress came to have the necessary authority to make statutory enactments pertaining to patents and copyrights. But the question would inevitably arise as to the extent to which the Framers in drafting the intellectual property clause intended to pre-empt the authority of the states to act in the same arena. It is an issue that remains with us to this day.

The first federal Congress was acutely aware that it was writing on a clean slate or as George Washington phrased it, walking "on untrodden ground,"[66] and that every time it engaged in constitutional interpretation to ascertain its own authority, it would be creating the judicial equivalent of a case of first impression. As a consequence, it tended to be conservative in its interpretations, and nowhere was this more in evidence than in regard to the interpretations it gave to the intellectual property clause. In fact, the clause presented the House of Representatives with one of its earliest issues of constitutional interpretation. But the issue was confused by the fact that James Madison, who most probably authored the clause, took inconsistent positions with regard to its interpretation in 1789 and 1790 and those positions were also inconsistent with his later views on constitutional interpretation.[67] Nonetheless, Madison's constitutional views had a major substantive impact on the interpretation of novelty under the new United States patent law and caused it to be viewed differently—and much more restrictively—than it had been defined under the European patent custom that had been extant for almost four centuries.

---

66. Letter from George Washington to Catherine Macaulay Graham (Jan. 9, 1790), *in* 30 THE WRITINGS OF GEORGE WASHINGTON at 495–96 (John C. Fitzpatrick ed., 1939).

67. For an interesting discussion of Madison's changing views on constitutional interpretation between 1789 and 1796, see Chapter XI, "Madison and the Origins of Originalism," *in* JACK N. RAKOVE, ORIGINAL MEANINGS: POLITICS AND IDEAS IN THE MAKING OF THE CONSTITUTION at 339–65 (New York 1996). *See also* E. C. WALTERSCHEID, ORIGINALISM AND THE INTELLECTUAL PROPERTY CLAUSE: THE PERSPECTIVES OF MADISON AND HAMILTON (manuscript on file with author).

H. Historiography

The interpretations given to the intellectual property clause are not static; they have evolved and changed with time. Because interpretation of the constitutional language inevitably affects the meaning of the patent and copyright law authorized by the clause, it is important that there be a clear understanding both of the origins of the clause and the nature of the interpretations given through time. As Oliver Wendell Holmes has noted, "[t]he history of what the law has been is necessary to the knowledge of what the law is."[68] Also as stated by Holmes:

> [H]istory is the means by which we measure the power which the past has had to govern the present in spite of ourselves, so to speak, by imposing traditions which no longer meet their original end. History sets us free and enables us to make up our own minds dispassionately whether the survival which we are enforcing answers any new purpose when it has ceased to answer the old.[69]

Explanations of the clause "must be historically well-informed if they are to be fully satisfying," bearing always in mind that "tradition is often a powerful explanatory tool."[70]

This is a work of history. Its intent is not so much to establish original meanings or current interpretations of the intellectual property clause as it is to demonstrate and analyze the various interpretational issues that have arisen during the more than two centuries that the clause has been in existence. A number of those issues are only of academic interest today, but in their time they were of major concern. Others are as topical today as they were when first raised.

I concur whole heartedly in the views expressed by David Currie "that in focusing so heavily on judicial decisions those who think about the Constitution from a legal perspective have paid too little attention to other sources of insights into its interpretation"[71] and that "[i]t was in the legislative and executive branches, not in the courts, that the original understanding of the

---

68. THE COMMON LAW at 33 (M. Howe ed., 1963).
69. Oliver Wendell Holmes, *Law in Science and Science in Law*, 7 HARV. L. REV. 444, 452 (1899).
70. Nance, *supra* note 42, at 760.
71. David P. Currie, *The Constitution in Congress: The Most Endangered Branch, 1801–1805*, 33 WAKE FOREST L. REV. 219 (1998).

Constitution was forged."[72] This perspective is particularly accurate with respect to the intellectual property clause. For this reason, a significant portion of the work addresses the interpretations placed on the clause by the early federal Congresses (especially by Madison in the House) and to a lesser extent the interpretations placed on it by those who also served early on in the executive branch, primarily Jefferson and Hamilton.

I emphasize once again that this work is not an attempt to establish original meanings, but rather an effort to understand the intellectual property clause as it has been perceived since its inception.[73] While I clearly have my own views concerning interpretation, I have sought to expressly delineate them as mine when they present themselves and to avoid substituting my views for those of others. Nonetheless, I find myself on occasion in disagreement with the views of various commentators and historians. Accordingly, at the end of each chapter dealing primarily with interpretational issues, there is a section which sets forth my perspective on the issues discussed in the chapter. The framework is topical; that is to say, each chapter attempts to deal with specific topics or issues of origin and interpretation. Within the chapters, there is generally but not always a chronological sequence from past to present. I have attempted to treat patent and copyright issues impartially and completely, but I recognize that there is somewhat more of an emphasis on patent-related matters, if for no other reason than that historically patent issues involving the interpretation of the clause have arisen more frequently than have those pertaining to copyright.

This is an appropriate time to first raise a cautionary note on the issue of comprehension that is reiterated at several points in this work. Although

---

72. DAVID P. CURRIE, THE CONSTITUTION IN CONGRESS: THE FEDERALIST PERIOD, 1789–1801, at 296 (1997).

73. I subscribe to the view that history is relevant to an understanding of the clause and that the relevant history is not simply that of the period at which it was drafted. *See, e.g.,* Erich J. Segal, *A Century Lost: The End of the Originalism Debate,* 15 CONST. COMMENT. 411, 438 (1998) ("a proper use of history in constitutional interpretation requires a study, not just of the original meaning of constitutional language, but of how that meaning has been applied over the full course of American history"); Larry Kramer, *Fidelity to History—and Through It,* 65 FORDHAM L. REV. 1627, 1628 (1997) ("while I believe that history matters very much in constitutional interpretation . . . the history that matters is not limited to Founding moments but must include subsequent developments as well"). *See also* Barry Friedman, *The Sedimentary Constitution,* 147 U. PA. L. REV. 1, 6–7 (1998) ("history is essential to interpretation of the Constitution, but the relevant history is not just that of the founding, it is all of American history").

in one sense, this is a work of constitutional history, in another sense it is a work of legal history. American legal history, unlike constitutional history, is almost exclusively written by lawyers (who may or may not be practicing historians). Indeed, the present work is no exception. Legal historiography, at least to the last several decades, has generally been marked by an emphasis on continuity and a corresponding de-emphasis on change.[74] It has been colored by the lawyer's devotion to finding the origins of doctrines presently enshrined in the law and to an advocacy of particular interpretations of those doctrines. The practical consequence, as has long been acknowledged, has been the "subservience of legal historian to practicing lawyer."[75]

In short, there is a propensity to "use history to justify and glorify the present,"[76] or at least a particular interpretation of the present. As a result, an understandable but frequently muddying and sometimes erroneous inclination exists for the legal profession and the judiciary to seek to apply current usages, idioms, interpretations, and definitions to historical analysis rather than to seek to determine and apply those in use at the time in question.[77] The net result is at best reliance on pseudohistory; and at worst history that is incorrect or has no relationship to the issue at hand.

This approach, at least in the context of the Constitution, is not a new phenomena. Writing in 1824, Madison complained:

> What a metamorphosis would be produced in the code of law if all its ancient phraseology were to be taken in its modern sense! And that the language of our Constitution is already undergoing interpretations unknown to its founders will, I believe, appear to all inquirers into the history of its origin and adoption.[78]

---

74. M. J. Horwitz, *The Conservative Tradition in the Writing of American Legal History*, 17 AM. J. LEG. HIST. 275, 276 (1973).
75. Daniel Boorstin, *Tradition and Method in Legal History*, 54 HARV. L. REV. 424, 428 (1941). He points out that the use of present legal categories as a framework for legal history almost of necessity defines the methods to be used as well as giving the study of legal history a more conservative function that it might otherwise have had. *Id.* at 426.
76. Horwitz, *supra* note 74, at 283.
77. A classic example of this approach was that of Justice Douglas concurring in Great Atl. & Pac. Tea Co. v. Supermarket Equip. Corp., 340 U.S. 147, 154–55 (1950). *See generally* Chapter Four, Part B, *infra*.
78. Letter, James Madison to Henry Lee, June 25 1824, *reprinted in* III THE RECORDS OF THE FEDERAL CONVENTION OF 1787, *supra* note 39, at 464.

When the Supreme Court engages in this practice, as it has been known to do, in its interpretation of the intellectual property clause, it effectively changes either the patent or the copyright law as the case may be, albeit not for the reasons the Justices necessarily intended or understood.[79] The point to be made here is that intellectual property law may on occasion evolve or change because of reliance on pseudohistory, e.g., an interpretation of historical events in a contemporaneous or anachronistic context rather than the context actually existing, or a juxtaposition of events or circumstances that is not historically accurate.[80] This does not mean that a new and differing interpretation of law has not occurred, but rather that the reasons ostensibly given do not support the interpretation given and thus call into question the underlying rationale for it.

Commentators on legal history are not immune to the practice either. Indeed, they are more likely to be susceptible to it as they seek to support or develop a particular point of emphasis by reference to the language of the past. I seek to point this out on occasion, and, more importantly, try to avoid doing it myself. But the reader should always bear in mind the difficulty of knowing with certainty the meaning of centuries old language, even in the context of that most studied of historical documents, the U.S. Constitution.[81]

Although my analysis is historical in nature, it is important to set forth the mode of constitutional interpretation I have sought to follow in treating the historical material. Tribe has recently set forth several points about constitutional interpretation which I have taken to heart and which I believe to be highly relevant to any understanding of the intellectual property clause and the manner in which it has been perceived over time. In any case, I have sought to employ them in this work.

According to Tribe:

> One basic point warrants special emphasis: Interpreting the Constitution's *text* requires close attention to linguistic *context*—that is, to

---

79. For an excellent analysis on this point, see Kenneth Burchfiel, *Revising the "Original" Patent Clause: Pseudohistory in Constitutional Construction*, 2 HARV. J. L. & TECH. 155 (1989).

80. In the modern era the Supreme Court has on several occasions relied on a highly erroneous historical interpretation of Thomas Jefferson's views as support for its interpretation of the patent provision of the clause. *See* Edward C. Walterscheid, *The Use and Abuse of History: The Supreme Court's Interpretation of Thomas Jefferson's Influence on the Patent Law*, 39 IDEA 195 (1999).

81. For a discussion on this point, see R. N. Clinton, *Original Understanding, Legal Realism, and the Interpretation of "This Constitution,"* 72 IOWA L. REV. 1177 (1987).

surrounding language; to how the relevant word or phrase is used elsewhere in the document; and to how it is used or what appeared in its
stead, in prior drafts of the Constitution or, indeed, in the Articles of
Confederation.[82]

As shown, all too often this precept has been ignored and words and
phrases in the clause have been sought to be interpreted in isolation, not
only from the remainder of the clause itself but from the broader language
of the Constitution.

A second point emphasized by Tribe has to do with

> an aspect of the Constitution that is particularly elusive yet indisputably
> central—its structure. The Constitution's "structure" is (borrowing
> Wittgenstein's famous distinction) that which the text *shows* but does
> not directly *say*.[83] Diction, word repetitions, and documentary organiz-
> ing forms (e.g., the division of the text into articles, or the separate
> status of the preamble and the amendments), for example, all contrib-
> ute to a sense of what the Constitution is about that is as obviously
> "constitutional" as are the Constitution's words as such. . . . [O]ne
> should not hesitate to take structural considerations with utmost
> seriousness as a source of authoritative insight into the Constitution's
> content, and thus into its implications for particular contested practices
> by the states or the federal government.[84]

As I demonstrate here, what the intellectual property clause shows but
does not directly say is critical to an understanding of the nature of the
clause. Determining what it shows is as much dependent on constitutional
structure as it is on context.

Structural analysis is increasingly being used by the Supreme Court to
evaluate the constitutionality of federal legislation. As then-Justice
Rehnquist put it in 1979, a constitution is necessarily "built on certain
postulates or assumptions" which in turn are predicated "on shared experience and common understanding." Sometimes these are obvious, but
sometimes they are not. In such circumstance, "when the Constitution is

---

82. LAURENCE H. TRIBE, I AMERICAN CONSTITUTIONAL LAW at 38–39 (3d
    ed. 2000).
83. LUDWIG WITTGENSTEIN, TRACTATUS LOGICO-PHILOSOPHICUS, ¶ 4.1212
    (1921) (1962 ed).
84. TRIBE, *supra* note 82, at 40–41.

ambiguous or silent on a particular issue,"[85] the Court not infrequently seeks to rely

> on notions of a constitutional plan—the implicit ordering of relationships within the federal system necessary to make the Constitution a workable governing charter and to give each provision within that document the full effect intended by the Framers. The tacit postulates yielded by that ordering are as much engrained in the fabric of the document as its express provisions, because without them the Constitution is denied force and often meaning.[86]

By focusing on both context and structure, the nature of the intellectual property clause is shown to be quite different than has been traditionally supposed. It provides a broader scope of authority to Congress than merely the power to create patents and copyrights, while at the same time it contains limitations on the patent and copyright power that are only in recent years coming to be understood. All in all, it is indeed a most unusual clause.

I. Synopsis of This Work

Chapter Two reviews both the immediate backdrop and the historical antecedents that came into play in the drafting of the intellectual property clause. It begins with a brief look at the Articles of Confederation and why they failed to give Congress authority to issue patents and copyrights. It then shifts to a discussion of how the concept of intellectual property originated. This is followed by a look at the patent custom prior to 1787. The emphasis here is on the English antecedents and to a lesser extent on the colonial and state patent custom prior to 1787. A similar approach is then taken with respect to the copyright practice that existed prior to 1787. The chapter closes with a brief mention of why it was deemed necessary to seek to give the new federal government authority with respect to patents and copyrights.

The drafting of the clause at the federal convention is the subject of Chapter Three. It begins with the calling of the convention and notes that giving power regarding patents and copyrights to the national government was not high on the priority list of issues faced by the delegates. It points out that despite some later contentions to the contrary the first governance

---

85. By this he meant when the *text* is silent or ambiguous.
86. Nevada v. Hall, 440 U.S. 410, 433 (1979) (Rehnquist, J., dissenting).

proposals presented to the convention said nothing about patents or copy-rights. It then addresses the question of why there is an intellectual property clause, first suggesting that the authority therein could have been developed by interpretation of the commerce clause. It then argues that the reason for the clause was a desire by the delegates to give Congress power to emulate the English patent custom and copyright practice and a concern that such would not be possible without an express authority, because patents and copyrights were viewed as monopolies. The proposals that ultimately were transformed into the clause are then set forth as is a discussion of who made the proposals and their apparent motivations. Finally, the manner in which the final clause came to be drafted is briefly reviewed.

Chapter Four begins with a look at the grammatical form of the clause with attention given to its balanced composition. It points out that both the judiciary and commentators take this balanced composition as evidence that the clause is the combining of two separate proposals, one for patent authority and the other for copyright authority, but suggests that the clause actually encompasses three of the proposals presented to the delegates, including most particularly the one for encouraging the advancement of useful knowledge and discoveries. It notes that there is confusion as to the actual purpose of the patent and copyright provisions of the clause and that the Supreme Court has contributed to this confusion. It then looks to the origins and contemporaneous interpretations of the terms "science" and "useful arts" as they appear in the clause and briefly reviews the anach-ronistic meaning given to "science" in the clause by two Supreme Court justices in the twentieth century. The lack of any contemporaneous justification other than that set forth in *The Federalist No. 43* is noted as is the early view that the exclusive rights authorized by the clause were intended as a reward for authors and inventors and that this was a primary purpose of the clause. Finally, the rationales that existed in England for patents and copyrights at the end of the eighteenth century are reviewed.

Chapter Five focuses on the powers and limitations in the clause. It analyzes the conflicting views expressed by the Supreme Court in this regard and notes that the patent and copyright power is not plenary despite what the Supreme Court said in this regard in the nineteenth century. It points out that the powers and limitations can—and indeed have been—viewed in different ways, with the "to" language at times being viewed as the grant of power and the "by" language deemed to be a limitation on that grant. At other times, the language has been treated just the reverse, with the "by" language treated as the grant of power and the "to" language as a limitation on that grant of power or—as frequently argued in the copyright context—as no limitation at all on congressional power. It suggests that the better interpretation of the clause is to treat the "to" language as the grant of power and the "by" language not as a limitation per se but rather as a means of assuring that the broad power to promote the progress of science and useful arts would include authority with regard to the limited-term monopolies known as patents and copyrights.

Chapter Six addresses the issue of whether the clause is intended to protect existing property rights or instead is intended to authorize Congress to create property rights in patents and copyrights. While it is generally accepted today that the rights are created rights, this was a hotly debated topic in the decades following the ratification of the Constitution. The issue revolved around the meaning to be given to the word "securing" in the clause and whether there was a common-law right to patents and copyrights which remained in effect when the United States became an independent nation.

Chapter Seven is directed to the nature of "the exclusive right" Congress is authorized to create under the clause. It notes that under the balanced composition of the clause "the exclusive right" should reasonably have read "exclusive rights" or "an exclusive right" and points out that the use of the singular with the definite article "the" nonetheless appears to have been deliberate by the Framers. It analyzes in considerable detail why the issue of whether patents and copyrights are monopolies is intimately intertwined with the interpretations that have been given to "the exclusive right" and "for limited times" in the clause. How Congress and the Supreme Court have interpreted both phrases is reviewed. The critical importance of the clause to the enlargement of the public domain of creative works is demonstrated. The remarkable and irrational disparity between the patent term and the copyright term that Congress has allowed to develop, particularly in the second half of the twentieth century, is analyzed and shown to be constitutionally suspect.

Chapter Eight reviews the treatment that has been given to the terms "inventors" and "discoveries" in the clause. It begins by analyzing the constitutional requirement for novelty for patentability and then discusses why the United States became the first nation to prohibit patents of importation despite its desperate need for imported technology at the end of the eighteenth century. It suggests that the clause does not forbid patents of importation, but that the prohibition came about because of a conservative congressional interpretation of the term "inventors" and the peculiar American emphasis on originality as a requirement for novelty. It reviews and questions the constitutional standard of invention declared by the Supreme Court in 1966. It notes that the requirement of utility for patentability is also derived from the clause. Finally, it addresses the extent to which the clause limits or circumscribes congressional discretion to define patentable subject matter.

Chapter Nine is an analog to Chapter Eight, addressing the interpretation given to the terms "authors" and "writings" in the clause. Unlike the situation with patents, Congress has authorized copyrights to issue to other than the literal authors of the work when the work is made for hire. Since the clause refers to "their writings," this chapter questions the constitutionality of legislation defining corporate owners of works made for hire as "authors." It then goes on to analyze in some detail the meaning given to authorship under the clause as well as the extremely broad Supreme Court interpretation given to "writings" under the clause. It challenges the view of several circuit courts that the introductory language of the clause does not place any limitation on congressional copyright power. It analyzes the requirements for originality and fixation said by the Supreme Court to reside in the terms "authors" and "writings." Finally, it addresses congressional authority to define copyrightable works, and the transformation of "writings" into "works" in modern copyright legislation.

The last chapter, Chapter Ten, examines the clause in an external rather than an internal perspective. It provides a perusal of the relationship of the clause to state patent and copyright authority and to other enumerated grants of congressional power. In so doing, it suggests that these relationships are in a state of flux with judicial guidance being decidedly mixed.

CHAPTER TWO
ANTECEDENTS

A. Introduction

Prior to the ratification of the Constitution by the requisite nine states on June 21, 1788, there was no federal patent or copyright law because under the Articles of Confederation each state retained "every power, jurisdiction and right, which is not expressly delegated to the United States, in Congress assembled."[1] Among the powers which the states failed to expressly delegate were the right to issue patents or otherwise grant rights with respect to inventions and discoveries, as well as the right to provide for copyright of writings.

In seeking to understand the origins of the United States patent and copyright law it is necessary to inquire into the foundations of the constitutional language. Why did the Framers believe it necessary to even mention inventors and authors in the Constitution, much less expressly empower Congress to grant them exclusive rights, albeit for limited times, in their respective discoveries and writings? The answer, of course, is that the constitutional language was not framed out of whole cloth. At the time the United States moved to the federal form of government, the patenting of inventions and copyrighting of literary works had been practiced for several centuries. Indeed, the legal forms of letters patent, at least in the English context, were not only time-honored but time-worn.[2] So too it was with copyright.[3]

---

1. Articles of Confederation, art. II.
2. Frank D. Prager, *Historic Background and Foundation of American Patent Law,* 5 AM. J. LEG. HIST. 309 (1961).
3. Patterson & Lindberg suggest, albeit incorrectly, that "[c]opyright may very well be the only law [judges] deal with that can be traced back to its origins in sixteenth-century England." *See* L. RAY PATTERSON & STANLEY W. LINDBERG, THE NATURE OF COPYRIGHT, A LAW OF USERS' RIGHTS at 6 (Athens 1991). As I demonstrate elsewhere, the American patent law also is predicated on law that had its origins in sixteenth-century England. See E. C. Walterscheid, *The Early Evolution of the United States Patent Law: Antecedents (Part 2),* 76 J. PAT. & TRADEMARK OFF. SOC'Y 849–62 (1994), and the sources cited therein.

The intellectual property clause was drafted against the immediate backdrop of the Articles of Confederation but within the overall framework of the English, colonial, and state practices regarding patents and copyright. To understand it in the context of its time, it is first necessary to look at how that backdrop came to be, then to briefly explore the overall framework of existing patent and copyright practice. Only then is it possible to obtain some insight into what the Framers did and why they did it.

B. The Articles of Confederation

In 1776 Americans gave precious little thought to any form of national government that might ensue if their revolt against Great Britain was successful. Indeed, at that time it is likely that the majority of the American colonists would have been content to remain under the British crown, if only some workable form of self-determination within a colonial framework could be worked out. Even after the Declaration of Independence, the fight was not thought by most Americans to be for some ill-defined and amorphous national entity but rather for their newly independent states.[4] To the extent that they thought about it, they were generally convinced that the one thing they did not want was to substitute a strong new central government—assumed almost certainly to be tyrannical—for the despotic British rule they were fighting to overcome.[5]

---

4. As pointed out by Jensen, "[t]he people, so far as they had fought for independence, had not fought for the independence of a vague entity known as the United States, but for the independence of their own particular states." M. JENSEN, THE NEW NATION: A HISTORY OF THE UNITED STATES DURING THE CONFEDERATION, 1781–1789, at 83 (New York 1962). Or as phrased by Schuyler, "the patriotism of many a sturdy Revolutionary was bounded by the limits of his own state." R. L. SCHUYLER, THE CONSTITUTION OF THE UNITED STATES—AN HISTORICAL SURVEY OF ITS FORMATION at 27 (1923).

5. To be sure, there were those who from the inception of the Revolution believed that a strong central American government would be necessary but they were in the minority. Nonetheless the words attributed to Rufus King, a delegate to the federal convention, should be remembered. According to T. E. Benton:

> He said: "You young men who have been born since the Revolution, look with horror upon the name of a King, and upon all propositions for a strong government. It was not so with us. We were born the subjects of a King, and were accustomed to subscribe ourselves 'His Majesty's most faithful subjects;' and we began the quarrel which ended in the Revolution, not

Nonetheless, they were pragmatic souls and recognized that the individual states could not go it alone, for to do so would simply invite piecemeal defeat by the British. They thus accepted—although not always gracefully—the need for the Continental Congress to take unto itself those powers necessary to achieve the ultimate goal of independence. The remarkable thing is that while the second Continental Congress early on called upon the states to set up their own governments and write their own constitutions,[6] it operated without any constitutional charter of its own for some seven years. When such a charter, the Articles of Confederation, was finally ratified by all the states in 1781, "Congress suffered a serious diminution of its authority and effectiveness as well as its prestige both at home and abroad."[7] The reason for this was that the Articles "were a constitution [only] in the most tenuous sense—they provided fundamental law, but they did not establish a government."[8]

While Congress managed to guide the fledgling United States through much of the Revolutionary War without a constitutional charter, it did not in fact intend to do so. Rather, the circumstance that no such charter existed was not the fault of Congress but rather of the recalcitrance of a single state, Maryland, which refused to ratify the Articles of Confederation until 1781.[9] Within a few months of the inception of the second Continental Congress on May 10, 1775, it began to receive proposals for

---

against the King, but against his parliament; and in making the new government many propositions were submitted which would not bear discussion; and ought not to be quoted against their authors, being offered for consideration, and to bring out opinions, and which, though behind the opinions of this day, were in advance of those of that day."

T. E. Benton, *I Thirty Year's View* at 58, *reproduced in* III THE RECORDS OF THE FEDERAL CONVENTION OF 1787, at 466 (Max Farrand ed., 1937).

6. The first Continental Congress met from September 5 to October 26, 1774, and the second met from May 10, 1775 to March 2, 1789. Exactly one year after the second Continental Congress came into being, it issued a resolution calling on the various colonies to form state governments. *See* RICHARD G. MORRIS, THE FORGING OF THE UNION, 1781–1789, at 55–59 (New York 1987).

7. MORRIS, *supra* note 6, at 80.

8. R. MIDDLEKAUF, THE GLORIOUS CAUSE at 621 (New York 1982).

9. Although all the states except Maryland signed the Articles of Confederation in 1778, ratification could not occur until all the states had signed, and Maryland did not actually sign until 1781. Maryland refused to sign until the states agreed in principle to disposition of the western lands by ceding state claims thereto to the United States. According to Morris, "the West would prove the most divisive issue delaying adoption of the Articles of Confederation." *Supra* note 6, at 87.

some form of confederation for the colonies, soon to be declared states. Indeed, some six different drafts of confederation proposals are now known to have been prepared in 1775 and 1776.[10]

These early proposals were in many respects quite nationalistic in tone and content and would have conferred upon Congress significant powers, some of which it never in reality would possess. Congress did not act directly on any of them, but instead some thirteen months after its inception finally appointed a committee of thirteen to draft what ultimately became the Articles of Confederation. This was only a month after the Congress had asked the various colonies to form state governments and create their own constitutional charters, but even then it was recognized that a fundamental issue in the formation of any central or national government would be the relative authority of the states and the Congress. At this early stage in the development of the United States it was largely assumed that Congress would have the primary if indeed not the exclusive role in any central government that was formed.[11]

If the states were to have governments of their own, then clearly power had to be divided between those state governments and Congress as the embodiment of the national government.[12] But where was the dividing line to lie? One approach was to give Congress a grant of authority to do all things necessary for the general good of the country. Needless to say any such grant of general authority would give Congress power to override the states on almost any issue it chose to act upon. An alternative approach was to strictly limit the authority of Congress to specifically enumerated powers. In the absence of a specific grant of power to Congress, it would be reserved to the states. An approach of this kind would severely restrict the authority of Congress because it would not be able to act in any

---

10. This discussion of the events leading up to the drafting of the Articles of Confederation is taken largely from MORRIS, *supra* note 6, at 80–91.

11. Some favored the formation of a strong executive authority, but they were in a distinct minority. It was precisely the claimed tyranny of a strong executive authority embodied in the English crown that the colonists were rebelling against. They were not predisposed to replace one strong executive authority with another. *But see* Benton, *supra* note 5.

12. The content of this paragraph is taken by analogy from C. COLLIER & J. L. COLLIER, DECISION IN PHILADELPHIA, THE CONSTITUTIONAL CONVENTION OF 1787, at 185 (New York 1986). Collier et al. write in the context of the federal convention in 1787, but the issue of the relative roles of the states and the national government—of whatever sort—was clearly understood by the Congress a decade earlier during the debates on the drafting of the Articles of Confederation.

situation wherein it had not received an express grant of power. At heart, the issue was one of sovereignty. Was it to remain with the newly established states or was it to be transferred to a national government?

For the most part, the members of the committee tasked to draft a proposed charter of national government were moderates and conservatives. As such, they were predisposed toward the first approach noted above.[13] The committee draft of proposed articles of confederation was reported to Congress on July 12, 1776, but it would not be accepted—and then only in substantially modified form—until November 15, 1777. Nonetheless, as initially presented, "[i]t was a constitution with great possibilities for centralization, for it contained few limitations on the power of Congress and no guarantees of power to the states."[14]

It made no mention of patents or copyrights or of the rights of inventors and authors.[15] Nonetheless, had it been accepted as presented, Congress would clearly have had power to protect intellectual property and the subsequent constitutional provision might well have never been included—if indeed any need for a U.S. Constitution was perceived at all. The key clause was Article III which stated:

> Each colony shall retain and enjoy as much of its present Laws, Rights and Customs as it may think fit, and reserve to itself the sole and exclusive regulation and Government of its internal Police, in all Matters that shall not interfere with the Articles [agreed upon] at this Confederation.[16]

This in effect would have given Congress supreme authority over the states, and such authority would have given Congress the ability to legislatively "promote the progress of science and useful arts" by whatever means it deemed appropriate, including the power to issue patents or grant other rights to inventors as well as provide for copyright of literary works.

But it was not to be. During the early intermittent debates on the draft, there seems to have been no recognition whatever that this third article in which the reserved power of the states was so vaguely defined would in essence transfer sovereignty in all significant matters to the national government, i.e., Congress. It was not until the early spring of 1777 that the issue was raised by a newly arrived delegate from North Carolina named

---

13. Jensen argues that "they believed in the need for a coercive, centralized government." *Supra* note 4, at 23.
14. JENSEN, *supra* note 4, at 24.
15. In the midst of the American Revolution concerns about such rights could not have been high on the list of priorities of Congress.
16. MORRIS, *supra* note 6, at 84.

Thomas Burke. Burke is not well known as one having any significant role in the development of constitutional government in the United States, yet he played a pivotal role in causing Congress to replace the third article of the draft Articles with what became the second article in the ratified Articles of Confederation. And it would be the limitations imposed on national government by the second article which ultimately more than anything else would result in the federal convention and change forever the form of government in the United States.

Initially, Burke seems to have been driven by concern that the third article as drafted would provide Congress with authority to control the western lands.[17] He also seems to have sincerely believed "that unlimited power was not to be safely entrusted to any man or set of men on earth."[18] In his view, the third article granted virtually unlimited power to Congress because it "expressed only a reservation of the power of regulating the internal police, and consequently resigned every other power."[19] He argued that unless the third article was drastically changed, Congress "could explain away every right belonging to the States and to make their own power as unlimited as they please."[20]

Accordingly, he proposed the language of what became the second article, i.e., "Each State retains its sovereignty, freedom and independence, and every power, jurisdiction and right, which is not by this confederation expressly delegated to the United States, in Congress assembled." The profound significance of this language seems to have caught the other delegates by surprise, and, as Burke noted in a letter to the governor of North Carolina, "[t]his was at first so little understood that it was sometime before it was seconded, and South Carolina first took it up."[21] Once understood, however, the concept of leaving the locus of sovereignty firmly

---

17. JENSEN, *supra* note 4, at 25. South Carolina, which Burke represented in the Congress, was one of those southern states having "seaboard to seaboard" charters, MORRIS, *supra* note 6, at 87. Attempts to place control of their rights to western land in a national government were vigorously opposed by them.
18. JENSEN, *supra* note 4.
19. *Id.*
20. MORRIS, *supra* note 6, at 88.
21. Letter from Thomas Burke to Richard Caswell (Apr. 29, 1777), *reproduced in* LETTERS OF DELEGATES TO CONGRESS, 1774–1789, at 671–773 (P. H. Smith, ed., 1980). Ironically, Burke began his letter by stating that he was not "able to communicate anything interesting."

with the states exercised a powerful attraction, with eleven states voting yes, Virginia no, and New Hampshire divided.[22]

The use of the term "expressly" in Article II was what made it so supremely restrictive of the authority of the national government, i.e., "the United States, in Congress assembled." For by the literal language of Article II, if the Articles did not expressly delegate a power, jurisdiction, or right, that authority could not be exercised by Congress. It was for this reason that the Continental Congress never attempted to issue patents or grant any form of exclusive rights to inventors in their inventions.[23] Nor did it attempt to provide copyrights, although it did encourage the states to enact their own copyright laws.[24] Nor did it attempt through any other particular means "to promote the Progress of Science and useful Arts." The power to do so was simply not delegated to Congress by the Articles.[25]

C. Originating the Concept of Intellectual Property

The idea of property, for example, some form of ownership of or control over an object or thing which gave the right to exclude others from using or having access to or control over it, originated in antiquity and may well have antedated organized society. A major impetus toward the development of concepts of laws involved the perceived need to create and protect

---

22. That Virginia should vote "no" was intriguing to say the least, because it was among the most powerful of the states and had the greatest claim to the western lands.

23. This, however, did not prevent inventors from on occasion seeking patent rights from the Congress. *See, e.g.,* Frank D. Prager, *The Steamboat Pioneers Before the Founding Fathers,* 37 J. PAT. OFF. SOC'Y 486, 493–95, 509 (1955); Frank D. Prager, *The Steamboat Interference 1787–1793,* 40 J. PAT. OFF. SOC'Y 611, 615 (1958).

24. *See infra* note 172 and accompanying text. Interestingly, the Continental Congress never suggested that the states take any legislative action concerning patents. The reason for this seems to have been that during the Confederation years authors sought protection for their writings from Congress more vigorously than inventors did.

25. Arguably, Congress was not expressly bound by the Articles until they were formally ratified by all the states, so that prior to 1781 it might have conceivably issued patents or something akin thereto. But as a practical matter, no one seems to have petitioned Congress for patent rights or for copyright during this period so the issue seems not to have been addressed.

rights in property. As systems of law developed, the property rights sought to be protected were rights in tangible things. It was only with the greatest difficulty that property rights in intangible things came slowly to be recognized and then only relatively late in the development of legal systems.[26]

The term "intellectual property" is a relatively recent one which first came to be used in the second half of the nineteenth century. In the context of technology, it is based on the legal premise that knowledge of craft processes and techniques and the development of technological innovations are forms of intangible property with commercial value separate and distinct from that of the physical manifestation of the use of such knowledge, e.g., products or devices.[27] Although the term is comparatively new, the concept itself is a development of the late Middle Ages, having come into existence at least with respect to invention by early in the fifteenth century.[28]

Despite occasional argument to the contrary, ancient law failed completely to recognize the concept of intellectual property.[29] While accusations of literary theft and plagiarism were common in both the Greek and Roman worlds, they were almost always tied to concerns about honor,

---

26. As noted by Armstrong:

> The growth of market society and the increasing attribution of market value to tangibles and eventually to intangibles tended to reify them, causing market participants to view as "things" entities that had previously been regarded as aspects of the whole. . . . This . . . process of reification . . . occurred earlier for land and chattels, and came later for inventive ideas.

G. M. Armstrong, FROM THE FETISHISM OF COMMODITIES TO THE REGULATED MARKET: THE RISE AND DECLINE OF PROPERTY, 82 NW. U. L. REV. 79 (1987).

27. Pamela O. Long, *Invention, Authorship, "Intellectual Property," and the Origin of Patents: Notes toward a Conceptual History*, 32 TECH. & CULTURE 846 (1991). For different definitions, see the text accompanying note 35, *infra*, and see note 39, *infra*.

28. Nonetheless, the term is frequently used anachronistically when referring to the early patent custom because it implies the existence of a property right where no such right in fact existed.

29. As Long points out, "[n]either Greek nor Roman laws included any notion of intellectual property." *Supra* note 27, at 854.

credit or fame. That, however, does not add up to a concept of intellectual property.[30] Before such could be developed, two prerequisites were necessary. The first was a clear understanding that invention or ideas could indeed be the product of the human intellect rather than the random gift of the gods or in the Christian era of God. The second which depended from the first was a recognition that the product of the intellect in its intangible form could also have commercial value.

While the first came to be well understood in both the Greek and Roman communities, the second was not. But after the fall of the Roman Empire, there was a profound retrogression in the understanding of the human intellect and its ability to influence the development and course of technology. It was the perception which arose during the Middle Ages that genius was a gift of God that largely precluded an earlier development of the concept of intellectual property. For how could one properly seek to obtain commercial value from that which was perceived to have been granted by the grace of God?

The argument has convincingly been made that the idea of intellectual property arose from the recognition by the guilds that craft knowledge in and of itself had commercial value and as a result ought to be protected. Since guilds existed in the Roman era, one may reasonably inquire as to why such recognition did not arise earlier. This, however, presupposes that an important guild function at that time was the protection and transmission of craft secrets through an apprenticeship process. There was to some degree an apprenticeship process for the imparting of techniques of the craft through on-the-job training. But there is little evidence of deliberate concealment of tradecraft for the purposes of creating or maintaining a commercial advantage. Roman guilds, at least, were primarily for religious and social purposes and, with few exceptions, did not exercise monopolies over trades or crafts.

The guilds that developed in the late Middle Ages were quite different than the Roman guilds. They arose in the context of medieval cities and the market economies that developed within and among them.[31] Perhaps

---

30. As Long puts it:

> Two essential elements are missing. The first is the explicit separation of tangible from intangible aspects of a work. The second is the notion that the intangible aspects of authorship consist of commercial property. The ancient theft of writings constituted a purloining of honor, fame, and reputation. It was never considered larceny of intangible commercial property.

Supra note 27, at 858.

31. This discussion of craft guilds is taken largely from Long, *supra* note 27, at 869–75.

because of this, they early began to develop proprietary attitudes toward craft knowledge. As a consequence:

> In promoting attitudes of ownership toward intangible property—craft knowledge and processes as distinct from material products—the guilds developed the concept of "intellectual property" without ever calling it that. The view that craft knowledge was intangible property with commercial value developed in this context quite apart from notions of individual authorship. Neither was it necessarily tied to innovation. "Intellectual property" became an aspect of corporate ownership— whether the corporation was more or less autonomous, or was closely tied to the government of the commune.[32]

Nowhere was this more apparent than in Italy and particularly in Venice.

The example of the glassmakers of Venice is particularly instructive. At the time of the Renaissance, Venetian glasswork was recognized as the finest in Europe. Glass making in Venice was restricted to guild members, and this guild, like those of other Venetian artisans, was closely controlled by the Venetian commune. There were detailed guild regulations covering a variety of matters, including legal workdays, election of guild officials, judicial procedures, apprenticeship, and relations between masters and patrons. Selling stolen, defective, or non-Venetian glass products was forbidden.

Surprisingly, there were only a few regulations which pertained specifically to the actual technical aspects of glassmaking, and these seem to have been directed more at quality control than anything else. Yet glassmaking was a complex and intricate process and there was much art involved. The quality, clarity, and strength of the product depended not only on a detailed knowledge of the proper ingredients but also of the proportions and ways of combining them as well as of the specific furnace temperatures required at various stages of the process. Knowledge of coloration formulas and techniques as well as of glassblowing added to the highly specialized nature of the craft. While a part of the superiority of Venetian glass derived from access to superior ingredients, the skill and knowledge of the glassmakers themselves was also a critical component in the fame which the glass acquired over Europe.

As the lucrative sale of its glass products throughout Europe convinced Venice of the great commercial importance of its glassworks, there also came a realization that the craft knowledge of the glassmakers was exceedingly valuable in its own right. With this also came the recognition that such craft knowledge was a communal property of both the state and the guild that

---

32. Long, *supra* note 27, at 870.

must be protected. As a consequence, the export of the craft itself was strictly forbidden. But this was easier said than done, and it served only to emphasize the commercial importance of knowledge of secret craft processes. This recognition that secret craft knowledge in certain specialized fields had intrinsic commercial value in its own right, separate and distinct from actual products, and could be used to effectively control lucrative industries, was an important precursor to the development of the patent custom.[33]

But there was another notion that was gradually taking shape that was also fully as important. This was the realization that while Venetian glassware was generally recognized as being of superior quality to other glass made in Europe, it was by no means of an absolutely uniform character. There were nuances that made some glass more valuable than the rest and certain masters within the guild were recognized more than others for the quality of their glass. Critical to the point at hand is that these masters from certain glassmaking families fully recognized this and zealously sought to protect their tradecraft secrets not only from those who were not members of the guild but from other guild members as well. As a consequence, specific formulas and specifications for making and coloring glass were often jealously guarded trade secrets even within the guild. Thus there was a rising awareness of an individual as well as a communal property interest in tradecraft. This too would serve as a backdrop to the development of the patent custom. Indeed, it may have been the critical factor for it brought into play the idea of seeking to award exclusive privileges to practice a particular tradecraft to individuals as opposed to groups or corporate entities.[34]

In the modern era patents are commonly referred to under the rubric of intellectual property which inherently presupposes some form of property right. Indeed, one working definition of intellectual property is "those property rights which result from the physical manifestation of original thought, either naturally or on compliance with statute."[35] Although this definition was originally developed in the context of copyright law and

---

33. This recognition was in no way unique to Venice or even the other Italian city-states, but the commercial value of encouraging the introduction of new tradecraft into the state was understood there earlier than elsewhere with direct consequences for the development of the patent custom.

34. As Cooper has emphasized, "[o]nly once individual authorship was recognized and legitimized by a society could the granting of a patent or copyright even be conceived." Carolyn C. Cooper, *Making Inventions Patent*, 32 TECH. & CULTURE 837, 838 (1991).

35. BRUCE BUGBEE, GENESIS OF AMERICAN PATENT AND COPYRIGHT LAW at 3 (Washington, D.C. 1967). *Cf.* the definition given in the text accompanying *supra* note 27, and in note 39 *infra*.

literary property, it is apparent that it is broad enough to read on rights arising out of invention and the patent law and indeed has been so interpreted.[36] It is also important to note that this definition refers to property rights which result from, not in, the physical manifestation of the idea or thought. The property rights are intangible or, as the English are wont to say, incorporeal. Finally, the definition encompasses rights which arise inherently or naturally as well as those set by statute. There is reason to return to this latter point because it would become an issue of considerable significance in interpreting the intellectual property clause.

Insofar as can be ascertained, the term "intellectual property" is a creature of the nineteenth and twentieth centuries, and there is no evidence it was actually used any earlier.[37] Nonetheless, it is not uncommon to see it used in modern works in referring to patents and copyrights of the seventeenth and eighteenth centuries and even earlier.[38] It is unfortunate to see it in the context of the early English patent custom because, despite arguments to the contrary, the custom did not involve the creation of a property right at common law.[39]

---

36. BUGBEE, *supra* note 35, at 4.

37. BUGBEE, *supra* note 35, at 3–4, notes the existence of a book published in 1878 entitled *Thoughts on the Nature of Intellectual Property and Its Importance to the State* which is a defense of the United States patent system as it then existed. Lubar cites an earlier work entitled *Law of Intellectual Property* published in 1855 which in essence is a strong attack on the antebellum United States patent system. *See* Steven Lubar, *The Transformation of Antebellum Patent Law*, 32 TECH. & CULTURE 932, 953 (1991).

38. *See, e.g.,* CHRISTINE MACLEOD, INVENTING THE INDUSTRIAL REVOLUTION, THE ENGLISH PATENT SYSTEM, 1660–1800, at 197–99 (Cambridge 1988); BUGBEE, *supra* note 35, at 12; Frank D. Prager, *Historic Background and Foundation of American Patent Law*, 5 AM. J. LEG. HIST. 309, 314 (1961); Frank D. Prager, *The Early Growth and Influence of Intellectual Property*, 34 J. PAT. OFF. SOC'Y 106 (1952); Frank D. Prager, *A History of Intellectual Property From 1545 to 1787*, 26 J. PAT. OFF. SOC'Y 711 (1944).

39. Prager was a leading exponent of the view that the concept of intellectual property in the form of patents and copyrights had existed from medieval times. See, for example, his articles referenced in note 38, *supra*. Indeed, he sought to define intellectual property as

> the idea that authors and inventors have inherent, exclusive rights in their works and inventions; that such rights are not created but only developed or limited by statutes on privileges, patents and copyrights; that such works are not lost by the mere publication of the work or invention, except when explicitly limited in such manner by statutes.

The sixteenth century English view was that property rights were given "by the law of man, not by the law of God or reason" and therefore the state could determine the limitations under which property could be acquired.[40] There was no inherent right to property. It is thus not surprising that there was no common law in favor of either patents or copyrights before or during the reign of Elizabeth I.[41] Patents were issued under the royal prerogative as a grant of a special privilege conferred by the crown upon the patentee which did not belong to the citizen as of common right.[42]

There are differing perspectives as to the legal nature of the privilege conferred by a patent during the sixteenth and seventeenth centuries. It has been argued that a patent was a franchise and since franchises were originally deemed to be special privileges they were not at first considered as property.[43] An alternative view is that the early patent grant was closely analogous to a franchise, and if it had arisen at an earlier stage in the history of the law it would most likely have been regarded as a franchise. However, at the time that patents came to be recognized as objects of property, franchises were "an obsolescent and decadent class of property."[44] This suggests that the franchise had in fact come to be recognized as a form of property, albeit one conferring limited rights.

Be that as it may, by the eighteenth century patents and copyrights had come to be classed as choses in action.[45] In English law a chose in action is

---

34 J. PAT. OFF. SOC'Y at 108. Clearly, under a definition of this type, the early English patents must be construed as involving property rights. But, as pointed out by E. G. Inlow in *The Patent Grant* (Baltimore 1950) at 34, neither the Statute of Monopolies nor Lord Coke, its foremost early commentator, made any mention of property rights in the context of letters patent. He also notes that none of the common-law cases decided to 1800 "mentioned or implied the fact that the patentee held a property in his patent." *Id.*

40. WILLIAM HOLDSWORTH, 4 A HISTORY OF ENGLISH LAW at 316 (London 1932).
41. Frank D. Prager, *A History of Intellectual Property From 1545 to 1787*, 26 J. PAT. OFF. SOC'Y 711, 740 (1944).
42. *See, e.g.,* E. G. INLOW, THE PATENT GRANT at 59 (Baltimore 1950); BUGBEE, *supra* note 35, at 35; H. G. FOX, MONOPOLIES: A STUDY OF THE HISTORY AND FUTURE OF THE PATENT MONOPOLY at 192 (Toronto 1947).
43. INLOW, *id.* at 60.
44. WILLIAM HOLDSWORTH, 7 A HISTORY OF ENGLISH LAW at 530 (London 1932).
45. *Id.* at 529–30.

"a known legal expression used to describe all personal rights of property which can only be claimed or enforced by action."[46] The law of contract was developing, and the legal concept of a chose in action had been extended to cover the documents which evidenced or proved the existence of such a right of action. Since many of these documents were effectively evidence of title to intangible property, it was easy to include in this category patent rights and copyrights which were the most obvious type of intangible property.[47]

If there was no common law right to a patent at the time of Elizabeth I, did such a right subsequently accrue at any time during the seventeenth and eighteenth centuries?[48] The short and simple answer is that neither by statutory provision nor by court decision was an inventor conceded to have a common law right to a patent by reason of his invention.[49] Insofar as can be ascertained, the issue seems never to have been addressed in any of the common law court opinions involving patents of invention issued in the eighteenth century.[50] The Statute of Monopolies sanctioned the use of the royal prerogative to grant patents of monopoly for invention, but it did not create a right to such a patent nor did it specify any procedure by which the inventor might obtain the privilege of the grant or defend it against infringers.[51]

Arguments for a common-law right to a patent are predicated almost entirely on copyright law as it developed in the seventeenth and eighteenth centuries.[52] The nature of these arguments is briefly reviewed in the discussion of copyright.[53] In the eighteenth century, the distinction

---

46. *Id.* at 516. Although uncertain of the legal context, Adam Smith wrote in 1762 that "the property one has in a book he has written or a machine he has invented, which continues by a patent in this country for fourteen years, is actually a real right." Quoted by MACLEOD, *supra* note 38, at 198.

47. HOLDSWORTH, *supra* note 44, at 516, 530.

48. Phrased somewhat differently, did the crown have a common law duty, along with the common law power, to issue a patent for invention? *See* Frank D. Prager, *Historic Background and Foundation of American Patent Law,* 5 AM. J. LEG. HIST. 309, 314 (1961).

49. *See, e.g.,* LYMAN RAY PATTERSON, COPYRIGHT IN HISTORICAL PERSPECTIVE at 195 (Nashville 1968); Prager, *supra* note 41, at 739.

50. But it was raised and discussed in the context of copyright. *See infra* text accompanying notes 151–158.

51. PATTERSON, *supra* note 49; BUGBEE, *supra* note 35, at 39.

52. *See, e.g.,* Prager, *supra* note 41, at 740–41; INLOW, *supra* note 42, at 64–68; MACLEOD, *supra* note 38, at 197–99.

53. For the nature of the arguments for and against, see text accompanying notes 164 and 165 *infra*.

between patents and copyright was in the process of being worked out and was as yet unclear. Indeed, early on in the century it appeared that the crown and its law officers had difficulty distinguishing between the two, at least in the context of determining property rights.[54]

D. Patents Prior to 1787

The concept of the state granting some form of exclusive rights in their inventions to inventors, which would ultimately come to commonly be known as patents of monopoly, originated first in Italy, primarily in Venice, during the early part of the fifteenth century. During the sixteenth century it spread relatively rapidly, in much the same form, to Germany, France, the Netherlands, and England.[55]

The European patent custom arose out of the desire of rulers to encourage the development of new industries within their realms.[56] There were basically two ways in which this might be done, i.e., by importation

---

54. INLOW, *supra* note 42, at 64. Citing the argument of Attorney General Thurlow in Tonson v. Collins, H. Bl. 301, 321 (K.B. 1760), in which he ridicules the notion of any distinction between property rights granted to authors and those of inventors.

55. *See generally* C. F. Greenstreet, *History of Patents in* MAINLY ON PATENTS 1 (F. Liebesny ed. 1972); H. Pohlmann, *The Inventor's Right in Early German Law*, 43 J. PAT. OFF. SOC'Y 121 (1961) (F. D. Prager trans.); G. Mandich, *Venetian Origins of Inventors' Rights*, 42 J. PAT. OFF. SOC'Y 378 (1960) (F. D. Prager trans.); R. A. Klitzke, *Historical Background of the English Patent Law*, 41 J. PAT. OFF. SOC'Y 615 (1959); F. D. Prager, *The Early Growth and Influence of Intellectual Property*, 34 J. PAT. OFF. SOC'Y 106 (1952); G. Mandich, *Venetian Patents (1450–1550)*, 30 J. PAT. OFF. SOC'Y 166 (1948) (F. D. Prager trans.); M. Frumkin, *The Origin of Patents*, 27 J. PAT. OFF. SOC'Y 143 (1945); F. D. Prager, *A History of Intellectual Property from 1545 to 1787*, 26 J. PAT. OFF. SOC'Y 711 (1944); E. W. Hulme, *The History of the Patent System Under the Prerogative and at Common Law*, 16 L. Q. REV. 44 (1900). *Cf.* P. J. Federico, *Origin and Early History of Patents*, 11 J. PAT. OFF. SOC'Y 292 (1929), which, while acknowledging that Venice must have had a fairly well-developed patent system, also states that nothing is known about it. He indicates that at that time (1929) knowledge of the history of the grant of patent monopolies on the continent is meager and limited to few details. Thanks to Prager, a great deal more would become known about the early development of the continental patent custom.

56. What came to be known in England as "native manufactures" (*see, e.g.,* HOLDSWORTH, 4 A HISTORY OF ENGLISH LAW at 344), and would be known in the Constitution as "useful arts."

of knowledge of new industries into the realm or by invention within the realm.[57] Initially, importation of new knowledge appears to have been the favored mode[58] if for no other reason than that existing trade knowledge suggested certain industries practiced abroad might be profitable if worked within the realm. The desirability of a particular foreign industry was known, or at least could be strongly inferred, from the profitability of the trade in its product or products. New invention might result in new industries, but this was more speculative. It was to be encouraged to be sure, but at first the safer road seemed to be to promote importation.[59]

In 1787 there were three sources of precedent that the Framers would have looked to in deciding whether to provide authority in the Constitution for the granting of some form of limited exclusive or monopoly right by the state (meaning the national government) to authors and inventors with respect to their writings and discoveries. These were: (a) the extant practice in Great Britain with regard to the issuance of both patents and copyright; (b) the colonial practice regarding what would now be termed patents; and (c) the practice of the various states during the Confederacy with regard to "patents" and copyright.

It was only near the end of the eighteenth century—indeed at the very time that the Framers were considering the question—that the term "patent" (short for letters patent) began to have a precise and technical meaning, i.e., a grant of monopoly power by the state over the commercial

---

57. The European patent custom, including that of England, did not distinguish between the two. The concept of novelty in its modern sense of new or original or never before used did not exist. For this reason, commentators who try to distinguish patents of monopoly for invention from those for importation, for example, and seek to apply the modern definition of novelty to invention in the European patent custom as it developed run into considerable difficulty in attempting to ascertain just when patents for "invention" were first granted. *See, e.g.,* BUGBEE, *supra* note 35, at 12–43.

58. In principle this might be done by sending out native artisans to learn the craft but there was always the problem of the reception of such artisans in a foreign country as well as the fact that most artisans were extremely reluctant to pass on their tradecraft to others outside of a guild. Indeed, in many states it was illegal for them to do so. Accordingly, the favored approach was somehow to induce foreign artisans to bring the new trade or industry and practice it for a sufficient time for it to become known and established.

59. For a discussion of the early continental patent custom, see E. C. Walterscheid, *The Early Evolution of the United States Patent Law: Antecedents (Part1),* 76 J. PAT. & TRADEMARK OFF. SOC'Y 697, 705–15 (1994).

exploitation of an invention for a limited time.[60] Prior to this time, the meaning attached to letters patent was much broader.

The kings of England did much of their state business by means of charters, letters patent, and letters close. At least initially, charters were used for their more solemn acts. Letters patent were used to set forth their public directives, of whatever sort, whereas letters close were used to provide private instructions to individuals. Royal charters and letters patent often were similar in content and differed only in their form.[61]

Separate records called "rolls"[62] were kept for these three types of state papers. Unlike the Close Rolls, the Patent Rolls contain a wide variety of documents intended to be open to public inspection. Initially, these documents related primarily to the royal prerogative, the revenue of the realm, and the various branches of judicature. But they also came to include documents relating to foreign affairs as well as grants and confirmations of office and privileges, pardons, charters, proclamations, and commissions.[63] As stated by Blackstone:

> The king's grants are also matter[s] of public record. . . . These grants, whether of land, honors, liberties, franchises, or aught besides, are contained in charters, or letters *patent,* that is, open letters, *literae patentes:* so called, because they are not sealed up, but exposed to open view, with the great seal pendant at the bottom; and are usually directed or addressed by the king to all his subjects at large.[64]

---

60. MACLEOD, *supra* note 38, at 10.
61. HOLDSWORTH, 2 A HISTORY OF ENGLISH LAW at 182. He states that the royal charters were addressed to the archbishops, bishops, earls, barons, etc. and were executed in the presence of witnesses, whereas letters patent were addressed "to all to whom these presents come" and were generally witnessed by the king himself. *Id.* at n.1.
62. From the fact that they literally were recorded on long strips of vellum or parchment initially and stored in rolls. As stated by Jeremy: "The patents, written and drawn on vellum, were sewn end to end to form rolls, each containing several dozen patents, the number depending on their length. Long patents before 1829 ran to twenty or thirty skins of descriptive matter, with perhaps fifteen to twenty skins of drawings." *See* DAVID J. JEREMY, TRANSATLANTIC INDUSTRIAL REVOLUTION: THE DIFFUSION OF TEXTILE TECHNOLOGIES BETWEEN BRITAIN AND AMERICA, 1790–1830S, at 45, 47 (1981). In Great Britain to this day, when a patent is officially made of record, it is said to be "enrolled."
63. HOLDSWORTH, *supra* note 61, at n.2.
64. WILLIAM BLACKSTONE, 2 COMMENTARIES ON THE LAWS OF ENGLAND at 316–17 (Oxford 1768).

It is the royal grants and confirmation of privilege by letters patent that are of particular interest here, for these were used as the vehicle for the crown to grant privileges to inventors concerning their inventions.[65]

The Statute of Monopolies[66] enacted in 1623 is frequently stated to be the legal foundation for the English patent system. Constitutional historians view the statute as the culmination of a long struggle between Parliament and the crown to place curbs on the royal prerogative.[67] For the purposes of this work, it is primarily of interest because in the eighteenth century it was the only statutory basis for the English patent practice.

In most respects, the statute simply was a recapitulation in statutory form of the existing common law. The first section declares as contrary to the law of the realm and utterly void, all monopolies, grants, licenses, and letters patent theretofore made or granted, or thereafter to be made or granted, to any person or persons, bodies politic or corporate, of or for the sole buying, selling, making, working, or using of anything within the realm. Section 2 provides that the force and validity of all monopolies, and all commissions, grants, licenses, charters, letters patent, proclamations, etc. tending toward monopoly, shall be determined in accordance with common law. Section 3 provides that no person, body politic, or corporation may use or exercise any monopoly right granted by any commission, grant, license,

---

65. For a detailed look at the evolution of the English patent practice as it existed prior to 1787, see E. C. Walterscheid, *The Early Evolution of the United States Patent Law: Antecedents (Part 2),* 76 J. PAT. & TRADEMARK OFF. SOC'Y 849 (1994); *(Part 3),* 77 J. PAT. & TRADEMARK OFF. SOC'Y 771, 847 (1995).
66. 21 James I, c. 3; VII Statutes at Large 255. The term "monopoly" first came into use in England during the sixteenth century. *See* H. G. FOX, MONOPOLIES: A STUDY OF THE HISTORY AND FUTURE OF THE PATENT MONOPOLY at 24–26 (Toronto 1947). Cornering the market in a particular commodity so as to control the price of that commodity, which was considered a monopoly practice, was variously known as "engrossing," "regrating," or "forestalling," and was generally an offence at common law. FOX, *id.* at 21–22, n.6. For a discussion of the nuances of these terms and of the law as set forth in an early patent treatise, see R. GODSON, A PRACTICAL TREATISE ON THE LAW OF PATENTS FOR INVENTION at 17–41 (London 1823).
67. *Cf.* Hulme's statement that

> [t]he choice of language employed by the framers of this statute appears to have been dictated not so much by a desire to restrain unduly the exercise of the prerogative as to avoid lending a semblance of legality to grants which in the future might be exercised to the public detriment.

See E. Wyndham Hulme, *The History of the Patent System Under the Prerogative and at Common Law,* 12 L. Q. REV. at 151–52 (1896).

charter, letters patent, proclamation etc. Section 4 grants any party aggrieved by a monopoly the right to recover treble damages and double costs in the common law courts. Sections 5 through 14 set forth a variety of exceptions to the mandate of the first section. Of specific interest here is section 6 which provides that

> any declaration before mentioned shall not extend to any letters patent and grants of privilege for the term of fourteen years or under, hereafter to be made, of the sole working or making in any manner of new manufactures within this realm, to the true and first inventor and inventors of such manufactures, which others at the time of making such letters patent and grants shall not use, so as also they be not contrary to law, nor mischievous to the State; the said fourteen years to be accounted from the date of the first letters patents, or grant of such privilege hereafter to be made, but the same shall be of such force as they should be if this Act had never been made, and of none other.

It was this language which sanctioned the extant English patent practice in 1787 and which provided the example for the patent provision of the intellectual property clause.

During the reign of Elizabeth I and James I, the common law established that novelty was a sine qua non for the granting of patents of invention.[68] This common law view was incorporated into the Statute of Monopolies. At the time the Constitution was drafted, novelty was considered to be synonymous with new, but new in what sense? This was not an academic question, for the interpretation given to novelty was not static and indeed had changed markedly from the advent of the English patent custom in the late sixteenth century to the first development of the United States patent law at the end of the eighteenth century.

---

68. Darcy v. Allin (also referred to as "Allen or "Allein"), 72 Eng. Rep. 830 (Moore 671), 74 Eng. Rep. 1131 (Noy 173), 11 Coke Rep. 86, 1 Abbott's P.C. 1 (K.B. 1602); The Clothworkers of Ipswich, Godbolt, 252, 78 Eng. Rep. 147 (K.B. 1615) ("[b]ut if a man hath brought in a new invention and a new trade within the kingdom, in peril of his life, and consumption of his estate or stock, &c., or if a man hath made a new discovery of any thing, in such cases the King of his grace and favour, in recompense of his costs and travail, may grant by charter unto him, that he shall use such trade or trafique for a certain time, because at first the people of the kingdom are ignorant, and have not the knowledge or skill to use it: but when that patent is expired, the King cannot make a new grant thereof: for when the trade is become common, and others have been found apprentices in the same trade, there is no reason that such should be forbidden to use it").

It is useful to remember that the early English patent custom arose out of a desire to create new industry in the realm primarily by importation and only secondarily by what would now be termed invention.[69] As a consequence, novelty—and hence patentability—was predicated on whether the subject matter of the grant was presently being worked in England. It mattered not whether the art or manufacture was known or practiced elsewhere or even whether it had previously been practiced or worked in England. Novelty thus had a very broad connotation. Originality was only peripherally involved, and the subject matter was considered new if it had not been worked in England within recent memory. The Statute of Monopolies did not change this despite much later American belief that its literal language[70] was such as to indicate that it had.[71]

---

69. For a more detailed discussion of novelty in the English patent custom, see E. C. Walterscheid, *Novelty in Historical Perspective*, 75 J. PAT. & TRADEMARK OFF. SOC'Y 689, 692–706 (1993).

70. In particular, the reference to "the true and first inventor or inventors."

71. In 1826 an American judge gave what was undoubtedly a general American view at the time:

> The received construction then, of the statute of [Monopolies], appears to me, to involve gross absurdities, and to be a palpable perversion of the terms and plain meaning of the act. It is a departure from its spirit, and defeats its avowed object. It is everywhere said that this prerogative power was left in the crown, for the purpose of rewarding the personal merit of ingenious men,—to stimulate their inventive powers. But this alleged object of the act is at war with its practical application and places the plagiarist and original inventor upon the same footing. This construction . . . has its origin, I am constrained to believe, in the policy of the government. Expediency and the policy of the state have, no doubt, contributed to uphold it. It has been uniformly adhered to, and is everywhere laid down as established law; but I have nowhere seen it supported as the true and grammatical construction of the language of the act. The policy may be good. It is not that I mean to condemn. But it ought to have been authorized and supported by a legislative provision, and not founded on a judicial perversion of the language of the act.

Thompson v. Haight, 23 F. Cas. 1040, 1044 (No. 13,956) (S.D.N.Y. 1826). Here the learned judge, while recognizing that a policy of the crown was to encourage new manufactures within the realm, either by importation or by invention, fails to accept that such was the policy at the time the Statute of Monopolies was enacted and that such was the intent of the Statute, regardless of grammatical niceties, but instead assumes that the only purpose was to reward original inventors.

The first common law case interpreting the statutory language had to do with the issue of novelty and whether a manufacture imported into England could be patented. In *Edgeberry v. Stephens,* decided in 1691, the court held that

> if the invention be new in England, a patent may be granted though the thing was practiced beyond the sea before; for the statute speaks of new manufactures within this realm; so that, if they be new here, it is within the statute; for the act intended to encourage new devices, useful to the kingdom, and whether learned by travel or by study it is the same thing.[72]

In other words, novelty was not affected by what was known or used outside England, and "true and first inventor" did not per se mean the original inventor. This remained the common law interpretation in 1787, but it would not be accepted in the United States.

Even so, in the second half of the eighteenth century, a significant change occurred in the common law definition of novelty. It began with the recognition in 1766 in *Dollond's Case* that a secret working within the realm would not preclude a patent to one who first publicly disclosed the invention.[73] Implicit in this holding was that it was the disclosure to the public or at least those working in the trade rather than the working itself that should be the consideration for the grant. In 1778 in *Liardet v. Johnson* this was made explicit. Henceforth under the common law, prior publication as well as prior public working could be used to show lack of novelty.[74] As is shown, this change in the interpretation of novelty, or more precisely of what constitutes an anticipation which shows a lack of novelty, would be incorporated into the American patent law, but not without interpretational difficulty. Although it was not immediately apparent, what the American law would not accept was the English interpretation of the limited relationship of originality to novelty.

Sometime after the beginning of the eighteenth century the English law officers[75] began to require a written specification as a condition of the patent grant and thereafter came to make this a routine requirement.[76]

---

72. 2 Salk. 447, 1 Abbott's P.C. 8 (K.B. 1691).
73. E. Wyndham Hulme, *On the History of the Patent Law in the Seventeenth and Eighteenth Centuries,* 18 L. Q. REV. at 283 (1902).
74. HOLDSWORTH, 11 A HISTORY OF ENGLISH LAW at 429.
75. The attorney general and the solicitor general.
76. Hulme indicates that compulsory disclosure, i.e., the requirement for a specification, can be traced back as early as 1716 but the uniform requirement for a specification did not occur until about 1740. *Supra* note 73, at 283. Davies,

When the specification became a formal requirement at common law, it had already been a condition of the grant in actual practice for decades. The importance which the crown placed on the specification can be adduced from the fact that in the first half of the eighteenth century it, through the law officers, caused the validity of the grant to be dependent on the provision within a stated time of a full specification. It did so by making a clause in substantially the following form a routine condition of the grant:

> Provided also that if the said A.B. shall not particularly describe and ascertain the nature of said invention and in what manner the same is to be performed, by an instrument in writing under his hand and seal and cause the same to be inrolled in our High Court of Chancery within six months next and immediately after the date of these our Letters Patent, then these our Letters Patent and all liberties and advantages whatsoever hereby granted shall utterly cease determine and become void.[77]

This clause makes clear that the specification did not have to be a part of the patent petition itself, but was required to be provided within the specified time after the patent was enrolled, or the patent would automatically be voided.

Through much of the eighteenth century few patentees knew what a specification was meant to do.[78] As first introduced, the specification seems

---

however, states that the filing of a specification became customary about 1734. D. Seaborne Davies, *The Early History of the Patent Specification*, 50 L. Q. REV. 86, 89 (1934).

Gomme says that

> when the patent specification became a feature of patent procedure about 1730 . . . it was the Law Officer's business to determine whether and in what precise form reference to it should appear in the Letters Patent, and therefore, very largely the position that the specification was to occupy in patent law in the future.

He goes on to indicate that "the practice became standardized" in 1734, and that the law officers were almost certainly responsible for requiring compulsory disclosure. *See* ALLAN A. GOMME, PATENTS OF INVENTION, ORIGIN AND GROWTH OF THE PATENT SYSTEM IN BRITAIN at 21, 34 (London 1946).

77. GOMME, *supra* note 76, at 25.
78. HAROLD I. DUTTON, THE PATENT SYSTEM AND INVENTIVE ACTIVITY DURING THE INDUSTRIAL REVOLUTION, 1750–1852, at 76 (Manchester 1984). As MacLeod has phrased it

> Since official and judicial guidance was lacking for most of the eighteenth century, it is doubtful whether patentees had any clear idea what the

primarily to have been intended to show the confines of the patentee's monopoly rights and the limits of the field others were prohibited from entering.[79] But "throughout the century, specifications were enrolled which could in no way have enabled those skilled in the art to carry out the invention, and which would have been valueless in an infringement action."[80] Simply put, they could be as informative or as evasive as the patentee saw fit.[81]

Nonetheless, as the century progressed, an at times subtle but nonetheless clear transition with regard to the crown's views on the consideration for the patent grant occurred. Specifically, the crown came increasingly to recognize that working the invention was no longer the consideration for the grant, but that instead wider dissemination of new skills to the public in general should be the desideratum. Just as importantly, the common law courts began to voice the same view.[82] In 1787 it was argued that "[t]he consideration, which the patentee gives for his monopoly, is the benefit the public are to derive from his invention after his patent is expired: and that

<hr>

function of a specification was or how full or accurate it ought to be. Like most other things about the system, it was left to the patentee's discretion. MACLEOD, *supra* note 38, at 50.

79. GOMME, *supra* note 76, at 26. Or as Hulme put it, "with the view of making the grant more certain." E. Wyndham Hulme, *On the Consideration of the Patent Grant, Past and Present*, 13 L. Q. REV. at 317 (1897). But Adams & Averley have challenged this view with the question, "[W]hy . . . are so many specifications vague and evasive if patentees were trying to make their grants more certain?" *See* John N. Adams & Gwen Averley, *The Patent Specification: The Role of Liardet v. Johnson*, 7 J. LEGAL HIST. 156, 161 (1986).

80. Adams & Averley, *supra* note 79, at 160.

81. MACLEOD, *supra* note 38, at 49.

82. The first reported common law patent case in the eighteenth century, *Dollond's Case*, more correctly styled *Dollond v. Champneys*, decided in 1766, seems to have anticipated this trend. *See supra* note 73 and accompanying text. Hulme states that this case "established that proof of priority of invention without publication will not invalidate a later patent to an inventor who has disclosed the invention." *Supra* note 73, at 283. It is not clear whether by "publication" Hulme meant also public use, but in a later article he states that "[t]he evidence of prior use by the manufacture and sale of [the first inventor's] object glasses was set aside." *See* E. Wyndham Hulme, *Privy Council Law and Practice of Letters Patent for Invention from the Restoration to 1794*, 33 L. Q. REV. at 292 (1917). MacLeod provides additional support for the view that it was lack of public knowledge of the prior invention which caused the later patent to be upheld, commenting "it was decided that the earlier production of such lenses did not obstruct the patent since it had not been taken beyond the laboratory." MACLEOD, *supra* note 38, at 70.

benefit is secured to them by means of a specification of the invention."[83] By 1795 Justice Buller could state unequivocally that "[t]he specification is the price the patentee is to pay for the monopoly."[84] In essence, there was a change in perception—from viewing the patent as a contract between the crown and the patentee to viewing it as a "social contract" between the patentee and society.[85]

It was in 1778 in *Liardet v. Johnson*[86] that the common law came to definitely and finally lay aside "the doctrine of the instruction of the public by means of the personal effects and supervision of the grantee . . . in favor of the novel theory that this function belongs to the patent specification."[87] There were actually two trials in *Liardet,* but from the perspective of the Framers the most important aspect was Lord Mansfield's charge to the jury[88] during the second trial[89]:

> There are three grounds that must be made out to your satisfaction: the first is . . . that the defendant did use that which the plaintiff claims to be his invention. If he did use it, the next point is . . . whether the invention was new or old, within the sense of the Act of Parliament [i.e., the Statute of Monopolies]. The third point is whether the specification is such as instructs others to make it. For the condition of giving encouragement is this: that you must specify upon record your invention in such a way as shall teach an artist, when the term is out, to make it—and to make it as well by your directions: for then at the end of the term, the public shall have benefit of it. The inventor has the benefit of it during the term, and the public have the benefit after. But if . . .

---

83. Turner v. Winter, 1 T. R. at 605, 99 Eng. Rep. at 1276 (1787).
84. Boulton v. Bull, 2 H. Bl. at 472, 126 Eng. Rep. at 656 (1795).
85. DUTTON, *supra* note 78, at 75. It would not be, however, until early in the nineteenth century that the common law courts would begin to expressly speak in terms of a patent being a contract.
86. The case is not officially reported. What is known about it comes to us from contemporaneous pamphlets and newspaper articles as well as notes of judges. Perhaps the most detailed information about it is provided in JAMES OLDHAM, 1 THE MANSFIELD MANUSCRIPTS AND THE GROWTH OF ENGLISH LAW IN THE EIGHTEENTH CENTURY at 748–57 (Chapel Hill 1992).
87. Hulme, *supra* note 79, at 318.
88. *Cf.* Adams & Averley who state that the case is primarily of interest for the way the outcome turned on the opinion of expert witnesses. *Supra* note 79, at 171.
89. Although Hulme stresses the importance of *Liardet* to the history of patent law, it is not at all clear that he was aware that there were actually two trials in this case and that the instructions to the jury that were subsequently published were for the second trial. *See* Adams & Averley, *supra* note 79, at n.175.

the specification of the composition gives no proportions, there is an end of his patent. . . . I have determined, several cases here, the specification must state, where there is a composition, the proportions; so that any other artist may be able to make it, and it must be a lesson and direction to him by which to make it. If the invention be of another sort, to be done by mechanism, they must describe it in a way that an artist must be able to do it.[90]

This is one of the earliest statements by an English judge that a specification must be enabling, i.e., it must teach one skilled in the art to which it pertains how to make and use the invention. It also establishes that the quid pro quo which the state receives for the patent grant is that enabling disclosure for which the public shall ultimately have the benefit. These principles would become foundation stones for the new American patent law but not without interpretational difficulties.

Several aspects of the English patent practice would have been noteworthy to the Framers. First of all, it was an exception to the general ban on monopolies, but one which was considered to be in the interest of the public at large because it was for the purpose of introducing new trades or industry into the realm. Secondly, the practice was entirely at the discretion of the crown, i.e., a patent was the creature of the royal prerogative.[91] The rights secured by the patent could be protected at common law, but there was no common law right to a patent. Nonetheless, by the second half of the eighteenth century the crown was routinely granting patents if the formalities were met and the requisite fees paid.

Thirdly, and perhaps most importantly, patents were beginning to be perceived as playing an increasingly important role in the industrial development of Great Britain. Patents of monopoly for invention had issued in England for more than 200 years. The official series begins from the year

---

90. Hulme, *supra* note 73, at 285.
91. As stated by Hindmarch in 1846, "inventors are *never entitled as of right* to letters patent, granting them the sole use of their inventions, but they must obtain them from the Crown by petition, and *as a matter of grace and favour* . . . " (emphasis in the original). *See* WILLIAM M. HINDMARCH, A TREATISE ON THE LAW RELATIVE TO PATENT PRIVILEGES FOR THE SOLE USE OF INVENTIONS at 2 (London 1846).

1617, although patents had issued for at least fifty years earlier.[92] Up to the Restoration in 1660 there are some 130 patents in the official series. The number of patents listed in each decade from 1660 to 1800 are[93]:

1660–1669	36	1710–1719	38	1760–1769	205
1670–1679	50	1720–1729	89	1770–1779	294
1680–1689	53	1730–1739	56	1780–1789	477
1690–1699	105	1740–1749	82	1790–1799	647
1700–1709	22	1750–1759	92		

The most obvious aspect of this data is the tremendous upsurge in the number of patents issued from 1760 onwards.[94]

A patent custom involving exclusive grants of privilege for limited terms with respect to invention and importation existed in a number of the American colonies and states prior to the drafting of the Constitution. That custom developed in parallel with that in England, albeit on a much more sporadic and less uniform scale. In principle, there were two sources of authority for the grant of monopoly patents of invention in the colonies, the royal prerogative as in England and the powers invested in the royal governors. Letters patent covering the American colonies in whole or in part were issued in England from time to time but they were not commonplace. There is little or no evidence that royal governors issued patents of monopoly. Instead the patent custom in the colonies—such as it was— came to be predicated largely on the activities of local assemblies and legislatures which, "while not formally invested with such sovereign power,

---

92. *See, e.g.,* Davies, *supra* note 76, at 86 n.1; Gomme, *supra* note 76, at 25. Both authors note that compilation of the official series did not actually commence until 1853. Gomme suggests that the official series may not be absolutely complete for the period that it covers and acknowledges that it lacks the hundred or so patents granted before 1617 and the eighteen patents known to have been granted during the Commonwealth and Protectorate, i.e., during 1649–1660. Gomme, *supra* note 76, at 37–38. Hulme points out that the official series is far from complete for the early years of the Restoration period. *See* Hulme, *supra* note 82, at 63.

93. Data taken from MACLEOD, *supra* note 38, at 150.

94. Holdsworth notes that "[t]he number of patents taken out between 1617 and 1760 was smaller than the number of patents taken out in the course of the following twenty-five years." 11 A HISTORY OF ENGLISH LAW at 426, n.1.

readily assumed the authority in practice."[95] After the Revolution, the state assemblies and legislatures—taking up where their colonial predecessors had left off—continued to exercise this self-assumed authority.[96]

These grants of exclusivity were private legislative acts of the assemblies or legislatures. It was precisely because they were private acts and not grants under the royal prerogative that it is something of a misnomer to call them patents as such, i.e., they were literally not letters patent, although what they had in common with English letters patent was the purported grant of exclusivity within the geographic area covered by the grant.

For a variety of reasons these exclusive grants were never sought in the colonies on anything like the scale that occurred in England.[97] The major reason was that the colonies were predominantly agrarian societies with never more than ten percent of the population engaged in manufacturing of any kind.[98] Such manufacturing as existed was mostly for local consumption and directed to supplying the essentials required for the maintenance of the community. There was no wide industrial base nor any extended markets over which the patent monopoly could be enforced. Another major disincentive was that there was very little evidence that it was worth the time, effort, and cost involved.[99] Competition among tradesmen and artisans in the

---

95. INLOW, *supra* note 42, at 36.
96. During the period between the Declaration of Independence and the ratification of the U.S. Constitution, each state had ratified its own constitution, and in some instances more than one constitution. Unlike the later federal Constitution, these state constitutions said not a word about giving authority to the legislative assembly to grant any form of limited-term exclusive rights in their writings and discoveries to authors and inventors.
97. At the time of the American Revolution nearly 1000 English patents had been issued. Because of the lack of adequate records, it is difficult to know with any degree of precision the number of monopoly grants actually issued in the various colonies which came to be included in the United States, but it is unlikely that it was much in excess of 50.
98. INLOW, *supra* note 42, at 37; P. J. Federico, *Colonial Monopolies and Patents*, 11 J. PAT. OFF. SOC'Y 358 (1929).
99. INLOW, *supra* note 42, at 38. Little is known about the actual costs and administrative complexities involved in obtaining patents in the various colonies. Clearly, these varied from colony to colony, but it is reasonable to assume that they never approached those in England. Nonetheless both cost and administrative requirements must have been adverse factors, because there was always less available specie in the colonies than in England and the legislatures only met at certain times of the year. Inlow also suggests that considerable graft was involved, which likely served to convince more than one would-be patentee that the game was not worth the candle. *Id.*

individual colonies was never on the scale that existed in England, and there were few examples to illustrate the worth of a patent. One indication of the relatively low value attached to patents is the fact that no record has been found of any litigation involving colonial patents of monopoly for invention in any colonial or English court.[100]

No state ever enacted a general patent statute ensuring the right of inventors to obtain exclusive rights in their inventions for some limited period of time. One state, however, did address the issue but in the context of its copyright statute. In 1784 South Carolina enacted a copyright law which contained the following clause: "The Inventors of useful machines shall have a like exclusive privilege of making or vending their machines for the like term of fourteen years, under the same privileges and restrictions hereby granted to, and imposed on, the authors of books."[101] No provision was made for any administrative procedure for implementing this clause so that a special act of the legislature was still necessary for the granting of each patent.[102]

Following the cessation of hostilities with Great Britain, there was a significant renewal of patenting activity. In particular, states which as colonies had little or no experience with the patent custom now found themselves actively granting patents although they were still not usually called such. As with colonial patents, it is difficult to know precisely how many state patents were actually granted prior to 1787, but it is unlikely that the total exceeded twenty.[103]

---

100. Inlow seems to have been the first to point this out with respect to colonial courts. He argues that "[t]o a people more than usually quick to seek recourse in the courts for evils done, this could only indicate a lack of sustained interest anywhere." INLOW, *supra* note 42, at 39. The remarkably litigious nature of the Americans has been noted by more than one historian. Thus, "Americans were constantly racing into court over their claims and counterclaims: it is safe to say that nowhere in the world were ordinary people so at home before judge and jury." COLLIER & COLLIER, *supra* note 12, at 212.
101. BUGBEE, *supra* note 35, at 93, citing PUBLIC LAWS OF THE STATE OF SOUTH-CAROLINA at 333–34 (J. F. Grimke, ed., Philadelphia 1790), and IV STATUTES AT LARGE OF SOUTH CAROLINA (T. Cooper, ed., Columbia S.C. 1837–68) at 618–20.
102. P. J. Federico, *State Patents,* 13 J. PAT. OFF. SOC'Y 166, 167 (1931); *see also* 18 J. PAT. OFF. SOC'Y 43, 44 (1936); BUGBEE, *supra* note 35, at 93.
103. Bugbee is the best extant source, and he lists some twenty-three state patents as having been granted between 1779 and 1791. *See supra* note 35, at 85–103. However, he limits his coverage to so-called patents of invention and excludes patents for importation even though during this period novelty was not

E. Copyright Prior to 1787

Unlike the term "patent," copyright had a literal connotation through the eighteenth century, namely, the right to copy. The rise of copyright is inextricably intertwined with the development of printing. In England it began in the same way as patents of monopoly for invention did, as an adjunct to the royal prerogative, but unlike the patent privilege which prior to 1852 was never treated as a right under the common law, copyright—as the very name implies—developed into something more than a mere privilege. It arguably became an inherent right at common law, and it certainly became a statutory right.

The history of the development of copyright in England, which paralleled that of the development of the patent custom, was nonetheless much more complex. Unlike the monolithic development of the patent custom, prior to 1787 four distinct forms of copyright had come into being. The first of these was the printing patent issued under the royal prerogative. The second was the stationers' copyright issued under a charter granted by the crown. The third was the statutory copyright created by the Statute of Anne in 1710. The fourth, common law copyright, was held to exist in *Millar v. Taylor* decided in 1769. These four forms of copyright show a marked transition primarily through judicial interpretation in the eighteenth century from what began as a protection of publishers' rights to what ultimately became the protection of authors' rights.

In England printing was introduced about 1476,[104] and by 1504 royal grants of privilege with respect to printing had commenced.[105] This practice continued throughout the sixteenth century,[106] with Elizabeth I in particular using it as a means of rewarding her favorites at no expense to the crown. These patent grants of printing monopolies with respect to a particular work or class of works were given to printers and booksellers (who were often one and the same) as well as to courtiers and other royal

---

precluded merely because the subject matter of the grant had previously been known or practiced elsewhere.

104. *See, e.g.,* PATTERSON, *supra* note 49, at 20; BUGBEE, *supra* note 35, at 49. *Cf.* R. C. DE WOLF, AN OUTLINE OF COPYRIGHT LAW at 2 (Boston 1925) (states that this occurred in 1474); JOHN FEATHER, PUBLISHING, PIRACY AND POLITICS, AN HISTORICAL STUDY OF COPYRIGHT IN BRITAIN at 10 (London 1994) (states the date was 1477).

105. FEATHER, *supra* note 104, at 11.

106. *See, e.g.,* FEATHER, *supra* note 104, at 11–14; BUGBEE, *supra* note 35, at 50; DE WOLF, *supra* note 104, at 2.

favorites who were obviously not printers in their own right and who farmed out the grant to a printer, for an appropriate fee of course.[107] Nowhere was there any recognition in these monopoly grants that the author might have property rights with respect to the works being printed.[108] The first known copyright to an author was issued in 1530 for seven years.[109]

In much the same manner as other patents of monopoly, these printing monopolies came to be looked upon with suspicion, and they gradually came to be restricted to the printing of books over which the crown claimed control by virtue of its authority as head of both state and church. In particular, the rise of printed matter threatened the predominance of the sovereign in both the political and religious arenas by for the first time giving a ready avenue for the wide dissemination of free speculation and criticism with respect to the existing order. It is not surprising therefore that developing a mechanism for the control of printed matter became a matter of some urgency for the crown.

Very early in the fifteenth century a craft guild was formed of those who wrote text letters and those who served as limners or illustrators as well as those who bound and sold books.[110] During this century those who made or dealt in books and were associated with this craft guild gradually came to be known as stationers. With the rise in printing in the latter part of the century the stationers naturally came to be those who bought from the printers the books which they bound and sold. In the order of things, the craft of printing quickly came to be allied to that of the stationers.[111]

In 1556 the crown chartered the company of stationers and granted it general supervision of the trades of printing, binding, publishing, and dealing

---

107. The commentators disagree as to who was most favored by these printing patents. Thus, for example, De Wolf states that "[s]ometimes they were given as a reward for meritorious enterprise to the printer, but oftener as a cheap way of benefiting some courtier or dependent," *supra* note 104, at 2–3. Holdsworth, on the other hand, states that in many instances these grants were made "to printers who were impoverished, owing to the fact that the most profitable copyrights had become property of the booksellers." *See* 6 A HISTORY OF ENGLISH LAW at 366.
108. DE WOLF, *supra* note 104, at 2. *Cf.* Feather's suggestion that "if a living author were the beneficiary of such grants, that was a purely coincidental consequence." *See* FEATHER, *supra* note 104, at 14.
109. BUGBEE, *supra* note 35, at 50.
110. Patterson states that in 1403 the mayor and aldermen of London granted a petition by such individuals to form a guild. *See supra* note 49, at 29.
111. HOLDSWORTH, 6 A HISTORY OF ENGLISH LAW at 362–63; PATTERSON, *supra* note 49, at 35–36.

in books.[112] In return for this right of supervision, the stationers agreed to royal censorship, supervision, regulation, and licensing of books to be printed. The stationers' company quickly established a register in which was recorded the works for which copying rights or privileges had been obtained. Unless a printer or publisher had obtained a printing patent from the crown, authorizing the printing of a particular book or class of books, the work to be printed had to be registered with the stationers' company.

This system of registry ultimately would result in the unintended and certainly unanticipated (at least by the crown) legal argument for a common law right of copyright. By registration the printer or publisher got an essentially exclusive copying right which in essence gave an incontestable title to the work being copied, i.e., printed. It gave substance to the idea of literary property which came to be known as copyright. The copyright was protected by imposition of penalties for infringement. It could be assigned, sold, settled, given in trust, and had all the various attributes of property. Moreover, unlike the privilege granted with printing patents, because the registration almost never carried a time limitation it came to be regarded as a perpetual form of property.

During the seventeenth century, a variety of ordinances and parliamentary acts were passed for the purposes of regulating printed works.[113] These appeared to tacitly if not specifically acknowledge a common law right of property in copyright.[114] The Statute of Monopolies expressly exempted the printing patents from its ban on monopolies.[115] The victory of Parliament during the interregnum put all the earlier ordinances and proclamations at risk since they were based solely upon the royal prerogative and the actions of the conciliar courts of Star Chamber and High Commission. But as Holdsworth points out, "[a] revolutionary government is peculiarly open to attack and peculiarly sensitive to criticism."[116] The Long Parliament therefore had

---

112. For a discussion of the stationers' company and how it operated, see PATTERSON, *supra* note 49, at 28–41. The content of this and the following paragraph are taken generally from BUGBEE, *supra* note 35, at 50–51, and HOLDSWORTH, 6 A HISTORY OF ENGLISH LAW at 363–65.

113. For a listing of this legislation, see Howard B. Abrams, *The Historic Foundation of American Copyright Law: Exploding the Myth of Common Law Copyright,* 29 WAYNE L. REV. 1119, 1137–38 (1983).

114. *See, e.g.,* BUGBEE, *supra* note 35, at 53; HOLDSWORTH, 6 A HISTORY OF ENGLISH LAW at 367–77.

115. 21 James I c. 3, § 10 states that the Statute does not extend to "any letters patent or grants of privilege heretofore made or hereafter to be made of, for, or concerning printing."

116. HOLDSWORTH, 6 A HISTORY OF ENGLISH LAW at 370.

a vested interest in pursuing policies similar to that of the crown when it came to the regulation of printing.

So too did the stationers for they stood to lose everything if unlicensed and unregulated printing were to prevail. In their petition to Parliament for a continuation of their rights, they were remarkably candid, stating: "It [publisher's rights] is not so much a free privilege as a necessary right to Stationers; without which they cannot at all subsist."[117] They went on to present one of the earliest known arguments in English legal history for a property right in ideas and intellectual thought, saying: "There is no good reason apparent why the productions of the Brain should not be assignable, and their interest and possession . . . held as tender in Law, as the right of any Goods and [or] Chattells, whatsoever."[118] Fortunately for them the ordinance enacted by Parliament in 1643 did not reap what they had sowed in presenting this remarkable theory for it largely continued in them the rights granted by the crown. But what they argued, whether in naivete or not, was that property rights in ideas and the expression of those ideas belonged fundamentally and originally to the author and not to the publisher.

The last of the licensing acts vesting rights in the stationers expired in 1694. The last years of the old century and the first years of the new one saw repeated attempts at the enactment of a new licensing act,[119] but it was not until 1710 that what has been denominated as the first true English copyright act[120] became law. This was the famous Statute of Anne.[121] It had two ostensible purposes: (a) to prevent the piracy of printed works, and

---

117. *Id.* at n.5.
118. *Id.* at n.6. *See also* MACLEOD, *supra* note 38, at 197. Holdsworth uses the phrase "goods and chattells" whereas MacLeod quotes it as "goods or chattels."
119. *See, e.g.,* HOLDSWORTH, 6 A HISTORY OF ENGLISH LAW at 375–77; BUGBEE, *supra* note 35, at 53. *See also* FEATHER, *supra* note 104, at 51–52; MARK ROSE, AUTHORS AND OWNERS, THE INVENTION OF COPYRIGHT (Cambridge 1993) at 34–36.
120. *Cf.* Patterson's view that "[t]he Statute of Anne was [not] the first copyright act in England." *See supra* note 49, at 143.
121. 8 Anne, c. 19. The Statute is reproduced in MELVILLE B. NIMMER & DAVID NIMMER, 8 NIMMER ON COPYRIGHT at App. 7-5–7-10 (New York, Rel. 34-12/93). There is frequent confusion as to the date of this statute. It was enacted in the calendar year 1709 and became effective April 10, 1710. But at this time the beginning of the year in England was March 25. It was not until 1752 that the first of January was designated as the beginning of the year in England. See the Calendar Act of 1750, 24 Geo. II, c. 23. By modern usage, the statute was both enacted and became effective in 1710. *See* PATTERSON, *supra* note 49, at 3, n.3.

(b) to encourage the writing of useful books. To accomplish these ends, it provided that authors, or their assigns, had the exclusive right for a limited period—twenty-one years for existing books, and fourteen years, with one fourteen-year right of renewal in the author, if still living, for new books—to print their works. Registration with the stationers' company of each book for which copyright protection was sought, along with any record of assignment or consent to copy, was still required; however, there was no requirement that registration be limited to members of the company.[122]

One of the more remarkable aspects of the Statute of Anne was that it was styled "An act for the encouragement of learning." Never before had copyright been declared to be for this purpose, either by the crown or by the stationers. Where then did this purpose originate? The preamble to the bill which became the Statute justified it by stating that piracy of printed works "is . . . a real discouragement to learning in generll [sic] which in all Civilized Nations ought to receive ye greatest Countenance and Encouragement. . . ."[123] The preamble to the Statute itself says merely that it is for the purpose of preventing piracy "and for the encouragement of learned men to compose and write useful books."[124] Nothing in the parliamentary record indicates why the emphasis on encouraging learning came about. Moreover, the petitions presented to Parliament during the debates make "no reference to, or even tacit support of, the encouragement of learning."[125] Rose, however, states that the "priority given to the encouragement of learning" was a direct result of a series of articles published in 1709 by Daniel Defoe and Joseph Addison arguing that the rights of authors had to be protected.[126] But irrespective of who was responsible for it, this justification for copyright quickly found favor with Parliament and would find its way into the intellectual property clause.

Regardless of its title, more than anything else, the Statute of Anne was a trade-regulation statute, aimed at controlling and limiting the rampant monopolies then extant in the book sellers trade. Its purpose was to act "in

---

122. But a provision was included which provided for an alternate method of registration in the event that the clerk of the Stationers' Company refused to enter the work in the Register. *See* ROSE, *supra* note 119, at 46.

123. FEATHER, *supra* note 104, at 59. Whether printing piracy encouraged or discouraged learning was a matter of perspective, depending on whether one was a reader seeking access to low-cost books or an author or publisher seeking a return on investment in the writing.

124. NIMMER & NIMMER, *supra* note 121, at App. 7-5.

125. FEATHER, *supra* note 104, at 60.

126. ROSE, *supra* note 119, at 42.

the interest of society by preventing monopoly, and in the interest of the publisher by protecting public works from piracy."[127] Although there is nothing to indicate that Parliament literally intended it as such, it would ultimately come to be judicially interpreted as providing for an author's right. It was in this interpretation that it would serve as an antecedent, along with the Statute of Monopolies, for the intellectual property clause.

One immediate consequence of the Statute was that "the traditional character of the stationers' copyright was radically altered by the introduction of a limited term." Not surprisingly, the stationers and booksellers strongly argued against the concept of a limited term, and:

> When the issue of limiting the term of protection arose, the booksellers objected that, if they had a property in their copies, they had it forever. This assertion rested on the claim that theirs was a common-law right based on ancient trade practice. Thus the question of whether a limited term was compatible with a common-law right was introduced.[128]

But almost six decades would pass before a common-law court would specifically be called upon to answer the twin questions of whether authors or their assigns retained a perpetual property at common law in their writings after their publication and what effect the Statute of Anne had on any such property right.[129] The case was *Millar v. Taylor*[130] decided in 1769. But before reviewing that case it is useful to briefly summarize why these issues were before the court.

Simply put, the stationers' company had acted so effectively to protect copyright over the long years that its registration system was in effect, that protection afforded by the registration had come to be perceived as a form of property.[131] Indeed, the power of the stationers to protect the rights afforded by the registration had been recognized by both crown ordinance and parliamentary act through almost all of the seventeenth century, such

---

127. PATTERSON, *supra* note 49, at 14.
128. ROSE, *supra* note 119, at 45.
129. The issue was clearly raised and argued in *Tonson v. Collins*. There were actually two hearings before King's Bench in this case, in 1759 and 1760, but the case apparently was dismissed as collusive without a final determination being made. *See* ROSE, *supra* note 119, at 76–78; FEATHER, *supra* note 104, at 83–86.
130. 4 Burrow, Reports 2302, 98 Eng. Rep. 201 (K.B. 1769). As the official reporter put it, at issue was an "old and oft-litigated question . . . [of which the case was] . . . the first determination which the question ever received, in this Court of King's Bench." Quoted by FEATHER, *supra* note 104, at 87.
131. The content of this and the next two paragraphs is taken largely from HOLDSWORTH, 6 A HISTORY OF ENGLISH LAW at 378–79.

that there was arguably good ground for holding that a right of copyright existed at common law.[132]

But the right to copy arose also from royal patents granting an exclusive right to print. These were dependent on the royal prerogative which conferred a privilege and not a common-law property right as such. The issue was further complicated by the fact that, as a practical matter, both the rights gained by registration and by patent were routinely sought to be protected in the early part of the seventeenth century by the courts of High Commission and Star Chamber,[133] and in the latter part of the century by the remedies provided under the licensing acts. This recourse to other than common-law remedies[134] gave rise to the view that copyright was not so much a right of property recognized at common law, as a right dependent upon royal grant, exercised directly in favor of a patentee, or indirectly through the powers conferred by the crown on the company.

During the seventeenth century at least, almost all the copyright cases reported turned on the rights of the royal patentees so that the right was rather straightforwardly treated by the courts as dependent on the royal grant. But the fact that there were no reported cases of common-law actions for infringement of copyright prior to the Statute of Anne[135] is not

---

132. Indeed, a fundamental aspect of the definition of common law is that it is law predicated on custom and usage as well as court decision. Patterson, in analyzing the Statute of Anne, however, presents an interesting argument that neither the custom and usage of the stationers' company with respect to the stationers' copyright nor the express language of the Statute provides support for the view that a common-law right to copyright came to exist in authors. *See* PATTERSON, *supra* note 49, at 143–50.

133. Both of which were crown [conciliar] courts and not common-law courts.

134. It should be recalled that until a common-law court actually held that a common-law property right existed, no common-law remedy could be applied. It would not be until the second half of the eighteenth century that a common-law court (in *Millar v. Taylor*) would so hold. More pragmatically, as was pointed out in the petitions seeking parliamentary protection of copyright in the first decade of the eighteenth century, an action for damages was a wholly inadequate remedy, "for by the common law, a book-seller can recover no more costs than he can prove damage; but it is impossible for him to prove the tenth, nay perhaps the hundredth part of the damage he suffers; because a thousand counterfeit copies may be dispersed into as many different lands, and he not be able to prove the sale of ten." Quoted by HOLDSWORTH, 6 A HISTORY OF ENGLISH LAW at 377, n.6.

135. Holdsworth notes a common law opinion in the middle of the nineteenth century which states that "no record of an action on the case for infringement of copyright prior to the statute of Anne, has been found" but suggests that

conclusive that such a remedy was not perceived to exist, but merely of the fact that more convenient remedies existed.

Be that as it may, by 1760 when the case of *Tonson v. Collins* was argued but not decided,[136] the debate on the meaning of copyright had become inextricably intertwined with more fundamental arguments concerning property itself. As has been nicely summarized:

> The gradual exploration of the meaning of the concept of copyright was therefore caught up in a wider debate about the nature of property itself. On the one hand, there was the prevalent view that property was a natural right, partially ceded to the state, which could be created and, having been created, existed in perpetuity. On the other, there was the view that all property derived from the Crown, and was therefore subject to the authority of the Crown and its agents, including laws made by the Crown-in-Parliament.[137]

Which concept of property would be controlling with respect to defining copyright?

The facts of *Millar v. Taylor* were straightforward. Millar who had been assigned the copyright to a particular book printed two thousand copies and placed them on sale. Taylor, at the expiration of the statutory copyright term, proceeded to print and sell the same book. Millar argued at trial that

> there is a real property remaining in authors, after publication of their works; and . . . they only, or those who claim under them, have a right to multiply the copies of such their literary property, at their pleasure for sale . . . this right is a common law right, which always has existed, and does still exist, independent of and not taken away by the statute.[138]

A majority of the four judges, including Lord Mansfield, held that a perpetual property right based on common law existed. Mansfield dismissed the Statute of Anne with the remark that "[w]e are considering the common law, upon principles before and independent of that Act."[139] For the first time, he used the term "incorporeal substance" to describe the property right found in copyright. He went on to state that "it is *just* that an

---

one or two cases are known to have been commenced without reported result. 6 A HISTORY OF ENGLISH LAW at 379, n.3.

136. *See supra* note 129.

137. FEATHER, *supra* note 104, at 86.

138. 4 Burr. at 2304, *quoted in* INLOW, *supra* note 42, at 64.

139. 4 Burr. at 2398, 98 Eng. Rep. at 252, *quoted in* DE WOLF, *supra* note 104, at 10.

author should reap the pecuniary profits of his own ingenuity and labour; it is *just* that another should not use his name without his consent."[140]

Just or not, five years later in *Donaldson v. Becket*[141] the House of Lords decided that whatever may have been the case originally at common law, the Statute of Anne effectively limited the term for which copyright could be enforced at common law to a maximum of twenty-eight years. During the debate in *Donaldson*, Lord Chief Justice De Grey could not accept the argument made by Mansfield in *Millar v. Taylor* that a perpetual property right should exist because it was just that it exist. According to De Grey, "[t]his idea of moral fitness is indeed an amiable principle and one cannot help wishing all claims derived from so pure a source might receive all possible encouragement." But "[b]eautiful as it may be in theory, to reduce it into the practice and execution of the common law would create intolerable confusion; it would make laws vain and judges arbitrary."[142]

To this day, what was actually decided in *Donaldson* remains a subject of considerable dispute among scholars and commentators. On a very pragmatic level, the House of Lords did "no more than to declare that copyright henceforth would be limited in term."[143] But there were other questions of significant interest:

> But on what basis did the peers make their determination? What understanding of the nature of copyright did they adopt? Were they persuaded that there never was a common-law right? Or did they believe that

---

140. 4 Burr. at 2398–99, 98 Eng. Rep. at 252, *quoted in* MACLEOD, *supra* note 38, at 199. MacLeod argues that with no custom to guide him, Lord Mansfield had turned to natural law. *Id. Cf.* Feather's contention that Mansfield "took a firm historically based view that all the precedents, both in Chancery and in King's Bench, supported the existence of property rights before publication." See FEATHER, *supra* note 104, at 88. De Wolf, while acknowledging the point that would later be made by Feather, favored the view later expressed by MacLeod. He states that "Lord Mansfield's opinion . . . while referring for support to the cases in Chancery in which injunctions had been granted, was based primarily upon that sense of justice and fitness of things which was the stronghold of the believers in natural law." *See* DE WOLF, *supra* note 104, at 9.
141. Also frequently referred to as *Beckett.* 4 Burr. 2408 (1774). *See also* COBBETT, 17 PARLIAMENTARY HISTORY OF ENGLAND at cols. 954–1003 (1774).
142. INLOW, *supra* note 42, at 67, quoting 17 PARLIAMENTARY HISTORY OF ENGLAND at 990.
143. ROSE, *supra* 119, at 103.

there was but that it ended with publication? Or that it was taken away by the statute?[144]

One commentator suggests that although the law lords did indeed discuss the principles involved, they couched their holdings in terms of precedent and not whether an inherent or natural law right ought to prevail.[145] Another argues that the lords "grounded their decision on the position that copyright had never existed as a right at common law."[146] Still a third implies that the issue is not so clear as the just quoted language would have it.[147] A fourth says merely that: "In general, all agreed that the 1710 act superseded whatever common law might have existed before that time."[148]

Of more immediate interest here is the manner in which *Donaldson* was perceived in the following decades when the Constitution was drafted and the American copyright law came into being. To understand this perception, it is useful to look at the facts of the case as well as how it was reported. Although not technically so, *Donaldson*, for all intents and purposes, was an appeal of the determination in *Millar v. Taylor.* Millar had sold his copyright at issue in *Millar v. Taylor* to Becket who had had it pirated by Donaldson. Becket immediately obtained an injunction against Donaldson, and the latter appealed to the House of Lords.[149]

The manner in which the House of Lords functioned at this time as a court of last resort has been nicely set forth:

> In 1774 the House of Lords decided cases by a general vote of the peers, lawyers and laymen alike. Great weight was usually given to the opinions of the lawyers, but the practice of lay peers not being recognized when the House of Lords set as a court had not yet been instituted. In important cases such as *Donaldson v. Becket,* however, the twelve common-law judges of the realm—the judges of King's Bench, Common Pleas, and the Exchequer—would be summoned to the House to hear the arguments of counsel and to give their advice on matters of law, after which the peers would debate the issue and vote.[150]

---

144. *Id.* at 102.
145. MACLEOD, *supra* note 38, at 199.
146. Abrams, *supra* note 113, at 1157.
147. ROSE, *supra* note 119, at 103.
148. FEATHER, *supra* note 104, at 92.
149. *See, e.g.,* ROSE, *supra* note 119, at 95; FEATHER, *supra* note 104, at 89.
150. ROSE, *supra* note 119, at 97–98.

This was exactly what occurred in *Donaldson*. The common-law judges were asked to answer five specific questions posed by the peers:

1. Whether at common Law, the Author of any Literary composition had the sole Right of printing and publishing the same for Sale, and could bring an Action against any Person for publishing the same, without his consent?
2. If the Author had such right originally, did the Law take it away upon his printing and publishing the said literary composition, or might any Person reprint and publish the said literary composition, for his own Benefit, against the Will of the Author?
3. If such Action would have laid at Common Law, is the same taken away by the statute of Anne? Or is an Author precluded by such Statute from any Remedy, except on the foundation of such Statute?
4. Whether the Author of any literary Composition, or his assigns, had the sole Right of printing and publishing the same in perpetuity by the Common Law?
5. Whether this Right is in any way impeached, restrained or taken away by the 8th of Anne?[151]

Eleven of the judges answered these questions. Mansfield, who was both a common-law judge and a peer, declined to do so but, because of the position he had taken in *Millar v. Taylor*, it generally was assumed that he would have answered them in a manner favoring a common-law right in perpetuity.[152]

Perhaps it was to be expected that the judges would split in their views. On the first question concerning whether a common-law right existed, eight voted affirmatively. On the second question as to whether publication adversely affected the right, seven answered affirmatively. On the third question, there is some confusion in the record. Both the Journal of the House of Lords and the standard and historical references indicate that by a slim majority of six to five the judges were of the opinion that the Statute took away the author's right at common law. But contemporary newspaper reports and other accounts indicate the vote was 6 to 5 the other way and that the clerk of the House made an error in tallying the votes.[153]

Modern commentators give conflicting views on what these answers and the accompanying advisory opinions by the judges meant, although they would undoubtedly all agree with the statement that "[d]etermining

---

151. FEATHER, *supra* note 104, at 90–91.
152. *See, e.g.,* ROSE, *supra* note 119, at 99.
153. ROSE, *supra* note 119, at 98–99.

the grounds for decision in *Donaldson v. Becket* is no simple task."[154] Thus, Patterson and Lindbergh indicate that based on these opinions, "American courts and commentators assumed that (and have since acted as if) the House of Lords had held that the author had a common-law copyright."[155] Abrams phrases it somewhat differently, saying that, based on the opinions, "*Donaldson* has been consistently interpreted as holding that copyright was recognized by the common law, but was 'impeached' or preempted by the Statute of Anne."[156] But, according to Feathers: "the judges were rather more decisive than some of the more ambiguous responses might suggest. In general, all agreed that the 1710 Act superseded whatever common law might have existed before that time."[157] Rose, however, has quite a different perspective, suggesting that "[h]ad Mansfield voted, the tally would have been a substantial seven to five in favor of the common-law right surviving the statute."[158]

All agree, however, that views expressed by the common-law judges were advisory only and not binding in any way on the lords. The decision was by vote of the entire House, and "the floor debate appears to have been very important."[159] But the nature of that debate was not officially reported, because the reporters were constrained by law from reporting it.[160] Thus, the most commonly cited report on the case, i.e., the fourth edition of *Burrow's Reports,* make no mention of the content of the debate, but instead reports only the arguments of counsel, the advisory opinions of the common-law judges, and the decision against the continuance of the injunction against Donaldson. The issue was further confused by the fact that Burrow appended his report on *Donaldson v. Becket* at the end of his much longer and much more detailed report on *Millar v. Taylor.*

There are three reports extant, however, which do include statements made during the debate by the peers.[161] They indicate that five of them actually spoke, with four of them arguing against any common-law

---

154. Abrams, *supra* note 113, at 1156.
155. L. RAY PATTERSON & STANLEY W. LINDBERG, THE NATURE OF COPYRIGHT, A LAW OF USERS' RIGHTS at 37 (Athens 1991).
156. Abrams, *supra* note 113, at 1156.
157. FEATHER, *supra* note 104, at 92.
158. ROSE, *supra* note 119, at 99.
159. *Id.* at 99.
160. As pointed out by Abrams, "[a]t the time of the *Donaldson* decision it was a contempt punishable by imprisonment to publish any statement made by a member of Parliament in the course of parliamentary business." *See* Abrams, *supra* note 113, at 1159.
161. *Id.* at 1159–60.

copyright and one speaking in favor of such a right. For reasons known only to him, Mansfield declined to voice his opinions. When the issue came to a vote in the House of Lords, the peers decisively supported a reversal of the Chancery decree upholding the injunction.[162] The literal effect was simply to reverse the ruling in *Millar v. Taylor*, but, as has been rather artfully stated, "when we ask what doctrine, precisely, the lords preferred to that which they thus cast aside, Clio (that coy muse) simply shrugs."[163]

What developed in the years after 1774 was the belief that *Donaldson* had established that there was indeed a common law property right in copyright, but one which had been merged into and could only be enforced in accordance with the Statute of Anne.[164] Be that as it may, based on perspectives of common law property right in copyright, arguments would be made that there is no logical distinction between literary work and invention, in that both involve the use of the mental faculty and the ideas that derive from such should result in similar property rights. But the life of the law is not always logic.[165] Thus, in *Donaldson* it was the *lack* of a common law property right in invention which provided a fixed point in the debate about common law property in copyright.[166] Those who argued for such property in perpetuity deemed themselves obligated to distinguish between literary

---

162. The vote commonly is stated as 22 to 11 in favor of reversing the decree, based on the report by Cobbett. *See* Abrams, *supra* note 113, at 1164, citing 17 Parl. Hist. Eng. 953, 1003 (H.L. 1774). Rose, while noting this report by Cobbett, states that "neither the *Journal of the House* nor the contemporary newspapers indicate a forma division of the House, and the *Public Advertiser* explicitly says there was no division (23 Feb. 1774)." He suggests that the decision was most likely rendered on a voice vote. ROSE, *supra* note 119, at 102.

163. John F. Whicher, *The Ghost of Donaldson v. Beckett: An Inquiry Into the Constitutional Distribution of Powers Over the Law of Literary Property in the United States*, 9 BULL. COPYRIGHT SOC'Y 102, 126 (1962). *Cf.* Abrams' unequivocal statement that "the holding of *Donaldson v. Becket* was clearly that the common law had not and did not recognize the existence of copyright." Abrams, *supra* note 113, at 1164.

164. ROSE, *supra* note 119, at 108–10; FEATHER, *supra* note 104, at 95. This certainly was the view set forth by Blackstone. *See infra* note 185.

165. OLIVER WENDELL HOLMES, THE COMMON LAW at 7 (M. Howe ed., 1963). What Holmes actually wrote is that "The life of the law has not been logic: it has been experience." But on occasion logic and experience have been known to produce the same result.

166. The same point was noted in *Millar v. Taylor* wherein Justice Yates, dissenting, argued that it was well known that no common law property right existed in mechanical inventions once they were published. 4 Burr. at 2386, 98 Eng. Rep. at 218.

work and invention, whereas those who denied it found themselves arguing that the two were analogous. While two of the law lords were prepared to admit the possibility that "previous to the monopoly statute, there existed a common law right, equally to an inventor of a machine and an author of a book," the only property right that existed after the Statute of Monopolies and once the invention was disclosed to the public was that granted by the crown for a limited time in the form of a patent.[167]

With this in mind, Baron James Eyre opined that the "Exactitude . . . of the Resemblance between a Book and any other mechanical invention" was clear:

> There is the same Identity of intellectual Substance; the same spiritual Unity. In a mechanic Invention the Corporeation of Parts, the Junction of Powers, tends to produce some one End. A literary Composition is an Assemblage of Ideas so judiciously arranged, as to enforce some one Truth, lay open some one Discovery, or exhibit some one Species of mental Improvement. A mechanic Invention , and a literary Composition, exactly agree in Point of Similarity; the one therefore is no more entitled to be the Object of Common Law Property than the other.[168]

In his view the Statute of Anne treated copyrights similarly to patents. Likewise, Lord Camden gave as his opinion that copyrights should not be distinguished from patents in that there was no real difference between authors and inventors, and both were beneficial to society. Because no common-law claim could be made for inventors, none should be made for authors.[169]

Beginning with *Tonson v. Collins* and continuing through *Donaldson v. Becket*, the arguments have been summarized as follows:

> First, the proponents of perpetual copyright asserted the author's natural right to own his creation. Second, their opponents replied that ideas could not be treated as property and that copyright could only be regarded as a limited privilege of the same sort as a patent. Third, the proponents responded that the property claimed was neither the physical book nor the ideas communicated by it but something else, an entity consisting of the style and sentiment combined.[170]

---

167. MACLEOD, *supra* note 38, at 198.
168. *The Cases of the Appellants and Respondents in the Cause of Literary Property, Before the House of Lords* (London 1774) *in* THE LITERARY PROPERTY DEBATE: SIX TRACTS 1764–1774, at 34 (Stephen Parks ed., New York 1974).
169. *Id.* at 53–54.
170. ROSE, *supra* note 119, at 91.

As a practical matter, those who argued that a copyright was similar to a patent ultimately prevailed, but this was not immediately apparent in the young United States.

For all intents and purposes, there was no colonial copyright practice.[171] Nor is there much evidence of any early state copyright practice. However, on May 2, 1783, the Continental Congress issued a resolution recommending that the various states enact copyright laws. It stated:

> That it be recommended to the several states, to secure to the authors or publishers of any new books not hitherto printed, being citizens of the United States, and to their . . . executors, administrators and assigns, the copyright of such books for a certain time, not less than fourteen years from the first publication; and to secure to said authors, if they shall survive the term first mentioned, and to their . . . executors, administrators and assigns, the copyright of such books for another term of time not less than fourteen years, such copy or exclusive right of printing, publishing and vending the same, to be secured to the original authors, or publishers, or . . . their executors, administrators and assigns, by such laws and under restrictions as the several states may deem proper.[172]

This resolution has been characterized as "the earliest known venture of the United States Government into the realm of intellectual property."[173] The committee which recommended this resolution reported that it was "persuaded that nothing is more properly a man's own than the fruits of his study, and that the protection and security of literary property would greatly tend to encourage genius, to promote useful discoveries and the general extension of arts and commerce."[174]

The May 2, 1783 resolution of the Continental Congress is limited to copyright and says nothing about letters patent for invention. Yet the rather

---

171. BUGBEE, *supra* note 35, at 106; PATTERSON, *supra* note 49, at 183 ("[c]opyright was not secured by law in colonial America"). *Cf.* Abrams' view that there was a limited form of copyright in colonial America, albeit one that "followed the English pattern of a monopoly on printing, based on censorship and royal prerogative." He acknowledges, however, that "it seems clear that the colonies had no concept of copyright as an author's right prior to the adoption of the Statute of Anne in 1710." Abrams, *supra* note 113, at 1171–72. He cites no example of any colonial copyright issued after 1710.
172. BUGBEE, *supra* note 35, at 113, quoting XXIV JOURNALS OF THE CONTINENTAL CONGRESS at 326–27. *See also* Abrams, *supra* note 113, at 1173.
173. BUGBEE, *supra* note 35, at 113.
174. *Id.* quoting XXIV JOURNALS OF THE CONTINENTAL CONGRESS at n.211, 326.

remarkable thing about the committee language quoted above is that if the phrase "literary property" is replaced with "property in invention" it would have provided an equally admirable justification for a congressional recommendation that the states protect the rights of inventors "by such laws and under such restrictions as the several states may deem proper."[175] Obviously, this did not occur, and one may reasonably ask why.

The most straightforward answer to this deceptively simple question is that authors seeking copyright protection lobbied for such a recommendation from the Congress whereas inventors did not. The *Journals of the Continental Congress* state that "sundry papers and memorials from different persons on the subject of literary property" had been submitted to the Congress by early in 1783.[176] One of those who was lobbying the Congress to recommend that the states adopt laws protecting literary property was the young Noah Webster, soon to be famed for his speller, grammar book, and dictionary. He would later write that "as Congress, under the confederation, had no power to protect literary property, certain gentlemen . . . presented a memorial to that body, petitioning them to recommend to the several states, the enactment of such a law."[177]

Between the beginning of 1783 and the close of 1786 twelve states enacted general copyright statutes,[178] although the suggestion has been made that these state statutes apparently never became operative in any real sense.[179] They were largely patterned after the Statute of Anne.[180] While neither the specific concepts nor their relative importance were expressly stated, Patterson suggests that four basic ideas ran through the state copyright statutes. Copyright was: (1) to protect author's rights; (2) to promote learning; (3) to provide order in the book trade as a government

---

175. *See supra* text accompanying note 172.
176. BUGBEE, *supra* note 35, at 112, quoting XXIV JOURNALS OF THE CONTINEN-TAL CONGRESS at 326.
177. BUGBEE, *supra* note 35, at 112, quoting NOAH WEBSTER, A COLLECTION OF PAPERS ON POLITICAL, LITERARY AND MORAL SUBJECTS, at 174 (New York 1843).
178. BUGBEE, *supra* note 35, at 117; PATTERSON, *supra* note 49, at 183–84. Six of these enactments occurred in 1783, with three of them, those of Connecticut, Massachusetts, and Maryland, actually preceding the congressional resolution. Only Delaware failed to comply with the congressional recommendation.
179. PATTERSON, *supra* note 49, at 181. Bugbee, however, points to several copyrights issued under the Connecticut statute and one issued under the South Carolina statute. *See* BUGBEE, *supra* note 35, at 110, 124.
180. The exceptions being those of Massachusetts, Rhode Island, New Hampshire, and Virginia. PATTERSON, *supra* note 49, at 184.

grant; and (4) to prevent harmful monopoly. Of primary importance in the state statutes was "[t]he idea that copyright is primarily for the benefit of the author."[181]

Most of the state statutes had preambles which set forth the rationales for copyright. They made clear that the purpose was to secure profits to the author so as to encourage authors to produce new works and thereby improve learning. The theory on which the exclusive right was based was that of the natural rights of the author.[182] Perhaps not surprisingly, the preambles reflected in no small measure the views of the congressional committee that had recommended the states adopt copyright law.[183]

The Massachusetts statute has an eloquent preamble which could fully as well have served as a justification for a patent statute. It read:

> Whereas the Improvement of Knowledge, the Progress of Civilization, the public Weal of the Community, and the Advancement of Human Happiness, greatly depend on the Efforts of learned and ingenious Persons in the various Arts and Sciences: As the principal Encouragement such Persons can have to make great and beneficial Exertions of this Nature must exist in the legal Security of the Fruits of their Study and Industry to themselves; and as such Security is one of the natural Rights of all Men, there being no Property more peculiarly a Man's own than that which is produced by the Labour of his mind.[184]

As has been noted, however, no state ever thought to apply such language to a general patent statute.

One may reasonably ask what the understanding was in the United States of the English copyright practice at the time of the federal convention. Did the Framers perceive there to be a common-law copyright independent of the statutory copyright set forth in the Statute of Anne? Whicher has presented a plausible argument that the Framers, and Madison in particular, were likely fully aware of the holding of *Millar v. Taylor* establishing common-law copyright, but either were not aware of *Donaldson v. Becket* or at best had a vague and imperfect understanding of what had occurred in that case.[185] Abrams, in turn, suggests that knowledge

---

181. PATTERSON, *supra* note 49, at 181–82.
182. *Id.* at 186. Abrams, *supra* note 113, at 1174.
183. *See supra* text accompanying note 174.
184. BUGBEE, *supra* note 35, at 114, quoting ACTS AND LAWS OF THE COMMONWEALTH OF MASSACHUSETTS (Boston 1781–1783) at 236.
185. He suggests that the primary source of information on recent English copyright developments would have been Blackstone's Commentaries. The fourth, fifth, and sixth editions, published in 1770, 1773, and 1774, all contained the

of *Donaldson v. Becket* was in fact available in the United States prior to 1787 and was, at least by implication, known to the Framers.[186] Be that as it may, the issue of whether the intellectual property clause was intended to give Congress authority to secure a common-law right or instead was for the purpose of giving Congress authority to enact legislation comparable to the Statute of Anne and the patent provision of the Statute of Monopolies was a very real one in the early republic.[187]

F. The Need for Change

Although the states in their individual capacities had sought to provide some form of limited-term exclusive rights in their writings and discoveries to inventors and authors, by early in 1787 the defects in the state copyright and patent custom were obvious.[188] The most singular defect was that states could only legislate with respect to their own territory. Thus, state patents and copyrights could be infringed with impunity in adjoining states. Getting multiple state patents or copyrights was time consuming, expensive, and frequently frustrating. Moreover, there was no certainty of consistency in terms and conditions from state to state. Some of the state

---

following footnote: "In the case of *Millar v. Taylor* . . . , it was determined (upon solemn argument and great consideration) by the opinion of three judges against one, that an exclusive copyright in authors subsists in the common law. . . ." In his seventh edition, published in 1775, and in all later editions, he added the following sentence: "But afterwards in the case of *Donaldson v. Becket,* before the house of lords, which was finally determined 2 Febr. 1774, it was held that no copyright subsists in authors, after the expiration of the several terms created by the statute of queen Anne." Whicher, *supra* note 163, at 126. Because of the American Revolution, the seventh and subsequent editions were not widely circulated in America before the federal convention, but a reprint of the fourth edition published by Robert Bell in Philadelphia in 1770–71, and reissued in 1774, did achieve wide circulation. It is on this basis that Whicher argues that the Framers were aware of the holding in *Millar v. Taylor,* but not that in *Donaldson v. Becket. Id.* at 135.

186.   Abrams, *supra* note 113, at 1177.

187.   *See infra* Chapter Six.

188.   As one observer at the time concluded, "a patent can be of no use unless it is from Congress, and not from them till they are vested with much more authority than they possess at this time." BUGBEE, *supra* note 35, at 90, citing communication from F. W. Geyer to Silas Deane, May 1, 1787, *quoted in* C. P. NETTELS, THE EMERGENCE OF A NATIONAL ECONOMY, 1776–1815, at n.101 (New York 1962). This conclusion was equally applicable to copyright.

copyright statutes declared that they would not come into force until all states had enacted similar laws, while the majority of them extended protection to residents of other states only on the basis of reciprocity.[189] With regard to patents at least, there was no guarantee of consistency from patent to patent even within a particular state because each patent required a private legislative act. Moreover, what a state could grant, it could also take away, and on occasion did so.[190]

The reasonable and straightforward solution appeared to be to amend the Articles of Confederation to expressly grant power to Congress to provide for patents and copyrights having national scope and coverage. Indeed, if the Framers assembled in convention in Philadelphia in the summer of 1787 had followed their express instructions received from Congress, this is quite possibly what would have happened. But they did not, and thus the basis for the United States patent and copyright law came to be the Constitution rather than the Articles of Confederation.

---

189. PATTERSON, *supra* note 49, at 192.
190. As happened to steamboat inventor John Fitch. Thus, on March 19, 1787 New York granted him a 14-year patent on the use of steam boats on all waterways within its jurisdiction. On March 27, 1798, however, this patent was revoked and the same rights granted to Robert R. Livingston for a term of 20 years. See Livingston v. Van Ingen, 9 Johns. R. 507-509 (N.Y. 1812).

CHAPTER THREE
THE FEDERAL CONVENTION

The antecedents have been reviewed. It is time now to look at the federal convention and how the Framers came to propose that Congress be authorized "To promote the Progress of Science and useful Arts, by securing for limited Times to Authors and Inventors the exclusive Right to their respective Writings and Discoveries."

A. The Immediate Background

On February 21, 1787, Congress, with considerable reluctance and after being importuned by several states, issued a formal resolution expressing "the opinion of Congress" that

> it is expedient that on the second Monday in May next, a convention of delegates, who shall have been appointed by the several states, be held at Philadelphia . . . for the sole and express purpose of revising the Articles of Confederation and reporting to Congress and the several legislatures such alterations and provisions therein as shall when agreed to by Congress and confirmed by the states render the federal constitution adequate to the exigencies of Government and the preservation of the Union.[1]

The events leading up to the calling of the federal convention have been chronicled in detail and are not repeated or even summarized here. Suffice it to say that there was nothing in those events to suggest that a lack of a power in Congress to issue patents or copyrights played any significant role in that decision.[2] Indeed, only one document is known to exist in which any

---

1. III THE RECORDS OF THE FEDERAL CONVENTION OF 1787, at 13–14 (Max Farrand ed., 1937).
2. In the rather extensive preface to his Notes of Debates in the Constitutional Convention, published in 1840, James Madison set forth a variety of reasons why a new constitutional scheme of government was required. Protection of intellectual property rights was not among them. *See* NOTES OF DEBATES IN THE FEDERAL CONVENTION OF 1787 REPORTED BY JAMES MADISON at 4–19 (Ohio University Press, Athens 1966).

delegate mentions prior to the convention, even in a peripheral way, the concerns that ultimately would result in the intellectual property clause.

In preparing in his methodical way to take part in that convention, James Madison, delegate from Virginia, set down in April 1787 "Observations by J. M." on the weaknesses of the existing Confederation.[3] Among those was a "want of concert in matters where common interest requires it" between state governments. In Madison's view, the resulting loss of "national dignity, interest, and revenue" was deplorable. Almost as an afterthought, he added "Instances of inferior moment are the want of uniformity in the laws concerning naturalization & literary property. . . ." The want of uniformity in the laws concerning patents or indeed the very absence of laws concerning patents seems not to have overly troubled him or any other delegate prior to the convention.

Nonetheless, various arguments continue to be presented that strong pressures existed on the delegates to encourage them to provide authorization for national patent and copyright laws. Bugbee, e.g., contends that the clause was not "accidental," and that it arose out "of the demand for patent and copyright protection." In his view, it was "the culmination of the provincial patent and copyright movements."[4]

Donner has argued that "the states felt a strong need for national copyright laws to secure to authors their property rights in their works" and that as a consequence there was a "strong desire of the Framers to include a copyright clause in the Constitution."[5] This considerably overstates the reality. Madison's concern about the lack of uniformity in state laws concerning literary property was by his own admission "of inferior moment." Moreover, there is no evidence whatsoever that any state instructed its delegates to seek a copyright clause in the Constitution.

As demonstrated by their actions, the Framers were certainly amenable to granting power to the Congress to enact both copyright and patent legislation, but that this was not high on their list of priorities is evidenced by (a) the fact that none of the general systems of governance debated by

---

3. The content of this paragraph is taken from BRUCE W. BUGBEE, GENESIS OF AMERICAN PATENT AND COPYRIGHT LAW at 124 (Washington, D.C. 1967), citing DEPARTMENT OF STATE, BUREAU OF ROLLS AND LIBRARY, IV DOCUMENTARY HISTORY OF THE CONSTITUTION OF THE UNITED STATES OF AMERICA, 1786–1870, at 128 (Washington 1894–1905).
4. BUGBEE, *supra* note 3, at 3, 128, 129.
5. Ira Donner, *The Copyright Clause of the U.S. Constitution: Why Did the Framers Include It With Unanimous Approval?* 36 AM. J. LEG. HIST. 361, 362, 365 (1992).

them included any such proposed delegation of authority,[6] and (b) when the enumerated powers of Congress were first actually proposed and initially debated, they did not include the powers set forth in the intellectual property clause.[7] Nothing in the records of the convention or in the commentary that followed it suggests that the powers granted by the clause were considered to be of any special importance or significance. Indeed, the impression is left that they were considered to be routine, last-minute additions to an enumeration of much more important powers.

The reality of the times is more accurately reflected by Patterson and Lindberg when they state:

> In retrospect, the presence of copyright in the Constitution is somewhat anomalous. Men in the process of establishing a central government for a new nation surely had more important concerns than drafting a provision to empower the new legislature to protect the rights of authors when there were so few authors to protect. Indeed, there was even an argument at that time that copyright legislation would be disadvantageous to a new country whose literature came mainly from foreign shores.[8]

While arguably a power in Congress to create patent legislation could be used to encourage the introduction of new manufacturing technology, either by original invention or by importation, there is nothing to indicate that this was considered to be of particular importance when the convention was convened.

B. First Governance Proposals

The assembly that would be known as the federal convention was originally scheduled to convene on May 14, 1787 but did not actually have a quorum of seven states represented until May 25th. Rather early on it would be presented with several proposals for schemes of national governance. These came to be called the Virginia Plan, the South Carolina Plan, the New Jersey Plan, and the New York Plan, depending on which delegation they arose from. The contention has been made, almost in passing, that "both the Virginia and New York plans originally included provisions

---

6. *See infra* text accompanying notes 9–13.
7. *See infra* text accompanying notes 78–80.
8. L. RAY PATTERSON & STANLEY W. LINDBERG, THE NATURE OF COPYRIGHT, A LAW OF USER'S RIGHTS at 53 (Athens, GA 1991).

stipulating the use of the letters patent for industrial inventions. . . ."[9] No evidence has been found which in any way supports this view, and it is almost certainly incorrect.[10]

In the early years after the Constitution was ratified, there was some confusion engendered by one of the delegates, Charles Pinckney, as to whether the South Carolina Plan had in fact contained a proposal to give Congress authority "to secure to authors the exclusive rights to their performances and discoveries." Pinckney, who authored the South Carolina Plan, wrote a pamphlet shortly after the convention describing that Plan as containing such a proposal.[11] As is shown, Pinckney deserves substantial credit for what ultimately became the intellectual property clause, but again there is no evidence—other than his own self-serving claim[12]—that he proposed the language quoted above as part of the South Carolina Plan.[13]

9. E. G. INLOW, THE PATENT GRANT at 46 (Baltimore 1950).
10. Various texts of the Virginia and the New York Plans are known. As succinctly stated by Fenning, "[i]n none of these is there any foundation for the portion of the Constitution with which we are interested [i.e., the intellectual property clause]." See Karl Fenning, The Origin of the Patent and Copyright Clause of the Constitution, 17 GEORGETOWN L.J. 109, 110–11 (1929) (reprinted in 11 J. PAT. OFF. SOC'Y 438, 439 (1929)).
11. CHARLES PINCKNEY, OBSERVATIONS ON THE PLAN OF THE GOVERNMENT SUBMITTED TO THE FEDERAL CONVENTION ON THE 28TH OF MAY, 1787. See RECORDS OF THE FEDERAL CONVENTION, supra note 1, at 106, 122. The pamphlet was published in New York by Francis Childs. Id. at 106. This suggests that it must have been published before October 14, 1787.
12. He was famous for his self-aggrandizement. He deliberately attempted to shave five years off his age so that he could claim to be the youngest member of the convention. As pointed out by Rossiter, he was known as "'Constitution Charlie' for his self-inflated opinion of his role in 1787, and scorned by Madison for continuing to falsify his age and for grossly exaggerating this role." CLINTON ROSSITER, 1787: THE GRAND CONVENTION at 327 (New York 1967). More recently, the Colliers have viewed Pinckney much more sympathetically. See C. COLLIER & J. L. COLLIER, DECISION IN PHILADELPHIA, THE CONSTITUTIONAL CONVENTION OF 1787, at 64–74 (New York 1986). Morris suggests that the Colliers give to the South Carolina Plan "a serious weight that tested scholarship rejects." See RICHARD G. MORRIS, THE FORGING OF THE UNION, 1781–1789, at 273 (New York 1987).
13. Fenning notes that the Journal of the Federal Convention shows that there was no such language included in the South Carolina Plan as originally submitted. He further points to various authoritative compilations which state that the quotation does not appear in the Plan as presented to the convention.

C. Why an Intellectual Property Clause?

Because there was nothing to suggest it in any of the plans of governance proposed by the delegates, the question naturally arises as to how the clause came to be included in the Constitution. Little has been written on the point. The reason for the dearth of commentary undoubtedly is the fact that so little is actually known about how its inclusion came about. Contemporaneous records such as Madison's Notes indicate that it was adopted nem. con.,[14] and without debate. Although most commentators on the origin of the United States patent and copyright law take this to mean that it met universal approbation, another interpretation is quite possible. It was agreed to by the delegates on September 5, 1787 after several months of intense and sometimes acrimonious debate on other more momentous issues, and it may well have been that the delegates were tired, wanted to go home, and simply did not perceive this particular grant of power to Congress to warrant any further debate,[15] regardless of whether they considered it to have any particular significance.[16]

Fenning, *supra* note 10, at 110 (reprinted in 11 J. PAT. OFF. SOC'Y at 439). Additionally, as pointed out by Bugbee, "no provision for the safeguarding of intellectual property can be found in a detailed draft which Pinckney supplied in 1818 to replace his earlier version, which was missing when the Convention papers were opened after a thirty-year interval." BUGBEE, *supra* note 3, at 193. *See also* text accompanying notes 95–98, *infra*.

14. Madison's shorthand for nemine contradicente, meaning "no one dissenting."
15. Levy makes this same point in the context of the contract clause, saying: "By that late date [September 12th] the Convention was winding up its work, and the delegates were eager to return home. They had lost their patience for controversy, despite the existence of unresolved substantive issues, and with slight changes they followed the recommendations of the Committee of Style." *See* LEONARD W. LEVY, ORIGINAL INTENT AND THE FRAMERS' CONSTITUTION, at 126 (New York 1988).
16. As noted by Sherwood:

> The absence of debate over the patent provision by the Founding Fathers has been taken as proof of their firm belief in patents as the best way to encourage socially beneficial innovation. However, it is more likely that the authors of the Constitution simply followed the English precedent and chose the patent without paying much attention to the subject, since they were also faced with the larger problems of how to structure the government, solve its fiscal difficulties, and defend the new nation.

M. Sherwood, *The Origins and Development of the American Patent System*, 71 AM. SCIENTIST 500 (1983).

This raises the rather intriguing question as to why the delegates considered it to be of sufficient import to be included in the Constitution at all. Indeed, a plausible argument can be made that the power to protect intellectual property rights is inherently subsumed in other powers granted to Congress so that there is in reality no need for a separate intellectual property clause. To understand the nature of this argument it is first necessary to briefly note two other grants of authority the delegates found appropriate to include in the Constitution.

The constitutional grants of authority to the Congress are set forth in eighteen clauses found in Section 8 of Article I. The content of half of those clauses can be traced back to the Articles of Confederation.[17] Of interest here are two clauses nowhere to be found in the Articles. Under these two clauses:

> The Congress shall have Power . . . To regulate Commerce with foreign Nations, and among the several States, and with the Indian Tribes . . . [and] To make all Laws which shall be necessary and proper for carrying into Execution the foregoing Powers and all other Powers vested by this Constitution in the Government of the United States or in any Department or Officer thereof.[18]

Since intellectual property in its various forms may be considered as articles of commerce both with foreign nations and among the several states, it would logically follow from these two clauses that patent and copyright laws constitute "laws necessary and proper for carrying into execution" the power of the Congress to regulate commerce. One may only speculate whether this is the approach that would have been taken had there been no intellectual property clause in the Constitution.

Many years after the federal convention in which he played such a primary role, Madison set forth language indicative that these two clauses might indeed be interpreted in accord with such an approach. Writing with respect to the commerce clause in 1829, he stated:

> That the encouragement of Manufactures, was an object of the power to regulate trade, is proved by the use made of the power for that object, in the first session of the first Congress under the Constitution; when among the members present were so many who had been members of the federal Convention which framed the Constitution, and of the State

---

17. Needless to say, the intellectual property clause was not one of them, although an occasional commentator so implies. *See, e.g.,* C. L. MEE, THE GENIUS OF THE PEOPLE at 256–57 (New York 1987).
18. U.S. CONST. art. I, § 8, cls. 3, 18.

Conventions which ratified it; each of these classes also consisting of members who had opposed & who had espoused, the Constitution in its actual form. It does not appear from the printed proceedings of Congress on that occasion that the power was denied by any of them.[19]

The "promotion of . . . useful arts" as set forth in the intellectual property clause and "the encouragement of Manufactures" under the commerce clause may be closely equated.

Madison was writing in the context of an argument over whether the commerce clause granted Congress the right to impose import duties. Several years later in 1832 he broadened his argument to suggest that even though the federal convention had rejected certain specific proposals with respect to congressional power, this did not mean that the delegates did not intend for Congress to have equivalent broad powers under the commerce clause to protect and encourage domestic manufactures. As he put it:

> The intention is inferred from the rejection or not adopting of particular propositions which embraced a power to encourage them [i.e., domestic manufactures]. But without knowing the reasons for the votes in those cases, no such inference can be sustained. The propositions might be disapproved because they were in bad form or not in order; because they blended other powers with the particular power in question; or because the object had been, or would be, elsewhere provided for. No one acquainted with the proceedings of deliberative bodies can have failed to notice the frequent uncertainty of inferences from a record of naked votes.[20]

Thus, in Madison's view—at least in his later years—the failure of the convention to include in the Constitution a congressional power "to establish public institutions, rewards, and immunities for the promotion of agriculture, commerce, and manufactures"[21] did not imply or suggest that Congress did not have broad powers to encourage manufactures, including by means of import duties on foreign manufactures. Arguably insofar as Madison was concerned, the absence of an intellectual property clause, or even the outright rejection of such a clause by the convention, would not per se have served as a constitutional ground for precluding Congress from granting patents under the commerce clause.

---

19. Communication from James Madison to J. C. Cabell (Feb. 2, 1829), *reproduced in* THE RECORDS OF THE FEDERAL CONVENTION OF 1787, *supra* note 1, at 477.
20. Letter from James Madison to Professor Davis, *reproduced in* THE RECORDS OF THE FEDERAL CONVENTION OF 1787, *supra* note 1, at 518, 520.
21. As initially proposed by Charles Pinckney. *See infra* text accompanying note 81.

Madison, however, held a very different view in 1790 when the bill that became the first patent statute was being debated. Then he was perfectly prepared to argue that rejection of a particular proposal by the convention precluded any authority by Congress to act in accordance with the proposal.[22] Moreover, it is not at all clear that the Framers in 1787 perceived the commerce clause as a mechanism for authorizing patents and copyright.[23] Had they done so, to include the intellectual property clause would have been simply to engage in a grant of redundant powers to the Congress, which was something they clearly were not disposed to do.

Be that as it may, there is an intellectual property clause, and the question is why. In the absence of any recorded debate on the point, any answer must to some degree be speculation. But there are intriguing clues which can be drawn from the backgrounds of the delegates themselves and the experiences on which they drew.[24] More than half of the fifty-five delegates were trained in the law.[25] Eight of them had signed the Declaration of Independence and two the Articles of Confederation.[26] Some forty had served in the Congress under the Confederation[27] and seven in the first Continental Congress. A number had been involved in the formation of their state constitutions[28] and seven had served as the chief executives of

---

22. *See infra* Chapter Five, notes 93–95 and accompanying text.
23. They certainly could not have envisaged the broad scope given to the commerce clause in the twentieth century.
24. ROSSITER, *supra* note 12, at 79–156. Gives not only a thumb-nail sketch of every delegate but also a composite picture of them.
25. Exactly how many were lawyers or had legal training is a point of some difference of opinion among various commentators. Thus, for example, Morris states that "although only about a dozen were practicing lawyers, three times that number had studied law," MORRIS, *supra* note 12, at 269. The Colliers are more specific, saying that "[t]hirty-one of the fifty-five men at the Convention had been trained in law," COLLIER & COLLIER, *supra* note 12, at 212–13. According to Warren, "[a]t least thirty-three had been lawyers, of whom ten had served as State Judges." *See* CHARLES WARREN, THE MAKING OF THE CONSTITUTION at 55 (Washington 1928).
26. Data taken from ROSSITER, *supra* note 12, at 144–46; WARREN, *supra* note 25, at 55; MORRIS, *supra* note 12, at 269.
27. Rossiter and Morris say 42 and Warren says 39.
28. Warren says eight and Rossiter says "perhaps twenty." However, the numbers keep getting larger with time. Thus, Banner states that "[a]t least thirty of them had participated in the drafting of various State Constitutions." *See* D. W. Banner, *An Unanticipated, Nonobvious, Enabling Portion of the Constitution: The Patent Provision—The Best Mode*, 69 J. PAT. & TRADEMARK OFF. SOC'Y 631, 632 (1987).

their states. Indeed, at the time of the convention, more than forty were involved with their state government either as chief executive, judge, or legislator. Needless to say, they were well aware of the political climate which had caused the convention to be called.

The observation has been made that "so very much of the Constitution was crafted on lessons drawn from the operations of the states as colonies, on the precedents provided by the state constitutions, and on the obvious examples of the inadequacies of the Articles of Confederation."[29] While undoubtedly true in the larger context, this point of view has only limited applicability to the intellectual property clause. It is certain that the state constitutions provided essentially no precedent of any sort for a clause of this type.[30] Indeed, the constitutions of two states, Maryland and North Carolina, actively discouraged any sort of monopoly, including limited term exclusive rights to authors and inventors.[31]

There is also nothing to suggest that the colonial patent custom played any significant role, although arguments to the contrary are occasionally presented. Thus, Bugbee has taken such a position, using the following logic: (a) "[a] majority of the fifty-five delegates to the Federal Convention were lawyers, members of a profession dedicated to a continuing search for precedent"; (b) "[m]ost of the men who framed the Constitution had acquired their political preparation in the colonial legislatures"' (c) "colonial and state development of legal protection for intellectual property was of fundamental importance as precedent upon which the founders of 1787 . . . could draw"; and (d) "the unanimously approved 'intellectual property' clause . . . was in large part the product of colonial and early state

---

29. MORRIS, *supra* note 12, at 267.
30. *See supra* Chapter Two, note 96. But if the clause had merely authorized Congress to promote the progress of science and useful arts without expressly stating how this was to be done, it would have found support in the Massachusetts Constitution of 1780, ch. V, § II, which stated that "it shall be the duty of legislatures . . . to cherish the interests of literature and sciences. . . ." *See* III THE FEDERAL AND STATE CONSTITUTIONS at 1907 (F. Thorpe ed., 1909) [hereinafter CONSTITUTIONS]. Similar language appeared in the New Hampshire Constitution of 1784, Part II The Form of Government, Encouragement of Literature. *See* IV CONSTITUTIONS at 2467–68.
31. According to the Maryland Constitution of 1776, § XXXIX, "monopolies are odious, contrary to the spirit of free government, and the principles of commerce; and ought not to be suffered." *See* CONSTITUTIONS, *supra* note 87, at 1690. Similarly, the North Carolina Constitution of 1776, § XXIII, stated "[t]hat perpetuities and monopolies are contrary to the genius of a free State, and ought not to be allowed." *See* V CONSTITUTIONS, *supra* note 30, at 2788.

experience."[32] While state experience may indeed have played a role in the incorporation of the clause into the Constitution, there is simply no contemporaneous record that supports Bugbee's premises that colonial political preparation had any significance or that the colonial patent custom was of fundamental importance as precedent. At best, it was part of the evolutionary background against which the precedent actually considered by the delegates could be viewed.

Also, Irons and Sears have quoted William Robinson in support of the view that colonial precedent played a role. According to them, Robinson in 1890 observed:

> When the Constitutional Convention met, its members had before them, there under consideration, the English idea, and a suggestion of a different idea, in the practice of the colonies. The English idea had been to encourage monopolies so that the introduction of a new trade or a new art was the essence of the law. The constitutional idea, however, was that of encouraging domestic invention, and in the first law of 1790, and in all subsequent amendments of that law, the basic idea has been to encourage original invention.[33]

While Robinson mightily confused the so-called "English idea,"[34] he also seemed to suggest that the language of the intellectual property clause was derived from colonial practice limiting the patent custom to the protection of original invention. Again, however, there is simply no contemporaneous evidence to indicate that the colonial patent custom was in fact limited to original invention or was intended to preclude patents of importation. Moreover, there is absolutely no evidence that the Framers in any way relied on the colonial patent custom in drafting the clause.[35]

---

32. BUGBEE, *supra* note 3, at 2, 3.
33. Edward S. Irons & Mary Helen Sears, *The Constitutional Standard of Invention—The Touchstone for Patent Reform*, 1973 UTAH L. REV. 653, 676, citing WILLIAM ROBINSON, PATENTS INTRODUCTION (11.4-5) (1890) (I have been unable to find the citation to which Irons & Sears refer).
34. The primary purpose of the English patent custom was to encourage the introduction of new trades or industry into the country either by original invention or importation through the granting of limited term monopolies. It was not in any way intended to encourage monopolies per se. *See supra* Chapter Two, note 69 and accompanying text.
35. Nor could they have, if for no other reason than that it was so heterodox and uneven. For a discussion on this point, see Edward C. Walterscheid, *The Early Evolution of the United States Patent Law (5 Part I)*, 78 J. PAT. & TRADEMARK OFF. SOC'Y 615, 623–31 (1996).

While the delegates would in all likelihood have been aware that Article II of the Articles of Confederation precluded the Congress from issuing patents or copyrights, this in and of itself would not have been sufficient for them to incorporate the clause into the Constitution. Rather, there must have been something that clearly warranted to them that Congress should as a matter of course have the power granted by the clause and that such power should be expressly set forth rather than merely being implied in the power to regulate commerce.[36]

There is nothing in the record of the convention or any subsequent statement by any Framer that indicates why a need was perceived for this type of clause, but the unusual fact of this particular detail in the clause in and of itself suggests a key to why the clause was included. It was intended not only as an express authority to promote the progress of science and the useful arts generally but also as a means of ensuring authority to do so in a particular way, namely, by securing exclusive rights for limited times to authors and inventors in their respective writings and discoveries. It is unique in being the only instance wherein the delegates prescribed a specific mode of accomplishing the particular authority granted.[37]

That they should do so is interesting because there are a variety of ways of promoting the progress of science and the useful arts which have nothing whatever to do with the granting of exclusive rights for limited

---

36. There is nothing to suggest that the delegates actually engaged in or even contemplated any analysis of the type set forth with regard to the commerce clause. *See supra* text accompanying notes 17 and 18.

37. It appears that this was deliberate and that other attempts to grant specific powers to Congress were rejected by the delegates. In this regard, Jefferson recorded the following as the result of a dinner conversation on March 11, 1798:

> Baldwin mentions at table the following fact. When the bank bill was under discussion in the House of Representatives, Judge Wilson came in, and was standing by Baldwin. Baldwin reminded him of the following fact which passed at the grand convention. Among the enumerated powers given to Congress, was one to erect corporations. It was, on debate, struck out. Several particular powers were then proposed. Among others, Robert Morris proposed to give Congress a power to establish a national bank. . . . [This] was rejected, as was every other special power, except that of giving copyrights to authors, and patents to inventors; the general power of incorporating being whittled down to this shred. Wilson agreed to the fact.

Reproduced in THE RECORDS OF THE FEDERAL CONVENTION OF 1787, *supra* note 1, at 375–76.

times in writings and inventions or discoveries.[38] Indeed, a strong movement would arise in Europe in the nineteenth century which would argue that this was precisely the wrong way to encourage industrial innovation.[39] Why then should the Constitution make specific reference to promoting the progress of science and the useful arts by securing exclusive rights in their writings and inventions to authors and inventors for limited times? The answer in no small measure seems to have been predicated on the fact that they desired to follow the English practice of granting exclusive rights through the issuance of patents and copyright or something similar[40] and were not at all certain that the Congress would have the power to do so without an explicit grant of authority. This unique departure from the general practice of the convention to specify general objects of congressional authority without specifying particular means for accomplishing the

---

38. Among those that had already been attempted by the time of the federal convention were medals, honorary titles, premiums, bounties, and other rewards of various types. As the attorney general pointed out in 1824, "there are a thousand other modes in which the progress of science and the useful arts may be promoted, as by establishing and endowing literary and philosophical societies, and many others that might be mentioned." Gibbons v. Ogden, 22 U.S. (9 Wheat.) 1, 166 (1824).

39. *See, e.g.,* M. Coulter, Property in Ideas: The Patent Controversy in Mid-Victorian Britain (unpublished Ph.D. Thesis, Indiana University, 1986); F. Machlup & E. Penrose, *The Patent Controversy in the Nineteenth Century,* 10 J. ECON. HIST. 1 (1950); V. M. Batzel, *Legal Monopoly in Liberal England: The Patent Controversy in the Mid-Nineteenth Century,* 22 BUS. HIST. 189 (1980).

40. This was certainly the assumption of commentators and the judiciary early in the nineteenth century. *See, e.g.,* JOSEPH STORY, II COMMENTARIES ON THE CONSTITUTION OF THE UNITED STATES § 1152 (Boston 1833) ("[i]t was doubtless to this knowledge of the common law and statutable rights of authors and inventors, that we are to attribute our constitutional provision"); Thompson v. Haight, 23 F. Cas. 1039, 1043 (No. 13,957) (S.D.N.Y. 1822) ("[i]t is this power in the British crown, as it existed and was understood at the time of the adoption of the constitution of the United States, which by that instrument is conceived to be vested in congress").

general object arose from the perception that the particular means would not be available to the Congress unless it was specified.[41]

But aside from familiarity with it why would they desire to perpetuate English institutions of this type? More than anything else their reason was purely a pragmatic one, namely, that this approach would cost the federal government the least to implement of the various schemes then being contemplated for encouraging the rise of manufacturing and the growth of knowledge while at the same time providing the desired pecuniary incentive to inventors and authors.[42] This was a critical consideration for a new federal government that would have to address the issue of taking over the state debts inherited from the Revolutionary War. Accordingly, from the perspective of delegates seeking to devise a form of governance for a fledgling, impecunious national government, granting limited-term exclusive rights in their works to authors and inventors seemed the perfect

---

41. As the Court of Customs and Patent Appeals put it:

> It is interesting to note that this particular grant is the only one of the several powers conferred upon the Congress which is accompanied by a specific statement of the reason for it. Its inclusion doubtlessly was due to the fact that those who formulated the Constitution were familiar with the long struggle over monopolies so prominent in English history, where exclusive rights to engage even in ordinary business activities were granted so frequently by the Crown for the financial benefits accruing to the Crown only. It was desired that in this country any Government grant of a monopoly for even a limited time should be limited to those things which serve in the promotion of science and the useful arts.

In re Shao Wen Yuan, 188 F.2d 377, 380 (C.C.P.A. 1951).

42. In the republican frame of mind that existed in the United States at this time, honorary titles were the last thing contemplated to encourage the promotion of science and the useful arts. Medals or plaques or something of the sort failed to excite the pecuniary interests of writers and inventors. For the views of a famous contemporary English inventor, James Watt, on this point, see HAROLD I. DUTTON, THE PATENT SYSTEM AND INVENTIVE ACTIVITY DURING THE INDUSTRIAL REVOLUTION, 1750–1852, at 109 (Manchester 1984). Simply put, in Watt's view, fame and honor were nice, but they were secondary considerations to the primary focus on profit. Other schemes being presented, such as bounties and monetary rewards, would all cost money while this approach was perceived as being almost entirely without cost to the new federal government. This did not prevent both "premiums" and "rewards" from being proposed as means for promoting the advancement of useful knowledge and discoveries as well as agriculture, trade, commerce, and manufactures. *See infra* text accompanying notes 79 and 80. But neither proposal saw the light of day in the Constitution as ratified.

solution to encouraging the progress of science and useful arts with the least expense.[43] Although no contemporaneous American exposition of this pragmatic economic reality has been found, it had recently been set forth in England.[44]

The practical monetary consequences of granting exclusive rights in lieu of other "rewards" is evidenced by the debate which took place in the first federal Congress with respect to the first inventor's petition presented to it. That petition sought not only an exclusive right but also "the patronage of Congress" to finance a voyage to Baffin's Bay for the inventor to conduct further experiments concerning his invention. The congressional committee which looked into the matter reported that it was reluctant to recommend "in the present deranged state of our finances, a precipitate adoption of a measure which would be attended by considerable expence."[45]

Several sources of precedent for this pragmatic approach that many if indeed not most of the delegates would have been aware of suggest themselves. The first would have been the English precedent embodied in the Statute of Monopolies and the English practice thereunder.[46] Because of their legal training, a majority of the delegates would have recognized that the Statute exempted patents for invention from its prohibition against monopolies. These same delegates would have generally been aware that

---

43. As noted about the British patent system in 1967, but fully applicable to the circumstances existing in 1787 in the newly independent United States, such an approach "makes no attempt to reward an inventor directly: the reward is of [the inventor's] own making." K. BOEHM & A. SIBERSTON, THE BRITISH PATENT SYSTEM at 1 (Cambridge 1967).

44. In 1785 Jeremy Bentham, comparing rewards by bonus payments with rewards by "exclusive privileges," took the view that the latter approach was "best proportioned, most natural, and least burdensome" in that "it produces an infinite effect and costs nothing." See JEREMY BENTHAM, III *A Manual of Political Economy, in* THE WORKS OF JEREMY BENTHAM at 71 (Bowring ed. 1843), as cited by Fritz Machlup, *An Economic Review of the Patent System, U.S. Senate Comm. on the Judiciary,* 85th Cong., 2d Sess. 19 (1958). While it is doubtful that more than a few of the Framers were aware of what Bentham had recently written, there is little question but that they as a group would have wholeheartedly endorsed his views.

45. *House of Representatives Journal, in* III DOCUMENTARY HISTORY OF THE FIRST FEDERAL CONGRESS OF THE UNITED STATES at 22 (Baltimore 1977). *See also Proceedings in Congress During the Years 1789 and 1790, Relating to the First Patent and Copyright Laws,* 22 J. PAT. OFF. SOC'Y 243–44 (1940).

46. Sherwood suggests this to be the case. *See supra* note 16.

such patents had been issued in England for more than a century and a half, although it would have been surprising if more than a very few were aware of the administrative details involved in obtaining an English patent.[47] Nonetheless, based on the English precedent, the concept of an exclusive patent for invention for a limited period of time was known and understood by them. The extent to which they understood that, under the English practice, a patent was a privilege rather than a right[48] is much less clear.

They would also have been aware that the purpose of the English patent custom and practice as authorized by the Statute of Monopolies was to encourage the introduction of new manufactures, trades, and industries into England both by importation and by invention. In this regard, they must have known that the common law had interpreted the phrase "true and first inventor" in the Statute of Monopolies to read on the first importer as well as the original inventor. There is nothing to suggest that in using the terms "inventors" and "discoveries" in the intellectual property clause, they intended in any way to depart from this English precedent and to preclude Congress from having authority to grant patents of importation. Yet this would immediately become an issue in the creation of the first American patent statute.

There is a natural tendency to suggest that the dramatic increase in patenting activity in England from 1760 onward[49] correlates well with the increase in economic and industrial activity resulting from the industrial revolution.[50] While no hard evidence has been developed that the Framers were in fact cognizant of such a correlation, nonetheless they undoubtedly were aware of the significant increase in industrial and economic activity in Great Britain and sought to provide a framework of governance which would permit the national government of the United States to provide

---

47. Most of them would likely have received their knowledge of the English common law from *Blackstone's Commentaries on the Law of England* first published in 1768. An American edition was printed in 1771–72 on a subscription basis for $16 a set. There were 840 American subscribers for 1,557 sets, which was an incredible response. *See* L. M. FRIEDMAN, A HISTORY OF AMERICAN LAW at 88–89 (1973). Blackstone provided a summary of the common law respecting copyright, but said almost nothing about patents. WILLIAM BLACKSTONE, BLACKSTONE'S COMMENTARIES ON THE LAW OF ENGLAND at 405–07 (1768).
48. *See supra* Chapter Two, note 91 and accompanying text.
49. *See supra* Chapter Two, text accompanying notes 93 and 94.
50. Dutton, for example, notes "that the trend of patenting grew almost exponentially throughout the industrial revolution." *See* DUTTON, *supra* note 42, at 176.

incentives similar to those perceived to be associated with the patent system of Great Britain.

They also were certainly aware of the Statute of Anne, but the extent to which they were aware of the recent English cases concerning the common law right to copyright is less clear.[51] Nonetheless, it has been argued that their knowledge of this perceived common law right may well have influenced the language actually used in the clause, specifically, the inclusion of the term "securing."[52] While this is doubtful,[53] it is certain that their knowledge of copyright in Great Britain influenced their decision to include copyright authority among the powers granted to Congress.

A second source of precedent, albeit in a very real sense a frustrating one, would have been the recognition by most of the delegates of the inability of the Continental Congress to act in both the patent and copyright arenas. Recall that a substantial majority of the delegates had served in the Continental Congress[54] and would have been aware of the various petitions for both patent and copyright which Congress had received and been unable to act upon. They would also have been aware of the May 2, 1783 resolution of the Congress recommending that the individual states enact copyright laws giving authors an exclusive copyright in their books not previously printed "for a certain time, not less than fourteen years from the first publication."[55] The close analogy between an exclusive right for a limited time granted to authors for their writings and a similar exclusive privilege granted to inventors for their discoveries would not have escaped them.

Finally, a third source of precedent would have been the actual experience of the states in issuing patents and enacting copyright legislation. The extent to which the various delegates would have been aware of this practice is uncertain, but there is every reason to believe that at least some

---

51. There is general consensus that they had knowledge of *Millar v. Taylor*, but the extent to which they were aware of and understood the holding in *Donaldson v. Becket* is a matter of considerable dispute. *See, e.g.,* Chapter Two, notes 185 and 186 and accompanying text *supra.*

52. Patterson, for example, certainly so argues ("[t]he use of the word 'securing' indicates that the statutory copyright was to affirm and protect an existing right, not create one"). *See* LYMAN RAY PATTERSON, COPYRIGHT IN HISTORICAL PERSPECTIVE at 194 (Nashville 1968). *Cf.* Bugbee's view that the use of "securing" implies that the clause was intended to protect natural, inherent rights of authors and inventors. *See* BUGBEE, *supra* note 3, at 129.

53. See Chapter Six, *infra,* for a discussion of the more likely meaning of "securing" as used in the clause.

54. *See supra* text accompanying note 27.

55. *See supra* Chapter Two, note 172 and accompanying text.

of them were cognizant of what their own and neighboring states were doing in this regard. Note that a majority of the delegates at the time of the convention were active in some capacity in their state governments.[56]

However, it is precisely because the delegates were familiar with the Statute of Monopolies either on legal or political terms that they were not about to give Congress any general power to create monopolies.[57] That was entirely too reminiscent of the power of the royal prerogative which was the last thing that any one wanted to grant to either the executive or the legislative branches contemplated by the proposed Constitution. While they were cognizant that the patent grant constituted an express exception to the general ban on monopolies that had existed in England for more than 150 years,[58] they also perceived patents to be monopolies, albeit of a limited and acceptable type. If therefore they were to give power to Congress to secure exclusive rights for limited times to inventors in their discoveries, it was necessary to do so expressly. This would have seemed so obvious to them as to merit almost no discussion.

Aside from the precedents known to the delegates, a point of interest is the extent to which authors, inventors, and others sought to influence the delegates to make some provision in the Constitution for granting limited term exclusive rights to authors and inventors for their writings and inventions. One noted commentator on the history of the patent law, Frank Prager, states unequivocally that this occurred, saying: "It was also recognized that federal rather than statewide legislation was needed in this field. Therefore, when the federal convention of 1787 came to consider questions of such legislation, provision for patents and copyrights was urged by a number of interested persons."[59]

---

56. *See supra* text following note 28. BUGBEE, *supra* note 3, at 128 (asserts that "[t]he major contributions of the state patent and copyright policies lay in the precedents which they had accumulated by that year [1787] and the 'education' which they had provided for men who soon left the states to play a national role").

57. Indeed, the failure of the draft Constitution to contain an express *prohibition* on monopoly would be raised as an objection to it. *See supra* text accompanying Chapter One, notes 31–33.

58. The ban in the Statute was not nearly as general as they—or most knowledgeable Englishmen for that matter—supposed, but they most certainly understood the intent of the Statute to curb the royal prerogative.

59. Frank D. Prager, *Historic Background and Foundation of American Patent Law*, 5 AM. J. LEG. HIST. 309, 317 (1961).

This is misleading in several respects. First of all, the members of the convention were not considering such legislation per se, but rather what the power of Congress should be to enact such legislation.[60] Secondly, there is nothing in the writings of the delegates or of those with whom the delegates corresponded which indicates that a constitutional provision for patents and copyrights was urged on the delegates by anybody outside the convention itself.[61] Although the assertion continues to be made,[62] no contemporaneous documentation has been found which provides any specific evidence that such a provision was in fact directly pressed on the delegates by anyone.

Nonetheless, there was quite likely an attempt, albeit in an indirect sense, to recommend to their deliberations that knowledge and invention be encouraged and rewarded by the state. In an address to the Pennsylvania Society for the Encouragement of Manufactures and the Useful Arts on August 9, 1787 in Philadelphia, Tench Coxe made express reference to the fact that the federal convention was then in session in that city and went on to state:

> We must carefully examine the conduct of other countries in order to possess ourselves of their methods of encouraging manufactories, and pursue such of them, as apply to our own situation, so far as it may be in our power. Exempting raw materials, dye-stuffs, and certain implements for manufacturing, from duty on importation, is a very proper measure. Premiums for useful inventions and improvements, whether foreign or American, for the best experiments in any unknown matter, and for the largest quantity of any valuable raw material, must have an

---

60. There is a tendency for commentators to confuse authority granted to Congress by the constitutional provision with some form of inherent constitutional authority. Thus, see, for example, J. B. Gambrell, *The Constitution and the In Personam Defense of First Invention*, 39 J. PAT. OFF. SOC'Y 791, 799 (1957) ("[t]he Constitutional provision, it is clear, established in the owner of a *valid* patent grant the right to exclude others from its use") Clearly, the constitutional provision did nothing of the sort, but instead merely gave the Congress the power to statutorily establish such a right in a patentee.

61. But even if this had actually occurred, the delegates were prevented by the secrecy rule adopted on May 29, 1787 from commenting on their deliberations outside the convention itself. For various contemporaneous views on the secrecy rule, see WARREN, *supra* note 25, at 134–39.

62. *See, e.g.*, Arthur H. Seidel, *The Constitution and a Standard of Patentability*, 48 J. PAT. OFF. SOC'Y 1, 23 (1966) ("it is believed that the various developers of steam boats and their supporters pressed members of the convention for a constitutional provision").

excellent effect. They would assist the efforts of industry, and hold out the noble incentive of honourable distinction to merit and genius. The state might with great convenience enable an enlightened society, established for the purpose, to offer liberal rewards in land for a number of objects of this nature. Our funds of that kind are considerable, and almost dormant. An unsettled tract of a thousand acres, as it may be paid for at this time, yields very little money to the state. By offering these premiums for useful invention, to any citizen of the union, or to any foreigner, who would become a citizen, we might often acquire in the man a compensation for the land, independent of the merit which gave it to him. If he should be induced to settle among us with a family and property, it would of more consequence to the state than all the purchase money.[63]

While purporting to address these remarks in the context of the concerns of the state of Pennsylvania, Coxe was also in a very real sense directing them toward the delegates working to draft the new form of government for the United States. There is good reason to believe that Madison was apprized of these remarks by Coxe for less than a fortnight later he would propose that the Congress be given authority "to encourage by premiums & provisions, the advancement of useful knowledge and discoveries."[64]

Donner has argued that Noah Webster's "close proximity to the Constitutional Convention coupled with his familiarity with the delegates makes it likely that he played some indirect role in the development of the copyright clause."[65] While the contemporaneous record makes clear that Webster had vigorously sought state copyright laws and was in favor of some form of national copyright law, there is no direct evidence to support the view that Webster either sought to influence, or in fact influenced, the delegates, with regard to the drafting of the intellectual property clause. In this regard, it should be noted that Webster in later life was not reticent in setting forth his role in the development of copyright law in this country, and he never made any allegation that he had influenced, either directly or indirectly, the content of the intellectual property clause.

---

63. Quoted from *An address to an assembly of the friends of American manufacture, convened for the purpose of establishing a society for the encouragement of manufactures and the useful arts, read in the university of Pennsylvania, on Thursday the 9th of August, 1787—by Tench Coxe, Esq. and published at their request*, 2 THE AMERICAN MUSEUM OR REPOSITORY OF ANCIENT AND MODERN FUGITIVE PIECES, ETC. at 249–55 (Philadelphia 1787).

64. *See infra* text accompanying notes 83–85.

65. Donner, *supra* note 5, at 372.

The contention that a provision for copyrights and patents was "urged by no one less than Washington" in the context of the federal convention[66] is simply wrong. What Washington actually did was to provide a certificate to the Congress in 1784 on behalf of James Rumsey, one of the early contestants for priority as the inventor of the steamboat, which stated that he believed that Rumsey had made a discovery of vast importance.[67] He made no request whatever that Rumsey be granted a patent or any other form of exclusive right in this discovery. Insofar as is known, Washington never said a word about the intellectual property provision of the proposed Constitution during the deliberations of the delegates.

Nor is there any clear record indicating that "[s]uch a provision was urged for instance by a man who operated a steamboat on the river a few blocks from Convention hall," as Prager has argued.[68] The man in question was John Fitch, who was Rumsey's chief protagonist in the quest for priority of invention with respect to steamboats. This is not to say that Fitch may not well have done so, but only that there is no specific evidence to show that he actually did so.[69] What is known is that he certainly had the chance to lobby the delegates for such a provision at a most opportune time.

Contemporaneous documents indicate that during the week of August 20, 1787 Fitch did demonstrate his steamboat to at least certain of the delegates to the convention.[70] This was not the later successful paddle-wheel version of the steamboat,[71] but rather a most ungainly contraption involving the use of twelve oars. Its method of operation had been described earlier in the December 1786 edition of *Columbia Magazine*: "Each revolution of the axletree moves twelve oars five and a half feet. As six oars

---

66. Prager, *supra* note 59, at 317.
67. The certificate is reproduced in Bugbee. BUGBEE *supra* note 3, at 95–96.
68. Prager, *supra* note 59, at 317.
69. According to Seidel, "[t]he Fitch developments are said to have furthered the adoption of the Constitutional provision." Seidel, *supra* note 62, at 23.
70. The content of this and the next paragraph is taken largely from Frank D. Prager, *The Steamboat Pioneers Before the Founding Fathers*, 37 J. PAT. OFF. SOC'Y 486, 517–18 (1955); and WARREN, *supra* note 25, at 510–12. There is some confusion as to the actual date with Warren stating it was August 22, 1787 and Prager saying it was August 20, 1787. Prager discusses the confusion as to dates and makes a persuasive argument that it was in fact August 20th. *See* Prager, *id.* at 518.
71. In 1787 neither Fitch nor Rumsey were attempting to build a paddlewheel version because of Benjamin Franklin's recent disparagement of the use of steam-actuated paddlewheels as a means of propulsion. *See* Prager, *supra* note 59, at 505–08.

come out of the water, six more enter the water, which makes a stroke similar to the paddle of a canoe." Ungainly as it was, and exceedingly prone to mechanical failure, it nonetheless successfully demonstrated that steam could be used to propel a boat against the current of a river.

The number of delegates who were actually present for the demonstration is uncertain, although three are specifically known by name. Fitch recorded in his journal that nearly all the members of the convention were present.[72] Whether any of the delegates actually rode on the boat is a matter of some dispute.[73] What was discussed between Fitch and the delegates is not known, but it can reasonably be supposed that he pressed his claims of priority with respect to the steamboat and further sought some form of exclusive recognition as the inventor of the steamboat. This was at a time when he was vigorously seeking state patents for his steamboat, and had become more than a little aware of the vagaries of obtaining such patents.[74] Thus, it is likely that he sought some means of obtaining exclusive rights through the federal government which at the time he would have perceived as Congress.

D. First Proposals

His timing was highly appropriate for on August 18, 1787 the convention received its first proposals for what would ultimately become the intellectual property clause. Before discussing those proposals, it is useful, however, to establish the background against which they were submitted. On July 24th, a five-member Committee of Detail had been appointed for the purpose of preparing a draft of a Constitution based on various resolutions which had been adopted by the convention to that point. On July

---

72. This according to Warren.WARREN, *supra* note 25, at 511. Prager, however, states that "it is not reported how big the group was." Prager, *supra* note 70, at 517.

73. Prager states that a group of delegates appeared "to take a sail" on Fitch's steamboat. Prager, *supra* note 70, at 517. Turner, however, rather vigorously contends that no delegate actually rode on the boat. *See* E. M. TURNER, JAMES RUMSEY: PIONEER IN STEAM NAVIGATION at 114–15 (Scottsdale Pa. 1930). Wescott, however, quotes an entry in the diary of the Rev. Ezra Stiles of New Haven, Connecticut, dated August 27, 1787, which states that Judge Ellsworth, a Connecticut delegate to the convention, newly returned to Connecticut, "was on board the boat, and saw the experiment succeed." *See* T. WESCOTT, LIFE OF JOHN FITCH at 192–93 (Philadelphia 1878).

74. *See* Prager, *supra* note 70, at 517–21.

26th several additional resolutions were given to the Committee. None of these made any reference to inventors or authors or any rights or privileges respecting inventions or written works. The resolution given to the Committee with respect to legislative powers stated only:

> That the National Legislature of the United States ought to possess the legislative Rights vested in Congress by the Confederation; and moreover to legislate in all Cases for the general Interests of the Union, and also in those Cases to which the States are separately incompetent, or in which the Harmony of the United States may be interrupted by the Exercise of individual Legislation.[75]

Although the details are vague (with the exception of the rights granted to Congress by the Articles of Confederation), this resolution certainly is sufficiently broad as to permit specific legislative authority to be set forth with respect to inventors and authors if that should be the course chosen. Alternatively, incorporation of its general language into the Constitution would also have given the Congress authority to legislate with respect to the rights of inventors and authors.

Neither approach was taken in the draft Constitution reported by the Committee on August 6th. While the Committee adopted the approach of enumerating specific powers to be granted to the Congress, it did not set forth any specific powers relating to the authority of Congress to legislate with respect to rights or privileges of inventors and authors. It did contain a grant of power "[t]o regulate commerce with foreign nations, and among the several states"; and "to make all laws that shall be necessary and proper for carrying into execution the foregoing powers, and all other powers vested, by this Constitution, in the government of the United States, or in any department or officer thereof."[76] Similar language appears in the Constitution as ratified, and, as has been suggested, an argument can be made that language of this type implicitly grants to the Congress the power to legislate with respect to patents and copyright.[77] But the subsequent course of events would lead the delegates down a different path.

The powers to be granted to Congress were enumerated in Article VII of the draft Constitution.[78] They were not taken up for discussion until

---

75. RECORDS OF THE FEDERAL CONVENTION OF 1787, *supra* note 1, at 131–32.
76. *Id.* at 181–82.
77. *See supra* text accompanying notes 17 and 18.
78. The printed copies given to the delegates inadvertently repeated Article VI as the heading. *See* RECORDS OF THE FEDERAL CONVENTION OF 1787, *supra* note 1, at n.181.

August 16th. They said nothing about inventors and patents or authors and copyrights. However, on August 18th a number of additional powers for the Congress were proposed and out of certain of these came the intellectual property clause.

This is where it gets both interesting and complicated. The Journal of the Convention[79] for August 18, 1787 lists twenty additional powers "proposed to be vested in the Legislature of the United States," among which were: To secure to literary authors their copy rights for a limited time; To encourage, by proper premiums and provisions, the advancement of useful knowledge and discoveries; To grant patents for useful inventions; To secure to authors exclusive rights for a certain time; [and] To establish public institutions, rewards and immunities for the promotion of agriculture, commerce, trades, and manufactures.[80] These proposals served as the genesis for the clause, but unfortunately the Journal says not a word about who offered them or why.

E. Who Made the Proposals

Madison's Notes are both more revealing and in some respects more enigmatic. The problem with his Notes is that he edited them after they were written and what was ultimately published in 1840 does not in some instances reflect what he initially wrote at the time of the events described. His notes for August 18, 1787 are among those he edited. Fortunately, his original notes are available in the Library of Congress and the nature of the editing is known. But that is precisely what produces the enigma.

As published, Madison's Notes for Saturday August 18th state:

> Mr. Madison submitted in order to be referred to the Committee of detail the following powers as proper to be added to those of the General Legislature . . . To secure to literary authors their copy rights for a limited time . . . To encourage by premiums & provisions, the advancement of useful knowledge and discoveries. . . .
>
> These propositions were referred to the Committee of detail which had prepared the Report and at the same time the following which was moved by Mr. Pinkney [sic]: in both cases unanimously. . . . To grant

---

79. As one of its first acts, the convention had chosen William Jackson as official secretary. This was a position for which Jackson had assiduously lobbied the other delegates; but he was a poor choice, because the Journal is at best a very incomplete record of what transpired at the convention.

80. RECORDS OF THE FEDERAL CONVENTION OF 1787, *supra* note 1, at 321–22.

patents for useful inventions[;] To secure to Authors exclusive rights for a certain time[; and] To establish public institutions, rewards and immunities for the promotion of agriculture, commerce, trades and manufactures . . . .[81]

They thus clearly establish that Madison and Pinckney made the proposals which ultimately led to the clause. They also suggest that Pinckney was the first to propose that the Congress explicitly have the power to grant patents for useful inventions, although not in the context of the South Carolina Plan as he later asserted.[82]

But Madison's unedited Notes reveal a different story.[83] His original entries began: "Mr. Pinkney proposed for consideration several additional powers which had occurred to him. [See Journal of Convention.]"[84] This was followed immediately by: "Mr. M. proposed the following,. to be referred to a Committee." Then came a list of ten numbered congressional powers which Madison had suggested, including the following: "6 to secure to literary authors their copy rights for a limited time. *7 to secure to the inventors of useful machines and implements the benefits thereof for a limited time.* . . . 9 to encourage by [proper][85] premiums and provisions, the advancement of useful knowledge and discoveries. . . ." At the end of this listing was the statement: "These motions were referred to the Committee of detail who had prepared the reports nem con." All of this material was subsequently crossed out and a paper, also in Madison's handwriting, pasted over it containing the material found in the printed version.

What is interesting and perplexing about this is that item 7 above is nowhere found in the printed version of Madison's Notes or in the Journal of the Convention.[86] Nor is it found in any of at least seven other sets of notes from the convention which have been printed. Why then did

---

81. RECORDS OF THE FEDERAL CONVENTION OF 1787, *supra* note 1, at 477–78.
82. *See supra* text accompanying notes 11–13.
83. This discussion is taken from RECORDS OF THE FEDERAL CONVENTION OF 1787, *supra* note 1, at 324; BUGBEE, *supra* note 3, at 193.
84. Farrand, who was normally quite meticulous in citing Madison's Notes, makes no reference to and does not disclose the bracketed sentence.
85. Farrand notes several changes in this list from the edited version but fails to note that the edited version does not contain the word "proper" in item 9 (emphasis supplied).
86. Fenning suggests or at least infers that Madison submitted two separate minutes to the Committee of Detail, one containing item 7 and the other not. *See* Fenning, *supra* note 10, at 112–13 (reprinted in 11 J. PAT. OFF. SOC'Y at 441–42). But there is nothing in Madison's Notes that indicates this to have been the case.

Madison put it in his original Notes and later edit it out? The suggestion has been made that he later came to believe "that Pinckney alone had made the suggestion that the future Congress be empowered to grant patents."[87] But Madison was meticulous about transcribing his short notes taken during the discussions into a more detailed product within a short time of when the discussion had actually occurred. Moreover, he must have been fully aware of what he had actually proposed as additional powers for Congress so that it is difficult to understand why he would insert into his original Notes a proposal that the Journal of the Convention does not indicate was ever presented. The situation would make more sense if he had deleted or misrepresented a proposal made by Pinckney, but this does not seem to have been the case.[88]

Thus, for whatever reason, Madison himself provides the best evidence that it was Pinckney who first proposed that the Constitution grant power to the Congress to issue patents for useful inventions. Nonetheless, the claim continues to be made that Madison was one of those responsible for suggesting that the Congress be given power to issue patents.[89] This is not to say that Madison played no significant role in the origination of the intellectual property clause; he obviously did. But it was in the context of protecting the rights of authors rather than those of inventors.

It must be remembered first and foremost that Madison during this period was of a most scholarly inclination. As such he was highly interested in protecting the interests of authors and of scholarship in general. He had served on the committee which in 1783 had drafted the congressional resolution recommending to the states that they adopt copyright laws.[90] In preparing for the convention he had expressed concern about the lack of uniformity in state laws concerning literary property.[91] It is thus not at all surprising that he should propose that Congress have power to grant copyrights for a limited time and to encourage the advancement of useful

---

87. BUGBEE, *supra* note 3, at 193.
88. Madison intensely disliked Pinckney, and the contention has been made that his failure to record anything about details of the South Carolina Plan into his Notes, and to claim that a later Pinckney version of it was incorrect or at worst a forgery, resulted from this dislike. *See* Collier & Colier, *supra* note 12, at 69–70. If this was indeed the case, it renders it even more difficult to understand why Madison would later in effect make an "admission against interest" that Pinckney had been the one to suggest that Congress have the power to grant patents. *See* BUGBEE, *supra* note 3, at 127.
89. *See, e.g.,* Prager, *supra* note 59, at 317–19; Fenning, *supra* note 10, at 113.
90. *See supra* Chapter Two, text accompanying notes 171–74.
91. *See supra* text accompanying and following note 3.

knowledge and discovery by "premiums and provisions." The latter proposal, while including invention within its ambit, is clearly not limited to invention. Rather, it has a Baconian sweep to it and is meant to encompass scholarship and discovery in their broadest sense.

Pinckney's motivations are less apparent. Unlike Madison, he was no scholar and never pretended to be. He, too, had served in the Continental Congress and was a strong nationalist. But in almost every other way, he differed markedly from Madison. Why then would he propose that Congress have power to grant patents for useful inventions, to secure to authors exclusive rights for a certain time, and to establish rewards and immunities for the promotion of agriculture, commerce, trades, and manufactures?

The most likely answer is that he was already a politician at a time when to be considered such was still abhorrent to most office holders.[92] As a politician, he had learned to be aware of the concerns of constituents, and he would think in terms of agriculture, commerce, trades, manufactures, and useful invention, whereas Madison did not. Pinckney's interests were at the pragmatic level of the practicing politician, whereas Madison's were—at least during this period—on a higher intellectual level. Moreover, Pinckney was from South Carolina which had enacted the only general state statute authorizing both copyrights and patents to be granted.[93] He had in fact been a member of the state legislature in 1784 when this statute was enacted. It might reasonably be inferred that his knowledge of this state statute played a role in the proposals he made on August 18, 1787.[94]

Unfortunately, Pinckney has confused the issue almost as much as has Madison, for like Madison he has left a conflicting record. It may be recalled that in a pamphlet published shortly after the federal convention ended, Pinckney alleged that in the South Carolina Plan he had proposed that the Congress have authority "to secure to authors the exclusive rights to their

---

92. Undoubtedly one of the reasons why Madison disliked him so much was that he acted as a politician when government was still considered by many if not most of those involved as a duty imposed upon gentlemen.

93. *See supra* Chapter Two, text accompanying notes 101 and 102.

94. As pointed out by Bugbee, however, "[t]he wording of Pinckney's patent and copyright suggestions of August 18 nevertheless bears little resemblance to any portion of this South Carolina law, which may have provided only inspiration." BUGBEE, *supra* note 3, at 127. But Pinckney may have deliberately simplified his proposals in accordance with the views prevalent among the delegates that a constitution should contain only "essential principles" and "general propositions." *See supra* Chapter One, text accompanying note 39.

performances and discoveries."[95] Thirty odd years later, however, when John Quincy Adams was preparing the Journal of the Convention for publication, he could not find a copy of the South Carolina Plan and accordingly ask Pinckney to supply him with one. Pinckney responded by stating:

> I have already informed you I have several rough draughts of the Constitution I proposed & that they are all substantially the same differing only in words & the arrangement of the Articles—at the distance of nearly thirty two years it is impossible for me now to say which of the 4 or 5 draughts I have was the one but enclosed I send you the one I believe was it—*I repeat however that they are substantially the same differing only in form & unessentials.*[96]

The version supplied shows twenty powers to be granted to the Congress[97] but does not include a power "to secure to authors the exclusive rights to their performances and discoveries" or any other power relating to the protection of intellectual property.[98]

Even if it is assumed that Pinckney had in fact sought in the original South Carolina Plan to give Congress power to protect the exclusive rights of authors, then like Madison he subsequently edited out this as apparently being an "unessential." But taking Pinckney at face value—inconsistency and all—it is clear that the South Carolina Plan never contained any reference to a power in Congress to grant patents or otherwise protect inventors with respect to their inventions.

---

95. *See* Pickney, *supra* note 11 and accompanying text.
96. THE RECORDS OF THE FEDERAL CONVENTION OF 1787, *supra* note 1, at 428, 595 (emphasis supplied).
97. THE RECORDS OF THE FEDERAL CONVENTION OF 1787, *supra* note 1, at 598.
98. Madison would subsequently point this out, noting that "[t]he pamphlet refers to the following provisions which are not found in the plan furnished to Mr. Adams as forming a part of the plan presented at the Convention: . . . 6. For securing exclusive rights of authors and discoverers." Letter from James Madison to W. A. Duer (June 5, 1835), *in* THE RECORDS OF THE FEDERAL CONVENTION OF 1787, *supra* note 1, at 534, 535. Madison erred somewhat here because the pamphlet published on behalf of Pinckney immediately after the convention did not speak in terms of granting power to Congress "for securing exclusive rights of authors and discoverers" but rather provided for a power in Congress "to secure to authors the exclusive rights to their performances and discoveries." *See supra* text preceding note 95.

F. The Nature of the Proposals

The August 18th proposals are interesting in several respects. First of all, they are not limited to merely authority to issue patents and copyrights. Indeed, two of them are much broader.[99] One in particular, that "to encourage, by proper premiums and provisions, the advancement of useful knowledge and discoveries," appeared on its face sufficiently broad to give Congress whatever power it deemed "proper" to promote what would quickly be called "the progress of science and useful arts," including by the issuance of patents and copyrights. But there was concern that more specific authority was required before Congress could grant even limited-term monopoly rights of a desirable type such as patents and copyrights.

Secondly, the reference to "patents" clearly indicates an intent to give Congress power to emulate and follow the British practice of granting limited-term rights to inventors in their inventions.[100] Unlike in the context of the copyright proposals, there is no specific reference to either "a limited time" or " certain time" as the term of a patent. The reason for this is that, unlike the case with copyright, there was no uncertainty as to whether the patent term was limited. The Statute of Monopolies clearly indicated that it was limited,[101] and there was thus no need to specifically require a limited time as long as there was a specific reference to "patent." But it was unclear to the Framers whether there was in fact a perpetual common-law property right in copyright or whether the Statute of Anne had limited the copyright term as set forth therein. What is clear is that both Pinckney and Madison did not want a perpetual copyright term but rather wanted something along the lines set forth in the Statute of Anne.

G. Creating the Final Clause

In any case, the proposals submitted by both Madison and Pinckney on August 18th were referred to the Committee of Detail which made a partial report on August 22nd but said nothing about those proposals from either gentleman relating to intellectual property. On August 31st, the delegates agreed to "refer such parts of the Constitution as have been postponed, and such parts of reports as have not been acted upon to a committee of a

---

99. *See supra* text accompanying note 80.
100. Recall that the state practice in this respect did not refer to these limited-term exclusive rights as "patents." *See supra* Chapter Two, text following note 96.
101. *See supra* Chapter Two, text preceding note 68.

member from each state.[102] Since Rhode Island had never sent delegates, and New York did not have its delegation present and hence could not vote, this became the Committee of Eleven. Madison was on it; Pinckney was not.[103]

On September 1st and 4th, this Committee of Eleven reported partially on the unfinished business presented to it. Again there was no reference to intellectual property matters. On September 5th the Committee reported five unresolved matters pertaining to the powers to be granted to the Congress. The fifth of these was what became the intellectual property clause, to wit: "To promote the progress of science and useful arts by securing for limited times to authors and inventors, the exclusive right to their respective writings and discoveries." As Madison reported, this clause was approved without debate.[104] There is no record to indicate how the intellectual property proposals submitted by Madison and Pinckney were transformed into this clause. Madison, being a member of the Committee that made the change, obviously knew but never said. Neither did any other member of the Committee. It is quite conceivable, however, that Madison was the author.[105]

On its face, the clause appears to be narrower than certain of the proposals out of which it came. Had it stated simply that Congress is given power "to promote the progress of science and useful arts," it would have encompassed essentially all of the proposals put forth by Madison and Pinckney and in addition could be interpreted to authorize Congress to grant patents and copyright. The inclusion of specific language authorizing patents and copyright occurred because the delegates were concerned that in the absence of specific authorization of this type, the general antipathy toward monopolies under the English common law which continued to be strongly felt in the new United States would preclude interpreting more

---

102. II THE RECORDS OF THE FEDERAL CONVENTION OF 1787, *supra* note 1, at 473, 481.

103. The other ten members were Gilman, King, Sherman, Brearley, Governeur Morris, Dickinson, Carrol, Williamson, Butler, and Baldwin.

104. THE RECORDS OF THE FEDERAL CONVENTION OF 1787, *supra* note 1, vol. II at 508–10. The only difference in the Journal report of this clause was the deletion of the comma between "inventors" and "the." *See* THE RECORDS OF THE FEDERAL CONVENTION OF 1787, *supra* note 1, vol. II at 505.

105. He had incentive to do so because he had clearly proposed that the Congress have power to secure copyrights for authors and because he was highly interested in protecting scholarly works. Moreover, his defense of the clause in *The Federalist No. 43*, while not conclusive on the point, is suggestive that he had more than a passing interest in it.

general language as authorizing the issuance of the limited-term monopolies known as patents and copyright. But the express inclusion of this specific authority could readily be interpreted as limiting the authority of Congress to promoting the progress of science and useful arts *only* through the issuance of patents and copyright.[106]

In private correspondence with Tench Coxe in March 1790, Madison, moreover, seemed to clearly indicate that the language of the clause was intended to be limiting and that the delegates (or at least those that served on the Committee of Eleven) expressly rejected any broader grant of authority.[107] However, he veered all over the place on this point. But he would rather quickly reject the view he espoused to Coxe that refusal of the delegates to adopt particular language precluded any interpretation of the actual language to include powers encompassed in the rejected language. Initially, at least, various members of Congress also expressed a concern of this type.[108]

If the language of the clause was indeed intended to be limiting, one may reasonably ask why the proposed broader grants of power were defeated in committee. There is little to indicate the nature of the debates in this regard, but Warren states that Governeur Morris, who was on the Committee with Madison, argued against the proposal "to establish public institutions, rewards and immunities for the promotion of agriculture, commerce, trades, and manufactures," observing: "[I]t is not necessary. The exclusive power at the seat of government will reach the object."[109] Exactly what Morris intended by this comment is unclear, but it rather strongly suggests a belief that the clause was not intended to limit the power of Congress "to promote the progress of science and useful arts" to only the issuance of copyright and patents, and that Congress (and presumably the executive branch) had other powers to accomplish this purpose.

There is another context in which the clause appears to be narrower than the proposals out of which it came. That is in its reference to the "writings" of "authors." While the copyright proposals put forth by both Madison and Pinckney referred to "authors," they did not mention "writings."[110] Moreover, at this time copyright in Great Britain covered

---

106. For a discussion of this point of view see Chapter Five.
107. *See infra* Chapter Five, notes 93–95 and accompanying text.
108. *See infra* Chapter Five, Part B.
109. CHARLES WARREN, THE MAKING OF THE CONSTITUTION at 702 (rev. 1937).
110. *See supra* text accompanying note 80.

more than simply "writings."[111] According to a congressional study written in 1956:

> The fact that the clause contained the word "writings" while the original proposals did not, permits opposing conjectures: (1) the word was used as a limitation upon the broad scope of all proposals; or (2) since the word was included by the committee on style and there was no consideration by the convention, it can be inferred that the change was not substantive but merely formal.[112]

Although the study got its committees wrong, it was essentially correct in suggesting that the issue raised by incorporation of "writings" in the clause was the extent to which it was intended to be a limitation on the copyright power of Congress.[113]

Be that as it may, September 8th saw the delegates appoint a Committee on "Stile and Arrangement" for the purpose of revising the style of and arranging the articles of the Constitution which had been agreed upon by the delegates. Madison was again a member of this Committee and Pinckney was not. On September 12th, the Committee reported a draft of the Constitution which left the intellectual property clause the same. The final draft of the Constitution was approved on September 17th with the clause remaining intact.

The final draft, however, on its face appears to have a last minute correction in the clause. As originally written in the September 17th draft the clause contains the phrase "for a limited time." This was corrected by drawing a line through the "a" and adding an "s" to "time" by a caret with the "s" above it. The impression is left from the document itself that this was a last minute change made to the clause for the purpose of permitting the right to be extended.[114] A look at the language of the clause proposed on September 5th and incorporated in the September 12th draft reveals, however, that the change was made to correct a typographical error in the final draft and to render the language consistent with that which had been earlier approved.

---

111. In addition to books and literary productions, it covered maps, charts, and engravings. For more on this see Chapter Nine.
112. Study No. 3, The Meaning of "Writings" in the Copyright Clause of the Constitution in Copyright Law Revision, Studies Prepared for the Subcommittee on Patents, Trademarks, and Copyrights of the Senate Committee on the Judiciary, 86th Cong., 1st Sess. (Washington 1960) at 71.
113. What evidence there is suggests that it was intended to limit copyright to literary expression. *See infra* Chapter Nine, Part E.
114. *See, e.g.,* G. Ramsey, *The Historical Background of Patents,* 18 J. PAT. OFF. SOC'Y 7, 14 (1936).

Thus, no attempt was made to change this clause at the close of the proceedings, even though the final draft may give such an impression.

H. Perspectives

Despite occasional argument to the contrary, the lack of authority in the Continental Congress to legislate with respect to patents or copyrights played no role whatsoever in the decision to call the federal convention. Indeed, the inclusion of the intellectual property clause in the draft Constitution was for all intents and purposes an afterthought, occurring after other more momentous decisions had been taken and acted upon. A cogent caution that should always be borne in mind is that almost nothing is known of the intent of the Framers in including the clause beyond that which is apparent on its face.[115] But what is supposedly apparent on its face has been a matter of substantial dispute, as is evidenced in subsequent chapters.

Ascertaining original intent is a notoriously difficult and frequently irrelevant exercise. Aside from the fact that the only known comments by any Framers relevant to the clause are those by Madison and Governeur Morris, there is nothing to per se indicate that their comments represented the views of any Framer other than themselves, much less that of a majority of the Framers. With the exception of Madison in *The Federalist No. 43,* no Framer ever offered any explanation of the clause or of why it was included in the draft Constitution.

Madison's brief comments in *The Federalist No. 43* are not so much an explanation of the clause as a justification for its inclusion in the Constitution. He wrote, in toto:

> The utility of this power will scarcely be questioned. The copyright of authors has been solemnly adjudged, in Great Britain, to be a right of the common law. The right to useful inventions seems with equal reason to belong to the inventors. The public good fully coincides in both cases with the claims of individuals. The States cannot separately make effectual provision for either of the cases, and most of them have anticipated the decision on this point, by laws passed at the instance of Congress.[116]

---

115. Howard B. Abrams, *The Historic Foundation of American Copyright Law: Exploding the Myth of Common Law Copyright,* 29 Wayne L. Rev. 1119, 1174–75 (1983).
116. THE FEDERALIST at 309 (B. Wright ed. 1961).

These statements are analyzed in more detail later in this work.[117] Suffice it to say here that the utility and the desirability of the authority granted by the intellectual property clause were not as unchallenged as Madison sought to indicate.[118]

Madison's key justification is that "the public good fully coincides in both cases with the claims of individuals." Implicit in this language is the view that the clause was intended not only as a broad express authority to promote the progress of science, i.e., learning, and the useful arts but also as a means of ensuring congressional authority to do so in a particular way, namely, by securing exclusive rights for limited times to authors and inventors in their respective writings and discoveries. The Framers did so because they desired to follow the English practice of granting limited term exclusive rights through the issuance of patents and copyright, which they viewed as the most pragmatic way of encouraging the public benefit at the least cost to the public fisc while at the same time protecting what they perceived to be a property interest of both inventors and authors. Because they viewed the limited-term exclusive rights as monopolies, they deemed it necessary to expressly grant Congress authority to legislate with respect to them.

In an essay written late in his life and published posthumously, Madison clearly explicated this understanding:

> Monopolies tho' in certain cases useful ought to be granted with caution, and guarded with strictness against abuse. The Constitution of the United States has limited them to two cases—the authors of Books, and of useful inventions, in both [of] which they are considered as compensation for a benefit actually gained to the community as a purchase of property which the owner might otherwise withhold from public use. There can be no just objection to a temporary monopoly in these cases; but it ought to be temporary because under that limitation a sufficient recompense and encouragement may be given.[119]

Thus, in Madison's view, the clause was included to ensure the authority of Congress to legislate with respect to the grant of limited-term monopoly

---

117. *See infra* Chapter Six, Part D.
118. As has been noted, Jefferson strongly challenged both the utility and the desirability of the clause as it was worded in the Constitution. *See supra* Chapter One, text accompanying notes 8–27.
119. James Madison, *Aspects of Monopoly One Hundred Years Ago*, 128 HARPER'S MAG. 489, 490 (1914). *See also* IRVING BRANT, 2 JAMES MADISON, 370–71 (New York 1948).

rights to authors and inventors as compensation for the public disclosure of their writings and inventions for the public benefit.

Crosskey suggests that "[r]eading the power, then, in light of the [S]tatute of Anne and the then recent decisions of the English courts, it is clear that this power of Congress was enumerated in the Constitution, *for the purpose* of expressing its limitations."[120] While I have no quarrel with the view that the Framers deliberately placed limitations on congressional power in the clause—and indeed strongly concur in such an interpretation—I disagree with the contention that the clause exists only for the purpose of expressing such limitations. Rather, the "by securing" portion of the clause was included to assure that Congress would indeed have power to legislate regarding the monopolies known as patents and copyrights, albeit within certain constraints set forth in the constitutional language.

One may reasonably speculate as to whether the Framers would have deemed it necessary to include the clause if its express grant of authority concerning limited-term monopoly rights had been excluded. The views expressed by Governeur Morris rather clearly suggest that he perceived there to be no need to set forth a broad authority to legislate with respect to the promotion of "science and useful arts" because "the exclusive power at the seat of government will reach the object."[121] It is questionable whether most of the Framers shared such a point of view. Indeed, the desire to avoid granting broad, unspecified powers to the Congress was exactly the reason why the powers given to Congress were enumerated. But they also accepted the premise that it was the duty of enlightened government to aid in the development of learning and new manufacturing technologies as deemed appropriate and feasible by Congress. Thus, even if they had accepted arguments against the limited-term monopolies known as patents and copyrights, such as those made by Jefferson, it is likely that a clause authorizing Congress "to promote the progress of science and useful arts would still have been included.[122]

The dearth of contemporaneous commentary by the Framers ought not to be taken as indicative that the wording of the clause was so clear as to require no exposition. Rather, the more likely explanation is that in the context of the much more momentous issues addressed during the

---

120. WILLIAM W. CROSSKEY, I POLITICS AND THE CONSTITUTION IN THE HISTORY OF THE UNITED STATES at 486 (1953).

121. *See supra* text accompanying note 109.

122. Even if it had not, it is likely that the broad interpretation of the general welfare clause discussed in Chapter Five ultimately would have produced essentially the same result.

ratification debates, the meaning to be attributed to this clause simply did not assume the relevance it soon would have when the Congress came to look at it and act under its authority. When this happened, it would quickly become apparent that the language was not so innocuous and unambiguous as it at first glance appeared. To understand the issues of interpretation that would quickly arise, it is useful now to parse that language.

CHAPTER FOUR
PARSING THE CLAUSE

Any attempt to come to an understanding of the intellectual property clause must commence with a careful look at its grammatical form as well as its language, and in particular the language setting forth its ostensible purpose.[1] It must also look not only to the justification given for including the clause in the Constitution but more fundamentally to the rationales that existed at the end of the eighteenth century for the limited-term monopoly rights known as patents and copyrights. It is only with the establishment of a contemporaneous baseline that the extent to which the meaning and interpretation of the clause has evolved in the succeeding two centuries can be ascertained and understood.

A. A Balanced Composition

With one exception, the clause exhibits a remarkably parallel or balanced structure.[2] In modern times, the Congress, the courts, and various commentators have on occasion sought to invoke this parallelism to interpret what have been termed the patent and copyright provisions of the clause. Just as often, however, the parallelism has been ignored. Nonetheless, to aid in understanding the clause, it is useful to turn first to its grammatical form,

---

1. That purpose of course is "to promote the progress of science and useful arts." This chapter examines the origin and meaning of the terms "science" and "useful arts" as understood at the end of the eighteenth century and as subsequently interpreted. There are other terms in the clause that also need to have their meanings carefully explored. The meaning attributed to "securing" is addressed in detail in Chapter Six. Chapter Seven analyzes the meanings given to "exclusive right" and "limited terms." Chapters Eight and Nine are devoted to gaining an understanding respectively of the interpretations given to "inventors and their discoveries" and "authors and their writings."
2. The exception is the use of the singular "the exclusive right," as opposed to "exclusive rights." This appears to have been deliberate on the part of the Framers, although most courts and commentators take the view that the use of the singular was inadvertent. *See infra* Chapter Seven, text accompanying notes 4 and 5.

because the aesthetics of the form may have in no small measure influenced the actual language used.

As it came forth from the Committee of Eleven the clause attempted, among other things, through a balanced style of composition much favored in the eighteenth century[3] to harmoniously combine the several proposals for congressional authority relating to exclusive rights in both invention and written works.[4] Although Rich characterizes it as "a consolidation of two proposals which got packaged together,"[5] in reality it encompasses two of the earlier proposals entirely, i.e., those put forth to provide for copyright and patents, and a significant part of a third one, i.e., "to encourage, by proper premiums and provisions, the advancement of useful knowledge and discoveries."[6] In essence it authorizes copyrights and patents for the purpose respectively of encouraging the advancement of useful knowledge and discoveries. But it does not—and was not intended to—limit the promotion of science and useful arts only to the issuance of copyrights and patents.

What is common to the balanced composition of the clause are the terms "promote," "progress," "securing," and "limited times." The usual interpretation is that Congress is given two separate powers involving the common use of these terms. In this view, it is given power (1) "to promote the progress of science . . . by securing for limited times to authors . . . the

---

3. For various discussions on this balanced style of composition in the context of the intellectual property clause, see, e.g., Arthur. H. Seidel, *The Constitution and a Standard of Patentability*, 48 J. PAT. OFF. SOC'Y 1, 9 (1966); Giles S. Rich, *The Principles of Patentability*, 42 J. PAT. OFF. SOC'Y 75, 77–78 (1962); Karl B. Lutz, *Patents and Science: A Clarification of the Patent Clause of the U.S. Constitution*, 32 J. PAT. OFF. SOC'Y 83, 84 (1952); R. I. Coulter, *The Field of the Statutory Useful Arts*, 32 J. PAT. OFF. SOC'Y 487, 491 (1952); R. C. DE WOLF, AN OUTLINE OF COPYRIGHT LAW at 15 (Boston 1925).

4. As is shown, however, this was easier said than done, because copyright and patents appeared to be treated quite differently under the common law and the use of the term "securing" with regard to the rights of both inventors and authors created a significant legal ambiguity. For a discussion on this point, see Chapter Six parts A and C, *infra*.

5. Rich, *supra* note 3, at 78. The manner in which the term "respective" is used in the clause lends credence to this interpretation, but it is not the only one possible. Prager, while acknowledging that "respective" may indeed serve "to correlate 'writings' with 'science' and 'discoveries' with 'useful arts,'" also suggests that it may mean instead or in addition "that each new creation be considered individually and with precision and that it be distinguished from the work of contemporaries or predecessors." Frank D. Prager, *Historical Background and Foundation of American Patent Law*, 5 AM. J. LEGAL HIST. 317 (1961).

6. *See supra* Chapter Three, text accompanying note 80.

exclusive right to their . . . writings," and (2) "to promote the progress of . . . useful arts by securing for limited times to . . . inventors the exclusive right to their . . . discoveries."[7] The balanced composition of the clause explains why the terms "patents" and "copyrights" do not appear therein.[8]

A careful comparison of the actual language of the clause with the proposals submitted by Madison and Pinckney suggests that the conventional wisdom is wrong, and that the clause is actually a consolidation and incorporation of three separate and distinct proposals presented by these gentlemen. The reference to securing to authors for limited times an exclusive right to their writings incorporates the essentially identical proposals first from Madison to secure to literary authors their copyrights for a limited time and second from Pinckney to secure to authors exclusive rights for limited times. The reference to securing to inventors for limited times an exclusive right to their discoveries incorporates Pinckney's proposal to grant patents for useful inventions. This much is generally accepted. What is not generally recognized is that the clause incorporates a third proposal, namely, that by Madison to encourage by proper premiums and provisions the advancement of useful knowledge and discoveries. This is closely similar to the actual language used, i.e., to promote the progress of science and useful arts. Clearly, this proposal by Madison is much broader in scope than the proposals to provide for patents and copyrights, and incorporation of language closely analogous to it[9] in the clause indicates that the Framers viewed the clause as providing much more than merely power to grant patents and copyrights.

---

7. *See infra* note 43 and accompanying text. *See also* In re Bergy, 596 F.2d 952, 958 (C.C.P.A. 1979) ("[s]cholars who have studied this provision, its origins, and its subsequent history have from time to time pointed out that it is really two grants of power rolled into one; first, to establish a copyright system and, second, to establish a patent system"). *Bergy* is a clear example of a prevalent judicial view that the grant of power resides only in the "securing" language of the clause.

8. To use them would literally have destroyed the balanced composition. *Cf.* Pollack's argument that the Framers deliberately refused to use the terms "patents" and "copyrights" because they did not want to limit or tie the clause to the technical meaning of these two terms. *See* Malla Pollack, *Unconstitutional Incontestability?: The Intersection of the Intellectual Property and Commerce Clauses of the Constitution: Beyond a Critique of Shakespeare Co. v. Silstar Corp.,* 18 SEATTLE U. L. REV. 259, 290 (1995). But Pollack cites no contemporaneous evidence for this view, and I know of none.

9. The deletion of "proper premiums & provisions" did nothing to change the broad import of this grant of power.

In this view, Congress is given two broad powers, one "to promote the progress of science . . . [including] by securing for limited times to authors . . . the exclusive right to their . . . writings,' and the other "to promote the progress of . . . useful arts [including] by securing for limited times to . . . inventors the exclusive right to their . . . discoveries." Obviously, the bracketed word "including" does not appear in the clause but there is nothing to indicate that the Framers intended to limit the promotion of science and useful arts solely to the mechanism of copyrights and patents, and in modern times it has not been considered as so limited. The most straightforward way to indicate that the promotion of science and useful arts is not limited to the issuance of copyrights and patents is to write the clause with the bracketed "including" incorporated into it.[10]

Be that as it may, this language posed several issues for the Congress. Should it seek to enact individual private laws granting exclusive patent rights and copyrights to inventors and authors as the states had done with respect to patents, or should it instead enact generic laws under the authority of the clause as the states sought to do with regard to copyrights?[11] If it decided on generic law, would that law encompass both the rights of authors and inventors or would those rights be treated separately?

Initially, both inventors and authors expected Congress to pass private laws securing their rights as the states had done with respect to invention,

---

10. The reasons for so doing are discussed in detail in Chapter Five. In 1979 Judge Rich argued that: "The only restraints placed on Congress [by the intellectual property clause] pertained to the *means* by which it could promote useful arts, namely, through the device of securing 'exclusive rights' which were required to be limited in time, a device known to governments for centuries." *In re Bergy*, 596 F.2d at 958 n.2. This followed from the statement by the Supreme Court in 1973 in *Goldstein v. California* that the clause "describes both the objective which Congress may seek and *the* means to achieve it" (emphasis supplied) 412 U.S. 546, 555 (1973). For the reasons set forth in Chapter Five, I believe that the grant of authority to Congress under the clause "to promote the progress of science and useful arts" is much more expansive than merely "by securing for limited times to authors and inventors the exclusive right to their respective writings and discoveries."

11. The constitutional language is broad enough to contemplate both approaches, but Prager, for one, has been inconsistent in interpreting what the Framers intended. In 1952, he wrote that: "The Constitution contemplates patents granted by Congress, not patent laws enacted by Congress." *See* Frank D. Prager, *Standards of Patentable Invention from 1474 to 1952*, 20 U. CHI. L. REV. 69, 94 (1952). But in 1961, he suggested that "[t]he philosophy of the Constitution seemed to favor uniform securement of rights rather than granting of individual favors." *See* Prager, *supra* note 5, at 320.

and numerous petitions were received from both authors and inventors asking that their rights be secured by private acts.[12] But it quickly became "evident that neither Congress nor the inventors could be burdened with the tedious and uncertain action of a special act for each case, and a general act providing for patents for inventions would be necessary."[13] What was true for inventors was also true for authors.

In enacting the first patent and copyright laws, the first and second federal Congresses certainly understood that the clause granted two separate and distinct powers, the one directed to promoting the progress of science and the other to promoting the progress of useful arts. Thus the title to the Patent Act of 1790 is "An Act to Promote the Progress of Useful Arts,"[14] whereas the title to the Patent Act of 1793 is ""An Act to promote the progress of useful arts; and to repeal the act heretofore made for that purpose."[15] Indeed, the term "science" is nowhere found in the Patent Act of 1790, and appears only once in the Patent Act of 1793.[16] The distinction between the two powers set forth in the clause was pointed out in 1834 by Justice Thompson, when he stated: "This article is to be construed distributively and must have been so understood; for when Congress came to execute this power by legislation, the subjects are kept distinct and very different provisions are made respecting them."[17]

In its 1966 opinion in *Graham v. John Deere Co.*, the Supreme Court sought carefully to distinguish between what it called the patent and copyright provisions of the clause. It noted that the federal patent power stems from the provision authorizing Congress "To promote the Progress of . . . useful Arts, by securing for limited Times to . . . inventors the exclusive Right to their . . . Discoveries" and pointed out that "this qualified authority . . . is limited to the promotion of advances in the 'useful

---

12. The first session of the first federal Congress received eighteen petitions seeking exclusive rights or privileges with respect to writings and invention. Four of these were from authors and fourteen from inventors. *See* EDWARD C. WALTERSCHEID, TO PROMOTE THE PROGRESS OF USEFUL ARTS: AMERICAN PATENT LAW AND ADMINISTRATION, 1787–1836, at 108 (Littleton, Co. 1998).

13. *Proceedings in Congress During the Years 1789 and 1790, Relating to the First Patent and Copyright Laws*, 22 J. PAT. OFF. SOC'Y at 243–44 (1940).

14. 1 Stat. 109.

15. 1 Stat. 318.

16. Section 3 of the Act requires the written description of the invention to be such as "to enable any person skilled in the art or science of which it is a branch, or with which it is most nearly connected, to make, compound, and use the same."

17. Wheaton v. Peters, 33 U.S. (8 Pet.) 684 (1834) (Thompson, J., dissenting).

arts.'"[18] It carefully pointed out that "[t]he [patent] provision appears in the Constitution with the copyright provision, *which we omit as not relevant.*"[19]

In like manner, the term "useful arts" does not appear in the first copyright statute, although interestingly neither does the term "science." Rather, that statute is entitled "An Act for the encouragement of learning, by securing the copies of maps, charts, and books, to the authors and proprietors of such copies, during the times therein mentioned."[20] The relevance of this title to the meaning to be attributed to "science" as used in the clause is discussed in the next part.[21] The critical point here, however, is that in enacting the first patent and copyright statutes the first and second federal Congresses clearly recognized that the power to promote the progress of science, for example, "learning," was separate and distinct from that to promote the progress of useful arts.

In 1973 Irons and Sears argued that the "patent clause" grants power to Congress "to promote the Progress of Science *and* useful Arts." They sought to avoid the distinction made by the Court in *Graham* and indeed by the first two federal Congresses by contending that it is merely the argument of "some writers," and "its footless character is perhaps best exposed by reference to section 3 of the Patent Act of 1793."[22] Specifically, they referred to the statutory language requiring that there be a "written description" of the invention "in such full, clear and exact terms, as to . . . enable any person skilled in the art or science, of which it is a branch, or with which it is most nearly connected, to make . . . and use the same."[23] They seem not to contemplate the possibility that as it appears in the 1793 patent statute, the term "science" is used in a much narrower and more utilitarian sense than it appears in the intellectual property clause. Nor do they mention that the 1793 statute defines patentable invention as "any new and useful art, machine, manufacture, or composition of matter, or any new and useful improvement on any art, machine, manufacture or composition of matter"[24] and does not include "science" within the ambit of patentable subject matter.

---

18. 383 U.S. 1, 5 (1966).
19. *Id.* at 6 (emphasis supplied).
20. Act of May 31, 1790, 1 Stat. 124.
21. *See infra* text accompanying notes 59 and 60.
22. Edward S. Irons & Mary Helen Sears, *The Constitutional Standard of Invention—The Touchstone for Patent Reform,* 1973 UTAH L. REV. 653.
23. Act of February 21, 1793, 1 Stat. 318, at § 3.
24. *Id.* at § 1. This was quite similar to the definition given in the Patent Act of 1790, with only "new and" being added before "useful art."

For a few years, members of the Court sought to observe the distinction set forth in *Graham*.[25] But in 1980 a majority of the Court ignored it in stating that the "subject-matter provisions of the patent law have been cast in broad terms to fulfill the constitutional and statutory goal of promoting 'the Progress of Science and the useful Arts. . . .'"[26] More recently in 1989, the Supreme Court, again referred to the patent provision as reflecting a requirement for "an advance in the 'Progress of Science and useful Arts.'"[27] This reflects a tendency by the judiciary, and indeed many commentators, to ignore the balanced composition of the clause and instead to assume that the patent provision is intended to promote the progress of both "science" and the "useful arts."[28] The fact that scientific discoveries frequently are patentable only adds to the confusion.[29] Indeed, it may be for this reason that some commentators appear to view these terms as interchangeable in their discussions of the patent provision.[30]

---

25. *See, e.g.*, Anderson's Black Rock, Inc. v. Pavement Salvage Co., 396 U.S. 57, 61 (1969) ("[t]he patent standard is basically constitutional, Article I, § 8, of the Constitution authorizing Congress '[t]o promote the Progress of . . . useful Arts' by allowing inventors monopolies for limited times"); Justice Douglas, dissenting in Shultz, dba Walt Shultz Equipment Co. v. Moore, 419 U.S. 930 (1974) ("[i]t bears repeating that patents derive from the specific constitutional authorization of Congress '[t]o promote the Progress of . . . useful Arts, by securing for limited Times to . . . Inventors the exclusive Right to their . . . Discoveries'"); Justices White and Brennan dissenting in Roanwell Corp. v. Plantronics, Inc., 429 U.S. 1079 (1976) ("[w]hether referred to as 'invention' or 'nonobviousness' the requirement is based on the constitutional command that patents be used 'to promote the Progress of . . . useful Arts'").

26. Diamond v. Chakrabarty, 447 U.S. 303, 315 (1980).

27. Bonito Boats, Inc. v. Thunder Craft Boats, Inc., 489 U.S. 141, 146 (1989).

28. As Judge Rich puts it: "Many people have been so conditioned by reading the constitutional clause uncritically, and by reading the plethora of judicial opinions reiterating the phrase, 'To promote the progress of Science and useful Arts. . . .' that they have come to think that that is the purpose of the patent system." *See* Rich, *supra* note 3, at 77.

29. *See, e.g.*, Rebecca S. Eisenberg, *Patents and the Progress of Science: Exclusive Rights and Experimental Use*, 56 U. CHI. L. REV. 1017 (1989) ("[t]he patent laws confer exclusive rights in inventions and discoveries in furtherance of a constitutional purpose 'To Promote the Progress of Science and useful arts'").

30. Thus, for example, Eisenberg cites the clause in stating that "[t]he United States Constitution posits an instrumental justification for patents, allowing Congress to enact patent legislation for the specific purpose of promoting scientific progress." *See* Eisenberg, *supra* note 29, at 1024. *Cf.* the views expressed by the Court of Customs and Patent Appeals that "the

As a corollary, it might reasonably be argued that the purpose of the copyright provision is also to promote the progress of both "science" and the "useful arts." While commentators tend to strongly reject such a notion,[31] the Supreme Court seems to have espoused it in recent years. Thus, e.g., in 1991 Justice Connor, speaking for the Court, stated: "The primary objective of copyright is . . . '[t]o promote the Progress of Science and useful Arts.'"[32] No mention was made of the careful dichotomy between the patent and copyright provisions of the clause set forth in *Graham v. John Deere*, and it is unclear whether Justice O'Connor and the Court actually intended to depart from it. The view expressed by Justice Souter for the Court in 1994 that "copyright's very purpose [is] '[t]o promote the Progress of Science and useful Arts'"[33] would seem to suggest that the Court has now departed from the dichotomy noted in *Graham v. John Deere*, but it may also be an artifact of the Court's continued failure to carefully distinguish between the copyright and patent provisions of the clause.

If the former, then it appears that the Court has moved toward the formerly dissenting views of Justices Brennan and Douglas. Thus, e.g., in a dissenting opinion in 1985 Justice Brennan assumed that the "promotion of science and the useful arts" precluded a copyrighted work from being

---

constitutionally stated purpose of granting patent rights to inventors for their discoveries is the promotion of progress in the 'useful Arts,' rather than in science." *See* In re Bergy, 596 F.2d 952, 958 (C.C.P.A. 1979). Likewise, the Court of Customs and Patent Appeals has pointed out "that the present day equivalent of the term 'useful arts' employed by the Founding Fathers is 'technological arts.'" *Id.* at 959.

31. *See, e.g.*, David Silverstein, *Patents, Science and Innovation: Historical Linkages and Implications for Global Technological Competitiveness*, 17 RUTGERS COMPUTER & TECH. L.J. 261, 291 (1991) ("'[s]cience' as used in the copyright portion of article I, section 8 refers not to the natural sciences as we would interpret science today but rather to artistic and literary creations. The patent provision is also not designed to promote science generally but only science that results in 'useful arts'"); Rich, *supra* note 3, at 79 ("[i]f the promotion of both 'Science and useful Arts' be ascribed as the object of the patent system, then the copyright system would have no stated object"); Coulter, *supra* note 3, at 492 ("obviously the advancement of 'useful Arts' is not a specific goal of the copyright system. Otherwise, copyrights could not be registered on products of the *fine* arts or on books on theoretical astrophysics, for instance"); Lutz, *supra* note 3.

32. Feist Publ'ns, Inc. v. Rural Tel. Serv. Co., 499 U.S. 340, 349 (1991) (cited with approval in Fogerty v. Fantasy, Inc., 510 U.S. ___, 127 L. Ed. 2d 455, 465 (1994)).

33. Campbell v. Acuff-Rose Music, Inc., 510 U.S. 569, 575 (1994).

directed to "concepts, ideas and facts."[34] Likewise, in 1971 Justice Douglas in a dissent argued that a copyright holder's "rights are limited to that which is necessary 'to promote the Progress of Science and useful Arts.'"[35]

The standard treatise on copyright, *Nimmer on Copyright*, suggests that the purpose of copyright is in fact "to promote the progress of science and useful arts," but that this introductory phrase of the clause does not create a rigid standard for copyright but rather at most suggests certain minimal requirements.[36] Nimmer and Nimmer point out that the confusion engendered by the Supreme Court as to whether copyright is intended to promote the progress of useful arts goes back at least to 1903. In that year according to them, the Court "indicated that it is the 'useful arts' that are the subject of copyright legislation under the Constitution."[37] This appeared to turn the balanced construction on its ear, although whether this was what the Court actually intended is doubtful.[38]

Generally, however, in recent years courts have declined to hold that the promotion of the progress of useful arts is a requirement placed on copyright by the clause. The issue tends to come up most frequently when issues of obscenity are raised.[39] Thus, e.g., the Fifth Circuit, in holding that obscenity of a motion picture is not a bar to copyright, has stated that "although Congress could require that each copyrighted work be shown to promote the useful arts," it is not constitutionally required to do so. It went on to conclude that "the [copyright] protection of all writings, regardless of their content, is a constitutionally protected means of promoting science

---

34. Justice Brennan, joined by Justices White and Marshall, dissenting in Harper & Row v. Nation Enterprises, 471 U.S. 539, 581–82 (1985).
35. Joyce Lee v. Senta Maria Runge, 92 S. Ct. 197 (1971).
36. MELVILLE B. NIMMER & DAVID NIMMER, 1 NIMMER ON COPYRIGHT §1.03 (1997 release) at 1–66.7. The merits of this position are addressed in Chapter Seven.
37. NIMMER & NIMMER, *supra* note 36, §1.03[A] n.1. The case was Bleistein v. Donaldson Lithographing Co., 188 U.S. 239 (1903).
38. Despite the views expressed by Nimmer & Nimmer, *Bleistein* also can reasonably be read as suggesting only that, to the extent that copyright may be for the purpose of promoting the useful arts, "the Constitution does not limit the useful to that which satisfies immediate bodily needs." 188 U.S. at 249. Thus, the Court upheld a copyright in circus posters.
39. Early cases seemed to indicate that obscenity could be a bar to copyright because immoral or obscene works do not promote either science or useful arts. *See, e.g.,* Martinetti v. Maguire, 16 F. Cas. 920 (No. 9173) (D. Cal. 1867); Barnes v. Miner, 122 F. 480 (S.D.N.Y. 1903).

and the useful arts."[40] Inherent in the Fifth Circuit's discussion is the presumption that copyright is intended to promote both science and the useful arts, and that essentially any original work, regardless of its content, meets that standard.[41]

This imprecision is not limited to commentators and the courts. Congress, too, has been susceptible to it. Thus in its report accompanying the comprehensive revision of the Copyright Act of 1909, the Judiciary Committee of the House of Representatives emphasized that "the enactment of copyright legislation by Congress under the terms of the Constitution" is predicated "upon the ground that the welfare of the public will be served and progress of science and useful arts will be promoted by securing to authors for limited periods the exclusive right to their writings. . . ."[42] But in enacting the Patent Act of 1952, both houses of Congress in their committee reports took a very different tack; saying in identical language:

> The background, the balanced construction, and the usage current then and later, indicate that the constitutional provision is really two provisions merged into one. The purpose of the first provision is to promote the progress of Science by securing for limited times to authors the exclusive right to their Writings, the word "science" in this connection having the meaning of knowledge in general, which is one of its meanings today. The other provision is that Congress has the power to promote the Progress of useful arts by securing for limited times to inventors the exclusive right to their Discoveries. The first patent law and all patent laws up to a much later period were entitled "Acts to promote the progress of useful arts."[43]

---

40. Mitchell Bros. Film Group v. Cinema Adult Theater, 604 F.2d 852, 860 (5th Cir. 1979), *cert. denied*, 445 U.S. 917 (1980).

41. One commentator has interpreted this to mean that while the clause applies to obscene works, it is to be interpreted by a "lenient standard." *See* Wendy J. Gordon, *An Inquiry into the Merits of Copyright: The Challenges of Consistency, Consent, and Encouragement Theory*, 41 STAN. L. REV. 1343, 1450n (1989).

42. H.R. REP. NO. 2222, 60th Cong., 2d Sess. (1909) at 7. This language was cited by the Court in Sony Corp. v. Universal City Studios, Inc., 464 U.S. 417, 429 (1984).

43. H.R. REP. NO. 1923, 82d Cong., 2d Sess. 4 (1952); S. REP. NO. 1979, 82nd Cong., 2d Sess. 3 (1952), U.S.C.C.A.N. 1952, pp. 2394, 2396, as quoted in In re Bergy, 596 F.2d 952, 958 (C.C.P.A. 1979). It is interesting to note that the Court in *Graham v. John Deere* failed to cite these reports, although they fully supported its interpretation of the balanced construction of the clause.

Despite the inconsistency between the congressional views expressed in 1909 and in 1952, at least as of 1966 when *Graham v. John Deere* was decided, it appears that both Congress and the Court viewed the balanced construction of the clause in the same manner.[44]

Because of his failure to appreciate the nature of the balanced composition found in the clause, science historian Bernard Cohen considers it to be "a curious hodgepodge," "confusing," and "puzzling." He notes that "a good case can perhaps be made that granting patents to inventors would promote 'the Progress of ... useful Arts,'" but finds it difficult to see how "such patents might equally promote 'the Progress of Science.'" He finds it "equally difficult to conceive how copyrights granted to authors could possibly 'promote' either 'the Progress of Science' or 'the Progress of . . . useful Arts.'"[45] His concern about how granting limited-term exclusive rights to authors could possible promote the progress of science is an interesting one which I shall return to, but first it is necessary to look to the origins of the terms "science" and "useful arts" in the clause and to the interpretations that have been argued for them.

B. Originating and Interpreting the Terms "Science" and "Useful Arts"

The terms "Science" and "useful Arts" are not to be found in any of the proposals set forth by Madison and Pinckney. How then did they find their way into the final product? The use of the term "science" is straight-forwardly explained by the fact that in the latter part of the eighteenth century it was synonymous with "knowledge" and "learning."[46] Recall that

---

44. The Federal Circuit, which has responsibility for hearing patent appeals, continues to apply the clear dichotomy set forth by the balanced construction. *See, e.g.,* Constant v. Advanced Micro-Devices, Inc., 848 F.2d 1560, 1564 (Fed. Cir. 1988) ("[t[he power to grant patents to inventors is for the promotion of the useful arts, while the power to grant copyrights to authors is for the promotion of "Science," which had a much broader meaning in the 18th Century than it does today").

45. I. BERNARD COHEN, SCIENCE AND THE FOUNDING FATHERS at 238–39 (New York 1995).

46. Samuel Johnson's *A Dictionary of the English Language* which was the most authoritative dictionary of the times gives "knowledge" as the first definition of "science." Seidel points out that in 1787 "science" meant learning or knowledge generally and in fact had had such a meaning since the times of Lord Coke. *See* Seidel, *supra* note 3, at 11–13. Cohen points out that in the

the promotion of "knowledge" had been part of the proposals placed on the table by Madison. Thus, if Madison was in fact the author as seems likely, it would have readily occurred to him to use the shorter and more succinct "science" in place of the term "knowledge" that he had originally proposed.[47] Moreover, in the context of the balanced style of composition used in the clause, the shorter word would have appeared more aesthetically pleasing.

The origin of the words "useful arts" can also plausibly be determined. In 1787 "useful arts" meant basically helpful or valuable trades. Thus to promote the progress of useful arts presupposed an intent to advance or forward the course or procession of such trades.[48] Less than a month before the intellectual property clause was first set forth by the Committee of Eleven, Philadelphia was the birthplace of a new group called the Pennsylvania Society for the Encouragement of Manufactures and the Useful Arts.[49] Its name was quite descriptive of its purpose.[50] The inaugural

---

eighteenth century, the word "science" was used to denote any branch of organized or demonstrated knowledge and had not acquired the present more restricted sense of the physical or biological or earth sciences. Cohen, *supra* note 45, at 281. Rich not only makes the same point, but emphasizes it by noting that the first copyright law in 1790 was entitled "An act for the encouragement of learning" and that the only word in the constitutional language corresponding to learning is "science." *See* Rich, *supra* note 3, at 78–80. Moreover, in modern times, the congressional interpretation of "science" as used in the clause is as meaning "knowledge." *See supra* text accompanying note 43. *Cf.* the view of the Federal Circuit as set forth in note 44 *supra*.

47. *See supra* Chapter Three, text accompanying note 81.
48. Seidel, *supra* note 3, at 10.
49. At the time the Society was formed the phrase "useful arts" seems to have been in rather common use. Thus, for example, in a letter dated January 25, 1783, George Washington spoke of the "liberal and useful Arts." *See* letter from George Washington to Christopher Colles (Jan. 25, 1783), *in* LIBRARY OF CONGRESS, GEORGE WASHINGTON PAPERS SERIES 3C VARICK TRANSCRIPTS, LETTERBOOK 5, images 3–5.
50. The justification for forming the Society was set forth in the following terms:

    In the various stages of her political existence, America has derived great advantages from the establishment of manufactures and the useful arts. Her present situation in the world calls her by new and weighty considerations, to promote and extend them. The [U]nited [S]tates, having assumed the station of an independent government, requires new resources to support their rank and influence, both abroad and at home. Our distance from the nations of Europe—our possessing within ourselves the materials of the useful arts, and articles of consumption and

meeting of the Society took place on August 9th and was well attended.[51] Consequently, there is good reason to believe that Madison and the other members of the Committee of Eleven were not only aware of its existence but conversant with its aims as well.[52] For much the same reason that "knowledge" was replaced with "science," "manufactures" as first proposed was replaced with "useful arts." It was more aesthetically pleasing and covered much the same territory.[53]

Cohen points out that in the eighteenth century lexicographers were puzzled about the exact sense to be given to "science" and "art" when they appeared in company.[54] He looks to several contemporaneous sources to review how these two terms were interpreted. He begins by noting that the seventh edition of Ephraim Chambers' *Cyclopaedia, or an Universal Dictionary of Arts and Sciences* published in London in 1752 was the foremost scientific dictionary in English at the time the Constitution was drafted, and that Chambers had difficulty in distinguishing the two terms.

---

commerce—the profusion of wood and water, (those powerful and necessary agents in all arts and manufactures)—the variety of natural productions with which this extensive country abounds, and the number of people in our towns, and most ancient settlements, whose education has qualified them for employments of this nature—all concur to point out the necessity of promoting and establishing manufactures among ourselves.

See 2 THE AMERICAN MUSEUM OR REPOSITORY OF ANCIENT AND MODERN FUGITIVE PIECES, ETC. at 167 (Philadelphia 1787) [hereinafter AMERICAN MUSEUM].

51. 2 AMERICAN MUSEUM, *supra* note 50, at 248.
52. As has been suggested, Madison may well have crafted one of his proposals for congressional authority based on his knowledge of the talk given at the inaugural meeting of the Society. *See supra* Chapter Three, text accompanying notes 63 and 64.
53. In this view, it may well have only been the adoption of the balanced structure discussed in the references set forth in note 3 *supra* that precluded the intellectual property clause from commencing, e.g., "to promote the progress of knowledge, learning, manufactures, and the useful arts." *Cf.* Lutz, who suggests that "useful arts" was deliberately used to broaden the field from "new manufactures" because "by the year 1787 it was being recognized even in Great Britain that the phrase 'new manufactures' was an unduly limited object for a patent system, since it seemed to exclude new processes." *See* Lutz, *supra* note 3, at 86. But there is no contemporaneous record to indicate that the Framers either understood or intended a distinction of the type suggested by Lutz.
54. The content of this and the next paragraph is taken from COHEN, *supra* note 45, at 306–08.

According to Chambers, "the precise notion of an art, and *science*, and their just adequate distinction, do not seem to yet be well fixed." He suggested, however, that science "is more particularly used for a formed system of any branch of knowledge comprehending the doctrine, reason, and theory, of the thing, without any immediate application thereof to any uses or offices of life," and in this sense, "the word is used in opposition to *art*." In turn, one of the definitions of "art" given in Samuel Johnson's *Dictionary of the English Language* published in London in 1755 was "trade."

Citing to the Oxford English Dictionary, Cohen goes on to suggest that the Framers were familiar with another sense of "science" intended to clearly distinguish from "art." In this view, "art" implies a skill "in doing anything" that is acquired by knowledge and practice and implies the use of human skill or human workmanship, whereas "science" is generally conceived to be concerned with general rules or "theoretic truth." Phrased more simply, "science" involves theory, whereas "art" refers to practical methods "for effecting certain results." Cohen goes on to note that in 1724 in his Logic Isaac Watts referred to the "remarkable distinction between an art and a science, viz. the one refers chiefly to practice, the other to speculation." According to Cohen, "this stress on practice rather than theory explains why the framers of the Constitution introduced 'practical arts' rather than simply 'arts.'"[55]

Although he chose not to, Cohen could readily have pointed to a 1789 letter by Thomas Jefferson to the President of Harvard College which rather clearly signifies the distinction between arts and science in almost exactly the manner contemplated by the Framers. Therein, Jefferson noted that: "In the arts, I think two of our countrymen have presented the most important inventions." He went on to discuss the inventions of Paine for an iron bridge and Rumsey for navigating by steam. He then turned to "knowledge in Geography, Botany, and Natural History" and closed by saying:

> It is for such as that over which you preside so worthily, Sir, to do justice to our country, its productions and its genius. It the work to which the young men, whom you are forming, should lay their hands. We have spent the prime of our lives in procuring them the precious blessing of liberty. Let them spend theirs in showing that it is the great

---

55. The Framers used the phrase "useful arts" rather than "practical arts," but presumably the meaning is similar.

parent of *science* and of virtue; and that a nation will be great in both, always in proportion that it is free.[56]

Jefferson's use of "art" in the context of invention and "science" in the context of learning was not incidental.

Cohen could also have referred to the language used by Washington in his address to Congress on January 8, 1790 on the state of the union. Among the recommendations presented to Congress were the following:

> The advancement of Agriculture, Commerce and Manufactures, by all proper means, will not, I trust, need recommendation. But I cannot forbear intimating to you the expediency of giving effectual encouragement as well to the introduction of new and useful inventions from abroad , as to the exertions of skill and genius in producing them at home. . . . Nor am I less persuaded that you will agree with me in opinion, that there is nothing which can better deserve your patronage than the promotion of science and literature.[57]

Here Washington was politely informing Congress that in its first session it had failed to enact either patent or copyright legislation, and was recommending that it promptly do so. He clearly delineated between encouragement of inventions in the useful arts for which patent legislation was needed and "the promotion of science and literature"[58] for which copyright legislation was needed.

---

56. Letter from Thomas Jefferson to Joseph Willard (Mar. 24, 1789), *in* 14 THE PAPERS OF THOMAS JEFFERSON at 697 (Julian P. Boyd et al. eds., Princeton, 1958).

57. III DOCUMENTARY HISTORY OF THE FIRST FEDERAL CONGRESS OF THE UNITED STATES OF AMERICA, HOUSE OF REPRESENTATIVES JOURNAL at 253 (Linda G. De Pauw et al. eds., Baltimore 1977). *See also Proceedings, supra* note 13, at 253–54.

58. Washington actually seems to have had several things in mind by his use of the phrase "the promotion of science and literature." In addition to demonstrating the need for copyright legislation, he also seems to have intended this language to encourage Congress to fund a national university. When a motion was made in the House on May 3, 1790 to refer this language to a select committee, Rep. Stone argued that the only constitutional authority given to Congress "in a business of this kind" was to enact copyright legislation which it was in the process of doing. Rep. Sherman in turn pointed out that although a proposal to vest Congress with power to create a national university was presented at the federal convention, it was "negatived" on the ground that such a power could and should be exercised by the states in their separate capacities. *See* XIII DOCUMENTARY HISTORY, *supra* note 57, at 1221.

Perhaps the major defect in Cohen's analysis of the term "science" as used in the clause is his failure to consider the manner in which the first federal Congress viewed it.[59] As has been previously noted, the first federal copyright statute enacted in 1790 did not make any reference to the term "science."[60] But its title, i.e., "An Act for the encouragement of learning...," clearly indicates that the first federal Congress equated the term "science" as it appears in the clause with "learning," or its equivalent, "knowledge." Thus, the first federal Congress interpreted "science" to have its broadest contemporary meaning, a point totally lost on Cohen.

Cohen, while acknowledging that the clause authorizes Congress to grant copyright, nonetheless has great difficulty in perceiving how copyright promotes the progress of science. He concludes that the juxtaposition of "science" and "useful arts" in the clause indicates that "what the framers sought to promote was not the progress of science at large, as we would understand the word 'science' to imply, but more narrowly and specifically those theoretical or general principles of practice that are associated directly with useful inventions or that lead to economic benefits or financial rewards."[61] In no small measure, this appears to be an attempt to read the copyright provision out of the clause, and is obviously at odds with the usual judicial interpretation of the language of the clause.

Cohen is certainly not alone in this regard. Two Justices of the Supreme Court, while not ignoring the copyright provision or reading it out of the constitutional language, had earlier on occasion sought to interpret the juxtaposition of "science" and "useful arts" in much the same fashion that Cohen proposes. Indeed, for all intents and purposes they ignored the existence of the term "useful arts" and instead contended that the term "science" in the clause must be defined in its modern context, and this modern definition in turn must control as to what is actually patentable under the constitutional language.

---

59. As Currie indicates, one of the best means of establishing contemporaneous meanings given to constitutional language at the time of the ratification are the debates and actions of the first federal Congresses. *See* DAVID P. CURRIE, THE CONSTITUTION IN CONGRESS: THE FEDERAL PERIOD 1789–1801, at 296 (Chicago 1997).

60. *See supra* text accompanying note 20.

61. COHEN, *supra* note 45, at 308.

Thus in 1950 Justice Douglas (with Justice Black agreeing), concurring in *Great Atlantic & Pacific Tea Co. v. Supermarket Equipment Corp.*,[62] stated:

> every patent case involving validity represents a question which requires reference to a standard written into the Constitution. Article I, Section 8 contains a grant to the Congress of the power to permit patents to be issued. But, unlike most of the specific powers which Congress is given, the grant is qualified. The Congress does not have free rein, for example, to decide that patents should be freely or easily given. The Congress acts under the restraint imposed by the statement of purpose in Art. I, § 8. The purpose is "To promote the Progress of Science and useful Arts. . . ." The means for achievement of that end is the grant for a limited time to inventors of the exclusive right to their inventions.
>
> Every patent is the grant of a privilege of exacting tolls from the public. The Framers plainly did not want those monopolies freely granted. The invention, to justify a patent, had to serve the ends of science—to push back the frontiers of chemistry, physics, and the like; to make a distinctive contribution to scientific knowledge. That is why through the years the opinions of the Court commonly have taken "inventive genius" as the test.[63] It is not enough that an article is new and useful. The Constitution never sanctioned the patenting of gadgets. Patents serve a higher end—the advancement of science. An invention need not be as startling as an atomic bomb to be patentable. But it has to be of such quality and distinction that members of the scientific field in which it falls will recognize it as an advance.[64]

Aside from its anachronistic interpretation of science in a manner never contemplated by the Framers,[65] this language demonstrates a total disregard for

---

62. 340 U.S. 147 (1950).

63. This was more than a bit misleading. The first reference by the Court to "inventive genius" as a constitutional test for patentable invention had occurred nine years earlier Cuno Eng'g Corp. v. Automatic Devices Corp., 314 U.S. 84, 91 (1941). Indeed, *Cuno* was the first indication by the Court that it perceived a constitutional standard to exist for determining patentable invention. *See infra* Chapter Eight, text accompanying notes 91 and 92. Moreover, no one had ever before contended that "a distinctive contribution to scientific knowledge" was the constitutional standard for patentability.

64. 340 U.S. at 154–55.

65. Burchfiel calls it "[p]erhaps the most egregious recent example of judicial '[f]ailure to recognize the difference between modern and circa-1800 usage,'" citing H. J. Powell, *The Original Understanding of Original Intent*, 98 HARV. L. REV. 885, 896 (1985). *See* Kenneth J. Burchfiel, *Revising the "Original" Patent Clause: Pseudohistory in Constitutional Construction*, 2 HARV. J. L. & TECH. 155, 214 (1989).

the balanced composition used in the clause. It also effectively reads "useful arts" out of the clause and substitutes in its place "science."

Not surprisingly, the views expressed by Justices Douglas and Black have been strongly criticized by most commentators.[66] Prager was perhaps most blunt, saying: "This was about as clearly wrong as a judicial opinion on an intricate matter can possibly be. It was based on a complete disregard for the constitutional promotion of the useful arts."[67] Undismayed and undeterred by the torrent of criticism, Justice Douglas would stand by his position for the remainder of his stay on the Court.[68]

Not all of those who have commented have been so negative. Irons and Sears, for example, call the views expressed by Justice Douglas "much maligned, but obviously correct."[69] In their minds, certain language from the 1833 Supreme Court opinion in *Shaw v. Cooper,* namely, "[i]n the progress of society, the range of discoveries in the mechanic arts, in science, and in all things which promote the public convenience, as a matter of course, will be enlarged,"[70] is indicative that the Court had long espoused the views held by Justices Douglas and Black. As they put it, "[t]he 1833 Court, like Justices Douglas and Black, understood that the Constitution authorized a patent system to promote *both* 'science' and the useful arts."[71]

Whether the quoted language from *Shaw v. Cooper* stands for such a proposition is open to question, particularly because Irons and Sears failed to quote the next sentence from the opinion, i.e., "This results from an aggregation of mind, and the diversity of talents and pursuits, which exist in every intelligent community." It is thus apparent that the Court in

---

66. *See, e.g.,* Burchfiel, *supra* note 65, at 214–15; Albert B. Kimball Jr., *An Analysis of Recent Supreme Court Assertions Regarding a Constitutional Standard of Invention,* 1 APLA Q. J. 204, 206 (1973); Seidel, *supra* note 3, at 7–8; Coulter, *supra* note 3, at 493; Karl B. Lutz, *Are the Courts Carrying Out Constitutional Public Policy on Patents?* 34 J. PAT. OFF. SOC'Y 766, 789 (1952); Prager, *supra* note 5, at 86.

67. Prager, *supra* note 5.

68. See, for example, his dissenting opinion in the memorandum case of Walt Shultz, d.b.a. Walt Shultz Equip. Co. v. Elton M. Moore, 419 U.S. 930 (1974) ("[w]riting against the backdrop of abuses by the Crown in granting monopolies, the Framers did not intend these 'exclusive rights' to be granted freely. To justify the toll exacted by exclusivity, the invention had to make a distinctive contribution to the advancement of scientific knowledge. Besides novelty and utility, a distinctive contribution expanding the frontiers of scientific and industrial knowledge was required").

69. Irons & Sears, *supra* note 22, at 657.

70. 32 U.S. (7 Pet.) 292, 320 (1833).

71. Irons & Sears, *supra* note 22.

making these comments was ranging much wider than simply the purpose of the patent system. Moreover, the year before Chief Justice Marshall, speaking for the court in another patent case and in the context of the purpose of the patent system, declared: "To promote the progress of useful arts is the interest and policy of every enlightened government."[72] He then quoted the clause as a whole, but did not by so doing, indicate or infer that the patent system was intended to promote both science and useful arts. Irons and Sears carefully refrain from noting this language of Justice Marshall or that of Justice Thompson in 1834 when he noted that the provisions of the clause must be construed "distributively" because the subjects are distinct with different provisions made for each of them.[73]

Remarkably, in the more than two hundred years that the clause has been in existence, the Supreme Court has never rendered an opinion as to the meaning of either "science" or "useful arts" as used therein.[74] It clearly had an opportunity to at least interpret the meaning of "useful arts" in 1966 in *Graham v. John Deere Co.*[75] when it opined on a constitutional standard of invention, but failed to do so. The views put forth by Justice Douglas (and agreed to by Justice Black) in *Great Atlantic & Pacific Tea Co.* implicitly suggest that they perceived "science" as used in the clause to mean natural science or, as Justice Douglas put it, "chemistry, physics, and the like." But their views have not been expressly adopted by the Court as a whole, and hopefully will not be, because they create major difficulties with long standing judicial interpretations of the meaning of the copyright provision of the clause.[76]

C. Justifying the Clause

The records of the federal convention, as well as the notes taken by the delegates, provide no indication whatever as to the reasoning or rationales for incorporating the intellectual property clause into the Constitution. The

---

72. Grant v. Raymond, 31 U.S. (6 Pet.) 218, 239 (1832).
73. *See supra* text accompanying note 17.
74. Yet the Court has seen fit to define the term "promote" as used in the clause. See Goldstein v. California, 412 U.S. 546, 555 (1973) ("As employed, the terms 'to promote' are synonymous with the words 'to stimulate,' 'to encourage,' or 'to induce'").
75. 383 U.S. 1 (1966).
76. In this regard, see Chapter Nine on authors and their writings.

only justification given for it by any Framer was that set forth by Madison in *The Federalist No. 43*, where he stated:

> The utility of this power will scarcely be questioned. The copyright of authors has been solemnly adjudged, in Great Britain, to be a right of common law. The right to useful inventions seems with equal reason to belong to the inventors. The public good fully coincides in both cases with the claims of individuals. The States cannot separately make effectual provision in either of the cases, and most of them have anticipated the decision on this point by laws passed at the instance of Congress.[77]

This was succinct and to the point, but it was also a bit misleading.[78] Not only could the utility of the power be questioned, but it had been questioned directly to him by none other than his good friend, Thomas Jefferson.[79] He also knew that many Americans shared Jefferson's strong aversion to monopolies, even of a beneficial kind which patents and copyrights presumably were. Moreover, he, in all probability, was aware that the Society of Arts in both England and the United States was strongly opposed to the issuance of patents.[80] Although he did not expressly so indicate, it is quite possible that Madison viewed "utility" in the context of cost effectiveness. That is to say, giving Congress authority with regard to the issuance of copyrights and patents was quite likely perceived by most Framers as the most pragmatic and least expensive way for the proposed new federal government to actually "promote the progress of

---

77. THE FEDERALIST NO. 43, at 303–04 (James Madison).
78. For a detailed analysis of this language in the context of the meaning to be given to "securing" in the clause, see Chapter Six, Part D, *infra*.
79. *See supra* Chapter One, text accompanying notes 11–13. It is possible, although unlikely, that at the time Madison prepared *The Federalist No. 43* he was unaware of Jefferson's opposition to the limited-term monopolies known as patents and copyrights.
80. According to Brooke Hindle:

> For the Constitutional Convention, the case was open and shut, but the opposition of the Society of Arts to the patent process had more meaning than usually perceived. That society refused to grant a premium for any device that had already been patented. It went further; it required recipients of its rewards to agree never subsequently to accept patents for their inventions. This restriction was a function of its deep-seated opposition to secrecy, and indeed the society had helped materially to breach traditional craft secrecy.

See BROOKE HINDLE, EMULATION AND INVENTION at 18 (New York 1981).

science and useful arts."[81] Abrams suggests that "[t]he stress on the 'utility' of the power and the 'public good' reinforced the notion of public interest as a justification for the copyright system" and presumably the patent system as well.[82]

The ordering of the language used by Madison in *The Federalist No. 43* also strongly suggests that a major—if not the primary—justification for the clause was to assure that Congress would in fact have authority to legislatively protect property rights of authors in their writings and inventors in their discoveries.[83] The idea that inventors had certain rights in their discoveries had exercised a strong attraction in the development of the English patent custom and would continue to do so in the early development of the United States patent system. A naturalized Italian, one Jacobus Acontius, is frequently stated to have been the first to have given specific reasons to the English crown for granting a monopoly patent for invention. In a petition for patent presumably filed in 1559, he is reported as saying: "Nothing is more honest than that those who, by searching, have found out things useful to the public should have some fruits of their rights and labors, as meanwhile they abandon all other modes of gain, are at much expense in experiments, and often sustain much loss. . . ."[84] Although the Framers had never heard of Acontius, there is every reason to believe that they would have agreed entirely with the sentiments he expressed.

Indeed, the idea that the patent system authorized by the clause was intended to supply a just reward to inventors was commonplace in the

---

81. For a discussion on this point, see *supra* Chapter Three, notes 42–45 and accompanying text.
82. Howard B. Abrams, *The Historic Foundation of American Copyright Law: Exploding the Myth of Common Law Copyright*, 29 WAYNE L. REV. 1119, 1176 (1983).
83. Whether the authority contemplated was for the purpose of creating property rights in authors and inventors with regard to their writings and discoveries or was instead for the purpose of assuring protection of existing property rights was a matter of considerable dispute for the next few decades, and the meaning of Madison's language in *The Federalist No. 43* was hotly argued. See Chapter Six in this regard.
84. *See, e.g.,* R. A. CHOATE ET AL., CASES AND MATERIALS ON PATENT LAW (3d ed., St. Paul 1987) at 65; Jeremy Phillips, *The English Patent as a Reward for Invention: The Importation of an Idea*, 3 J. LEG. HIST. 71 (1982); R. A. Klitzke, *Historical Background of the English Patent Law*, 41 J. PAT. OFF. SOC'Y 615, 633 (1959); H. G. FOX, MONOPOLIES: A STUDY OF THE HISTORY AND FUTURE OF THE PATENT MONOPOLY at 27 (Toronto 1947); E. Wyndham Hulme, *The History of the Patent System under the Prerogative and at Common Law*, 12 L. Q. REV. 148 (1896).

United States at the end of the eighteenth century and early in the nineteenth century. Inventors certainly thought that this was the case.[85] Certain members of Congress seem to have held the same view.[86] In 1807 while serving as President, Jefferson clearly recognized both a societal interest and the interest of the inventor in a "profitable" return on invention. In that year, he informed inventor Oliver Evans that "[c]ertainly an inventor ought to be allowed a right to the benefit of his invention for some certain time." He went on to state: "Nobody wishes more than I do that ingenuity should receive a liberal encouragement. . . ."[87]

For the first three decades of the nineteenth century, administrative patent practice in the United States reflected the philosophy of one remarkably strong-willed individual, William Thornton,[88] concerning the nature of the patent system authorized by the clause and the role it should play in protecting the interests of the inventor as opposed to that of the public. This is not to suggest that Thornton did not also seek to protect against the issuance of invalid patents and their use to defraud and dupe the public—he did. But he, like many of his contemporaries, and quite in opposition to modern economic theory, viewed the patent system not so much as being imbued with a public interest, but rather as a mechanism for rewarding legitimate inventors and protecting their rights.[89] When the public interest

---

85. *See, e.g.,* JOSEPH BARNES, TREATISE ON THE JUSTICE, POLICY, AND UTILITY OF ESTABLISHING AN EFFECTUAL SYSTEM OF PROMOTING THE PROGRESS OF USEFUL ARTS, BY ASSURING PROPERTY IN THE PRODUCTS OF GENIUS (Philadelphia 1792); ADDRESS OF THE ADVOCATE OF THE PATENTEES, INVENTORS OF USEFUL IMPROVEMENTS IN THE ARTS AND SCIENCES; PETITIONERS TO CONGRESS FOR REDRESS OF GRIEVANCES (Washington 1806); NEWENGLAND ASSOCIATION OF INVENTORS AND PATRONS OF USEFUL ARTS, REMARKS ON THE RIGHTS OF INVENTORS (Boston 1807); OLIVER EVANS, THE YOUNG MILL-WRIGHT AND MILLER'S GUIDE (2d ed. 1807) at appendix; OLIVER EVANS, EXPOSITION OF PART OF THE PATENT LAW BY A NATIVE BORN CITIZEN OF THE UNITED STATES (Philadelphia 1816).

86. *See, e.g.,* Chapter Six, text accompanying note 111, *infra.*

87. Letter from Thomas Jefferson to Oliver Evans (May 2, 1807), *in* XI THE WRITINGS OF THOMAS JEFFERSON at 200–02 (Andrew A. Lipscomb et al. eds., Washington 1904).

88. Who served as the first Superintendent of Patents from 1802 to 1828.

89. As Machlup points out, this idea that the patent system is intended to secure "a just reward for the inventor is entirely absent from modern economic literature." *See* Fritz Machlup, *An Economic Review of the Patent System, U.S. Senate, Committee on the Judiciary,* 85th Cong., 2d Sess. at 29 (1958). But five years earlier that was exactly what the Supreme Court had declared with regards to both authors and inventors. *See* Mazer v. Stein, 347 U.S. 201, 219

could be perceived as conflicting with that of legitimate inventors, more often than not he came down on the side of the inventors. Nowhere was this more evident than in his policy of keeping issued patents secret and in his informal caveat and reissue practices.[90] He was not adverse to acting independently of statutory authority—and frequently did so—when he perceived such action necessary to protect the interests of inventors.

Certain members of the judiciary also perceived the purpose of the patent system authorized by the clause to be to assure reward to the inventor. Thus, e.g., in 1826 an American judge assumed that the only purpose of the Statute of Monopolies was to reward original inventors, saying: "It is everywhere said that this prerogative power was left in the crown [by the Statute], for the purpose of rewarding the personal merit of ingenious men,—to stimulate their inventive powers."[91] Left unsaid but clear was the presumption that the patent provision of the clause was for the purpose also "of rewarding the personal merit of ingenious men." A few years later, Justice Baldwin, acting in his capacity as circuit judge, made the point clear by stating that "congress have declared the intention of the law to be to promote the progress of useful arts by the benefits granted to inventors; not by those accruing to the public."[92]

That was a bit much for the other members of the Supreme Court for it seemed to run counter to the express language of the clause, and perhaps more importantly to a recent pronouncement of the Court on the purpose of the patent law. Thus, in 1829 in *Pennock v. Dialogue,* Justice Story speaking for the Court had stated:

> While one great object was, by holding out a reasonable reward to inventors, and giving them an exclusive right to their inventions for a limited period, to stimulate the efforts of genius; the main object was 'to promote the progress of science and useful arts;' and this could be

---

(1953) ("[t]he economic philosophy behind the clause empowering Congress to grant patents and copyrights is the conviction that encouragement of individual effort by personal gain is the best way to advance public welfare through the talents of authors and inventors in 'Science and useful Arts.' Sacrificial days devoted to such creative activities deserve rewards commensurate with the services rendered").

90. These administrative practices, which strongly favored inventors and were not sanctioned by statute, are discussed in detail in WALTERSCHEID, *supra* note 12, at 265–68, 275–78, 281–304.

91. Thompson v. Haight, 23 F. Cas. 1040, 1044 (Case No. 13, 956) (C.C.S.D.N.Y. 1826).

92. Whitney v. Emmett, 29 F. Cas. 1074, 1082 (Case No. 17,585) (E.D. Pa. 1831).

done best by giving the public at large a right to make, construct, use, and vend the thing invented, at as early a period as possible having a due regard to the rights of the inventor.[93]

Moreover, as of 1831, Congress had in fact made no such declaration.[94] Accordingly, the Court now sought again to emphasize that there were dual motivations for the patent system authorized by the clause. Thus in 1833, Justice McLean stated for a unanimous Court in *Shaw v. Cooper:* "The patent law was designed for the public benefit as well as the benefit of inventors."[95] Presumably such was also the case with respect to the copyright law. The idea that patent and copyright laws authorized by the clause were intended for the benefit of inventors and authors was alive and well in the early republic, and in Madison's view in *The Federalist No. 43* was a major justification in itself for the inclusion of the clause in the Constitution.[96] To the very limited extent that the clause was publicly mentioned by others during the ratification period, this was also assumed to be the purpose of the authority granted by it.[97]

Aside from the views expressed by Madison, there was no attempt made either by any other Framer or by the first federal Congresses to give political, legal, or economic rationales for the patent and copyright systems authorized by the clause.[98] Perhaps in the context of the many more

---

93. 27 U.S. (2 Pet.) 1, 19 (1829).
94. Rather Justice Baldwin inferred this to be the intent of Congress. As he put it:

> This is most evident from their imposing as conditions, that the invention must be new to all the world, and the patentee be a citizen of the United States. If public benefit had been the sole object, it was immaterial where the invention originated, or by whom invented; but being for the benefit of the patentee, the meritorious cause was invention, not importation, and the benefit was not extended to foreigners, in which respects the law had been otherwise settled in England.

> 29 F. Cas. at 1082. But this was more than a bit misleading. Nothing in the statutory language required that an invention must be new to all the world, thereby precluding patents of importation. Rather, this had been a judicial gloss put on the statutory language. Moreover, the Patent Act of 1800, 2 Stat. 37, had given resident aliens the right to obtain patents.

95. 32 U.S. at 320.
96. This is self evident from his statement in *The Federalist No. 43* that "[t]he public good fully coincides in both cases with the claims of individuals."
97. *See supra* Chapter One, text accompanying notes 34–36.
98. Nor was there any attempt to clarify, explain, or interpret what was intended by "to promote the progress of science and the useful arts" as used in the clause. Perhaps the language was thought so clear as to require no explanation

momentous issues facing the fledgling federal government, none was thought necessary. But rationales there were, and rationales there would be. It is to these we now turn.

D. Rationales

If at the end of the eighteenth century there were no American rationales advanced for the patent and copyright systems authorized by the clause, such were being presented in Great Britain. They could be broadly divided between the "social benefit" rationales and the "reward for creativity" justifications. It might be supposed that the combination of patents and copyrights authority in one constitutional clause occurred because the rationales for patents and copyrights were the same. But this was not the case at all.

As the English patent custom transitioned into a bona fide patent system and that system was increasingly exposed to what was perceived to be a hostile court system in the last quarter of the eighteenth century,[99] theoretical and pragmatic rationales for the system came to be advanced by a wide variety of individuals.[100] What is intriguing is that the crown, while perfectly prepared to continue to administer the system, felt little or no need to defend or support it or to rationalize its existence. But others did, and they did so out of a growing understanding not only that invention could and was affecting the economic well-being of the country but also out of a perception that the very concept of invention had changed.[101]

---

or interpretation. If so, this was most unfortunate, for the Supreme Court would have no appropriate contemporaneous record to rely on when it came to interpret this language in the middle of the twentieth century. *See infra* Chapter Eight, Part D.

99. Dutton provides some interesting evidence on this point. *See* HAROLD I. DUTTON, THE PATENT SYSTEM AND INVENTIVE ACTIVITY DURING THE INDUSTRIAL REVOLUTION 1750–1852, at 77–79 (Manchester 1984).

100. These included political economists, lawyers, engineers, patent agents, inventors, manufacturers, and "those who regarded the market for inventions—not parliament, or other 'invisible hand'—as the fairest arbiter of reward." DUTTON, *supra* note 99, at 17; CHRISTINE MACLEOD, INVENTING THE INDUSTRIAL REVOLUTION, THE ENGLISH PATENT SYSTEM, 1660–1800, at 75–114 (Cambridge 1988).

101. Their arguments concerning the purpose of the patent system were predicated on an understanding of the system as it then existed and not as it had originated. As Boehm & Silberston note: "It is always difficult to input

This latter point was important and in no small measure predicated on the first one. The economics of technological change was of ever increasing interest as the century came to an end. This was in marked contrast to the seventeenth century wherein "discussions of invention were rare and couched largely in metaphysical terms,"[102] and invention was deemed to be more an act of Providence than of man.[103] Although the term "invention" could be—and occasionally was—used in its modern sense, it was more frequently used to mean discovery of something that had been there all along. For all intents and purposes, it had not changed much from its Elizabethan meaning.[104] Importation was generally deemed more important than actual creation of new manufacture by an intellectual process; where necessary the technical know-how and crafts imported from Europe could be improved upon, but such improvements were not perceived in any legal sense to warrant patent protection.

---

objectives to ancient institutions—at least with any accuracy. This is particularly true where the origins of the institutions and hence their original objectives have not be established with complete authority." *See* K. BOEHM & A. SILBERSTON, I THE BRITISH PATENT SYSTEM at 6 (Cambridge 1967).

102. MACLEOD, *supra* note 100, at 201.

103. This discussion of the changing concept of invention is taken largely from MacLeod. MACLEOD, *supra* note 100, at 201–22.

104. Care must be taken not to associate any modern definition of "invent," i.e., to conceive of or devise first or to originate, with the manner in which the term "invention" was used in Elizabethan times. As stated by Getz, "'invention' in the modern sense of the word, as a result of a special creative ingenuity, was neither the ground nor the condition of the grant." L. Getz, *History of the Patentee's Obligations in Great Britain*, 46 J. PAT. OFF. SOC'Y 62, 75 (1964). *See also* E. Wyndham Hulme, *On the History of the Patent Law in the Seventeenth and Eighteenth Centuries*, 18 L. Q. REV. 280–81 (1902). Moreover, as Hulme points out, "the modern distinction between invention, discovery, and the acquisition of knowledge by other than mental effort had no existence in the language of the sixteenth and seventeenth centuries." E. Wyndham Hulme, *The History of the Patent System Under the Prerogative and at Common Law, A Sequel*, 16 L. Q. REV. 44, 52 (1900). Rather, invention denoted primarily a physical act rather than a mental process. E. Wyndham Hulme, *The History of the Patent System Under the Prerogative and at Common Law*, 12 L. Q. REV. 141, 151 (1896). It could encompass the attainment of knowledge of a new manufacture by the simple expedient of procuring foreign workmen to practice the new art within the realm. Hulme, *History of the Patent System*, 16 L. Q. REV. at 44. It is undoubtedly for this reason that the term "manufactures" took on such significance in the Statute of Monopolies.

All that changed as the eighteenth century progressed. Discussions of invention became more numerous, and the context was increasingly economic. Economic theory was beginning to come into its own, but it did not lead the way. Rather, it began to seek to take into account the arguments of capitalists, manufacturers, and others who acted out of self interest. At some time in the century, the view became accepted that inventors were more than just agents of Providence; they were perceived to be creative in their own right as individuals, going beyond what God had wrought in nature. Invention had come to be viewed in terms of synthesis instead of merely analysis; it had begun to take on its modern meaning.

This new understanding of invention, coupled with the recognition that the patent system to be justified must exist to protect and encourage not only invention but the commercial development of inventions, led to the development of five separate rationales for the existence of the patent system at the end of the century.[105] The first of these, the natural-law thesis, was predicated on the assumption that individuals had a natural or inherent right of property in their own ideas. That being the case, society has an obligation to protect against the improper use of one persons ideas by another without some form of compensation. The patent system is one means by which ones inherent rights in ones own invention may be protected by society for a limited period. Indeed, under this reasoning the state is required to issue patents to enforce the personal and exclusive property right which the inventor has in his or her invention.[106] In England, the common-law tradition

---

105. These various rationales were in wide circulation by early in the nineteenth century, but all were developed in some fashion or another, albeit perhaps crudely, by the end of the eighteenth century. The discussion of these rationales is based to a considerable extent on Dutton. DUTTON, *supra* note 99, at 17–23.
106. This seems indeed to have been the raison d'etre for the French patent law of 1791 which provided among other things:

> 1. Any discovery or new invention, in any kind of industry, is the property of its author. Consequently, the law guarantees to him the full and complete enjoyment thereof, in the manner and for the time hereinafter determined.
>
> . . .
>
> 7. In order to secure to any inventor the property and temporary enjoyment of his invention, there shall be delivered to him a title or patent, according to the form indicated in the Regulations which shall be made for the carrying out of this decree.

See Frank D. Prager, *A History of Intellectual Property From 1545 to 1787*, 26 J. PAT. OFF. SOC'Y 711, 756–57 (1944).

with its reliance on custom and precedent posed an instinctive barrier to natural-rights theories, and justification of the patent system on the basis of this thesis was never very common in England.

In contrast, the reward-by-monopoly thesis was widely argued as a rationale for the patent system. It was predicated on the notion that inventors deserved to be rewarded according to how useful their inventions were to society. Because ordinary market forces do not assure this happy outcome, the state intervenes to provide a temporary monopoly. Adam Smith, that most ardent of political economists, favored this view for two reasons, one of which, taken alone, might more reasonably be viewed as damnation by faint praise. That reason was that patents were generally harmless and occasionally might do some good. His second reason, however, was more substantive and offered an explanation of why patents might on occasion be worthwhile. The temporary monopoly garnered by the patent might permit a return on ingenuity, investment, and effort to the inventor while at the same time precluding competitors from obtaining a free ride without paying the developmental costs borne by the inventor. Moreover, because the patented invention was subject to the laws of supply and demand, the reward received by the inventor, either in the form of royalties or direct sales, would be proportionate to the value of the invention to society. The alternative of a monetary reward to the inventor was unsatisfactory because "they would hardly ever be so precisely proportioned to the merit of the invention as this is."[107]

Inventors and their supporters quite naturally tended to favor this rationale. In 1774 the argument was presented that parliamentary monetary awards "would almost always run the risk of being inadequate" and that patents were "the most plausible and politic method of bestowing that encouragement . . . by which the eventual utility of such inventions[s] is made the measure of the reward."[108] This refrain would be repeated again and again.[109]

---

107. ADAM SMITH, AN INQUIRY INTO THE NATURE AND CAUSES OF THE WEALTH OF NATIONS at 593 (R. H. Campbell, A. S. Skinner & W. B. Tood eds., 1976); ADAM SMITH, LECTURES ON JURISPRUDENCE at 83, 472 (R. L. Meek, D. D. Raphael & P. G. Stein eds., 1978). Smith's views on patents are more clearly delineated in the Lectures than in the Wealth of Nations.
108. W. KENDRICK, AN ADDRESS TO THE ARTISTS AND MANUFACTURERS OF GREAT BRITAIN RESPECTING AN APPLICATION FOR THE ENCOURAGEMENT OF NEW DISCOVERIES AND USEFUL ARTS at 118, 120 (1774), quoted by MACLEOD, *supra* note 100, at 196; DUTTON, *supra* note 99, at 20.
109. MACLEOD, *supra* note 100, at 196–97; DUTTON, *supra* note 99, at 20.

The third rationale, called the monopoly-profit-incentive thesis, is to some extent a variation on the reward-by-monopoly thesis. However, it focuses not so much on reward for the inventor, although that is a part of it, as on the assumptions that (a) economic growth is inherently desirable; (b) an increase in the supply of invention favorably affects economic growth, and (c) the supply of invention would be less than it would otherwise be if patents were not used to protect the inventor. Believing this was one thing and proving it was another, but few bothered with any attempted proof. By the end of the eighteenth century there was ever increasing belief that there was a causal link between patents, inventions, and industrial development.

The fourth rationale put forth in favor of the patent system, the exchange-for-secrets thesis, was based on the eighteenth-century idea of contract whereby the inventor in return for the temporary monopoly disclosed to the public the secret of the invention. It grew out of the views expressed by Lord Mansfield in *Liardet v. Johnson* that the specification of the patent must be enabling, i.e., it must teach one skilled in the art how to make and use the invention.[110] Under this rationale, an essential purpose of the patent system is to assure dissemination to the public of technical information which would otherwise be held in secrecy. Again, it was assumed that progress and invention were causally linked. The earliest known published statement that a patent represents a contract between the inventor and the public in the United States or for that matter Great Britain appears to have been made by Joseph Barnes in 1792 in Philadelphia.[111] As he put it,

> a system for securing property in the products of genius, is a *mutual* con-tract between the *inventor* and the *public*, in which the *inventor* agrees, on *proviso* that the public will secure to him his property in, and the exclusive use of his discovery for a limited time, he will, at the expira-tion of such time, *cede* his right in the same to the public; thenceforth

---

110. *See supra* Chapter Two, text accompanying notes 86–90.
111. It was not until the beginning of the nineteenth century that the English courts would expressly set forth this view. Although Inlow contends that by about 1780 "the idea of the contract in the patent grant was being previewed," he cites no authority for this view and none has been found. He incorrectly states that "[t]he equitable concept of contract was first actually advanced by Lord Eldon in *Cartwright v. Amatt* in 1800." *See* E. G. INLOW, THE PATENT GRANT at 63, 68 (Baltimore 1950). The correct reference should be to *Cart-wright v. Eamer*. No report of this case has been found, but it is mentioned in Harmer v. Playne, 11 East Reports, 1 Abbott's P. C. 171 (K.B. 1809).

the discovery is common right, being the compensation required by the public, stipulated in the contract, for having thus secured the same.[112]

Although Barnes did not so indicate, under this contract thesis, the consideration for the grant was the enabling disclosure provided in the specification.

The fifth rationale, which may be termed the protection of investment thesis, was predicated on the view that patents were necessary to stimulate the capital investment needed to assure that a new trade or industry based on new inventive concepts could in fact be successfully commercially developed. The new class of manufacturing entrepreneurs arising in England in the second half of the eighteenth century increasingly advocated this rationale. Interestingly, it was perhaps best set forth by Alexander Hamilton in 1791 in his *Report on the Subject of Manufactures.*

Hamilton pointed out that industry, if left to itself, tended to be inherently conservative. As he put it: "Experience teaches that men are often governed by what they are accustomed to see and practice, that the simplest and most obvious improvements, in the [most] ordinary occupations, are adopted with hesitation, reluctance and by slow gradations."[113] Moreover:

> The apprehension of failing in new attempts is perhaps a more serious impediment. There are dispositions apt to be attracted by the mere novelty of an undertaking—but these are not always those best calculated to give it success. To this, it is of importance that the confidence of cautious sagacious capitalists both citizens and foreigners, should be excited. And to inspire this description of persons with confidence, it is essential, that they should be made to see in any project, which is new, and for that reason alone, if, for no other, precarious, the prospect of such a degree of countenance and support from government, as may be capable of overcoming the obstacles, inseparable from first experiments.[114]

---

112. JOSEPH BARNES, TREATISE ON THE JUSTICE, POLICY, AND UTILITY OF ESTABLISHING AN EFFECTUAL SYSTEM OF PROMOTING THE PROGRESS OF USEFUL ARTS, BY ASSURING PROPERTY IN THE PRODUCTS OF GENIUS (Philadelphia 1792) at 25.
113. X THE PAPERS OF ALEXANDER HAMILTON at 266 (Harold C. Syrett et al. eds., New York 1966).
114. PAPERS OF ALEXANDER HAMILTON *id.* at 267.

In England at the end of the eighteenth century patents were increasingly seen as a form of "countenance and support from government" upon which "cautious sagacious capitalists" could rely in investing in new industries.

The classic example was the case of James Watt and his famous improvement in the steam engine. In 1765 when Watt hit upon the idea of a separate condenser to evacuate the cylinder, it took him only three days to develop a working model. Yet it would take eleven years and major expenditure before his perfected steam engine was ready for the market-place.[115] As Scherer has noted, the existence of a patent system had little or no influence on Watt's invention, i.e., he seems to have made it out of simple scientific curiosity, but its ultimate successful commercial development was in no small measure dependent on a massive expenditure of capital by Matthew Boulton who entered into partnership with Watt only after Watt's patent term was extended by Parliament for twenty-five years in 1775.[116]

While there was some overlap, the rationales put forth for the copyright system in England at the end of the eighteenth century of necessity varied from those offered for the patent system. The differences in perspective came about because of the differences in the intangible property being protected as well as the different treatment of copyrights and patents under the common law. Copyright had come to be viewed as a form of property right arising out of the tangible expression of an idea. The copyright is in the expression of the idea rather than in the idea itself. At the end of the eighteenth century, this was most commonly thought to be a printed literary work. A patent on the other hand was a form of property in an idea that could be reduced to practice in any of a variety of "manufactures," which was coming to be understood to include compositions of matter as well as arts, i.e., methods and processes. Whereas a patent was entirely a creature of the royal prerogative, i.e., that was no legal right to a patent, there was perceived to be a legal right to a copyright under the common law, albeit one that could only be enforced in accordance with the Statute of Anne.

Just as the perception of invention had changed, so too the rationale for copyright changed markedly between the seventeenth and eighteenth centuries. The stationers' copyright came into being purely and simply as

---

115. ERICH KAUFER, THE ECONOMICS OF THE PATENT SYSTEM at 20 (New York 1988).
116. F. M. Scherer, *Invention and Innovation in the Watt-Boulton Steam-Engine Venture*, 6 TECH. & CULTURE 165, 182–86 (1965). *See also* George E. Frost, *Watt's 31-Year Patent*, 71 J. PAT. & TRADEMARK OFF. SOC'Y 136, 143–45 (1991).

a means for the crown to regulate and censor printed works. The best way to do this was to establish a monopoly in the stationers who in turn acted for the crown in the exercise of censorship and control. The rights granted under the stationers' copyright were in the publisher and not the author. With the advent of the eighteenth century and the Statute of Anne, the emphasis shifted to authors and the purpose became to promote the progress of learning, or at least so the statute said. But in the eighteenth century in England there was a major dichotomy in rationale presented by the emphasis on the one hand on the promotion of learning and, on the other hand, the idea that the property right derives from authorship.

Unlike the most frequently cited rationales for the patent system, those proposed for the copyright system had very little to do with the economic well-being of England.[117] Perhaps the most straightforward rationale for the English copyright system at the end of the eighteenth century was that copyright was perceived to be a right a common law.[118] In other words, the perceived existence of a legal right based on long tradition and practice was in and of itself deemed a sufficient justification for copyright without more.

Patterson has emphasized that the Statute of Anne "was a trade-regulation statute enacted to bring order to the chaos created in the book trade by the final lapse in 1694 of its predecessor, the Licensing Act of 1662, and to prevent a continuation of the bookseller's monopoly."[119] But almost as an afterthought, it set forth another rationale for copyright, namely, "for the encouragement of learned men to compose and write useful books," or as stated in the title, "for the encouragement of learning."[120] Feather suggests that "[t]he 'encouragement of learning' may have originally been little more than a blanket of respectability to cover the naked commercialism of the late seventeenth- and early eighteenth-century booksellers, but it had become the core of the argument about [and in favor of] literary property by the mid-1770s."[121] That is to say, the

---

117. While the advancement of learning could arguably be stated to have some economic benefit, no one seems to have seriously argued such benefit as a justification for the copyright system.
118. Madison certainly seemed to endorse this rationale in *The Federalist No. 43. See supra* text accompanying note 77.
119. LYMAN RAY PATTERSON, COPYRIGHT IN HISTORICAL PERSPECTIVE at 143 (Nashville 1968).
120. The statute is reproduced in 8 NIMMER & NIMMER, *supra* note 36, at App. 7-5.
121. JOHN FEATHER, PUBLISHING, PIRACY AND POLITICS: AN HISTORICAL STUDY OF COPYRIGHT IN BRITAIN at 122 (London 1994).

rationale for copyright was that it provided a societal benefit through the encouragement of learning.

By its reference to "authors" the Statute of Anne also provided the impetus for what became the third major rationale for copyright at the end of the eighteenth century, namely, that an author had an inherent property right in his writings stemming from the very act of creation. Under this view, which was similar to the natural law rationale for the patent system, the state is obligated to protect the rights of the author arising out of authorship, and copyright is an appropriate means for protecting this property right. The fact that copyright, unlike the patent privilege, was perceived to be a common-law right only gave additional impetus and support to this rationale. As Abrams points out, this rationale was perhaps most concisely and eloquently stated by Benjamin Disraeli when he argued in Parliament concerning literary works:

> They were works requiring great learning, great industry, great labour, and great capital in their preparation. . . . [T]hey constituted a species of property better than any other. The tenure of that property was not fictitious; it was primitive; it was the most natural and least liable to be disputed. It was a tenure by creation. . . .[122]

Initially at least, this rationale seems to have been equated with the direct labor of the author in creating the work. As William Enfield succinctly put it in 1774: "Labour gives a man a natural right of property in that which he produces: literary compositions are the effect of labour; authors have therefore a natural right of property in their works."[123] One consequence was that early English cases under the Statute of Anne focused on this labor component and, as a consequence, limited the author's copyright to the actual text at issue. Thus, e.g., a translation was ruled to be a new work not covered by the copyright,[124] as was an

---

122. 42 Parl. Deb. (3d Ser.) 575 (1838), as quoted by Abrams, *supra* note 82, at 1122.

123. William Enfield, *Observations on Literary Property* (London 1774) *in* THE LITERARY PROPERTY DEBATE: EIGHT TRACTS, 1774–1775, at 21 (Stephen Parks ed., New York 1974). This was a straightforward extension of John Locke's theory of property to literary works. *See* John Locke, *Second Treatise of Government, in* TWO TREATISES OF GOVERNMENT (P. Laslett rev. ed. 1963) (3d ed. 1698). There are numerous discussions of Lockean theory in the context of intellectual property; *see, e.g.,* Justin Hughes, *The Philosophy of Intellectual Property,* 77 GEO. L.J. 287 (1988); Adam D. Moore, *A Lockean Theory of Intellectual Property,* 21 HAMLINE L. REV. 65 (1997).

124. Burnett v. Chetwood, 35 Eng. Rep. (1720).

abridgment.[125] Perhaps because of this, there was a subtle addition to this rationale, namely, that a literary work was somehow inextricably tied up not only with the labor of the author but with the whole *persona* of the author and for this additional reason must be viewed as inherently the property of the author.[126] Blackstone put it in the following way:

> Style and sentiment are the essentials of a literary composition. These alone constitute its identity. The paper and print are merely accidents, which serve as vehicles to convey that style and sentiment to a distance. Every duplicate therefore of a work, whether ten or ten thousand, if it conveys the same style and sentiment, is the same identical work, which was produced by the author's invention and labour.[127]

Not surprisingly, authors in the United States would find this argument in favor of "style and sentiment" as the very basis of the property right set forth in copyright to be highly persuasive.

E. Perspectives

There are three interests subsumed in the language of the intellectual property clause, two of which are explicit. The first, and indeed the primary one, is the public interest encompassed in the phrase "to promote the progress of science and useful arts" and the requirement that "the exclusive right" be "for limited times only." It is the public interest that is ultimately served by placing the subject matter of patents and copyrights in the public domain.[128] The second explicit interest is that of the authors and inventors who receive the limited-term exclusive right authorized by the clause. A third interest, not mentioned in the clause but nonetheless perhaps the most powerful interest of all (at least in modern times), is that of those "proprietors" of an interest in "the exclusive right," either through assignment or license.[129] Because the public interest and these private

---

125. Gyles v. Wilcox, 26 Eng. Rep. 490 (1740).
126. For a discussion of this perspective, see MARK ROSE, AUTHORS AND OWNERS, THE INVENTION OF COPYRIGHT at 113–29 (Cambridge 1993).
127. Tonson v. Collins, 96 Eng. Rep. 189 (1760).
128. For a discussion of the public domain, see Chapter Seven, Part D, *infra*.
129. Patterson & Lindberg suggest that the exclusion of any mention of this third interest "is probably explained by concern [at least in the case of copyright] for the perceived potential of a booksellers' monopoly in this country." See L. RAY PATTERSON & STANLEY W. LINDBERG, THE NATURE OF COPYRIGHT, A LAW OF USERS' RIGHTS at 54 (Athens, Ga. 1991). I question this as a reason

interests are almost always at odds, Madison dissembled more than bit with his statement in *The Federalist No. 43* that "[t]he public good fully coincides in both cases [i.e., patents and copyrights] with the claims of individuals."

It would have been abundantly clear to the Framers in 1787 that it was the duty of every enlightened government "to promote the progress of science and useful arts." Indeed, this would have seemed so clear to them as to require no explanation whatever for its inclusion among the powers granted to Congress. But they went further and incorporated specific language that would ensure authority in Congress to do so in a particular way, i.e., by the issuance of the limited term exclusive rights known as copyrights and patents. I have earlier suggested that they did so not only as an express authority to promote the progress of science and useful arts but also to ensure that it could in fact be done in this particular way.[130] They did so for pragmatic reasons; they were familiar with the English institutions of copyrights and patents and considered them to be the most straightforward and least expensive mechanism by which the new federal government created by the Constitution could effectively promote the progress of science and useful arts.[131] If Madison's views expressed in *The Federalist No. 43* are indicative of their intent, they also perceived that authors and inventors *should* be given certain rights with respect to their writings and discoveries. As discussed in Chapter Six, they did not believe that authors and inventors in the United States had inherent property rights in their writings and discoveries after publication under either natural or common law, absent some power expressly vested in Congress to create such rights.

The combination of the authority to issue copyrights with the authority to issue patents in the same clause suggests that the Framers considered the rights created and protected by copyrights and patents as well as their purposes to be similar in nature.[132] As set forth by Patterson in 1968, there were four basic purposes perceived for copyright in 1787, namely, that

---

for the exclusion, since the Framers clearly perceived patents and copyrights to be monopolies no matter who owned them. I do agree, however, with the view expressed by Patterson & Lindberg that "[t]he exclusion of publishers [from the constitutional language] can be said to have constitutionalized the fiction of copyright as an author's right, with substantial, albeit subtle, consequences for copyright." *Id.*

130. *See supra* Chapter Three, text accompanying notes 38–41.

131. *See supra* Chapter Three, text accompanying notes 42–53.

132. The use of the singular "the exclusive right" in the intellectual property clause also supports this view. *See infra* Chapter Seven, text accompanying notes 3–9.

copyright is: (a) to protect the author's rights; (b) to promote learning; (c) to provide order in the book trade as a government grant; and (d) to prevent harmful monopoly. In his view, "[t]he idea that copyright is primarily for the benefit of the author was central to the state statutes; [and] that copyright is necessary for learning was central to the constitutional provision."[133]

It is doubtful that items (c) and (d) above played any role in the creation of the intellectual property clause. Unlike the situation that had existed in England, there was only a modest book trade in the United States, and certainly no pronounced concern about disorder regarding that trade. Moreover, the clause was included, not to prevent harmful monopoly, but rather to assure that the presumably socially beneficial limited-term monopolies known as copyrights and patents could in fact be granted by Congress.

More recently, Patterson has considerably modified his views, now saying that the language of the clause

> manifests three policies for copyright: the promotion of learning (because the language so states), the preservation of the public domain (because after a limited time all writings go into the public domain), and the protection of the author (because to achieve the larger goals the author is given an exclusive right). [Moreover,] [t]he ordering of the policies in the clause indicates their priority: the first is that copyright promote learning; the second is that it preserve the public domain; and the third is that it encourage the creation and distribution of works by benefiting the author.[134]

Although I have one caveat, I am in general agreement with these later perspectives of Patterson regarding the purpose and intent of the copyright provision of the clause. My caveat is that copyright is not so much to preserve the writings in the public domain as it is to ultimately enlarge the reservoir of writings in the public domain. I also believe that the Framers intended the same type of policy considerations to apply to the patent provision of the clause. That is to say, the Congress was authorized to grant patents: first to promote the progress of useful arts, secondly, to preserve and enlarge the public domain of useful arts and discoveries, and thirdly, to benefit inventors for a reasonable time as recompense for their expense and effort. It is the similarity in purposes for both copyrights and patents

---

133. LYMAN RAY PATTERSON, COPYRIGHT IN HISTORICAL PERSPECTIVE at 181 (Nashville 1968).
134. PATTERSON & LINDBERG, *supra* note 129, at 49.

that justifies the combination of the copyright and patent provisions in the same clause.

Nonetheless, a careful reading of the clause as well as a parsing of its balanced style of composition indicates that, while similar, the purposes of the copyright and patent provisions are not identical. Moreover, there is nothing to indicate that the Framers intended their purposes to be identical. Unfortunately, over time, a lax and less than careful reading of the clause has caused both the judiciary and the Congress, as well as numerous commentators to join and equate the purpose of the two provisions as being one and the same, i.e., to promote the progress of *both* science *and* useful arts. The changing definition of the term "science" over time has only added to the confusion.

There is little question but that the Framers viewed copyrights to be for the purpose of promoting "science," i.e., learning, and patents to be for the purpose of promoting "useful arts," or, as they have been more recently defined, the technological arts. While any valid patent inherently adds to the sum of learning, many, if not most, copyrighted works do nothing to promote the progress of useful arts. Nor are they intended to. Rather, as understood by the Framers, copyright had an inherently cultural aspect in its emphasis on the form of presentation rather than the factual content of the work. Indeed, the promotion of literature and the fine arts and the dissemination of works of literature and of fine art were primary purposes of copyright. Fiction has no place in the world of patents, but traditionally has held pride of place in the world of copyright.

Finally, there is a point which cannot be over-emphasized. Not only is the clause intended to promote the progress of science and useful arts, but it is also intended to assure the subject matters of both patents and copyrights ultimately become a part of the public domain, i.e., become the property of no one and the property of everyone. This purpose of adding to the public domain is addressed in much more detail in Chapter Seven.

CHAPTER FIVE
A GRANT OF POWER AND A LIMITATION

In 1966 in *Graham v. John Deere Co.* the Supreme Court declared that the patent provision of the clause "is both a grant of power and a limitation."[1] The Court was speaking in the context of the view that the patent provision contains an inherent constitutional standard of invention,[2] but at the same time it indicated that the clause precludes Congress from authorizing "the issuance of patents whose effects are to remove existent knowledge from the public domain, or to restrict free access to materials already available."[3] In 1989, the Court reiterated these points, and noted a further limitation, namely, that "Congress may not create monopolies of unlimited duration."[4] These views of the Court are of interest because the clause contains several grants of power and several limitations. The difficulty is in ascertaining just exactly what the grants of power are and what the limitations are. As shown in this chapter, they sometimes have been confused, and it has not always been obvious what the limitations are or how they should be treated.

---

1. 383 U.S. 1, 5 (1966).
2. That supposed standard is addressed in detail in Chapter Eight.
3. 383 U.S. at 6. This view that the clause absolutely precludes Congress from issuing patents that "remove existent knowledge from the public domain" is more restrictive than that held by the Court in the first half of the nineteenth century. In 1815 the Court upheld the validity of an act of Congress authorizing the reissue to Oliver Evans for an additional term of 14 years of a patent that had expired three years earlier. *See* Evans v. Jordan, 13 U.S. (9 Cranch) 199 (1815). Based on such authority, through much of the nineteenth century term renewals and extensions authorized after the original patent had expired and the subject matter was in the public domain were judicially upheld. *See, e.g.,* Agawam Woolen Co. v. Jordan, 74 U.S. (7 Wall.) 177, 183-84 (1869); Blanchard v. Sprague, 3 F. Cas. 648, 650 (D. Mass. 1839) (Case No. 1,518).
4. Bonito Boats, Inc. v. Thunder Craft Boats, Inc., 489 U.S. 141, 146 (1989). The meaning of the phrase "for limited times" in the clause is addressed in Chapter Seven.

A. Powers and Limitations

In the nineteenth century, the Supreme Court on a number of occasions set forth inconsistent views on the scope of congressional authority to set the terms and conditions of patents and copyrights. In this regard, several opinions suggested that congressional power under the clause was plenary, i.e., without qualification.[5] Thus, for example, in 1843 in *McClurg v. Kingsland* the Court stated "the powers of Congress to legislate upon the subject of patents is plenary by the terms of the Constitution, and as there are no restraints on its exercise, there can be no limitation of their right to modify [the patent laws] at their pleasure, so [long as] they do not take away the rights of property in existing patents."[6] In 1899, it declared:

> Since, under the Constitution, Congress has power "to promote the progress of science and useful arts, by securing for limited times to authors and inventors the exclusive right to their respective writings and discoveries," and to make all laws which shall be necessary and proper for carrying that expressed power into execution, it follows that Congress may provide such instrumentalities in respect of securing to inventors the exclusive right to their discoveries as in its judgment will be best calculated to effect the object.[7]

Unfortunately, in making these pronouncements, the Court let itself be carried away by its rhetoric, for the power of Congress respecting patents and copyrights is not plenary, but rather is qualified and restricted by certain express language of the intellectual property clause as well as such other constitutional limitations as may exist.[8] Thus, on several other occasions in the

---

5. *Black's Law Dictionary* (6th ed. 1990) defines "plenary" as "full, entire, complete, absolute, perfect, unqualified."
6. 42 U.S. (1 How.) 202, 206 (1843).
7. United States v. Duell, 172 U.S. 576, 583 (1899).
8. Nonetheless, the idea that the patent and copyright power, if not plenary, was the next thing to it was commonplace in the nineteenth century. In his magisterial patent treatise published in 1890, for example, Robinson states:

> The authority thus conferred on Congress [by the intellectual property clause] is unrestricted as to the method of its exercise. The subject of the exclusive right must be a writing or discovery of the person to whom the right is granted, and the period during which the right may be enjoyed must be determined by the letter of the grant. As to all other matters Congress is supreme. It may refuse all privileges whatsoever. It may bestow them with or without conditions. It may establish such a period for their duration as it deems expedient. It may exhaust its powers by special

nineteenth century, it had expressly recognized this to be the case. For example, in 1829 in *Pennock v. Dialogue* it declared that the constitutional language "contemplates . . . that the exclusive right shall exist but for a limited time."[9] In 1856 it held that the power granted to Congress by the clause "is domestic in its character and is necessarily confined within the limits of the United States."[10] In 1878 it held that the exclusive property right authorized by the clause and encompassed within the patent grant does not preempt the authority of a state to regulate the sale of patented material under the reasonable exercise of its police power.[11] Despite these cases, one modern commentator still argues that there was an "early judicial conviction that the intellectual property clause grants plenary power to Congress in patent matters, rather than sets limits to the exercise of the power."[12] What there was early on was a less than critical analysis of the qualified nature of the power actually granted to Congress.

The *Graham* Court sought to avoid any such impression by citing to *McClurg* in support of its view that "[w]ithin the scope established by the Constitution, Congress may set out conditions and tests for patentability."[13] While such a statement is clearly correct, it is not supported by *McClurg* where the Court stated that the congressional patent power was plenary, i.e., unqualified or unlimited.[14] The *Graham* Court would have better served all concerned by simply acknowledging that the views expressed in *McClurg* were overbroad, and then emphasizing that the congressional patent power of necessity is qualified by the language of the intellectual property clause.

Any analysis of the qualified nature of that power ought to begin by looking to the form and language of the clause and comparing them to the

---

grants to individual authors and inventors, or by a general law award to all a uniform protection. Its action may be retrospective or prospective, as long as vested rights are not impaired.

WILLIAM C. ROBINSON, I THE LAW OF PATENTS FOR USEFUL INVENTIONS (Boston 1890) at § 46. *See also* Graham v. Johnston, 21 Fed. Rep. 40, 42 (1884) ("the constitutional power of Congress for securing to them the exclusive right to their inventions has only one restriction, viz.: that it shall be for limited times").

9. 27 U.S. (2 Pet.) 1, 16–17 (1829).
10. Brown v. Duchesne, 60 U.S. (19 How.) 183, 195 (1856).
11. Kentucky v. Patterson, 97 U.S. 501 (1878).
12. Kenneth J. Burchfiel, *Revising the "Original" Patent Clause: Pseudohistory in Constitutional Construction*, 2 HARV. J. L. & TECH. 155, 175 (1989).
13. 383 U.S. at 6.
14. *See* 42 U.S. (1 How.) 202, 206 (1843). *See also supra* text accompanying note 6.

form and language of the other constitutional clauses granting power to Congress.[15] This is simply an application of the long-standing maxim of in pari materia.[16] With the exception of the intellectual property clause, all of the granting clauses provide for generic grants of power to the Congress to do specifically enumerated tasks without setting forth a particular mode of accomplishing the task. Thus, for example, Congress is given power "to lay and collect taxes," "to borrow money," "to regulate commerce," "to coin money," "to declare war, "to provide and maintain a navy," etc.[17] In each instance, the Congress is given authority to accomplish the enumerated task without limitation or with broad limitation as to how it is to be accomplished.

The intellectual property clause sets forth particular authority "to promote the progress of science and useful arts," but it goes further and prescribes a specific mode of accomplishing this authority, i.e., "by securing for limited times to authors and inventors the exclusive right to their respective writings and discoveries." I have earlier suggested that the clause taken as a whole was intended not only as an express authority to promote the progress of science and useful arts generally but also as an express authority to do so in a particular way, namely, by securing exclusive rights for limited times to authors and inventors in their respective writings and discoveries.[18] The question then arises, which part of the clause is the grant of authority and which is a limitation on that grant of authority? Or, in a very real sense, are they *both* grants of authority *and* limitations?[19]

It is useful to begin with the views expressed by Chief Justice Marshall first in *Marbury v. Madison*[20] in 1803 and later, in 1824, in *Gibbons v. Ogden.*[21]

---

15. In construing the clause in another context, the Supreme Court early on stated: "There is no mode by which the meaning affixed to any word or sentence, by a deliberative body, can be so well ascertained, as by comparing it with the words and sentences with which it stands connected." Wheaton v. Peters, 33 U.S. (8 Pet.) 591, 661 (1834).
16. Defined as "upon the same matter or subject." BLACK'S LAW DICTIONARY (6th ed. 1990).
17. U.S. CONST. art. I, § 8.
18. *See supra* Chapter Three, text accompanying note 37.
19. In construing the meaning to be given Section 5 of the Fourteenth Amendment, the Supreme Court has recently noted "that the same language that serves as the basis for [an] affirmative grant of congressional power [can also serve] to limit that power." *See* Kimel v. Florida Board of Regents, 120 S. Ct. 631, 644 (2000).
20. 5 U.S. (1 Cranch) 137 (1803).
21. 22 U.S. (9 Wheat.) 1 (1824).

In *Marbury* he noted that "[i]t cannot be presumed, that any clause in the constitution is intended to be without effect,"[22] and then declared:

> The powers of the legislature are defined and limited: and that those limits may not be mistaken or forgotten, the constitution is written. To what purpose are powers limited, and to what purpose is that limitation committed to writing , if these limits may, at any time, be passed by those intended to be restrained? The distinction between a government with limited and unlimited powers is abolished, if those limits do not confine the persons on whom they are imposed, if acts prohibited and acts allowed are of equal obligation.[23]

The import of this is that powers are both granted and limited in the Constitution, and that limitations may not be ignored.

In *Gibbons* he emphasized his opposition to any narrow construction of the enumerated powers and went on to state:

> As men, whose intentions require no concealment, generally employ the words which most directly and aptly express the ideas they intend to convey, the enlightened patriots who framed our constitution, and the people who adopted it, must be understood to have employed words in their natural sense, and to have intended what they have said. If from the imperfections of human language, there should be serious doubts respecting the extent of any given power, it is a well-settled rule that the objects for which it was given, especially when those objects are expressed in the instrument itself, should have great influence in the construction. . . . We know of no rule for construing the extent of such powers, other than is given by the language of the instrument which confers them, taken in connection with the purposes for which they are conferred.[24]

In the context of the intellectual property clause, these views have added significance, for they clearly indicate that in 1824 the Court was of the view that a statement of purpose or objects "should have great influence" on its

---

22. 5 U.S. at 174. In 1822 President Monroe would make the same point, saying: "no part of the Constitution can be considered useless; no sentence or clause in it without meanings." See James Monroe, *Views of the President of the United States on the Subject of Internal Improvements, May 4, 1822,* as reproduced in II MESSAGES AND PAPERS OF THE PRESIDENTS, 1789–1908, at 144, 163 (James D. Richardson ed., 1909) (I am indebted to Daniel Preston for bringing this paper by President Monroe to my attention).
23. 5 U.S. at 176.
24. 22 U.S. at 187–88.

interpretation. Phrased somewhat differently, the statement of purpose, i.e., "to promote the progress of science and useful arts," constitutes a limitation on the extent or scope of the clause which must be taken into account when interpreting it. We shall have cause to return to this important point.

An early expert on constitutional interpretation, Justice Joseph Story, in his Commentaries on the Constitution of the United States, concurred fully with the views expressed by Marshall. Story strongly opposed strict construction of the Constitution. As he put it, if

> we are to give a reasonable construction to this instrument, as a constitution of government established for the common good, we must throw aside all notions of subjecting it to a strict interpretation, as if it were subversive of the great interests of society, or derogated from the inherent sovereignty of the people.[25]

Perhaps his basic rule of interpretation was that "every clause ought, in all events, to be construed according to its fair intent and objects, as disclosed in its language."[26]

Story quoted with favor the view expressed by President James Monroe in 1822 that:

> The order generally observed in grants [of power], an order founded in common sense, since it promotes a clear understanding of their import, is to grant the power intended to be conveyed in the most full and explicit manner; and then to explain or qualify it, if explanation or qualification should be necessary. This order has, it is believed, been invariably observed in all the grants contained in the constitution.[27]

Story set forth a straightforward rule for interpreting a grant of power, namely, that "all the ordinary and appropriate means to execute it are to be deemed a part of the power itself." He argued that this "results from the very nature and design of a constitution" which in granting the power "does not intend to limit it to any one mode of exercising it, exclusive of all others."[28]

---

25. JOSEPH STORY, I COMMENTARIES ON THE CONSTITUTION OF THE UNITED STATES § 423 (Boston 1833).
26. *Id.* § 407, n.10.
27. II STORY, *supra* note 25, § 977. Story did not provide a citation for the quoted language but it is from Monroe's *Views of the President of the United States on the Subject of Internal Improvements,* dated May 4, 1822. *See* II MESSAGES AND PAPERS OF THE PRESIDENTS, *supra* note 22, at 163.
28. STORY, *supra* note 25, § 430.

He pointed out that "if the power only is given, without pointing out the means, how are we to ascertain, that any one means, rather than another, is exclusively within its scope?"[29] This was a highly relevant question, but Story failed to address another highly relevant question, namely, where a means is in fact set forth, is it to be construed as the exclusive means, i.e., as a limitation on the power? This was, of course, the issue presented by the wording of the intellectual property clause. Story clearly considered the power granted by the clause to be that "to promote the progress of science and useful arts,"[30] but he was silent as to whether that power was limited to the granting of copyrights and patents.[31] Nonetheless, he clearly did not believe this to be the case.[32]

In modern times it is commonly assumed that the grant of power is to legislate with respect to copyrights and patents, or, in essence, the constitutional grant of power is that set forth in the "by" portion of the clause.[33] Thus, e.g., in 1973 in *Goldstein v. California*, Chief Justice Burger stressed that the clause "describes both the objective which Congress may seek and *the* means to achieve it. The objective is to promote the progress of science and the useful arts."[34] Implicit in the language used by Chief Justice Burger is the assumption that the object or purpose of the clause is set forth in the "to" portion, and the only means available to Congress to accomplish that object or purpose is set forth in the "by" portion.[35]

If this was indeed what was intended, then it was sharply at odds with the view expressed by Justice White for a Court majority a year earlier in *Deepsouth Packing Co. v. Laitram Corp.*: "The direction of Art. I is that *Congress* shall have the power to promote the progress of science and the useful arts. When, as here, the Constitution is permissive, the sign of how

---

29. STORY, *supra* note 25, § 431.
30. STORY, *supra* note 25, vol. II, § 968.
31. For reasons not known, he failed to address this point in his discussion of the intellectual property clause, although his views on it can be inferred from his discussion of the general welfare clause.
32. *See infra* text accompanying notes 189 and 190.
33. Whicher, for example, refers to the introductory phrase as "the purposive phrase" and the "by" phrase as "the substantive phrase." *See* John F. Whicher, *The Ghost of Donaldson v. Beckett: An Inquiry Into the Constitutional Distribution of Powers Over the Law of Literary Property in the United States*, 9 BULL. COPYRIGHT SOC'Y 228 (1962).
34. 412 U.S. 546, 555 (1973) (emphasis added).
35. In this regard, note that the Court did not say that the clause sets forth "a" means or "one" means, but rather interpreted it as setting forth "the" means. *See also supra* Chapter Four, note 10.

far Congress has chosen to go can come only from Congress."[36] In this interpretation of the clause, the introductory "to" portion is not simply a statement of object or purpose, but rather is a generic grant of power in its own right. For the reasons discussed in detail in the remainder of this chapter, I believe that this is the correct interpretation and that the clause is not limited to a grant of authority to Congress to legislate concerning patents and copyrights. Moreover, the introductory language is not only a grant of generic power, it is also a limitation on that grant of power.[37]

The "to" portion of the clause is sometimes referred to as the preamble,[38] particularly by those addressing copyright issues, and is argued to be intended merely as a statement of purpose or object which does not limit the authority given to Congress. As Nimmer and Nimmer put it, "the phrase 'To promote the progress of science and useful arts . . .' must be read as largely in the nature of a preamble, indicating the purpose of the power but not in limitation of its exercise."[39] This in essence reads the introductory language out of the clause and renders it meaningless. It is also very much at odds with modern pronouncements of the Supreme Court pertaining to the effect of the introductory language on the patent power granted to Congress and earlier pronouncements of the Court concerning the effect of that language on the copyright power.

Somewhat surprisingly the meaning to be attributed to the "to" language had been only occasionally addressed by the Court prior to *Graham v. John Deere Co.*[40] in 1966. One context in which the Court had

---

36. 406 U.S. 518, 530 (1972).
37. In construing the meaning to be given Section 5 of the Fourteenth Amendment, the Supreme Court has recently noted "that the same language that serves as the basis for [an] affirmative grant of congressional power [can also serve] to limit that power." *See* Kimel v. Florida Board of Regents, 120 S. Ct. 631, 644 (2000).
38. *See, e.g.,* Paul J. Heald & Suzanna Sherry, *Implied Limits on the Legislative Power: The Intellectual Property Clause as an Absolute Constraint on Congress,* 2000 ILL. L. REV. 1119, 1153; MELVILLE B. NIMMER & DAVID NIMMER, 1 NIMMER ON COPYRIGHT § 1.03[A] (Rel. 44-12/97); Wendy J. Gordon, *An Inquiry into the Merits of Copyright: The Challenges of Consistency, Consent, and Encouragement Theory,* 41 STAN. L. REV. 1343, 1449 (1989).
39. NIMMER & NIMMER, *id. Cf.* the view expressed by Heald & Sherry that: "Some of the constraints on Congress's power over intellectual property are self-evident: grants of rights should 'promote the Progress of Science and useful Arts' and be made only 'for limited times.'" Heald & Sherry, *supra* note 38, at 1120.
40. *See* 383 U.S. 1, 5 (1966).

looked at it in some detail were the so-called patent non-use cases. The issue was first brought before the Court in 1908 in *Continental Paper Bag Co. v. Eastern Paper Bag Co.* wherein it was argued that an injunction against patent infringement could not lay because non-use of the patent by its owner violated the constitutional purpose of promoting the progress of useful arts.[41] For whatever reason, the Court declined to specifically address whether the statement of purpose in the intellectual property clause obligated a refusal to enjoin infringement, but instead held only that Congress had selected another policy and had continued that policy for a number of years. The Court simply assumed that such a policy had been beneficial and was appropriate.[42]

Nonetheless, implicit in *Continental Paper Bag* was an assumption by the Court that the introductory language did not obligate Congress to ensure that the subject matter of a patent would be put in use during the term of the grant of the exclusive right. A divided Court thereafter would make the point clear in *Special Equipment Co. v. Coe* decided in 1945 by reversing a lower court opinion invalidating a patent on the ground that non-use was contrary to the constitutional purpose.[43] The majority noted congressional awareness of non-use and that Congress could predicate patent validity upon use of the patented subject matter if it so chose.[44] But, emphasized the majority, "it by no means follows" that a patent grant not so conditioned "is an inconsistent or inappropriate exercise of the constitutional authority of Congress 'to promote the Progress of Science and useful Arts' by securing to inventors 'the exclusive Right to their . . . Discoveries.'"[45] Rather, Congress "could have concluded that the useful arts would be best promoted" by the statutory requirement of a full disclosure of the invention and the manner of making and using it.[46] In other words, it was not use but full disclosure in a published patent that could be viewed as conforming to the constitutional purpose.

A dissent by Justice Douglas[47] argued that: "The purpose 'to promote the progress of science and useful arts' . . . provides the standards for the

---

41. 210 U.S. 405, 422–23 (1908).
42. *Id.* at 429–30.
43. 324 U.S. 370, 377 (1945).
44. *Id.* at 378. The majority pointed out that Congress had in fact chosen to do so in the Patent Act of 1832, when it conditioned patents to aliens upon the use of the patented invention. *Id.*
45. *Id.*
46. *Id.*
47. Joined by Justices Black and Murphy.

exercise of the power and sets the limits beyond which it may not go."[48] In his view, non-use was irreconcilable with this purpose. He seems to have been influenced in no small measure by his view that "[o]f the various enumerated powers it [the intellectual property clause] is the only one which states the purpose of the authority granted to Congress."[49] But even a cursory glance at the enumerated powers shows that each contains a statement of purpose explicit or implicit in the grant of power.[50]

In 1966 in *Graham v. John Deere Co.* the Court would agree with Douglas that the introductory language of the clause contains a standard that Congress may not violate. But it would do so to support its view that there is a constitutional standard of invention that must be met in order for there to be patentability. It began by noting that the qualified authority given to Congress with regard to the issuance of patents "is limited to the promotion of advances in the 'useful arts,'" and went on to state that "Congress in the exercise of the patent power may not overreach the restraints imposed by the stated constitutional purpose." According to the Court, "'promot[ing] the Progress of . . . useful Arts' . . . is the *standard* expressed in the Constitution and it may not be ignored."[51]

The import of this is that, in the patent context, the Court has most emphatically stated that the "to" language of the clause is a limitation which sets forth a constitutional standard for the issuance of patents. Nothing similar has been expressed in the context of copyright, although why this language should be perceived to set forth a constitutional standard with respect to patents but not with respect to copyrights is unclear.[52] Yet there was case law out of the nineteenth century, including from the Supreme Court, that clearly indicated that the "to" language limited the copyright power of Congress.[53] Indeed, in 1829 in one of the earliest

---

48. 324 U.S. at 381.
49. *Id.* He seems to have taken this view on the assumption that the grant of power resides only in the "by" portion of the clause. Such an assumption is of course strongly challenged in the present work.
50. *See, e.g.,* text accompanying note 17, *supra.*
51. 383 U.S. at 5–6.
52. The constitutional standard of originality required for copyright supposedly is found not in the "to" language, but rather from the interpretation given to "authors" and "writings." *See, e.g.,* Feist Publ'ns v. Rural Tel. Serv., 499 U.S., 340, 346 (1991). *See also* The Trademark Cases, 100 U.S. 82, 94 (1879); Burrow-Giles Lithographic Co. v. Sarony, 111 U.S. 53, 58 (1884).
53. Yet copyright commentators invariably ignore the language of this case law indicating that the "to" language of the clause limits the copyright power of Congress, with Nimmer & Nimmer being the classic example.

reported copyright cases, Justice Thompson in his capacity as circuit judge held that this language of the clause did in fact limit the type of subject matter that could be copyrighted.[54] In 1879 the Supreme Court in *Baker v. Selden* quoted with approval the views expressed by Justice Thompson in 1829.[55] In 1891 in *Higgins v. Keuffel,* the Court clearly indicated that the meaning to be given to "writings" in the clause was limited by the "to" language of the clause.[56] Nonetheless, in recent years the lower courts have refused to treat the "to" language as placing any limitation of the power of Congress to issue copyrights.[57]

Part of the problem arises out of the fact that power granted to Congress by the clause is discretionary rather than compulsory.[58] In noting this fact in a patent case in 1972, the Court used language which suggests that Congress has a great deal of discretion as to what patent and copyright policy it adopts.[59] In so doing, however, it failed to reference the point it had earlier made in *Graham v. John Deere Co.* that the grant of authority does not permit Congress to go beyond, or act outside of, the stated constitutional purpose,[60] or the views it had expressed in *Baker v. Selden* and *Higgins v. Keuffel.*[61] It has thus created considerable uncertainty as to what limits, if any, the "to" language of the clause places on congressional power.[62]

Nonetheless, *Graham v. John Deere Co.* makes clear that congressional discretion is not unbounded, i.e., Congress may act only within the limits imposed by the stated constitutional purpose.[63] The statement of purpose set forth in the intellectual property clause is both a general grant of power and a constitutional limitation on the authority granted to Congress with

---

54. Clayton v. Stone, 5 F. Cas. 999 (No. 2,872), 13 Copyright Dec., 1789–1909, at 64 (C.C.S.D.N.Y. 1829). For more on this case, see Chapter Nine, text accompanying notes 166–69, *infra.*
55. 101 U.S. 99, 105 (1879).
56. 140 U.S. 428, 430 (1891).
57. For a discussion of these lower-court cases see Chapter Nine, text accompanying notes 55–67, *infra.*
58. Article I, section 8 of the Constitution begins: "Congress shall have power to" rather than "Congress shall."
59. Deepsouth Packing Co. v. Laitram Corp., 406 U.S. 518, 530 (1972).
60. *See supra* text accompanying note 51.
61. *See supra* notes 55 and 56 and accompanying text .
62. This point is addressed in some detail in Chapter Seven. The extent to which Congress has discretion to treat copyrights and patents differently is addressed in a number of places in this work.
63. It is accordingly fully consistent with the views expressed by Chief Justice Marshall in 1824 in *Gibbons v. Ogden. See supra* text accompanying note 24.

respect to copyrights and patents.[64]   Because he disagrees with the nature of the constitutional standard suggested by the Court in *Graham v. John Deere Co.*,[65] Burchfiel argues that in interpreting several other enumerated congressional powers the Court has rejected the view that a statement of purpose in an enumerated congressional power should be construed to express an implied limit on congressional exercise of the power.[66] But in each example he cites, the Court has not held that a statement of purpose places no restriction on the exercise of particular congressional power, thereby rendering the statement of purpose essentially meaningless. Rather in each instance, the Court has adopted an expansive definition of the statement of purpose, rather than holding that it creates no limitation on the exercise of the particular power.

Because it is relevant to the subject matter of this chapter, let me cite to one of Burchfiel's examples, the general welfare clause.[67] He notes that in *United States v. Butler*[68] the Court held that while congressional authority to spend public moneys for public purposes is not absolute, neither is it limited to the direct grants of legislative powers found in the

---

64. I fundamentally disagree with the statement by Lavigne that "the Copyright Clause is one of only a few portions of the entire Constitution to recite a purpose" and that "[t]his gives copyright a special place in the framework of the Constitution." *See* Joseph A. Lavigne, *Comment: For Limited Times? Making Kids Richer via the Copyright Term Extension Act of 1996*, 73 U. DET. MERCY L. REV. 311, 319 (1996). Contrary to this view, every enumerated power granted to Congress by the Constitution literally contains a statement of purpose. What makes the intellectual property clause unusual is that it is the only enumerated power to set forth a particular mode of carrying out the power granted. It does so to assure that the power to grant copyrights and patents is included in the congressional authority to promote the progress of science and useful arts.

65. I also disagree with the nature of this standard, but for reasons quite different than those espoused by Burchfiel. *See infra* Chapter Eight, text accompanying notes 268–277.

66. Kenneth J. Burchfiel, *The Constitutional Intellectual Property Power: Progress of Useful Arts and the Legal Protection of Semiconductor Technology*, 28 SANTA CLARA L. REV. 473, 518–19 (1988). Kimball has gone even further and argued that "it is an inherently self-contradictory statement, and contrary to recognized meanings of the terms, to assert that a restraint is imposed by a statement of purpose." Albert J. Kimball Jr., *An Analysis of Recent Supreme Court Assertions Regarding a Constitutional Standard of Invention*, 1 AM. PAT. L. ASS'N Q. J. 204, 206 (1973).

67. *See* note 77 *infra*.

68. 297 U.S. 1 (1936).

Constitution.[69] He argues, however, that in *Butler* and its progeny the Court "stressed the breadth of the power to promote the general welfare and the constitutional discretion of Congress, without recognizing a judicially inforceable internal limit in the language of the grant."[70] This statement is simply incorrect. In *Butler,* for example, the Court majority expressly stated: "That the qualifying phrase [i.e., "the general Welfare"] must be given effect all advocates of broad construction admit."[71] In other words, the phrase "the general welfare" has meaning as a limitation on the power to tax and spend.[72] So too does "to promote the progress of science and useful arts" on the power of Congress to create copyrights and patents.[73]

Regardless of the differences between the modern judicial treatment of the introductory language with regard to patents and copyrights, in both instances there is a basic presumption that the grant of power resides in the phrase introduced by "by." Many members of the first federal Congresses, however, tended to view the matter quite differently. From their perspective, the introductory phrase was in actuality the grant of power, and the phrase introduced by "by" was considered to be a limitation on that grant of power. They were not alone in holding this view.[74]

---

69. *See infra* the text accompanying note 167.
70. Burchfiel, *supra* note 66, at 522–23.
71. 297 U.S. at 66.
72. *See, e.g.,* South Dakota v. Dole, 483 U.S. 203, 207–10 (1987).
73. Elsewhere I have discussed in detail the relationship between the general welfare clause and the intellectual property clause and whether the intellectual property clause serves as an independent constitutional bar in some respects to the broad interpretation of the general welfare clause. *See* Edward C. Walterscheid, *Conforming the General Welfare Clause and the Intellectual Property Clause,* 13 HARV. J. L. & TECH. 87 (2000).
74. Indeed some modern commentators hold such a view. *See, e.g.,* Jeffrey T. Renz, *What Spending Clause? (Or the President's Paramour): An Examination of the Views of Hamilton, Madison, and Story on Article I, Section 8, Clause 1 of the United States Constitution,* 33 J. MARSHALL L. REV. 81, 102 (1999) ("[c]lause 8 sets forth the object of promoting the progress of arts and sciences, but limits the scope of that power by setting forth the means, for example, granting of patents and copyrights").

B. Early Interpretations, Congressional and Otherwise

The meaning to be given to the intellectual property clause was one of the earliest issues of constitutional interpretation faced by the first federal Congress. On April 15, 1789 John Churchman petitioned the House of Representatives for an exclusive right with respect to his invention for determining longitude based on the magnetic variation at places of known latitude. He also requested that the House fund a voyage to Baffin's Bay to aid in further development of the invention.[75] This is the first known request for federal funding of what would now be known as research and development. Debate on this request for funding rather quickly raised the question whether the exclusive right provision of the clause was intended to be the exclusive mode granted to Congress for promoting the progress of science and useful arts.[76] Two years later, Alexander Hamilton would provide a strong constitutional argument that other means such as bounties could be used for this purpose under the general welfare clause.[77]

Arguments of this type had yet to be made in 1789, however. Although Madison spoke in favor of funding the voyage, he made no mention whatsoever of what authority Congress might have to provide such funding.[78] Brant argues that Madison's support for the voyage "could only be justified by a sweeping interpretation of the power to spend for the general welfare."[79] Likewise, Levy states that "Madison supported an expenditure justifiable only upon a breathtaking interpretation of the general welfare clause."[80] Alternatively, Currie suggests that Madison was "conjur[ing] up the

---

75. *See* III THE DOCUMENTARY HISTORY OF THE FIRST FEDERAL CONGRESS OF THE UNITED STATES at 28–29 (Linda De Pauw et al. eds., Baltimore 1977) [hereinafter DOCUMENTARY HISTORY].
76. For the debates on Churchman's petition, see X DOCUMENTARY HISTORY, *id.* at 211–20.
77. For Hamilton's argument see text accompanying notes 96–103 *infra*. The general welfare clause states that: "Congress shall have Power To lay and collect Taxes, Duties, Imposts and Excises, to pay the Debts and provide for the common Defence and general Welfare of the United States." *See* U.S. CONST. art. I, § 8, cl. 1.
78. *See* X DOCUMENTARY HISTORY, *supra* note 75, at 211–12 and 217–18.
79. IRVING BRANT, JAMES MADISON: THE FATHER OF THE CONSTITUTION at 332 (Indianapolis 1950).
80. LEONARD LEVY, ORIGINAL INTENT AND THE FRAMERS' CONSTITUTION at 9 (New York 1988).

ubiquitous Commerce Clause."[81] There is no evidence to support either of these perspectives, because at this early stage in congressional debate no one, including Madison, had proposed a broad reading of either the commerce clause or the general welfare clause. Moreover, the context of the debate makes clear that it was conducted under the supposition that what was at issue was the authority given by the intellectual property clause.

Rather, it appears that initially Madison gave little thought to the constitutional implications of Churchman's request,[82] although he soon thereafter would admonish the House "that constitutional issues should be given 'careful investigation and full discussion' because '[t]he decision that is at this time made, will become the permanent exposition of the constitution.'"[83] Instead, he was prepared to accept an expansive interpretation of the clause which did not read the inclusion of a particular mode of practicing the power as limiting Congress to only that mode.[84] Several other Representatives, however, expressed doubt as to whether Congress had power under the clause to do anything other than merely secure to inventors for limited times the exclusive rights to their discoveries.[85] They

---

81. David P. Currie, *The Constitution in Congress: Substantive Issues in the First Federal Congress*, 61 U. CHI. L. REV. 775, 799 (1994). The commerce clause states that "Congress shall have Power To regulate Commerce with foreign Nations, and among the several States, and with the Indian Tribes." *See* U.S. CONST. art. I, § 8, cl. 3.
82. Without intending to do so (his analysis is in the context of the interpretation given to the general welfare clause), Lynch provides support for this view by pointing out that Madison spoke in favor of the voyage as a favor to a friend and did not argue when constitutional objections were raised. *See* JOSEPH M. LYNCH, NEGOTIATING THE CONSTITUTION: THE EARLIEST DEBATES OVER ORIGINAL INTENT at 260 (Ithaca 1999).
83. DAVID P. CURRIE, THE CONSTITUTION IN CONGRESS 1789–1801, at 116 (Chicago 1997), citing 1 ANNALS OF CONGRESS 514. Little did Madison realize how much constitutional interpretation would change in just two centuries.
84. Madison soon would change his mind on any expansive interpretation of the intellectual property clause. For his views on this topic one year later, for example, in 1790, see note 94 *infra* and accompanying text.
85. *See* X DOCUMENTARY HISTORY, *supra* note 75, at 213–14, 220 . Rep. Tucker
   expressed a doubt whether the Legislature has power, by the Constitution, to go further in rewarding the inventors of useful machines, or discoveries in sciences, then merely to secure to them for a time the right of making, publishing and vending them: in case of a doubt, he thought it best to err on the safe side.
   Id. at 220.

believed that the specific inclusion of particular means for promoting the progress of science and useful arts was intended to limit the authority of Congress to this particular means. As a result, no action was taken on Churchman's request.

When Churchman renewed his efforts to obtain federal funding for the voyage, a committee report dated January 6, 1791 stated that the issue of funding the voyage "involves an inquiry into the Constitutional powers of Congress," which the committee was not prepared to do.[86] In 1796 a congressional committee made the point even more clearly, saying: "That it is their opinion that application to Congress for pecuniary encouragement of important discoveries, or of useful arts, cannot be complied with, as the constitution of the United States appears to have limited the powers of Congress to granting patents only. . . ."[87] Clearly, the early federal Congresses interpreted the grant of authority to promote the progress of science and useful arts in the "to" portion to be limited to the particular modes set forth in the remainder of the clause, i.e., the issuance of patents and copyrights.[88] In this way of interpreting the clause, the "by" portion is treated as a limitation on the power set forth in the "to" portion.

Currie contends that the congressional doubts "were solidly supported by the text of the provision" and that the Constitution confers "not a general power 'to promote the progress of science and useful arts,' but instead only the power to grant limited exclusive rights in order to accomplish that

---

86. *See* IV DOCUMENTARY HISTORY, *supra* note 75, at 530–31.

87. American State Papers, Miscellaneous, Doc. No. 74, 4th Cong., 1st Sess. (1796). One House member said that he was "sorry to have it established as a principle, that this Government cannot Constitutionally extend its fostering aid to the useful arts and discoveries," but he did not make an issue of it. *See* ANNALS OF CONGRESS, Feb. 3, 1796 (4th Cong., 1st Sess. 1796), at 288.

88. As stated by Dupree:

> the tide ran clear and strong against the establishment of any power in the government to subsidize science directly. The failure of the patent clause to become what it might have been—a basis for scientific activity of all sorts—well illustrates the reluctance of the Congress in this period to become active in science, even where, as in the case of patents themselves, they had to make no appropriation. The people's representatives settled into a silent groove of strict construction of the Constitution concerning a subject where popular enthusiasm did not measure up to the cost of action both in controversy and money.

A. HUNTER DUPREE, SCIENCE IN THE FEDERAL GOVERNMENT, A HISTORY OF POLICIES AND ACTIVITIES TO 1940, at 14 (Cambridge, Mass. 1957).

goal."[89] Although Currie did not cite to him, St. George Tucker, one of the earliest commentators on the Constitution interpreted the clause in exactly the same way, saying: "For the constitution not only declares the object, but points out the express mode of giving encouragement; viz. 'by securing for a limited time to authors and inventors, the exclusive right to their respective writings and discoveries.' Nothing could be more superfluous, or incompatible with the object contended for, than these words, if it was, indeed, the intention of the constitution to authorize congress, to adopt any other mode which they might think proper."[90] As is shown, this view would prevail during much of the first half of the nineteenth century.

Interestingly, early in 1790 Madison would adopt a similar conservative perspective, albeit for what appeared a somewhat different reason. To understand why, a bit of background is necessary. Speaking in early August 1787 in Philadelphia while the federal convention was in progress Tench Coxe suggested that as one means of encouraging manufactures in the United States "[p]remiums for useful inventions and improvements, whether foreign or American . . . must have an excellent effect." He suggested that the granting of tracts of land would serve as effective premiums.[91] Although he was speaking in the context of what other countries did to encourage manufactures, he failed to mention patents. It is quite possible that this talk influenced Madison's proposal to the convention that Congress be given power "to encourage by premiums & provisions, the advancement of useful knowledge and discoveries."[92]

On March 21, 1790 Coxe wrote to Madison seeking support for his efforts to encourage the diffusion of European technology to the United States through his scheme of offering land premiums for the importation

---

89. Currie, *supra* note 81, at 799, 822. *See also* CURRIE, *supra* note 83, at 93.
90. ST. GEORGE TUCKER, 1 BLACKSTONE'S COMMENTARIES: WITH NOTES OF REFERENCE TO THE CONSTITUTION AND LAWS OF THE UNITED STATES; AND OF THE COMMONWEALTH OF VIRGINIA, ETC. at Appendix, Note D (Philadelphia 1803).
91. *An address to an assembly of the friends of American manufacture, convened for the purpose of establishing a society for the encouragement of manufactures and the useful arts, read at the university of Pennsylvania, on Thursday, the 9th of August, 1787—by Tench Coxe, Esq. and published at their request,* 2 AMERICAN MUSEUM at 249–55 (Philadelphia 1787).
92. Many years later, Coxe stated that copies of this address "were provided to general Washington and the other members of the federal convention then sitting in Philadelphia." *See* J. E. COOKE, TENCH COXE AND THE EARLY REPUBLIC at 104 (Chapel Hill, N.C. 1978).

of such technology.[93] In his response a week later, Madison now gave short shrift to such an idea, saying:

> Your idea of appropriating a district of territory to the encouragement of imported inventions is new and worthy of consideration. I cannot but apprehend however that the clause in the constitution which forbids patents for this purpose will lie equally in the way of your expedient. Congress seems to be tied down to the single mode of encouraging inventions by granting the exclusive benefit of them for a limited time, and therefore to have no more power to give a further encouragement out of a fund of land than a fund of money. The Latitude of authority wished for was strongly urged and expressly rejected.[94]

There is no contemporaneous record which expressly indicates why Madison took the position that the clause limits the means by which the federal government could encourage invention and, more generically, "the progress of the useful arts," only to the grant of limited-term exclusive rights.[95]

---

93. Letter from Tench Coxe to James Madison (Mar. 21, 1790), *in* 13 THE PAPERS OF JAMES MADISON at 111–14 (Charles F. Hobson et al. eds., Charlottesville 1981). Coxe argued that the creation of new technology in the United States would

> save great sums of Money, raise our character as an intelligent Nation, and encrease [sic] the comforts of human life and the most pure & dignifying Enjoyments of the mind of man. No man has a higher confidence than I, in the talents of my Countrymen & their ability to attain these things by their native strength of mind, but I would nevertheless draw upon the great fund of skill & knowledge, particularly of the useful Arts, wch. Europe possesses.

94. Letter from James Madison to Tench Coxe (Mar. 28, 1790), *in* THE PAPERS OF JAMES MADISON, *supra* note 93, at 128.

95. Nonetheless, the language used by Madison implicitly suggests that this construction was predicated on the rejection by the convention of broader powers that both he and Pinckney had proposed. Recall that he had proposed that Congress have power "to encourage by proper premiums & provisions, the advancement of useful knowledge and discoveries," and Pinckney had proposed that Congress be authorized "to establish public institutions, rewards and immunities for the promotion of agriculture, commerce, trades, and manufactures." *See supra* Chapter Three, text accompanying note 81.

   Coxe's land-premium scheme obviously fell within the scope of either of these proposals. Within a few years, Madison would expressly reject as the basis for constitutional interpretation the fact that a particular proposal was rejected by the convention. *See* Chapter IX, *Madison and the Origins of Originalism, in* JACK N. RAKOVE, ORIGINAL MEANINGS: POLITICS AND IDEAS IN THE

This, of course, is what is now termed the narrow view of the spending power of Congress, namely, that it is limited to that specifically authorized in the enumerated powers given to Congress. Hamilton, however, had appeared to propose a much broader view of the spending power under the welfare clause,[96] one that at first glance appeared not in any way limited by any other enumerated power. In the *Report on the Subject of Manufactures*[97] submitted to Congress December 5, 1791, Hamilton argued that the federal government had constitutional authority under the general welfare clause to issue "pecuniary bounties" as an encouragement to the development of manufacturing in the United States. He contended that under this clause

> the power to *raise money* is *plenary*, and *indefinite;* and the objects to which it may be *appropriated* are no less comprehensive, than the payment of the public debts and the providing for the common defence and *"general Welfare."* The terms *"general Welfare"* were doubtless intended to signify more than was expressed or imported than those which Preceded; otherwise numerous exigencies incident to the affairs of a Nation would have been left without a provision. The phrase is as comprehensive as any that could have been used; because it was not fit that the constitutional authority of the Union, to appropriate its revenues should have been restricted within narrower limits than the "general Welfare" and because this necessarily embraces a vast variety of particulars, which are susceptible neither of specification nor of definition.
>
> It is therefore of necessity left to the discretion of the National Legislature, to pronounce, upon the objects, which concern the general Welfare, and for which under that description, an appropriation of money is requisite and proper. And there seems to be no room for a doubt that whatever concerns the general Interests of *learning* of *Agriculture* of *Manufactures* and of *Commerce* are within the sphere of the national Councils *as far as regards an application of Money.*[98]

Having established to his satisfaction that under the general welfare clause Congress had broad constitutional authority to appropriate and spend money for a wide variety of purposes, Hamilton went on to propose a

---

MAKING OF THE CONSTITUTION at 339–65 (New York 1996). Be that as it may, he would henceforth hew to a narrow interpretation of the intellectual property clause.

96. For the general welfare clause, *see supra* note 77.

97. *Alexander Hamilton, Report on the Subject of Manufactures, December 5, 1791, reproduced in* X THE PAPERS OF ALEXANDER HAMILTON at 230–340 (Harold C. Syrett et al. eds., New York 1966).

98. *Id.* at 303.

specific scheme. He recommended that Congress appropriate an annual sum to be spent by a Board of Commissioners empowered among other things "to induce the prosecution and introduction of useful discoveries, inventions and improvements by proportionate rewards, judiciously held out and applied—to encourage by premiums both honorable and lucrative the exertions of individuals."[99] From the context it appears that Hamilton was not actually recommending that Congress fund research and development but rather that in certain cases of successful discovery and invention it reward the individuals responsible, presumably thereby encouraging others to make similar efforts.[100]

Although he used quite broad language in setting forth this scheme, it appears that his primary intent was to set up a mechanism "for promoting the introduction of foreign improvements" into the United States.[101] In this regard, he was aware that Congress believed that there was a constitutional impediment to the granting of patents of importation for inventions known and used in other countries.[102] His proposed solution was to pay premiums for the introduction of foreign inventions into the country. In so doing, however, he failed to make any mention of the intellectual property clause or to discuss how or in what manner this approach would be acceptable in light of its express language.

Hamilton seems to have been fully aware that his broad interpretation of the general welfare clause could—and indeed would—be challenged on the ground that it rendered the limitations either expressly specified or inherent in the following seventeen grants of power essentially meaningless. He sought to meet an anticipated challenge of this kind by in essence

---

99. THE PAPERS OF ALEXANDER HAMILTON, *supra* note 97, at 338.
100. This idea of using premiums to encourage invention had been specifically proposed in the federal convention by Madison and indirectly by Pinckney. *See supra* Chapter Three, text accompanying notes 80 and 81. But in 1790 Madison argued to Tench Coxe that the refusal of the convention to include premiums as a means of encouraging invention in the Constitution was evidence that the use of such premiums was unconstitutional. *See* PAPERS OF JAMES MADISON *supra* note 93 and accompanying text. One only can speculate as to whether Hamilton was aware of the position taken by Madison but chose simply to ignore it. It is quite possible, however, that Coxe had informed him of it, particularly since Coxe was an assistant secretary of the Treasury during the period that the *Report* was being prepared.
101. THE PAPERS OF ALEXANDER HAMILTON, *supra* note 97, at 308.
102. For a discussion of this concern, *see infra* Chapter Eight, text accompanying notes 27–53.

arguing that the limitations of the other enumerated grants of power would still be in effect, saying:

> No objection ought to arise to this construction on a supposition that it would imply a power to whatever else should appear to Congress conducive to the General Welfare. A power to appropriate money with this latitude which is granted too in *express terms* would not carry a power to do any other thing, not authorized in the constitution, either expressly or by fair implication.[103]

Presumably it was his view that the use of premiums to promote the progress of science and useful arts was authorized "by fair implication," despite the language of the intellectual property clause. Unfortunately, the *Report* was totally silent as to what the nature of that "fair implication" might be. Nonetheless, this could be termed the broad interpretation of the intellectual property clause.

Albeit in a different context, Washington, as president, seems to have held a more expansive view of the intellectual property clause than did the early federal Congresses.[104] Washington's interest was in the promotion of "science" in its broad meaning of learning or knowledge, as he made clear in his first annual message to Congress on January 8, 1790:

> Nor am I less persuaded, that you will agree with me in opinion, that there is nothing which can better deserve your patronage, than the promotion of Science and Literature. Knowledge is in every Country the surest basis of public happiness. In one, in which the measures of Government receive their impression so immediately from the sense of the Community as in our's, it is proportionably essential. To the security of a free Constitution it contributes in various ways: By convincing those, who are entrusted with the public administration that every valuable end of Government is best answered by the enlightened confidence of the people: And by teaching the people themselves to know and to value their own rights; to discern and provide against invasions of them; to distinguish between oppression and the necessary exercise of lawful authority; between burthens proceeding from an disregard of their convenience and those resulting from the inevitable exigencies of Society; to discriminate the spirit of liberty from that of licentiousness, cherishing the first, avoiding the last, and uniting a speedy, but temperate vigilence [sic] against encroachments, with an inviolable respect to the laws.

---

103. THE PAPERS OF ALEXANDER HAMILTON, *supra* note 97, at 303–04.
104. I am indebted to William C. diGiacomantonio for helpful discussions on Washington's views.

> Whether this desirable object will be best promoted by affording
> aids to Seminaries of Learning already established—by the institution
> of a national University—or by any other expedients, will be well
> worthy of a place in the deliberations of the Legislature.[105]

In proposing federal aid to existing schools and the establishment of a
national university, Washington clearly did not perceive the intellectual
property clause to limit the promotion of "science" by Congress to merely
the issuance of copyrights.[106]

The House debate on May 3, 1790 on this aspect of Washington's
message demonstrated an ambivalence concerning whether constitutional
authority existed to proceed as proposed by Washington. When a motion
was made to refer Washington's proposal to a select committee:

> Mr. Stone enquired what part of the Constitution authorised Congress to
> take any steps in a business of this kind—for his part he knew of none.
> We have already done as much as we can with propriety—We have en-
> couraged learning, by giving to authors an exclusive privilege of vending
> their works—this is going as far as we have power to, by the Constitution.
>
> Mr. Sherman said that a proposition to vest Congress with power
> to establish a National University was made in the General Conven-
> tion—but it was negatived—It was thought sufficient that this power
> should be exercised by the States in their separate capacity.[107]

---

105. DOCUMENTARY HISTORY, *supra* note 75, at 253–54. *See also* I THE STATE OF
     THE UNION MESSAGES OF THE PRESIDENT, 1790–1966, at 3 (Fred L. Israel
     ed., New York 1967).
106. *Cf.* Lynch's argument that "the founding of a university was not within the
     enumerated powers" and his suggestion that in seeking congressional support
     for a national university Washington "was a secret believer in the sweeping
     powers of the Necessary and Proper Clause." LYNCH, *supra* note 82, at 258.
     Lynch obviously fails to consider a broad interpretation of the intellectual
     property clause as set forth herein.
107. Sherman's view that the negativing of a proposal by the constitutional conven-
     tion, i.e., the refusal to incorporate it into the Constitution, rendered the
     subject matter of the proposal unconstitutional was similar to that taken by
     Madison to Tench Coxe some weeks earlier with regard to Coxe's proposal to
     use land premiums to encourage invention. *See* PAPERS OF JAMES MADISON,
     supra note 93, at 128. *See also* text accompanying note 94, *supra*. Charles
     Pinckney had proposed to the federal convention on May 28, 1787 that the
     draft Constitution include a provision "to establish a Federal University." *See*
     3 RECORDS OF THE FEDERAL CONVENTION OF 1787, at 122 (Max Farrand
     ed., New Haven 1937). This provision was among the "additional powers
     proposed to be vested in the Legislature" on August 18, 1787 and referred to

Mr. Page observed, that he was in favor of the motion. He wished to have the matter determined whether Congress has or has not a right to do anything for the promotion of science and literature—He rather supposed they had such a right—but if on investigation of the subject, it shall appear that have not, I should consider the circumstance said he, as a very essential defect in the Constitution—and should be for proposing an amendment—for on the diffusion of knowledge and literature depend the liberties of this country, and the preservation of the Constitution.[108]

The House declined to act on the motion. Its refusal to take up the proposal was likely predicated on a combination of constitutional concern and pragmatic reluctance to propose anything that was likely to cost money and not be deemed essential to the operation of the new federal government.

Washington was content to let the issue lie until near the end of his administration when he once again raised it in his eighth annual message to Congress. He had enlisted the aid of Hamilton in the preparation of his farewell message and on September 1, 1796 asked him to draft a section for the message which would once again recommend that Congress fund a national university. Hamilton responded by stating that "[t]he idea of the university is one of those which I think will be most properly reserved for your speech at the opening of the session," i.e., Washington's eighth annual message to Congress. He thereafter prepared a draft which was

---

the Committee of Detail. *See* 2 RECORDS OF THE FEDERAL CONVENTION OF 1787, *id.* at 321. On that same day, Pinckney proposed somewhat different language to grant Congress the power "to establish seminaries for the promotion of literature & sciences." Both proposals failed to make the final draft submitted to the convention on September 12, 1787. On September 14th, Madison and Pinckney moved to add this authority to the enumerated list of congressional powers. James Wilson supported the motion but Governeur Morris thought "it was not necessary" because "the exclusive power at the Seat of Government, will reach the object." 2 RECORDS OF THE FEDERAL CONVENTION OF 1787, *id.* at 616. In essence, he was arguing that Congress could do whatever it wanted to in the proposed federal district, in the absence of any express constitutional prohibition. Whether because of this or some other argument (now unknown), the motion was defeated. *See* 2 RECORDS OF THE FEDERAL CONVENTION OF 1787, *id.* at 616. Sherman had been one of those voting against the motion at the convention.

108. XIII DOCUMENTARY HISTORY, *supra* note 75, at 1221.

incorporated with some variations into Washington's message delivered to Congress on December 7, 1796.[109]

Neither Washington nor Hamilton made any mention of constitutional issues, but it is apparent that Washington endorsed Hamilton's broad interpretation of the general welfare clause, albeit not as strongly as Hamilton would have hoped. Thus, Hamilton had sought to begin the recommendation for a national university with the comment that Congress "will not doubt that the extension of science and knowlege [sic] is an object primarily interesting to our national [read, 'general'] welfare."[110] Washington replaced this with a statement that Congress "is too enlightened not to be fully sensible how much a flourishing state of the Arts and Sciences contributes to National Prosperity and reputation."[111] He incorporated Hamilton's argument that state institutions of learning were inadequately funded "to command the ablest Professors" but added the argument that "a primary object of such a National Institution should be, the education of our Youth in the science of *Government*."[112]

Washington also incorporated Hamilton's effort to get Congress to fund his proposal for premiums to encourage invention, although in the context of promoting agriculture, saying that of the means adopted for this purpose,

> none have been attended with greater success than the establishment of Boards composed of proper characters charged with collecting and diffusing information, and enabled by premiums, and small pecuniary aids, to encourage and assist a spirit of discovery and improvement. This species of establishment contributes doubly to the increase of improvement; by stimulating to enterprise and experiment, and by drawing to a common centre, the results everywhere of individual skill and observation; and spreading them thence over the whole Nation.

---

109. Letter from George Washington to Alexander Hamilton (Sept. 1, 1796); letter from Alexander Hamilton to George Washington (Sept. 4, 1796); letter from Alexander Hamilton to George Washington (Nov. 10, 1796) (enclosing Hamilton's draft), *in* 20 THE PAPERS OF ALEXANDER HAMILTON (H. C. Syrett et al. eds., New York 1974), at 311–14, 316, 381–85.

110. Hamilton's draft in PAPERS OF ALEXANDER HAMILTON, *supra* note 109, at 384.

111. George Washington, *Eighth Annual Message to Congress, December 7, 1796, in* GEORGE WASHINGTON WRITINGS at 982 (John Rhodehamel, ed. 1997). *See also* STATE OF THE UNION MESSAGES, *supra* note 105, at 35.

112. GEORGE WASHINGTON WRITINGS, *supra* note 111, at 982–83; STATE OF THE UNION MESSAGES, *supra* note 111, at 35.

Experience accordingly has shewn, that they are very cheap Instruments, of immense National benefits.[113]

It is doubtful that premiums or pecuniary rewards were nearly as widespread or as useful to promote discovery as Washington seemed to think,[114] but it is apparent that he did not perceive a constitutional impediment to their use. Contrary to various members of Congress he did not view the intellectual property clause as limiting the promotion of knowledge by the federal government to the issuance of copyrights.

Regardless of Washington's views, both Jefferson and Madison rather quickly challenged Hamilton's broad interpretation of the spending authority under the general welfare clause,[115] and Congress was not generally disposed to adopt it for the purpose of either creating a national university or funding research and development, as evidenced by the 1796 congressional report earlier noted.[116] In any case Congress largely ignored the *Report on the Subject of Manufactures* and failed to either create the Board of Commissioners or appropriate funds as recommended by Hamilton. A patent bill, H.R. 166, introduced March 1, 1792 , did contain a provision providing that among other things the fees collected for patents should be "appropriated for the expense of procuring and importing useful arts or machines from foreign countries."[117] This provision was promptly challenged by American inventors and did not survive into the Patent Act

---

113. GEORGE WASHINGTON WRITINGS, *supra* note 111, at 982; THE STATE OF THE UNION MESSAGES OF THE PRESIDENT, 1790–1966, *supra* note 105, at 34–35.

114. For a discussion on this point, *see* EDWARD C. WALTERSCHEID, TO PROMOTE THE PROGRESS OF USEFUL ARTS: AMERICAN PATENT LAW AND ADMINISTRATION, 1787–1836, at 149–50 (Littleton, CO 1998).

115. *See, e.g.,* Letter from James Madison to Henry Lee (Jan. 21, 1792) *in* 14 THE PAPERS OF JAMES MADISON, at 193–94 (Robert A. Rutland et al. eds., Charlottesville 1983). Jefferson argued to Washington in a private meeting on February 29, 1792 that to accept Hamilton's interpretation was to grant unlimited power to the federal government. Apparently in preparation for this meeting he prepared *Notes on the Constitutionality of Bounties to Encourage Manufacturing* wherein he stated that "the general govmt. has no powers but what are given by the Constn. [and] that of Levying money on the people to give out premiums is not among the powers in that instrument, nor necessary to carry any of the enumerated powers into [existence]." *See* 23 THE PAPERS OF THOMAS JEFFERSON, at 172–73 (C. T. Cullen ed., Princeton 1990).

116. *See supra* text accompanying note 87.

117. *See* WALTERSCHEID, *supra* note 114, at 473–77.

of 1793.[118] Either out of parsimony or constitutional objections or a combination thereof, Congress simply ignored Washington and Hamilton's later effort in 1796 to promote invention through premiums and to fund a national university.

Hamilton's broad view of the spending power would be increasingly argued in the decades preceding the Civil War, but it would not be until 1936 that the Supreme Court would ultimately declare it to be a correct interpretation of the general welfare clause.[119] As now shown, the constitutionality of federal funding of research and development would continue to be raised through the early part of the antebellum period.

C. Antebellum Views

According to Nathan Reingold:

> The Constitution ostensibly gives the federal government only two explicit authorizations for the support of science and technology, the patent clause and the authority to fix standards of weights and measures. The absence of constitutional authority was often raised as an objection to scientific and technological programs. On a number of occasions constitutional issues even carried the day. . . . [But w]hen stimulated by proper pressures, constitutional qualms were easily bypassed and constitutional justifications confidently propounded.[120]

Although Reingold made no mention of it, part of the constitutional concern was not merely the absence of express authorization to Congress to engage in such programs but the apparent limitation of the intellectual property clause to only patents and copyrights as the permitted means to promote the progress of science and useful arts. During the administrations

---

118. *See, e.g.,* JOSEPH BARNES, TREATISE ON THE JUSTICE, POLICY, AND UTILITY OF ESTABLISHING AN EFFECTUAL SYSTEM OF PROMOTING THE PROGRESS OF USEFUL ARTS, BY ASSURING PROPERTY IN THE PRODUCTS OF GENIUS at 20 (Philadelphia 1792). The challenge seems not to have been on constitutional grounds, but rather on the assumption that importing foreign inventions was somehow unfair to American inventors. It should be noted that the bill did not contemplate an appropriation for the purpose of importing foreign inventions, such as Hamilton had contemplated, but instead obligated a portion of the patent fee to be used for this purpose.
119. *See* Section D *infra.*
120. Nathan Reingold, *Introduction,* 1 THE NEW AMERICAN STATE PAPERS SCIENCE AND TECHNOLOGY at 12 (Wilmington 1973).

of both Jefferson and Madison, the perceived constitutional qualms did in fact carry the day and it would be several decades before they would be as easily bypassed as Reingold suggests.

Hamilton's interpretation of the general welfare clause certainly appeared broad enough to authorize the federal government to fund research and development, but during his presidency Jefferson would have none of it. His views were set forth in the 1798 Kentucky Resolutions, which he drafted:

> *Resolved,* That the construction applied by the General Government (as is evidenced by sundry of their proceedings[121]) to those parts of the Constitution of the United States which delegate to Congress a power "to lay and collect taxes, duties, imports, and excises, to pay the debts, and provide for the common defence and general welfare of the United States," and "to make all laws which shall be necessary and proper for carrying into execution the powers vested by the Constitution in the government of the United States, or any department thereof,"[122] goes to the destruction of all limits prescribed to their power by the Constitution: that words meant by the instrument to be subsidiary only to the execution of limited powers, ought not to be so construed as themselves to give unlimited powers, nor a part to be so taken as to destroy the whole residue of that instrument: that the proceedings of the General Government under color of these articles, will be a fit and necessary subject of revisal and correction, at a time of greater tranquility....[123]

In other words, the spending power of Congress was limited by the express provisions set forth in the enumerated powers. Jefferson construed the intellectual property clause literally to mean that the only mechanism constitutionally available to Congress to promote the progress of science and useful arts was the issuance of copyrights and patents. This narrow interpretation would soon cause Jefferson to engage in some interesting subterfuge. The occasion was the Lewis and Clark Expedition.

Prior to becoming president, Jefferson had long had a scientific interest in the land to the west of the United States and had actively encouraged its exploration.[124] As president, he could do more than encourage, he could

---

121. Jefferson failed to indicate the specific nature of those sundry proceedings.
122. U.S. CONST. art. I, § 8, cl. 18. During the course of the debates on the constitutionality of incorporating a national bank in 1791 Hamilton had also invoked this clause as granting wide latitude to the Congress.
123. 17 THE WRITINGS OF THOMAS JEFFERSON at 379, 385 (Andrew A. Lipscomb et al. eds., Washington 1904).
124. STEPHEN E. AMBROSE, UNDAUNTED COURAGE at 68–71 (New York 1996).

initiate active efforts in this regard. He was spurred to action by the publication of a book in 1801 in London describing the explorations of Alexander Mackenzie across Canada, culminating in his arrival at the Pacific Ocean on July 22, 1793. What really got Jefferson's attention was Mackenzie's argument in favor of setting up regular trading establishments across the continent and on the Pacific coast, with an emphasis on the Columbia River (which had recently been discovered) as the most likely river route into the continent from the Pacific.[125] The idea of British control of much of the Pacific coast as well as the headwaters of the Missouri River did not sit well with Jefferson, and he determined to do something about it.

It was not until the summer of 1802 that Jefferson actually obtained a copy of Mackenzie's book, but when he did he discussed its contents in detail with his private secretary, Captain Meriwether Lewis. That fall he determined on the expedition with Lewis to command it. There were three ostensible purposes: to forestall British (or possibly Spanish or French) control of this vast unknown area, to engage in scientific exploration to determine not only the geography but the flora, fauna, and minerals of the region as well as the customs of its native inhabitants, and to seek to develop the fur trade with the various Indian tribes throughout the area. Because of his narrow views on constitutional interpretation, Jefferson determined that he could seek congressional approval to fund the exploration only under the commerce clause.

Because at this time Louisiana still was under the control of Spain, Jefferson discussed the proposed expedition with the Spanish minister to the United States, Carlos Martinez de Yrujo. As Martinez reported to his government on December 2, 1802, Jefferson asked whether Spain would have any objection to a small group of travelers exploring the Missouri River with "no other view than the advancement of geography." According to Martinez, Jefferson stated that he would

> give it the denomination of mercantile, inasmuch as only in this way would Congress have the power of voting the necessary funds; it not being possible to appropriate funds for a society, or a purely literary [i.e., scientific] expedition, since there does not exist in the constitution any clause which would give it the authority for this effect.[126]

---

125. ALEXANDER MACKENZIE, VOYAGES FROM MONTREAL, ON THE RIVER ST. LAWRENCE, THROUGH THE CONTINENT OF NORTH AMERICA, TO THE FROZEN AND PACIFIC OCEAN (London 1801).
126. I LETTERS OF THE LEWIS AND CLARK EXPEDITION, WITH RELATED DOCUMENTS: 1803–1854, at 5 (Donald Jackson ed., 2d ed. Urbana 1978).

When he sought congressional approval to fund the expedition, Jefferson reversed the emphasis, arguing that its primary purpose was to gain control of the fur trade on the upper Missouri, but that Spain and France would consider it a mere "literary pursuit." He concluded his request somewhat disingenuously by saying: "The interests of commerce place the principal object within the constitutional powers and care of Congress, and that it should incidentally advance the geographical knowledge of our own continent can not but be an additional gratification."[127] Indeed as Dupree puts it, "science as the objective was for foreign ears; commerce as an objective was for Congress; and the real purpose, which had to do with the claims of empires, was carefully screened by the ambiguous title to the act."[128]

On February 10, 1806, William Tatham wrote a letter to the Speaker of the House which addressed various means of promoting the U.S. economy and science in general. It contained a far-sighted proposal, namely, that the government should establish a Department of Works and Public Economy.[129] A House committee report regarding Tatham's proposal stated:

> It would appear from the letter referred to your committee, that it is the wish of Colonel Tatham that the public should purchase the whole of his collection, in order to form the basis of a national institution under the control of the executive branch of the Government, in the nature of a department of public economy. Your committee can have no doubt of the utility of such a plan, particularly if connected with other branches of general science. By it the American youth might have an opportunity of enjoying the best kind of instruction, that which unites theory with practice, which adds to an acquaintance with principles a knowledge of the best means of bringing those principles into actual use.

Having said that, the committee expressed strong doubts about the ability of the country to fund such a project and went on to state:

> Doubts have also been suggested respecting the powers of the General Government to contribute to any actual improvement of the means of internal intercourse, unless requested by the individual states, or

---

127. *Confidential Message Recommending a Western Exploring Expedition, January 18, 1803 in* 3 THE WRITINGS OF THOMAS JEFFERSON at 489, 493 (Andrew Lipscomb et al. eds., Washington 1904).
128. DUPREE, *supra* note 88, at 26.
129. For the letter, *see* 1 NEW AMERICAN STATE PAPERS SCIENCE AND TECHNOLOGY at 15 (Wilmington 1971).

confined to the existing roads; and this improvement seems to be no minor object in the proposition of Colonel Tatham. Without expressing any opinion on this last subject, but from a deliberate review of all the circumstances connected with the matter referred to them, your committee would not recommend the present adoption of a plan such as suggested in the letter.[130]

There was indeed no need for the House to engage in any discussion of constitutional objections; they knew that Jefferson would veto any bill proposing such a department, should they have the temerity to present one for his signature.

Not that Jefferson was opposed to the use of federal funds to promote the progress of science, i.e., learning, and the useful arts. Rather, because of his strict views on constitutional construction, he believed that such funds could only be authorized by a constitutional amendment. In his second inaugural address on March 4, 1805, he suggested that once the national debt was retired, "the revenue thereby liberated may, by a just repartition of it among the States and a corresponding amendment to the Constitution, be applied in time of peace to rivers, canals, roads, arts, manufactures, education and other great objects within each State."[131] In his sixth annual address to Congress on December 2, 1806, he proposed the application of federal funding

> to the great purposes of public education, roads, rivers, canals, and such other objects of public improvement as it may be thought proper to add to the constitutional enumeration of Federal powers. . . . I suppose an amendment to the Constitution, by consent of the States, necessary, because the objects now recommended are not among those enumerated in the Constitution, and to which it permits the public moneys to be applied.[132]

Two years later, however, he let a bit of doubt as to the necessity for a constitutional amendment creep into his views. In his last annual message to Congress on November 8, 1808, he asked rhetorically whether, when surplus revenue became available, it should be "appropriated to the improvements of roads, canals, rivers, education, and other great foundations of prosperity and union under the powers which Congress may

---

130. *Id.* at 26.
131. I MESSAGES AND PAPERS OF THE PRESIDENT 1787–1897, *supra* note 22, at 378–79.
132. THE STATE OF THE UNION MESSAGES OF THE PRESIDENT, 1790–1966, *supra* note 105, at 87–88.

already possess or such amendment of the Constitution as may be approved by the States?"[133] As Currie notes, he was now at least prepared to consider the possibility that Congress might have constitutional authority to tax and spend for these purposes.[134] He gives no indication, however, of where such authority might lie, but it is just possible that he was now prepared to consider a broader interpretation of the intellectual property clause.

It is ironic that Jefferson, with the strongest scientific credentials of any early president, was the one least disposed, because of constitutional scruples, to permit the federal government to play a role in funding research and development or a national university. Madison, in turn, was more pragmatic and less doctrinaire than Jefferson when it came to constitutional interpretation, but he too, as president, took a narrow view of the spending power. He indirectly but clearly made the point in his first inaugural address when he pledged: "To support the Constitution, which is the cement of the Union, *as well in its limitations* as in its authorities."[135]

Madison was not opposed to federal funding of internal improvements and in fact favored it, but only if an appropriate constitutional amendment could be brought about. Indeed, he somewhat obtusely recommended such an amendment in his seventh annual message to Congress, saying "it is a happy reflection that any defect of constitutional authority which may be encountered can be supplied in a mode which the Constitution itself has providently pointed out."[136]

Nonetheless, that Madison continued to hew to his narrow interpretation of the spending power throughout his presidency is evidenced by one of his last acts as president, namely, the veto of a federal public works bill as being unconstitutional.[137] In his veto message, Madison noted that the act pledged funds "for constructing roads and canals, and improving the navigation of water courses, in order to facilitate, promote, and give security to internal commerce among the several States, and to render more easy and less expensive the means and provisions for common defense." In essence,

---

133. MESSAGES AND PAPERS OF THE PRESIDENT 1787–1897, *supra* note 22, at 456.

134. David P. Currie, *The Constitution in Congress: Jefferson and the West, 1801–1809,* 39 WM. & MARY L. REV. 1441, 1493 (1998).

135. IRVING BRANT, JAMES MADISON THE PRESIDENT 1807–1812, at 18 (New York 1956) (emphasis supplied).

136. THE STATE OF THE UNION MESSAGES OF THE PRESIDENT, 1790–1966, *supra* note 105, at 138–39.

137. James Madison, veto of "An act to set apart and pledge certain funds for internal improvements" (Mar. 3, 1817).

the Congress sought to ground the constitutionality of the act on the commerce clause and the common defense clause, the latter being coupled with the general welfare clause which Hamilton had broadly interpreted.

Madison argued that the power proposed to be exercised under the bill was not among the enumerated powers granted to Congress and that the power to regulate commerce among the several States did not encompass it. Of more interest in the present context was his discussion of the clause "to provide for common defense and general welfare." In his view:

> To refer the power in question to [this] clause . . . would be contrary to the established and consistent rules of interpretation, as rendering the special and careful enumeration of powers which follow the clause nugatory and improper. Such a view of the Constitution would have the effect of giving to Congress a general power of legislation instead of the defined and limited one hitherto understood to belong to them, the terms "common defense and general welfare" embracing every object and act within the purview of a legislative trust. It would have the effect of subjecting both the Constitution and the laws of the several States in all cases not specifically exempted to be superseded by laws of Congress, it being expressly declared "that the Constitution of the United States shall be the supreme law of the land, and the judges of every state shall be bound thereby, anything in the constitution or laws of any State to the contrary notwithstanding." Such a view of the Constitution, finally, would have the effect of excluding the judicial authority of the United States from its participation in guarding the boundary between the legislative powers of the General and the State Governments, inasmuch as questions relating to the general welfare, being questions of policy and expediency, are unsusceptible of judicial cognizance and decision.[138]

It is apparent that Madison's argument was fully applicable to any attempt by the federal government to fund research and development, and he undoubtedly would have vetoed any such attempt on the same grounds. None seems to have been made, however.

Madison did believe that he had found a way around the constitutional issue with regard to the funding of a national university. The solution was to place it in the Federal District (which would soon be known as the District of Columbia) where Congress had sole jurisdiction and could constitutionally do as it wished without infringing on the states. In his second annual message to Congress he invited "attention to the advantages of superadding to the means of education provided by the several States a

138. *Id.*

seminary of learning instituted by the National Legislature within the limits of their exclusive jurisdiction."[139] In his eighth annual message he again stated his recommendation that Congress establish "a university within this District on a scale and for objects worthy of the American nation."[140] Once again Congress failed to act.

Nonetheless there was developing a strong pragmatic appeal to the concept of federal funding of scientific support for both geographic exploration and the development of internal resources under the aegis of what would commonly be called "internal improvements"[141] and funding for both would be sought during the presidency of James Monroe. This did not mean that he did not have constitutional concerns on the matter. In his first annual message to Congress he strongly recommended internal improvements but went on to state that:

> A difference of opinion has existed from the first formation of our Constitution to the present time among our most enlightened and virtuous citizens respecting the right of Congress to establish such a system of improvement. Taking into view the trust with which I am now honored, it would be improper after what has passed that this discussion should be revived with an uncertainty of my opinion respecting the right. Disregarding early impressions I have bestowed on the subject all the deliberation which its great importance and a just sense of my duty required, and the result is a settled conviction in my mind that Congress do not possess the right. It is not contained in any of the specified powers granted to Congress, nor can I consider it incidental to or a necessary means, viewed on the most liberal scale, for carrying into effect any of the powers which are specifically granted.[142] In communicating this result I cannot resist the obligation which I feel to suggest to Congress the propriety of recommending to the States the adoption of an amendment to the Constitution which shall give to Congress the right in question.[143]

---

139. THE STATE OF THE UNION MESSAGES OF THE PRESIDENT, 1790–1966, *supra* note 105, at 108.
140. *Id.* at 142.
141. GEORGE H. DANIELS, SCIENCE IN AMERICAN SOCIETY at 176 (New York 1971).
142. This sentence certainly seems to suggest that Monroe did not interpret the intellectual property clause broadly.
143. THE STATE OF THE UNION MESSAGES OF THE PRESIDENT, 1790–1966, *supra* note 105, at 154.

No such amendment was forthcoming, but Monroe continued to push for one. In his sixth annual message he stated:

> Believing that a competent power to adopt and execute a system of internal improvement has not been granted to Congress, but that such a power confined to great national purposes and with proper limitations, would be productive of eminent advantage to our Union, I have thought it advisable that an amendment of the Constitution to that effect should be recommended to the several States. A bill which assumed the right to adopt and execute such a system having been presented for my signature at the last session, I was compelled, from the view which I have taken of the powers of the General Government, to negative it, on which occasion I thought it proper to communicate the sentiments which I had formed, on mature consideration, on the whole subject.[144]

The narrow constitutional construction of the Jeffersonian democrats was still alive and well. Indeed, in 1824 the Attorney General argued that while "Congress has the power to promote the progress of science and the useful arts," it may do so "only in one mode, viz. by securing, for a limited time, to authors and inventors, the exclusive right to their respective writings and discoveries."[145]

In 1825, however, John Quincy Adams for the first time argued strongly for federal funding of a wide variety of scientific research and development along with internal improvements. Unlike Monroe who had continued to argue the narrow construction, Adams met the constitutional issue head on and suggested that federal funding of both science and internal improvements was amply supported by the Constitution. He ignored any discussion of the intellectual property clause and instead implied that such funding was clearly authorized by various other enumerated powers granted to Congress.

According to Dupree, Adams' first annual message to Congress "was the clearest statement ever made by a President of the government's duty

---

144. *Id.* at 198. He was referring to the paper he had submitted to Congress along with his veto message on the Cumberland Road bill, dated May 4, 1822. See MESSAGES AND PAPERS OF THE PRESIDENTS, 1789–1908, *supra* note 22. This was the paper in which he had set forth his views on the order observed in the enumerated grants of powers, i.e. "to grant the power intended to be conveyed in the most full and explicit manner; and then to explain or qualify it, if explanation or qualification should be necessary." *See* STORY, *supra* note 25 and accompanying text.

145. Gibbons v. Ogden, 22 U.S. (9 Wheat.) 1, 165–66 (1824).

toward knowledge."[146] In addition to calling for federal support of internal improvements such as roads and canals, he elevated support of science to the highest of governmental priorities. He made a number of specific recommendations, among other things asking again for a national university and also seeking support for an astronomical observatory. He suggested a new executive department to plan and supervise internal improvements and various scientific projects.[147]

In this latter respect, he was reiterating to a considerable degree the proposal first advanced by William Tatham nineteen years earlier,[148] but now he was advancing the view that science and scientific research and development were not only desirable but clearly authorized by the Constitution. He seemed to suggest that his ambitious program was authorized by the congressional powers over the District of Columbia, to tax for the common defense and general welfare, to regulate commerce, to fix the standards of weights and measures, to establish post offices and post roads, to make rules concerning territories and other property, and to make all laws necessary and proper to carry out these powers.[149] This was the Hamiltonian view at its broadest. He argued that if "these powers and others enumerated in the Constitution may be effectually brought into action by laws promoting the improvement of agriculture, commerce and manufactures, the cultivation and encouragement of the mechanic and of the elegant arts . . . and the progress of the sciences, ornamental and profound," then to fail to do so would be to hide "in the earth the talent committed to our charge—would be treachery to the most sacred of trusts."[150]

---

146. DUPREE, *supra* note 88, at 39.
147. THE STATE OF THE UNION MESSAGES OF THE PRESIDENT, 1790–1966, *supra* note 105, at 232–49.
148. *See supra* text accompanying notes 129 and 131.
149. This was certainly the way that Dupree read him. *See* DUPREE, *supra* note 88, at 40. But Adams was also careful to state that

> After full and solemn deliberation upon all or any of the objects which, urged by an irresistible sense of my own duty, I have recommended to your attention should you come to the conclusion that, however desirable in themselves, the enactment of laws for effecting them would transcend the powers committed to you by that venerable instrument which we are all bound to support [i.e., the Constitution], let no consideration induce you to assume the exercise of powers not granted to you by the people.

THE STATE OF THE UNION MESSAGES OF THE PRESIDENT, 1790–1966, *supra* note 105, at 248.
150. THE STATE OF THE UNION MESSAGES OF THE PRESIDENT, 1790–1966, *supra* note 105, at 248.

Adams' proposals were over bold and his rhetoric overblown and absolutely nothing happened.[151] Several friendly committees in Congress issued favorable reports, and one, acting contrary to his wishes according to Dupree, went so far as to propose a comprehensive constitutional amendment to assure the power of Congress to "make surveys. . . to construct roads. . . to establish a National University . . . and to offer and distribute prizes for promoting agriculture, education, science, and the liberal and useful arts."[152] Implicit in this proposed amendment was a presumption that the intellectual property clause limited the promotion of the progress of science and useful arts to the issuance of copyrights and patents.

Nothing came of this proposed amendment, and although constitutional objections would occasionally still arise, from the administration of Andrew Jackson onward federal funding of research and development, although fitful and slow to develop, became an accomplished fact.[153] In 1833 Story would write:

> Appropriations have never been limited by congress to cases falling within the specific powers enumerated in the constitution, whether those powers be construed in their broad, or their narrow sense. And, in an especial manner appropriations have been made to aid internal improvements of various sorts, in our roads, our navigation, our streams, and other objects of a national character and importance.[154]

---

151. His cabinet had in essence warned him of this likely result. Moreover, his Secretary of State, Henry Clay, was concerned about a constitutional objection to the proposed national university. *See* DUPREE, *supra* note 88, at 41.

152. DUPREE, *supra* note 88, at 41–42, citing ANNALS OF CONGRESS (19th Cong., 1st Sess.) (Dec. 13, 1825), at 802.

153. One of the earliest examples of federal funding of research and development which was indeed intended to promote the progress of useful arts was the use of government funds for materials in a study of steam engine explosions by the Franklin Institute during the early 1830s. *See* DUPREE, *supra* note 88, at 50. In 1842 Congress appropriated $30,000 to build a telegraph line between Washington and Baltimore to test the viability of Samuel Morse's recently invented electric telegraph. Dupree suggests that the commerce clause and the post office clause were the main constitutional justifications. *Id.* at 48. In 1849 Congress granted $20,000 to Charles G. Page to develop an electric motor. *Id.* at 49. But as late as 1850 constitutional objections were still being raised in the Senate to such funding. *See* RICHARD C. POST, PHYSICS, PATENTS, AND POLITICS at 95 (New York 1976).

154. II STORY, *supra* note 25, § 988.

The broad interpretation attributed to Hamilton had de facto, if not de jure, prevailed.

D. The Modern Judicial Interpretation

After the Civil War arguments that federal funding of research and development was unconstitutional seem to have disappeared, but it was not until 1988 that the issue of whether the intellectual property clause precluded such funding was actually raised in a judicial setting. Unfortunately, the plaintiff who raised the issue was acting pro se and did not attempt to give any historical perspective on the interpretation given to the clause. As a consequence, the Court of Appeals for the Federal Circuit in *Constant v. Advanced Micro-Devices, Inc.*[155] rather summarily rejected the argument.[156] According to the Federal Circuit, the intellectual property clause

> does not state that the Government may promote the progress of the useful arts *only* through the patent and copyright system.[157] Ample constitutional power for Government funding of research and development can be found in art. I, § 8, cl. 1 (provide for the common Defense and general Welfare), cl. 3 (Commerce), cl. 12 (Army), cl. 13 (Navy) and cl. 18 (necessary and proper clause). It is also settled that art. I, § 8 authorizes Congress to spend money to promote the "general welfare," and that the definition of the general welfare and decisions concerning how to promote it are within the discretion of Congress [citations omitted].[158]

---

155. 848 F.2d 1560 (Fed. Cir. 1988).
156. Constant had argued that "Government sponsorship of research and development offends the 'Science Clause' of the Constitution," i.e., the intellectual property clause. The Federal Circuit began its analysis by pointing out: "The power to grant patents to inventors is for the promotion of the useful arts, while the power to grant copyrights to authors is for the promotion of 'Science,' which had a much broader meaning in the 18th Century than it does today." 848 F.2d at 1564.
157. *Cf.* the view expressed by the Court of Customs and Patent Appeals nine years earlier that: "The only restraints placed on Congress [by the intellectual property clause] pertained to the *means* by which it could promote useful arts, namely, through the device of securing 'exclusive rights' which were required to be limited in time. . . ." In re Bergy, 596 F.2d 952, 958 n.2 (1979).
158. Helvering v. Davis, 301 U.S. 619, 640 (1937); Buckley v. Valeo, 424 U.S. 1, 90–91 (1976).

Government support for research and development is well within this discretionary power.[159]

It is apparent from this language that the Federal Circuit viewed the issue not so much as one of whether the clause precluded federal funding of research and development as one of whether other discretionary constitutional authority exists for such funding. By its summary view that the clause does not expressly state that promotion of the useful arts can occur *only* through the patent and copyright system, the Federal Circuit arbitrarily concluded that it could not reasonably be interpreted in such a limiting fashion.[160] Yet this is precisely the way it was repeatedly interpreted by both Congress and the Executive during the first half century of its existence.[161]

In his analysis of the constitutional authority for federal funding of science, Goldberg argues that "from the framers' point of view, three areas of congressional authority—the military, coinage weights and measures, and patents—were the most important in bringing about government support for science." He goes on to state that in modern times "a fourth power—to spend for the general welfare—has outstripped all others in this respect."[162] While acknowledging that "awarding patents does not involve the government directly in funding or choosing precise areas of research,"[163] he nonetheless contends that the intellectual property clause is a source of authority for federal funding of research, albeit without providing any rationale for this interpretation. Goldberg, like the Federal Circuit, fails completely to acknowledge that in the first decades of its

---

159. 848 F.2d at 1565.
160. Nor did the Federal Circuit apparently contemplate the result of such an argument applied to a whole host of constitutional clauses which have been interpreted to have limiting provisions. In essence, such an approach renders limiting provisions meaningless unless there is an express statement (which nowhere appears) that the limiting provision is intended to be the *only* way the clause can be interpreted.
161. Despite the lack of any analytical or historical discussion of the basis for the holding in *Advanced Micro-Devices, Inc.*, a leading copyright treatise has nonetheless cited it as authority for the view that: "*Obviously*, the preamble does not limit the United States Government to promoting science and the useful arts exclusively through patent and copyright law. . . ." *See* NIMMER & NIMMER, *supra* note 38, § 1.03[A], n.11.1 (emphasis supplied). Yet a literal reading of the language suggests exactly that, and, as I have shown, it was frequently so interpreted during its early existence.
162. STEVEN GOLDBERG, CULTURE CLASH at 32 (New York 1994).
163. *Id.* at 34.

existence, the intellectual property clause was interpreted as a constitutional barrier to federal funding of research and development.[164]

The ultimate resolution to the issue has resided in the interpretation given not to the intellectual property clause but rather to the clause granting authority to Congress to provide for the general welfare. Indeed, it was two Supreme Court cases interpreting this clause that the Federal Circuit cited in *Advanced Micro-Devices*.[165] The leading case is *United States v. Butler*[166] which for some reason the Federal Circuit failed to cite. There the Court stated:

> The Congress is expressly empowered to lay taxes to provide for the general welfare. Funds in the Treasury as a result of taxation may be expended only through appropriation. They can never accomplish the objects for which they were collected, unless the power to appropriate is as broad as the power to tax. The necessary implication from the terms of the grant is that the public funds may be appropriated "to provide for the general welfare of the United States." . . .
>
> Since the foundation of the Nation, sharp differences of opinion have persisted as to the true interpretation of the phrase. Madison asserted it amounted to no more than a reference to the other powers enumerated in the subsequent clauses of the same section; that, as the United States is a government of limited and enumerated powers, the grant of power to tax and spend for the general national welfare must be confined to the enumerated legislative fields committed to the Congress. In this view the phrase is mere tautology, for taxation and appropriation are or may be necessary incidents of the exercise of any of the enumerated legislative powers. Hamilton, on the other hand, maintained the clause confers a power separate and distinct from those later enumerated, is not restricted in meaning by the grant of them, and Congress consequently has a substantive power to tax and to appropriate, limited only by the requirement that it shall be exercised to provide for the general welfare of the United States. . . . Mr. Justice Story, in his Commentaries, espouses the Hamiltonian position. . . . [We] conclude that the reading advocated by Mr. Justice Story is the correct one. While therefore, the power to tax is not unlimited, *its*

---

164. He acknowledges that there were "constitutional objections," without saying what they were or what they were predicated on. *Id.* at 36. As a practical matter, they could only have been based on a narrow reading of the intellectual property clause.

165. 848 F.2d 1560 (Fed. Cir. 1988) (citing Helvering v. Davis, 301 U.S. 619, 640 (1937); Buckley v. Valeo, 424 U.S. 1, 90–91 (1976)).

166. 297 U.S. 1 (1936).

confines are set in the clause which confers it, and not in those of section 8 which bestow and define the legislative powers of Congress.[167] It results that the power of Congress to authorize expenditure of public moneys for public purposes is not limited to the direct grants of legislative power found in the Constitution.[168]

The Court provided no citation of authority for the views attributed to Hamilton and Madison, but Goldberg argues that in adopting the Hamiltonian view it "relied on the very passage in the *Report on the Subject of Manufactures* in which Hamilton supported premiums for scientific advances."[169] As a practical matter, the Court relied not so much on Hamilton's views per se as on Story's exposition of them.[170]

Goldberg makes the interesting observation that the brief for the government in *United States v. Butler* urged the Court to interpret the general welfare clause expansively "in part so that federal science spending programs would not be endangered."[171] This appears to have been a tacit admission of a concern by the Solicitor General not only that the intellectual property clause provides no explicit constitutional authority for federal funding "to support the progress of science and useful arts," but that it actually could be interpreted to preclude such funding.[172]

E. Perspectives

Contrary to early assertions by the Supreme Court the power granted to Congress by the intellectual property clause is not plenary or unqualified. Rather, there are certain limitations on congressional power inherent in the clause. The most obvious is that set forth the phrase "for limited times." Thus, Congress does not have plenary power to grant either patents or copyrights in perpetuity. Another apparent limitation is that Congress may only issue patents and copyright to authors and inventors for "*their* respective

---

167. The Court somewhat muddied the water here because the power to tax is in fact a legislative power of Congress that is in fact set forth in art. I, § 8. That is to say, it is itself a direct grant of legislative power.
168. 297 U.S. at 65–66 (emphasis supplied).
169. GOLDBERG, *supra* note 162, at 37.
170. Indeed, it noted that "Mr Justice Story, in his Commentaries, espouses the Hamiltonian position." 297 U.S. at 66. It primarily cited Chapter XIV in Vol. II of the Commentaries. *See* STORY, *supra* note 25.
171. GOLDBERG, *supra* note 162, at 37.
172. As this chapter has sought to show, this was a recurring argument during the first 50 years of the Constitution.

writings and discoveries."[173] The introductory language of the clause also constitutes a limitation on congressional power, although not in the manner that *Graham v. John Deere Co.* customarily has been interpreted.[174]

Discussions of the meaning and interpretation of the intellectual property clause by both constitutional commentators and the judiciary almost invariably view it in isolation rather than in the context of the other enumerated powers given to Congress. The result has been a failure to understand the broad grant of power that is actually encompassed within the clause.[175] In seeking to ascertain the scope and meaning of the clause, I have taken to heart the concern expressed by Akhil Reed Amar about "how much is lost by the clausebound approach that now dominates constitutional discourse." I concur fully in his view that we should never forget "that our Constitution is a single document, and not a jumble of disconnected clauses—that it is a Constitution we are expounding."[176]

For many years, the judiciary, including the Supreme Court, and constitutional commentators have misapprehended and improperly narrowed the grant of power set forth in the clause. They characterize it as the power to issue the limited-term exclusive rights known as patents and copyrights. While this is certainly a part of the grant of power set forth, it is not the grant of power. Rather, the generic grant is power "to promote the progress of science and useful arts," and the power to issue a limited-term exclusive right to authors and inventors is intended to be incorporated into and made a part of the generic grant.

The misapprehension as to the scope of the grant set forth in the clause arises out of the propensity to look at it in isolation and to ignore the fact that it is part and parcel of article I, § 8, enumerating the various grants of

---

173. Congress has always required patents to issue in the name of the inventors, but beginning with the Copyright Act of 1909 it has authorized "works made for hire" to be copyrighted in the name of the proprietor of the work. For a discussion of the constitutionality of such a practice, see Chapter Nine, Part A (emphasis supplied).

174. These views are addressed in more detail in Chapters Seven and Eight.

175. Thus, for example, in their excellent analysis of implied limits in the clause Heald & Sherry assume without discussion that the grant of power in the clause is limited to authority regarding the issuance of patents and copyrights. *See* Heald & Sherry, *supra* note 38.

176. AKHIL REED AMAR, THE BILL OF RIGHTS: CREATION AND RECONSTRUCTION at 124–25 (New Haven 1998). Professor Amar was referring to the famous statement by Chief Justice Marshall that "we must never forget that it is a Constitution we are expounding." McCulloch v. Maryland, 16 U.S. (4 Wheat.) 316, 407 (1819).

power to Congress. A look at that section quickly reveals a uniform parallel grammatical construction of the grants and that those grants all follow the standardized format noted by President Monroe in 1822, namely, a grant of power is first set forth "in the most full and explicit manner," which is followed by an "explanation or qualification" if such is thought necessary."[177] Justice Story strongly agreed that this was the mode followed in enumerating the powers given to Congress.[178]

Thus, rather than being "clausebound," any analysis of the scope of the power granted by the intellectual property clause ought to begin by comparing the form and language of the clause to the form and language of the other clauses granting powers to Congress.[179] With the exception of the intellectual property clause, all of the granting clauses provide for generic grants of power to Congress to do specifically enumerated tasks without setting forth a particular mode of accomplishing the task. For example, Congress is given power "to lay and collect taxes," "to borrow money," "to declare war," and "to provide for a navy."[180] In each instance, Congress is given the authority to accomplish the enumerated task without limitation or with broad limitation as to how it is to be accomplished. If there is a limitation or explanation, that limitation or explanation follows the generic grant in each instance.[181]

The intellectual property clause is no different. It begins with a generic grant of power and follows it with an explanation. That explanation is that the generic grant of power "to promote the progress of science and useful arts" includes the power to authorize limited-term exclusive rights, more commonly known as copyrights and patents, to authors and inventors. Unfortunately, in drafting the clause, the Framers inartfully phrased what was for them a very pragmatic consideration, namely, to assure that among the various means for promoting the progress of science and useful arts, this particular approach would in fact be included. They did so because they

---

177. *See supra* text accompanying note 27.
178. *Id.*
179. *See* Wheaton v. Peters. 33 U.S. (8 Pet.) 591, 661 (1834). *See also supra* text accompanying notes 15 and 16.
180. Landry terms these "a series of infinitive verb forms expressing the function that Congress is [authorized] to perform." *See* Thomas K. Landry, *Constitutional Invention: A Patent Perspective,* 25 RUTGERS L.J. 67, 94–95 (1993).
181. The general welfare clause provides a good example. It first authorizes Congress to lay and collect taxes, duties, imposts, and excises and then follows with an explanation that such shall be for the purpose of paying the debts and providing for the common defense and general welfare of the country. *See supra* note 77.

wanted to adopt the same general approach set forth in the English Statute of Monopolies, i.e., refusing authority to create monopolies in general, but nonetheless providing a specific exception in the case of the limited-term monopolies that came to be known as patents and copyrights.[182]

The Framers seem to have taken for granted the eighteenth century view that it was the duty of enlightened government to promote what they called the progress of science and useful arts. But in their effort to assure that this could be done through the issuance of patents and copyrights they used language that, as pointed out by commentators from St. George Tucker in the early nineteenth century[183] to Currie in the late twentieth century,[184] appeared to place an express limitation on any general authority of Congress to promote the progress of science and useful arts. As I have sought to show here, this was certainly an oft repeated concern during the first fifty years after the Constitution was ratified.

Although it is doubtful that there was any general intent by the Framers to preclude Congress from authority to promote the progress of science and useful arts by other than the grant of limited-term monopolies to authors and inventors,[185] nonetheless in 1790 two of the Framers, Madison and Sherman, put forth a constitutional argument that seemed to endorse such a view. By arguing in effect that the failure of the federal convention to incorporate particular proposals for congressional authority into the Constitution effectively precluded Congress from exercising such authority after the Constitution was ratified, they placed a narrow construction on the intellectual property clause. Thus, for example, in March 1790 Madison informed Tench Coxe that the refusal of the convention to include premiums as means of encouraging invention in the Constitution after such had been proposed was evidence that the use of premiums for this purpose was unconstitutional.[186] In like manner, Sherman argued in May 1790 that the failure of the convention to include a provision authorizing Congress to establish a national university or seminaries for the promotion of literature and sciences was evidence that a national university was unconstitutional.[187] Neither view would have been tenable under a broad

---

182. *See, e.g.,* Chapter Three, note 41 and accompanying text.
183. *See supra* note 90, and accompanying text.
184. *See supra* note 81. See also text accompanying note 89.
185. No rationale has ever been advanced which provides a convincing argument why the Framers should have favored such a restriction on congressional authority.
186. Letter from James Madison to Tench Coxe (Mar. 28, 1790), *in* THE PAPERS OF JAMES MADISON, *supra* note 93, at 128. *See supra* text accompanying note 94.
187. *See supra* note 107 and accompanying text.

interpretation of the intellectual property clause. Some forty years later, in his old age, Madison would expressly reject the view that he had espoused in 1790 and would argue that the refusal of the convention to incorporate a particular proposal was not evidence that Congress did not have equivalent powers under language actually incorporated into the Constitution.[188]

Although neither Hamilton nor Washington ever discussed the intellectual property clause per se, their views on congressional authority to fund both premiums to encourage invention and a national university could only be consonant with a broad interpretation of the clause.[189] That broad interpretation read the clause in effect as: "To promote the progress of science and useful arts [including] by securing for limited times to authors and inventors the exclusive right to their respective writings and discoveries." It is apparent that Story too read the clause in this fashion. How else could he have raised the following rhetorical question: "Take the power to promote the progress of science and useful arts; might not a tax be laid on foreigners, and foreign inventions, in aid of this power, so as to suppress foreign competition, or encourage domestic science and arts?"[190]

Moreover, Story laid a clear framework for this type of interpretation in his analysis of the general welfare clause. He began by pointing out that in order to understand the nature and extent of the power conferred by this clause, it is necessary to settle its grammatical construction. In this regard he asked:

> Do the words "to lay and collect taxes, duties, imposts, and excises," constitute a distinct substantial power; and the words "to pay debts and provide for the common defence and general welfare of the United States" constitute another distinct and substantial power? Or are the latter words connected to the former, so as to constitute a qualification upon them?[191]

He stated that the reading he would follow "in these commentaries" is "that which makes the latter words a qualification of the former." To do this, he would supply certain words necessarily understood by such interpretation: "The congress shall have power to lay and collect taxes, duties, imposts, and excises *in order to* pay the debts, and to provide for the common defence and

---

188. *See supra* Chapter Three, note 20 and accompanying text.
189. *See supra* text accompanying notes 109–114.
190. STORY, *supra* note 25, vol. II, § 968.
191. *Id.* § 904.

general welfare of the United States."[192] This is the approach given judicial sanction by the Supreme Court in *United States v. Butler*.[193]

Under the narrow interpretation of the intellectual property clause which was either expressly or implicitly raised during the first decades of the federal government, the "to" phrase was considered to be the grant of power and the "by" portion of the clause was treated as a limitation of the grant to the particular mode set forth therein. Under the broad interpretation, both portions of the clause were considered as grants of power and the "by" portion was not treated as a limitation on the "to" portion, but rather as an expansion of the general power granted to assure that it would include the power to grant the limited-term monopolies known as copyrights and patents. The broad interpretation appears most consonant with both the intent of the Framers and the actual legislative and judicial constructions of the constitutional powers of Congress, taken as a whole, that have occurred in the twentieth century.

In the modern era both commentators and the courts have tended to treat the grant of authority as residing in the "by" portion,[194] with the "to" portion being viewed as a limitation on the scope of the authority granted, although to a much lesser extent with regard to copyrights than with regard to patents. Indeed, those appellate courts which have addressed the issue have tended to minimize almost to the point of meaningless any limitation on copyrights in the "to" portion. On what basis there can be a constitutional standard of patentable invention set forth in the "to" portion as enunciated in *Graham v. John Deere Co.*, but not a constitutional standard for copyright is simply not clear. Contrary to the contention of Nimmer and Nimmer,[195] a statement of purpose is inherently a limitation on a grant of power in the Constitution.

In light of the literal language of the intellectual property clause, it is remarkable that no judicial challenge to the constitutionality of federal funding of research and development based on this clause seems to have occurred

---

192. STORY, *supra* note 25, vol. II, § 905 (emphasis supplied).
193. Admittedly, the approach taken by Story can be read as a qualification on the power to tax or in essence a limitation on the power to tax, whereas the interpretation proposed for the intellectual property clause is in essence a broadening of the power granted by the clause, but the principle of interpretation is the same in both cases, i.e., the inclusion of a word or words which renders clear the interpretation that appears to conform to the general intent of the Constitution taken as a whole.
194. To the extent the Supreme Court has addressed the issue, it has taken inconsistent positions. *See supra* text accompanying notes 34–37.
195. *See* NIMMER & NIMMER, *supra* note 38 and accompanying text.

until 1988. The Federal Circuit's argument in *Constant v. Advanced Micro-Devices, Inc.* that the intellectual property clause does not limit the promotion of the progress of science and useful arts *only* to patents and copyrights because there is no express statement to that effect in the clause[196] is a sophism which if taken at face value renders essentially meaningless any limitation set forth in the Constitution because nowhere does that document contain an express statement that a particular limitation is the only permitted interpretation. Applied literally, this argument would effectively remove the constitutional limitations on the power to tax "to pay the Debts and provide for the common Defence and general Welfare of the United States" because these quoted limitations are not expressly stated to be the *only* purposes for taxation.[197] Yet as expressly stated by the Supreme Court in *United States v. Butler* "[t]hat the qualifying phrase must be given effect all advocates of broad construction must admit."[198]

Unfortunately, the Court's opinion in *United States v. Butler* is not an example of pristine judicial logic in its own right. It argued that the Madisonian view that the qualifying phrase amounts to no more than a reference to the other powers enumerated in the subsequent clauses in the same section amounted to "mere tautology, for taxation and appropriation are or may be necessary incidents of the exercise of any of the enumerated legislative powers."[199] But this "tautology" logic arguably cuts both ways, because if all of the subsequently enumerated powers are encompassed within the power to tax and appropriate, then they too can be viewed as mere tautological expressions without meaning outside the qualifying phrase with regard to taxation and appropriation in the first clause of the enumerated powers. Obviously, the Court has never taken such a view, and Story argued vigorously against it.[200] As but one of a number of examples, he asked rhetorically, would the power to tax for the general welfare "confide to Congress the power to grant patents for inventions?" He answered: "The constitution itself upon its face refutes any such notion. It gives the power to tax, as a substantive power; and gives others, as equally substantive and independent."[201]

The Court's statement that Hamilton maintained that the general welfare clause conveys a power separate and distinct from those later

---

196. *See supra* text following note 156.
197. *See supra* note 77.
198. 297 U.S. at 66.
199. *Id.*
200. STORY, *supra* note 25, vol. II, §§ 915–922.
201. *Id.* § 920.

enumerated and "is not restricted in meaning by the grant of them"[202] does not appear consistent with Hamilton's statement in the *Report on the Subject of Manufactures* that the power to appropriate money under the general welfare clause "would not carry a power to do any other thing, *not authorized in the constitution, either expressly or by fair implication.*"[203] This language rather strongly suggests that Hamilton did in fact believe that the limitations set forth in the other enumerated powers were relevant and could in fact limit the power to tax and appropriate under the general welfare clause. While Hamilton did indeed argue, as did Story, that the power to tax and appropriate was independent and substantive, neither argued that taxation and appropriation in support of one of the enumerated powers was not constrained by constitutional limitations imposed on particular powers.[204]

In this context it is apparent that Hamilton did not view the intellectual property clause as being a constitutional barrier to the use of premiums to encourage invention and thereby promote the progress of useful arts. His failure to provide any discussion on this point either in the

---

202. 297 U.S. at 65.
203. THE PAPERS OF ALEXANDER HAMILTON, *supra* note 97 (emphasis supplied). *See also supra* text accompanying note 103.
204. *Cf.* the views recently expressed by Renz that:

> If we assume that the power to tax is also the power to spend, then many of the limitations in the clauses that follow lose their meaning. Story's view enlarges powers that are expressly limited. For example, Congress has the power to promote the sciences and arts, but that power is limited to a system of patents and copyrights. Story's interpretation enlarges the power by authorizing Congress to give money to artists and scientists, doing violence to the express limitation of the clause.

> Renz, *supra* note 74, at 128. Renz does not address the conclusion that would seem to follow from these views, namely, that it is unconstitutional for the federal government to support and fund educational programs, the arts, and research and development. I do not believe that Hamilton or Story argued that the power to tax and spend under the general welfare clause was not restricted by limitations set forth in the other enumerated powers. Rather, in the case of the intellectual property clause they espoused the broad interpretation of the clause, namely, that the power to promote the progress of science and useful arts given therein included by was not limited to the power to issue patents and copyrights. Because Congress was broadly authorized "to promote the progress of science and useful arts," it could tax and spend under the general welfare clause for this purpose, including funding education and research and development. *See supra* Walterscheid, note 73.

Report or in any of his other writings leaves his reasoning unknown. It is likely, however, that he viewed the clause in the broad sense that I have discussed, i.e., that it is intended to provide Congress with a broad authority to promote the progress of science and useful arts and that the inclusion of the specific authority to issue patents and copyrights was intended merely to ensure this specific constitutional authority for Congress as an exception to a general prohibition against the granting of monopolies rather than as a specific limitation on the manner of promoting the progress of science and useful arts. It is a broad interpretation of the intellectual property clause coupled with a broad interpretation of the general welfare clause that authorizes the broad range of federal support of education and research and development that exists in the United States today.

CHAPTER SIX
INHERENT OR CREATED RIGHTS

Much has been written about the preoccupation of the Framers with the protection of property.[1] As noted by Jennifer Nedelsky: "For the Framers, property was both a natural and a positive right, and it was a right that could not simply be declared to be beyond the reach of government because it required government (and therefore was the origin of government)."[2] Surprisingly, constitutional scholars and legal historians who readily discuss every other aspect of the constitutional language in the context of its supposed relationship to property rights have almost nothing to say about the intellectual property clause.[3]

Even so, there long has been a school of thought which argues that the intellectual property clause was not intended to empower Congress to statutorily create intellectual property but rather was intended to obligate it to secure, confirm, and implement property rights of authors and inventors already existing under common law or natural law.[4] Perhaps the

---

1. *See, e.g.,* JENNIFER NEDELSKY, PRIVATE PROPERTY AND THE LIMITS OF AMERICAN CONSTUTIONALISM (1990); Laura S. Underkuffler, *On Property: An Essay,* 100 YALE L.J. 127 (1990); Mark V. Tushnet, *The Constitution as an Economic Document,* 56 GEO. WASH. L. REV. 106 (1987); RICHARD HOFSTADTER, THE AMERICAN POLITICAL TRADITION AND THE MEN WHO MADE IT (2d ed. 1973); CHARLES A. BEARD, AN ECONOMIC INTERPRETATION OF THE CONSTITUTION OF THE UNITED STATES (2d ed. 1935).
2. JENNIFER NEDELSKY, PRIVATE PROPERTY AND THE LIMITS OF AMERICAN CONSTUTIONALISM at 152 (1990).
3. This is all the more surprising because, as the Ninth Circuit has noted, "[t]he founding fathers recognized a critical difference between intellectual and other forms of property, by specifying in the Constitution that patents can be granted only 'for limited times.'" *See* International Techs. Consultants, Inc. v. Pilkington PLC, 137 F.3d 1382, 1392 (9th Cir. 1998).
4. As has been previously noted, one of the rationales put forth for the English patent system in the eighteenth century was that it was intended to protect the natural, inherent right of inventors in their inventions. *See supra* Chapter Four, text accompanying notes 105 and 106. Similarly, as has been noted, one of the eighteenth-century rationales for the English copyright system was that common law had established a right of authors in their writings. *See supra* Chapter Four, text accompanying notes 117 and 118.

foremost exponent of this view in recent times has been Frank D. Prager, who contended that "common law had binding force in America in and before 1787."[5] Prager argues that Madison perceived such a common law right to exist when he wrote in *The Federalist* in 1788 with respect to the intellectual property clause:

> The utility of the power will scarcely be questioned. The copyright of authors has been solemnly adjudged in Great Britain to be a right of Common Law. The right to useful inventions seems with equal reason to belong to inventors. ... The public good fully coincides in both cases with the claims of individuals.[6]

According to Prager, the text of the intellectual property clause "is consistent with these views of *The Federalist*" and "[n]o known document of the convention period is to other effect."[7]

Prager was certainly not alone in this view. Those who argued in favor of common-law copyright in the United States of necessity also espoused it.[8] In their minds, "[t]he common law of England was regarded as a precious American heritage. ..."[9] The purpose of this chapter is to explore the merits of this school of thought in the context of early commentary on the intellectual property clause and the Constitution.

A. Intellectual Property Rights Under the Common Law in the Eighteenth Century

As has been noted, the Statute of Monopolies is generally considered to be the legal foundation for the English patent system,[10] and in the eighteenth century it was the only statutory basis for the English patent practice.[11] A critical aspect of the Statute was that it permitted but did not require the

---

5. Frank D. Prager, *Historic Background and Foundation of American Patent Law*, 5 AM. J. LEG. HIST. 309, 318–19 (1961).
6. *Id.* at 318 (*quoting The Federalist No. 43*).
7. *Id.* at 319.
8. *See, e.g.,* John F. Whicher, *The Ghost of Donaldson v. Beckett: An Inquiry into the Constitutional Distribution of Powers over the Law of Literary Property in the United States—Part I,* 9 BULL. COPYRIGHT SOC'Y 102 (1962); J. TAUBMAN, COPYRIGHT AND ANTITRUST (1960).
9. Whicher, *supra* note 8, at 115.
10. *See generally* Edward C. Walterscheid, *The Early Evolution of the United States Patent Law: Antecedents (Part 2),* 76 J. PAT. & TRADEMARK OFF. SOC'Y 874 (1994).
11. *See* Chapter Two, text following note 67.

crown to issue patents of monopoly for invention. Such patents were considered to be exceptions to the general ban on monopolies because they were deemed to be in the interest of the public at large. The practice was entirely at the discretion of the crown, with a patent being solely the creature of the royal prerogative.[12] The rights secured by patent could be protected at common law, but there was no common law right to a patent. In the absence of a patent an inventor had no means at common law of protecting any perceived "rights" in invention. Without patent, such rights were at best deemed to be inchoate.

Copyright developed very differently under the common law. Although Abrams has argued that "[t]here is no historical justification whatsoever for the claim that copyright was recognized as a common law right of an author,"[13] that was not the way it was perceived in both the United States and England at the end of the eighteenth century.[14] The various ordinances and regulations enacted in the seventeenth century for the regulation of printing appeared to tacitly acknowledge a common law right of property in copyright. The Statute of Anne enacted in 1710 and its subsequent interpretation in 1769 in *Millar v. Taylor* and in 1774 in *Donaldson v. Becket* were taken as having established in the last quarter of the eighteenth century that there was indeed a common law property right in copyright but that it could only be enforced in accordance with the Statute of Anne.[15]

As indicated by his statements in *The Federalist No.43,* Madison was well aware that in 1787 there was no common law right to patent, but that such a right was in fact perceived to exist with respect to copyright.[16] Perhaps because he took it as a given that the common law did not apply in the United States,[17] it seems never to have dawned on him that this

---

12. WILLIAM M. HINDMARCH, A TREATISE ON THE LAW RELATIVE TO PATENT PRIVILEGES FOR THE SOLE USE OF INVENTIONS at 3 (Harrisburg 1846). Hindmarch stated: "[I]nventors are *never entitled as of right* to letters patent, granting them the sole use of their inventions, but they must obtain them from the Crown by petition, and *as a matter of grace and favour. . . .*" *Id.* at 4.

13. Howard B. Abrams, *The Historic Foundation of American Copyright Law: Exploding the Myth of Common Law Copyright,* 29 WAYNE L. REV. 1119, 1128 (1983).

14. The most obvious statement of this perception was set forth by Madison in *The Federalist No. 43. See supra* text accompanying note 6.

15. For a general overview in this regard, see Chapter Two, Part E.

16. *See supra* the text accompanying note 6.

17. He was fully aware that a number of states had adopted the common law either by statute or constitutional provision, but he simply did not believe that this could have any effect on either the interpretation of the Constitution or

differing common law perspective on patents and copyrights would create significant interpretational difficulties regarding the purpose of the intellectual property clause.

B. The Common Law in America

Prager's unequivocal statement that "[c]ommon law had binding force in America in and before 1787"[18] does not accord with the actual state of affairs. While Americans in the colonies in general desired to have the common law apply to them (although with the right to modify it to fit their particular circumstances),[19] there is a massive difference between simply desiring and actually having the common law in effect as a legal reality.

Nonetheless, because of this general desire the issue was an important one, and as Brown puts it, "[i]n the years preceding the American Revolution, the British Crown's refusal to concede that the colonies were entitled to the common law of England was a rankling sore point."[20] Indeed, the high value which the colonies placed on the use of both common law and English statutes is evidenced by a resolution contained in the Declaration

---

the interpretation of federal law authorized by the Constitution. *See infra* text accompanying notes 89 and 90.

18. Prager, *supra* note 5, at 319. He contends that William W. Crosskey demonstrates this to be the case as to the patent law. WILLIAM W. CROSSKEY, I POLITICS AND THE CONSTITUTION at 421 (Chicago 1952). All Crosskey in fact does is rely on Blackstone for the view that the English crown had authority under the royal prerogative to issue patents, and state that in the Constitution the authority to issue patents which historically existed in England under the executive, i.e., the crown, was shifted to Congress. While Crosskey is a strong advocate of the view that the common law existed in America, contrary to the assertion made by Prager he does not show that there was a common law right of inventors in America or indeed for that matter in England. Moreover, Prager is one of the few commentators to take seriously Crosskey's work. As Currie puts it, "Crosskey's work, after a barrage of devastating reviews, has been profoundly ignored." *See* DAVID P. CURRIE. THE CONSTITUTION IN THE SUPREME COURT, THE FIRST HUNDRED YEARS, 1789–1888, at 170n. (Chicago 1985). But after having made this crushing comment, Currie does nonetheless cite Crosskey in a variety of differing contexts.

19. *See, e.g.,* MORTON J. HORWITZ, THE TRANSFORMATION OF AMERICAN LAW, 1780-1860, at 5–9 (Cambridge, Mass. 1977); CROSSKEY, *supra* note 18, at 578–609.

20. Elizabeth G. Brown, *The Views of a Michigan Territorial Jurist on the Common Law,* 15 AM. J. LEG. HIST. 307 (1971).

of Rights issued by the Continental Congress in 1774: "the respective colonies are entitled to the common law of England . . . [and] they are entitled to the benefit of such of the English statutes as existed at the time of their colonization; and which they have, by experience, respectively found to be applicable to their several and local circumstances."[21] It is not too much to say that the refusal of the crown to concede these points was a significant factor leading up to the American Revolution.

The position of the crown may be summarized as follows.[22] From the time of the Norman conquest onward, the crown had held non-English possessions. The King in Council issued orders or acts relating to these possessions, with an order for one entity being typically limited to that entity alone on the logical premise that a decree well suited to Acquitaine, for example, might well be unsuited for England and vice versa. When the King in Council became the King in Parliament, the crown took the position that Parliament had no authority over the crown's non-English possessions. It was the crown's prerogative to govern its non-English holdings, and an act of Parliament would not extend to such dominions unless the crown specifically authorized it. At the time the first American colonies were settled,

> it was an accepted proposition by the Crown lawyers that English laws were not necessarily in force in non-English Crown dominions and that an act of the King in Parliament did not extend to non-English possessions unless specifically declared to extend thereto. While Englishmen going to uninhabited regions carried the laws of England with them, those going to inhabited ones did not. The Crown lawyers held that the "old American colonies" were settled in "inhabited countries" and thus, absent an affirmative act by the Crown, the colonists did not carry with them the laws of England.[23]

While it seems to have been acknowledged that acts of Parliament would not apply to the American colonies unless such acts specifically mentioned them, the applicability of the common law itself remained muddled.[24]

---

21. I JOURNALS OF THE CONTINENTAL CONGRESS (1774) 63, 69 (1904).
22. This discussion is taken from Elizabeth G. Brown, *British Statutes in the Emergent Nations of North America 1606–1949*, 7 AM J. LEG. HIST. 95, 96–101 (1963).
23. Brown, *supra* note 22, at 96.
24. As Morris has pointed out,

    the whole issue of the applicability of English law to the colonies was confused by Calvin's Case, 7 Coke Rep. 1 (1608), which distinguished acquisition of territory by conquest from a Christian king, where the laws

Thus, for example, Lord Coke had stated that: "The common law is sometimes called Right, sometimes Common Right, and sometimes Common Justice."[25] If this was indeed the case, then it was difficult to perceive how common law should not apply to all dominions of the English crown and particularly to the new colonies in America. Indeed, in 1720 the English Attorney General Richard West acknowledged that

> the common law of England is the common law of the [American] plantations and all statutes in affirmance of the common law, passed in England antecedent to the settlement of a colony, are in force in that colony, unless there is some private act to the contrary; though no statutes, made since those settlements, are thus in force unless the colonists are particularly mentioned.[26]

This certainly seemed to suggest that the common law applied to all English colonial subjects no matter in which English dominion they resided.

But taken at face value, Attorney General West's acknowledgment that the statutory law applicable to a particular colony depended on its date of settlement meant that the English law applicable in the American colonies must of necessity vary from colony to colony, something somehow antithetical to the concept of a "common law."[27] Moreover, to say the common law is in effect is not quite the same thing as setting forth the

---

> remained unaltered subject to the will of the king, and conquest from an infidel, where the laws were abrogated and the inhabitants governed by the king; but once he introduced them, they could not be altered without express reference to Parliament. The courts could not refrain from further refinements. Holt (C.J.), is reputed to have said that in the case of an uninhabited country newly discovered by English subjects, all the laws of England were in force there.

Earl of Derby's Case, 2 And. 116; Holt 3; 2 Salk. 411; 4 Modern 222; Comberback 228. RICHARD B. MORRIS, THE FORGING OF THE UNION, 1781–1789 (New York 1987) at 343.

25. SIR EDWARD COKE, 1 INSTITUTES OF THE LAWS OF ENGLAND, at 142 (London 1644).

26. HORWITZ, *supra* note 19, at 6, quoting ST. G. SIOUSSAT, THE ENGLISH STATUTES IN MARYLAND at 21 (1903).

27. Horwitz, for example, seeks to carefully distinguish between common law and statutory law as applied to the American colonies, arguing that common law is customary law arising out of natural principles of justice. As he puts it, "common law doctrines were derived from natural principles of justice, statutes were acts of will; common law rules were discovered, statutes were made." HORWITZ, *supra* note 19, at 21.

legal effect of such a pronouncement. American views as to what constituted the common law were not necessarily in agreement with those in England. The net result was that, as set forth in a famous 1803 American edition of Blackstone, it would be "in vain" to "attempt, by a *general theory*, to establish an uniform authority and obligation in the common law of England, over the American colonies, at any period between the first migrations to this country, and that epoch, which annihilated the sovereignty of the crown of England over them." The differences between rules of English common law and those of the American colonies as well as the diversity of the colonies themselves were so great that "it would require the talents of an Alfred to harmonize and digest into one system such opposite, discordant, and conflicting municipal institutions, as composed the codes of the several colonies of the period of the revolution."[28]

The charters of the various colonies were to be patterned—with some variation—after those of Virginia. There were three Virginia charters. The first in 1606 provided that the English subjects of the colony "shall HAVE and enjoy all Liberties, Franchises, and Immunities within any of our other Dominions, to all Intents and Purposes, as if they had been abiding and born, within this our Realm of *England,* or any other of our said Dominions."[29] The second charter in 1609 authorized a council to govern the colony "according to such Orders, Ordinances, Constitutions, Directions, and Instructions as by our said Council as aforesaid, shall be established. . . . So always as the Said Statutes, Ordinances and Proceedings as nearly as conveniently may be, be agreeable to the Laws, Statutes,

---

28. HORWITZ, *supra* note 19, at 11, quoting 1 BLACKSTONE, COMMENTARIES: WITH NOTES OF REFERENCE TO THE CONSTITUTION AND LAWS OF THE FEDERAL GOVERNMENT OF THE UNITED STATES AND OF THE COMMONWEALTH OF VIRGINIA 429–30 (St. George Tucker ed., 1803). Blackstone himself had stated that

> the common law of England, as such, has no allowance or authority there [i.e., in the American plantations]; they being no part of the mother country, but distinct (though dependent) dominions. They are subject however to the control of the parliament; though (like Ireland, Man, the rest) not bound by any acts of parliament, unless particularly named.

See WILLIAM BLACKSTONE, 1 COMMENTARIES ON THE LAW OF ENGLAND 105 (Oxford 1765). The problem of attempting to define what the common law meant in the United States would become even more pronounced after the Revolution. *See* text accompanying notes 32–36 *infra.*

29. Brown, *supra* note 22, at 96–97, citing 7 AMERICAN CHARTERS, CONSTITUTIONS, AND ORGANIC LAWS 3783, 3788 (Thorpe, ed. 1909).

Government and Policy of this our Realm of *England*."[30] The third charter of 1611–1612 provided for the holding of "one, greate, general, and solemn Assembly" four times each year to make laws for the welfare of the colony "So *always*, as the same be not contrary to the Laws and Statutes of this our Realm of *England*. . . ."[31]

The American colonists would later seek to rely on such language as imputing a grant of the laws of England to them. But if this language is interpreted in the sense in which it was used by those who drafted it, i.e., the crown lawyers, then no such imputation is warranted. Indeed, this seems to have been recognized by certain of the colonies for on several occasions colonial assemblies sought to re-enact English statutes by reference to them. The crown did not look kindly on such endeavors and on two occasions specifically disallowed such re-enactments by Orders in Council.

The problem of attempting to define what the common law meant in the United States would become even more pronounced after the Revolution. In the period following the Declaration of Independence, nine states had declared either by constitutional provision or legislative enactment that the common law was in effect within their jurisdictions.[32] But it was one thing to say that the common law was in effect and quite another to determine exactly what was meant by such a pronouncement:

> Was it the common law of England or the common law as had been practiced in the courts of a particular colony? The common law of what date—the first emigration, the Declaration of Independence? Was it the common law without any statutory modification, the common law with statutory modification prior to a given date, the common law as modified by all subsequent statutes?[33]

These were questions that could not be answered at the state level, much less at the federal level. Indeed, as is shown, shortly after the Constitution had been drafted and signed, Madison set forth some very pronounced views on why, under the proposed Constitution, the common law could have no applicability.[34]

---

30. Brown, *supra* note 22, at 97, citing 7 AMERICAN CHARTERS, CONSTITUTIONS, AND ORGANIC LAWS 3790, 3801 (Thorpe, ed. 1909).
31. *Id.*, citing 7 AMERICAN CHARTERS, CONSTITUTIONS, AND ORGANIC LAWS 3802, 3806 (Thorpe, ed. 1909).
32. Brown, *supra* note 22, at 307.
33. *Id.* at 308.
34. *See* text accompanying notes 89 and 90 *infra*.

Because the Statute of Monopolies and the Statute of Anne made no express reference to the American colonies, they were by crown interpretation not automatically applicable to all those colonies. For this reason, English patents and copyrights did not automatically cover the American colonies.[35] Yet under the common law the only basis for granting exclusive rights to inventors and authors for their respective discoveries and writings had been determined to be these two statutes. If they did not automatically cover the colonies prior to the Revolution, how could they be said to provide any basis for exclusive rights in discoveries and writings in the United States after it had become an independent nation?[36] No one who has argued for a common law property right in literary works or invention in this country has ever satisfactorily answered this question.

Nonetheless, a point which must have impressed itself on federal judges at the beginning of the nineteenth century was that any patent law case they heard was likely to be a case of first impression. They recognized that they were moving in uncharted territory, and they were apt to move cautiously, relying on their views of the literal language of the statute, i.e., the Patent Act of 1793. Initially, there was little attempt to rely by analogy on common law cases even where they may have been perceived to be relevant. But as the United States moved well into the era of registration under the Patent Act of 1793 the common law opinions in Great Britain would come to exercise considerable influence.[37] For a number of years both the federal courts and the counsel that appeared before them would

---

35. Thus, Fenning is incorrect in stating that "[o]f course, copyright and invention patent protection were extended to the colonies by the English Laws . . . ." *See* Karl Fenning, *The Origin of the Patent and Copyright Clause of the Constitution,* 17 GEO. L.J. 109, 116 (1929) (reprinted in 11 J. PAT. OFF. SOC'Y 438, 444 (1929)).

36. Arguably, there was a common law right to copyright that existed independently of the Statute of Anne, but it was generally acknowledged at the end of the eighteenth century that if such right existed it was limited by the terms of the Statute of Anne. *See* Chapter Two, text accompanying note 164.

37. Writing in 1826, prominent Philadelphia attorney Peter Browne noted:

With respect to the intricacy of the subject, it is necessary to observe that in discussing the patent law of the United States, I shall be led to take considerable notice of the laws of England on the same subject. This course will be found to be indispensable; the laws of the two countries are so interwoven together, that a perfect understanding of the former, is much aided by a general knowledge of the latter.

Peter A. Browne, *Mechanical Jurisprudence—No. VII,* 2 J. FRANKLIN INST. at 20 (1826).

have easier access to the reported patent law opinions in Great Britain than they would have to those in the United States.[38]

A critical point is that these British cases, while providing useful interpretation with respect to issues common to both the British and the United States patent law, were not viewed as constituting binding precedent in the American courts. This was a major departure from earlier practice, because "the overwhelming fact about American law through most of the eighteenth century is the extent to which lawyers believed that English authority settled all questions for which there was no legislative rule."[39] As the judges in the first two decades of the nineteenth century came to increasingly see themselves as agents of legal change, reliance on precedence and particularly English precedent was seen as limiting their roles in promoting change. Consequently, "adherence to precedent was thought of as necessary only to the extent it allowed private parties to calculate in advance on the consequences of particular courses of conduct."[40]

During this period, the extent to which any case law, foreign or domestic, was relied upon depended more on the predilection of the individual judge than on anything else. Indeed, one familiar with the plethora of case citations in modern patent opinions is immediately struck by the almost total lack of such citations in the early United States case law, particularly by the judges.[41] Justice Bushrod Washington, who presided over a number of the earliest reported patent cases, apparently thought so little of case citation that in certain later cases he failed to mention his earlier opinions, although they were in the same circuit and directly in

---

38. The reason for this is not so much that there were more reported English cases (although this was true), but rather that they occurred earlier than the American cases, and the English reports were actually easier to obtain in the United States than were the American reports. In the first edition of the first American patent treatise, published in 1810, Thomas Greene Fessenden cited 11 patent cases, only three of which were American. In his second edition, published in 1822, he cited 35 patent cases, of which 15 were American.
39. HORWITZ, *supra* note 19, at 8.
40. *Id.* at 26.
41. Then, as now, counsel sought to rely on all available case authority of which they were aware, but even with respect to argument of counsel there is little evidence of any extensive citation to case law in the early reported patent cases. The first known extensive citation to both United States and English case law with regard to a reported patent case occurs not in a federal case but rather in the New York state case of Livingston v. Van Ingen, 9 Johns. R. 507 (N.Y. 1812).

point.[42] It is not surprising, therefore, that it is only in his later reported patent cases that he makes much mention of American or English case law.

Justice Joseph Story, however, was a judge of a different stripe. Very early in his legal career he was taught to rely upon and use the common law where appropriate,[43] and he would follow this credo throughout his life. He would adopt and adapt the case law as he found it, whether American or English, in his patent opinions as in his other opinions. That is to say, he was prepared to use the common law when it suited his purposes, and to ignore it or rephrase it in peculiarly American terms when it did not.

In 1818 he published an anonymous note entitled *On the Patent Laws*[44] which outlined his understanding of the current state of the patent law. He began by stating:

> The patent acts of the United States are in a great degree, founded on the principles and usages which have grown out of the English statute on the same subject. It may be useful, therefore, to collect together the cases which have been adjudged in England, with a view to illustrate the corresponding provisions of our own laws; and then bring in review the adjudications of the courts of the United States.[45]

He carefully refrained from any suggestion that the common law cases were binding in the United States, but this did not preclude him from being cited at the end of the nineteenth century for the view that the common law of patents was binding in the United States.[46]

Just as the common law of patents was not considered as binding precedent in the United States, neither was the common law pertaining of

---

42. Thus, for example, in Evans v. Eaton, 8 F. Cas. 846, 853 (Case No. 4,559) (D. Pa. 1816), Justice Washington stated that for an invention to be novel and hence patentable "it must not have been known or used before in any part of the world." In so doing, he failed to note that he had expressed essentially the same view a dozen years earlier in Reutgen v. Kanowrs, 20 F. Cas. 555 (Case No. 11,710) (D. Pa. 1804) and eight years earlier in Dawson v. Follen, 7 F. Cas. 216 (Case No. 3,670) (D. Pa. 1808).
43. RICHARD NEWMYER, SUPREME COURT JUSTICE JOSEPH STORY: STATESMAN OF THE OLD REPUBLIC at 42 (Chapel Hill 1985).
44. 16 U.S. (3 Wheat.) 13 (1818). This note can be viewed as a sort of unofficial dissent to an opinion published by Chief Justice Marshall. See Frank D. Prager, *The Influence of Mr. Justice Story on American Patent Law*, 5 AM. J. LEG. HIST. 254, 256 (1961). The case in question was Evans v. Eaton, 16 U.S. (3 Wheat.) 454 (1818).
45. 16 U.S. (3 Wheat.) 13 (1818).
46. *See* text accompanying note 147, *infra*.

copyrights. The point was decided once and for all in 1834 in *Wheaton v. Peters* wherein the Supreme Court held with regard to copyright that "[t]he common law could be made a part of our federal system only by legislative adoption."[47]

C. The Ambiguous Meaning of "Securing"

No delegate to the federal convention has left any record concerning the interpretation or meaning placed on the intellectual property clause by the delegates themselves.[48] It may well be that they perceived no comment to be necessary in that the clause was considered on its face to be self-explanatory. If so, this was most unfortunate because of the ambiguity inherent in several of its key terms.[49] Nonetheless, the one thing that distinguishes the intellectual property clause during the ratification process is the almost total lack of comment with respect to it within any state. It simply was not an issue, and there is almost no discussion to be found concerning it in any extant documentation. The only real attempt to justify the clause was that set forth by Madison in *The Federalist No. 43*.[50] Short and succinct, Madison's comments represented a carefully crafted argument in favor of the clause, but they did little to actually explain its content and were in reality more than a bit disingenuous.

Before analyzing Madison's argument, it is helpful to turn once again to the grammatical form of the intellectual property clause, because the aesthetics of the form may have in no small measure influenced the actual language used. As has been indicated, the clause is generally taken as an example of the balanced style of composition much favored in the eighteenth century, and viewed as "a consolidation of two proposals which

---

47. *See infra* note 135 and accompanying text.
48. Writing in 1966, Seidel noted that "[n]o historical writings or events have been found analyzing the [clause]." *See* Arthur H. Seidel, *The Constitution and a Standard of Patentability*, 48 J. PAT. OFF. SOC'Y 1, 10 (1966). Madison's views expressed in *The Federalist No. 43* are not so much an explanation of the clause as an argument in favor of its inclusion in the Constitution. *See* Part D *infra* and Chapter Four, text accompanying notes 77–82, *supra*.
49. Such as "securing," "inventors," "discoveries," "authors," and "writings." The treatment afforded "inventors" and "discoveries" is analyzed in Chapter Eight. That afforded to "authors" and "writings" is reviewed in Chapter Nine.
50. *See supra* Chapter Four, note 77 and accompanying text.

got packaged together."[51] The manner in which the term "respective" is used in the clause lends substantial credence to this interpretation.[52] In essence, Congress is given two separate powers with regard to copyrights for authors and patents for inventors which involve the common use of the terms "promote," "progress," "securing," and "limited times."

The problem created by the used of "securing" in the intellectual property clause was that "to secure" had two very different meanings in the eighteenth century when used in connection with "rights." One meaning was "to obtain" or "to provide" which in essence would mean a grant of authority to create property rights with respect to patents and copyrights. A second meaning had a decidedly legal connotation, to wit, "to insure" or "to affirm and protect" which in turn suggested not an authority to create a right but rather an obligation to protect an existing right in the writings of authors and the discoveries of inventors.[53]

In attempting to understand the meaning of "securing" in the intellectual property clause, it is helpful to note that the question of the meaning of the term "securing" had in fact been raised in England in the context of the Statute of Anne, although Madison and the rest of the Framers may well have been unaware of it. The issue arose out of the fact that the title to the bill that became the Statute had been changed. Its original title was "A bill for the Encouragement of Learning and for Securing the Property of the Copies of Books in the Rightful Owners thereof." This was amended to read "A Bill for the Encouragement of Learning by Vesting the Copies of Printed Books in the Authors, or Purchasers, of such Copies, during the Times therein Mentioned." The removal of the key word "securing" and its replacement with "vesting"

---

51. Giles S. Rich, *The Principles of Patentability*, 42 J. PAT. OFF. SOC'Y 75, 77–78 (1960). But, as I pointed out earlier, it in reality is a packaging together of three earlier proposals. *See* Chapter Four, text between notes 8 and 10.

52. But it is not the only one that is possible. Prager, while acknowledging that "respective" may indeed serve "to correlate 'writings' with 'science' and 'discoveries' with 'useful arts,'" also suggests that may mean instead or in addition "that each new creation be considered individually and with precision and that it be distinguished from the work of contemporaries and predecessors." Prager, *supra* note 5, at 317.

53. An extreme version of this view was presented by a patentee in Constant v. Advanced Micro-Devices, Inc., 848 F.2d 1560 (Fed. Cir. 1988) who argued that "securing" as used in the intellectual property clause meant that any issued patent must be presumed to be conclusively valid and not subject to administrative or judicial challenge. 848 F.2d at 1564. The Federal Circuit's response was that "[t]his novel interpretation is obviously erroneous." *Id.*

seemed to suggest that instead of an extant right being confirmed, a new right was being conferred.[54]

As Rose points out, however, the language of the Statute is inconsistent, because "although 'vesting' is used in the title, 'securing' is employed in the preamble to the second section, where the act defines its intent to ensure that property in books 'be secured to the Proprietor or Proprietor thereof.'" He notes that this phrasing was unchanged from the original draft of the bill and indicates that "[l]ater in the century the proponents of perpetual copyright would seize on this inconsistency and argue that the use of 'securing' in the body of the act had more force than the use of 'vesting' in the title."[55] In *Millar v. Taylor*, the issue of the meaning of the term "securing" in the context of the title of the Statute of Anne was raised. But as stated therein:

> Great stress has been laid by counsel for the defendant, upon the change of the title and the word "vesting" instead of "securing."
> The restraining of the provisions of the bill to a term,[56] necessarily occasioned an alteration of the title. "Securing for a term" would not import that there was a common-law right beyond the term: and "vesting for a term" does not import that there is no common-law right.[57]

Although the majority in *Millar v. Taylor* held that there was indeed a common-law right to copyright, they clearly were not disposed to predicate any such holding on the meaning of "securing" or "vesting" as used in the Statute of Anne.

With this background, it is important to note that the symmetry of the balanced construction is destroyed if the term "securing" is not used to mean the same thing in the context of an exclusive right for both authors *and* inventors. If "securing" had a particular legal connotation of "to insure" or "to affirm and protect" certain existing rights as arguably it did at the time the Constitution was drafted and if this legal connotation was in fact intended, the balanced construction would only be justified if this legal connotation of "securing" was in fact applicable to the rights of both authors

---

54. MARK ROSE, AUTHORS AND OWNERS at 46 (Cambridge, Mass. 1993).
55. *Id.*
56. The original bill had contained no term limitation for copyright.
57. 98 Eng. Rep. at 218, 4 Burr. at 2334.

and inventors.[58] But such was not the case at common law. Thus, if they actually intended "securing" to be used with this legal connotation, then by using a balanced composition of this type, the Framers effectively created an interpretational approach to the intellectual property clause not justified by the existing common law. Madison, being the erudite fellow that he was, may well have known this to be the case.[59] It is most unlikely, however that the other delegates were aware for the potential for inconsistency created by the balanced composition of the intellectual property clause.

Alternatively, "securing" may be interpreted in a manner having nothing whatever to do with the then existing common law treatment of patents and copyrights. As is suggested, this approach removes any inconsistency in meaning as applied to the rights of authors and inventors. Nonetheless, the ambiguity inherent in the phrase "securing . . . the exclusive right" has created substantial argument among commentators as to the actual intent of the Framers.

The point has been made that "[t]he early Colonial writings usually associate the word 'secure' with the word 'rights.'"[60] The same can be said for that most famous of early American documents, the Declaration of Independence, which states in its second paragraph that: "We hold these truths to be self evident, that all men are created equal; that they are endowed by their Creator with certain *inalienable rights.* Among these are life, liberty and the pursuit of happiness; that *to secure* these *rights* Governments are instituted among men."[61] Clearly, if men are endowed with certain rights that are "inalienable," then "to secure" them cannot mean "to obtain" or "to provide" them but rather must mean "to insure" or "to affirm and protect" existing rights.

This language is frequently cited as demonstrating the natural law and natural rights precepts on which the Declaration is in no small measure predicated. But a word of caution is in order, if it is presumed that these

58. As pointed out by Seidel, *supra* note 48, at 9: "The division of a balanced sentence was a rule of construction at common law. *Reddendo Singula, Singulis,* meaning literally to refer each to each, as each phrase or expression to its appropriate object."
59. As a practical matter, this potential interpretational conundrum did not concern Madison, because, as is shown, it is highly unlikely that he perceived "securing" as used in the clause to have any pre-existing legal connotation.
60. G. Ramsey, *The Historical Background of Patents,* 18 J. PAT. OFF. SOC'Y 7, 15 (1936).
61. Emphasis supplied.

lines somehow demonstrate that the rights to be secured are inherent. For these lines are not what Jefferson initially drafted. Instead:

> Jefferson had written "endowed by their Creator with inherent and inalienable rights." The Congress deleted "inherent" and added "certain." Since inherent rights are natural rights, the deletion by Congress diminishes, and by some interpretations even eliminates, the idea that the rights proclaimed in the Declaration exist by nature.[62]

This would seem to suggest that any automatic assumption that the use of "secure" with "rights" in the Declaration means that the rights to be secured are inherent ones is not entirely tenable.

But even if such an assumption is deemed correct with regard to the Declaration, this does not mean that it also applies concerning similar language used in the Constitution. Two critical distinctions must be borne in mind in any comparison of the language of the Constitution and the Declaration. The Declaration is above all else a political document whereas the Constitution is the quintessential legal document of the land, setting forth as it does the legal framework of the national government. The Constitution is the result of a long and studied drafting process, and there is a considerable record to indicate the intent of the Framers.[63] The Declaration was written in a few days, and there are no notes to indicate Jefferson's intent in his draftsmanship,[64] or the intent of Congress in making the changes that it did. Reliance on language from the Declaration to provide meaning to a term in the Constitution is thus a dubious process at best.[65]

Be that as it may, it ought not to be forgotten that the verb "secure" is used elsewhere in the Constitution in a manner that can reasonably be

---

62. CHARLES A. MILLER, JEFFERSON AND NATURE at 166 (Baltimore 1988).
63. Although unfortunately not with respect to the intellectual property clause.
64. G. WILLS, INVENTING AMERICA: JEFFERSON'S DECLARATION OF INDEPENDENCE at xxv (New York 1978).
65. Nonetheless, modern commentators continue the practice with respect to the intellectual property clause. Thus, for example, Forman states that the use of the term "secure" in the clause constitutes "a tacit recognition of the fact that inventors inherently owned all rights to their inventions, and that the government was only furnishing them with a means of protecting those rights by law," and that this tacit recognition "is consistent with similar language in the Declaration of Independence that 'all men are endowed by their creator with certain inalienable rights' and that governments exist to secure those rights." See H. I. Forman, *Two Hundred Years of American Patent Law, in* AMERICAN BAR ASSOCIATION, TWO HUNDRED YEARS OF ENGLISH AND AMERICAN PATENT, TRADEMARK AND COPYRIGHT LAW 27–28 (Chicago 1976).

interpreted to mean "to insure" or "to affirm and protect."[66] It is not surprising, therefore, that it should in more recent times be argued to have the same meaning in the context of the intellectual property clause.[67] This was all well and good with respect to securing the rights of authors since the right to copyright had been held to exist at common law,[68] and a case could be presented that this right should continue to exist in the United States.[69] But the same could not be said for the rights of inventors because the right to a patent simply did not exist at common law.[70] That was the dilemma inherent in the use of the balanced composition and one which Madison had somehow to address in his justification for the intellectual property clause in *The Federalist No. 43.*

Those who have commented on Madison's passage have frequently assumed that he understood the use of the term "securing" in the

---

66. Thus the Preamble states:

    We, the people of the United States, in order to form a more perfect union, establish justice, insure domestic tranquility, provide for the common defense, promote the general welfare and *secure* the blessings of liberty to ourselves and to our posterity, do ordain and establish this Constitution of the United States

    (emphasis supplied).

67. *See, e.g.,* Ira Donner, *The Copyright Clause of the Constitution: Why Did the Framers Include It With Unanimous Approval?* 36 AM. J. LEG. HIST. 361, 362 (1992); Donald W. Banner, *An Unanticipated, Nonobvious, Enabling Portion of the Constitution: The Patent Provision—The Best Mode,* 69 J. PAT. & TRADEMARK OFF. SOC'Y 631, 637–38 (1987); Forman, *supra* note 65, at 27–28; Prager, note 5, at 318; L. RAY PATTERSON, COPYRIGHT IN HISTORICAL PERSPECTIVE (Nashville 1968) at 194; BRUCE BUGBEE, THE GENESIS OF AMERICAN PATENT AND COPYRIGHT LAW at 129–30 (Washington D.C. 1967); Ramsey, *supra* note 60, at 15–16; J. L. MacAuliffe, *Patents and Their Purpose,* 14 J. PAT. OFF. SOC'Y 253, 258 (1932).

68. In the celebrated case of *Millar v. Taylor.*

69. Any such argument of necessity had to presume that the common-law of copyright had existed in the colonies prior to the Revolution, which was a doubtful presumption at best. *See supra* Part B. Madison certainly was of the view that the Constitution did not make the common law the law of the land. *See* text accompanying notes 85 and 86, *infra.*

70. Neither by statutory provision nor by court decision was an inventor conceded to have a common-law right to a patent by reason of his invention. *See, e.g.,* PATTERSON, *supra* note 67, at 195; Frank D. Prager, *A History of Intellectual Property from 1545 to 1787,* 25 J. PAT. OFF. SOC'Y 711, 739 (1944). Moreover, this point was clearly understood in the United States at the end of the eighteenth century. *See* text accompanying note 108 *infra.*

intellectual property clause to mean that inventors have certain basic pre-existing rights with respect to their inventions which the state is obligated to protect.[71] Bugbee, however, has gone further and suggested that Madison's defense of the intellectual property clause against Jefferson's objections also indicates a belief by Madison that intellectual property rights were inherent.[72] Madison had argued that the limited-term monopolies authorized by the intellectual property clause were acceptable, even though they were "sacrifices of the many to the few," because in the United States the power was in the many rather than the few and it was "much more to be dreaded that the few will be unnecessarily sacrificed to the many."[73] Bugbee suggests that this is clear evidence of "Madison's fear for the safety of property against a predatory and leveling majority."[74]

Madison clearly believed that both inventors and authors should have their rights protected by a grant of exclusivity, at least for a limited time, but it is much less certain whether he believed that such rights inherently existed or were conferred by the common law, absent congressional action. Moreover, he was fully aware that while both he and Pinckney had used "to secure" in the context of their proposals for protecting the rights of authors, Pinckney had used the quite different "to grant" in his proposal respecting the rights of inventors.[75] If the right to a patent either inherently existed or existed at common law, why would Pinckney not have also used

---

71. As phrased by Banner, "there were rights that the inventor inherently possessed and which the Congress had the power to recognize and 'secure.'" *Supra* note 67, at 637. Or as Inlow put it, "James Madison, for example, had been certain that there was a common law right to patents." *See* E. G. INLOW, THE PATENT GRANT at 70 (Baltimore 1950). In Prager's view, Madison had interpreted the intellectual property clause "as saying that Congress will, by patent act, secure, confirm and implement the right already existing under the common law." Prager, *supra* note 5, at 318. *Cf.* Bugbee's statement that "Like Madison's and Pinckney's suggestions, [certain earlier but unspecified] enactments—both general and private—had expressly set forth the concept of *securing* certain rights to individuals, with the implication that such rights were inherent." BUGBEE, *supra* note 67, at 129.

72. BUGBEE, *supra* note 67, at 130–31. *See also* Wendy J. Gordon, *An Inquiry into the Merits of Copyright: The Challenges of Consistency, Consent, and Encouragement Theory*, 41 STAN. L. REV. 1343, 1448–1449 (1989).

73. *See supra* Chapter One, note 17, and accompanying text.

74. BUGBEE, *supra* note 67, at 130–31.

75. *See supra* Chapter Three, text accompanying note 81.

"to secure" with regard to inventors as well as authors?[76] An even more fundamental objection involved the constitutional limitation on the term of the property right. If it was in fact inherent, how could the Constitution limit it in duration?[77]

Nonetheless, the language of the first copyright statute, enacted in 1790, rather strongly suggests a perception by Congress that it was not creating a right but rather affirming and protecting an existing right. Thus, it refers to the "copyright" of maps, charts, and books already printed within the United States and to those who have "legally acquired the copyright of any such map, chart, book or books."[78] This reference to an existing "copyright" is almost certainly to a perceived common-law right.[79] Although the D.C. Circuit has stated that the "First Congress made the Copyright Act of 1790 applicable to subsisting copyrights arising under the

---

76. Patterson suggests that "the language of Pinckney's recommendations, 'To grant patents. . .' and 'To secure to authors. . .' indicates that the choice of words was made advisedly." He also argues that "[t]he use of the word 'securing' indicates that a statutory copyright was to affirm and protect an existing right, not create one." But he argues just as firmly that an inventor never had a common-law right "to a monopoly of manufacture by reason of his invention." PATERSON, *supra* note 67, at 194–95. Patterson fails to address the obvious dichotomy and inconsistency presented by the use of "securing" in the context of both authors and inventors if "securing" is indeed intended to "affirm and protect and existing right."

77. Whicher, for one, has argued that it could not and did not. *See* Whicher, *supra* note 8, at 151. Abrams, in turn, states: "The constitutional provision for 'limited Times' is perhaps the most obvious argument against the theory that a perpetual common law copyright was adopted in the constitutional clause." *See* Abrams, *supra* note 13, at 1177.

78. Act of May 31, 1790, 1 Stat. 124.

79. The titles of the Patent Act of 1790 and the Copyright Act of 1790 are indicative that the first federal congress assumed that it was creating an exclusive right with respect to patents but securing an existing common-law right in copyright. Thus the Patent Act is simply titled "An Act to promote the progress of useful arts" whereas the Copyright Act is titled "An Act for the encouragement of learning, by securing the copies of maps, charts, and books to the authors and proprietors of such copies, during the times therein mentioned." *See* Act of April 10, 1790, 1 Stat. 109, and Act of May 31, 1790, 1 Stat. 124. The inclusion of the "by securing" phraseology in the title of the Copyright Act suggests a congressional intent to protect and affirm a perceived existing common-law right, albeit for a limited time, rather than the creation of a new right, since otherwise there would have been no reason whatever to include it in the title.

copyright laws of the several states,"[80] there is no contemporaneous evidence to support such a view.[81]

D. Interpreting The Federalist No. 43

Consider now what Madison wrote in *The Federalist No. 43*.[82] "The utility of this device will scarcely be questioned." This is a nice rhetorical technique whereby the basic premise that he seeks to demonstrate is set forth almost as a given not subject to challenge.[83] But the arguments used to support the premise are indeed questionable, unless Madison was in fact interpreting "securing" as meaning "to provide" rather than "to insure" or "to affirm." In that case, they make a great deal of sense.

"The copyright of authors has been solemnly adjudged in Great Britain, to be a right at common law." This was correct, insofar as it went, because copyright in Great Britain had indeed been adjudged a common law right in *Millar v. Taylor*, although *Donaldson v. Beckett* had in practical effect limited any common-law copyright to the statutory terms set forth in the Statute of Anne. But care should be taken not to read more into this statement than is actually there. It does not give any indication whatever concerning Madison's views concerning whether common-law copyright was deemed to be perpetual or limited to the terms set forth in the Statute of Anne. Indeed, from his perspective, the term of common-law copyright was not particularly relevant because he did not view the intellectual property clause as adopting or authorizing common-law copyright. Rather, all he intended by this statement was to indicate that, just as in Great Britain, the intellectual property clause was intended to give Congress authority to create a legal right to copyright as opposed to a mere privilege.

To the extent this statement is taken as an affirmation that Madison interpreted "securing" as meaning "to insure or affirm" then also implicit

---

80. Eldred v. Reno, 239 F.3d 372, 379 (D.C. Cir. 2001).

81. If Congress had intended this to be a reference to state copyrights, it is reasonable to suppose that it would have expressly so stated, as it did in the patent context. Thus, the Patent Act of 1793 made express reference to certain existing state patents and declared that they were "relinquished" upon the filing for a federal patent for the same invention. *See* Section 7, Act of February 23, 1793, 1 Stat. 318.

82. The content of *The Federalist No. 43* was discussed in Chapter Four, text accompanying notes 77–83.

83. But it was in fact almost immediately challenged by Thomas Jefferson. *See* Chapter One, Part B.

in it is a presumption that rights under the common law carried over and were operative under the new Constitution. Yet the Constitution as initially drafted says not a word about the common law.[84] Indeed, this was one of the reasons given by Virginia delegate George Mason for refusing to sign the Constitution. As he put it, "Nor are the people secured even in the enjoyment of the benefit of the common law [which stands here upon no other foundation than its having been adopted by the respective acts forming the constitutions of the several States]."[85] Mason had a point because the applicability of the common law in the American colonies had been a matter of great contention between the crown and the colonies.[86] Moreover, not all states had adopted the common law,[87] and there was great confusion as to exactly what had been adopted.[88]

Shortly after the federal convention, Madison raised the subject of Mason's concerns about the common law to George Washington, saying:

> What can he mean by saying that the Common law is not secured by the new Constitution, though it has been adopted by the State Constitutions. The Common Law is nothing more than the unwritten law, and is left by all the Constitutions equally liable to legislative alterations. I am not sure that any notice is particularly taken of it in the Constitutions of the States. If there is, nothing more is provided than a general declaration that it shall continue along with other branches of law to be in force until legally changed. The Constitution of Virga. drawn by Col Mason himself, is absolutely silent on the subject. An *ordinance* passed during the same Session, declared the Common Law as heretofore & all Statutes of prior date to the 4 of James I. to be still the law of the land, merely to obviate pretexts that the separation from G. Britain threw us into a State of nature, and abolished all civil rights and obligations.[89]

---

84. The only reference to the common law in the Constitution is in the seventh amendment which has to do with a right to trial by jury.
85. II THE RECORDS OF THE FEDERAL CONVENTION OF 1787, at 637 (Max Farrand ed., New Haven 1937). Farrand points out that the material in brackets was not in Mason's original written comments but was added later by Mason when his reasons for not signing were printed in pamphlet form.
86. *See, e.g.,* HORWITZ, *supra* note 19, at 5–9; CROSSKEY, *supra* note 18, at 578–609; Brown, *supra* note 22; MORRIS, *supra* note 24, at 343.
87. *See supra* text accompanying note 32.
88. *See supra* text accompanying note 33.
89. Letter from James Madison to George Washington (Oct. 18, 1787), *in* III THE RECORDS OF THE FEDERAL CONVENTION OF 1787, at 129–30 (Max Farrand ed., New Haven 1937).

He then went on to forcefully argue why the convention simply could not have made the common law the law of the land saying:

> If they had in general terms declared the Common law to be in force, they would have broken in upon the legal Code of every State in the most material points: they wd. have done more, they would have brought over from G. B. a thousand heterogeneous & anti-republican doctrines, and even the *ecclesiastical Hierarchy itself,* for that is a part of the Common Law.[90]

Crosskey contends that "the men of the Convention apparently considered the standing national law of the United States to be 'the common law of England,' in all of its applicable portions."[91] As has been shown by the foregoing discussion this was clearly not the case. Rather, there were those, such as Mason, who believed that it should be declared the law of the land by the Constitution. Obviously, such views did not prevail during the debates over constitutional language.

But if the common law was deliberately not made applicable under the Constitution as Madison most emphatically seemed to be stating, what then was the relevance to "securing" the rights of authors of his statement that "The copyright of authors has been solemnly adjudged, in Great Britain, to be a right of common law"? Either Madison was arguing in a quite inconsistent legal fashion with regard to the position he had taken earlier with Washington, or he intended the term "securing" to mean "to obtain" or "to provide" rather than "to insure" or "to affirm and protect." That he clearly contemplated and used the term to mean "to obtain" or "to provide" is amply supported by his later discussion with Jefferson

---

90. *Id.*
91. CROSSKEY, *supra* note 18, at 549. He later states that there is no possibility of understanding the enumeration of congressional powers in the Constitution,

> except upon the assumption—fully warranted by its perfect fit and its rationalizing effect upon a great multitude of otherwise unruly facts—that, to the extent of their applicability to American conditions, the various branches of the Common Law, and the British statutes in amendment thereof, were deemed to be "Laws of the United States" when the Constitution was drawn and adopted.

CROSSKEY, II POLITICS AND THE CONSTITUTION, *supra* note 18, at 1166. He acknowledges, however, that his views are at almost total variance with accepted scholarship and legal history; contending only that "the actual, historic meaning" of the Constitution as determined by him "is a matter unknown, alike, to our accepted constitutional law and our conventional American histories." *Id.* at vii.

concerning the intellectual property clause wherein he refers not to a common-law right but rather to a privilege.[92]

Those who contend that Madison interpreted the intellectual property clause as providing for a common-law copyright ignore these points entirely. They assume that this statement in *The Federalist No. 43* is indicative that Madison (and the Framers as a whole) believed that a common law copyright in perpetuity was desirable and that they were authorizing something closely akin to it in the intellectual property clause and that this form of copyright was predicated on a "natural rights" theory.[93] All that the statement on its face can be taken to indicate is that Madison assumed there to be a common law copyright, not that such copyright was binding in the United States or that it should be perpetuated in the United States.[94]

Look now at his next sentence: "The right to useful inventions seems with equal reason to belong to inventors." This suggests a rather clear understanding by Madison of the existing state of the common law whereby a right to copyright existed but a right to a patent did not. He very carefully refrains from contending that there is a common-law right to a patent, but instead says only that "with equal reason" inventors should have similar rights as authors are adjudged to have at common law. However, saying that an inventor should have a right is not the same thing as saying that the right inherently exists, as would be necessitated if "securing" is interpreted by him to mean "to insure" or "to affirm and protect" an existing right. Rather, Madison is saying that the intent of the intellectual property clause is to treat patents and copyrights similarly as legal rights for limited periods.

"The public good fully coincides in both cases with the claims of individuals." This sounds impressive, but it is doubtful that Madison literally believed this to be the case. He was fully aware from his earlier public life that the claims of individuals not infrequently conflict with the public good, and that government is in a constant effort to balance the claims of individuals with the public interest. He gave no indication of where the balance should lie between the public interest and the rights of individuals, apparently assuming that such would be left to the discretion of Congress and the courts.

---

92. *See supra* Chapter One, text accompanying note 17.
93. *See, e.g.,* Whicher, *supra* note 8, at 115, 134, 136.
94. Madison's biographer, Irving Brant, strenuously argues that Madison was a life-long opponent of perpetual rights in intellectual property. *See* IRVING BRANT, 2 JAMES MADISON at 370–71 (1948).

Nonetheless, even if the premise is assumed that the interests of individuals and the public are the same insofar as the intellectual property clause is concerned, it does not necessarily follow that there is any inherent right to either a copyright or a patent or any other form of exclusive right for either an author or an inventor. Rather, once again it can be interpreted as meaning that to create a right in both instances coincides with the public good. That this is in fact what was intended is further evidence by Madison's use of the phrase *"claims of individuals"* rather than "rights of individuals."

Madison did not explain what he meant by the "claims of individuals," and it is unclear whether he viewed the "claims" of inventors as a demand to protect an inherent, natural right to what they viewed as their mental property or as the petitioning for a form of reward for the risks taken in developing and practicing new useful arts.[95] Irrespective of how he viewed the claims of inventors, Madison implicitly recognized that under the constitutional language, an exclusive right to an invention could only be made legally cognizable by an express act of Congress. This was also true with regard to an exclusive right to a writing in that, as Madison expressly indicated, the only other legal basis for such an exclusive right was the common law which was not made applicable by the Constitution.

"The States cannot separately make effectual provision in either of the cases, and most of them have anticipated the decision on this point by laws passed at the instance of Congress." As pointed out by Abrams, this statement on its face is indicative of a great deal of skepticism concerning the existence of common-law copyright in the United States. If the states could not make "effective provision" for it, it must have most insubstantial attributes.[96]

---

95. Early on in both England and the United States inventors would present both arguments as a justification for the patent grant. The courts in either country never accepted the view that a natural, inherent property right in invention existed, although they did long favor the view that one purpose of granting patents was to reward inventors for taking entrepreneurial risk. As noted by Machlup, however, "[t]he argument that the patent monopoly secures a just reward for the inventor is entirely absent from modern economic literature." *See* Fritz Machlup, *An Economic Review of the Patent System*, U.S. Senate, Comm. on Judiciary, 85th Cong., 2d Sess. at 29 (1958). *Cf.* MacLeod's statement that "in 1790–91 . . . both France and the United States had established patent systems . . . embodying the concept of an inventor's natural right to his intellectual property." *See* Christine MacLeod, *The Paradoxes of Patenting: Invention and Its Diffusion in 18th- and 19th-Century Britain, France, and North America*, 32 TECH. & CULTURE 885, 888 (1991).

96. Abrams, *supra* note 13, at 1177.

This statement is also internally inconsistent and a misstatement of what the states had actually done. If the states "have anticipated the decision on this point" by enacting laws, how is this consistent with the argument that they cannot effectively act with regard to protecting the rights of either authors or inventors? Moreover, contrary to the clear impression left by Madison, the states most certainly had not enacted patent laws "at the instance of Congress." With the exception of South Carolina, none of them had enacted a general patent law, and the Congress had never asked them to do so.[97] What Madison was referring to was the copyright laws enacted by all the original thirteen states except Delaware at the suggestion of the Second Continental Congress in 1783.[98] He was correct in his view that these laws were largely ineffectual, but he failed to indicate why they were ineffectual.[99] What Madison was really arguing was that national law as opposed to state law was needed to effectively grant exclusive rights in their writings and discoveries to authors and inventors.

It is thus seen that Madison's arguments in *The Federalist No. 43* can best be understood if it is assumed that he interpreted "securing" to mean "to create" or "to provide." This view is also consistent with that of at least some inventors during this same time frame. As but one example, John Fitch, of steamboat fame, "was convinced of the natural pre-existence of his inventor's rights,"[100] but was also pragmatic enough to realize that this was not going to get him much. So in a petition to Congress in 1786, first drafted for an exclusive "right," the word "right" was changed to "privilege."[101]

Lutz suggests that

> according to the best evidence of contemporary usage the phrase "securing . . . the exclusive right" meant merely *the issuance of a patent.* See the petition filed in New Hampshire by Benjamin Dearborn in 1786 which prayed "that an *exclusive right* of making, and selling said press and scales, and of printing and vending said guide . . . may be *secured* to him . . . for the term of twenty-one years."[102]

---

97. BUGBEE, *supra* note 67, at 93.
98. *See supra* Chapter Two, text accompanying notes 172–184.
99. For the reasons for their ineffectiveness, see Chapter Two, text accompanying notes 188–191.
100. Frank D. Prager, *The Steamboat Pioneers Before the Founding Fathers,* 37 J. PAT. OFF. SOC'Y 486, 519 (1955).
101. Prager, *id.* at 519, citing FITCH PAPERS, LIBRARY OF CONGRESS, f. 1762.
102. Karl B. Lutz, *Are the Courts Carrying Out Constitutional Public Policy on Patents?* 34 J. PAT. OFF. SOC'Y 766, 772 (1952) (emphasis added).

From this perspective, "securing . . . the exclusive right" plausibly can be taken to mean creation of a new right rather than protection of an existing one.

As Madison wrote late in his life:

> Monopolies tho' in certain cases useful ought to be granted with caution, and guarded with strictness against abuse. The Constitution of the United States has limited them to two cases—the authors of Books, and of useful inventions, in both [of] which they are considered as compensation for a benefit actually gained to the community as a purchase of property which the owners might otherwise withhold from public use. There can be no just objection to temporary monopolies in these cases; but it ought to be temporary because under that limitation a sufficient recompense and encouragement may be given.
>
> . . .
>
> Perpetual monopolies of every sort are forbidden not only by the Genius of free Governments, but by the imperfections of human foresight.[103]

Evidence that Madison held similar views in 1788 is evidenced in his exchange of correspondence with Jefferson in that year concerning the intellectual property clause.[104]

E. A Question of Property

The intellectual property clause does not speak in terms of property rights. Nor does it in and of itself create either a property right in invention or writings or protect or insure an existing property right under either natural law or the common law.[105] Instead, all that it does is authorize Congress to create and protect for authors and inventors an exclusive right, whether or

---

103. Madison, as quoted in *Aspects of Monopoly One Hundred Years Ago,* 128 HARPER'S MAG. 489, 490 (1914). *See also* Brant, *supra* note 94.
104. *See* Chapter One, text accompanying notes 14–17.
105. But arguments would continue to be made that under the intellectual property clause there was a pre-existent common law right to property in invention. *See, e.g.,* Gibbons v. Ogden, 22 U.S. (9 Wheat.) 1, 44–51, 141–52 (1824). As noted, modern commentators still occasionally raise this argument. *See supra* text accompanying notes 4–9.

not denominated property,[106] in their writings and discoveries for a limited time.[107] It did not obligate the Congress to do this, but only gave it authority to do so. If there was some inherent right of authors and inventors in their writings and discoveries as understood by the Framers, then it is difficult to understand why they would not have perceived themselves obligated to require Congress to protect such right. Yet they did not.[108]

Contemporaneous commentary urging that invention and writings should be treated as property did not suggest that the intellectual property clause had in fact created a property right in either invention or writings. Thus, e.g., Noah Webster's published comments in February 1788, after the Constitution had been drafted but before it had been ratified, argued that "the want of some regulation for this purpose [i.e., protecting inventions and writings as property] may be numbered among the defects of the American government."[109] He said nothing, however, about the intellectual property clause in the proposed Constitution.

Nonetheless, there would quickly be arguments contending for some inherent property right either perceived to be created by the intellectual property clause or which the intellectual property clause was seen as obligating to be protected.[110] One of the earliest of these was presented by Rep. William Murray during debate on what became the Patent Act of

---

106. It was not until the Patent Act of 1793 that Congress saw fit to denominate patents as a means of creating a property right with regard to invention.

107. Some who should have known better have even managed to confuse the issue in the same paragraph. Thus, in the introduction to the *Outline of the History of the United States Patent Office*, published on the centennial of the Patent Act of 1836, Richard Spencer, a former First Assistant Commissioner of the Patent Office, first correctly stated with respect to the intellectual property clause that in only one instance did the Constitution grant Congress authority "to create private property rights." Two sentences later, he incorrectly stated that "these were the only private property rights *created by the Constitution*" (emphasis supplied). See *Centennial Number*, 18 J. PAT. OFF. SOC'Y at 13 (July 1936). In this regard, compare the text accompanying note 152, *infra*.

108. Note that article I, § 8 commences with the phrase "Congress shall have power to . . ." rather than simply "shall."

109. Frank D. Prager, *Proposals for the Patent Act of 1790*, 36 J. PAT. OFF. SOC'Y 157 (1954), quoting front page of the February 1788 issue of *American Magazine*.

110. Recall that the language of the Copyright Act of 1790 rather clearly suggested a perception by Congress that with regard to copyright it was not creating a right but rather affirming and protecting an existing common-law right. See *supra* text accompanying notes 78–81.

1793. On January 30, 1793, in speaking for certain amendments to the pending patent bill, he commented:

> [English] patents are derived from the grace of the Monarch, and the exclusive enjoyments of the profits of a discovery is not so much a right inherent as it is a privilege bestowed and an emanation of the prerogative. Here, on the contrary, a citizen has a *right* in the inventions he may make, and he considers the law but as the mode by which he is to enjoy their fruits.[111]

This certainly seemed to imply the existence of some inherent right protected under the intellectual property clause.

The basis for this argument, although not expressly articulated, is an assumption that individuals have a natural or inherent right of property in their own ideas, which society has an obligation to protect. This so-called natural law thesis ran up against the common-law tradition in England and was never widely accepted.[112] It is not surprising, however, that early on in the United States various inventors should seek to apply it,[113] and in particular to argue that the intellectual property clause "seem[s] also to acknowledge the right of the inventor to his mental property."[114] In 1812

---

111. ANNALS OF CONGRESS 855 (2d Cong., 2d Sess.), quoted in Ramsay, *supra* note 60, at 16. *See also* Banner, *supra* note 67, at 638 (emphasis in the original).

112. As Armitage notes: "There was no question of the inventor having a natural right to the fruits of his expression. Such enlightened notions, inspired by 18th-century revolutionary thinking, found expression in the United States and France but not in England." *See* Edward Armitage, *Two Hundred Years of English Patent Law, in* AMERICAN BAR ASSOCIATION, TWO HUNDRED YEARS OF ENGLISH AND AMERICAN PATENT, TRADEMARK AND COPYRIGHT LAW at 4–5 (Chicago 1976). *See also* CHRISTINE MACLEOD, INVENTING THE INDUSTRIAL REVOLUTION, THE ENGLISH PATENT SYSTEM, 1660–1800, at 199 (Cambridge 1988); HAROLD I. DUTTON, THE PATENT SYSTEM AND INVENTIVE ACTIVITY DURING THE INDUSTRIAL REVOLUTION, 1750–1852, at 17–23 (Manchester 1984).

113. *See, e.g.,* NEW ENGLAND ASSOCIATION OF INVENTORS AND PATRONS OF THE USEFUL ARTS, REMARKS ON THE RIGHTS OF INVENTORS AND THE INFLUENCE OF THEIR STUDIES IN PROMOTING THE ENJOYMENTS OF LIFE AND PUBLIC PROSPERITY at 10 (Boston 1807) ("[o]ne feature of an aristocratic case, is however apparent in patent-laws, and only this the power assumed therein of confiscating the inventor's *natural* right, without the shadow of a crime in the proprietor to merit it").

114. Address of the Advocate of the Patentees, Inventors of Useful Improvements in the Arts and Sciences; in Defence of Mental Property at 9 (Philadelphia, Dec. 19, 1806). Writing in 1792 Joseph Barnes was somewhat more

counsel would argue in *Livingston v. Van Ingen*[115] that: "The patent merely *secures* the property to the inventor for a certain time. It proceeds as to authors, on the common law notion; as to inventors, on natural rights."[116] It would not be too long before a lawyer would unequivocally state: "In the United States, it [a patent] is a CONSTITUTIONAL RIGHT, which the citizen may *demand,* and which the officers of government have no power to withhold."[117] But Congress chose not to adopt such a view, for neither the Patent Act of 1790 nor that of 1793 required that a patent issue merely upon demand.

It is not surprising that the thesis that inventions are somehow, in nature, a subject of property should exert such a powerful attraction to inventors at a time when no clear distinction between a property right in invention and one in a patent had been made.[118] But in 1813 Jefferson provided an articulate rebuttal of this view, saying:

> It has been pretended by some, (and in England especially,) that inventors have a natural and exclusive right to their own inventions, and not merely for their own lives, but inheritable to their heirs.[119] But

---

circumspect, saying "each American citizen has a *constitutional* right to claim his property in the products of his genius, should be secured by the National Legislature." *See* JOSEPH BARNES, TREATISE ON THE JUSTICE, POLICY, AND UTILITY OF ESTABLISHING AN EFFECTUAL SYSTEM OF PROMOTING THE PROGRESS OF USEFUL ARTS, BY ASSURING PROPERTY IN THE PRODUCTS OF GENIUS at 16 (Philadelphia 1792).

115. 9 Johns. R. 507 (N.Y. 1812).

116. *Id.* at 533.

117. Peter A. Brown, *Mechanical Jurisprudence—No. XIV*, 3 J. FRANKLIN INST. at 176 (1827). According to Browne, the purpose of the intellectual property clause

> is to *secure,* not to *grant,* the right. A *grant* implies a property in the thing granted in the grantor, or person making the grant: but the framers of the Constitution never meant to invest Congress with the private property which every citizen has in his own invention and discoveries. The right . . . is in the inventor, before the patent is granted. To *secure,* means only to protect, and insure, a pre-existing right.

2 J. FRANKLIN INST. at 228–29 (1826).

118. Indeed, as Machlup point out in 1958 "it is almost embarrassing how often the controversial idea of a property right in *invention* is confused with the noncontroversial idea of a property right in a *patent." See* Machlup, *supra* note 95, at 53.

119. The reference to England in this sentence is merely another example of Jefferson's well-known anglophobia. Not only was this natural right theory never accepted in England, but what Jefferson was actually addressing was the rights of inventors in the United States and not in England.

while it is a moot question whether the origin of any kind of property is derived from nature at all, it would be singular to admit a natural and even a hereditary right to inventors. . . . Stable ownership [of property] is the gift of social law, and is given late in the progress of society. It would be curious, then, if an idea, the fugitive fermentation of an individual brain, could, of natural right, be claimed in exclusive and stable property. If nature had made any one thing less susceptible than all others of exclusive property, it is the action of the thinking power called an idea, which an individual may exclusively possess as long as he keeps it to himself; but the moment it is divulged, it forces itself into the possession of every one, and the receiver cannot dispossess himself of it. Its peculiar character, too, is that no one possesses the less, because every other possesses the whole of it. He who receives an idea from me, receives instruction himself without lessening mine; as he who lights his taper at mine, receives light without darkening me. That ideas should freely spread from one to another over the globe, for the moral and mutual instruction of man, and improvement of his condition, seems to have been peculiarly and benevolently designed by nature, when she made them, like fire, expansible over all space, without lessening their density at any point, and like the air which we breathe, move, and have our physical being, incapable of confinement or exclusive appropriation. *Invention then cannot, in nature, be a subject of property.* Society may give an exclusive right to the profits arising from them, as an encouragement to men to pursue ideas which may produce utility, but this may or may not be done, according to the will and convenience of the society, without claim or complaint from anybody.[120]

Jefferson thus eloquently denied the existence of any natural property right in invention, while at the same time fully acknowledging the power of the state (society) at its discretion to give an exclusive right for some limited period. Interestingly, Jefferson makes no reference to the intellectual property clause, although the views he expresses are clearly an interpretation of it.[121]

---

120. Letter from Thomas Jefferson to Isaac McPherson (Aug. 13, 1813), *in* 13 THE WRITINGS OF THOMAS JEFFERSON at 333–34 (A. A. Lipscomb ed., Washington 1903) (emphasis supplied).

121. Eisenberg cites the last several sentences of Jefferson's language quoted above as being indicative that the Framers rejected the notion that inventors have a natural property right in their inventions. *See* Rebecca S. Eisenberg, *Patents and the Progress of Science: Exclusive Rights and Experimental Use,* 56 U. CHI. L. REV. 1017, 1024 (1989). Jefferson of course was not a Framer and he set forth these views more than a quarter century after the Constitution was drafted. While there is nothing to suggest that what he wrote is not consonant

Several months earlier Justice Marshall had stated that "[t]he constitution and law, taken together, give to the inventor, from the moment of invention, an inchoate property therein, which is completed by suing out a patent."[122] The views expressed by Jefferson and Marshall are not inconsistent, although they at first glance appear to be. While Marshall speaks of an inchoate property right in invention, he makes clear that this inchoate right arises out of—and not independently of—the Constitution and the patent law. Secondly, because it is inchoate, it cannot be protected until a patent actually issues. In other words, the legally cognizable property right arises out of the issuance of the patent and not out of the act of invention itself.[123]

F. The Supreme Court Speaks Out

Although Jefferson's views in this regard rather quickly became known in the United States,[124] they were not universally accepted.[125] One who did not accept them was Thomas Jones, editor of the *Journal of the Franklin Institute* and former Superintendent of Patents who in 1830 stated: "The patent law is not intended to confer any right, but to confirm those already existing."[126]

Another was Noah Webster's younger kinsman, Daniel Webster, who was perhaps the most eminent trial attorney in the United States in the first half of the nineteenth century. Webster tried many patent and copyright cases and argued vigorously that there was a pre-existing right under the common law for both authors and inventors in their writings and

---

with the views of the Framers, neither is there anything to expressly suggest that it is in fact representative of their views. My point is only that care should be taken in any assumption that Jefferson spoke for the Framers.

122. Evans v. Jordan, 8 F. Cas. 872, 873 (Case No. 4,564) (D. Va. 1813).

123. The Supreme Court sought to make this point clearer in 1832 by stating that the exclusive right conferred by the patent law "can only be secured by a substantial compliance with every legal requisite. His [the inventor's] exclusive right does not rest alone upon his discovery; but also upon the legal sanctions which have been given to it, and the forms of law with which it has been clothed." Shaw v. Cooper, 32 U.S. (7 Pet.) 292, 320 (1832).

124. His letter to McPherson was soon published in an addendum to vol. 5 of *Nile's Register* in Baltimore and almost immediately thereafter it appeared in 1 THE EMPORIUM OF ARTS AND SCIENCES at 446–53 (New Series) (1814).

125. *See, e.g., supra* note 117.

126. 10 J. FRANKLIN INST. at 116–17 (Thomas P. Jones ed., 1830).

discoveries.[127] He was one of the counsel for Gibbons in *Gibbons v. Ogden*[128] which ultimately was decided by the Supreme Court in 1824 on the basis of the interpretation given to the commerce clause but wherein both parties contended that the intellectual property clause was intended to read on a pre-existing common law property right in invention.[129] In *Pennock v. Dialogue*[130] he modified the argument slightly, contending that "[u]nder the provisions of the laws of the United States, the right is created by the invention, and not by the patent."[131] This in essence was the same contention that Jones would make, i.e., that the patent laws are for the purpose of protecting an inherent right in invention that exists independent of the patent laws.

In 1834 Webster as co-counsel would argue in *Wheaton v. Peters*[132] for the intellectual property clause being predicated on a common-law property right in copyright,[133] and the Supreme Court would give short shrift to such argument. In so doing, the Court would also provide a specific interpretation of the meaning to be given to "securing" as used in the intellectual property clause. Justice McLean, speaking for the majority, stated:

> The counsel for the complainants insist that the term, as used, clearly indicates an intention, not to originate a right, but to protect one already in existence.
>
> There is no mode by which the meaning affixed to any word or sentence, by a deliberative body, can be so well ascertained as by comparing it with the words and sentences with which it stands connected. By this rule the word "secure" as used in the Constitution, could not mean the protection of an acknowledged legal right. It refers to inventors as well as authors, and it has never been contended by anyone, either in this country or in England, that an inventor has a perpetual right, at common law, to sell the thing invented.[134]

He went on to indicate that the term "securing" as used in the intellectual property clause refers only to a grant of authority to Congress to create a future right and not to the protection of an existing right.

---

127. INLOW, *supra* note 71, at 70–71.
128. 22 U.S. (9 Wheat.) 1 (1824).
129. *See* 22 U.S. at 49, 146.
130. 27 U.S. (2 Pet.) 1 (1829).
131. *Id.* at 7.
132. 33 U.S. (8 Pet.) 591 (1834).
133. *Id.* 652–53.
134. 33 U.S. at 661–62.

He also did away with any notion that the common law was somehow valid in the United States, saying:

> It is clear that there can be no common law of the United States. . . . There is no principle which pervades the Union and has the authority of law that is not embodied in the Constitution or the laws of the Union. The common law could be made a part of our federal system only by legislative adoption.[135]

It thus had taken the Supreme Court more than four decades before it reached a definitive interpretation as to whether the intellectual property clause insured or protected an existing common law right or whether it merely provided Congress with authority to create a future property right. When it did so, however, it interpreted the clause as granting an authority to create a future right rather than an authority to protect an existing one.

The view that the intellectual property clause was intended to protect existing rights died hard, however. The second United States patent treatise, published in 1837 three years after *Wheaton v. Peters* was decided, clearly acknowledges that there is no natural inherent exclusive right of an inventor to an invention,[136] but then goes on to state:

> Though *property* in a discovery, therefore, like that in land, originates in and is created by legislation, the *right* to such property exists in an imperfect degree, independently of the positive laws. In this view Mr. Rawle remarks, that upon the provisions of the constitution of the United States on this subject, that it was not intended thereby to create rights, but merely to regulate those already existing.[137] The inventor has

---

135. *Id.* at 658. It is frequently forgotten that the same point had been made 36 years earlier by Justice Chase in 1798 when he declared that there could be no common law of the United States, since "the whole of the common law of England has been no where introduced" into this country and since "the common law . . . from one State, is not the common law of another." HORWITZ, *supra* note 19, at 12, *quoting* United States v. Worrall, 2 Dall. 384 (1798).
136. WILLARD PHILLIPS, THE LAW OF PATENTS FOR INVENTION at 4 (Boston 1837). In coming to this conclusion, he ignores the earlier views of Jefferson on the point, and instead relies on an argument presented in a French patent treatise, *See* A. C. RENOUARD, TRAITE DES BREVETS D'INVENTION, &C. (Paris 1825).
137. Citing WILLIAM RAWLE, A VIEW OF THE CONSTITUTION OF THE UNITED STATES at 102 (Philadelphia 1825). According to Rawle,

> that as from the nature of our Constitution, no new rights can be considered as created by it, but its operation more properly is the organization and distribution of a conceded power in relation to rights already existing, we must regard these provisions [i.e., the intellectual property clause] as

a *right* to keep his secret, and if he discloses it he has a just claim to remuneration and reward, according to the amount of his expenditure, and the importance of his improvement.[138]

This despite the fact that the Supreme Court just three years earlier had held expressly opposite to the view set forth by Rawle.

In 1988 an argument was presented to the Federal Circuit that the term "securing" in the intellectual property clause meant that the issuance of patent meant that it was conclusively valid and not subject to judicial challenge.[139] The court gave short shrift to this argument, saying that "judicial review of patent validity was accepted by members of Congress and presidents who were themselves framers of the Constitution," and the courts have consistently construed the intellectual property clause as permitting judicial review of patents.[140]

G. Perspectives

It is not surprising that in enacting the Copyright Act of 1790 Congress should perceive that it was affirming and protecting an existing common-law copyright in authors.[141] Moreover, it was perhaps inevitable that in the late eighteenth and early nineteenth century authors and inventors and their representatives would argue that they had an inherent property right in their writings and inventions which the intellectual property clause was intended to protect. Some contended that the right arose out of natural law, while others argued that it was a common-law right which Congress was compelled to protect under the Constitution. These two arguments, while occasionally used together and at other times confused, were in fact quite different, in that the common law tended to be antithetical to any view that property rights arose out of natural law.[142]

---

at least the evidence of opinion, that such a species of property, both in the works of authors and in the inventions of artists, had a legal existence.

Id. Rawle provides no citation of authority for his assertion that "from the nature of our Constitution, no new rights can be considered as created by it." It is generally accepted today that the intellectual property clause did in fact authorize the creation of a new species of property.

138. PHILLIPS, *supra* note 136, at 8–9.
139. Constant v. Advanced Micro-Devices, Inc., 848 F.2d 1560, 1564 (Fed. Cir. 1988).
140. *Id.*
141. *See supra* text accompanying notes 78–81.
142. *See supra* Chapter Four, text accompanying and following note 106.

Jefferson in 1813, quite effectively showed that there could be no natural law basis for any right in invention. Although he did not speak expressly to literary works, implicit in his discussion was the view that the argument was the same irrespective of whether the intellectual property involved was writings or invention. While it is probable that the views of the Framers were similar to those expressed by Jefferson, there is nothing to expressly indicate that this was the case, and it should be noted that Jefferson wrote twenty-six years after the Constitution was drafted. Jefferson also never made any reference whatever to the intellectual property clause when he set forth his views.

Without reference to the views of Jefferson, a congressional report in 1894, incident to a general codification of the patent laws, expressly rejected any natural law theory of property rights in invention or writings, arguing that the intellectual property clause simply cannot be read to state or imply a natural, inherent property right to invention or writings:

> The object to be attained and the reason for the constitutional grant of power are imbedded in the grant itself. They are to "promote the progress of science and the useful arts." There is nothing said about any desire or purpose to secure to the author or inventor his "natural right to his property." The monopoly given to him is avowedly given, not primarily for his benefit, but for the benefit of society at large. The claims made so often, especially in recent years, that the author or inventor has a natural right to the exclusive use of his production, and is therefore entitled, as of course, to legislation securing to him the full enjoyment of this right, does not seem to have been specifically passed upon by the fathers; but one thing is absolutely certain, they did not make this constitutional grant of power upon any such ground. Much confusion of thought has arisen from the assertion of this right as an innate, absolute right existing in the individual, and a contemporaneous neglect to examine the limitation of the power given in the premises to Congress.
>
> It is perhaps safe to say that for the past twenty or thirty years no Committee on patents has had an existence which has not had the fortune to listen to long and very interesting arguments claiming the existence in the author or inventor of this right, and the duty of Congress to give by legislative enactment full and complete enjoyment of that right. Whatever may be the correct conclusion to the existence of any such right, the duty of Congress is measured by its power, and that power can be no broader than the words conferring it.

> . . . It is sufficient to read the words of the grant in their plain every-
> day meaning to discover that the good of society was the only thing
> provided for, or intended to be provided for. . . .[143]

This interpretation would continue to be emphasized by House committees into the twentieth century.[144]

Those who favored the argument that the intellectual property clause
was intended to implement the common law as it applied to property rights
in invention and writings made two basic assumptions, both of which
would ultimately be shown to be invalid. The first was that the common
law applied to the federal system set up by the Constitution. The second
was that there was in fact a common law right in both writings and invention; that is to say, there was a common-law right to both copyrights and
patents. While the common law did establish a right to copyright (or at least
was perceived to do so, which is essentially the same thing), it never before
or during this period held that a right to a patent existed.

Nonetheless, an argument could be—and indeed was—made that the
specific language used in the intellectual property clause, specifically the
term "securing" of necessity compelled a conclusion that the constitutional
language was intended to protect existing property rights in both writings
and invention. Read superficially and without reference to other contemporaneous views expressed by him, Madison's comments in *The
Federalist No. 43* could indeed be taken as supporting this view. But when
the issue was presented to the Supreme Court in 1834, it chose to interpret
the meaning given to "securing" in quite a different light, namely, as
merely a grant of authority to Congress to create a right.

In 1890 in his magisterial patent treatise William Robinson ignored
both this Supreme Court interpretation and the fact that the common law
had never established a right to a patent. Instead, he argued:

> The disposition to regard the rights and remedies of inventors as resting
> entirely upon the Constitution and the Acts of Congress . . . is . . .
> improper. These rights and remedies were recognized by the common
> law before the [Statute of Monopolies] was enacted. They were
> acknowledged and enforced by the individual states before the adop-
> tion of the Federal Constitution. Our patent acts have always depended
> upon common-law principles for their construction, and until recently

---

143. H.R. REP. NO. 1494, 52d Cong., 1st Sess. (1894).
144. *See, e.g.,* H.R. REP. NO. 2222, 60th Cong., 2d Sess. (1909).

have been uniformly treated as a part of this great body of theoretical and practical jurisprudence.[145]

The majority holding in *Wheaton v. Peters*, which has never been disavowed or modified by the Court in all the subsequent years, is completely at variance with the views expressed by Robinson.[146]

The only authority cited by Robinson for his sweeping generalizations was Story's note *On the Patent Law* provided as an appendix to *Evans v. Eaton* in 1818.[147] That note provides no support for Robinson's view that the rights and remedies of inventors rest on something more than the Constitution and the patent laws. Story makes no mention whatever of any common-law right prior to the Statute of Monopolies, but instead limits himself to the "principles and usages" that have grown out of that Statute. Nor does Story say a word about what the individual states did with respect to the issuance of patents before the Constitution was adopted.

Moreover, there is no historical record of any sort that suggests that the states in issuing patents were in effect acknowledging a common-law right of inventors. Nor is there any historical record to indicate that any state actually made any attempt to enforce (judicially or otherwise) patent rights granted by it prior to the adoption of the Constitution.[148] Even more to the point is the total irrelevance of such action, had it occurred, to the issue addressed by Robinson, namely, whether the Constitution and the federal patent laws are controlling as to the rights and remedies of inventors.

Story did suggest that the patent acts of the United States were founded "in a great degree" on the customs and usages that had grown out of the Statute of Monopolies and that accordingly the English cases might be useful to illustrate the corresponding provisions of the United States law.[149] He did *not* indicate that the American "patent acts have always depended upon common-law principles for their construction" as stated by Robinson, and indeed as is shown in Chapter Eight this statement is patently[150] false. Nor did he suggest that the American patent laws were a

---

145. WILLIAM C. ROBINSON, 1 THE LAW OF PATENTS FOR USEFUL INVENTIONS at 15 (Boston 1890).
146. *See supra* text accompanying notes 132–135.
147. *See supra* note 44 and text accompanying notes 44 and 45.
148. For a discussion of the state patent custom prior to the adoption of the Constitution, see BUGBEE, *supra* note 67, at 84–103; Edward C. Walterscheid, *The Early Evolution of the U.S. Patent Law: Antecedents (5, Part II)*, 78 J. PAT. (& TRADEMARK) OFF. SOC'Y 665–85 (1996).
149. *See supra* text accompanying note 45.
150. Pun at least partially intended.

part of the common law. Indeed, no judicial or legislative pronouncement to this effect during the nineteenth century has been found.

To this day there are those who argue that the intellectual property clause protects certain inherent rights of authors and inventors rather than merely giving the Congress power to create exclusive rights for a limited period of time.[151] They almost invariably cite Madison's commentary in *The Federalist No. 43* and ignore the Supreme Court opinion in *Wheaton v. Peters*.[152] Their interpretation of Madison is perhaps not surprising, for the dissent in *Wheaton v. Peters* interpreted him similarly,[153] but their historical objectivity is open to question when they fail to look at Madison's commentary in the light of his other correspondence at the time and also fail to acknowledge that the Supreme Court, when given the opportunity, refused to interpret the intellectual property clause as protecting any existing right under the common law in either authors or inventors.[154]

It is of interest to note the views expressed for the Court by Justice Stewart in 1972: "Property interests . . . are not created by the Constitution. Rather, they are created and their dimensions are defined by existing rules or understanding that stem from an independent source. . . ."[155] Thus the exclusive rights embodied in patents and copyrights are created and defined by federal statutes authorized by the intellectual property clause rather than by the clause itself. In the absence of the federal statutes, they are simply inchoate rights.

---

151. *See, e.g.,* the commentators in note 67 *supra. Cf.* J. B. Gambrell, *The Constitution and the In Personam Defense of First Invention,* 39 J. PAT. OFF. SOC'Y 791, 804–05 (1957) ("[a]t most, in the United States, the courts have held that an inventor holds an 'inchoate right' of property in his invention which is perfected by the issuance of a patent"); Edward S. Irons & Mary Helen Sears, *The Constitutional Standard of Invention—The Touchstone of Patent Reform,* 1973 UTAH L. REV. 653, 670 ("[o]n its face this theory of a 'natural property right in ideas' has little logic").

152. *See, e.g.,* R. A. CHOATE, ET AL., CASES AND MATERIALS ON PATENT LAW at 70 (3d ed. St. Paul 1987) ("[d]oes an inventor have a right to his invention at common law? Madison . . . and perhaps the Federal Constitution itself, imply that this right exists").

153. 33 U.S. at 685 (Thompson, J., dissenting).

154. Prager, for example, dismisses *Wheaton v. Peters* with the casual statement that the opinion therein was issued "without adequate historic analysis and with questionable legal arguments." *See* Prager, *supra* note 5, at 319.

155. Board of Regents v. Roth, 408 U.S. 564, 577 (1972).

CHAPTER SEVEN
THE NATURE OF THE EXCLUSIVE RIGHT

The intellectual property clause authorizes Congress to create an exclusive right for limited times with respect to two distinct forms of property, patents and copyrights. In each instance, the exclusive right is for quite a different form of intangible property, one involving the creation of a useful embodiment of an idea and the other involving the form of expression of an idea. Because the intangible property rights thus authorized were deemed to be monopolies,[1] the clause prohibits the creation of perpetual rights in this property. Whether these intangible property rights are to be actually treated as monopolies has been a subject of ongoing dispute to the present day. This, in turn, has influenced the interpretation that has been given to the phrase "for limited times" in the clause, although Congress has not been disposed to view the clause as placing any particular limitation on the term of either patents or copyrights, other than that the term must be finite. Here we explore the meaning of the phrases "the exclusive right" and "for limited times." I suggest that "for limited times" must be read in the context of the overall language of the clause and not in isolation.[2]

A. A Deliberate Singularity

A peculiarity of the intellectual property clause is that the provision authorizing patents and copyrights speaks in the plural with but one exception. Thus, this provision is phrased in terms of "authors," "inventors," "writings," "discoveries," and "limited times," but rather than "exclusive rights" it speaks of "the exclusive right." Was the use of the singular in this regard deliberate or inadvertent? Taken literally the use of the singular with regard to the right granted seems to suggest that the exclusive right granted with regard to both patents and copyrights is the same right with no distinction between the two forms of intangible property.

---

1. *See* note 11 *infra*.
2. But as is seen in Part E *infra* there are courts and commentators that dispute such a view.

Although the Framers in their subsequent correspondence and documentation seem never to have addressed the point, contemporaneous evidence in the form of the final draft of the Constitution itself indicates that the use of the singular "the exclusive right" was deliberate. That evidence is found in the fact that in the final draft the intellectual property clause shows a correction changing "a limited time" to read "limited times." I have earlier indicated that the change was made to correct an error and render the final language consistent with that which had been earlier approved.[3] The change of "a limited time" to "limited times" in the final draft with retention of "the exclusive right" instead of a change to "exclusive rights" is indicative that the singular usage in this particular instance was deliberate, for if it had been inadvertent or in error there is no reason to suppose that it would not have been corrected in the same manner that "a limited time" was changed to "limited times."

Nonetheless there is no apparent reason in the clause itself why it should confer an authority to create an "exclusive right" (in the singular) "for limited times" (in the plural). As Pollack notes, "the modern notion of parallelism suggests that 'right' should have been 'rights.'"[4] And indeed that is the way that some commentators and courts have interpreted the language.[5] But the difficulty with this approach is the application of "modern notion[s]" to language drafted more than two centuries ago, for in 1787 there was indeed a good reason for using the singular rather than the plural. That reason had to do with the dichotomy in existing British treatment of patents and copyrights at the time the Constitution was drafted.

Recall that under the British practice patents conferred a privilege rather than a property right protected by common law. Patents were a creature of the royal prerogative, and the privilege could be given or taken

---

3. *See supra* Chapter Three, note 114 and accompanying text.
4. Malla Pollack, *Unconstitutional Incontestability? The Intersection of the Intellectual Property and Commerce Clauses of the Constitution: Beyond a Critique of Shakespeare Co. v. Silstar Corp.*, 18 SEATTLE U. L. REV. 259, 286 (1995).
5. For example, that is the way Pollack has subsequently interpreted it. *See* Malla Pollack, *The Right to Know?: Delimiting Database Protection at the Juncture of the Commerce Clause, the Intellectual Property Clause, and the First Amendment,* 17 CARDOZO ARTS & ENT. L.J. 47, 60 (1999) ("the Clause discusses 'exclusive rights' of 'authors' and 'inventors' in 'writings' and 'discoveries'"). *See also* Paul J. Heald & Suzanna Sherry, *Implied Limits on the Legislative Power: The Intellectual Property Clause as an Absolute Constraint on Congress,* 2000 ILL. L. REV. 1119, 1195 ("[w]e have previously noted the ambiguity inherent in the term 'exclusive rights' in the Intellectual Property Clause").

away at the discretion of the crown.[6] Copyrights, however, were viewed at the very least as a statutory right if not a common law right.[7] But at the time the Constitution was drafted strong arguments had appeared in England that there was no logical distinction between literary work and inventions, in that both involved the use of the mental faculty, and the ideas from both should result in similar limited-term property rights.[8] Because they accepted this view, the Framers saw fit to combine the patent authority and the copyright authority in the same clause and to use the singular "the exclusive right" to ensure that no such dichotomy as existed in Great Britain would come into being in the United States.[9]

B. A Question of Monopoly

The issue of monopoly is intimately intertwined with the interpretations that have been given to "the exclusive right" and "for limited times." This may seem surprising in that no American copyright or patent statute has ever made any reference to monopoly. Nonetheless, the "exclusive" or "sole" rights granted by these statutes would rather quickly come to be referred to as monopoly rights. Although not limited to patents per se, the question of monopoly rights has been more frequently addressed in the context of patents rather than has copyrights.

The Constitution contains no prohibition against monopolies. The lack of an express prohibition was a matter of concern during the ratification process.[10] Nonetheless, a majority of the Framers appear to have assumed that in the absence of an expressly enumerated power to do so, Congress would have no authority to issue or grant monopolies. Indeed, it was for this very reason that they deemed it necessary to expressly grant Congress

---

6. *See supra* Chapter Two, note 91 and accompanying text.
7. *See supra* Chapter Two, text accompanying note 164.
8. *See supra* Chapter Two, text accompanying notes 164–169.
9. While they were successful in this respect, they were much less successful in assuring that "the exclusive right," however defined, would be similar for both patents and copyrights. Nowhere is this more apparent than in the disparity that has arisen between the length of the patent term and that of copyright. *See* Part E *infra*.
10. Jefferson viewed the lack of such a prohibition as a significant defect in the Constitution as did George Mason, a Framer who cited the lack as one of the reasons for his refusal to sign the Constitution. Several of the ratifying conventions thought that it should be amended to add such an express prohibition. *See supra* Chapter One, Parts B and C.

authority in the intellectual property clause with regard to patents and copyrights. They clearly viewed these limited-term grants as monopolies, albeit of a desirable and acceptable type.[11] Nonetheless, there would soon be fierce arguments—which have continued to this day—as to whether "the exclusive right" authorized by the intellectual property clause in both patent and copyright results in monopoly. Those who argued patents and copyrights to be monopolies tended to favor a more restrictive interpretation of the patent and copyright laws,[12] while those who contended that they were not monopolies generally did so for the purpose of advocating a more liberal interpretation of those laws. Those who argued that they were monopolies tended to favor the view that the patent and copyright laws were intended to be in the public interest whereas those who avoided the use of the term "monopoly" generally argued that an important purpose of these laws was to reward inventors and authors for their efforts.

The Statute of Monopolies[13] enacted in 1623 may be the best known of all the legislative enactments of Parliament. It certainly is among the longest running. It purported to ban all monopolies (with a number of exceptions including patents for invention) "for the sole buying, selling, making,

---

11. The exchange of correspondence between Madison and Jefferson shortly after the Constitution had been drafted renders abundantly clear that patents and copyrights were contemporaneously viewed as monopolies. *See supra* Chapter One, Part B. *Cf.* Dreyfuss' view that "[a]t the time of the Constitutional Convention, exclusive rights were not conflated with the notion of monopoly because theorists understood monopolies as privatizing matter already in use by the public while exclusive rights were for new developed material." *See* Rochelle Cooper Dreyfuss, *A Wiseguy's Approach to Information Products: Muscling Copyright and Patent into a Unitary Theory of Intellectual Property*, 1992 Sup. Ct. Rev. 195, 231. It was not what theorists such as Lord Coke thought or supposedly understood, but rather what was understood by the public at large and the Framers in particular. They understood or perceived patents and copyrights to be monopolies.

12. A classic example of this point of view occurred in one of the earliest Attorney General's Opinions concerning patents. In 1802, Attorney General Levi Lincoln declared that "[t]he [patent] privilege is a monopoly in derogation of common right, and, as it is not, ought not to be extended to foreigners." 1 Ops. Atty. Gen. 110 (May 26, 1802).

13. 21 James I, c.3, VII Statutes at Large 255. The Statute is reproduced in H. G. Fox, Monopolies: A Study of the History and Future of the Patent Monopoly at 339–43 (Toronto 1947); A. W. Deller, 1 Walker on Patents at 18–21 (Deller's ed., New York 1937).

working, or using of anything within the realm."[14] Although it exempted printing patents from its coverage, it said nothing about copyrights.[15]

The Statute as enacted inadvertently created a touchy legal point, which Lord Coke in his subsequent analysis did nothing to dispel.[16] Section 2 of the Statute provided that the validity of any monopoly should be determined in accordance with common law. Section 6, however, stated that "any declaration before mentioned shall not extend to" patents of invention meeting the requirements set forth therein.[17] Did this mean that the declaration of Section 2 did not apply to patents of invention? And if it did not apply, were patents of invention monopolies as that term was used in Section 1? It was with regard to this latter question that Coke clouded the issue by his definition of monopoly.

In his Institutes of the Laws of England, Coke states that in the Statute Parliament adjudged monopolies to be against the ancient and fundamental law of the kingdom,[18] and accordingly it is necessary to define what a monopoly is. Being nothing remiss, he promptly proceeded to supply a definition, to wit, "[a] monopoly is an institution or allowance by the king by his grant, commission, or otherwise to any person or persons, bodies politic or corporate, of or for the sole buying, selling, making, working, or using of any thing, whereby any person or persons, bodies politic or corporate, are sought to be restrained of any freedom *that they had before*, or hindered in their lawful trade.[19] It would be the emphasized

---

14. *See supra* Chapter Two, text following note 67. For the background of the Statute and its relationship to the development of the patent law, see Edward C. Walterscheid, *The Early Evolution of the United States Patent Law: Antecedents (Part 2),* 76 J. PAT. & TRADEMARK OFF. SOC'Y 849 (1994).

15. The concept of copyright had yet to be fully developed and the Statute of Anne was more than 85 years in the future. *See supra* Chapter Two, text accompanying notes 103–121.

16. A contemporaneous exposition of the Statute was given by Lord Coke soon after it was enacted. *See* EDWARD COKE, 3 INSTITUTES OF THE LAWS OF ENGLAND (London 1644). Coke was a major participant in the development of the law relating to monopolies in the first quarter of the seventeenth century. *See* CHRISTINE MACLEOD, INVENTING THE INDUSTRIAL REVOLUTION, THE ENGLISH PATENT SYSTEM, 1660–1800, at 18 (Cambridge 1988).

17. *See supra* Chapter Two, text preceding note 68.

18. I have elsewhere questioned this statement by Coke and argued that there is nothing in the Statute which specifically so states or even infers. *See* Walterscheid, *supra* note 14, at 875.

19. COKE, *supra* note 16, at 181 (emphasis supplied).

language that down to modern times has resulted in learned and exhaustive argument as to whether a patent of invention is a monopoly.[20]

Rich makes several interesting points concerning patents and the Statute of Monopolies as well as Coke's definition of monopoly. First of all, he notes that the Statute does not declare that patents for inventions are not monopolies, but rather merely exempts them from the general ban on monopolies set forth. Secondly, he emphasizes that Coke's definition was so phrased "as to include illegal monopolies and exclude lawful monopolies."[21] If that was indeed what Coke intended, his definition seemed to emphasize the point by suggesting that patents and copyrights were not literally monopolies, because they did not take away or restrain "any freedom or liberty" previously held.

Be that as it may, the common-law court opinions in the late eighteenth century which addressed patent issues made no reference to Coke's definition but instead referred to patents as monopolies.[22] It is thus somewhat surprising that the earliest United States patent cases made no reference to patents as monopolies.[23] The first published federal case to do so was decided in 1820, and there is another such reference in 1821.[24] State

---

20. *See, e.g.,* WILLIAM C. ROBINSON, 1 THE LAW OF PATENTS FOR USEFUL INVENTIONS at 16–67 (Boston 1890); Deller, *supra* note 13, at 22–28; Giles S. Rich, *The Relationship Between Patent Practices and the Anti-Monopoly Laws,* 24 J. PAT. OFF. SOC'Y 85 (1942).
21. Rich, *supra* note 20, at 94–95.
22. *See, e.g.,* Liardet v. Johnson, 1 Web. 53, 54 (1778) ("[t]he law relative to patents requires, as a price the individual should pay the people for his monopoly . . . "); Rex v. Arkwright, 1 Web. 64, 66 (1785) ("[i]t is clearly settled at law that a man, to entitle himself to the benefit of a patent for a monopoly, must disclose his secret . . . "); Turner v. Winter, 1 Web. 77, 80 (1787) ("[a]s every patent is calculated to give a monopoly to the patentee . . . ").
23. One of the earliest discussion of patents in the context of monopoly occurs in the New York state case of Livingston v. Van Ingen, 9 Johns. R. 53 (N.Y. 1812).
24. Kneass v. Schuylkill Bank, 14 F. Cas. 746, 749 (C.C.D. Pa. 1820) (No. 7,875) ("[w]ithout the specification, there would, in most cases be a total failure of the consideration for which the monopoly is granted"); McGaw v. Bryan, 16 Fed Cas. 96, 97 (S.D.N.Y. 1821) (Case No. 8,793) ("[b]ut in consequence of the fundamental differences in the principle of the English and American patent law, and of the still wider difference in the manner of granting these exclusive rights or monopolies . . . ").

courts also started to refer to patents as monopolies during this period.[25] In 1822 a federal judge actually quoted Coke's definition of monopoly, but still referred to patents as monopolies.[26]

The earliest United States patent treatise by Thomas G. Fessenden, first published in 1810 and in a second edition in 1822, refers to "patent monopolies" while at the same time quoting Coke's definition of monopoly.[27] Fessenden makes no attempt to use Coke's definition to suggest that a patent is not literally a monopoly within that definition. The second United States patent treatise, published in 1837 by Willard Phillips, makes no reference to Coke's definition, but instead simply states that a patent "is a monopoly of the invention."[28]

As the nineteenth century progressed, the lower courts would have some difficulty in deciding whether to treat a patent as a monopoly or not. Increasingly, judges would argue that patents should be liberally construed, which seemed inconsistent with the view that a patent is a monopoly. Thus, Robinson in 1890 suggested that in the earliest case to discuss this issue in any detail, *Whitney v. Emmett* decided in 1831,[29]

> the court adopted . . . three fundamental principles, which have been followed in all subsequent decision [to 1890]: (1) That a patent creates a contract between the inventor and the public, and that each party is bound to exercise good faith toward the other; (2) That a patent is not granted to an inventor as a favor, but as a matter of right on his complying with the conditions prescribed by law; (3) That being intended for his benefit, both the patent and the law are to be construed in favor of the patentee.[30]

25. *See, e.g.,* Stearns v. Barrett, 1 Pick 443, 18 Mass. 443, 450 (Mass. 1823) ("[b]eing the inventors of these machines, the parties may obtain valid patents for them; or, without thus securing a monopoly, they might reasonably expect to enjoy it in fact by means of their superior skill").
26. Thompson v. Haight, 23 F. Cas. 1039, 1043 (D.C.S.D.N.Y. 1822) (No. 13,957).
27. THOMAS G. FESSENDEN, AN ESSAY ON THE LAW OF PATENTS FOR NEW INVENTIONS at 42–43 (Boston 1810).
28. WILLARD PHILLIPS, THE LAW OF PATENTS FOR INVENTIONS at 2 (Boston 1837).
29. 29 F. Cas. 1074 (D. E. Pa. 1831) (No. 17,585).
30. ROBINSON, *supra* note 20, at 31.

Two years later, in *Ames v. Howard*, Circuit Justice Story made the last point even more specifically, saying:

> Patents for inventions are not to be treated as mere monopolies, odious in the eyes of the law and therefore not to be favored; nor are they to be construed with the utmost vigor, as *strictissimi juris*. . . . [I]t has always been the course of the American courts . . . to construe these patents fairly and liberally, and not to subject them to any overly-nice and critical refinements.[31]

Story considerably overstated his point in the last quoted sentence, because early on American courts had indeed subjected patents to "overly-nice and critical refinements" in finding them invalid.[32]

Nonetheless, the lower courts would increasingly seek to argue that a patent is not a monopoly because it does not take away from the public that which it had before.[33] This, of course, is the essence of Lord Coke's definition, although that definition typically was not mentioned at all.

What appears to be the earliest reference to monopoly in a Supreme Court opinion concerning the patent right occurs in *Pennock v. Dialogue* in

---

31. 1 F. Cas. 755, 756 (C.C.D. Mass. 1833) (No. 326).
32. *See, e.g.,* Evans v. Chambers, 8 F. Cas. 837 (C.C.D. Pa. 1807) (No. 4,555).
33. *See, e.g.,* Brooks v. Jenkins, 4 F. Cas. 275, 277 (C.C.D. Ohio 1844) (No. 1,953) ("[t]his law gives a monopoly, but not in an odious sense. It takes nothing from the community at large, but secures to them the greatest benefits"); Parker v. Haworth, 18 F. Cas. 1135, 1136 (C.C.D. Ill. 1848) (No. 10,738) ("[i]t is not a monopoly the inventor receives. Instead of taking anything away from the public, he confers on it the greatest benefits"); Bloomer v. Stolley, 3 F. Cas. 729, 731 (C.C.D. Ohio) 1850) (No. 1,559) ("[i]t is said that monopolies are odious; but a patent right, that shall compensate the inventor, is not a monopoly in the general sense of that term. The inventor takes nothing from society").

1829.[34] This was followed a few years later by another such reference in *Shaw v. Cooper*.[35] But it was in *Wilson v. Rousseau*,[36] decided in 1846, that Justice Nelson, speaking for the majority, repeatedly referred to the exclusive right granted by a patent as a monopoly.[37] Justice Woodbury, in dissent, took a different view, namely, that rather than being an "odious monopolist" a patentee is simply seeking to protect a right in his own property.[38] Nonetheless, in the next few years, in *Gayler v. Wilder*[39] and *Bloomer v. McQuewan*,[40] Chief Justice Taney, speaking for the Court,

---

34. Therein Justice Story stated for the Court:

> If an inventor should be permitted to hold back from the knowledge of the public the secrets of his invention; if he should for a long period of years retain the monopoly, and make, and sell his invention publicly, and thus gather the whole profits of it, rely upon his superior skill and knowledge of the structure; and then, and then only, when the danger of competition should force him to secure the exclusive right, he should be allowed to take out a patent, and thus exclude the public from any farther use than what should be derived under it during his fourteen years; it would materially retard the progress of science and the useful arts, and give a premium to those who should be least prompt to communicate their discoveries.

> 27 U.S. (2 Pet.) 1, 19 (1829).

35. 32 U.S. (7 Pet.) 292, 320 (1833) ("it would be extremely impolitic to retard or embarrass this advance, by withdrawing from the public any useful invention or art, and making it a subject of a private monopoly").
36. 45 U.S. (4 How.) 646 (1846).
37. *See, e.g.,* 45 U.S. at 681–82.
38. As he put it:

> While other countries, and Congress, and our own State courts are adopting a more liberal course yearly towards such public benefactors as inventions [inventors], I should regret to see this high tribunal pursue a kind of construction open to imputation of an opposite character, or be supposed by anyone to evince a feeling towards patentees which belongs to other ages than this (and which I am satisfied is not cherished), as if patentees were odious monopolists of the property and labor of others, when in truth they are only asking to be protected in the enjoyment and sale of their own—as truly their own as the wheat grown by the farmer, or the wagon built by the mechanic.

> 45 U.S. at 708.

39. 51 U.S. 477 (1850).
40. 55 U.S. 539 (1852).

referred to the patent right as a monopoly.[41] Again in 1858 and 1863, the Court referred to the patent right as a monopoly.[42]

But in 1863 and again in 1870 Justice Clifford, speaking for the Court, took a very different tack. He argued that patents were "not to be treated as mere monopolies, and therefore odious in the eyes of the law."[43] Rather, they were to be regarded

> as public franchises granted to inventors of new and useful improvements for the purpose of securing to them, as such inventors, for the limited term therein mentioned, the exclusive right and liberty to make and use and vend to others to be used, their own inventions, as tending to promote the progress of science and the useful arts, for their labor, toil and expense in making the inventions, and reducing the same to practice for the public benefit, as contemplated by the Constitution and sanctioned by the laws of Congress.[44]

If a patent was considered no longer to be a monopoly, did this imply that the Court would now treat patents significantly differently than it had in the past fifty-five years? The answer was, not really, at least in the near term. The argument that a patent should not be treated as a monopoly was advanced by George Ticknor Curtis in his patent treatise first published in 1849 and in succeeding editions in 1854, 1867, and 1873.[45] Regardless of whether a patent was called a monopoly or something else, for much of the nineteenth century neither the courts nor the Congress nor the Patent Office as a practical matter treated patents as monopolies in the pejorative sense, i.e., as "odious."

But as William Robinson would point out in his massive patent treatise published in 1890, "[t]he question whether a patent privilege is a monopoly is not merely a question of words."[46] Contrary to the views expressed by Curtis and in many judicial opinions, Robinson believed that patents were indeed monopolies, albeit desirable ones, and he devoted some fifty

---

41. *See* 51 U.S. at 493; 55 U.S. at 548.
42. Kendall v. Winsor, 62 U.S. 322 (1858); Burr v. Duryee, 68 U.S. 531 (1863).
43. Turril v. Michigan S. &c., R.R. Co., 68 U.S. 491, 17 L. Ed. 668, 672 (1863). *See also* Seymour v. Osborne, 78 U.S. 516, 20 L. Ed. 33, 35 (1870).
44. 20 L. Ed. at 35.
45. GEORGE TICKNOR CURTIS, A TREATISE ON THE LAW OF PATENTS FOR USEFUL INVENTIONS, AS ENACTED AND ADMINISTERED IN THE UNITED STATES OF AMERICA at xix (Boston 1849) ("[a] patent for a useful invention is not, under our law, or the law of England, a grant of a monopoly in the sense of the old common law").
46. ROBINSON, *supra* note 20, at 18.

pages to a discussion of the relevance of such a view. His analysis is worth repeating in some detail here. He began by noting that:

> In legislative bodies, which recognize a patent right as a monopoly, the interests of the public will naturally be preferred to those of the inventor; legislation on the subject will be cautious and conservative; and the powers conferred upon the patentee will be subordinated to the free enjoyment by all other citizens of every privilege that is not inconsistent with the protection to which his inventive skill and genius are entitled. In courts where the same theory prevails such rules will be followed as tend to limit the monopoly of the inventor to the exact letter of his grant, and hold him to a strict compliance with all its conditions as an essential requisite to its validity.[47]

But if a patent is not treated as a monopoly, it is considered favorably by the law, with the following consequences:

> Being intended principally, if not entirely, for the benefit of the grantee, and conflicting with no public interest either actual or possible, the law construes it liberally in order to secure to the grantee all the advantage which the grantor might have proposed to bestow upon him. And hence, where legislatures and the courts adopt this theory of the exclusive privilege created by a patent, and lose sight of its true character as a monopoly, legislative acts in favor of the inventor will be sweeping and extravagant, and the decisions of the courts will sustain him in claims which seriously abridge the rights of others, and will afford him a protection and redress far beyond that which justice and the public interest demand.[48]

Although using extravagant language, Robinson made clear that whether a patent was actually treated as a monopoly, as opposed to simply being called one, depended in no small measure whether the intent of the grant was perceived to be primarily for the benefit of the public or primarily for the benefit of the patentee.[49] What was true with regard to patents was also true regarding the treatment of copyrights.

Although Robinson makes no mention of it, William Thornton, who served as Superintendent of Patents from 1802 until his death in 1828,

---

47. *Id.* at 19–20.
48. *Id.* at 20.
49. As Robinson put it: "That the purpose of the patent law is to benefit the inventor is one principle. That the purpose of the law is to secure to the public the advantages of the invention by compensating the inventor for its disclosure, is an entirely different principle." *Id.* at 33.

strongly believed that the primary purpose of the patent system was to reward inventors.[50] Although he may have done so, I have been unable to find any instance wherein Thornton referred to a patent as a monopoly. Rather, he clearly perceived a patent to be a reward to the proper inventor, as his administrative approach to patents amply demonstrated. It was Thornton who first created the administrative practice of reissuing patents to correct defects therein even though there was no statutory basis for so doing.[51]

Thornton's approach to reissuing patents first received judicial sanction in 1824 in *Morris v. Huntington.*[52] While acknowledging that there was nothing whatever in the existing patent statutes which authorized reissues, nonetheless the Supreme Court in 1832 in *Grant v. Raymond* stated that the issue must be decided on whether such practice was within "the general spirit and object of the law."[53] It held that reissues were based on well-settled administrative practice, were not contrary to law, and that such administrative practice "is required by justice and good faith."[54] That same year Congress specifically authorized reissues in the Patent Act of 1832.[55]

Robinson argued that reissues were a departure from the view that patents were monopolies.[56] He also stated that the "marked regard for the welfare of the patentee" by Congress exhibited in various patent statutes was also a departure from such a view.[57] In particular, Congress departed from such a view when it "freely exercised its powers of granting to patentees an extension of the period of their monopoly, at first by special acts and later under general laws, until the act of 1861 which prohibited extensions and increased the ordinary period to seventeen years."[58] In Robinson's view,

> the development of the theory that an inventor is necessarily a public benefactor, and that the means adopted for his protection and encouragement are in themselves promotive of the public good . . . has

---

50. *See supra* Chapter Four, text accompanying notes 88–90.
51. *See* EDWARD C. WALTERSCHEID, TO PROMOTE THE PROGRESS OF USEFUL ARTS: AMERICAN PATENT LAW AND ADMINISTRATION, 1787–1836, at 265–67 (1998).
52. 17 F. Cas. 818 (C.C.D. N.Y. 1824) (No. 9,831).
53. 31 U.S. (6 Pet.) 218, 241 (1832).
54. 31 U.S. at 244.
55. Act of July 3, 1832, § 3, 4 Stat. 559.
56. ROBINSON, *supra* note 20, at 33.
57. *Id.* at 34.
58. *Id.* at 36.

produced its legitimate results in the constant increase of his exclusive privileges and the corresponding limitation of the public rights.[59]

Robinson set forth his premise succinctly, namely, "that a patent privilege is a true monopoly, but that it approaches very nearly to an odious monopoly in its restriction of the pre-existing public right."[60] Implicit in this statement is the view that a patent is indeed a monopoly as defined by Lord Coke in that it does in fact restrict or limit that which the public had before. Robinson's premise was that in the absence of some defined property right set by society an idea once communicated to the public is freely available for use by the public, and an inventor has no right or power to restrain its use by the public.[61] By granting a right or power to restrain the use of an invention by the public, a patent, Robinson contended,

> is a true restriction of pre-existing public rights. It may not, and ordinarily it does not, take away from the people the actual enjoyment of any benefit which they already had in their possession, but it does prohibit their immediate exercise of that perpetual and natural right by virtue of which every new discovery, when openly practised or proclaimed, becomes at once the possession and property of all.[62]

While patents are granted to stimulate inventive activity and to reward inventors, "[t]he duty which the state owes to the people to obtain for them, at the earliest moment, the practical use of every valuable invention in the industrial arts is, however, a higher and more imperative duty than any which it owes to the inventor."[63]

---

59. *Id.*
60. *Id.* at 37.
61. *Id.* at 38. Although Robinson made no reference to him, Thomas Jefferson had articulated and persuasively argued much the same point in 1813. *See supra* Chapter Six, note 120 and accompanying text.
62. ROBINSON, *supra* note 20, at 42–43.
63. *Id.* at 57. In other words, the term of a patent is—and should be—constitutionally limited to that required to actually "promote the progress of . . . useful arts," and there is no proper basis for making it any longer. A modern commentator, Carolyn Cooper, makes the same point, saying:

> From the point of view of a society intending to encourage invention by rewarding inventors, it is important that the reward be sufficient for such encouragement, but not excessive. It is also important that particular inventions not disappear, but become part of society's available stock of technology. Thus, the optimal social system to satisfy these criteria is one that holds the maximum credible prospect of reward to a potential inventor, in order to induce that person to make an invention and to share

He concluded "[t]hat the patent privilege is a true monopoly, granted in derogation of the common right," but that it is nonetheless appropriate, "because, upon the whole, it is conducive to the public good."[64] Writing a half century after Robinson, Rich found Robinson's views in this regard to be "sound."[65] He emphasized, however, that the argument as to whether a patent is or is not a monopoly had now extended well into the twentieth century. In particular, he pointed to statements in the 1937 edition of Walker on Patents that "A patent is not a monopoly" and "an inventor is not a monopolist, but a public benefactor."[66] He also noted that on one occasion in 1933 the Supreme Court appeared to follow Lord Coke's definition of monopoly[67] when Justice Roberts for the Court stated:

> Though often so characterized a patent is not, accurately speaking, a monopoly, for it is not created by the executive authority at the expense and to the prejudice of the community except the grantee of the patent. ... The term monopoly connotes the giving of an exclusive privilege

---

it with society, but one that then gives the inventor the minimum actual reward consistent with continued credibility.

See CAROLYN C. COOPER, SHAPING INVENTION, THOMAS BLANCHARD'S MACHINERY AND PATENT MANAGEMENT IN NINETEENTH-CENTURY AMERICA at 29–30 (New York 1991). Her view that the purpose of the patent system is to encourage invention is one that was prevalent in first half of the nineteenth century, but one which has been largely discredited today. Nonetheless, her point that the patent system ought to give "the inventor the minimum actual reward consistent with continued credibility" is a valid one. The length of the patent term is certainly a critical factor in making this determination.

64. *Id.* at 67.
65. Rich, *supra* note 20, at 90. Rich would later amplify why he believed it necessary to declare a patent a monopoly:

> It is essential to keep in the forefront of our thinking the fact that a patent is a monopoly because its only value as an incentive depends upon securing to the owner monopoly power over the invention. That is the only thing that gives the possibility of profit. The economic power of monopoly is the mainspring of the patent system, a system whose ultimate purpose is the public good. Weaken or destroy the monopoly and you weaken or destroy the system.

Giles S. Rich, *Infringement Under Section 271 of the Patent Act of 1952*, 35 J. PAT. OFF. SOC'Y 476, 479 (1953).
66. Rich, *supra* note 20, at 91.
67. Although it cited the definition of "monopoly" found in *Webster's New International Dictionary.*

for buying, selling, working or using a thing which the public freely enjoyed prior to the grant. Thus a monopoly takes something from the people. An inventor deprives the public of nothing which it enjoyed before his discovery, but gives something of value to the community by adding to the sum of human knowledge.[68]

With this exception, however, during the twentieth century the Court routinely and regularly described patents as monopolies.[69]

Even so, in 1978 the Sixth Circuit suggested that "[t]he loose application of the pejorative term 'monopoly' to the property right of exclusion represented by a patent, can be misleading. Unchecked, it can also destroy the constitutional and statutory scheme reflected in the patent system."[70] Since then the Federal Circuit has gone further and on several occasions

---

68. United States v. Dubilier Condenser Corp., 289 U.S. 178, 186 (1933).
69. *See, e.g.,* Bement v. National Harrow Co., 186 U.S. 70, 91 (1902) ("[t]he very object of [patent] laws is monopoly"); Continental Paper Bag Co. v. Eastern Paper Bag Co., 210 U.S. 405, 423 (1908) ("language of complete monopoly has been used"); Henry v. A. B. Dick Co., 224 U.S. 1, 27 (1912) ("It is a true monopoly . . . "); Motion Picture Patents Co. v Universal Film Mfg. 243 U.S. 502, 510 (1917) ("monopoly"); Crown Die & Tool Co. v Nye Tool & Mach. Works, 261 U.S. 24, 36–37 (1923) ("[a] patent confers a monopoly"); Morton Salt Co. v. G.S. Suppiger Co., 314 U.S. 488, 492 (1942) ("granted monopoly"); United States v. Univis Lens Co., 316 U.S. 241, 250 (1942) ("limited monopoly"); Precision Instrument Mfg. Co. v. Automotive Maint. Mach. Co., 324 U.S. 806, 816 (1945) ("patent monopolies"); Sears, Roebuck & Co. v. Stiffel Co., 376 U.S. 225, 229–30 (1946) ("patent monopoly"); Transparent-Wrap Mach. Corp. v. Stokes & Smith Co., 329 U.S. 488, 492 (1947) ("double monopoly"); Brulotte v. Thys Co., 379 U.S. 29, 32 (1965) ("patent monopoly"); Graham v. John Deere Co., 383 U.S. 1, 6 (1966) ("patent monopoly"); Zenith Radio Corp. v. Hazeltine Research, Inc., 395 U.S. 100, 135 (1969) ("legal monopoly"); Blonder-Tongue Labs, Inc. v. University of Illinois Found., 402 U.S. 313, 343 (1971) ("patent monopoly"); Dann v. Johnston, 425 U.S. 219, 229 (1976) ("patent monopoly"); Bonito Boats, Inc. v. Thunder Craft Boats, Inc., 489 U.S. 141, 146 (1989) ("patent monopolies"); Cardinal Chemical Co. v. Morton Int'l, Inc., 508 U.S. 83, 101 (1993) ("monopoly privileges"); Pfaff v. Wells Electronics, Inc., 525 U.S. 55, 63 (1999) ("exclusive monopolies").
70. Panduit Corp. v. Stahlin Co., 575 F.2d 1152, 1160 (6th Cir. 1978).

instructed counsel not to refer to patents as monopolies.[71] The rationales for such instruction have been:

> (1) the patent statute does not use the word "monopoly"; (2) a patent is just like any other property right which may be used to violate the antitrust laws; (3) the antitrust laws were enacted long after the patent laws and deal with the appropriation of what should belong to others while a valid patent gives the public what it did not earlier have; (4) it is an "obfuscation" to describe a patent as an exception to the general rule against monopolies; and (5) the description of a patentee as a monopolist is pejorative and should be avoided because the term monopoly is used in a different sense in the patent and antitrust laws.[72]

Clearly, the Supreme Court and certain of the federal circuits take differing perspectives on whether a patent should be characterized as a monopoly.

It is interesting to note that although *Wheaton v. Peters*[73] decided in 1834 has been viewed as establishing the principle that copyright is the grant of a limited statutory monopoly,[74] the Supreme Court in that case never mentioned the word "monopoly." The issue of whether a copyright should be construed as a monopoly seems not to have been a topic of concern to the Court, probably because of an assumption that copyrights were indeed monopolies.[75] Through much of the nineteenth century it made no mention of monopoly in its copyright cases. That changed in 1884 when the Court stated that "the monopoly which is granted to [authors] is called a copyright."[76] Since then the Court has periodically referred to copyrights as monopolies.[77]

---

71. *See, e.g.,* Carl Schenek, A.G. v. Norton Corp., 713 F.2d 782, 784 (Fed. Cir. 1983); Union Carbide Corp. v. American Can Co., 724 F.2d 1567, 1574 n.4 (Fed. Cir. 1984); Jamesbury Corp. v. Litton Indus. Prods., Inc., 756 F.2d 1156, 1159 (Fed. Cir. 1985); In re Kaplan, 789 F.2d 1574, 1578 n.3 (Fed. Cir. 1986).
72. Allan A. Littman, *Monopoly, Competition and Other Factors in Determining Patent Infringement Damages,* 38 IDEA 1, 10–11 (1997).
73. 33 U.S. (8 Pet.) 591 (1834).
74. L. RAY PATTERSON & STANLEY W. LINDBERG, THE NATURE OF COPYRIGHT, A LAW OF USER'S RIGHTS at 61–62 (Athens, GA. 1994).
75. Although why the issue of whether patents were to be considered monopolies was an issue thought fit to be addressed by the Court on occasion, but the same issue with respect to copyright seems not to have been raised is unclear.
76. Burrow-Giles Lithographic Co. v. Sarony, 111 U.S. 53, 55 (1884).
77. *See, e.g.,* Holmes v. Hurst, 174 U.S. 82, 85 (1899); Straus v. American Publisher's Ass'n, 231 U.S. 234 (1913); Jewell-La Salle Realty Co. v. Buck, 283 U.S. 202, 204 (1931); Washingtonian Pub. Co. v. Pearson, 306 U.S. 30, 56 (1939); Mazer v. Stein, 347 U.S. 201, 220 (1954); Sony Corp. of Am. v. Universal City

At the beginning of the twentieth century Congress was also perfectly prepared to consider copyrights as monopolies. Thus, the House report accompanying the 1909 Copyright Act noted that in enacting a copyright law Congress must consider "how much will the monopoly granted be detrimental to the public." It emphasized that any such legislation must confer "a benefit upon that public that outweighs the evils of the temporary monopoly."[78] In more recent times congressional reports on copyright legislation have made almost no mention of monopoly.[79] This is perhaps not surprising in view of the major expansion of author's rights under copyright that Congress has authorized in recent years.[80] Although there is an occasional exception,[81] most commentators do not challenge references to copyright as a monopoly.

C. Identifying the Exclusive Right

As with other language of the intellectual property clause, there is no contemporaneous documentation to suggest exactly what the Framers contemplated by the phrase "the exclusive right." Although the clause makes no reference to either patents or copyrights, it has always been treated by both Congress and the courts as the constitutional grant of authority for statutory protection of both forms of intellectual property. On occasion commentators have suggested that the phrase "the exclusive

---

Studios, Inc., 464 U.S. 417, 429 (1984); Harper & Row Publishers, Inc. v. Nation Enters., 471 U.S. 539, 546 (1985); Stewart v. Abend, 495 U.S. 207, 229 (1990); Fogerty v. Fantasy, Inc., 510 U.S. 517, 526 (1994).

78. H.R. REP. NO. 2222, 60th Cong., 2d Sess. (1909), *reproduced in* MELVILLE B. NIMMER & DAVID NIMMER, 8 NIMMER ON COPYRIGHT at App.13-11 [Rel. 34-12/93].

79. One exception is the 1988 reference to a Supreme Court statement that "the monopoly privileges that Congress may confer on creators of intellectual property 'are neither unlimited nor primarily designed to provide a special private benefit.'" *See* H.R. REP. NO. 100-609, 100th Cong., 2d Sess. (1988), reproduced in 9 NIMMER & NIMMER, *supra* note 78, at App. 32-22.

80. Whether one aspect of this expansion, the significant lengthening of the copyright term, exceeds the bounds of the constitutional mandate, is addressed in Part G, *infra*.

81. Whicher, for example, argues that patents are monopolies, but that copyrights are not. *See* John F. Whicher, *The Ghost of Donaldson v. Beckett: An Inquiry Into the Constitutional Distribution of Powers Over the Law of Literary Property in the United States,* 9 BULL. COPYRIGHT SOC'Y 102, 203–14 (1962).

right" is intended to encompass something more than simply the type of exclusivity provided by patents and copyrights. Thus, in 1929 Fenning tentatively concluded that the terms "patents" and "copyrights" were not used in the clause "possibly lest the power be limited to the particular forms . . . at that time known as copyrights and patents."[82] In 1995 Pollack made the point more forcibly, saying: "The only logical conclusion from the Framers' choice to use these words is that they did not want to tie the Clause to the technical meaning of 'patent' and 'copyright.'"[83]

Pollack may be right, but it is more likely that the Framers sought to avoid the political and legal ramifications of the term "patent" under the extant British practice in 1787. At that time a patent was entirely a creature of the crown prerogative, and could be issued or denied solely at the discretion of the crown. Because they wanted to assure that Congress would be authorized to provide an exclusive right as opposed to merely a privilege, and to avoid any connotation of prerogative, they chose to use "the exclusive right" in place of "patents."[84] Moreover, in 1787 the term "patent" in the United States most commonly meant a land grant and not a property right with respect to invention.[85] It was only at the end of the eighteenth century that the meaning of the term was shifting to a precise and technical meaning of "a grant of monopoly power by the state over the commercial exploitation of a new invention."[86]

Be that as it may, in 1979 in *In re Bergy*, Judge Rich declared that "although the Constitution does not mention patents . . . history shows that the authors of the Constitution had patents in mind as the means for securing exclusive rights to inventors." He went on to emphasize that the clause "neither gave to nor preserved in inventors (or authors) any rights . . . but merely empowered Congress, if it elected to do so, to secure to

---

82. Karl Fenning, *The Origin of the Patent and Copyright Clause of the Constitution*, 11 J. PAT. OFF. SOC'Y 438, 445 (1929).
83. Pollack, *supra* note 5, at 290.
84. *See supra* Part A.
85. The term "patent" seems almost never to have been used in either the colonial or the state practice of granting limited-term exclusive rights to inventors prior to the ratification of the Constitution. The colonial grants could not be called patents because to do so would be to usurp the royal prerogative. Perhaps as a holdover from the colonial practice the early state grants before ratification of the Constitution were also almost never called patents. *See* Edward C. Walterscheid, *The Early Evolution of the United States Patent Law: Antecedents (Part 5)*, 78 J. PAT. & TRADEMARK OFF. SOC'Y 615, 616 n.4 (1996).
86. CHRISTINE MACLEOD, INVENTING THE INDUSTRIAL REVOLUTION, THE ENGLISH PATENT SYSTEM, 1660–1800, at 10 (Cambridge 1988).

inventors an 'exclusive right' for an unstated 'limited time' for the stated purpose of promoting useful arts."[87] Judge Rich was only reiterating what the Supreme Court has said a few years earlier with respect to both patents and copyrights, namely that the grant of power is discretionary, and Congress could have declined to exercise it.[88] Because of the discretionary nature of the grant, it has been argued that "[i]nasmuch as Congress manifestly has the power to grant complete or no protection at all, it would seem that it may properly invoke protection somewhere between these two polar positions."[89] It is questionable whether the clause gives Congress authority to grant "complete exclusivity" if by this is taken to mean complete freedom from any form of state regulation.[90]

To the extent that Congress does indeed have broad discretionary power to define the nature of "the exclusive right," the literal language of the clause is such as to suggest that since the right is set forth in the singular, whatever Congress determines it to be must be the same for both patents and copyrights.[91] Moreover, the balanced composition of the clause[92] argues in favor of a generic phrase that encompasses both grants. But it also arguably suggests that "the exclusive right" should properly have read "exclusive rights." There is nothing to suggest that the Framers by using the singular form meant to require that the exclusive right granted by patents and copyrights be literally the same.[93] What they did want to ensure was that however "the exclusive right" was defined, it would indeed be a "right" and not a privilege for both forms of grant rather than merely copyright.

---

87. 596 F.2d 952, 958–59 (C.C.P.A. 1979).
88. Deepsouth Packing Co. v. Laitram Corp., 406 U.S. 518, 530 (1972) ("[t]he direction of Art. I is that *Congress* shall have the power to promote the progress of science and the useful arts. When, as here, the Constitution is permissive, the sign of how far Congress has chosen to go can come only from Congress"). *See also* Goldstein v. California, 412 U.S. 546, 555 (1973).
89. MELVILLE B. NIMMER & DAVID NIMMER, 1 NIMMER ON COPYRIGHT § 1.07 (Rel. 44-12/97).
90. *See, e.g.,* text accompanying notes 107–111 *infra.*
91. I have been unable to find any commentary that specifically addresses this point.
92. *See supra* Chapter Four, Part A.
93. They were fully cognizant of the fact that copyrights were intended to create property in the form of expression of an idea whereas patents were intended to create property in a useful embodiment of an idea, and that these were two quite different concepts.

Despite this, little attempt has been made to analyze what "the exclusive right" as used in the clause actually means.[94] According to Patterson, "there is no question as to its 1787 meaning: the right of authors to publish and vend their writings."[95] He provides no citation of authority for this view[96] and conveniently ignores that the phrase also refers to "the exclusive right" of inventors in their discoveries. The use of the definite article "the" presupposes an intent that the exclusive right, however defined, be similar for both patents and copyrights.[97] If so, that is not how the patent and copyright law has developed.

In the patent context at least, the phrase "the exclusive right" engendered much confusion for more than 160 years.[98] During that period Congress, through statutory enactment, said it meant one thing, and the Supreme Court, beginning in 1852, said it meant something quite different. It was not until 1952 that Congress finally got around to defining "the exclusive right" in the same fashion as the Court.

It is reasonable to suppose that the Framers intended that Congress have power to provide for both patents and copyrights in accordance with the prevailing British practice, albeit with discretion to vary therefrom. The first federal Congress certainly assumed this to be the case for in enacting the first patent and copyright statutes in 1790 it rather closely paralleled this British practice. Thus, the first patent act described the patent grant as "the sole and exclusive right and liberty of making, constructing, using and vending to others to be used the said invention or said discovery."[99] The Act of 1793 repeated this language,[100] as did the Act of 1836.[101] The Act of 1871 modified it somewhat to read "the exclusive right to make, use, and vend the said invention or discovery throughout the United States and the Territories thereof."[102] This language remained in effect until 1952.

---

94. As Patterson puts it, "'the exclusive right' has received little attention." *See* L. Ray Patterson, *Copyright and "the Exclusive Right" of Authors*, 1 J. INTELL. PROP. L. 1, 3 (1993).
95. *Id.*
96. Instead he merely states that "there is abundant evidence for this view." *Id.*
97. Had the intent been otherwise, the Framers could easily have made this clear by using either the plural "exclusive rights" or the singular "an exclusive right."
98. *Cf.* In re Bergy, 596 F.2d 952, 959 n.3 (C.C.P.A. 1979) ("[t]he term 'exclusive right' is one which caused much confusion in thinking throughout much of the early history of patent law . . . ").
99. Act of April 10, 1790 at § 1, 1 Stat. 109.
100. Act of February 21, 1793 at § 1, 1 Stat. 318.
101. Act of July 4, 1836 At § 5, 4 Stat. 577.
102. 16 Stat. 198 at § 22.

According to the first copyright statute in 1790, a copyright gave "the sole right and liberty of printing, reprinting, publishing and vending [the copyrighted work]."[103] This language was repeated in the Act of 1831.[104] It was modified in 1870 to read "the sole liberty of printing, reprinting, publishing, completing, copying, executing, finishing, and vending [the copyrighted work]."[105] This was expanded substantially in 1909 to provide the exclusive right:

(a) To print, reprint, publish, copy, and vend the copyrighted work;

(b) To translate the copyrighted work into other languages or dialects, or make any other version thereof, if it be a literary work; to dramatize it if it be a nondramatic work; to convert it into a novel or other nondramatic work if it be a drama; to arrange or adapt it if it be a musical work; to complete, execute, and finish it if it be a model or design for a work of art;

(c) To deliver, authorize the delivery of, read, or present the copyrighted work in public for profit if it be a lecture, sermon, address or similar production, or other nondramatic literary work; to make or procure the making of any transcription or record thereof by or from which, in whole or in part, it may in any manner or by any method be exhibited, delivered, presented, produced, or reproduced; and to play or perform it in public for profit, and to exhibit, represent, produce, or reproduce it in any manner or by any method whatsoever. . . .

(d) To perform or represent the copyrighted work publicly if it be a drama or, if it be a dramatic work and not reproduced in copies for sale, to vend any manuscript or any record whatsoever thereof; to make or to procure the making of any transcription or record thereof from which, in whole or in part, it may in any manner or by any method be exhibited, performed, represented, produced, or reproduced; and to exhibit, perform, represent, produce, or reproduce it in any manner or by any method whatsoever;

(e) To perform the copyrighted work publicly for profit if it be a musical composition; and for the purpose of public performance for profit, and for the purposes set forth in subsection (a) hereof, to make any arrangement or setting of it or of the melody of it in any system of notation or any form of record in which the thought of an author may be recorded and from which it may be reproduced . . . [and]

---

103. Act of May 31, 1790 at § 1, 1 Stat. 124.
104. Act of February 3, 1831 at § 1, 4 Stat. 36.
105. Act of July 8, 1870 at § 85, 16 Stat. 212.

> (f) To reproduce and distribute to the public for sale or other transfers of ownership, or by rental, lease, or lending, reproductions of the copyrighted work if it be a sound recording. . . .[106]

Whereas the language of the exclusive patent right remained substantially the same until 1952, the language of the exclusive right under copyright became much more expansive, particularly as evidenced by the Act of 1909.

In 1824 Daniel Webster argued before the Supreme Court in *Gibbons v. Ogden*[107] that under the patent and copyright acts then in effect, copyright gives "the same right to the author as the patent grants to the inventor" and that "[i]n both cases, they depend on the same constitutional right." He went on to emphasize that the exclusive right in each instance is not absolute but "only convey[s] a right to prevent others from using or publishing without his [the author or inventor] consent, but not to enable him to use or publish without restraint."[108] Webster was arguing that the exclusive right provided in the intellectual property law did not preempt state control over the right to regulate the use, sale, or publication, as the case might be, of a patented or copyrighted article. His argument would find favor in the Supreme Court[109] in the context of patents but much less so in regard to copyrighted material where First Amendment rights would increasingly be argued to preclude state regulation.[110]

Thus, in 1878 the Court held that the federal patent law does not grant an absolute right to sell a patented material and that states for purposes of protecting the health and safety of their citizens may properly regulate and in appropriate instances preclude the sale of patented materials for certain purposes deemed harmful by the state.[111] This certainly was evidence of a limitation on any absolute right to sell, make, use or vend the patented invention, but a quarter century earlier in 1852 the Court had issued an even more remarkable holding, namely, that the patent grant was not at all

---

106. Act of July 1, 1909, 35 Stat. 1075.
107. 22 U.S. (9 Wheat.) 1 (1824).
108. 22 U.S. at 56.
109. Although not in *Gibbons v. Ogden* which was decided on an interpretation of the commerce clause.
110. With regard to copyrighted materials, the issue would almost always arise in the context of the work being argued to be offensive to public morals, with obscenity being the big issue in the twentieth century.
111. Patterson v. Kentucky, 97 U.S. 501 (1878). In this instance, the Court upheld the right of Kentucky to issue regulations which effectively precluded the sale of a patented coal distillate for illumination purposes, on the ground that it was unsafe for such purposes.

what the statute said it was, and despite the literal statutory language, a patent did *not* grant the patentee any right to make, use, sell or vend the patented invention.

Rather, in *Bloomer v. McQuewan,* the Court stated: "The franchise which the patent grants, consists altogether in the right to exclude everyone from making, using, or vending the thing patented, without the permission of the patentee. That is all that he obtains by the patent."[112] In so stating, the Court made no attempt whatever to explain the basis for this remarkable holding which appeared on its face so contradictory to the statutory language. While the Court thereafter repeatedly upheld this view,[113] it was not until 1952 that Congress got around to conforming the statutory language by modifying it to read: "Every patent shall contain . . . a grant to the patentee, his heirs or assigns . . . of the right to exclude others from making, using or selling the invention throughout the United States."[114]

In 1937 Stringham emphatically condemned the failure of Congress to change the wording of the statute from a positive grant to make, use or vend the invention covered by the patent to a negative one of merely the right to exclude others from so doing. He contended that the false nature of the positive grant "is patent law's most notorious scandal" and argued that the grant of necessity was only a negative one in that the patent gives (1) "no right to exercise the invention covered by a dominant patent having an effective earlier date"[115]; (2) "no exemption from liability under

---

112. 55 U.S. 539, 549 (1852).
113. *See, e.g.,* Patterson v. Kentucky, 97 U.S. at 508 ("[t]he sole operation of the statute is to enable him [the patentee] to prevent others from the products of his labors except with his consent"); United States Shoe Mach. Corp. v. United States, 258 U.S. 451, 463 (1922) ("[f]rom an early day it has been held by this court that the franchise secured by a patent consists only in the right to exclude others from making, using or vending the thing patented without the permission of the patentee"); Ethyl Gasoline Corp. v. United States, 309 U.S. 436, 456 (1940) ("[t]he patent law confers on the patentee a limited monopoly, the right or power to exclude all others from manufacturing, using or selling his invention").
114. Act of July 19, 1952, 66 Stat. 804, 35 U.S.C. § 154.
115. A dominant patent is one which would be infringed by the practice of the invention covered by the subsequent patent. The issue of a dominant patent most frequently arises when the subsequently patented invention is an improvement on the earlier patented invention.

anti-trust laws"[116]; and (3) "no right to carry on buying, [or] selling of patent rights or of patented things, this being a matter subject to state laws."[117]

The fact that since 1952 both the statutory language and the Supreme Court have agreed that "the exclusive right" is a negative one to exclude rather than a positive right to make, use, or vend the patented invention does not per se mean that the patentee has no right to make, use, or vend the patented invention but only that such right may be subject to legal restriction as, for example, in the three instances noted by Stringham. That is to say, there is not an absolute right to make, use, or vend the invention, even though it is patented.

Of course, neither is there an absolute right to preclude others from so doing, although the negative right to exclude is more nearly absolute than any positive right held by the patentee. An absolute right to exclude means that the patentee can literally exclude anyone else from making, using or vending the patented invention, as opposed to merely seeking damages for unauthorized making, using or vending. The way in which this is accomplished is by injunction, but early on neither a patentee nor a copyright holder had any right to an injunction. It was not until 1819 that such a right was created by statute.[118] Moreover, in modern times both patentees and copyright holders have been statutorily precluded from enjoining the federal government from making or using a patented invention or copying a copyrighted work. Rather, the only remedy in such circumstance is a suit for damages.[119]

There is another limited circumstance wherein the right to exclude is not absolute, and a patented invention may be practiced without infringement. That is the experimental use exception. As early as 1813, Justice Story in his capacity as a circuit judge observed that "it could never have been the intention to punish a man, who constructed a [patented] machine merely for philosophical experiments, or for the purpose of ascertaining the sufficiency of the machine to produce its described effects."[120] Although the experimental use exception has long been recognized, its use is

---

116. This was a "Johnny-come-lately" rationale, because at the time that *Bloomer v. McQuewan* was decided, there were no anti-trust laws which could provide any basis for treating the patent right as a negative as opposed to a positive right.

117. Rich, *supra* note 20, at 168–69, quoting STRINGHAM, OUTLINE OF PATENT LAW at § 4050 (1937).

118. Act of February 15, 1819, 3 Stat. 481.

119. *See* 28 U.S.C. § 1498.

120. Whittemore v. Cutter, 29 F. Cas. 1120, 1121 (D. Mass. 1813) (No. 17,600).

narrowly circumscribed.[121] In particular, courts are reluctant to accept such an exception to the patent monopoly except in "pure" research instances, i.e., where there are no commercial implications involved.[122]

The point of this discussion has been to demonstrate that "the exclusive right" as used in the patent context in the intellectual property clause has been judicially interpreted in ways that at first glance appear at odds with its literal meaning. So too it has been with "the exclusive right" provided by copyrights, although to a lesser extent that with that associated with patents. Interestingly, the most widely known American treatise on copyright, *Nimmer on Copyright,* discusses the meaning of "the exclusive right" only in the context of whether the compulsory licensing provisions of the copyright statute[123] are unconstitutional, and does not address the issue of whether in the copyright context "the exclusive right" is a positive or a negative right. Although there are apparently no cases raising the constitutionality of compulsory copyright licensing, *Nimmer on Copyright* argues that such is constitutional on the grounds that Congress has discretion whether to enact copyright legislation at all, and accordingly may appropriately determine the extent of the exclusive right.[124] The treatise concludes "that the phrase 'the exclusive right' imports words of authority, but not of limitation."[125]

In 1824 Webster had argued that the phrase "the exclusive right" could not give authority to create an absolute right because the intellectual property clause did note preempt state control over the right to regulate the use, sale, or publication, as the case might be, of a patented or copyrighted article.[126] While the Supreme Court thereafter upheld this view in the patent context,[127] there seems to have been no comparable case involving copyright. Nonetheless, the right of a state to regulate a patented or copyrighted article is in principle the same, so that "the exclusive right" grants only a negative right to exclude others from printing, publishing, copying, or vending the copyrighted work, rather than an affirmative right in the

121. Rebecca S. Eisenberg, *Patents and the Progress of Science: Exclusive Rights and Experimental Use,* 56 U. CHI. L. REV. 1017, 1023 (1989) ("[s]ubsequent courts have consistently recognized the existence of an experimental use defense in theory, although the defense has almost never succeeded in practice").
122. *See, e.g.,* Roche Prods. v. Bolar Pharm. Co., 733 F.2d 858 (Fed. Cir. 1984).
123. These provisions occur at 17 U.S.C. §§ 111(d), 115, 116(a), 118.
124. NIMMER & NIMMER, *supra* note 89.
125. *Id.*
126. *See supra* text accompanying notes 107–110.
127. *See* Patterson v. Kentucky, 97 U.S. 501 (1878).

author to engage in such activity.[128] In other words, "the exclusive right" as used in the intellectual property clause is not absolute but instead authorizes the grant of a negative property right as opposed to a positive property right with respect to both patents and copyrights.

But as the negative right to exclude is not absolute with regard to patents, neither is it absolute with regard to copyrights.[129] Thus, for example, just as there is an experimental use exception with regard to "the exclusive right" granted by patents, so too there is a "fair use" exception to "the exclusive right" granted by copyrights. Justice Story, in his capacity as circuit judge, was also largely responsible for the judicial development of this exception. As he put it in 1841 in *Folsom v. Marsh*:

> [A] reviewer may fairly cite largely from the original work, if his design be really and truly to use the passages for the purposes of fair and reasonable criticism. On the other hand, it is clear, that if he thus cites the most important parts of the work, with a view, not to criticize, but to supersede the use of the original work, and substitute the review for it, such a use will be deemed a piracy.[130]

Fair use traditionally has been defined as "a privilege in others than the owner of the copyright to use the copyrighted material in a reasonable manner without his consent."[131]

In the 1976 Copyright Act Congress got around to statutorily recognizing the "fair use" exception to the exclusive rights granted by copyrights, saying:

> the fair use of a copyrighted work, including such use by reproduction in copies or phonorecords or by any other means specified . . . , for purposes such as criticism, comment, news reporting, teaching (including multiple copies for classroom use), scholarship, or research, is not an infringement of copyright. In determining whether the use made of the

---

128. Gordon notes that: "Copyright gives authors only what trespass law gives to landowners: Authors have the right to exclude others from what they own." *See* Wendy J. Gordon, *An Inquiry into the Merits of Copyright: The Challenges of Consistency, Consent, and Encouragement,* 41 STAN. L. REV. 1343, 1370 (1989).

129. Gordon provides a listing of limitations on the exclusive right to exclude. *Id.* at 1370–72.

130. 9 F. Cas. 342, 344–45 (C.C.D. Mass. 1841) (No. 4,901). For an historical account of the development of the fair use doctrine, *see* WILLIAM PATRY, THE FAIR USE PRIVILEGE IN COPYRIGHT LAW at 1–61 (1985).

131. Harper & Row v. Nation Enters., 471 U.S. 539, 549 (1985), citing H. BALL, LAW OF COPYRIGHT AND LITERARY PROPERTY at 260 (1944).

work in any particular case is a fair use, the factors to be considered shall include—

(1) the purpose and character of the use, including whether such use is of a commercial nature or is for nonprofit educational purposes;
(2) the nature of the copyrighted work;
(3) the amount and substantiality of the portion used in relation to the copyrighted work as a whole; and
(4) the effect of the use upon the potential market for or value of the copyrighted work.[132]

The intent of the statutory language was simply to incorporate into the copyright statute the existing judicial doctrine of fair use without changing, narrowing, or enlarging it in any way.[133]

To this point, the limitations identified with respect to "the exclusive right" have been associated with actions of the judiciary or Congress. But there is another limitation on this phrase that is inherent in the phrase "for limited times" in the intellectual property clause. In order to understand why this is so, it is first necessary to address the meaning of the public domain in the context of the patent and copyright law.

D. The Public Domain

Although Congress in recent years has given little thought to the public domain, particularly in the copyright arena, it does on occasion recognize its importance. Thus, for example, a 1984 House report declared that it is important to keep in mind the following admonition:

> Copyright is an amalgam of property law principles bent to the service of a rather simple bargain. A limited term of protection against copying is granted to an author's original expression in exchange for the dedication of that expression to the public domain at the end of the term. The public ordinarily benefits at least twice from this bargain: once, when the original expression is first created, and then again when the expression is added to the public domain from which anyone may borrow freely to fashion new works. Although a copyright belongs to an author during its term, the ultimate purpose of this bargain is not to protect authors but rather to enrich the public domain. The cardinal

---

132. 17 U.S.C. § 107.
133. Campbell v. Acuff-Rose Music, Inc., 510 U.S. 569, 577, (1994), citing H.R. REP. NO. 94-1476 (1976) at 66.

principal [sic] in copyright law, then, is that any decision to extend the law or to recognize new interests ought to be based on a realistic expectation that one day the public domain will bear new fruit.[134]

Unfortunately, as is shown later, Congress repeatedly has failed to heed this admonition.

The intellectual property clause does not speak in terms of "the public domain" but implicit in the phrase "for limited times" therein is the presumption that at some point in time the subject matter of both patents and copyrights is intended to go into the public domain, i.e., patents and copyrights do not—and cannot—create a perpetual property right in inventors and authors. But there were those in the early republic who vigorously argued that authors and inventors had inherent property rights in their writings and inventions which were perpetual, despite any language to the contrary in the intellectual property clause. The Supreme Court disposed of this view in *Wheaton v. Peters* in 1834 when it held that the property rights authorized by the intellectual property clause were created rights not inherent rights.[135]

The ultimate purpose of patents and copyrights authorized by the clause is to enlarge the public domain of creative works by authors and inventors, thereby promoting "the progress of science and useful arts." An initial issue, which has long since been resolved, was whether there was any distinction between a property right in tangible property and that in the intangible property represented by the creative efforts of authors and inventors, such that Congress could transfer this intangible property into the public domain after some defined term.[136] Today, the primary issue is not whether patented and copyrighted subject matter should go into the public domain, but when it should enter the public domain. A corollary issue is whether there should be any inherent distinction made between the creative efforts of authors and inventors in determining when the subject matter of their creative work should go into the public domain.

In this work, I define the phrase "public domain" narrowly. It is that which is owned by everyone, and consequently by no one. The phrase has

---

134. H.R. REP. NO. 92-487, 92th Cong., 1st Sess. (1984) (*reproduced in* 9 NIMMER & NIMMER, *supra* note 78, at App. 30-7).

135. These issues and their resolution have been discussed in detail in Chapter Six.

136. *Wheaton v. Peters* clearly demonstrated that any property rights authorized by the clause were created rights. It followed that the property rights in the intangible grants known as patents and copyrights were distinguishable from property rights in tangible objects, and could be limited and controlled by act of Congress.

frequently been used to describe lands owned and managed by the federal government, such as national forests and national parks.[137] This public land is regulated and controlled by the federal government, and there is no automatic right of access and use in any and all contexts by the public. But as nicely and succinctly put by Patterson and Lindberg:

> The public domain is not a territory, but a concept: there are certain materials—the air we breathe, sunlight, rain, ideas, words, numbers— not subject to private ownership. The materials that compose our cultural heritage must be free for all to use no less than matter necessary for biological survival.[138]

In the public domain I define, the government does not have a right of control or regulation over the use of what constitutes it, except in the narrowest sense.[139] The right of public access and use is near absolute.[140]

In the case of land, an absolute right of access and use by all leads almost inevitably to what has famously been called "the tragedy of the commons."[141] "The classic example" is

> that of a common pastureland in an English village, where any villager had a right to put as many animals on the pasture as he wanted. Whatever benefit came of that—milk, beef or whatever—belonged to him as private property. The problem with this arrangement is that it

---

137. According to Littman speaking in the copyright context:

> The term public domain gained widespread use in the late nineteenth century when the Berne Convention adopted the term domaine public from the French. In the U.S., we had already been using the phrase "public domain" (apparently derived from the British Royal demesne) to describe lands owned by the federal government intended for sale, lease, or grant to members of the public.

Jessica Littman, *The Public Domain*, 39 EMORY L.J. 965, 975 (1990).

138. L. RAY PATTERSON & STANLEY W. LINDBERG, THE NATURE OF COPYRIGHT, A LAW OF USERS' RIGHTS at 50 (Athens, Ga. 1991).

139. Through the use of its police power the government may in some circumstances restrict public access and use of material in this public domain, but only to the degree that it may likewise do so to similar private property.

140. According to Benkler: "Information is 'in the public domain' to the extent that no person has a right to exclude anyone else from using the specified information in a particular way. Information is in the public domain if all users are equally privileged to use it." Yochai Benkler, *Free as the Air to Common Use: First Amendment Constraints on Enclosure of the Public Domain*, 74 N.Y.U. L. REV. 354, 360 (1999).

141. Garrett Hardin, *The Tragedy of the Commons*, 162 SCIENCE 1243 (1968).

"commonizes" costs and "privatizes" profits, so that it becomes possible for the individual to be paid and to mistreat the commons because he gets all the benefits without having to pay the costs.[142]

Such use of land results in an almost irresistible urge to be among the first to abuse the commons and overgraze from concern that others sooner or later will do so. This traps individuals "in a system that pays them to act irresponsibly."[143]

There are two ways out of the dilemma. The first is to privatize the commons and give individuals portions thereof. They control the right of access to and use of their private portion, pay the cost of upkeep and maintenance, as well as taxes, and reap any benefits from their use or rental of the land. There is no limit on the length of time the private portion can be held. The second approach is basically what the federal government does with its public lands. The property remains with the public as a whole, but a manager is appointed to control and regulate the use of the land. Public access and use is controlled by specific regulation intended to avoid overuse or improper use and presumably to maximize the public benefit derived from access to and use of the land. Whether the regulations governing the use of such public land actually are in the public benefit may be—and not infrequently is—a much debated question, but it is important to understand that this public land is not "public domain" as I have defined the phrase.

If unregulated and uncontrolled access and use of land in the public domain leads to irresponsible action and diminished value, the same cannot be said for knowledge in the public domain. Access and use by all does not diminish its value to individuals or to society. Indeed, it is precisely the unregulated and uncontrolled nature of knowledge in the public domain that renders it valuable to society. Patents and copyrights are deemed to be for the public good precisely because they are intended to enlarge the intellectual commons of knowledge available to all.[144]

---

142. Interview, *The Commons in Crisis: Garrett Hardin*, CALYPSO LOG 17 (Apr. 1988).

143. *Id.*

144. The Supreme Court made this point in the patent context as early as 1829 when it stated:

> the main object was 'to promote the progress of science and useful arts;' and this could be done best by giving the public at large a right to make, construct, use, and vend the thing invented, at as early a period as possible having a due regard to the rights of the inventor.

Pennock v. Dialogue, 27 U.S. (2 Pet.) 1, 19 (1829).

A critical point is that unlike property rights in land, the incorporeal (the British term) or intangible (the American term) property rights known as patents and copyrights are not perpetual or unlimited in term but are intended from their creation to cease to exist at some point in time so that their subject matter may be ultimately transferred to—and enlarge—the public domain as I have defined it.[145] One reason for this is that from their earliest creation in England to the present they have generally been considered as monopolies, albeit desirable ones. They are permitted only because their term is in fact limited. They are intended only as incentives to enlarge the intellectual commons which aids and abets the public well being, not to mention the work of future authors and inventors.[146]

In the two decades preceding the drafting of the U.S. Constitution in 1787, it had been firmly established in Great Britain that inventors had no inherent or common law property right in the subject matter of their inventions or discoveries once that subject matter had been published, i.e.,

---

145. As Justice Brandeis phrased it more than 80 years ago:

> The general rule of law is, that the noblest of human productions—knowledge, truths ascertained, conceptions, and ideas—become, after voluntary communication to others, free as the air to common use. Upon these incorporeal productions the attribute of property is continued after such communication only in certain classes of cases where public policy has seemed to demand it.

> International News Serv. v. Associated Press, 248 U.S. 215, 250 (1918) (Brandeis, J., dissenting). Patents and copyrights do of course place the attribute of property upon the intangible production of ideas, albeit in different ways, but only for a limited time, so that the subject matter thereof, as a matter of public policy, is intended to go into the public domain, i.e., be "free as the air to common use."

146. As Littman aptly puts it, "the public domain is the law's primary safeguard of the raw material that makes authorship [and inventorship] possible." Littman, *supra* note 137, at 967. The limited-term monopoly is permitted because in economic terms

> this body of law grants creators a bundle of exclusive property rights devised to overcome the 'public good' problem arising from the intangible, indivisible and inexhaustible nature of intellectual creations, which allows them to be copied by second comers who have not shared in the costs and risks of the economic endeavor.

> J. H. Reichman, *Charting the Collapse of the Patent-Copyright Dichotomy: Premises for a Restructured International Intellectual Property System*, 13 CARDOZO ARTS & ENT. J. 475, 485–86 (1995).

made publicly known. Once published, and without patent protection, the subject matter was truly in the public domain.

> A critical aspect of the Statute of Monopolies was that it permitted but did not require the crown to issue patents of monopoly for invention. Such patents were considered to be exceptions to the general ban on monopolies, but were deemed to be in the interest of the public at large. The practice was entirely at the discretion of the crown; a patent was the creature of the royal prerogative.[147] The rights secured by patent could be protected at common law, but there was no common law right to a patent. In the absence of a patent an inventor had no means at common law of protecting any perceived "rights" in invention. Without patent such rights were at best deemed inchoate.[148]

The Statute of Monopolies declared that a property right created by a patent in a physical embodiment of an idea, called a discovery or an invention, was a creature of the state and could be controlled by the state. Most importantly, the property right could exist only for a limited time and then passed into the public domain.[149] A prominent commentator on the British patent law argues that "[t]he statutory limitation of the term of the grant to fourteen years . . . was avowedly based upon the consideration that the patent should not operate in restraint of trade."[150]

Despite the existence of the Statute of Anne, the issue was much more complicated with respect to the works of authors. The Statute seemed clearly to state that the copyright term was for fourteen years, with a right of renewal for another fourteen years if the author was still living at the end of the first term. But this statutory term limitation was thrown into complete disarray in 1769 in *Millar v. Taylor*[151] wherein a majority of the four-judge panel held that a perpetual property right in literary works

---

147. *See, e.g.,* W. R. HINDMARCH, A TREATISE ON THE LAW RELATIVE TO PATENT PRIVILEGES FOR THE SOLE USE OF INVENTIONS at 3 (1846). As he put it, "[i]nventors [in Great Britain] are *never entitled as of right* to letters patent, granting them the sole use of their inventions, but they must obtain them from the Crown by petition, and *as a matter of grace and favour. . . .*" *Id.* at 4.
148. Edward C. Walterscheid, *Inherent or Created Rights: Early Views on the Intellectual Property Clause,* 19 HAMLINE L. REV. 81, 83–84 (1995).
149. Despite being an ardent Anglophobe, Thomas Jefferson nonetheless whole-heartedly accepted this view. *See supra* Chapter Six, note 120 and accompanying text.
150. E. Wyndham Hulme, *The History of the Patent System Under the Prerogative and at Common Law,* 12 L. Q. REV. 141, 153–54 (1896).
151. 98 Eng. Rep. 201 (K.B. 1769).

based on common law existed. Five years later in *Donaldson v. Becket*,[152] however, the House of Lords decided that whatever may have been the case originally at common law, the Statute of Anne effectively limited the term for which copyright could be enforced at common law to a maximum of twenty-eight years.

Although the Framers were aware of the holding of *Millar v. Taylor*, there is considerable dispute as to whether they were aware of *Donaldson v. Becket* or exactly what the holding was therein.[153] Be that as it may, as evidenced by the content of the intellectual property clause, they clearly intended to limit the temporal term of both patents and copyrights and to have the subject matter of both enter into the public domain after some limited period of exclusive right in the patentee or copyright holder. We turn now to a closer look at the interpretation to be given to "for limited times" in the clause.

E. For Limited Times

If Congress had discretion to create the exclusive right encompassed by patents and copyrights, then presumably it also had discretion to set or modify the length of the grant of such right. While it was precluded from creating a perpetual property right, were there any other limitations in the intellectual property clause which affected the interpretation to be given to "for limited times"? In particular, to what extent, if any, is the phrase controlled and limited by the purpose of the intellectual property clause, i.e., "to promote the progress of science and useful arts"? Congress and the courts have largely ignored these questions, but the wide disparity that presently exists between the patent term and the copyright term has caused them to be highly relevant. Here we look to constitutional limitations relevant to interpreting "for limited times" and the interpretations relevant to an understanding of those limitations.[154]

Just as the Framers deliberately used the singular "the exclusive right," so too they deliberately used the plural "for limited times." This is evidenced by the correction in the final draft of the Constitution that

---

152. 4 Burr. 2408 (1774). *See also* Cobbett, 17 PARL. HIST. ENG. at cols. 954–1003 (H.L. 1774).
153. *See supra* Chapter Two, text accompanying notes 185 and 186.
154. Whether the copyright term as presently set exceeds the constitutional authority of Congress is discussed in Part G *infra*.

changed "for a limited time" to "for limited times."[155] Although no contemporaneous documentation exists which explains the use of the plural
"for limited times," it can only be assumed that their intent was to give
Congress some flexibility in setting both the patent and the copyright term,
while at the same time assuring that neither the patent grant nor the
copyright grant could be in perpetuity. They likely took it for granted that
Congress would set the term of the exclusive right along the lines followed
in the British practice with respect to both patents and copyrights.[156] In any
case, they determined that ultimately the subject matter of both the patent
grant and the copyright grant must become a part of the public domain.

The Framers must be presumed to have been aware of the British
practice of granting patent term extensions and of the term renewal for
copyright authorized by the Statute of Anne.[157] It can safely be assumed
that by using the phrase "for limited times" they contemplated that
Congress should have similar authority. Thomas Jefferson certainly
assumed this to be the case and didn't like it at all. Thus in August 1789 he
informed Madison that he preferred a provision in the proposed Bill of
Rights stating: "Monopolies may be allowed to persons for their own
productions in literature and their own inventions in the arts for a term not
exceeding—years but for no longer term and no other purpose."[158] Such
language would clearly have precluded term extension and term renewal.
Jefferson also assumed that Congress had discretion in setting the term of
patents and copyrights. Thus, only a month later in September 1789, for
reasons peculiarly his own he asked Madison to seek to have the patent

---

155. *See supra* Chapter Three, text accompanying note 114.
156. As Story put it: "It is doubtless to [their] knowledge of the common law and
     statutable rights of authors and inventors, that we are to attribute this
     constitution provision [i.e., the intellectual property clause]." *See* JOSEPH
     STORY, II COMMENTARIES ON THE CONSTITUTION OF THE UNITED STATES
     § 1152 (Boston 1833).
157. The Statute of Monopolies gave the crown discretion to issue a patent for any
     term not exceeding fourteen years. Parliament, however, had authority to
     extend the term and not infrequently did. The most famous British patent
     term extension was that granted to James Watt in 1775 which extended the
     term of his "fire engine" patent to thirty-one years. *See, e.g.,* George E. Frost,
     Watt's 31 Year Patent, 71 J. PAT. & TRADEMARK OFF. SOC'Y 136 (1991). Under
     the Statute of Anne, the British copyright term was set at 14 years, with a right
     of renewal for another 14 years if the author was still living at the time the
     initial term expired.
158. Letter from Thomas Jefferson to James Madison (Aug. 28, 1789), *in* 1 THE
     REPUBLIC OF LETTERS at 630 (James Morton Smith ed., 1995).

and copyright term in the new United States law be longer than that set forth in the contemporaneous British practice "by securing the exclusive right for 19[,] instead of 14[,] years."[159]

The phrase "for limited times" is clearly a limitation on the power to grant an exclusive right to authors and inventors in their writings and discoveries. There is obviously some term of the grant beyond which Congress cannot constitutionally proceed.[160] But what is it and how is it to be determined? The Supreme Court has addressed the meaning to be given to "for limited times" only in an indirect sense. In 1829 in *Pennock v. Dialogue*[161] Justice Story referred to this language, saying: "It contemplates . . . that this exclusive right shall exist but for a limited time, and that the period shall be subject to the discretion of Congress."[162] In more recent times, the Court has stated that "Congress may not create monopolies of unlimited duration."[163]

---

159. *Id.* at 631–36.
160. This is to be contrasted to the congressional resolution four years earlier on May 2, 1783, to wit:

> That it be recommended to the several states, to secure to authors or publishers of any new books not hitherto printed, being citizens of the United States, and to their . . . executors, administrators and assigns, the copyright of such books for a certain time, not less than fourteen years from the first publication; and to secure to said authors, if they shall survive the term first mentioned, and to their . . . executors, administrators and assigns, the copyright of such books for another term of time not less than fourteen years, such copy or exclusive right of printing, publishing and vending the same, to be secured to the original authors, or publishers, or . . . their executors, administrators and assigns, by such laws and under restrictions as the several states may deem proper.

> *See* BRUCE BUGBEE, GENESIS OF AMERICAN PATENT AND COPYRIGHT LAW at 113 (Washington 1967), quoting XXIV JOURNALS OF THE CONTINENTAL CONGRESS at 326–27. Perhaps the most striking feature of this congressional resolution is that it recommends a floor of at least 14 years for the term of the copyright but suggests no ceiling whatever. Apparently, insofar as the Continental Congress was concerned, there was no objection if a state wanted to issue a copyright in perpetuity; the concern was that the copyright term not be too short, rather than that it might be too long. This is a significant distinction from what would be incorporated into the Constitution four years later, namely, the power to enact laws securing to writers the exclusive right to their works "for limited times."

161. 27 U.S. (2 Pet.) 1 (1829).
162. *Id.* at 16–17.
163. Bonito Boats, Inc. v. Thunder Craft Boats, Inc., 489 U.S. 141, 146 (1989).

Nonetheless, the discretion afforded to Congress with respect to the patent and copyright term is not unbounded, and Justice Story does not provide support for any view that courts may not interpret the meaning to be given to "for limited times." In *Pennock* he made the following point:

> The words of our statute[164] are not identical with those of the statute of James,[165] but it can scarcely admit of doubt, that they must have been within the contemplation of those by whom it was framed, as well as the construction which has been put on them by Lord Coke.[166]

Although these words refer to the language of the patent statute, there is little doubt but that they are fully applicable to the language of at least the patent provision of the intellectual property clause. It is thus useful to recall what Lord Coke had to say about the patent term as set forth in the Statute of Monopolies. He argued that the patent privilege was proper as long as it was for "a convenient time"[167] which he perceived as the time required to bring a "new manufacture" into free practice in the realm.[168] Simply put, Story agreed with Coke that the intellectual property clause should be interpreted as providing a term adequate to encourage the social progress at the root of the patent system,[169] but no longer. In his Commentaries, published four years after his *Pennock* opinion, Story made the point clear with regard to both the patent and the copyright term by his statement that short terms are beneficial in that they "admit the people at large, *after a short interval*, to the full possession and enjoyment of all writings and inventions without restraint."[170]

A basic issue in determining the upper bounds of constitutionally permissible patent and copyright terms is the extent, if any, to which the stated purpose of the intellectual property clause acts as a limitation on the discretion of Congress to set patent and copyright terms. In his *Pennock* opinion, Story rather clearly indicated that it did, saying that:

> the main object was "to promote the progress of science and useful arts;" and this could be done best by giving the public at large a right

---

164. He was referring to the Patent Act of 1793.
165. The Statute of Monopolies.
166. 27 U.S. at 20–21.
167. *See* EDWARD COKE, 3 INSTITUTES OF THE LAWS OF ENGLAND at 184 (London 1644).
168. *Id.*
169. Coke could not—and did not—speak to the copyright system because that system had yet to be created by the Statute of Anne.
170. *See Story, supra* note 156 (emphasis supplied).

to make, construct, use, and vend the thing invented, *at as early a period as possible*; having a due regard to the rights of the inventor.[171]

While not specifically addressing this issue, commentators have argued that the statement of purpose in the clause does not create any limitation on the power of Congress to act with respect to patents and copyrights.[172] Thus, e.g., Nimmer and Nimmer in the copyright context state "the phrase 'To promote the progress of science and useful arts . . .' must be read largely in the nature of a preamble, indicating the purpose of the power but not in limitation of its exercise.'"[173] The only authority cited for this view is *Jacobson v. Massachusetts* wherein the Supreme Court stated only that the preamble to the Constitution itself "has never been regarded as the source of any substantive power conferred on the government of the United States, or on any of its departments."[174] But the intellectual property clause is in fact a substantive grant of power to Congress, and the "to" portion thereof may not be read out of it and rendered meaningless.

In the patent context, Burchfiel has presented a similar argument, contending that in interpreting several other enumerated congressional powers the Supreme Court has rejected the view that a statement of purpose should be construed to express an implied limit on congressional exercise of the power.[175] But, in each example he cites, the Court adopted an expansive definition of purpose, rather than holding that the purpose places no limitation on the exercise of the particular power.

Moreover, from early in the republic the Court has accepted the view that a statement of purpose is highly relevant in construing the nature and extent of powers granted to Congress. Thus, for example, in 1824 in *Gibbons v. Ogden*, Chief Justice Marshall stated:

> As men, whose intentions require no concealment, generally employ the words which most directly and aptly express the ideas they intend to convey, the enlightened patriots who framed our constitution, and the

---

171. 27 U.S. at 19 (emphasis supplied).
172. Indeed one commentator argues that "it is an inherently self-contradictory statement, and contrary to recognized meanings of the terms to assert that a restraint is imposed by a statement of purpose." *See* Albert A. Kimball Jr., *An Analysis of Recent Supreme Court Decisions Regarding a Constitutional Standard of Invention*, 1 APLA Q. J. 204, 206 (1972).
173. NIMMER & NIMMER, *supra* note 78, § 1.02(A).
174. 197 U.S. 11, 23 (1904).
175. Kenneth J. Burchfiel, *The Constitutional Intellectual Property Power: Progress of Useful Arts and the Legal Protection of Semiconductor Technology*, 28 SANTA CLARA L. REV. 473, 518–19 (1988).

people who adopted it, must be understood to have employed words in their natural sense, and to have intended what they have said. If from the imperfections of human language, there should be serious doubts respecting the extent of any given power, it is a well settled rule that the objects for which it was given, especially when the objects are expressed in the instrument itself, should have great influence on the construction. ... We know of no rule for construing the extent of such powers, other than is given by the language of the instrument which confers them, taken in connection with the purposes for which they are conferred.[176]

In the context of the intellectual property clause these views have particular significance, for they clearly indicate that a statement of purpose or objects set forth in the clause itself "should have great influence" on the interpretation of the clause. Phrased somewhat differently, the statement of purposes, i.e., "to promote the progress of science and useful arts," constitutes a limitation on the power of Congress granted by the clause which must be taken into account in interpreting it.

Indeed, the Supreme Court has expressly recognized this in both the patent context and the copyright context. Thus, in 1966 in *Graham v. John Deere Co.* the Court relied heavily on the "to" language of the clause to support its view that there is a constitutional standard of invention that must be met for there to be patentability. It began by noting that the qualified authority given to Congress with regard to the issuance of patents "is limited to the promotion of advances in the 'useful arts,'" and went on to state that "Congress in the exercise of the patent power may not overreach the restraints imposed by the stated constitutional purpose." According to the Court, "'promot[ing] the Progress of ... useful Arts' ... is the *standard* expressed in the Constitution and it may not be ignored."[177]

Although the Court has never expressly stated that the "to" language sets a standard for the copyright power, it has on several occasions used language clearly indicating a belief that this language limits the copyright power of Congress. In 1879 in *Baker v. Selden* it quoted with approval the views that had been expressed by Justice Thompson in 1829 that this language limited the type of subject matter that could be copyrighted.[178] In 1891 in *Higgins v. Keuffel* it clearly indicated that the meaning to be given to "writings" in the clause was limited by this language.[179]

---

176. 22 U.S. (9 Wheat.) 1, 187–88 (1824).
177. 383 U.S. at 5–6.
178. 101 U.S. 99, 105 (1879).
179. 140 U.S. 428, 430 (1891).

The import of this is that, with regard to patents, the Court has most emphatically stated that the "to" language is a limitation which sets forth a constitutional standard that Congress may not ignore. This is as true with respect to the patent term as it is with respect to the nature and type of invention that may be protected. Simply put, there is a term beyond which the progress of useful arts is no longer promoted and beyond which such progress may actually be said to be hindered. It is at that point that discretion of Congress to set the patent term becomes constitutionally limited. The Court also made this point implicitly in 1975 in *Twentieth Century Corp. v. Aiken* by noting the competition or tension that exists between the public interest and the interest of authors when it comes to issuance of copyrights.[180] At some copyright term, the public interest must predominate over that of the author, and Congress does not have constitutional authority to grant a longer term.

Despite the views expressed by the Supreme Court in *Gibbons, Baker, Higgins, Graham,* and *Aiken,* several circuit courts have declined to treat the "to" language of the clause as a limitation on congressional power regarding copyrights.[181] Although they were not addressing the specific issue of whether this language containing the statement of purposes acts as a limitation on the power of Congress in setting the copyright term, the language they used is sufficiently broad as to indicate they would hold that it is not a restriction or limitation on the length of the copyright term.[182] Indeed, the D.C. Circuit has now expressly so ruled.[183]

As we shall now see, Congress has never been disposed to treat the "to" language as placing any limitation on its discretion to set the term of patents and copyrights.

---

180. *See infra* note 281 and accompanying text.
181. *See, e.g.,* Schnapper v. Foley, 667 F.2d 102, 112 (D.C. Cir. 1981), *cert. denied,* 455 U.S. 948 (1982) ("we cannot accept appellant's argument that the introductory language constitutes a limitation on congressional power"); Hutchinson Tel. Co. v. Fronteer Directory Co., 770 F.2d 128, 130–31 (8th Cir. 1985) (the purposes of the introductory phrase "do not limit Congress' power to legislate in the field of copyright").
182. This is to be contrasted with the express congressional view at the beginning of the twentieth century that the introductory language of the intellectual property clause does indeed limit the power of Congress regarding copyright. *See infra* text accompanying notes 257–260.
183. Eldred v. Reno, 239 F.3d 372, 378 (D.C. Cir. 2001).

F. Congressional Action in Setting the Term of Patents and Copyrights

The initial statutory terms of the copyright and patent grants were simply copied from the existing British law, both because this was the easiest thing to do, and because Congress had no basis on which to make any determination that American conditions were sufficiently different from British conditions as to justify the setting of different lengths of the terms. But the constitutional language did not preclude term extension or renewal and in the case of copyright the statute early on expressly provided for term renewal. I turn now to what Congress has actually done and the factors which have influenced the length of the patent and copyright term from 1790 to the present.

The first patent statute, the Patent Act of 1790, authorized the issuance of a patent "for any term not exceeding fourteen years."[184] This was exactly equivalent although not identical to the language of the Statute of Monopolies.[185] The patent board authorized under the Act of 1790 to issue patents[186] determined on a standard term of fourteen years.[187] It quickly became apparent that having high government officials responsible for issuing patents was an inefficient and ineffective way to proceed, particularly in view of the fact that these officials had to determine whether the invention was deemed "sufficiently useful and important" to warrant a patent, and less than three years later Congress opted for a registration system under which a patent would automatically issue if the fees were paid and the ministerial requirements met. This Patent Act of 1793 also provided "for a term not exceeding fourteen years,"[188] but the Secretary of State, who was responsible for seeing that the ministerial requirements were met, quickly established a standard term of fourteen years which

---

184. Act of April 10, 1790, 1 Stat. 109.
185. The Statute of Monopolies authorized a "term of fourteen years or under."
186. Consisting of the Secretaries of State and the Department of War and the Attorney General, a majority of which could determine whether a patent issued.
187. Although the board could clearly have issued patents with a term of less than 14 years, all patents issued under the Act of 1790 had a term of 14 years. At least one commentator has incorrectly assumed from this that the Act of 1790 "provided for a uniform duration of exclusive rights." *See* Kenneth Burchfiel, *Revising the "Original" Patent Clause: Pseudohistory in Constitutional Construction*, 2 HARV. J. L. & TECH. 173 (1989).
188. Act of February 21, 1793, 1 Stat. 318.

would be the term during the forty-three years that the Act of 1793 remained in effect.

The language of the Acts of 1790 and 1793 seemed literally to indicate that no patent could have a term in excess of fourteen years. Congress, however, would interpret the statutory language as placing a limitation on the executive branch from issuing a patent with a term of more than fourteen years, but not on congressional ability to extend or renew the term of an issued patent beyond fourteen years as it saw fit. The issue of congressional authority in this regard was for all intents and purposes moot until 1804 when the first patents issued under the Act of 1790 expired.

The issue was brought to the attention of Congress by Oliver Evans who in 1791 obtained the third United States patent for his invention concerning improvements in the milling of flour. His improvements constituted a major advance in the art of milling. Not only did they materially increase the efficiency of the milling process and thereby lower costs, they also produced a more uniform and cleaner product. Although his improvements were slow to catch on, by 1804 many millers were licensing his invention and many others were infringing his patent.

Evans, like most inventors of his time, thought that the fourteen-year term of a federal patent was too short, and that, at the very minimum, each patent holder should have an automatic right of renewal for some period of time.[189] Beginning in December 1804 he repeatedly petitioned Congress for a term extension but was unsuccessful in obtaining one. In recognition that Evans was simply the first of what were likely to be many patentees seeking term extension, a bill was prepared to amend the patent law to expressly allow for term extensions but it was rejected by the House.[190] It would not be until 1832 that Congress would pass any general legislation pertaining to term extension.[191]

---

189. In light of what had been established in the copyright law, there was certainly some justification for this view. *See infra* note 240 and accompanying text. For contemporaneous views of other inventors in this regard, *see, e.g.,* THOMAS GREENE FESSENDEN, ESSAY ON THE LAW OF PATENTS FOR NEW INVENTIONS at 214 (1st ed. 1810). *See also* JOSEPH BARNES, TREATISE ON JUSTICE, POLICY, AND UTILITY OF ESTABLISHING AN EFFECTUAL SYSTEM OF PROMOTING THE PROGRESS OF USEFUL ARTS, BY ASSURING PROPERTY IN THE PRODUCTS OF GENIUS at 6 (Philadelphia 1792); NEW ENGLAND ASSOCIATION OF INVENTORS AND PATRONS OF USEFUL ARTS, REMARKS ON THE RIGHTS OF INVENTORS at 11–12 (1807).

190. *See* ANNALS OF CONGRESS at 1002–03, 1180–81 (8th Cong., 2d Sess.); No. 186, American State Papers (Miscellaneous) (8th Cong., 2d Sess.).

191. *See* note 209, *infra,* and accompanying text.

While Evans was seeking to have his patent term extended, he was also litigating an infringement action that had been commenced prior to the expiration of the term. The action did not come to trial until October 1807 when Justice Bushrod Washington in his capacity as circuit judge invalidated the patent on the ground that it failed to fully recite the suggestions and allegation of that portion of the invention known as the hopperboy in Evan's original petition for patent.[192] Evans was stunned, because the content of the patent had been defined by the patent board, and he had had no control over the description set forth therein.[193] Nonetheless, he immediately took advantage of this turn of events and petitioned Congress, protesting the inequity of having the patent invalidated through no fault or action of his. Congress agreed,[194] and it now passed a special act authorizing renewal of the patent for a term of fourteen years, and Jefferson signed it into law on January 21, 1808, late in his administration.[195]

By authorizing a new renewal patent three years after the original patent had expired, the special act created a major contretemps. A fundamental premise of the patent law, and one inherent in the "for limited times" portion of the intellectual property clause, is that once a patent expires, the public has a right to freely use the invention. Clearly, during the intervening three years anyone, including those who had earlier licensed the patent rights, now had the right to use the invention free of charge. Could Congress constitutionally remove from the public domain that which had been in it for three years and renew the exclusive right for an additional term of fourteen years?

Evans would have been well advised to voluntarily limit the scope of his patent rights to those who installed his patented improvements after the date of the renewal patent. He chose instead to take a hard line and sought license fees or damages from anyone using the patented improvements, regardless of when they were installed. The result was extensive litigation.

---

192. Evans v. Chambers, 8 F. Cas. 837 (C.C.D. Pa. 1807) (No. 4,444).
193. The description of the invention set forth in the patent was actually prepared by a clerk in the State Department and approved by the patent board. Many years later in Hogg v. Emerson, 47 U.S. (6 How.) 437 (1848), the Supreme Court would rule that a patent could not be invalidated because of a failure of government officials to properly perform their ministerial functions.
194. For the congressional action, see ANNALS OF CONGRESS (10th Cong., 1st Sess.) at 80, 83, 86, 1384, 1409. See also No. 231, American State Papers (Miscellaneous) (10th Cong., 1st Sess.).
195. Act for the Relief of Oliver Evans, January 21, 1808, 6 Stat. 70.

In 1813 Jefferson sharply criticized what he termed the "retrospection" given to the Act for the Relief of Oliver Evans that authorized the renewal patent. He strongly disagreed with the judicial interpretations by the circuit courts for Pennsylvania and Maryland[196] that this Act was not an ex post facto law repugnant to the Constitution, and that Evans was legally authorized to claim royalties under the renewed patent for machinery installed during the three-year period when his improvements were in the public domain, but only from the date that infringing millers had received notice of the issuance of the new patent.[197] Two years later, the Supreme Court upheld the views expressed by the circuit courts.[198]

Interestingly, no one, including Jefferson, seems to have argued that Congress did not have constitutional authority to remove the subject matter of an invention from the public domain once it had clearly entered the public domain. This did not prevent courts from holding that it did. As Justice Story in his capacity as circuit judge would put it in 1839:

> The power is general, to grant to inventors; and it rests in the sound dis-
> cretion of congress to say, when and for what length of time and under
> what circumstances the patent for an invention shall be granted. There
> is no restriction, which limits the power of Congress to enact, [only to]
> where the invention has not been known or used by the public.[199]

Story thus seemed to emphatically deny that the intellectual property clause placed any limitation on the power of Congress to remove an invention from the public domain and give it back to the inventor. This is to be contrasted with the view expressed by the Supreme Court in 1966 and again in 1989 that the clause precludes Congress from authorizing "the issuance of patents

---

196. *See* Evans v. Weiss, 8 F. Cas. 888 (C.C.D. Pa. 1809) (No. 4,572); Evans v. Robinson, 8 F. Cas. 886 (C.C.D. Md. 1813) (No. 4,571).
197. *See* letter from Thomas Jefferson to Isaac McPherson (Aug. 13, 1813), *in* 13 WRITINGS OF THOMAS JEFFERSON (A. A. Lipscomb ed., Washington 1903) at 326–27. While recognizing that the constitutional prohibition on ex post facto laws applied literally only to criminal cases, Jefferson nonetheless contended that "they are equally unjust in civil as in criminal cases, and the omission of a caution which would have been right, does not justify the doing of what is wrong." In his view, the retrospective construction was "contrary to natural right," and any such laws "should be restrained by vigorous construc-tions within their narrowest limits." *Id.*
198. Evans v. Jordan, 13 U.S. (9 Cranch) 199, 203–04 (1815).
199. Blanchard v. Sprague, 3 F. Cas. 648, 650 (C.C.D. Mass. 1839) (No. 1,518).

whose effects are to remove existent knowledge from the public domain, or to restrict free access to materials already [publicly] available."[200]

The saga of Evans' renewal patent is instructive in several respects. First of all, it indicates an early reluctance by Congress to statutorily authorize any general form of term extension or renewal for patents, despite the fact that it had done this for copyrights.[201] Secondly, it demonstrates an ambivalence concerning term extension or renewal. Finally, it suggests that Congress would predicate any term extension or renewal on whether the inventor was perceived to have received a fair profit or reward for his inventive effort.[202]

Sometime after he left the presidency in 1817, Madison expressed the view that while there could be no objection to a temporary patent monopoly, it was important that it be temporary. Although he did not expressly so state, it is apparent that he opposed term extensions, because as he put it inventions "grow so much out of preceding ones that there is the less merit in the authors: and because for the same reason, the discovery might be expected in a short time from other hands."[203] In 1833 Justice Story wrote that the intellectual property clause was beneficial "to the public, as it would promote the progress of science and the useful arts, and admit the people at large, after a short interval, to the full possession and enjoyment of all writings and inventions without restraint."[204] But his judicial holdings appeared to belie this language, because he was perfectly prepared to find that Congress had authority not only to extend the "short interval," but to take from the public domain and give back to the inventor an exclusive right in an invention that had entered to the public domain.[205]

---

200. Graham v. John Deere Co., 383 U.S. 1, 6 (1966); Bonito Boats, Inc. v. Thunder Craft Boats, Inc., 489 U.S. 141, 146 (1989).
201. *See* note 241, *infra,* and accompanying text.
202. There was nothing to preclude an argument that term extension or renewal was required in order to assure adequate investment in commercializing the invention which presumably was in the public interest under a social benefit rationale. Indeed, this was the argument chiefly relied upon by James Watt in obtaining his term extension in 1775 in England. As a practical matter, however, arguments for term extension or renewal in the United States would usually be predicated on the contention that the inventor had not been adequately compensated, rather than that more time was needed to assure investment in developing and commercializing the invention.
203. E. Fleet, *Madison's "Detatched Memoranda,"* 3 WM. & MARY Q. 534, 551 (1946).
204. Story, *supra* note 156.
205. Graham v. John Deere Co., 383 U.S. 1, 6 (1966); Bonito Boats, Inc. v. Thunder Craft Boats, Inc., 489 U.S. 141, 146 (1989). *See supra* text accompanying note 200.

During this period, Congress exhibited no interest whatever in either statutorily extending the term of the patent grant or providing for a statutory right of renewal.[206] Quite possibly because of the furor that the renewal of the Evans patent had caused, Congress thereafter exhibited considerable caution in granting term extensions, and between 1808 and 1836 only six additional term extensions were granted.[207] Gradually inventors came to accept this, although they never came to like it. Finally, in response to numerous petitions for extension or renewal, Congress in 1832 statutorily established the conditions under which it would consider such petitions.[208]

This statute clearly indicated that the basis for any extension or renewal would be whether the inventor was considered to have received an adequate monetary compensation for his inventive effort. Thus, the petition for renewal or extension was required to "be accompanied by a statement of the ascertained value of the discovery, invention, or improvement, and of the receipts and expenditures of the patentee, so as to exhibit the profit or loss arising therefrom."[209] It did not give any assurance that the petition for extension or renewal would be granted. In any case, extension or renewal still necessitated a special act of Congress.

In 1836 Congress completely revised the patent law, changing the system from one of registration to one of examination and creating both the modern patent office and the beginnings of the modern examination process. The statutory term of the Act of 1793 was retained, for example, "a term not exceeding fourteen years,"[210] but an administrative mechanism for term extension for seven years was added which did not require a private act of Congress. Instead, the statutory language stated

> the Secretary of State, the Commissioner of the Patent Office, and the Solicitor of the Treasury shall constitute a board to hear and decide upon the evidence produced before them both for and against extension. . . . The patentee shall furnish to said board a statement, in writing, under oath, of the ascertained value of the invention, and of his receipts and expenditures, sufficiently in detail to exhibit a true and faithful account

---

206. Although on several occasions bills were introduced providing for a statutory right of renewal for a specified term, nothing came of them.
207. *See* C. P. Benagh, *The History of Private Patent Legislation in the House of Representatives, Subcommittee on Courts, Civil Liberties, and the Administration of Justice of the House Committee on the Judiciary*, 96th Cong., 1st Sess. (Washington 1979).
208. Act of July 3, 1832, § 2, 4 Stat. 559.
209. *Id.*
210. Act of July 4, 1836, § 5, 5 Stat. 117.

of loss and profit in any manner accruing to him from and by reason of said invention. And if, upon a hearing of the matter, it shall appear to the full and entire satisfaction of said board, having due regard to the public interest therein, that it is just and proper that the term of the patent should be extended, by reason of the patentee, without neglect or fault on his part, having failed to obtain, from the use and sale of his invention, a reasonable remuneration for the time, ingenuity, and expense bestowed upon the same, and the introduction thereof into use, it shall be the duty of the Commissioner to renew and extend the patent, by making a certificate thereon of such extension, for the term of seven years from and after the expiration of the first term; which certificate, with a certificate of said board of their judgment and opinion as aforesaid, shall be entered on record in the Patent Office; and thereupon the said patent shall have the same effect in law as though it had been originally granted for the term of twenty-one years.[211]

Although lip service was paid to the public interest, the clear import of this statutory language was that whether the patentee was perceived to have received "reasonable remuneration" during the original term would be determinative as to whether an extension would be granted. How or on what basis the board was to determine what was reasonable was not stated. Nonetheless, during the following decade, some ten term extensions were granted under this language.[212]

The meaning to be given to this term-extension language was addressed by the Supreme Court in 1846 in *Wilson v. Rousseau*. At issue was a patent issued to William Woodworth in 1828. Shortly after the patent issued Woodworth had assigned all rights to it to several other parties. In 1839 Woodworth died, and in 1842 the administrator of his estate sought and obtained a seven-year extension of the patent. At issue in *Wilson v. Rousseau* was whether the term of a patent could be extended after the patentee died, and, if so, whether the term extension would adhere to the benefit of the assignees. A divided Court answered both questions affirmatively.

Justice Nelson, speaking for the majority, stated:

The statute is not founded upon the idea of conferring a mere personal reward and gratuity upon the individual, as a mark of distinction for a great public service, would terminate with his death; but of awarding to him an enlarged interest and right of property in the invention itself,

---

211. *Id.* § 18. This language was not in the original bill that became the Patent Act of 1836 but was added by Senate amendment. *See* Wilson v. Rousseau, 45 U.S. (4 How.) 646, 701 (1846) (Woodbury, J., dissenting).
212. 45 U.S. at 708.

with a view to secure to him, with greater certainty, a fair and reason-able remuneration. And to the extent of this further right of property thus secured, whatever that may be, it is of the same description and character as that held and enjoyed under the patent for the first term. In its nature, therefore, it continues, and is to be dealt with after the decease of the patentee, the same as an interest under the first, and passes with other rights of property belonging to him, to the personal representative, as part of the effects of the estate.[213]

The several dissents had no difficulty with a term extension occurring after the death of the patentee, but rather strongly opposed the holding that the term extension accrued to the benefit of assignees under the original term of the patent.[214]

Having provided an administrative mechanism for term extension, it might reasonably be supposed that Congress would now cease to consider petitions for this purpose presented to it. For the next decade, with limited exception this seems to have been exactly what occurred. In 1844, for example, the House Committee on Patents received a petition from Stephen McCormick seeking extension of his patent "on the grounds that lawsuits and the failure of the public to accept his patented reaper had prevented his receipt of adequate compensation."[215] The petition was adversely reported because the Patent Appeals Board had denied the request.[216]

---

213. 45 U.S. at 675. Prager argues that "the government's power to grant reissues and renewals to the inventor's heir seemed questionable." *See* Frank D. Prager, *The Changing Views of Justice Story on the Construction of Patents,* 4 AM. J. LEGAL HIST. 1, 18 (1960). The difficulty arose from the fact that Section 18 pertaining to term extension spoke only of the patentee and not of his or her "heirs, assigns, or administrators" as did several other sections of the statute. But the Court simply dismissed this as irrelevant. *See* 45 U.S. at 676–76.

214. *See, e.g.,* 45 U.S. at 692–709 (Woodbury, J., dissenting). The primary concern was that assignees under the original term of the patent had paid no consideration for the added benefit obtained by the term extension. But in the *Wilson* case, although not expressly stated in the record, it is apparent that Woodworth's son, as administrator of his estate, received a significant added consideration from the assignees for seeking and obtaining the term extension. The argument was also made that future assignees of various patents would pay added consideration in the hopes that a term extension would be obtained.

215. Benagh, *supra* note 207, at 8, citing H.R. REP. No. 431, 28th Cong., 1st Sess. (1844).

216. The Act of 1836 provided for an administrative appeal from any adverse act or decision of the Commissioner of patents affecting patent rights.

And, the

> committee would not feel at liberty to report a bill for his relief, believing that it would be unwise to establish a precedent, that numerous persons, who now have and may hereafter obtain patents, if their expectations of profit are not fully realized, might, by applying to Congress, have their exclusive right prolonged from time to time, until their invention should fully remunerate them for their time and trouble.[217]

These words were prophetic for what was soon to occur. Beginning in 1848, in the 30th and 31st Congresses some twenty bills of this nature were given do-pass recommendations, but only a few actually resulted in term extensions or renewals.[218] But private legislation of this type did result in two full term renewals to Thomas Blanchard, giving him a patent with an ultimate term of forty-two years,[219] which appears to be the longest term ever accorded to any United States patent.[220] Blanchard seems to have succeeded in this effort by a combination of astute lobbying and arguments that he had not been adequately compensated for his invention, a dubious proposition at best.

The failure of both Congress and the Supreme Court to consider the constitutional implications of term extension reached an absurd extreme in *Agawam Woolen Co. v. Jordan* decided in 1869.[221] The case involved a seven-year extension of a patent first issued in 1826 with the extension authorized by a special act of Congress in 1862, twenty years *after* the original patent had expired. The rationale for the term extension was that because of erroneous information provided by the Commissioner of Patents, the inventor had failed to seek a renewal within the time and in

---

217. Benagh, *supra* note 207, at 8.
218. *Id.* at 8, 9.
219. Blanchard received his patent for an irregular wood-turning lathe in 1819. It was renewed by Act of Congress, 6 Stat. 589, in June 1934, five months after the original patent had expired. Even though the subject matter of the patent had gone into the public domain, Justice Story in his capacity as circuit judge upheld the validity of the renewal patent. *See supra* text accompanying note 200. In 1848 Blanchard succeeded in having the patent renewed for third full term. 9 Stat. 683. For a discussion of Blanchard's patent management and litigation under it, see CAROLYN C. COOPER, SHAPING INVENTION, THOMAS BLANCHARD'S MACHINERY AND PATENT MANAGEMENT IN NINETEENTH-CENTURY AMERICA at 39–56 (New York 1991).
220. I have been unable to find any other U.S. patent with a term extending beyond 28 years.
221. 74 U.S. (7 Wall.) 177 (1869).

accordance with the manner specified in the Patent Act of 1836.[222] Apparently neither Congress nor the Court thought there was anything odd, remiss, or unconstitutional in the person to whom the invention was assigned waiting twenty years after the original patent had expired to obtain a term extension.

In 1879, however, the House Committee on Patents became much more hostile to arguments for term extension that patentees had failed to receive adequate remuneration for their inventive efforts. In that year it took the position that term extension should be determined "solely in its effects on the public interests."[223] Thereafter, the number of petitions for term extension predicated on personal or financial considerations dropped rapidly. The last favorable report to extend the term of a patent based on inadequate compensation to the patentee was issued in 1916.[224] As Benagh reports, "[t]here was a period in the mid-19th century when the Congress attempted to assure adequate compensation to every inventor with the device of private legislation, but the concept of guaranteed income proved to be too time-consuming and open to frivolous claims."[225] It also paid short shrift to the public interest inherent in the intellectual property clause.

In 1870 the patent statutes were substantially revised. The Patent Act of 1870 extended the term of patents to seventeen years.[226] It retained the term-extension provisions of the Act of 1836, but with an important proviso, namely, that a seven-year term extension could only be sought for patents issued prior to March 2, 1861.[227] Four years later the Act of 1870 was repealed and its provisions incorporated into the Revised Statutes.[228] Because the term-extension section stated that no extension could be issued after the expiration of the original term, this provision had an effective sunset provision of March 2, 1875 built into it. It is likely that Congress perceived the creation of a seventeen-year term as being sufficient to remove the need for any administrative extension process.[229] It is

---

222. 74 U.S. at 183–84.
223. Benagh, *supra* note 207, at 9, quoting from H.R. 195, 45th Cong. 3rd Sess. (1879).
224. Benagh, *supra* note 207, at 10.
225. *Id.* at 14.
226. Act of July 8, 1870, § 22, 16 Stat. 198.
227. *Id.* § 63.
228. The 17-year term was now set by § 4884 of the Revised Statutes and the 7-year term extension provision now appeared at § 4924 of the Revised Statutes.
229. The 17-year term resulted from a compromise between the House which wanted to retain the earlier 14-year term plus 7-year extension, and the Senate which wanted to eliminate the statutory term extension. C. Michael White, *Why a Seventeen-Year Patent?* 38 J. PAT. OFF. SOC'Y 839 (1956). To the extent that a

also apparent that Congress was now questioning its earlier assumption that a primary role of the patent system was to reward inventors as opposed to promoting the public interest.[230]

Another major revision of the patent law occurred with the Patent Act of 1952.[231] This Act retained the seventeen-year term,[232] but made no provision for term extension. Within several decades there would be a significant lobbying effort for term-extension legislation, not in the context of rewarding patentees but rather in the context of extending the term of patent wherein regulatory review and approval of the patented product or process delayed its commercial availability after the patent term had commenced.[233] The purpose of the proposed term extension was to in essence make up for the period while the product or process was patented but could not be sold or used because of lack of regulatory approval. In 1984 Congress enacted two forms of such extension.[234] Subsequently, any such term extension has been limited to a period not exceeding five years.[235]

Patent harmonization came upon the scene in the 1990s, and a part of this process was conforming the term of U.S. patents to that set by international treaty. Certain changes in U.S. law were required when the United States became a signatory to the General Agreement on Tariffs and Trades, specifically by the agreement known as the Trade Related Aspects of Intellectual Property Rights, and these were made in 1994 through the Uruguay Rounds Agreement Act (URAA).[236]

---

patentee could show genuine hardship, he or she could still resort to private patent legislation to obtain a term extension. But, as has been indicated, Congress rather quickly became reluctant to enact such private legislation.

230. *See supra* text accompanying notes 210, 212.

231. Act of July 19, 1952, 66 Stat. 792.

232. *Id.* § 154.

233. *See, e.g.,* James J. Wheaton, *Generic Competition and Pharmaceutical Innovation: The Drug Price Competition and Patent Term Restoration Act of 1984,* 35 CATH. U. L. REV. 433, 435 (1986) ("[f]or years, the brand-name pharmaceutical industry lobbied Congress to enact patent extension legislation, claiming the lengthy drug approval process had eroded the effective patent protection for new drug products far below the seventeen-year grant contemplated by the federal patent statute").

234. *See* Pub. L. No. 97-414, § 11(a), 96 Stat. 2065 (Jan. 4, 1983); Pub. L. No. 98-127, § 4(a), 97 Stat. 832 (Oct. 13, 1983).

235. *See* 35 U.S.C. § 156.

236. Pub. L. No. 103-465 (Dec. 8, 1994).

The patent term is now defined as

> beginning on the date on which the patent issues and ending 20 years
> from the date on which the application for the patent was filed in the
> United States or, if the application contains a specific reference to an
> earlier filed application or applications under section 120, 121 or 365(c)
> of this title [Title 35], from the date on which the earliest application
> was filed.[237]

The URAA also set forth certain circumstances for extending the term
because of delays in the issuance of the patent. Thus, under U.S. law as it
now exists, term extension of up to five years may be obtained for delays
in the issuing the patent, and term extension of up to five years for
regulatory delay is also possible.[238] Conceptually this means that a term
extension of up to ten years is possible if both rationales are accepted, but
in most instances a term extension because of delay in the issuance of the
patent will offset the consequences of regulatory delay. As a consequence,
it would be a most unusual circumstance to have a patent term extending
more than twenty-five years from the date the application was filed.

Although patent extensions for drugs are rare, the extraordinary profits
derived from certain patented drugs have caused their manufacturers to
spend literally millions of dollars and engage in strenuous lobbying efforts
to obtain patent extensions through private congressional acts. They have
also on occasion sought to attach patent extensions to totally unrelated bills
and to have the patent statutes modified to better protect their business
interests by making patent extensions easier to obtain.[239] Such activities
make very good pragmatic business sense, but they are constitutionally
suspect in that they do absolutely nothing to promote the progress of
science and useful arts.

Just as with the patent term, Congress initially opted to use the British
term for copyright. Thus, the Copyright Act of 1790 was patterned after the
Statute of Anne and provided an initial term of fourteen years with a right of
renewal for another fourteen years, provided that an author was living at the
expiration of the first term.[240] But in the next two centuries the copyright

---

237. 35 U.S.C. § 154(a)(2).
238. The mechanics of both types of extension are now spelled out in 35 U.S.C.
§ 156.
239. *See, e.g.,* Jim Drinkard, *Drug Firm Seeking Rider on Flood Relief; Hoffman-LaRoche
Finds Friends in Senate,* CINCINNATI INQUIRER, May 3, 1997 at B10; Viveca
Novak, *How One Firm Played the Patent Game,* TIME, Nov. 22, 1999, at 42.
240. Act of May 31, 1790, § 1, 1 Stat. 124.

term would be extended much more than the patent term. For much of that period it would also provide express mechanisms for term extension.[241]

During the nineteenth century almost two-hundred copyright bills were introduced,[242] and some twenty of these were enacted into law in some form or another.[243] The only one to actually change the statutory term of copyright became law in 1831. It extended the initial term to twenty-eight years "from the time of the recording of the title thereof" and authorized a living widow or children of a deceased author to seek a renewal for fourteen years.[244] The rationale for doubling the initial term has received no discussion in the literature,[245] but several differing arguments were presented during the congressional debate[246] and yet another in the legislative history.[247]

---

241. Express statutory provision for term renewal should arguably have precluded any term renewal or extension by private act or indeed the issuance of copyright by private act. Although rare, private copyright acts have occurred. At the end of the nineteenth century, only nine such acts had been passed by Congress. The only other such act in the twentieth century was Private Law 92-60 passed in 1971. *See* United Christian Scientists v. First Church of Christ, Scientist, 829 F.2d 1152, 1169 (D.C. Cir. 1987).

242. LYMAN RAY PATTERSON, COPYRIGHT IN HISTORICAL PERSPECTIVE at 213 (Nashville 1968).

243. For a listing of these statutory enactments, see MELVILLE B. NIMMER & DAVID NIMMER, 8 NIMMER ON COPYRIGHT at App.7-45–7-95[Rel. 34-12/93].

244. Act of February 3, 1831, §§ 1, 2, 4 Stat. 36.

245. Patterson, for example, simply notes it without providing any explanation of why it occurred. *See* PATTERSON, *supra* note 242, at 201.

246. The first was it "would enhance the literary character of the country by holding forth to men of learning and genius additional inducements to devote their time and talents to literature and the fine arts." The second was that copyright was "merely the legal provision for a protection of a natural right." *See* 7 GALES AND SEATON'S REGISTER OF DEBATES IN CONGRESS at cols. 423–24 (21st Cong., 2d Sess. 1831). If there was an inherent, natural property right in the works of authors, then it was entirely reasonable to extend the term of copyright to afford a legal action for infringement. Three years later in *Wheaton v. Peters* the Supreme Court would give short shrift to such an argument, but it may well have carried the day in 1831.

247. According to the House Judiciary Committee's report, the change in term was intended "to place authors in this country more nearly on an equality with authors in other countries." It noted that most European nations had adopted much longer periods of protection for copyrighted works, and that the United States was "very far behind" other countries in protecting such work. 7 REGISTER OF DEBATES IN CONGRESS, 21st Cong., 2d Sess., App. CXIX (Dec. 17, 1830).

In 1834 in *Wheaton v. Peters*[248] the Supreme Court issued a copyright opinion that had a great deal of relevance to the interpretation to be given to "for limited times" in the intellectual property clause. Simply put, one of the questions raised and decided was whether in the United States an author has a common-law copyright in perpetuity after publication occurs. It is immediately apparent that if such a copyright were held to exist then the phrase "for limited times" in the clause is meaningless, at least in the copyright context. The justices split four to two on the issue.

Patterson summarizes the relevant issues and opinions as follows:

> Subsidiary to this point were the questions of whether a federal common law existed; whether the common-law copyright existed in England; and whether, assuming its existence, Pennsylvania incorporated the common-law copyright in its common law. The majority held that no federal common law existed; the dissenters took the position that this was irrelevant to the case, as the law of Pennsylvania applied. As to the existence of the common-law copyright in England, the majority thought this was very much in doubt, and the dissenters argued that it existed without question. The majority did not think that Pennsylvania, assuming the existence of a common-law copyright in England, had incorporated that right into its common law; and the dissenters took the opposite view.[249]

What Patterson failed to note is that the case also involved an interpretation of the meaning of "securing" as it appears in the clause.

As a part of the argument in favor of a perpetual common-law right, it was contended that "securing" in the clause "clearly indicates an intention not to originate a right, but to protect one already in existence."[250] Not so, said the majority, because the meaning of the term must be determined in the context of "the words and sentences with which it stands connected." In this light, "securing" could not mean the protection of an acknowledged legal right because "[i]t refers to inventors as well as authors, and it has never been pretended by anyone, either in this country or in England, that an inventor has a perpetual right, at common law, to sell the thing invented."[251] In other words, any right to copyright under the intellectual property clause was a created rather than an inherent right.[252] According to the dissent, however, any such analysis is in the nature of a non sequitur,

---

248. 33 U.S. (8 Pet.) 591 (1834).
249. PATTERSON, *supra* note 242, at 208.
250. 33 U.S. at 661.
251. *Id.*
252. For a detailed discussion on this point, see *supra* Chapter Six.

because the "article [i.e., the clause] is to be construed distributively, and must have been so understood."[253]

Ever since *Wheaton v. Peters*, copyright in published works has been understood to be a creature of statute. The statute in turn must conform to the mandate of the intellectual property clause that the exclusive right be secured for limited times. A point that has been largely ignored by both Congress and the judiciary is that the majority opinion in *Wheaton v. Peters* suggested that the rights of inventors and the rights of authors were similar and ought to be treated similarly.[254] This does not mean that the terms of copyright and patent should be identical, but it does support the view that disproportionate differences in the terms of these two property rights are constitutionally suspect.

The Copyright Act of 1909 maintained the initial term of twenty-eight years but provided that the term should run "from the date of first publication," and extended the renewal term to twenty-eight years.[255] This was at a time when the patent term had been set at seventeen years; there was no statutory basis for extension of the patent term, and Congress was exhibiting extreme reluctance to extend patent terms by private act.[256] As a consequence, it was now routinely possible to obtain a copyright term that was typically more than three times the length of the patent term.

The House report accompanying the 1909 Act is of considerable interest because of its discussion of the constitutional aspects of copyright law.[257] It points out that the intellectual property clause limits the power of Congress by several conditions, one of which is that "[t]he object of all legislation must be . . . to promote science and the useful arts." Accordingly, "the spirit of any act which Congress is authorized to pass must be one which would promote the progress of science and the useful arts, and

---

253. 33 U.S. at 684.
254. Justice McLean, for the majority, stated:

> In what respect does the right of an author differ from that of an individual who has invented a most useful and valuable machine? In the production of this, his mind has been as intensely engaged, as long, and perhaps, as usefully to the public, as any distinguished author in the composition of his book. The result of their labors may be equally beneficial to society and in their respective spheres they may be alike distinguished for mental vigor.

> 33 U.S. at 657–58.

255. Act of March 4, 1909, ch. 320, §§ 23, 24, 35 Stat. 1075.
256. *See supra* text accompanying notes 226–230.
257. H.R. REP. NO. 2222, 60th Cong., 2d Sess. (1909), *reproduced in* NIMMER & NIMMER, *supra* note 243, at App.13-1–App. 13-31.

unless it is designed to accomplish this result and is believed, in fact, to accomplish this result, it would be beyond the power of Congress."[258] This to be contrasted with the view of some modern commentators and several circuit courts that the introductory language of the intellectual property clause is not limiting in any way on the authority of Congress.[259]

The report went on to emphasize that copyright is "[n]ot primarily for the benefit of the author, but primarily for the benefit of the public." Thus, "[i]n enacting a copyright law Congress must consider . . . two questions: First, how much will the legislation stimulate the producer and so benefit the public; and, second, how much will the monopoly granted be detrimental to the public." Any such legislation must confer "a benefit upon the public that outweighs the evils of the temporary monopoly."[260]

Although it was argued that there should be a single term of life plus fifty years,[261] the report rejected this proposal on the ground that it was distinctly advantageous to the author to have a right of renewal. According to the report the doubling of the renewal term to twenty-eight years, taken together with the original term of twenty-eight years, "ought to be long enough to give the author the exclusive right to his work for such a period that there would be no probability of its being taken away from him in his old age, when, perhaps, he needs it the most."[262] The relevance of such an argument to the constitutional purpose of copyright was not stated, nor was there any indication as to why authors were thought deserving of an original term plus a renewal term that was more than three time longer than that statutorily authorized for patents. One is left with the question of why authors needed to be statutorily protected in their old age but inventors did not.

During the 1960s there was a renewed effort for a major revision of the copyright law, including modifying and lengthening the term. Pending this revision, Congress passed a number of laws effectively extending the renewal terms of copyrights subsisting after September 19, 1962 or prior to December

---

258. *Id.* at App. 13-10.

259. *See supra* notes 172–175 and accompanying text.

260. NIMMER & NIMMER, *supra* note 243, at App. 13-11.

261. The report gives no indication of the basis for this argument, but it likely was predicated on grounds that certain other nations had set such a term for copyright. As early as 1774 Samuel Johnson had recommended a copyright term of life of the author plus 30 years. *See* 2 JOHNSONIAN MISCELLANIES at 444–45 (George Birkbeck Hill ed., 1907). In 1842 Parliament extended the term of British copyright to life of the author plus 7 years or 42 years from publication. *See* MARK ROSE, AUTHORS AND OWNERS, THE INVENTION OF COPYRIGHT at 111 (Cambridge 1993).

262. NIMMER & NIMMER, *supra* note 243, at App. 13-21–App. 13-22.

31, 1971 until December 31, 1976.[263] In 1976 the long-anticipated revision occurred, and with it another broadening of the copyright term. Effective as of January 1, 1978, a unitary term for copyright beginning at the date of the work's creation and continuing for the life of the author plus fifty years after his or her death was established.[264] But for anonymous or pseudonymous works or works made for hire, a unitary term of seventy-five years from the date of first publication or one-hundred years from the date of creation, whichever expires first.[265] The 1976 Act also extended the renewal term for works statutorily copyrighted prior to January 1, 1978 to forty-seven years,[266] thus providing a total term of seventy-five years for such copyrights. The result of this was that the copyright term was now almost always at least three times that of the patent term, and could on occasion be four times or more that of the patent term.

What were the rationales for these changes in the copyright term? The legislative history is set forth in essentially identical language in House and Senate reports.[267] A remarkable aspect of these reports is that, unlike the 1909 House report, they make almost no mention of the limitations imposed on the power of Congress by the intellectual property clause.[268] Specifically, the issue of whether there is a constitutional problem with a copyright term of life-plus-fifty years is never raised, much less addressed.

The legislative history emphasizes that "authors and their representatives stressed that the adoption of a life-plus-50 term was by far their most important legislative goal in copyright law revision" and that the Register

---

263. *See* Pub. L. No. 87-668, 76 Stat. 556 (Sept. 19, 1962); Pub. L. No. 89-142, 79 Stat. 581 (Aug. 28, 1965); Pub. L. No. 90-141, 81 Stat. 464 (Nov. 16, 1967); Pub. L. No. 90-416, 82 Stat. 397 (July 23, 1968); Pub. L. No. 91-147, 83 Stat. 360 (Dec. 16, 1969); Pub. L. No. 91-555, 84 Stat. 1441 (Dec. 17, 1970); Pub. L. No. 92-170, 85 Stat. 490 (Nov. 24, 1971); Pub. L. No. 92-566, § 1, 86 Stat. 1181 (Oct. 25, 1972); Pub. L. No. 93-573, title I, § 104, 88 Stat. 1873 (Dec. 31, 1974).
264. 17 U.S.C. § 302(a).
265. *Id.* § 302(c).
266. *Id.* § 304(a).
267. H.R. REP. NO. 94-1476, 94th Cong., 2d Sess. (1976) reproduced in NIMMER & NIMMER, *supra* note 243, at App.4-2–4-216; Senate Report reproduced *id.*, at 4A-2–4A-255.
268. For the only mention of constitutional issues in the legislative history of the 1976 Act, *see supra* Chapter Nine, notes 85–88 and accompanying text.

of Copyrights regards such a term as the foundation of the revisions.[269] Seven rationales are set forth which have been summarized as follows.

1. The 56-year term under the 1909 Act was not long enough to assure an author and his dependents a fair economic return, given the substantial increase in life expectancy.

2. The growth in communication media has substantially lengthened the commercial life of a great many works, particularly serious works which may not initially be recognized by the public.

3. The public does not benefit from a shorter term, but rather the user groups derive a windfall, as prices the public pay for a work often remain the same after the work enters the public domain.

4. A system based upon the life of the author avoids confusion and uncertainty, because the date of death is clearer and more definite than the date of publication, and it means that all of a given author's works will enter the public domain at the same time instead of seriatim as under a term based on publication.

5. The renewal system is avoided with its highly technical requirements which often cause inadvertent loss of copyright.

6. A statutory term of life-plus-50 years is no more than a fair recompense for those who under the 1909 Act owned common law copyrights which continued in perpetuity as long as a work remained unpublished.

7. A majority of the world's countries have a term of life plus fifty. To adopt the same term expedites international commerce in literary properties, and opens the way for membership in the Berne Convention.[270]

Even a cursory look at these rationales reveals a congressional view that, rather than being for the public benefit as stated in the intellectual property clause, copyright is intended (a) almost entirely for the benefit of an author, and (b) for the purpose of expediting international trade.

Twelve years later, the House took a very different approach in its report on the Berne Convention Implementation Act of 1988.[271] Now the constitutional purpose was very much in evidence:

> Sound copyright legislation is necessarily subject to other considerations in addition to the fact that a writing be created and that the exclusive right be protected only for a limited term. Congress must weigh the

---

269. NIMMER & NIMMER, *supra* note 243, at App. 4-132.
270. 3 NIMMER & NIMMER, *supra* note 243, § 9.01[A][2] (Rel. 38-12/95).
271. H.R. REP. NO. 100-609, 100th Cong., 2d Sess. (1988), *reproduced in* 9 NIMMER & NIMMER, *supra* note 243, at App. 32-1–App. 32-65.

public costs and benefits derived from protecting a particular interest. "The constitutional purpose of copyrights is to facilitate the flow of ideas in the interest of learning." . . . [T]he primary objective of our copyright laws is not to reward the author, but rather to secure for the public the benefits from the creations of authors.[272]

Moreover, the view expressed in the 1909 House report that copyright is "[n]ot primarily for the benefit of the author, but primarily for the benefit of the public" was now quoted with approval.[273] It was perhaps inevitable that the strong commercial interest in certain copyrights would result in extensive efforts in recent years to extend the term of these copyrights. The result has been the Sonny Bono Copyright Term Extension Act of 1998 which provides that "[a]ny copyright still in its renewal term at the time the Sonny Bono . . . Act becomes effective shall have a copyright term of 95 years from the date copyright was originally secured."[274] Recall that the 1976 Act authorized renewal of copyrights existing prior to January 1, 1978 to provide for a total term of seventy-five years.[275] The net effect of this was that in the next decade some highly profitable copyrights would expire and the works go into the public domain in the absent of further term extension.[276] Not now. Instead, the industries controlling these copyrights will continue to obtain major royalties for the use of the works covered by them for twenty years longer than they had any reasonable basis, other than their lobbying skills, to expect.

G. Perspectives

Although the use of the singular "the exclusive right" in the intellectual property clause has occasionally been noted, the intent behind this singular usage has been almost entirely ignored, and instead the patent and

---

272. *Id.* at App. 32-22.
273. *Id.*
274. Pub. L. No. 105-298 (1998), 112 Stat. 2827, 2828.
275. *See supra* text accompanying note 267.
276. Among the works that would have entered the public domain were the Disney characters Mickey Mouse, Pluto, Goofy, and Donald Duck, music written by George and Ira Gershwin, Cole Porter, Irving Berlin, Hoagy Carmichael, and a host of others, and early novels of Ernest Hemingway and William Faulkner. *See* Teresa Ou, *From Wheaton v. Peters to Eldred v. Reno: An Originalist Interpretation of the Copyright Clause* at 5 (manuscript available online at <http://cyber.law.harvard.edu/eldredvreno/legal.html>).

copyright provisions have been interpreted as though the clause read "exclusive rights." But as I have shown the Framers deliberately used the singular in an effort to avoid the dichotomy in the existing British practice whereby patents were a privilege, i.e., a product of the prerogative, and copyrights were at minimum a statutory right if not a common-law right. It is reasonable to suppose that by using the singular "the exclusive right" and combining authority to create both patents and copyrights in the same clause, the Framers intended that the legal consequences of both the patent grant and the copyright grant to be similar, if not identical.

The Framers clearly viewed patents and copyrights as monopolies and assumed that they would be treated as such. As a result, the need for them to be limited in time was so obvious as to need no explanation. While they assumed that the temporal scope of both the patent grant and the copyright grant would at least initially be patterned after the British practice (as indeed it was), they also recognized that Congress should have discretion in setting the term of both patents and copyrights. But they took care to assure that such discretion was not unbounded, and that ultimately the subject matter of both the patent grant and the copyright grant would be in the public domain to be used by all.

Perhaps because neither the Constitution nor the intellectual property statutes make any reference to monopoly, the question of whether patents are to be considered as monopolies has been a recurring one. Strangely enough, it has rarely if ever been raised concerning copyrights, although the issues are basically identical. Robinson pointed out in his 1890 treatise that when a patent is treated as a monopoly, the interests of the public are typically thought to take precedence over those of the inventor, whereas just the reverse tends to occur when patents are deemed not to be monopolies.[277] Although in the last century the Supreme Court has regularly referred to both patents and copyrights as monopolies,[278] the circuit courts on occasion have sought to avoid this usage, and indeed, in some instances have instructed counsel not to refer to patents as monopolies.[279]

In the context of the copyright provision, in 1975 the Supreme Court in *Twentieth Century Corp. v. Aiken* emphasized that:

> The limited scope of the copyright holder's statutory monopoly, like the limited copyright duration required by the Constitution, reflects a balance of competing claims upon the public interest: Creative work is

---

277. *See supra* text accompanying notes 47–49.
278. *See, e.g.,* notes 69 and 77 *supra.*
279. *See, e.g.,* notes 70 and 71 *supra.*

to be encouraged and rewarded, but private motivation must ultimately serve the cause of promoting broad public availability of literature, music, and the other arts.[280]

In so stating, the Court noted that Lord Mansfield's statement of the problem, now more than 200 years ago, bears repeating:

> [W]e must take care to guard against two extremes equally prejudicial; the one, that men of ability, who have employed their time in the service of the community, may not be deprived of their just merits, and the reward of their ingenuity and labour; the other, that the world may not be deprived of improvements, nor the progress of the arts retarded.[281]

The views expressed by the Court in *Aiken* are remarkable in several respects. First of all, they accept and adopt the views that were becoming prevalent in England at the time the Constitution was drafted, namely, that there are two separate and competing rationales for both the patent and the copyright systems and that the patent and copyright terms are derived from a balancing of the tensions between these two competing justifications. The first justification, which emphasizes the public interest, may broadly be called the "social benefits" rationale, and the second, which emphasizes the interest of the inventor or author, can be termed the "reward for creativity" rationale. Secondly, the Court assumed without any citation of authority that these competing rationales were also the justifications for— and indeed the purposes of—the intellectual property clause.

This is all the more strange because the Court could have cited several of its own opinions in the first third of the nineteenth century which certainly seemed to suggest that this was the case. Thus, for example, in 1829 in *Pennock v. Dialogue*, Justice Story speaking for the Court had declared:

> While one great object was, by holding out a reasonable reward to inventors, and giving them an exclusive right to their inventions for a limited time, to stimulate the efforts of genius; the main object was "to promote object the progress of science and useful arts;" and this could be done best by giving the public at large a right to make, construct, use, and vend the thing invented, at as early a period as possible having a due regard to the rights of the inventor.[282]

---

280. 422 U.S. 151, 156 (1975).
281. 426 U.S. at 156, citing *Sayre v. Moore*, cited in a footnote to Cary v. Longman, 1 East 368, 362(b), 102 Eng. Rep. 138 (1801).
282. 27 U.S. at 19.

Again in 1833 Justice McLean for a unanimous Court stated in *Shaw v. Cooper*: "The patent law was designed for the public benefit as well as the benefit of inventors."[283]

More remarkably, the Court in *Aiken* made no reference whatever to the language of the clause taken as a whole. Even a cursory look indicates that its purpose is "to promote the progress of science and useful arts." Nothing in it states that securing a property right or rewarding creativity (or genius, for that matter) is its purpose. Yet from the earliest days of the republic this has been assumed to be a purpose, if not the primary purpose, of the clause.[284] Such an assumption, however, appears to confuse the means with the end and appears at odds with the literal language of the clause. Thus, the purpose is clearly stated to be to provide benefits for society by promoting the progress of science and useful arts. No other purpose is set forth. A means for achieving the stated purpose is expressly stated to be creation of limited-term exclusive rights in authors and inventors. While this means may also be viewed as an incentive or reward for the creations of genius, i.e., inventions or writings, the clause does not in any way state that providing such incentive or reward is the purpose of the grant of authority to Congress.[285]

Be that as it may, in the context of defining a constitutional boundary for the term of patents and copyrights, which justification for the limited-term exclusive right is accepted as paramount in no small measure determines what length of term will be considered to be constitutionally acceptable. Thus, e.g., if the "social benefits" rationale is considered more important, then "limited times" should be interpreted to be that length of term which provides an appropriate incentive to authors and inventors "to promote the progress of science and useful arts" but is not so long that this purpose ceases to be met or is actually deterred. In this view, ultimate removal of the writing or invention into the public domain is the more critical factor, and long copyright and patent terms will be considered constitutionally suspect. Alternatively, if "reward for creativity" is considered the more important rationale, then there is a pronounced tendency to lengthen the term of

---

283. 32 U.S. at 320.
284. Nowhere was this more evident than in the patent statutes through the middle of the nineteenth century where term extension was made dependent on whether the patentee had been suitably rewarded during the initial term of the patent. *See supra* text accompanying notes 209–230.
285. The Court has expressly rejected an argument that the purpose of the clause is to secure and protect an inherent property right of authors in their writings. Wheaton v. Peters, 33 U.S. (8 Pet.) 591 (1834).

patents and copyrights to better assure that the "reward" actually will occur. Long terms will not be constitutionally suspect, and the property interest of authors and inventors becomes more important than the public interest in promoting the progress of science and useful arts.

In the last few decades there has been increasing discussion by various commentators concerning the patent and, in particular, the copyright term.[286] Much of this discussion has been engendered by the substantial increases in the copyright term that occurred in the last quarter of the twentieth century. While the length of the statutory patent and copyright term have both increased in the two centuries since the first patent and copyright statutes were enacted in 1790, the increase in the copyright term has been quite disproportionate to the increase in the patent term. A simple comparison shows the extraordinary disparity in treatment between the two terms. Thus, in 1790 both the patent and the copyright statutory term were set at fourteen years. At the beginning of the new millennium, the statutory patent term is twenty years and the statutory copyright term is life in being plus seventy years (or for certain works, if the life of the author cannot be ascertained, for ninety-five years after publication or 120 years after creation, whichever is shorter). Thus, in two centuries the statutory patent term has increased by 43% but the statutory copyright term has increased by almost 580%.[287] Where they were once the same, the copyright term now is typically between four and five times longer than the patent term.

This extraordinary disparity in terms raises the question of the extent to which the language of the intellectual property clause sets a constitutional limit on the terms of patents and copyrights and whether that limit has been reached or exceeded in the case of copyright.[288] In addressing this

---

286. *See, e.g.,* ROBERT L. BARD & LEWIS KURLANTZICK, COPYRIGHT DURATION: DURATION, TERM EXTENSION, THE EUROPEAN UNION, AND THE MAKING OF COPYRIGHT POLICY (San Francisco 1999). This book provides a detailed bibliography of books and articles addressing various issues relevant to both the patent and the copyright term.

287. Using as a baseline 95 years for the copyright term.

288. The issue of whether an ultimate copyright term of 140 years violated the intellectual property clause was raised but not reached in United Christian Scientists v. First Church of Christ Scientist, 829 F.2d 1152 (D.C. Cir. 1987). But the court did make the following points:

> The copyright Congress conferred upon First Church through Private Law 92-60 is, however, far from ordinary . . . [and] is exceptional in scope and duration. Even if not construed as a copyright in perpetuity, it purports to confer rights of unprecedented duration; the term of protection for the 1906 edition of Science and Health, which would have expired in 1981 if treated

issue, it is important to note what the Supreme Court has called "the historic kinship between patent law and copyright law" and "the basic similarities between copyrights and patents."[289] While the Court has stated that "the two areas of the law . . . are not identical twins" and that caution must be used in applying doctrine formulated in one area to the other,[290] it nonetheless has frequently done so. It would thus appear that the criteria used for setting the term of patents ought to have relevance to setting the term of copyright and vice versa. As has been demonstrated, however, Congress has applied quite different standards in the two areas, and, as a result, has set quite different terms.

Any judicial determination as to the meaning to be given to the phrase "for limited times" in the intellectual property clause cannot look at the phrase in isolation. Rather, it must be interpreted in the context of the language of the clause taken as a whole. As the Supreme Court has made clear in 1834 in *Wheaton v. Peters* with regard to copyright, the meaning of a word or phrase in the clause must be determined in the context of the "words and sentences with which it stands connected."[291] Moreover, the Court observed as early as 1824 in *Gibbons v. Ogden* that the objects for which a congressional power is given "especially when the objects are expressed in the instrument itself, should have great influence on the construction." As the Court put it, the extent of congressional powers is to be construed by the language of the instrument which confers them taken together with the purposes for which they are conferred.[292]

The purposes or objects of the intellectual property clause are *not* "to secure for limited times to Authors and Inventors the exclusive Right to their respective Writings and Discoveries." The grant of exclusive rights for limited times is simply a means authorized in the clause to accomplish the stated objects, i.e., "To promote the Progress of Science and useful Arts." All too frequently both Congress and the judiciary have confused the two. If the objects of the clause were merely to secure exclusive rights for

---

under the general copyright laws, is now until 2046; and numerous editions of Science and Health which . . . were in the public domain because their copyrights had expired [or were] . . . never copyrighted, are now subject to the long-term copyright First Church derived from Private Law 92-60. Scant authority, if any, exists for such a dramatic departure from copyright practice.

892 F.2d at 1169–70.
289. Sony Corp. v. Universal City Studios, 464 U.S. 417, 439 (1984).
290. *Id.*
291. 33 U.S. at 261.
292. 22 U.S. at 188.

limited times, Congress would indeed have very broad and almost unbounded discretion to set the term of both patents and copyrights. But Justice Story's statement in *Pennock v. Dialogue* in 1829 that the term of the exclusive patent right "shall be subject to the discretion of Congress"[293] cannot be read in this manner for he was fully cognizant that congressional discretion is bounded by the stated objects of the intellectual property clause.[294] Indeed, he expressly stated this to be case in his *Pennock* opinion when he went on to declare that the "main object" of the patent system authorized by the intellectual property clause

> was "to promote the progress of science and useful arts;" and this could be done best by giving the public at large a right to make, construct use, and vend the thing invented, *at as early a period as possible* having a due regard to the rights of the inventor.[295]

As Bard and Kurlantzick have rather nicely phrased it:

> Without doubt Congress has considerable latitude in deciding how to comply with the Constitution's injunction that protection be for "limited times." At some point, though, an ever-lengthening term crosses a line beyond which the constitutional provision's prescription about "limited times" and its underlying purposes are mocked as the term becomes limited in form and name only.[296]

There are thus some terms beyond which the stated objects of promoting science and the useful arts not only are no longer met but actually may be negated.[297]

Although the point is almost totally ignored in modern commentary and judicial opinions, the Supreme Court in the latter part of the nineteenth century clearly indicated that the "to" language of the clause was

---

293. 27 U.S. at 26–27.
294. Nowhere is this more clearly indicated than in his Commentaries on the United States Constitution published four years after *Pennock* wherein he emphasized that short patent and copyright terms are beneficial in that they "admit the people at large, *after a short interval*, to the full possession and enjoyment of all writings and inventions without restraint." *See* Story, *supra* note 156 (emphasis supplied).
295. 27 U.S. at 19 (emphasis supplied).
296. BARD & KURLANTZICK, *supra* note 286, at 75.
297. Lessig makes the point quite well when he states that "increasing intellectual property's protection is not guaranteed to 'promote the progress of science and useful arts'—indeed, often doing so will stifle it." LAWRENCE LESSIG, CODE AND OTHER LAWS OF CYBERSPACE at 134 (1999).

a limitation on the power of Congress regarding what could be copy-righted.[298] Moreover, there is highly relevant modern language of the Supreme Court in 1966 in *Graham v. John Deere Co.* on the subject of congressional discretion in interpreting the limitations set forth in the intellectual property clause. The Court began its discussion by noting that the clause sets forth not any absolute authority to Congress but instead only a "qualified authority." It went on to state that "Congress in the exercise of the patent power may not overreach the restraints imposed by the stated constitutional purpose." It then emphasized that "'promot[ing] the Progress of . . . useful Arts' . . . is the *standard* expressed in the Constitution and it may not be ignored." Finally, it concluded that "*within the limits of the constitutional grant*, the Congress may, of course, implement the stated purpose of the Framers by selecting the policy which in its judgment best effectuates the constitutional aim."[299] In other words, congressional discretion regarding the patent power is bounded by "the limits of the constitutional grant." Precisely the same limitations apply to the copyright power.[300]

Three years later the Court reiterated a point it had made in *Graham v. John Deere Co.*, namely, that under the authority granted by the intellectual property clause "Congress may not 'enlarge the patent monopoly without regard to the . . . social benefit gained thereby.'"[301] The same is true with respect to copyright. Extending or lengthening the term of either patents or copyrights is equivalent to enlarging the monopoly created by these grants of exclusive rights.

---

298. *See supra* notes 178 and 179 and accompanying text.
299. 383 U.S. at 5–6 (emphasis supplied).
300. It is interesting to note that Nimmer & Nimmer suggest that based on this language from *Graham v. John Deere Co.* the intellectual property clause limits the constitutional authority of Congress to extend the term of existing copyright as does the language of the First Amendment. *See* 1 NIMMER & NIMMER, *supra* note 89, § 1.10 [C][1] [rel. 50-12/99]. In the latter regard, see Chapter Ten, text accompanying notes 151–162. Nimmer & Nimmer note the existence of a number of nineteenth-century patent cases holding that Congress may constitutionally extend the term of a patent, in some instances even after the patent had expired, but suggest that *Graham* opinion may portend that a different view would be taken today. A point that may distinguish these cases is that in none of them was the language of the intellectual property clause argued to constitutionally limit the power of Congress to extend the term of existing patents or to take out of the public domain that which had entered it.
301. Anderson's-Black Rock, Inc. v. Pavement Salvage Co., Inc., 396 U.S. 57, 61 (1969), citing *Graham v. John Deere Co.*, 383 U.S. at 6.

Several circuit courts, however, have chosen to simply ignore the views expressed by the Supreme Court on statements of purpose as set forth in the Constitution. Thus, for example, in *Schnapper v. Foley*[302] the argument was presented "that the purposive language of the Copyright Clause constitutes a substantial limitation on Congress' legislative power."[303] In rejecting this argument, the D.C. Circuit adopted views earlier expressed by the Fifth Circuit:

> Congress has authority to make any law that is "necessary and proper" for the execution of the enumerated Article I powers, . . . including its copyright power, and the courts [sic] role in judging whether Congress has exceeded its Article I powers is limited. The courts will not find that Congress has exceeded its power so long as the means adopted by Congress for achieving a constitutional end are "appropriate" and "plainly adapted" to achieving that end. *McCulloch v. Maryland . . . .* It is by the lenient standard of *McCulloch* that we must judge whether Congress has exceeded its constitutional powers in enacting an all-inclusive copyright statute.[304]

It concluded that "we cannot accept . . . that the introductory language of the Copyright Clause constitutes a limit on congressional power."[305]

Most recently the D.C. Circuit has relied on this conclusion to hold that the "to" language of the Clause does not constrain Congress from further extending the term of copyrights, both those already extant and those to come.[306] In so doing, the court made no attempt to analyze views expressed by the Supreme Court regarding the interpretation to be given to the language of the clause taken as a whole or the interpretation given to its introductory language as a qualifier of congressional power.

The difficulty with such an approach is that not only is it inconsistent with the views expressed by the Supreme Court in *Gibbons v. Ogden, Wheaton v. Peters, Baker v. Selden, Higgins v. Keuffel,* and *Graham v. John Deere Co.*, but it literally reads the "to" language out of the intellectual property clause and instead treats the clause as: "To secure for limited times to Authors and Inventors the exclusive Right to their respective Writings and Discoveries." But that is not the language of the clause. The "lenient standard of *McCulloch*" does not contemplate that express language of the

---

302. 667 F.2d 102 (D.C. Cir. 1981).

303. *Id.* at 111.

304. 667 F.2d at 112, citing Mitchell Bros. Film Group v. Cinema Adult Theater, 604 F.2d 852, 860 (5th Cir. 1979).

305. 667 F.2d at 112.

306. Eldred v. Reno, 239 F.3d 372, 378 (D.C. Cir. 2001).

intellectual property clause can be ignored in the cavalier fashion of the Fifth and D.C. Circuits.[307] The Supreme Court has made the point abundantly clear in recent times by emphasizing that: "The primary objective of copyright is not to reward the labor of authors, but '[t]o promote the Progress of Science and useful Arts.'"[308]

While acknowledging this to be the case,[309] Congress has not seen fit, at least in the copyright context, to address the introductory language as any form of restriction or limitation on its discretion to set the term of the grant. Yet implicit in the introductory language is the presumption that beyond some term not only is the progress of science, i.e., education and learning, not met, but rather it may actually be inhibited. But the rationales presently set forth for the statutory copyright term simply do not address this point. Perhaps nowhere is this more evident than when those rationales are applied to the statutory patent term. Indeed, with but one exception Congress has never applied those rationales to the patent term.[310] But if as pointed out in *Wheaton v. Peters*, the rights of authors and inventors are similar and ought to be treated similarly,[311] then the patent and copyright terms ought to be comparable rather than exhibiting their present remarkable disparity.

Neither Congress nor the courts now suggest that the patent system has as a purpose, much less a primary purpose, rewarding inventors for their creative efforts. Rather, the modern view is that "[t]he patent law is directed to the public purposes of fostering technological progress, investment in research and development, capital formation, entrepreneurship, innovation, national strength, and international competitiveness."[312] Contrast this with the congressional view that a primary rationale for extending the copyright term is to assure authors and their dependents "a fair

---

307. The so-called "lenient standard of *McCulloch*" is in essence a reliance on the necessary and proper clause to exclude any limitation on congressional power inherent in the introductory language of the intellectual property clause. For a discussion of the preclusive effect of express limitations in the intellectual property clause on congressional reliance on other enumerated grants of power, see Chapter Ten, Part B *infra*.
308. *See* Feist Publ'ns, Inc. v. Rural Tel. Serv. Co., 499 U.S. 340, 349 (1991); Twentieth Century Music Co. v. Aiken, 422 U.S. 151, 156 (1975).
309. *See supra* notes 272 and 273 and accompanying text.
310. The sole exception is the argument for harmonization which has been applied with respect to both the patent and the copyright term.
311. *See supra* note 254 and accompanying text.
312. Hilton Davis Chem. Co. v. Warner-Jenkinson Co, 62 F.3d 1512, 1536 (Fed. Cir. 1995) (quoting Newman, Cir. J. concurring).

economic return."[313] In continuing to expand the term of copyright,
Congress has totally ignored the societal benefit purposes set forth in the
introduction to the intellectual property clause and which the Supreme has
stated must be met before the monopoly may be enlarged,[314] and instead
viewed copyright as primarily for the benefit of authors. Yet as recently as
1991 the Supreme Court has emphasized that "the primary objective of
copyright is not to reward the labor of authors" but to benefit the public
through "promot[ing] the Progress of Science and useful Arts."[315]

If the present statutory patent term of twenty years is presumed "to
promote the Progress of Science and useful Arts," what then is the constitutional justification for a copyright term that is typically four to five times
longer? What is so different about the works of authors that requires a term
so much longer than is deemed necessary to meet the constitutional objects
with regard to the discoveries of inventors? Congress has chosen to address
neither of these issues. Rather, in setting the copyright term, it has chosen
to simply ignore the constitutional issues raised by the objects of the
intellectual property clause. Those objects are for the purpose of promoting
the public interest by enhancing the intellectual public domain rather than
restricting it. If under the intellectual property clause there is indeed a
balance between the public interest and the interest of individual authors
and inventors, as both the Supreme Court and Congress state there is, then
the time has come for the courts to delineate the constitutional factors
which affect such a balance and to determine whether the present copyright term is in accord with those factors.

Under the constitutional scheme "[i]t is evident that as rights are
strengthened, they need run, *and can be endured*, only for a correspondingly
shorter period."[316] This is as true of copyrights as it is of patents. The
broader the right granted, the more intrusive it is on the public domain.
The comprehensive broadening of the property rights encompassed by

---

313. *See supra* text accompanying note 270; Ou, *supra* note 276, at 7, citing
comments by Senator Hatch in the *Congressional Record*. According to Hatch
the issue of copyright term extension in 1995 was one of "whether the current
term of copyright adequately protects the interests of authors." He further
stated that an extension of the copyright term beyond that provided by the
Copyright Act of 1976 would allow "authors to reap the full benefits to which
they are entitled from the exploitation of their creative works." *See* 141 CONG.
REC. § 3390 (1995).
314. *See supra* note 301 and accompanying text.
315. *See supra* note 308.
316. BENJAMIN KAPLAN, AN UNHURRIED VIEW OF COPYRIGHT at 114 (1967)
(emphasis supplied).

copyright in the twentieth century compels the realization that the term of copyright is too long and unconstitutionally restricts the public domain. Just as with patents,[317] the term of a copyright is constitutionally limited to that required to actually "promote the progress of science."

---

317. *See supra* note 63.

CHAPTER EIGHT
INVENTORS AND THEIR DISCOVERIES

The clause authorizes Congress to secure to "Inventors the exclusive Right to *their* . . . Discoveries. . . ."[1] Regardless of the definition given to either inventors or discoveries, this language clearly limits congressional authority to the issuance of patents to inventors only for *their* inventions or discoveries. It is for this reason that patents are always applied for and issued in the name of the inventor regardless of who or what entity may actually own the rights to the patent.[2]

For terms that are so fundamentally important to the patent law, it is remarkable that the Supreme Court has never attempted to define what is meant by the terms "inventors" and "discoveries" as used in the clause.[3]

---

1. U.S. CONST. art. I, § 8, cl. 8 (emphasis supplied).
2. *See* 35 U.S.C. §§ 111, 116, 117, 118, 151, 152 (1994). *See also* Kennedy v. Hazelton, 128 U.S. 667 (1888). Robinson made the point expressly in his magisterial patent treatise published in 1890. *See* WILLIAM ROBINSON, 1 THE LAW OF PATENTS § 363 (Boston 1890) ("[w]ithout a change in the language of the Constitution, no patent could be conferred except upon an inventor, and for his own invention or discovery"). More recently, the D.C. Circuit has expressly declared that the intellectual property clause contemplates the grant of a patent only to the true inventor "either directly or through his assignee." *See* A. F. Stoddard & Co. v. Dann, 564 F.2d 556, 562 (D.C. Cir. 1977).
3. The Court early on had an opportunity to address the meaning to be given to these terms but declined to do so. *See* Evans v. Eaton, 16 U.S. (3 Wheat.) 454, 513 (1818). Burchfiel suggests that Justice Black's dissent in Exhibit Supply Co. v. Ace Patents Corp., 315 U.S. 126, 137 (1942) is predicated "upon an essentially semantic argument that the constitutional terms 'inventors' and 'discoveries' may be redefined according to individual justices' views of the intrinsic worth of the invention." *See* Kenneth J. Burchfiel, *Revising the "Original" Patent Clause: Pseudohistory in Constitutional Construction*, 2 HARV. J. L. & TECH. 155, 170 (1989). Justice Black had stated that: "The Constitution authorizes the granting of patent privileges only to inventors who make 'discoveries.' . . . To call the device here an invention or discovery such as was contemplated by the Constitution . . . is, in my judgment, to degrade the meaning of those terms." 315 U.S. at 138. But Justice Black did not attempt any definition of the meaning to be given to "inventors" and "discoveries" as used in the Constitution.

Neither for that matter has the Congress, although in the Patent Act of 1952 it did define "invention" to mean "invention or discovery."[4] Aside from being more than a bit circular and unhelpful,[5] the congressional definition of "invention" ignores the fact that in the early republic there was a considerable dispute as to whether "discovery" and "invention" were to be considered synonymous.[6] Moreover, the Framers seem not to have contemplated that the terms "inventors" and "discoveries" could—and would quickly—be viewed in a restrictive light by Congress and the courts. The result would be an interpretation of patentable novelty much narrower than existed in the contemporaneous British patent practice. The immediate consequence would be that the United States would become the first country with a patent system to preclude the issuance of patents of importation—and this at a time when the United States was vigorously seeking the transfer of European, and particularly British, technology being created by the industrial revolution.

A. A Constitutional Requirement of Novelty

Implicit in the use of the terms "inventors" and "discoveries" in the intellectual property clause is the premise that before an exclusive right can be granted, the discovery to be patented must be novel. Novelty is also implicit in the statement of purpose, i.e., "to promote the progress of . . .

---

4. Act of July 19, 1952, c. 950, 66 Stat. 797; see also 35 U.S.C. § 100(a). A more meaningful definition would have been something along the following lines: "An invention, in the sense of the patent law, means the finding out, the contriving, the creating of something which did not exist, and which was not known before, and which can in some real sense be made useful and advantageous to society." *See* Koppe v. Burnstingle, 29 F.2d 923, 925 (D.R.I. 1929).

5. It is akin to saying "a rose is a rose is a rose," but without the aesthetic value. According to Federico (who along with Giles Rich was largely responsible for drafting the Patent Act of 1952), that Act was intended to clarify that "invention" is a neutral term that can be applied either to "discoveries" that meet the statutory requirements of novelty and nonobviousness or to those that do not. P. J. Federico. *Commentary on the New Patent Act*, 35 U.S.C.A. §§ 1, 17 (1954). In this view, the terms "inventors" and "discoveries" as they appear in the intellectual property clause have little or no relevance in the determination constitutionally of patentable subject matter.

6. This point is discussed in Parts A–C *infra*.

useful arts."[7] Simply put, novelty is a constitutional requirement.[8] Interestingly, it was not until 1966 that the Supreme Court so held, albeit in an indirect sense, when it stated: "Congress may not authorize the issuance of patents whose effects are to remove existent knowledge from the public domain, or to restrict free access to materials already [publicly] available."[9] The requirement in the first U.S. patent legislation that to be patentable a discovery be "not before known or used,"[10] simply is an incorporation of the constitutional requirement of novelty.

Regardless of whether a constitutional statement of purpose is viewed as a limitation on the grant of authority, the constitutional requirement that an invention must be novel to be patentable clearly arises out of the definitions of "inventors" and "discoveries" that were in common use in 1787. Seidel points out that the most authoritative English dictionary of its day was Samuel Johnson's *A Dictionary of the English Language* and that the fourth edition of this dictionary, published in 1818, "carried the word meanings of the late 1700's."[11] Johnson defined "inventor" as "one who produces something new; a devisor of something not known before"[12]; and "discovery" as "the act of finding anything hidden, the act of revealing or disclosing a secret."[13]

At the end of the eighteenth century then, novelty was synonymous with new, but new in what sense? Under the British practice at the time the Constitution was drafted, novelty meant new in the realm. The fact that a particular art or manufacture was known or practiced outside Great Britain did not preclude its patentability, provided only that it was not known in the country. Novelty thus had a very broad connotation, and originality was involved only peripherally. This, of course, was what permitted patents of importation under the English practice.[14]

---

7. Although certain commentators dispute it, a statement of purpose does indeed constitute a constitutional limitation on patentability. See generally the discussion in Chapter Five, Part A.

8. *See* Kenneth J. Burchfiel, *Revising the "Original" Patent Clause: Pseudohistory in Constitutional Construction*, 2 HARV. J. L. & TECH. at 162 (1989). *Cf.* Federico, *supra* note 5.

9. Graham v. John Deere Co., 383 U.S. 1, 6 (1966).

10. Act of April 10, 1790, § 1, 1 Stat. 109.

11. Arthur H. Seidel, *The Constitution and a Standard of Patentability*, 48 J. PAT. OFF. SOC'Y 5, 10 (1966).

12. *Id.* at 13.

13. *Id.* at 15.

14. *See supra* Chapter Two, text accompanying notes 68–72.

In 1846 Hindmarch summarized the English law relating to novelty in the following manner:

> If the public once becomes possessed of an invention by any means whatever, no subsequent patent for it can be granted, either to the true and first inventor himself, or any other person, for the public cannot be deprived of the right to use the invention, and a patentee of the invention could not give any consideration to the public for the grant, the public already possessing every thing he could give.[15]

He went on to state:

> The want of this requisite novelty in an art or invention may . . . be established in any way which shows the public had a *knowledge of the invention, or the means of knowing it before the date of the patent.* Public knowledge of an invention may be shown by the existence of some public record, or the publication of some work or paper before the date of the patent, containing a description of the invention—or by some public use of the invention prior to the grant of the patent.[16]

This was the law in Great Britain at the time the Constitution was drafted. Novelty of an invention was determined not by what was known or used or published in the rest of the world but by what was in public use, available to the public, or published within Great Britain itself.

No delegate has left any record as to what the convention intended "inventors" and "discoveries" to mean. As shown later, Madison engaged in private correspondence which appeared to suggest that he narrowly interpreted these terms, but his rationale was less than clear.[17] The lack of any specific interpretation by the delegates themselves is unfortunate because the argument has been made that "[t]he statement that patents are to issue to 'inventors' for 'their discoveries' was clearly meant to prevent grants for imported technology, the English 'patents of importation.'"[18] It is not at all obvious, however, that such a narrow scope of novelty was what the Framers intended or even contemplated.

There is no reason to believe that they were not conversant with the fact that the common law had interpreted "true and first inventor" as it appeared in the Statute of Monopolies to include the first importer.

---

15. WILLIAM HINDMARCH, A TREATISE ON THE LAW RELATING PATENT PRIVILEGES FOR THE SOLE USE OF INVENTION at 21 (Harrisburg 1847).
16. *Id.* at 66 (emphasis in the original).
17. *See* text accompanying notes 53–56 *infra.*
18. Karl B. Lutz, *Are the Courts Carrying Out Constitutional Public Policy on Patents?* 34 J. PAT. OFF. SOC'Y 766, 773 (1952).

Moreover, they had chosen not to use the words "true and first" to modify "inventors." Thus, on its face, the constitutional language seemed to suggest that an exclusive right could be granted to someone who fell within the definition of "inventor," but who was in actuality not the literal "true and first" inventor. In addition, the commonly accepted definitions of "inventor" and "discovery" in the late eighteenth century did not per se require novelty in the modern sense. Simply put, there is nothing in the constitutional language which obligated Congress to use statutory language that would obligate an interpretation of novelty in any way materially different than the contemporaneous British view that novelty was dependent on what was known and used within the country.

Yet, as now is seen, Congress thought it did. As a consequence, although it was not immediately apparent, the new American patent law would not accept the English interpretation of the limited relationship between originality and novelty. Instead, to be patentable in the United States a discovery had to be original to the inventor, i.e., not known or used anywhere in the world and not merely in the United States.

B. The Prohibition on Patents of Importation

Prior to the American Revolution, British mercantile policy sought to treat the North American colonies as primarily sources of agricultural goods and raw materials and as markets for English manufactures. After the United States gained its independence, pragmatic economic considerations suggested to both France and Great Britain that while the United States would continue to serve as an excellent source of raw materials, it would now be an even better customer for manufactured goods. At least in the near term, it was thus in the interest of both countries to seek to discourage the development of manufacturing in the United States.

The new federal government that came into being in 1789 was well aware of this. One consequence was that manufacturing and the role the government should play with respect to it became a topic of conversation in both official and unofficial circles. By 1791 a tenuous sort of recognition had been reached between President George Washington, Secretary of the Treasury Alexander Hamilton, and Secretary of State Thomas Jefferson not only of the need to encourage new manufactures in the United States but of the desirability of transferring European and particularly British manufacturing technology to the United States. Jefferson, who the decade before had staunchly opposed manufacturing in favor of agriculture, and still strongly favored an economy based on agriculture, would now state, albeit reluctantly, that "the risk of hanging our prosperity on the fluctuating counsels & caprices of others renders it wise to us to turn seriously to manufactures; and if Europe will not let us carry our provisions to their manufactures we must endeavor to bring their manufactures to our provisions."[19]

The question, of course, was how best to bring European manufacturing technology to the United States, for this was far easier said than done. Time, effort, and considerable risk were involved. Those taking the risk would reasonably want some assurance that they could have exclusive rights to the technology for some period of time in order to recover their investment and hopefully profit from it. The most obvious and straightforward way to encourage such investment while at the same time minimizing the cost to the government[20] was to grant patents of importation[21] to those who introduced new technology into the country. The British policy of obtaining new technology by this means was perceived to be highly successful.[22] Moreover, it was recognized as such in the United States. But as Hamilton would rather quickly point out there was difficulty with this approach in that it was not at all clear that the government had authority to issue such patents.

---

19. Letter from Thomas Jefferson to David Humphreys (June 23, 1791), *in* VI THE WORKS OF THOMAS JEFFERSON (P. L. Ford ed., 1904) at 272–73. Humphreys was at this time the U.S. minister to Portugal.
20. This latter point was highly important to a government that was contemplating assuming state debts from the Revolutionary War and found itself in a very tight fiscal situation.
21. Patents for technology known and used elsewhere, but not in the country issuing the patent.
22. *See* Doron Ben-Atar, *Alexander Hamilton's Alternative: Technology Piracy and the Report on Manufactures*, 52 WM. & MARY Q. 411 (1995); *cf.* MacLeod who states that it is unclear how many patents of importation were actually commercialized in England. *See* Christine MacLeod, *The Paradoxes of Patenting: Invention and Its Diffusion in 18th- and 19th-Century Britain, France, and North America*, 32 TECH. & CULTURE at 895 (1991). In 1826 Peter Browne noted that "John Davis, of the Rolls Chapel Office . . . remarks that . . . 'many patents are granted to persons resident in England, for inventions communicated to them from abroad, it being only necessary, under the words of the statute, that they should be new within the realm.'" *See* P. A. Browne, *Mechanical Jurisprudence No. IX*, 2 FRANKLIN J. 231 (1826). Interestingly, American inventors rather quickly came to believe that this British policy encouraged the pirating of their inventions to England (as indeed it did) and sought a change in the American patent law to include a prohibition of the exportation of patented American technology without the express approval of the patentee or assignee. *See* ANNALS OF CONGRESS at 967 (11th Cong., Feb. 1811).

Both the intellectual property clause and the Patent Act of 1790 had as a purpose the promotion of the progress of the useful arts. The terms "useful arts" and "manufactures" were used virtually synonomously during this period.[23] Nonetheless, the more common expression was "manufactures," and "promoting the progress of useful arts" was contemporaneously understood to mean promoting the development of manufacturing.[24]

In his address to Congress on January 8, 1790 Washington raised the issue of manufactures in the context of the common defense, saying that the safety and interest of a free people "require that they should promote such manufactories, as tend to render them independent on others for essential, particularly, for military supplies."[25] In response, the House on January 15th ordered the Secretary of the Treasury to prepare and report a plan as to how this recommendation could best be met.[26] Hamilton seized on the opportunity and, although it took him well over a year to complete, the resultant *Report on the Subject of Manufactures* communicated to the House on December 5, 1791 set forth in detail both a pragmatic and theoretical justification for the development of manufacturing in the United States.[27]

Hamilton adverted to eleven particular means which he stated had been employed with success by governments in other countries for the purpose of supporting manufactures. There is no indication that he attempted to rank them in order of importance, although it is reasonably apparent that he preferred some over others. Of particular interest to the present work is his eighth means, set forth as "The encouragement of new inventions and discoveries at home, and of the introduction into the United States of such as may have been made in other countries; particularly those which relate to machinery." Under this heading, he noted that such encouragement "is among the most useful and unexceptionable of the aids which can be given to manufactures," and the "usual means" for accomplishing it "are pecuniary awards, and, for a time, exclusive privileges." He pointed out that while patent and copyright laws had been enacted, "it is desirable . . . to be able to extend the same benefits to introducers, as well as authors and inventors; a policy which has been practiced with advantage

---

23. *See supra* Chapter Four, note 50, and text accompanying notes 48–53.
24. *But see* Chapter Four, note 53.
25. III DOCUMENTARY HISTORY OF THE FIRST FEDERAL CONGRESS OF THE UNITED STATES OF AMERICA 252 (L. G. De Pauw et al. eds., Baltimore 1979).
26. *Id.* at 265.
27. The *Report* is reproduced in full in 10 THE PAPERS OF ALEXANDER HAMILTON at 231–340 (H. C. Syrett et al. eds., New York 1966).

in other countries." But, "there is cause to regret that the competency of the authority of the National Government to the good which might be done, is not without question." Accordingly, if Congress could not do "all that might be wished" in this regard, he was prepared to offer other "[m]eans for promoting the introduction of foreign improvements, though less efficaciously than might be accomplished with more adequate authority," i.e., the ability to grant patents of importation.[28] That other means was a proposal to use bounties.

What meaning did Hamilton have in mind by his rather ambiguous statement "that the competency of the authority of the National Government to the good which might be done, is not without question"? From the context it is apparent that the "good" he contemplated was the ability to grant patents of importation. What is not so clear, however, is the nature of the lack of authority in question. At a pragmatic and indeed mundane level he could simply have been pointing out that Congress in its questionable wisdom had determined not to expressly authorize such patents in the Patent Act of 1790. Alternatively, he may have been suggesting that there was a fundamental question whether Congress even had authority to enact legislation providing for such patents.[29]

In seeking to resolve this issue it is helpful to step back for a moment and review the background against which Hamilton prepared the *Report*. In the years immediately preceding 1791, Tench Coxe was perhaps the best known advocate of the need for American manufactures.

Quite possibly because Coxe was such a strong advocate for American manufactures, Hamilton appointed him as an Assistant Secretary of the Treasury. In this capacity, Coxe prepared a first draft of what ultimately became the *Report on the Subject of Manufactures*.[30] This draft was prepared in late 1790 or early 1791, many months after the Patent Act of 1790 had become law. In it Coxe stresses the need to encourage the importation of technology from abroad. He acknowledges the existence of the Patent Act of 1790 only in the most indirect sense and makes no comment whatever on what effect it might presumably have on encouraging the development of manufacturing in the United States. Nonetheless, he implicitly recognizes that it does not contemplate patents of importation. But he also implicitly suggests that Congress has power through private acts to issue

---

28. *Id.* at 307–08
29. The latter view received support from his comment that "the Legislature of the Union cannot do all the good that might be expected."
30. PAPERS OF ALEXANDER HAMILTON, *supra* note 27, at 10–12.

the equivalent of patents of importation and recommends that in appropriate circumstances it should do so.[31]

In support of this last point he made the quite reasonable argument that to the extent that importation benefits society to the same degree that invention does, it ought to be rewarded by exclusive rights in a similar manner. Moreover, he accurately pointed out that the principal manufacturing nations of Europe successfully used patents of importation to promote their own manufacturing. Hamilton certainly accepted these views, but he questioned the basic premise that Congress had authority through private acts to issue patents of importation. He went through five drafts in preparing the *Report*. In his first draft, he accepted Coxe's view that private acts might be used to encourage importation by the grant of limited-term exclusive rights, but added an important provision, "if within the compass of the powers of government" to do so.[32] Here unlike Coxe he is suggesting that there may in fact be a limit on the power of "government," i.e, Congress, to create patents of importation, even by private act. He gives no intimation of who is suggesting that such a limitation may exist on or what it may be based.

His second draft is an incomplete one which never actually reached the stage of addressing the issue. His third draft, however, is much more specific. After pointing out that it would be useful to grant patents of importation to "introducers, though not authors nor inventors," he states "there is cause to regret that there is room for a question whether the constitutional authority of the United States is competent to the good which might be done by aiding industry and promoting a variety of internal improvements of primary magnitude."[33] Here he makes clear that there may be more than merely a statutory impediment to patents of importation, and instead the problem may reside in the language of the Constitution itself.

There is nothing in the *Report* to indicate whether he developed this concern on his own or whether he was merely reporting views expressed by others. What is significant, however, is that he gave credence to it.[34] Ben-Atar strongly challenges any such interpretation, arguing that Hamilton was no strict constructionist and that he "doubted not the constitutionality of patents of importation but [rather] the 'competency' of

---

31. He had more than an academic interest in this point. *See* text accompanying notes 44 and 45 *infra*.
32. PAPERS OF ALEXANDER HAMILTON, *supra* note 27, at 37.
33. *Id*. at 114.
34. *See* E. C. Walterscheid, *Communications*, 53 WM. & MARY Q. 425 (1996).

the national government."[35] In so stating, he conveniently chooses to ignore that Hamilton's express statement in the final *Report* referred "to the competency of the *authority*" of the national government (emphasis supplied). While Hamilton undoubtedly favored patents of importation, nowhere in the final *Report* did he argue that the patent law should be amended to authorize them.[36] It is precisely because he was no strict constructionist that his failure to provide any argument in favor of the constitutionality of patents of importation is in itself strong evidence of his constitutional concern.

Hamilton was not reticent in the final *Report* to vigorously contend for the constitutionality of bounties and premiums as a means of encouraging manufacturing in the United States. Since he incorporated that argument into the final *Report*,[37] why then did he not provide at least a summary of his concerns about the constitutionality of patents of importation? Had he done so, he would have provided valuable insight into early views on the interpretation of the intellectual property clause. But he did not, nor does it appear did anyone else, and thus only speculation is left. There seems to be nothing in extant dictionary definitions or in the English common law opinions concerning the terms "inventor," "invention," and "discoveries" that would compel the view that the constitutional language precludes patents of importation.[38] Moreover, the use of the phrase "not before known or used" in the Patent Act of 1790 suggests a conscious attempt to

---

35. Doron Ben-Atar, *Communications*, 53 WM. & MARY Q. at 429 (1996).
36. *Cf.* Ben-Atar's assertions that in the *Report* Hamilton retained "introducer monopoly," "came out strongly in favor of granting an inventor monopoly to introducers of technology," and "urged Congress to revise the Patent Act of 1790." *See* Ben-Atar, *supra* note 22, at 403–05. But he cites no specific language in the final *Report* which in any way supports these assertions, and I have been able to find none.
37. PAPERS OF ALEXANDER HAMILTON, *supra* note 27, at 302–04.
38. The common law interpreted the phrase "true and first inventor" in the Statute of Monopolies to include the first introducer as well as the original inventor. *See* Chapter Two, note 72 and accompanying text. Moreover, as Cohen notes, "the framers of the Constitution were generally fluent in Latin and . . . the Latin word 'inventor' means 'one who finds out, a contriver, author, discoverer' (from the verb 'invenio" meaning sensu stricto, 'I come upon,' 'I find,' 'I discover'). . . ." *See* I. BERNARD COHEN, SCIENCE AND THE FOUNDING FATHERS at 241 (New York 1995). Originality seems not to have been a requirement. For the American emphasis on originality, see Part C *infra*.

further restrict the meaning of "discoveries" as used in the Constitution.[39] Until recently, the best that could be said was that Hamilton's remarks in the *Report* were enigmatic and likely to remain so.[40] However, it now appears that Hamilton predicated his concerns on the fact that the House deleted from the bill that became the Patent Act of 1790 language that expressly authorized patents of importation primarily because of a belief that such patents were unconstitutional.

But if, as Hamilton argued, patents do encourage the development of manufacturing and the importation of European manufacturing technology was highly important, why then did the Patent Act of 1790 not expressly provide for patents of importation? As has been discussed, Hamilton thought that Congress believed there was a constitutional impediment to the granting of such patents. As shown later, Washington obviously entertained no such view, and neither did the House committee that drafted the bill that ultimately became the Patent Act of 1790. We turn now to why the United States became the first country wherein patents of importation were deemed to be expressly precluded by law.

Although a combined patent and copyright bill, H.R. 10, was introduced in the first session of the first federal Congress, it failed to even be considered.[41] At the commencement of the second session, Washington in his address to Congress on January 8, 1790 stated among other things that:

> The advancement of Agriculture, Commerce and Manufactures, by all proper means, will not, I trust, need recommendation. But I cannot forebear intimating to you the expediency of giving effectual

---

39. *See* E. C. Walterscheid, *Novelty in Historical Perspective*, 75 J. PAT. & TRADE-MARK OFF. SOC'Y at 777–78 (1995).

40. Although Hamilton was a delegate to the federal convention, he was absent when the proposals that resulted in the intellectual property clause were presented and he took no part in the debates with respect to them. He thus had no first-hand knowledge of what the delegates intended the clause to encompass.

41. The bill was introduced on June 23, 1789, read for a second time the next day, and "ordered to be committed to a committee of the whole House on Monday se'ennight." However, on July 6th the House deferred action "until tomorrow." The postponement was repeated from day to day until August 17th when the House decided to postpone action "until the next session of Congress." The reason for delaying into the second session was later stated to be "the multiplicity of other important business." *See* DOCUMENTARY HISTORY OF THE FIRST FEDERAL CONGRESS OF THE UNITED STATES OF AMERICA *supra* note 25, at 94, 150. *See also Proceedings in Congress During the Years 1789 and 1790 Relating to the First Patent and Copyright Laws*, 22 J. PAT. OFF. SOC'Y (1940) at 249, 250, 252, 257.

encouragement as well to the introduction of new and useful inventions from abroad, as to the exertions of skill and genius in producing them at home.[42]

Here Washington seemed clearly to be suggesting that whatever legislation was enacted for securing exclusive rights to inventors for their discoveries, such legislation should also be such as to encourage new and useful inventions from abroad. That is to say, such legislation should cover patents of importation as well as those for what would now be termed true invention.[43]

Washington was not alone in this view. Tench Coxe had earlier sought and apparently failed to obtain models and drawings of Richard Arkwright's fabulously successful cotton processing machinery from England, but now thought he would be successful in this regard. On January 17, 1790 he wrote to George Clymer[44] that "we" are about to apply for a patent for various items of Arkwright's machinery. He acknowledged that "we" were not original inventors of this machinery, and accordingly urged Clymer to use his influence to have the patent bill, H.R. 10, which he thought was

---

42. DOCUMENTARY HISTORY OF THE FIRST FEDERAL CONGRESS OF THE UNITED STATES OF AMERICA, *supra* note 25, at 253; *Proceedings, supra* note 41, at 253–54.

43. An unnamed commentator, who almost certainly is P. J. Federico, has argued against this view, saying:

> Washington's complete passage mentions such a variety of different objects in the same sentence and paragraph that it is obvious that the same kind of encouragement was not intended for each. Washington was only advising Congress of the objects to be sought; the particular manner of accomplishing them was not specified in any case.

Centennial Number, *The Patent Act of 1793,* 18 J. PAT. OFF. SOC'Y 77, 79 (1936). Nonetheless, it appears clear from the context of Washington's statement that he perceived no impediment to the granting of patents of importation if Congress was disposed to enact such legislation. The House certainly thought he was asking for such legislation when it instructed the committee drafting the proposed patent bill to "insert a clause or clauses for giving effectual encouragement to the introduction of useful arts from foreign countries." *See* DOCUMENTARY HISTORY OF THE FIRST FEDERAL CONGRESS OF THE UNITED STATES OF AMERICA, *supra* note 25, at 278; 18 J. PAT. OFF. SOC'Y at 260 (1936).

44. Clymer was associated with him in the Pennsylvania Society for Promoting Manufactures and the Useful Arts.

still pending before Congress amended to allow patent privileges for those who "introduced" valuable foreign machinery.[45]

The patent bill, H.R. 41, which ultimately became the Patent Act of 1790, was first read in the House on February 16, 1790.[46] As introduced, the phrase "not before known or used" therein was modified by "in the United States" thereby clearly indicating that an invention known or used outside the United States could be patented in the United States. To make this point unequivocally, a section 6 was added expressly stating that the first importer of any art, machine, engine, device or invention, or any improvement thereon should be treated as if he or she were the original inventor or improver within the United States. As introduced therefore, H.R. 41 was exactly what Tench Coxe wanted.

But this language would be short-lived, because during subsequent debate the House and the Senate would delete both section 6 and "in the United States." The congressional record is totally silent as to why these deletions occurred. Historians have largely ignored this major—and in its time radical—departure from the European patent custom and practice and have failed totally to recognize that it was initiated in the House.[47] They have also failed to address the question of why Congress chose to ignore Washington's recommendation in so doing.[48] But some of Tench Coxe's

45. A. F. C. Wallace & D. J. Jeremy, *William Pollard and the Arkwright Patents*, 34 WM. & MARY Q. 404, 409–11 (1977). For who the "we" were, see note 52 *infra*.
46. Earlier commentators had been unable to find any copy of H.R. 41 as introduced. *See, e.g.,* 18 J. PAT. OFF. SOC'Y at 264 (1936). However, more recently a copy found in the Broadside Collection, Rare Book Room, Library of Congress, has been reproduced in VI DOCUMENTARY HISTORY OF THE FIRST FEDERAL CONGRESS OF THE UNITED STATES OF AMERICA *supra* note 25, at 1626–32.
47. Thus, Ben-Atar, for example, gives a misleading impression in stating that "[t]he House . . . version of the bill [version passed by the House] followed English law in giving to the first importer of technology the monopoly privileges accorded to original inventors." Ben-Atar, *supra* note 22, at 403. It is quite possible that if the Senate had not deleted "within the United States" as a modifier to "not before known or used" the courts would have interpreted this language as permitting patents of importation, but Ben-Atar fails to note that the House deleted section 6 which would have expressly authorized patents of importation and in so doing it clearly intended to preclude patents of importation. For a detailed discussion of the enactment of the Patent Act of 1790, see E. C. Walterscheid, *Charting a Novel Course: The Creation of the Patent Act of 1790,* 25 AIPLA Q. J. 445 (1997).
48. Ben-Atar actually raises the question but only in a rhetorical sense. *See supra* note 22, at 404.

correspondence suggests that it came about primarily because of a concern expressed by Madison that patents of importation were unconstitutional.

On March 7, 1790, the day the House deleted section 6 from H.R. 41, Rep. Thomas Fitzsimmons of Philadelphia wrote to Coxe, describing the proceedings of the day. He stated in relevant part:

> The bill for promoting Useful Arts has been so farr gon thr. To be new Engrossed-& will probably go to the senate in a day or two. Many alterations in Stile & some in Substance has been made-Among which are some Suggested in your Leter to me the 6th Section, allowing to Importers, was left out, the Constitutional power being Questionable-but if it is not the inconvenience is too Manifest of Admitting Patents in such Cases except some better guards could be provided.[49]

Fitzsimmons thus makes clear section 6 was deleted primarily because of concerns raised about the constitutionality of patents of importation. He does not indicate who raised the constitutional concerns or what their nature was. But closely contemporaneous correspondence between Coxe and Madison several weeks after the House action suggests that Madison was largely—if not primarily—responsible for the refusal of Congress to specifically authorize patents of importation in the Patent Act of 1790.

Two weeks after section 6 was deleted from H.R. 41 by the House, Coxe wrote to Madison, saying:

> I saw with regret the truth of your apprehension, that the benefits of a patent could not be constitutionally extended to imported objects-nor indeed, if it were within the verge of the powers of Congress, do I think that any clause [meaning statutory provision] to that effect could be safely modified. Private acts would be wise and safe, if they could be thought constitutional; but I think they cannot without an Amendment, by

---

49. The letter is found in COXE PAPERS, Incoming Box 20, Pennsylvania Historical Society. Coxe's letter to Fitzsimmons is missing, but the one thing Coxe did not desire was the deletion of section 6 from H.R. 41.

striking out all of the clause that follows the word "by" in the 8th parag. of the 8th Sec. of the first Article[50]—or something for that purpose.[51]

How did Coxe know of Madison's concern that patents of importation were unconstitutional, and why did he refer to "any clause to that effect"? The answer is that he was closely following the progress of H.R. 41 because of his interest in obtaining patents of importation,[52] and thus was fully apprized of the House action with respect to section 6.

In his response to Coxe on March 28th, Madison acknowledged his view that patents of importation were unconstitutional.[53] There is no contemporaneous record which expressly indicates what Madison's rationale was for this view, and unfortunately neither Madison nor Coxe, nor apparently anyone else, has set forth Madison's reasoning. Nowhere in his voluminous writings did Madison indicate that the convention had ever addressed the issue of patents of importation, and there is nothing in the records of the convention, including Madison's Notes, which in any way suggests that the Framers consciously intended to preclude Congress from having authority to grant patents of importation. Nor does Madison ever seem to have stated or otherwise indicated that the granting of patents of importation would not promote the progress of useful arts and manufactures.

Rather, implicit in his letter to Coxe is that his reasoning was predicated on the perceived rejection by the convention of certain broader powers that he and Charles Pinckney had proposed.[54] If so, it was a short-lived

---

50. He was referring to the intellectual property clause.

51. Letter from Tench Coxe to James Madison (Mar. 21, 1790), *in* 13 THE PAPERS OF JAMES MADISON at 111–14 (Charles F. Hobson et al. eds., Charlottesville 1981). Less than a year later, he would take a different tack and argue in his draft of the *Report on the Subject of Manufactures* that Congress did indeed have authority by private acts to grant patents of importation. *See supra* text accompanying note 31. He never gave any explanation for his change in view, but it is likely that it was self-serving in that he still wanted to obtain patents of importation.

52. *See supra* text accompanying notes 44 and 45. Indeed, in his letter to Madison he candidly states that he possesses several objects, "some of wch. are not inventions, but importations." *Id.* at 113. He also tells Madison that "the Artist, who undertook to make the machine for spinning flax, hemp & wool by water has completed the model & . . . it is now in my hands ready for an application for a patent, which he will make as soon as the law shall pass." *Id.* at 112. The "artist" was George Parkinson, who was one of the "we" mentioned in Coxe's letter to Clymer on January 17th. *See supra* note 44 and accompanying text.

53. *See supra* Chapter Five, note 94 and accompanying text.

54. *See supra* Chapter Five, note 95.

approach to constitutional interpretation. Within a few years, he would expressly reject as the basis for constitutional interpretation the fact that a particular proposal had been rejected by the convention.[55] Several decades later, in 1832, he suggested that even though the convention had rejected certain specific proposals with respect to congressional power, this did not mean that the delegates did not intend for Congress to have broad equivalent powers to protect and encourage domestic manufacture.[56] Although Madison was speaking in the context of authority under the commerce clause to place import duties on foreign manufactures, his argument is just as applicable to interpreting the intellectual property clause in the context of authority to create patents of importation.

In 1790 and 1791, however, he seems to have been quite willing to predicate constitutional interpretation on rejection of particular language by the convention, with the result that the future course of the United States patent law was fundamentally changed. But being the erudite fellow that he was, he quite likely was aware that the common law had interpreted "true and first inventor" in the Statute of Monopolies as reading on one who first imports as well as one who first invents. Why then did he refuse to accept this common law interpretation and apply it to the constitutional language? The most likely reason is that he was convinced that the Constitution had not incorporated the common law as the law of the land,[57] as indeed it had not,[58] and he was not about to depend on the common law

---

55. *Id.*
56. As he put it:

> The intention is inferred from the rejection or not adopting of particular propositions which embraced a power to encourage them [i.e., domestic manufactures]. But without knowing the reasons for the votes in those cases, no such inference can be sustained. The propositions might be disapproved because they were in bad form or not in order; because they blended other powers with the particular power in question; or because the object had been, or would be, elsewhere provided for. No one acquainted with the proceedings of deliberative bodies can have failed to note the frequent uncertainty of inferences from a record of naked votes.

Letter from James Madison to Professor Davis, *in* III RECORDS OF THE FEDERAL CONVENTION OF 1787, at 518, 520 (Max Farrand ed., New Haven 1937).
57. See letter from James Madison to George Washington (Oct. 18, 1787), *in* RECORDS OF THE FEDERAL CONVENTION OF 1787, *supra* note 56, at 129–30.
58. *Cf.* Crosskey's view that "the men of the Convention apparently considered the standing national law of the United States to be the 'common law of England,' in all of its applicable portions." WILLIAM W. CROSSKEY, I POLITICS AND THE CONSTITUTION at 549 (1952).

for an interpretation of the meaning of any of the terms used in the intellectual property clause.[59]

As passed by the House, H.R. 41 retained the qualifier "in the United States" to the phrase "not before known or used." The reason for this seems to have been that in the press of business Madison and possibly others addressed their concerns about constitutionality of patents of importation only to section 6, apparently not realizing that retention of the qualifying phrase would also authorize patents of importation. Because it agreed with the House that the new patent statute should not authorize patents of importation, the Senate deleted the qualifier.[60] Aware that the House had acted with insufficient precision, the Senate seems to have viewed this amendment as merely one of house-keeping to implement the intent of the House with which it concurred.

The result was that the first federal patent legislation did not contain express language authorizing patents of importation, but neither did it contain language expressly precluding such patents. The Act of 1790 was replaced with new patent legislation which also provided no express authorization for patents of importation, although it too did not expressly preclude them. Instead, it retained the ambiguous language from the Act of 1790 that for an invention to be patentable it must be "not before known or used." At the end of the eighteenth century, all other countries with patent systems granted patents of importation as a means of promoting the development of new industries within their borders. It was only in the United States that such patents were being argued to be precluded by law. Although there had as yet been no reported judicial interpretation that

---

59. Although the wording of his views on the clause in *The Federalist No. 43* could be interpreted as suggesting that the common law was indeed applicable to interpreting the clause. For a discussion on this point, *see supra* Chapter Six, text accompanying notes 82–93.

60. Its reasons for doing so are nowhere found. It may have simply agreed with the constitutional concerns. Alternatively, it may have believed there were other good and sufficient reasons why the United States should not issue such patents. In this regard, note that Fitzsimmons had indicated to Coxe that even in the absence of constitutional concerns, "the inconvenience is too manifest of admitting patents in such cases except some better guards could be provided." *See supra* text accompanying note 49. Moreover, the Senate had received a copy of a petition by one Richard Wells which strongly objected to patents of importation, primarily because he believed they would make it more difficult to pirate English inventions. For a discussion of this petition, see E. C. Walterscheid, *Patents and Manufacturing in the Early Republic*, 80 J. PAT. & TRADEMARK OFF. SOC'Y 855, 875–77 (1998).

either the Act of 1790 or the Act of 1793 prohibited patents of importation, that conclusion would soon be drawn from the interpretation given to novelty under these Acts.[61]

It is interesting to note that at least part of the language of the Act of 1793 appears to have been intended by its sponsor to allow United States citizens to obtain patents of importation, while precluding foreigners from doing so. While the Act of 1790 had permitted anyone, citizen or not, to obtain a patent, the Act of 1793 restricted patents to American citizens. Maryland Congressman William H. Murray, who proposed this change, candidly stated that its purpose was to prevent foreigners from obtaining patents in the United States for inventions for which they had already obtained patents in Europe "by which means the citizens of the United States might be prevented from obtaining patents for the same or similar inventions."[62] Inherent in this view was the supposition that U.S. citizens might indeed properly obtain patents for inventions that had already been patented by others in Europe.

There never would be a federal judicial opinion expressly holding that patents of importation were unconstitutional.[63] But there was a state opinion indicating this to be case. In 1812 in *Livingston v. Van Ingen*[64] a unanimous appellate court in New York held that federal patents of importation were forbidden by the Constitution, but that this ban did not apply to state patents of importation. The judges argued that the term "inventors" as used in the Constitution was what precluded such patents,[65]

---

61. Conversely, however, for several decades to come arguments would be presented that the United States should indeed grant patents of importation because it was in her economic interest to do so. *See, e.g.,* THOMAS GREENE FESSENDEN, AN ESSAY ON THE LAW OF PATENTS FOR NEW INVENTIONS at 213–16 (Boston 1810); JOSEPH COOPER, THE EMPORIUM OF ARTS AND SCIENCES at 436 (New Series) (Philadelphia 1813); I. L. SKINNER, THE AMERICAN JOURNAL OF IMPROVEMENTS IN THE USEFUL ARTS, AND MIRROR OF THE PATENT OFFICE OF THE UNITED STATES at 34 (Washington 1828).

62. ANNALS OF CONGRESS at 855–56 (2d Cong. Jan. 30, 1793).

63. The first reported United States patent case, decided in 1804, held that patents of importation were precluded by American law, but gave no basis whatever for this holding. *See* note 77 *infra* and accompanying text. Subsequent cases would base such a holding on an interpretation of statutory language in the Patent Act of 1793.

64. 9 Johns. 507 (N.Y. 1812).

65. Thus, Chief Justice Kent stated that

> it seems to be admitted that Congress are authorized to grant patents only to *inventors* of the useful art. . . . There cannot, then, be any aid or

although there is nothing to indicate that the Framers intended a more narrow definition than that encompassed in the common law.[66]

As late as 1824, however, the Attorney General of the United States replied that there was nothing in the intellectual property clause that forbade federal patents of importation. As he put it:

> But it was argued that the power of Congress is limited to inventors, and that the power to encourage by patents the introduction of foreign discoveries, stands clear of this constitutional grant. If it were necessary, this doctrine might be questioned. The statute of [monopolies] uses the same word with the constitution, "inventors;" and the decisions upon the construction of this statute might be referred to, in order to show that it has been considered as embracing discoveries imported from abroad.[67]

But without any citation of authority, Story in his Commentaries published in 1833 stated with respect to the intellectual property clause: "The power, in its terms, is confined to authors and inventors; and cannot be extended to the introducers of any new works or inventions."[68] He thus accepted the view that the literal language of the Constitution, i.e., its use of the term "inventors," precluded patents of importation.

C. The American Emphasis on Originality

If patents of importation were precluded by the literal language of the intellectual property clause as Story indicated, a New York court opined, and Madison and Hamilton appeared to believe,[69] then the clause obligated

---

    encouragement, by means of an exclusive right under the law of the United States, to importers from abroad of any useful invention or improvement.

    Id. at 583.

66. *See supra* note 38.

67. Gibbons v. Ogden, 22 U.S. (9 Wheat.)1, 173 (1824).

68. JOSEPH STORY, COMMENTARIES ON THE CONSTITUTION OF THE UNITED STATES § 1153 (Boston 1833).

69. Although Madison's letter to Coxe seemed to indicate that his belief that patents of importation were unconstitutional was predicated on the rejection by the convention of proposals that were sufficiently broad to encompass such patents, implicit in any such view was that the terms "inventors" and "discoveries" as used in the clause must be construed to refer only to one who is the first and original discoverer of the subject matter for which an exclusive right is sought. Otherwise, there was nothing to prevent "inventor" to be defined as including the first introducer or importer.

a narrow interpretation of novelty and a broad interpretation of what constitutes an anticipation precluding patentable novelty. While early judicial opinions would indeed conclude that novelty under the United States patent law meant new and original with respect to the world at large, and not merely the United States, they would do so on the basis of an interpretation of certain language of the Patent Act of 1793 and not on any interpretation of "inventors" and "discoveries" as used in the intellectual property clause.

Several provisions of the Act of 1790 could be interpreted in the context of novelty. Thus, it required the petition for patent to state that the invention was "not before known or used." It also required the specification "to distinguish the invention or discovery from other things before known or used." These requirements seemed clearly to indicate that prior knowledge or use would effect novelty and hence patentability, but they did not provide any indication as to where the invention must not be "before known or used," i.e., in the United States only or in the world as a whole. Another provision that appeared to affect novelty was the statement that in any infringement act, the patent or specification itself should "be prima facie evidence" that the patentee was "the first and true inventor" of the thing patented.

The Act of 1793 changed the fledgling United States patent system from one of examination, albeit of a limited sort, to one of registration and thereby made it more closely akin to its English counterpart. While the petition was still required to state that the invention was "not before known or used," the inventor was now required to "swear or affirm that he does verily believe that he is the true inventor or discoverer" of the subject matter sought to be patented. The intent was clearly to seek to avoid having others than "the true inventor" obtain patents. But what defined "the true inventor"? The issue was further confused by the fact that the language indicating that the specification was prima facie evidence that the patentee was "the first and true inventor" was removed[70] and replaced with a proviso that in any infringement action the patent could be declared void if it was shown "that the thing thus secured by patent was not originally

---

70. Twenty-three years later Oliver Evans would argue with considerable justification that this represented a substantive change between the two Acts in that various individuals could independently invent the same thing and thus all be true inventors, although only one of them could be the first true inventor. *See* OLIVER EVANS, EXPOSITION OF PART OF THE PATENT LAW BY A NATIVE BORN CITIZEN OF THE UNITED STATES at 29–34 (Philadelphia 1816). *See also* text accompanying notes 82–84 *infra*.

discovered by the patentee." As would be emphasized many years later, the phrase "originally discovered" was susceptible to several meanings.[71]

The Act of 1800[72] introduced yet another provision affecting novelty. It granted certain resident aliens the right to obtain patents provided that they swore or affirmed that the invention had not "been known or used in this or any foreign country." It further provided that if it were subsequently shown that the invention "had been known or used previous to such application for patent, [the patent] shall be utterly void." But it failed to amend the Act of 1793 to modify "know or used" with "in this or any foreign country," and thereby arguably sought to distinguish between resident aliens and citizens in the context of what could be treated as prior art, i.e., "known or used."

It was against the background of these statutory provisions, and not as a result of judicial interpretation of the constitutional language, that novelty in the United States would come to have quite a different meaning than it had under the existing common law. Specifically, originality would be interpreted to be a fundamental component of novelty in the United States, i.e., the invention would have to be both new and original, not only in the United States but in the entire world.

The legislative history of the Patent Act of 1790 seemed to suggest that the phrase "not before known or used" was intended to mean not before known or used *anywhere in the world* and not simply in the United States.[73] But this legislative history was not known or reported, and even if it had been would not have been considered relevant under the rules of statutory construction then in vogue.[74] Instead, the courts would ultimately rely upon other language in the Act of 1793, i.e., "not originally discovered by the patentee,"[75] to hold that what is now termed "prior art" is not limited to that known or used in the United States.

Although it is difficult to imagine today, for more than a decade after enactment of the Act of 1793 there was no reported patent case law.[76] The

---

71. Evans took great pains to emphasize this point in 1816. *Id.* at 32–41, 45.
72. Act of April 17, 1800, 2 Stat 37.
73. Walterscheid, *supra* note 47.
74. *See, e.g.,* H. J. Powell, *The Original Understanding of Original Intent,* 98 HARV. L. REV. 885, 897 (1985) ("[t]he modern practice of interpreting a law by reference to its legislative history was almost entirely nonexistent . . . ").
75. Act of February 21, 1793, § 6, 1 Stat. 318.
76. This is not to suggest that during this period there was no litigation concerning patents, but rather that it was not reported in any formal sense and thus was not generally known.

earliest reported United States patent case, *Reutgen v. Kanowrs,* decided in 1804, did address the issue of novelty, although it made no reference to either constitutional or statutory language. Therein Justice Washington, in his capacity as circuit judge, stated that:

> if the invention as brought over [from Europe], that is, if it appears that the plaintiff was not the original inventor, in reference to other parts of the world as well as America, he is not entitled to a patent. This point has been decided otherwise in England, in consequence of the expressions of the Statute of Jac. I [i.e., the Statute of Monpolies], which speaks of new manufacture, within the realm.[77]

In *Dawson v. Follen,* decided in 1808, he instructed the jury that in an action for patent infringement, for the plaintiff to recover it must be satisfied that he was the original inventor, not only in relation to the United States but to other parts of the world.[78] Again, there was no reference to specific statutory or constitutional language, although he did indicate that "the act of congress [the Act of 1793] differed from the law of England on this subject."

Although he made no mention of it, it is likely that Justice Washington relied on the old common-law case of *Edgeberry v. Stephens* for his statement in *Reutgens* that the "expressions" of the Statute of Monopolies "which speaks of new manufacture, within the realm" serve as the authority for patents of importation under the common law.[79] His reference to these "expressions" suggests that he believed that the absence of "in the United States" or something akin to "within the realm" in the Acts of 1790 and 1793 was dispositive of the issue.

It should be noted, however, that the court in *Edgeberry* had engaged in a bit of judicial sophistry[80] to avoid having to deal directly with an interpretation or definition of "true and first inventor" as it appeared in the Statute of Monopolies.[81] The reference to "within this realm" in the Statute had nothing whatever to do with defining novelty but instead referred merely to the jurisdictional authority of the crown to grant patents for invention "of the sole working or making of any manner of new manufacture within this realm." As such, it was a tautological expression in

---

77. 20 F. Cas. 555, 556 (D. Pa. 1804) (No. 11,710).
78. 7 F. Cas. 216 (D. Pa. 1808) (No. 3,670).
79. *See supra* Chapter Two, note 72 and accompanying text.
80. An American judge in 1826 would call it "a judicial perversion of the language of the [Statute of Monopolies]." *See supra* Chapter Two, note 71.
81. *See* Section 5 of the Statute as set forth in Chapter Two, text preceding note 68.

that the crown clearly had no authority to grant such patents outside the realm. But Justice Washington was perfectly prepared to engage in the same bit of sophistry to distinguish the English law from what he interpreted the American law regarding novelty to be.

The federal case law does not reveal any further reference to novelty in the context of originality until 1816 when the issue was once again discussed by Justice Washington in his capacity as circuit judge. In *Evans v. Eaton* counsel for Oliver Evans had argued that:

> It is not necessary that the plaintiff should be the first discoverer, if he was a real bona fide discoverer, without knowing that a similar discovery had previously been made; this is clearly the meaning of the word "true"in the tenth section [of the Act of 1793],[82] with which the word "original" in the sixth section is synonymous.[83] The word "first" is used in the statute of [Monopolies], and was no doubt dropped intentionally by congress.[84]

In essence, Evans was contending that all that was required was that he be an actual and independent inventor who had not derived the invention from someone else, and that it mattered not that he might not be the first discoverer.

Evans had earlier publicly argued that the American patent laws cannot be construed

> to impede [the progress of science and useful arts], nor can [they] have effect beyond the limits of their territories. Therefore words *not known or used before*, must mean in, and apply to, the *United States and Territories*, and not to China or Tartary. For it is no benefit to the United States, no improvement in the arts here, for a thing to be known and used in any other country.[85]

He now took the opportunity of the *Evans v. Eaton* litigation to expand on this argument and vigorously contend that prior foreign usage or

---

82. The tenth section provided that "if it shall appear that the patentee was not the true inventor or discoverer, judgment shall be rendered by such Court for the repeal of such patent."
83. The sixth section provided that if it was proven that "the thing thus secured by patent was not originally discovered by the patentee, but had been in use, or had been described in some public work anterior to the supposed discovery of the patentee, . . . the patent shall be declared void."
84. 8 F. Cas. 846, 850 (D. Pa. 1816) (No. 4,559).
85. OLIVER EVANS, THE YOUNG MILL-WRIGHT AND MILLER'S GUIDE at 141–42 (2d ed. Philadelphia 1807).

publication did not serve to negate patentability of an act of true invention in this country. That is, he viewed patentable novelty under the Act of 1793 to extend to any act of independent invention made in this country regardless of whether the invention was known or used elsewhere in the world. He acknowledged and indeed applauded that prior knowledge and use in the United States would defeat the right to a patent but strongly contested any view that the Act of 1793 permitted a patent to be voided merely because it could be shown that there had been prior foreign knowledge or use. In his literal reading of the Act, it required only that the patentee be a *true* inventor, not that he or she be the *original* inventor.

His argument was predicated on three premises, none of which addressed the constitutional language. The first was that there was no express language in the Act of 1793 indicating that prior foreign knowledge or use bars patentability and that "not before known or used" and "but had been in use, or had been described in some public work" could and should reasonably be interpreted to mean "in the United States."[86]

His second premise was closely attuned to the first, namely, that in the Act of 1793 Congress chose not to use language that it had incorporated into the Act of 1790 and the Act of 1800, and that this decision must be deemed to have been deliberate by Congress. Thus he noted that whereas the Act of 1790 had spoken of "the first and true inventor," the Act of 1793 spoke only of "the true inventor." The import of this, he argued, was that it demonstrated a congressional intent to deliberately extend the right of a patent "to any or either of the *true inventors*," and not merely to the first

---

86. He drew this conclusion from the fact that no "other country than the United States is *alluded* to; no other being mentioned, no other could be intended by saying less than *in this or any other country*." *See* Evans, *supra* note 70, at 19. As he also stated,

> the words in section 1, "not known or used," and in the 6th section, "but had been in use, or had been described in some public work," can have no allusion to any country but the United States because they have not said "in this *or any foreign country*," which are the words used in section 1 of the act of 1800, to express their intention with respect to patents to foreigners; for they, too, must be *the true inventors or discovers* designated by law, and therefor shall not patent the improvements they import.

> *Id.* at 45. He seems to have been totally unaware that in the bill which became the Act of 1790, the limiting phrase "in the United States" had in fact been added and then subsequently deleted. Nonetheless, there was a rational basis for his argument.

or original inventor.[87] In other words, the Act of 1793 permitted an independent inventor in the United States to patent an invention irrespective of whether it had been earlier invented somewhere else in the word, provided only that it was not known or used in the United States prior to the independent invention in the United States.

In this same vein he noted that the Act of 1800 which extended the right to patent to resident aliens under certain conditions required them to affirmatively state that their invention was not "not known or used in this *or any foreign country.*" This too, he argued, was convincing evidence that the Act of 1793 had never been intended to permit prior knowledge or use in a foreign country to preclude or void a patent to a true inventor in the United States having no knowledge of the prior foreign publication or use.

His third premise went further and suggested that the Act of 1793 should be interpreted to permit patents of importation. He predicated this view on the fact that the patent laws spoke of both invention and discovery and inventors and discoverers. He argued that these terms are not synonymous and that discovery can occur without invention. In his view, the natural consequence was that inventions known and practiced in foreign countries could be "discovered" by an enterprising person and imported into and patented in the United States.[88]

---

87. *Id.* at 29.
88. As he put it:

> What ideas then do the terms invention or discovery, inventor or discoverer, as used in the patent laws, convey? They certainly are not synonymous, for may not a thing be discovered without invention? Certainly it can; a plant unknown may be discovered, or a new use of a known plant, by diligence and search, without invention. A new and useful principle or law in nature may, by expensive and laborious researches or experiments, be discovered, though the aid of invention may be necessary to apply them to useful purposes. A man may travel over Europe, Asia and Africa at great expense, on purpose to discover what improvements are in used there, "*not known or used*" in the United States, and in case he introduces them for the benefit of his country, did neither the framers of the constitution, nor congress, contemplate a reward for such expensive and patriotic labours to promote the welfare of his fellow citizens? Certainly they did intend to secure to the discoverers of things new and useful, *in the United States*, the exclusive right to their respective discoveries, for limited times.

Evans, *supra* note 70, at 60–61.

In *Evans v. Eaton,* however, Justice Washington refused to accept Evans' expansive view of novelty, saying:

> The discovery must not only be useful, but new; it must not have been known or used before in any part of the world. It is contended by plaintiff's counsel, that the title to the patentee cannot be impeached, unless it is shown that he knew of a prior discovery of the same art, machine, &c. And that true and original are synonymous, in the intention of the legislature. As it is not pretended that true and original mean the same thing in common parlance, I proceed to enquire whether the legislature intended to use them as such. As to this, there can scarcely be two opposed opinions. The first section, referring to the allegations of the applicant for a patent, speaks of the discovery as something not known or used before the application. And in the sixth section it is declared, that the defendant may give in evidence that the thing secured by patent, was not originally discovered by the patentee, but had been in use or had been described in some public work, anterior to the supposed discovery. Now if original does not mean first; the preceding expressions in the first and sixth sections most certainly do.[89]

In other words, as he interpreted the statutory language, novelty was defeated if it could be shown that the patentee was not the original or first inventor of the subject matter anywhere in the world.

When *Evans v. Eaton* was appealed to the Supreme Court, Chief Justice Marshall in 1818 agreed that the sixth section of the Act of 1793 required an invention to be both new and original to be patentable. As he put it:

> Without a critical inquiry into the accuracy with which the term invention or discovery may be applied to other than the first inventor, the court considers this question as completely decided by the 6th section of the general patent act. That declares, that if the thing was not originally discovered by the patentee, but had been in use, or had been described in some public work, anterior to the supposed discovery by the patentee, judgement shall be for the defendant, and the patent declared void.
>
> Admitting the words "originally discovered" to be explained or limited by the subsequent words, still, if the thing had been in use, or had been described in a public work, anterior to the supposed discovery, the patent is void.[90]

---

89. 8 F. Cas. at 853.
90. Evans v. Eaton, 16 U.S. (3 Wheat.) 454, 513–14 (1818).

While "anywhere in the world" is not mentioned, it is clear that Marshall viewed the sixth section of the Act of 1793 as requiring an invention to be both new and original throughout the world in order for it to be patentable in the United States. Henceforth, this would be the definition of novelty required for patentability in the United States.

Neither Justice Washington nor Chief Justice Marshall predicated their holdings on any supposed common definition of "inventors" and "discoveries" in the manner that the New York judges had in *Livingston v. Van Ingen* (9 Johns. 507 (N.Y. 1812)) in 1812 when they declared that the intellectual property clause precluded federal patents of importation.[91] If either Justice Washington or Chief Justice Marshall had believed that "in common parlance" the terms "inventors" and "discoveries" as used in the Constitution precluded any expansive definition of patentable novelty, it would have been extremely easy for them to say so, but they did not. Indeed, Marshall expressly refused to address the meaning to be given to these terms, and instead relied on other language in the statute to require that patentable invention be both new and original.

D. A Constitutional Standard of Invention

Accepting that novelty is a constitutional requirement for patentability, is there any higher standard set forth in the intellectual property clause than simple novelty with regard to what may be declared to be patentable invention? In the middle third of the twentieth century, Justices of the Supreme Court began, for the first time, to argue that there was.[92] The first intimation of this view occurred in 1941 in *Cuno Engineering Corp. v. Automatic Devices Corp.* (314 U.S. 84 (1941)) where Justice Douglas for the Court declared the invention in question not to be patentable because the inventor's "skill in making this contribution" failed to reach "the level of inventive genius which the Constitution (art. I, § 8) authorizes Congress to reward."[93] He pointed to no particular language of the intellectual property clause obligating a specific "level of inventive genius" before a patent could be proper.

---

91. *See supra* text accompanying notes 63–66.
92. This despite the fact that in 1891 the Court had declared that the term "invention" "cannot be defined in such a manner as to afford any substantial aid in determining whether an particular device involves an exercise of the inventive faculty or not." McClain v. Ortmayer, 141 U.S. 419, 427 (1891).
93. 314 U.S. 84, 91 (1941).

A year later, Justice Black, joined by Justice Douglas, dissenting in *Exhibit Supply Co. v. Ace Patents Corp.* (315 U.S. 126, 137 (1942)) seemed to suggest that the constitutional meaning of "inventors" and "discoveries" were somehow dependent on how individual justices viewed the intrinsic worth of the particular invention.[94] But it was in 1950 that Justices Douglas and Black, concurring in *Great Atlantic & Pacific Tea Co. v. Supermarket Equipment Corp.* (340 U.S. 147 (1950)), really got the attention of the patent bar, with their constitutional theory that every patent case involving validity represents a question which requires reference to a standard written into the Constitution. In their view, that standard is imposed by the statement of purpose in the intellectual property clause.[95] Had they stopped there, their views would have been controversial, but not historically absurd.

But they went much further and argued that constitutionally, an

> invention, to justify a patent, had to serve the ends of science—to push back the frontiers of chemistry, physics, and the like; to make a distinctive contribution to scientific knowledge. . . . The Constitution never sanctioned the patenting of gadgets. Patents serve a higher end—the advancement of science.[96]

The only supposed authority cited for this view was certain earlier references by members of the Court to variations on the phrase "inventive genius" in a number of earlier opinions.[97] But until *Cuno* the Court never had suggested that "inventive genius" was a constitutional standard for patentability, and even then there had been no suggestion that "advancement of science" was a constitutional requirement for patentability.

Such a view had never seriously been suggested by anyone,[98] and besides reading the phrase "useful arts" out of the clause, it relied on a totally anachronistic interpretation of "science" as used in the clause.[99] Quite likely for these reasons, the Court has declined to read into the clause any requirement that scientific advancement is a predicate for patentability.

---

94. *See supra* note 3.
95. *See supra* Chapter Four, notes 62–64 and accompanying text . They actually initially had taken this position five years earlier in Special Equip. Co. v. Coe, 314 U.S. 370, 381 (1945) ("[t]he purpose 'to promote the progress of science and useful arts' . . . provides the standards for the exercises of the power and sets the limits beyond which it may not go").
96. *See supra* Chapter Four, text accompanying note 64.
97. See the cases noted in 340 U.S. at 155, n.1.
98. *See* Chapter Four, note 63.
99. *See* Chapter Four, note 65 and accompanying text.

It has, however, accepted their view that the "to" language of the clause sets forth a constitutional standard of patentability. Thus, in 1966 in *Graham v. John Deere Co.* the Court relied heavily on the "to" language of the clause to support its view that there is a constitutional standard of invention that must be met for there to be patentability. It began by noting that the qualified authority given to Congress with regard to the issuance of patents "is limited to the promotion of advances in the 'useful arts,'" and went on to state:

> The Congress in the exercise of the patent power may not overreach the restraints imposed by the stated constitutional purpose. Nor may it enlarge the patent monopoly without regard to the innovation, advancement or social benefit gained thereby. Moreover, Congress may not authorize the issuance of patents whose effects are to remove existent knowledge from the public domain, or to restrict free access to materials already available. Innovation, advancement, and things which add to the sum of useful knowledge are inherent requisites in a patent system which by constitutional command must "promote the Progress of . . . useful Arts." This is the *standard* expressed in the Constitution and it may not be ignored. And it is in this light that patent validity "requires reference to a standard written into the Constitution."[100]

In so stating, the Court accepted the earlier view of Justices Douglas and Black that the intellectual property clause sets forth a constitutional standard of patentability but "clearly rejected any reading of the intellectual property clause that would require that an invention advance the frontiers of natural science."[101]

In 1969 the Court reiterated the views it had expressed in *Graham v. John Deere Co.* but did not amplify on them or explain them.[102] Nor has it done so since then. In the Court's view something more than simple novelty is constitutionally required, but what that something is—aside from encompassing "innovation, advancement, and things which add to the sum of useful knowledge"—is unclear. Needless to say, these terms are not particularly helpful in defining a constitutional standard of invention.

---

100. 383 U.S. 1, 5–6 (1966), citing the concurring opinion of Justices Douglas and Black in Great Atl. & Pac. Tea Co. v. Supermarket Equip. Corp., 340 U.S. 147 (1950).
101. Burchfiel, *supra* note 8, at 164.
102. Anderson's Black Rock, Inc. v. Pavement Salvage Co., 396 U.S. 57, 61 (1969).

Despite the Court's failure to give any indication what is intended by the quoted language, commentators[103] have generally assumed that it elevated to constitutional status the "general condition for patentability"[104] first stated in 1851 in *Hotchkiss v. Greenwood*.[105] There the Court declared that "unless more ingenuity and skill . . . were required . . . than were possessed by an ordinary mechanic acquainted with the business, there was an absence of that degree of skill and ingenuity which constitute essential elements of every invention."[106] As the *Graham* Court pointed out: "In practice, *Hotchkiss* has required a comparison between the subject matter of the patent, or patent application, and the background skill of the calling. It has been from this comparison that patentability was in each case determined."[107]

In 1952 Congress first set forth the present statutory requirement that to be patentable the subject matter of an invention must be nonobvious, saying:

> A patent may not be obtained . . . if the differences between the subject matter sought to be patented and the prior art are such that the subject matter as a whole would have been obvious at the time the invention was made to a person having ordinary skill in the art to which said subject matter pertains.[108]

In *Graham* the Court concluded that this language "was intended merely as a codification of judicial precedents embracing the *Hotchkiss* condition, with congressional directions that inquiries into the obviousness of the subject matter sought to be patented are a prerequisite to patentability."[109] If the *Hotchkiss* "condition" is a constitutional requirement, as various commentators have inferred,[110] then it followed that the language "innovation, advancement, and things which add to the sum of useful knowledge" in *Graham* was intended to mean that the statutory requirement of unobviousness for patentability was also a constitutional requirement.

---

103. *See, e.g.,* Burchfiel, *supra* note 8; Edward S. Irons & Mary Helen Sears, *The Constitutional Standard of Invention—The Touchstone for Patent Reform,* 1973 UTAH L. REV. 653; Albert B. Kimball Jr., *An Analysis of Recent Supreme Court Assertions Regarding a Constitutional Standard of Invention,* 1 AM. PAT. L. ASS'N Q. J. 204 (1973); Joel Rosenblatt, *The Constitutional Standard for "Ordinary Skill in the Art,"* 64 J. PAT. OFF. SOC'Y 435 (1972).
104. 383 U.S. at 7.
105. 52 U.S. (11 How.) 248 (1851).
106. *Id.* at 267.
107. 383 U.S. at 7.
108. 35 U.S.C. § 103.
109. 383 U.S. at 17.
110. *See supra* note 103.

While not expressly so stating, the Court certainly seemed to infer this when it declared "[t]he emphasis on nonobviousness is one of inquiry, not quality,[111] and, as such, comports with the constitutional strictures."[112]

Congress, however, has not interpreted *Graham* as setting forth a constitutional requirement for nonobviousness. Thus in 1996 it amended the patent statute to eliminate the nonobviousness requirement for some biotechnological processes.[113] Heald and Sherry, while conceding that nonobviousness was not a requirement for patentability under British law at the time the Constitution was drafted, nonetheless argue that something more than mere novelty was required and that this something more was incorporated into the intellectual property clause.[114] They are correct, but that something more was a constitutional requirement for utility which is subsequently discussed.[115]

In otherwise setting forth a statutory requirement that an invention be unobvious in order to be patentable, Congress had gone further and also stated that "[p]atentability shall not be negatived by the manner in which the invention was made."[116] The *Graham* Court noted that it "seems apparent that Congress intended" by this language "to abolish the test it believed this Court announced in the controversial phrase 'flash of creative genius,'" in *Cuno*.[117] If there was a certain "level of creative genius" required by the Constitution as Justice Douglas' opinion in *Cuno* certainly seemed to suggest then Congress clearly did not have authority to negate such a requirement by statutory enactment, and any statutory language seeking to do so would be unconstitutional.

To avoid this problem, the *Graham* Court now sought to "explain" *Cuno* as nothing more than a "rhetorical embellishment" which "merely

---

111. This certainly seemed to indicate disagreement with the views of Justices Douglas and Black that "advancement of science" was a constitutional requirement. *See supra* note 96 and accompanying text.
112. 383 U.S. at 17.
113. According to 35 U.S.C. § 103(b)(1), a "biotechnological process using or resulting in a composition of matter that is novel under section 102 and nonobvious under subsection (a) of this section shall be considered nonobvious if [the composition of matter and process are claimed in the same patent application and are owned by the same person]."
114. Paul J. Heald & Suzanna Sherry, *Implied Limits on the Legislative Power: The Intellectual Property Clause as an Absolute Constraint on Congress*, 2000 ILL. L. REV. 1119, 1186–87.
115. *See* Part E, *infra*.
116. 35 U.S.C. § 103.
117. 383 U.S. at 15.

rhetorically restated the requirement that the subject matter sought to be patented must be beyond the skill of the calling." According to the *Graham* Court, in *Cuno* "[i]t was the device, not the invention, that had to reveal the 'flash of creative genius.'"[118] Never mind that in *Cuno* the device *was* the invention.[119] Be that as it may, the *Graham* Court sought to indicate that the *Cuno* standard and the one it was pronouncing were basically the same. In essence, invention did not depend on the state of mind of the inventor, i.e., invention could be made accidentally as well as deliberately, and invention, regardless of how made, was patentable as long as it was unobvious to one of ordinary skill in the art.

This was well and good, but what was the basis for the *Hotchkiss* test as originally set forth in 1851? The *Hotchkiss* Court cited no authority, judicial or statutory, for the test it set forth, as indeed it could not for there was none.[120] Moreover, the *Hotchkiss* Court made no reference to any constitutional basis for the test. The *Graham* Court thus found itself in a quandary in attempting to establish a historical basis for its interpretation of the intellectual property clause as establishing a constitutional standard of invention beyond simple novelty. It had no contemporaneous documentation by any of the Framers to set forth their interpretation of the "to" language of the clause, nor did it have any other contemporaneous documentation relating to that language. Consequently, it turned to an imaginative—and in many ways incorrect—reconstruction of the views of Jefferson based on letters written over a period of twenty-six years as somehow representing the views and intentions of the Framers with regard to interpretation of the intellectual property clause.[121]

---

118. 383 U.S. at 15, n.7.

119. Instead of engaging in such semantics (some would call it sophistry), the Court would have been better served by never having included this supposed distinction between "the device" and "the invention."

120. The *Graham* Court noted that the ultimate determination in *Hotchkiss*, namely, that substitution of porcelain or clay for wood or metal in doorknobs did not constitute a patentable invention "flows directly" from one of the rules followed by the Patent Board under the Act of 1790. *See* 383 U.S. at 11, n.4. What the Court failed to note was that that particular "rule" never was publicly disclosed while it supposedly was in effect, and never had been incorporated into any subsequent statutory enactment nor ever been followed in any judicial opinion at the time that *Hotchkiss* was decided. Indeed, it is highly unlikely that the *Hotchkiss* Court even was aware that any such rule had ever existed during the brief period that the Patent Act of 1790 was in effect.

121. 383 U.S. at 7–11.

The gist of its argument was that Jefferson (and presumably the Framers) favored a high standard of patentability,[122] that Jefferson and the patent board which issued patents under the Act of 1790 believed "that the courts should develop additional conditions for patentability," and that Congress apparently agreed with such an approach.[123] This argument that Congress agreed that interpretation of the constitutional standard of invention should be determined by judicial activism was developed by negative implication, namely, that despite numerous other changes to the patent statutes between 1790 and 1950 Congress set no statutory requirements for patentability "beyond the bare novelty and utility tests reformulated" in the Act of 1793.[124] Why the failure of Congress to set a higher standard of patentability than merely novelty and utility was deemed to be proof that Congress had chosen to defer to judicial activism to set additional standards of patentability was not apparent or obvious. In any case, the relevance of this to the delineation of a constitutional standard of invention was not indicated.

The *Graham* Court's reliance on the supposed views of Thomas Jefferson has been sharply challenged.[125] The challenge has been on three levels. The first is that with the exception of his exchange of correspondence with Madison in 1788 and 1789,[126] none of his letters pertaining to patent matters ever mention the intellectual property clause, much less seek to interpret it. Secondly, there is nothing whatever to indicate that the views held by Jefferson were those of the Framers themselves or those of either the first federal Congresses or the early federal judiciary,[127] or for that matter the general populace.[128] In this regard, the *Graham* Court completely ignored the rejection by the second federal Congress of Jefferson's proposal that a good defense to infringement should be that the invention

---

122. As the Court put it: "Jefferson did not believe in granting patents for small details, obvious improvements, or frivolous devices. His writings evidence his insistence upon a high level of patentability." 383 U.S. at 9.

123. 383 U.S. at 10.

124. *Id.*

125. *See* Edward C. Walterscheid, *The Use and Abuse of History: The Supreme Court's Interpretation of Thomas Jefferson's Influence on the Patent Law*, 39 IDEA 195 (1999); Burchfiel, *supra* note 8, at 165–67, 209, 212.

126. *See* Chapter One, Part B.

127. Burchfiel, *supra* note 8, at 166, 167.

128. As Burchfiel put it, "By basing analysis of the privately expressed personal views of a single historical figure and by extending those views to the historical American populace in general, the Court acted as if it were in possession of an eighteenth-century opinion poll without margin for error." *Id.* at 212.

"is so unimportant and obvious that it ought not to be the basis of an exclusive right."[129] Thirdly, in a number of instances the Court either misstated Jefferson's role[130] or took his views out of context or attributed views to him that he did not hold. Thus, for example, contrary to the conclusion reached by the Court, Jefferson did not think "that the courts should develop additional conditions for patentability."[131] Rather, his views were just the opposite, and he clearly thought that judges were ill-equipped for this responsibility.[132] Perhaps most critically, the *Graham*

---

129. EDWARD C. WALTERSCHEID, TO PROMOTE THE PROGRESS OF USEFUL ARTS: AMERICAN PATENT LAW AND ADMINISTRATION, 1787–1836, at 200–06 (Littleton, CO 1998). According to Burchfiel, "[t]he legal evidence is uncontradicted that in rejecting Jefferson's proposals, including a statutory nonobviousness standard, the second Congress disavowed the proposition that a high standard of patentability was required by the plain meaning of the patent clause or by the original intent of the constitutional framers." Burchfiel, *supra* note 8, at 209.

130. Contrary to the Court's repeated assertion, Jefferson did not draft the Patent Act of 1793. *See* Walterscheid, *supra* note 125, at 202–12.

131. 383 U.S. at 10.

132. In 1813 Jefferson wrote:

> Instead of refusing a patent in the first instance as the board was author-ized to do, the patent now issues of course, subject to be declared void on such principles as should be established by the courts of law. This business, however, is but little analogous to their course of reading, since we might in vain turn over all the lubberly volumes of the law to find a single ray which would lighten the path of the mechanic or the mathema-tician. It is more within the information of a board of academical pro-fessors, and a previous refusal of a patent would better guard our citizens against harassment by lawsuits.

Letter from Thomas Jefferson to Isaac McPherson, *in* XIII THE WRITINGS OF THOMAS JEFFERSON at 337–38 (Andrew A. Lipscomb et al. eds, 1903). A year later, he would emphasize the point, arguing that "when so new a branch of science has been recently engrafted on our jurisprudence, one which its professors have till now had no call to make themselves acquainted, one bear-ing little analogy to their professional education or pursuits," one or two decisions before inferior and local tribunals should not act as precedent to "forever foreclose the whole of the new subject." *See* letter from Thomas Jefferson to Oliver Evans (Jan. 14, 1814), *id.* vol. XIV, at 67.

Court's assertion that Jefferson "clearly recognized the social and economic rationale of the patent system" is belied by the historical record.[133]

The view that the "to" language of the intellectual property clause serves to limit or qualify congressional patent power in any way, much less establish a constitutional standard of invention as stated by the *Graham* Court, has also been strongly challenged.[134] Pragmatically, the effect of such an argument is to read the "to" language out of the clause and to render it meaningless. It is also contrary to the well-established principle that, to the extent possible, the Constitution must be read so as to give effect to all of its parts without doing violence to any.[135] But saying that the "to" language qualifies the congressional patent power does not per se suggest that it creates a constitutional standard of invention above and beyond the requirement of novelty. It does suggest, however, that it

---

133. While the Court clearly recognized that in 1788 and 1789 Jefferson had opposed the intellectual property clause (*Graham*, 383 U.S. at 7–8), it failed completely to note that more than two decades later, in 1813 and 1814, he was still not convinced of either the usefulness or the desirability of the patent system. In 1813, he expressed skepticism about the value of patents in the following terms: "generally speaking, other nations have thought that these monopolies produce more embarrassment than advantage to society; and it may be observed that the nations which refuse monopolies of invention, are as fruitful as England in new and useful devices." XIII THE WRITINGS OF THOMAS JEFFERSON, *id.* at 334. In 1814 he reiterated his concern that, on balance, the abuses of the patent system through the issuance of what he called "frivolous" patents outweighed its benefit. Letter from Thomas Jefferson to Thomas Cooper (Jan. 16, 1814), *in* XIV THE WRITINGS OF THOMAS JEFFERSON, *id.* at 62.

134. *See* Burchfiel, *supra* note 8; Kenneth J. Burchfiel, *The Constitutional Intellectual Property Power: Progress of Useful Arts and the Legal Protection of Semiconductor Technology*, 28 SANTA CLARA L. REV. 473 (1988); Albert B. Kimball Jr., *An Analysis of Recent Supreme Court Assertions Regarding a Constitutional Standard of Invention*, 1 AM. PAT. L. ASS'N Q. J. 204 (1973).

135. *See, e.g.,* Mastro Plastics v. NLRB, 350 U.S. 270 (1956); United States v. Alpers, 338 U.S. 680 (1950); United States v. American Trucking Ass'ns, Inc., 310 U.S. 534 (1940); United States v. Boisdore's Heirs, 49 U.S. (8 How.) 113 (1850).

qualifies congressional power in other ways.[136] We turn now to one way it does so, namely, by creating a constitutional requirement for utility.

E. Utility

In the patent law, "utility" is synonymous with "usefulness." In 1966 in *Brenner v. Manson* the Supreme Court stated that it is indisputable that "one may patent only that which is 'useful'" and

> the concept of utility has maintained a central place in all of our patent legislation, beginning with the first patent law in 1790 and culminating in the present laws provision that "Whoever invents or discovers any new and useful process, machine, manufacture, or composition of matter, or any new and useful improvement thereof, may obtain a patent therefor, subject to the conditions and requirements of this title."[137]

It emphasized that "[t]he basic quid pro quo contemplated by the Constitution and the Congress for granting a patent monopoly is the benefit derived by the public from an invention with substantial utility."[138]

We shall look more carefully at what the Court meant by "substantial utility"; suffice it for the moment to note that it indicated that utility is a constitutional requirement and not merely a statutory one. In so indicating, however, it failed to suggest what language of the intellectual property clause created such a requirement. In his dissent, however, Justice Harlan certainly inferred that the requirement resides in the introductory language "[t]o promote the Progress of Science and useful Arts."[139] In other words, to promote the useful arts requires the patented invention to have utility, but what kind of utility? To quote the *Brenner* majority, "a simple, everyday word [i.e., "useful"] can be pregnant with ambiguity when applied to the facts of

---

136. One specific way it does so is by limiting the term which Congress may grant for patents. Indeed, Justice Story made this point as early as 1829 in *Pennock v. Dialogue* when he stated that the "main object" of the patent system authorized by the clause "was 'to promote the progress of science and useful arts'"; an object that could best be accomplished by giving the invention to the public "at as early a period as possible." 27 U.S. at 19. This point has been discussed in detail in Chapter Seven, Part E.
137. 383 U.S. 519, 528–29 (1966), citing various patent acts beginning with the Act of April 10, 1790 to 35 U.S.C. §101 (1964). This definition remains the law today.
138. 383 U.S. at 534.
139. *Id.* at 536.

life."[140] The difficulty was that Congress had never sought to define what it (or the Constitution for that matter) meant by "useful."

The question of the meaning of "useful" seems to have been first raised in 1817 when it was argued that it meant "of general utility," i.e., better than existing devices of the type patented. Not so, said Justice Story in his capacity as circuit judge:

> By useful invention, in the statute, is meant such a one as may be applied to some beneficial use in society, in contra-distinction to an invention, which is injurious to the morals, the health, or the good order of society. It is not necessary to establish, that the invention is of such general utility, as to supercede all other inventions now in practice to accomplish the same purpose. It is sufficient, that it has no obnoxious or mischievous tendency, that it may be applied to practical uses, and that so far as it is applied, it is salutary. . . . The law . . . does not look to the degree of utility; it simply requires that it shall be capable of use, and that the use is such as sound morals and policy do not discountenance or prohibit.[141]

Story's view that the utility must be socially beneficial, that is to say, not illegal, immoral, or adverse to public policy,[142] was generally followed into the twentieth century, primarily in two areas: gambling devices (including inventions that could be used as a part of such a device)[143] and inventions (including medicines) intended to defraud.[144] Also falling into this broad

---

140. 383 U.S. at 529.
141. Bedford v. Hunt, 3 F. Cas. 37 (D. Mass. 1817) (Case No. 1,217). *See also* Lowell v. Lewis, 15 F. Cas. 1018, 1019 (D. Mass. 1817) (Case No. 8,568). Story repeated his views in an appendix to Evans v. Eaton, 16 U.S. (3 Wheat.) 12, 24 (1818).
142. As examples, he stated "a new invention to poison people, or to promote debauchery, or to facilitate private assassination, is not a patentable invention." 15 F. Cas. at 1019.
143. *See, e.g.,* Meyer v. Buckley Mfg. Co., 15 F. Supp. 640 (N.D. Ill. 1936); Brewer v. Lichtenstein, 278 F. 512 (7th Cir. 1922); Schultze v. Holtz, 82 F. 448 (N.D. Cal. 1897); National Automatic Device Corp. v. Lloyd, 40 F. 89 (N.D. Ill. 1889).
144. *See, e.g.,* Scott & Williams v. Aristo Hosiery Co., 7 F.2d 1003 (2d Cir. 1925) (seamless stocking with structure on the back that imitated a seamed stocking); Richard v. Du Bon, 103 F. 868 (2d Cir. 1900) (process for making cigar wrapper resemble a higher quality tobacco leaf). For a discussion of the higher standard of utility imposed in health-related inventions, see Brand, *Utility in a Pharmaceutical Patent*, 39 FOOD DRUG COSM. L.J. 480 (1984).

category are the utterly worthless or frivolous[145] patents, e.g., those sought for perpetual motion machines.[146] There has, however, in recent years been a marked reluctance of courts to invalidate patents for lack of utility based on social benefit or morality arguments.[147]

In 1999 the Federal Circuit cited *Brenner* as support for the view: "The threshold of utility is not high: An invention is 'useful' . . . if it is capable of providing some identifiable benefit."[148] Unfortunately, *Brenner* does not support any such view, stating as it does a constitutional requirement of "substantial utility."[149] Until *Brenner*, Story's conclusion that as long as the invention has some utility, it does not have to accomplish its purpose better than taught in the existing art was treated as the law.[150] But *Brenner*'s statement that "substantial utility" is required for patentability under the Constitution seemed to challenge this conclusion. But if "substantial utility" was required by the Constitution, *Brenner* provided no indication of how such a standard was to be defined.[151] As a practical matter in the years since *Brenner* courts have made no attempt to apply the "substantial

---

145. This was a popular term of derision for worthless patents in the early nineteenth century.
146. *See, e.g.*, Newman v. Quigg, 877 F.2d 1575 (Fed. Cir. 1989) (perpetual motion machine); In re Perrigo, 48 F.2d 965 (C.C.P.A. 1931) (method and apparatus for accumulating and transforming ether electric energy); Ex parte Heicklin, 16 U.S.P.Q.2d 1463 (B.P.A.I. 1990) (method to retard the aging process).
147. *See, e.g.*, Juicy Whip, Inc. v. Orange Bang, Inc., 185 F.3d 1364 (Fed. Cir. 1999) (rejecting argument that claimed invention was immoral because it was designed to make people believe something that was not true); In re Murphy, 200 U.S.P.Q. 801 (Bd. App. 1977) (overturning rejection predicated solely on the ground that the device sought to be patented was useful solely for gambling purposes). The Federal Circuit in *Juicy Whip* declared that "the principle that inventions are invalid if they are principally designed to serve immoral or illegal purposes has not been applied broadly in recent years." 185 F.3d at 1366.
148. *Juicy Whip*, 185 F.3d at 1366.
149. *See Brenner*, 383 U.S. at 534. *See supra* text accompanying note 138.
150. The *Brenner* majority dismissed Story's views as requiring it to do no more than to decide whether the invention is "frivolous and insignificant" which it believed no easier to decide than the one it was addressing. 383 U.S. at 533.
151. It is interesting to note that *Brenner* and *Graham v. John Deere Co.* both were decided by the same Court in 1966 and both failed to indicate the nature of the heightened standard for patentability said to be required by the Constitution.

utility" criterion set forth therein or to require that an invention must somehow have more utility than taught in the existing art.[152]

The terms "useful" and "discoveries" as they appear in the intellectual property clause are susceptible of very broad meanings or interpretations. In the absence of any indication that the Framers intended them to be narrowly interpreted, it is reasonable to suppose that how broadly they were to be interpreted was left to the discretion of Congress. While Congress from the inception of the patent law has made some attempt to define "discoveries" at least indirectly through a definition of patentable subject matter,[153] it has never sought to provide any definition whatever of "useful" aside from the requirement that an invention be useful to be patentable. Thus in the absence of any indication to the contrary, a presumption exists that Congress intended "useful" to be read as broadly in the patent statutes as it appears in the intellectual property clause.[154]

The *Brenner* majority, however, applied just the opposite presumption. In its view, if utility or usefulness is read so broadly "as to allow the patenting of any invention not positively harmful to society, it places such a special meaning on the word 'useful' that we cannot accept it in the absence of evidence that Congress so intended."[155] The Court carefully failed to note that this supposedly "special" meaning of "useful" is in fact fully in accord with the dictionary definition of the term, and instead drew the remarkable conclusion that in the absence of specific evidence that

---

152. *See, e.g.,* Custom Accessories v. Jeffrey-Allan Indus., 807 F.2d 955, 960 n.12 (Fed. Cir. 1986) ("[i]t is possible for an invention to be less effective than existing devices but nevertheless meet the statutory criteria for patentability").
153. *See supra* text accompanying note 137.
154. Justice Harlan, concurring in part and dissenting in part in *Brenner*, certainly so argued. 383 U.S. at 536–37. Kreiss argues that the "useful arts" subject matter requirement is distinct from the constitutional requirement that an invention be "useful" to be patentable. In his view, both the Patent Office and judges have "confused and conflated" the two. In particular, he suggests that Judge Newman, dissenting in In re Schrader, 22 F.3d 290, 297 (Fed. Cir. 1994), improperly equated the two by stating that patentable subject matter must be within the "technological arts" before the claimed subject matter could be demonstrated to be "useful." *See* Robert A. Kreiss, *Patent Protection for Computer Programs and Mathematical Algorithms: Constitutional Limitations on Patentable Subject Matter,* 29 N.M. L. REV. 31, 74–75 (1999). But the only basis for a constitutional utility requirement for patentability is the constitutional language requiring the purpose of a patent to be to promote the progress of the useful arts.
155. 383 U.S. at 533.

Congress intended to use the term in accordance with its dictionary definition, such a definition of the term could not apply to it as used in the patent statute. This, of course, is the exact opposite of the usual approach taken to interpreting statutory language.

Be that as it may, the specific holding in *Brenner* was that a new and unobvious process for creating a chemical compound did not have patentable utility in the absence of a showing of patentable utility for the compound thus created. It is important to note that holding was predicated on statutory interpretation and not on interpretation of the constitutional meaning of "useful" in the intellectual property clause.

F. Patentable Subject Matter

To what extent, if any, does the intellectual property clause limit or circumscribe congressional discretion to define patentable subject matter? In the absence of any Supreme Court interpretation of the meaning to be given to either "inventors" or "discoveries" as these terms appear in the clause or of any record as to what the Framers intended these terms to mean,[156] it is reasonable to turn to the definitions of these terms used at the end of the eighteenth century when the Constitution was ratified. Those definitions were exceedingly broad,[157] and in and of themselves gave Congress wide and apparently unlimited discretion to define patentable subject matter.[158]

But if, as I have earlier suggested, terms in the clause cannot be read or interpreted in isolation, and if the introductory language qualifies the patent power given to Congress as the Supreme Court in *Graham v. John Deere Co.* most emphatically stated it does,[159] then a plausible argument can be made that the power of Congress to define patentable subject matter is

---

156. Seidel, for example, notes that "[n]o historical writings or events have been found analyzing the [clause]." *See supra* Seidel, note 11.

157. *See supra* text accompanying notes 11–13.

158. I use the phrase "patentable subject matter" in the same manner that Adelman et al. use "patent-eligibility," namely, "to describe the subject matter open to patenting, as opposed to the word 'patentability.' The latter term implies not just that the subject matter is appropriate under the statute, but that the invention has been approved following an individual determination of novelty, nonobviousness and the other requisites." MARTIN J. ADELMAN, RANDALL R. RADER, JOHN R. THOMAS, & HAROLD C. WEGNER, CASES AND MATERIALS ON PATENT LAW at 83 (St. Paul 1998).

159. *See supra* text accompanying note 100.

not plenary, but rather is constrained "to the promotion . . . of useful arts." That is to say, patentable subject constitutionally must be that which promotes the useful arts. This in turn requires a closer look by what is meant by "useful arts" in the clause.[160]

Again, however, the Framers provided no indication of what they meant by this term.[161] Seidel suggests that in 1787 it meant useful or helpful trades.[162] According to Coulter, "[i]t seems clear that 'useful arts' (as a unitary technical term) embraced the so-called industrial, mechanical and manual arts of the 18th century. . . ."[163] Lutz, in turn, thinks it is just as clear "that 'useful arts' meant what we now call 'technology,' or 'applied science.'"[164] He argues that the words "useful arts" were deliberately used to broaden the field of patentable subject matter from "new manufactures" as used in the Statute of Monopolies because "by the year 1787 it was being recognized even in Great Britain that the phrase 'new manufactures' was an unduly limited object for a patent system, since it seemed to exclude new processes."[165] Lutz may be correct in this regard,[166] but there is no contemporaneous documentation to indicate that the Framers either understood or intended a distinction of this type.

The statutory definition of patentable subject matter has changed but little since the Patent Act of 1790. That Act authorized patents for "any useful Art, Manufacture, Engine, Machine, or Device, or any improvement

---

160. The point was made as early as 1952 when Coulter emphasized that: *"The starting point of inquiry as to the field of subject matter embraced by the statutory proviso should be this Constitutional reference to 'useful Arts'"* (emphasis in original). Robert I. Coulter, *The Field of the Statutory Useful Arts*, 34 J. PAT. OFF. SOC'Y 487 (1952). More recently the Supreme Court has stated that: "The subject matter provisions of the patent law have been cast in broad terms to fulfill the constitutional and statutory goal of promoting 'the Progress of Science and the useful Arts. . . .'" Diamond v. Chakrabarty, 447 U.S. 303, 315 (1980).

161. I have earlier suggested that the words "useful arts" were suggested to the Framers by the creation of a new group called the Pennsylvania Society for the Encouragement of Manufactures and the Useful Arts in Philadelphia during the time the federal convention was meeting there. *See supra* Chapter Four, text accompanying notes 49–54.

162. Seidel, *supra* note 11, at 10.

163. Coulter, *supra* note 160, at 496.

164. Lutz, *supra* note 18, at 771.

165. Karl B. Lutz, *Patents and Science: A Clarification of the Patent Clause of the U.S. Constitution*, 32 J. PAT. OFF. SOC'Y 83, 86 (1950).

166. *See* text accompanying notes 202–210, *infra*.

therein."[167] The Act of 1793 changed this to read "any useful art, machine, manufacture, or composition of matter, or any new and useful improvement [therein]."[168] This definition of patentable subject matter was retained until 1952 when the term "art" was replaced with "process."[169] The Supreme Court has never attempted to define the words "useful arts" as they appear in the intellectual property clause, but has on a number of occasions sought to interpret the statutory language. The Court of Customs and Patent Appeals, however, has several times "pointed out that the present day equivalent of the term 'useful arts' employed by the Founding Fathers is 'technological arts.'"[170]

Let us return for a moment to the interpretation of "invention" and "discoveries" in the context of the clause. Obviously, the term "invention" does not appear therein, but if an inventor is one who invents then clearly an inventor is one who makes an invention. It thus is relevant to ascertain whether there is any distinction between "invention" and "discovery" for the purposes of determining whether there is a constitutional limitation (aside from novelty and utility as already discussed) on what constitutes patentable subject matter.

The Framers never indicated what they meant by the terms "inventors" and "discoveries" but they appear to have viewed the terms 'invention" and "discovery" as synonymous. In any case, Congress certainly seems to have assumed them to be synonymous,[171] As I have indicated, the definition of discovery at the end of the eighteenth century was exceedingly broad,[172] so that at least in principle the definition of patentable subject matter allowed by the Constitution was also exceedingly broad. The issue was further complicated at the end of the eighteenth century by the frequent reference to the "principles" of an invention, whatever that was intended to mean.

The Constitution says not a word about what quid pro quo, if any, the inventor is required to provide in return for the limited-term exclusive right encompassed by a patent. It was only in the decade immediately preceding the federal convention that the common law courts had decided that an

---

167. Act of April 10, 1790 at § 1, 1 Stat. 109.
168. Act of February 21, 1793 at § 1, 1 Stat. 318.
169. *See* 35 U.S.C.A § 101.
170. In re Bergy, 596 F.2d 952, 959 (1979); In re Waldbaum, 457 F.2d 997, 1003 (1972) (Rich, J., concurring); In re Musgrave, 431 F2d. 882, 893 (1970).
171. The Patent Act of 1793 refers to "invention or discovery." *See* Act of April 10, 1790, § 1, 1 Stat. 109. *See also* text accompanying note 4 *supra*.
172. *See supra* text accompanying note 13.

inventor was required to provide a patent specification containing an enabling disclosure, i.e., one teaching those skilled in the art with which the invention was most closely identified to make and use the invention.[173] Prior to this time, it was not at all clear what the purpose of a patent specification was, other than to identify the invention in some general sense.

Much of the confusion about the differences, if any, between discovery, invention, and principles arose out of this fact and was generated by none other than that most famous of English inventors, James Watt. Watt's patent on his major improvement in the steam engine issued in 1769 but not before he had spent considerable time and effort trying to decide what should be included in his specification.[174] He clearly considered the specification an important matter, but it is unlikely that either he or those he consulted thought that it would have to be fully enabling in the manner set forth by Mansfield nine years later in *Liardet v. Johnson*.[175] But they were not entirely certain on the point. Thus, in February 1769 he received advice that

> you should neither give drawings nor descriptions of any particular machinery, (if such omission would be allowed at the office) but specify in the clearest manner that you can, that you have discovered some principles, and thought of new applications of others, by means of both which joined together, you intend to construct steam engines of much greater powers, and applicable to a much greater number of useful purposes than any which hitherto have been constructed, that to effect each particular purpose you design to employ particular machinery, every species of which may be ranged in two classes. One class for producing reciprocal motions, and another for producing motions round axes. As to your principles, we think they should be enunciated (to use an hard word) as generally as possible, to secure you as effectually against piracy as the nature of your invention will allow.[176]

---

173. The case most frequently cited as setting forth this requirement is *Liardet v. Johnson* decided by Lord Mansfield in 1778. Although the case was not officially reported, knowledge of it survives through a number of newspaper accounts and pamphlets contemporaneously published. For a discussion of it, see Edward C. Walterscheid, *The Early Evolution of the United States Patent Law: Antecedents (Part 3)*, 77 J. PAT. & TRADEMARK OFF. SOC'Y 793–97 (1995).
174. Robinson states that several drafts of his first specification in his own hand still exist. *See* Eric Robinson, *James Watt and the Law of Patents*, 13 TECH. & CULTURE 115, 119 (1972).
175. *Id.*
176. *Id.* at 120–21.

This emphasis on "principles" as opposed to description of specific embodiments seems peculiar today but it was not in the context of the times. It has been argued that this advice badly served Watt for two reasons, because in consequence thereof he failed to provide drawings as a part of the specification and he sought to patent "a principle of action and not an application of a principle."[177] But in the eighteenth century, seeking to patent only "an application of a principle" was perceived as fraught with difficulties by both patentees and those from whom they sought legal advice.

This was in an era when the concept of mandatory specification was relatively new, and it had never been laid down either by statute or common law exactly what a specification should do. It would be well into the next century before the idea of using claims as a means of defining the invention would be developed. As a patentee wrote in 1784, some six years after *Liardet v. Johnson* had been decided and after consulting with Watt and others viewed as specialists in patents,

> they all agreed in saying that there was no need of particular descriptions and drawings, because the patent was taken upon the principle which may be applied to numberless shapes and forms, whereas giving particular description and drawings would be confining ourselves to these particular forms and enabling others to use the same principle under other forms.[178]

This language rather accurately describes the dilemma patentees perceived themselves to be in. Provide an insufficient description of the invention and the courts would invalidate the patent; provide too detailed a description of particular embodiments and the courts would construe the invention to be limited to the particular embodiments described. This in turn would permit others through minor change or modification to practice the invention without infringing the patent. It was to avoid what patentees perceived to be piracy of their inventions through such minor change or modification that they sought to describe the inventions in terms of general principles rather than specific embodiments. It would take many years for the common law to disabuse them of the idea that a patent covered the general principles under which the invention was perceived to operate.[179]

---

177. *Id.* at 120, quoting H. W. DICKINSON, JAMES WATT, CRAFTSMAN AND ENGINEER at 52 (Cambridge 1936).
178. *Id.* at 121.
179. Indeed the idea still seems to have been prevalent as late as 1829, although by that time there seems to have been a consensus that patents "could not be granted on abstract principles." Robinson, *supra* note 174, at 123.

By special act of Parliament in 1775, the term of Watt's patent was extended to 1800.[180] This extraordinary extension coupled with the significant commercial success of the new steam engines based on the patent led almost inevitably to extensive litigation. One of these cases, *Boulton v. Bull*,[181] decided in 1795, would have an impact on the early development of both British and American patent law. It is of interest here because of the views expressed therein by the judges on what constitutes patentable invention under the Statute of Monopolies.

This was part of the continuing effort by the common law courts to deal with the issue of the meaning to be given to the phrase "any manner of new manufactures" in the Statute.[182] An initial article of faith, which would continue to be given a great deal of lip service but which was honored more in the breach than in reality, was that the Statue was an enactment of existing common law and should be interpreted as such. A classic example had to do with the treatment of improvement inventions.

Coke had expounded the common law view, predicated on a holding in *Bircot's Case*, that the Statute forbade the granting of a patent for any improvement in an existing manufacture.[183] As a practical matter, by early in the eighteenth century the law officers had come to realize that many of the inventions for which patents were sought could be characterized as improvements over or in existing manufactures, but they chose at least tacitly to ignore this in recommending that patents be granted for these inventions. It was not surprising that when infringement actions were attempted at equity (as opposed to actions at common law which came later), the defense was frequently that the invention was merely an improvement over existing technology and hence the patent was invalid.[184] When the matter came before Lord Mansfield in 1776 in *Morris v. Bramson*[185] which seems to have been one of the first common law cases to address the issue, he accepted the practical reality and held that

---

180. The Fire Engine Act, 15 George III, c. 61 (1775).

181. 126 Eng. Rep. 651 (C.P. 1795).

182. For the relevant portion of the Statute and its wording, *see supra* Chapter Two, text accompanying notes 67–69.

183. *See* Edward C. Walterscheid, *The Early Evolution of the United States Patent Law: Antecedents* (Part 2), 76 J. PAT. & TRADEMARK OFF. SOC'Y 878 (1994).

184. MacLeod cites several instances of this that occurred before 1750. *See* CHRISTINE MACLEOD, INVENTING THE INDUSTRIAL REVOLUTION, THE ENGLISH PATENT SYSTEM, 1660–1800, at 64–68 (Cambridge 1988).

185. 1 Carp. P.C. 30, 1 Abbott's P.C. 21 (K.B. 1776). This case also frequently is cited as *Morris v. Branson*.

improvement inventions were patentable. In his view, to hold otherwise "would go to repeal almost every patent that ever was granted."[186]

This was all well and good insofar as it went, but what did the term "manufacture" as used in the Statute mean? What did it actually encompass? The definitions given in the various opinions in *Boulton v. Bull* are interesting if only partially illuminating. Boulton[187] and Watt argued that "manufacture" meant "any thing made or produced by art."[188] This seemed to suggest that some form of skill or special trade needed to be involved. It also seemed to imply that nothing discovered by accident could be the subject of a patent because it would not have been "made or produced by art." Justice Buller refused to accept any such contention, saying "whether the manufacture be . . . produced by accident or by art, is immaterial."[189] He also stated, however, that:

> The word manufacture is descriptive either of the practice of making a thing by art, or of the thing when made. The invention therefore of any instrument used in the process of making a thing by art, is a manufacture, and the subject of a patent within the statute, because such an instrument is itself a thing made by art.[190]

Justice Heath was of the view that patentable manufactures fell into two classes:

> The first class includes machinery, the second class substances (such as medicines) formed by chemical or other processes, where the vendible substance is the thing produced, and that which operates preserves no permanent form. In the first class, the machine, and in the second the substance produced, is the subject of the patent.[191]

Moreover, "[t]hat which is the subject of a patent . . . ought to be that which is vendible, otherwise it cannot be a manufacture."[192] Finally, Chief Justice Eyre noted that "[i]t was admitted in the argument at the bar, that the word 'manufacture' in the statute . . . applied not only to things made,

---

186. 1 Abbott's P.C. at 22.
187. Boulton was Watt's senior partner and owned a two-thirds interest in Watt's patent.
188. 2 H. Bl. at 468, 126 Eng. Rep. at 653.
189. 2 H. Bl. at 486, 126 Eng. Rep. at 663.
190. 2 H. Bl. at 471, 126 Eng. Rep. at 655.
191. 2 H. Bl. at 481–82, 126 Eng. Rep. at 660–61.
192. *Id.*

but to the practice of making, to principles carried into practice in a new manner, to new results of principles carried into practice."[193]

Although a modern analyst of the English patent system has stated that "[a]ccording to the Statute of Monopolies a patent could not be granted for an abstract or a philosophical principle,"[194] there was no language in the Statute that could literally be so interpreted. Moreover, Lord Coke, who was deemed to be the earliest authority on the Statute and provided the first detailed analysis of it,[195] is totally silent on the point. In the eighteenth century, patentees and those who gave advice concerning patents were certainly of the view that the Statute did not preclude the patenting of general principles of operation.[196]

As has been noted, Watt in 1769 was advised to specify that he had discovered "some principles" and to enunciate them as generally as possible in his specification.[197] He followed this advice,[198] and as a result found himself confronted with the argument in *Boulton v. Bull* that his patent was invalid because it was for a principle rather than particular embodiments pertaining to his improved steam engine.[199] Nonetheless, he must have felt reasonably comfortable that his approach would withstand common law scrutiny because in 1776 Chief Justice Eyre had suggested that a "principle" could be the subject of a patent.[200]

---

193. 2 H. Bl. at 492, 126 Eng. Rep. at 666.
194. HAROLD I. DUTTON, THE PATENT SYSTEM AND INVENTIVE ACTIVITY DURING THE INDUSTRIAL REVOLUTION (Manchester 1984) at 73.
195. *See* Walterscheid, *supra* note 183, at 876–79.
196. MacLeod, for example, suggests that as early as 1720 patents were being granted for general principles of operation. *See* MACLEOD, *supra* note 184, at 63–64.
197. *See supra* text accompanying notes 174–176.
198. But from time to time, he seems to have had some difficulty in defining what he meant by his "principles." In at least certain of his works, his defining principles of how various steam engines operated come very close to a description of simple natural forces. *See* Robinson, *supra* note 174, at 122–23, n.22.
199. Bull's counsel argued that:

> The reason seems obvious why this privilege of a monopoly which is to be granted by the Crown should not be granted merely for the principle or for the first idea which may occur to an ingenious mind because if that is the case he is to reserve to himself the sole power of every possible improvement which may be made upon that idea in bringing it forward to perfection in the shape of a complete instrument.

Robinson, *supra* note 174, at 123.
200. DUTTON, *supra* note 194, at 73.

Imagine his dismay then when the four judges hearing the case, including Chief Justice Eyre, unanimously held that an abstract principle could not be the subject of a patent.[201] Fortunately for him two of them were prepared to accept the view that his specification taught more than merely the application of a principle of nature. Although there would continue to be some argument about it for several decades, the common law view at the end of the eighteenth century was that a principle of nature could not be patented, because this amounted to patenting knowledge of the physical universe which should be available for all to use.

If at the end of the century it had become the common law that "any manner of new manufactures" as used in the Statute encompassed improvement inventions but did not cover principles of nature (although there would remain considerable dispute as to what constituted a principle of nature), there was mass confusion as to the extent to which this phrase covered so-called "method" or "process" inventions. Again Watt's experience is worthy of note. Despite the fact that his improved steam engines were obviously an article of manufacture, he chose to obtain his patent for a "Method of diminishing the consumption of fuel in fire-engines."[202] He did this because he believed that a patent for a method provided broader protection than one directed to a steam engine per se. His approach seems

---

201. WILLIAM HOLDSWORTH, 11 A HISTORY OF ENGLISH LAW at 429 (London 1932). As quoted by Holdsworth, Chief Justice Eyre stated that a patent was given "not for a principle, but for a process." Justice Buller argued that:

> The very statement of what a principle is, proves it not to be a ground for a patent. It is the very first ground and rule for arts and sciences, or in other words the elements and rudiments of them. A patent must be for some new production from those elements, and not for the elements themselves.

Id. at n.7. Robinson quotes Chief Justice Eyre as also stating that "[u]ndoubtedly there can be no Patent for a mere Principle but for a Principle so far embedded and connected with corporeal Substances so as to be in a condition to act . . . I think there may be a patent for." Robinson, *supra* note 174, at 123.

202. In the eighteenth century the term "fire engine" was used to denote what would today be called a steam engine.

to have been a common one in the eighteenth century, and numerous patents for "methods" were granted by the crown.[203]

But could any sort of "method" be construed as "any manner of new manufactures" as contemplated by the Statute? At the end of the eighteenth century there was no consensus whatever among the common law judges that such a construction was appropriate. As early as 1776 Chief Justice Eyre had taken the position that a method could properly be patented,[204] but in 1795 in *Boulton v. Bull* two of the judges had contended that no patent could be granted for a method unless a new and vendible substance was produced.[205] This caused Watt thereafter to take a different tack and argue in 1799 in *Hornblower v. Boulton*[206] that his invention was really an improvement over earlier steam engines.[207]

In *Hornblower v. Boulton* Lord Kenyon stated that "having now heard every thing that can be said on the subject, I have no doubt in saying that this is a patent for a manufacture, *which I understand to be something made by the hands of man.*"[208] This clearly was a broader definition of "manufacture" than even Watt had argued for four years earlier in *Boulton v. Bull*. It did not require "art" to be involved and thus was at least suggestive of the view that patentable invention could occur by accident. Nor did it require that an invention be "vendible" in order to be considered a manufacture. It implicitly seemed to indicate that products of nature were not patentable since not "made by the hands of man."

Lord Kenyon's definition of "manufacture" did not specifically address the issue of whether "methods" fell within the ambit of "manufactures" as used in the Statute of Monopolies. Rather, he was of the view that Watt was actually claiming "a monopoly for an engine or machine, composed of material parts, which are to produce the effect described,"[209] despite the fact that the patent was clearly titled to be for a method. In essence, he

---

203. Robinson, *supra* note 174, at 120, 123. In *Boulton v. Bull*, Chief Justice Eyre stated his belief that two-thirds to three-fourths "of all patents granted since the statute passed, are for Methods of operating and of manufacturing, producing no new substances, and employing no new machinery." 2 H. Bl. at 494–95, 126 Eng. Rep. at 667. Both Robinson and Dutton quote Eyre to the same effect but with somewhat different language. Robinson, *id.* at 123, n.54, DUTTON, *supra* note 194, at 73.
204. DUTTON, *supra* note 194, at 73.
205. Robinson, *supra* note 174, at 123; DUTTON, *supra* note 194, at 74.
206. 8 T. R. 95, 101 Eng. Rep. 1285 (K.B. 1799).
207. DUTTON, *supra* note 194, at 74.
208. 8 T. R. at 99, 101 Eng. Rep. at 1288 (emphasis supplied).
209. *Id.*

argued that a patent ostensibly for a method was really a patent for the substance produced by the method or for the apparatus which produced the effect intended by the method of operation.

Nonetheless, to the extent the judges were prepared to accept that certain methods involving new and vendible substances or apparatus were patentable, this did not mean that there was consensus that any and all methods were patentable. Indeed, as noted above, two of the judges in *Boulton v. Bull* were clearly of the view that there could be no patent for a new process of producing an old product. As one of the earliest texts on the patent law stated in 1806: "most of the patents now taken out, are by name, for the method of doing particular things: and where the patent is for only a method, if it be not affected or accompanied by a manufacture, it *seems* the patent is not good."[210] By this was apparently meant "affected or accompanied by a manufacture *which was novel and patentable in its own right.*" This inability to clearly distinguish between method or process and apparatus or product would present grave difficulties for the English patent law in the years to come.[211] Those same difficulties would also appear in the early U.S. patent law.

Watt was perhaps as expert as anyone on the state of the patent law in England as the eighteenth century came to a close, but when it came to what constituted patentable invention he was as uncertain as any other inventor or lawyer of the times. Sometime about 1795 he summed up his "Doubts and Queries upon Patents" as follows:

[1] Whether the King can grant a patent for a method of doing or performing any mechanical process
[2] Whether in such case patent would be valid without a description of an *organized* machine
[3] Whether a man improving his invention after patent granted, does not invalidate his patent
[4] Whether a patentee refusing to add his improvement to an old machine does not render patent void
[5] Whether a patentee asking more than a fair provid [sic] does not invalidate
[6] Whether a patent for an improvement on an old invention is valid

---

210. DUTTON, *supra* note 194, at 74, quoting WILLIAM HANDS, THE LAW AND PRACTICE OF PATENTS FOR INVENTIONS at 6 (1806).
211. It was not until 1842 that it was finally settled that "manufacture" as used in the Statute of Monopolies includes "processes" within its ambit. *See* Crane v. Price, 1 Web. P.C. 393, 134 Eng. Rep. 239 (1842).

[7] Whether patent for new mode of using old instruments is valid

[8] Whether a patent for a chemical process is valid[212]

Although it has been argued that none of these questions had been satisfactorily answered by the common law in 1795,[213] the answer to query [6] was reasonably clear. The others, however, were still very much up in the air. The infant United States found these and many other questions unanswered when it turned to the common law to interpret its own brand new patent law.

At the end of the eighteenth and the beginning of the nineteenth century there was a marked tendency for American inventors, just as English inventors, to speak of the "principles" of their invention. The reasoning was the same as in England, namely, a desire to avoid being literally limited to particular embodiments described in the specification. Thus, e.g., in 1792 Joseph Barnes suggested that any new patent law should provide that "a person shall be entitled to obtain a patent, provided he shall have discovered a new principle in case of machines, or shall have discovered an improvement in the principle of any machine which is free or patented. . . ."[214] This language was at least partially incorporated into the Patent Act of 1793.[215]

The earliest American patent case to discuss a meaning to be attributed to "principle" was *Whitney v. Carter*[216] decided in 1810. Eli Whitney had sued Carter for infringement of his cotton ginning patent. In defense, Carter alleged that Whitney's gin was not novel, in that an earlier machine was the same "in principle" as Whitney's gin. In response Whitney's counsel made two distinct arguments. The first was that even if the "principle" of the two machines was the same, Whitney had applied it in an entirely new fashion

---

212. Robinson, *supra* note 174, at 131.

213. *Id.*

214. JOSEPH BARNES, TREATISE ON JUSTICE, POLICY, AND UTILITY OF ESTAB-LISHING AN EFFECTUAL SYSTEM OF PROMOTING THE PROGRESS OF USEFUL ARTS, BY ASSURING PROPERTY IN THE PRODUCTS OF GENIUS; TO WHICH ARE ADDED, OBSERVATIONS ON THE DEFICIENCY OF, AND EXCEPTIONS TO THE BILL REPORTED IN MARCH 1792, at 30–31 (Philadelphia 1792).

215. Section 2 of the Act provided

that any person who shall have discovered an improvement in the prin-ciple of any machine . . . which shall have been patented, and shall have obtained a patent for such improvement, he shall not be at liberty to make, use, or vend the original discovery, nor shall the first inventor be at liberty to use the improvement.

216. 29 F. Cas. 1070 (D. Ga. 1810) (No. 17,583).

and for a distinct purpose that was patentable. Secondly, he contended that the "principle" of the two machines was entirely different.[217]

Of particular interest to the present discussion is that:

> He defined the term "principle," as applied to the mechanic arts, to mean the elements and rudiments of those arts, or, in other words, the first grounds and rule for them. That for a mere principle a patent cannot be obtained. That neither the element, nor the manner of combining them, nor even the effect produced can be the subject of a patent; and that it can only be obtained for the application of this effect to some new and useful purpose.[218]

The court agreed "that the legal title to a patent consists, not in a principle merely, but in an application of a principle, whether previously in existence or not, to some new and useful purpose."[219]

In 1813 Justice Story in his capacity as circuit judge amplified the point when he declared:

> So if the principles of the machine are new, either to produce a new or an old effect, the inventor may well entitle himself to the exclusive right of the whole machine. By the principles of a machine, (as these words are used in the statute) is not meant the original elementary principles of motion, which philosophers and science have discovered, but the modus operandi, the peculiar device or manner of producing any given effect.[220]

Five years later, he would state: "The true legal meaning of the principle of a machine, with reference to the patent act, is the peculiar structure or constituent parts of such machine."[221]

In essence, the courts sought to distinguish between physical or scientific principles in the abstract and the applications of such principles to produce a useful result. Taken in the abstract, scientific or physical principles were held not to be patentable. But because they viewed the application of such principles to produce useful technological result as a promotion of the progress of the useful arts (although they almost never phrased it in this fashion), they held that such application could indeed be

---

217. 29 F. Cas. at 1071.
218. *Id.*
219. 29 F. Cas. at 1072–73.
220. Whittemore v. Cutter, 29 F. Cas. 1123, 1124 (D. Mass. 1813) (No. 17,601).
221. Barrett v. Hall, 2 F. Cas. 914, 923 (D. Mass. 1818) (No. 1,047).

patentable, but this generally required some change or improvement in the means used to effect the application.[222]

Nonetheless, even in the middle of the nineteenth century, the Supreme Court found itself addressing general problems of the patentability of "principles":

> The word *principle* is used by elementary writers on patent subjects, and sometimes in adjudications of courts, with such a want of precision in its application, as to mislead. It is admitted that a principle is not patentable. A principle, in the abstract, is a fundamental truth; an original cause; a motive; and these cannot be patented, as no one can claim in either of them an exclusive right. Nor can an exclusive right exist to a new power, should one be discovered in addition to those already known. . . . A new property discovered in matter, when practically applied, in the construction of a useful article of commerce or manufacture, is patentable; but the process through which the new property is developed and applied, must be stated, with such precision as to enable an ordinary mechanic to construct and apply the necessary process.[223]

Oliver Evans was the first in the United States to make a serious attempt to define what constituted patentable subject matter. In 1813 he posed the question: "What is the original discovery in a new and useful improvement in any art, machine, manufacture, or composition of matter?" and answered:

> It is the new and useful effect or result produced by the characteristic principles of the machine and may consist of
>
> 1. The discovery of the application of a new principle by means of old and known machines, to produce a new and useful result.[224] In this case the application of the principle and result will be secured.
> 2. The discovery of a new machine to produce a known effect or result, with less labour or expense. In this case the patent will be for the machine.

---

222. For an interesting early discussion of these issues, *see* WILLARD PHILLIPS, THE LAW OF PATENTS FOR INVENTIONS; INCLUDING THE REMEDIES AND LEGAL PROCEEDINGS IN RELATION TO PATENT RIGHTS at 95–108 (1837).
223. Le Roy v. Tatham, 55 U.S. (14 How.) 156, 175 (1852).
224. Thomas Jefferson parted company with Evans on this point and absolutely refused to acknowledge that a new use of an old machine was patentable. For Jefferson's views on the patent law in the first two decades of the nineteenth century, see Edward C. Walterscheid, *Patents and the Jeffersonian Mythology*, 29 J. MARSHALL L. REV. 269, 298–311 (1995).

3.   The discovery of a new combination of known machines to pro-
     duce a new and useful result.[225] In this case, the combination will
     be secured by patent, as well as the new result.

4.   The application of known principles to produce a new and useful
     result. In this case the result will be secured.

5.   The discovery of the application of a known machine, to a new
     use.[226] Here the new application will be secured, if it be useful, by
     producing the effect with less labour or expense.

6.   The discovery of an improvement on a known machine, to fit it for
     applying to a new use, to produce a useful result. Here the im-
     provement and new application will be secured.

7.   The discovery of a new and useful improvement in the process of
     any art or manufacture, although on experiment no means may yet
     be known, by which the improvement may be carried into effect
     with profit by the manufacturer. Here the improvement in the
     process will be secured, although the use can hardly be ascertained.

8.   The discovery of a new machine that was necessary to carry a new
     process into effect that has been discovered by another. Here the
     machine is the discovery, and will be secured for all purposes for
     which it will apply.

9.   The discovery of a new and improved process in any art or manu-
     facture, and also a set of machines, some improved, others
     altogether new, and their combination, to carry the improved pro-
     cess into effect to produce a new and useful result. In this case, the
     new improved process, and the new result in the discovery, will be
     secured; also the improved and new machines are discoveries, and
     will be secured for all the uses to which they apply.

10. The discovery of the application of a known power or principle to
     a new and useful purpose, as the extension of the application to
     move a known machine with greater force, by the discovery of a
     new and improved form of the machine, rendering it susceptible of
     the new or extended application, so as to produce a greater effect,
     or a new or more useful result, or at a less expense. In this case the
     original discovery consists in the new or extended application, and
     in the change of or improved form of the machine, both will be
     secured either jointly or separately.

11. The discovery of an unknown principle, applicable to useful pur-
     poses without discovering the means of profitable application.

---

225. Here, too, Jefferson initially disagreed, but after more thought changed his
     mind. *Id.*
226. Jefferson strongly disagreed. *Id.*

Here the principle discovered will be secured by our laws, differing from British.

12. The discovery of the means of profitably applying a useful principle, discovered by another, to a useful purpose. Here the means of application will be secured, subject to the prior right of the discoverer of the principle.

13. The discovery of an improvement in the mode or means of the application of a principle. Here the improvement will be secured, subject to the prior right of the discoverer of the principle, also to the first discoverer of the means of application; for no prior right shall be *discharged or lessened* by a subsequent grant of protection.

14. The discovery of an unknown plant and its uses. Here the plant will be secured, and all the uses that are specified by the patentee.

15. The discovery of new uses of a known plant. Here the new uses will be secured, subject to the prior right of the discoverer of the plant, during the patent term.[227]

Evans was well ahead of his time with regard to certain of these items, e.g., plant patents, and others would never be judicially interpreted to constitute patentable subject matter, e.g., the discovery of a new scientific principle. Nevertheless, it is apparent that Evans had given more serious thought to what might constitute patentable subject matter than had anyone else in the country. But he still had some difficulty in coming to grips with the idea that methods should be patentable, although he was certainly amenable to it.

Although the Supreme Court has stated that "a process has historically enjoyed patent protection because it was considered a form of 'art' as that term was used in [the Patent Act of 1793],"[228] it was not at all clear in 1793 that the phrase "useful art[s]" as it appeared in the intellectual property clause or the 1793 Act encompassed processes within the ambit of patentable invention. While the 1793 Act made reference to "the process of any composition of matter,"[229] no one knew for certain what that was intended to mean. Jefferson, for one, could never conceive of a process or

---

227. OLIVER EVANS (writing under the pseudonym of P. N. I. Elisha), PATENT RIGHT OPPRESSION EXPOSED; OR, KNAVERY DETECTED. IN AN ADDRESS TO UNITE ALL GOOD PEOPLE TO OBTAIN A REPEAL OF THE PATENT LAWS at 137–39 (Philadelphia 1813). Much of this work was intended as a satire on those opposed to the patent laws, but he incorporated his views on what the patent law should be in it.

228. Diamond v. Diehr, 450 U.S. 175, 182 (1981).

229. Patent Act of 1793 at § 2.

method of doing something as being patentable.[230] *Boulton v. Bull*, decided in 1795, set the common law view that certain processes or methods were patentable, but the issue was not early addressed in the American judicial determinations.

It was not until 1854 that the Supreme Court declared that "A process, eo nomine, is not made the subject of a patent in our act of congress [but rather] is included the general term 'useful art.'" In a confusing vein, the Court went on to state that "[a] new process is usually the result; a machine, of invention," thereby inferring some distinction between the terms "discovery" and "invention" in the patent law. Be that as it may, it concluded that:

> It is for the discovery or invention of some practical method or means of producing a beneficial result or effect that a patent is granted, and not for the result or effect itself. It is when the term process is used to represent the means or method of producing a result that it is patentable, and it will include all methods or means which are not effected by mechanism or mechanical combinations.[231]

Ever since it has been clear that processes and methods for producing a useful result, if novel and unobvious, are patentable subject matter. In 1952 Congress finally got around to declaring processes to be statutorily patentable subject matter.[232]

The Supreme Court has repeatedly reiterated that laws of nature, natural phenomena, or abstract ideas do not constitute patentable subjects,[233] without stating what constitutional objection, if any, exists to

---

230. For Jefferson's varying and sometimes inconsistent views on the patent law, see Edward C. Walterscheid, *Patents and the Jeffersonian Mythology*, 29 J. MARSHALL L. REV. 269 (1995).

231. Corning v. Burden, 15 How. 252, 267–68 (1854).

232. *See supra* note 169 and accompanying text.

233. *See, e.g.*, Diamond v. Diehr, 450 U.S. 175, 185 (1981) ("[e]xcluded from such patent protection are laws of nature, natural phenomena, and abstract ideas"); Gottschalk v. Benson, 409 U.S. 63, 67 (1972) ("[p]henomena of nature, though just discovered, mental processes, and abstract intellectual concepts are not patentable, as they are the basic tools of scientific and technological work"); Funk Bros. Seed Co. v. Kalo Co., 333 U.S. 127, 130 (1948) ("patents cannot issue for the discovery of the phenomena of nature. . . . They are manifestations of laws of nature, free to all men and reserved exclusively to none. He who discovers a hitherto unknown phenomenon of nature has not claim to a monopoly of it which the law recognizes"); MacKay Radio & Tel. Co. v. Radio Corp. of Am., 306 U.S. 86, 94 (1939) ("[w]hile a scientific truth, or the

treating them as patentable "discoveries" within the meaning of the intellectual property clause. Kreiss argues that the Court predicated these holdings on its interpretation of the term "discoveries" as used in the intellectual property clause. From this he concludes that "discoveries" is a term of art and that "since 'discoveries' and 'useful arts' are integrally related concepts, one must infer that 'useful arts' is also a term of art."[234]

He acknowledges, however, that as he puts it "it is hard to know whether the Court correctly interpreted the word 'discoveries' in the Constitution, either on linguistic or on policy grounds."[235] This assumes, incorrectly I believe, that either the definition of "discoveries" or policy grounds forms the basis for these holdings by the Court. Since the Court has never indicated the constitutional basis for the holdings, and it is in fact rather clear that they are not predicated on either linguistic interpretation of the term "discoveries" or on policy considerations,[236] it is reasonable to look elsewhere in the intellectual property clause to ascertain the basis for these holdings. Simply put, a rationale for these holdings resides in the interpretation of the terms "useful arts" in the clause.[237] As Kreiss puts it, "the subject matter of patents is limited to the 'discoveries' which must be in the 'useful arts.'"[238]

If to be patentable a discovery must promote the progress of the useful arts, then the phrase "to promote the progress of . . . useful arts" in the

---

mathematical expression of it, is not patentable invention, a novel and useful structure created with the aid of knowledge of scientific truth may be"); Rubber-Tip Pencil Co. v. Howard, 87 U.S. (20 Wall.) 498, 507 (1874) ("[a]n idea of itself is not patentable . . . "); O'Reilly v. Morse, 56 U.S. (15 How.) 62, 116 (1853) ("the discovery of a principle in natural philosophy or physical science, is not patentable"); Le Roy v. Tatham, 55 U.S. (14 How.) 156, 175 (1852) ("[a] principle, in the abstract, is a fundamental truth; an original cause; a motive; these cannot be patented, as no one can claim in either of them an exclusive right").

234. Kreiss, *supra* note 154, at 67.

235. *Id.*

236. Kreiss admits that when the Constitution was drafted the meaning of "discover" included the finding of natural phenomena. *Id.* Moreover, in our system of government, it is not the usual role of the judiciary, including the Supreme Court, to set policy, and there is nothing to suggest that in making these holdings the Court viewed itself as in any way setting policy as opposed to interpreting the law.

237. Indeed the Court has expressly stated that "it is only useful arts—arts which may be used to advantage—that can be made the subject of a patent." The Telephone Cases, 126 U.S. 1, 533 (1888).

238. Kreiss, *supra* note 154, at 63.

clause serves as a limitation on any broad interpretation of "discoveries" as used therein to include natural phenomena, laws of nature, or abstract ideas.[239] In other words, natural phenomena, laws of nature, or abstract ideas, without more, are not considered to be "useful arts." However, if they are employed in such a fashion as to produce a useful technological result, then patentable "discovery" resides in the embodiment or process that makes use of them to produce the useful result, and not in them apart from such embodiment or process.

One problem with interpreting the words "useful arts" as they appear in the intellectual property clause, and hence what falls within the ambit of patentable "discovery" is that, despite what courts and commentators have said,[240] "useful arts" as the phrase appears in the clause encompasses more than merely the technological arts. Moreover, the interpretation as to what is covered by "useful arts" of necessity changes with time. Nowhere is this more apparent than in the changing judicial view on the patentability of natural products and so-called business methods.

As early as 1813, Oliver Evans argued that the discovery of an unknown plant and its uses could be patented.[241] The extent to which life forms and their products were sought to be patented in the nineteenth

---

239. Without referring to the clause, the Supreme Court has stated:

> [A] new mineral discovered in the earth or a new plant found in the wild is not patentable subject matter. Likewise, Einstein could not patent his celebrated law that $E=mc^2$, nor could Newton have patent his law of gravity. Such discoveries are "manifestations of . . . nature, free to all men and reserved exclusively to none."

Diamond v. Chakrabarty, 447 U.S. 303, 309 (1980).

240. *See, e.g.,* In re Bergy, 596 F.2d 952, 959 (C.C.P.A. 1979) ("the present day equivalent of the term 'useful arts' employed by the Founding Fathers is 'technological arts.'"); In re Waldbaum, 457 F.2d 997, 1003 (C.C.P.A. 1972) ("whether appellant's process is 'statutory' depends upon whether it is within the 'technological arts.'"); In re Musgrave, 431 F.2d 882, 893 (C.C.P.A. 1970) ("[a]ll that is necessary . . . to make a sequence of operational steps a statutory 'process' within 35 U.S.C. § 101 is that it be in the technological arts so as to be in consonance with the Constitutional purpose to promote the progress of 'useful arts.'"); 1 DONALD S. CHISUM, CHISUM ON PATENTS (1998) at glossary 23 (identifying "technological arts as being synonymous with "useful arts"); Vincent Chiapetta, *Patentability of Computer Software Instruction as an "Article of Manufacture": Software as Such is the Right Stuff,* 17 J. MARSHALL J. COMPUTER & INFO. L. 89, 129–30 (1998) (stating that the "useful arts" involve "technology" or "industrial arts").

241. *See* Evans, *supra* note 227 and accompanying text.

century is unclear.[242] However, in 1889 in refusing to authorize a patent for the natural fibers of a particular tree, the Commissioner of Patents declared: "I am not aware of any instance in which it has been held that a natural product is the subject of a patent, although it may have existed from creation without being discovered."[243] In 1980 in reviewing why plant patents had been refused prior to 1930 the Supreme Court indicated that this decision "came to 'se[t] forth the general stand taken in these matters' that plants were natural products not subject to patent protection."[244]

The reason the Court limited its discussion to the period before 1930 was that in that year Congress enacted the Plant Protection Act which afforded patent protection to certain asexually reproduced plants.[245] In so doing, Congress argued "that the work of the plant breeder 'in aid of nature' was patentable invention."[246] Although neither the Supreme Court nor the Congress addressed the patent protection afforded by the Plant Protection Act, and later by the Plant Variety Protection Act,[247] in the context of any interpretation of the intellectual property clause, it is reasonable to suggest that prior to 1930 the creation or discovery of new plant varieties was not deemed to promote the progress of useful arts, whereas from 1930 on it has been viewed as doing so. In this mode of looking at things, the interpretation of what constitutes a useful art in the clause had changed.

But in 1948 in *Funk Brothers Seed Co. v. Kalo Inoculant Co.*,[248] the Supreme Court took the position that a novel and unobvious[249] combination of naturally occurring strains of bacteria useful for fixing nitrogen in leguminous plants was unpatentable. The prior art had taught that

---

242. But such patents were occasionally issued. Thus, for example, in 1873 Louis Pasteur received a United States patent which included a claim for: "Yeast, free from organic germs of disease, as an article of manufacture." *See* ROBERT PATRICK MERGES, PATENT LAW AND POLICY at 177 (2d ed. 1997), citing *Louis Pasteur's Patents*, SCIENCE, Oct. 8, 1937.

243. Ex parte Latimer, 1889 Comm'n Dec. 123, 127 (1889). *But see* note 242, *supra*.

244. Diamond v. Chakrabarty, 447 U.S. 303, 311 (1980), citing Thorne, *Relation of Patent Law to Natural Products*, 6 J. PAT. OFF. SOC'Y 23, 24 (1923).

245. *See* 35 U.S.C. § 161. In the Plant Variety Protection Act of 1970 Congress extended patent protection to novel varieties of sexually reproduced plants. *See* 7 U.S.C. § 2402(a).

246. 447 U.S. at 312, citing S. REP. NO. 315, 71st Cong., 2d Sess. (1930) at 6–8; H.R. REP. NO. 1129, 71st Cong., 2d Sess. 91930) at 7–9.

247. *See supra* note 245.

248. 333 U.S. 127 (1948).

249. At least from the teaching of the prior art.

different strains of bacteria useful for fixing nitrogen in particular leguminous plants could not be combined in one inoculant suitable for a variety of leguminous plants because the various strains were mutually inhibitive on each other. The inventor had discovered that there were in fact strains of the bacteria that were not mutually inhibitive and hence could be combined in a single inoculant for several legumes. The combination of strains with this highly valuable property was not found in nature.

Nonetheless, according to the Court, the qualities of the bacteria

> are the work of nature. Those qualities are of course not patentable. For the patents cannot for the discovery of the phenomena of nature. The qualities of these bacteria, like the heat of the sun, electricity, or the qualities of metals, are part of the storehouse of knowledge of all men. They are manifestations of the laws of nature, free to all men and reserved exclusively to none. He who discovers a hitherto unknown phenomena of nature has no claim to a monopoly of it which the law recognizes. . . . [T]here is no invention here unless the discovery that certain strains of the several species of these bacteria are non-inhibitive and may thus be safely mixed is invention. But we cannot so hold without allowing a patent to issue on one of the ancient secrets of nature now disclosed.[250]

The difficulty with this approach is spelled out by the Court in a 1981 decision when it declared that such an analysis "would, if carried to its extreme, make all inventions unpatentable because all inventions can be reduced to underlying principles of nature which, once known, make their implementation obvious."[251]

Be that as it may, in 1980 in *Diamond v. Chakrabarty* the Court once again expressly stated that "a new plant found in the wild is not patentable subject matter" regardless of what useful properties it might have.[252] It did, however, note that in enacting the Patent Act of 1952 Congress intended

---

250. 333 U.S. at 130–32.

251. Diamond v. Diehr, 450 U.S. 175, 189, n.12 (1981). Although the quoted language was in the context of an argument that a mathematical algorithm must be assumed to be within the prior art, it would seem to be applicable to the Court's statement in *Funk Bros.* that to permit the patenting of the combination of bacterial strains set forth therein would be to permit the patenting of "one of the ancient secrets of nature." Interestingly, the Court in *Diehr* cited *Funk Bros.* for the proposition that: "It is now commonplace that an application of a law of nature or mathematical formula to a well known structure or process may be deserving of patent protection." 450 U.S. at 187–88.

252. *See supra* note 239.

"statutory subject matter" to "include everything under the sun that is made by man."[253] According to the Court, "Congress . . . recognized that the relevant distinction was not between living and inanimate things, but between products of nature, whether living or not, and human-made inventions."[254] This seemed to suggest that, in the Court's view, there is a distinction between "discovery" and "invention" with patentable invention being limited to something "made by man." Since such a distinction is not found in the Patent Act of 1952,[255] its origin must arguably reside in the constitutional language, but as I have earlier suggested, there was not a clear distinction between "invention" and "discovery" at the time the Constitution was drafted.[256] Nonetheless, since *Chakrabarty* it has been commonly assumed that a new life form created by man is patentable whereas a new life form merely discovered is not.

The judicially created doctrine that business methods are not patentable seems to have originated in dictum in a 1908 Second Circuit opinion, namely: "A system for transacting business disconnected from the means for carrying out the system is not, within the most liberal interpretation of the term, an art."[257] Here the court was referring to "art" as it appeared in the patent statute rather than as it appeared in the intellectual property clause. Nonetheless, this view generally held sway until 1998 when the Federal Circuit gave short shrift to it in *State Street Bank & Trust Co. v. Signature Financial Group.*[258] Instead the Federal Circuit gave its wholehearted approval to the following guidelines set forth by the Patent Office in 1996: "Office personnel have had difficulty in properly treating claims directed to methods of doing business. Claims should not be categorized as methods of doing business. Instead such claims should be treated like any other process claims."[259]

The court also stressed that "[t]he question of whether a claim encompasses statutory subject matter should not focus on *which* of the four categories of subject matter a claim is directed to—process, machine,

---

253. 447 U.S. at 309, citing S. REP. NO. 1979, 82d Cong., 2d Sess. (1952) at 5; H.R. REP. NO. 1923, 82d Cong., 2d Sess. (1952) at 6.
254. 447 U.S. at 313.
255. The Patent Act of 1952 declares that "invention" means "invention or discovery." *See* 35 U.S.C. § 100(a).
256. *See supra* Part A.
257. Hotel Security Checking Co. v. Lorraine, 160 F. 467, 469 (2d Cir. 1908).
258. 149 F.3d 1368 (Fed. Cir. 1998).
259. *Id.* at 1377 (citing U.S. Patent and Trademark 1996 Examination Guidelines for Computer Related Inventions).

manufacture, or composition of matter—but rather on the essential characteristics of the subject matter, in particular, its practical utility."[260] Phrased somewhat differently, whether a discovery covers patentable subject matter depends on whether it promotes the progress of useful arts, i.e., its practical utility.

Kreiss, for one, is not happy with this state of affairs, and believes that business methods should not be patentable. He strives hard to find some constitutional basis for refusing patentability to such methods, but finds none. Instead, he argues that such methods should not be patentable because "the repeated comments made by courts, commentators and the PTO over the years to the effect that business methods are not patentable subject matter should be taken as strong evidence that business systems are perceived to be outside the bounds of the useful arts."[261] This view, however, seems to be contrary to his own earlier contention that patentable "discoveries" in the "useful arts" should be generally limited to things that are "functional." He states that a work is "functional if it performs some utilitarian task other than to inform, entertain, or portray an appearance to human beings."[262] Clearly, business methods are functional within this interpretation and hence should be patentable, provided they are novel and unobvious.

G. Perspectives

Without realizing it, the Framers created a significant interpretational problem when they chose to use the term "discoveries" in the intellectual property clause. While they quite likely viewed "discovery" as synonymous with "invention," its eighteenth century definition was sufficiently broad to read on the finding out of something which previously existed but had yet to be revealed. While invention arguably could be interpreted as limited to the creation of something new, discovery encompassed more than simply a creative act. Clearly, the searching for and finding out of the laws of nature and the phenomena of nature such as previously unknown

---

260. 149 F.3d at 1375.
261. Kreiss, *supra* note 154, at 85–86. In so stating, he conveniently ignores the point made in *State Street* that the courts primarily responsible for hearing patent issues, namely, the Court of Custom and Patent Appeals and its successor, the Federal Circuit, have never held an invention to be unpatentable on the ground that it is directed to a method of doing business. *See* 149 F.3d at 1375.
262. *Id.* at 79.

life forms or minerals constituted discovery, although nothing new was in fact created. Thus the use of the term "discoveries" in the intellectual property clause gave Congress very broad discretion as to what it might deem to be patentable discovery.[263]

In order to be patentable, the constitutional language clearly required that a discovery be new, or novel in the jargon that would develop, but new in what sense? Today, in an era of rapid world-wide communication, such a question would be treated as largely academic, but it was one of real import in the late eighteenth and early nineteenth century. Recall that a primary reason for incorporating the intellectual property clause in the Constitution was to assure that Congress would have authority to engage in something akin to the British patent and copyright practice as it existed near the end of the eighteenth century.[264]

A primary reason for seeking to adopt and adapt the British patent custom was that it was perceived to be an important factor in the rapid industrialization of Great Britain that had recently commenced. Authority for the British patent practice was the Statute of Monopolies which exempted patents for new manufactures from the ban on monopolies. Bear in mind that the early English patent custom arose out of a desire to create new industries in the realm primarily by importation and only secondarily by what would now be termed invention. Thus, the phrase "true and first inventor" in the Statute of Monopolies had been interpreted under the common law to include not only the first inventor but the first importer as well. At the time of the drafting of the Constitution novelty was defined in Great Britain by whether the subject matter of the invention was known or used within the country, and it was immaterial whether it was known or used elsewhere. It was the introduction of the invention in Great Britain that defined novelty and not originality per se.[265]

There is nothing whatever to indicate or suggest that in drafting the intellectual property clause the Framers intended it to encompass a narrower view of patentable novelty than that which existed in Great Britain. Yet the first Congress assumed this to be case and refused to authorize patents of importation on the grounds that such were

---

263. In 1974 the Supreme Court quoted with approval the view that: "Quite clearly discovery is something less than invention." *See* A. O. Smith Corp. v. Petroleum Iron Works Co., 73 F.2d 531, 538 (6th Cir. 1934), *quoted in* Kewanee Oil Co. v. Bicron Corp., 416 U.S. 470, 476 (1974).
264. *See supra* Chapter Three, text accompanying notes 46–58.
265. These points are discussed in more detail in Chapter Two, text accompanying notes 66–94.

constitutionally precluded. Moreover, it would include language in the Patent Act of 1793 which the Supreme Court interpreted in 1818 as requiring an invention to be not only new but original throughout the world in order to be patentable in the United States.[266] But in so doing, the Court would expressly decline to interpret the meaning to be given to the terms "invention" or "discovery" in either the patent statute or the intellectual property clause.

In light of this narrow view of novelty, it might be assumed that any publication or use of the invention or discovery which placed it in the public domain would automatically preclude patentability, but this was not the case in at least one context through the nineteenth century. Thus on a number of occasions Congress authorized and the courts upheld patent term extensions or renewals that occurred after the original patent had expired and the subject matter had gone into the public domain.[267] The rationale given by Congress for so doing was that such was necessary to assure an adequate reward to the inventor. Never mind that the clause spoke only of promoting the progress of useful arts and that it was difficult to see how extending or renewing a patent after it had expired served in any way to promote such progress. More recently, however, the Supreme Court has concluded that the clause precludes Congress from issuing patents that remove knowledge from the public domain.[268] The constitutional requirement of novelty would seem to require such a conclusion, even though an original inventor may be involved.

Although the contemporaneous interpretation given to the terms "inventors" and "discoveries" clearly indicated a constitutional requirement of novelty before a patent could issue, the statement of purpose in the clause can also be construed as placing constitutional limitations on the power of Congress to issue patents.[269] That it also suggests a constitutional requirement of novelty and utility in order for patentability to exist can also be inferred from its language. But in 1966 in *Graham v. John Deere Co.* the Supreme Court declared that the introductory language of the clause sets forth a constitutional standard of invention[270] as an additional condition for

---

266. *See supra* note 90 and accompanying text.

267. *See, e.g.,* Chapter Seven, text accompanying notes 209–223.

268. Graham v. John Deere Co., 383 U.S. 1, 6 (1966); Bonito Boats, Inc. v. Thunder Craft Boats, Inc., 489 U.S. 141, 146 (1989).

269. *See* Chapter Five. I have earlier suggested that it places a limitation on the duration of patent and copyright terms that can be set by Congress. *See* Chapter Seven, Part E.

270. *See supra* note 100 and accompanying text.

patentability. In the Court's view, something more than novelty is constitutionally required for patentability, but what that something is is unclear. Most commentators have assumed that this constitutional standard refers to the unobviousness requirement first set forth by the Court in 1851 in *Hotchkiss v. Greenwood* and made statutory in 1952.[271] While Congress has wide discretion to set standards of patentability and has indeed set unobviousness as a standard, it is questionable at best whether such a standard is required by the intellectual property clause. In this regard, it is of interest to note that the *Hotchkiss* Court made no attempt to use the language of the clause to justify its conclusion that patentability required the application of a higher standard of skill than that "possessed by an ordinary mechanic acquainted with the business."[272]

The Court's rationale for holding that a constitutional standard of invention exists was not predicated in any way on a specific analysis of the actual language of the clause nor on any contemporaneous interpretation of clause language by the Framers, but instead was based almost entirely on an erroneous and misleading interpretation of Thomas Jefferson's role in the early development of the patent law and his views on it. The difficulty with this approach is that aside from being a misrepresentation of Jefferson's role and views, it ignores the fact that Jefferson never expressed any views on interpretation of the intellectual property clause after his early exchange of correspondence with James Madison in 1788 and 1789.

Contrary to the Court's assertion, Jefferson most definitely did not believe that the courts should develop conditions for patentability over and above those set forth by statute,[273] but even if he had such a belief, it is not relevant to constitutional interpretation of the language of the clause. The Court's assertion that Congress agreed by negative implication with the view that courts are authorized to set standards of patentability because it failed to set a higher standard of patentability between 1790 and 1950 than merely utility and novelty[274] is wholly without merit. Nothing in the clause grants such authority to courts, and it is just as likely that the failure of Congress to set a higher statutory standard of patentability was predicated on the view that none was required by the constitutional language or needed as a practical matter. Indeed, if the *Hotchkiss* test is predicated on a constitutional standard, and Congress understood it as such, it is difficult

---

271. *See supra* text accompanying notes 103–112.
272. *See supra* text accompanying notes 105–107.
273. *See supra* note 132.
274. *See supra* text accompanying notes 123, 124.

to understand why it took a century for such an unobviousness standard to be incorporated into the patent statute.

The answer, of course, is that in the intervening period between *Hotchkiss* and the enactment of the Patent Act of 1952 no court held that the *Hotchkiss* test was constitutionally required, and Congress most certainly did not perceive it to be constitutionally required for patentability. In this regard, the legislative history of the 1952 Act declares that Section 103 thereof, setting forth an unobviousness requirement for patentability "for the first time in our statute, provides a condition which exists in the law and has existed for more than 100 years, *but only by reason of decisions of the courts.*"[275] If there is a clear constitutional mandate that sets a higher standard of patentability than merely utility and novelty, then it is indeed the duty of the Court to so determine, but the Court is without authority to substitute its judgment for that of Congress absent a clear constitutional mandate. No such clear mandate exists in the intellectual property clause.[276]

While Jefferson undoubtedly had high standards for patentability as the Court declared, his standards were not those of the Framers or the first and second federal Congresses. Thus, in enacting the Patent Act of 1793, the second Congress which contained a number of Framers expressly declined to incorporate his proposal set forth in a draft patent bill in 1791 for a statutory nonobviousness standard.[277] If there is indeed a constitutional standard of invention set forth in the intellectual property clause, it is difficult to understand why the first patent acts did not incorporate such a standard.[278]

If the Court's holding that a constitutional standard of invention is required by the clause is based on a false reading of the historical record, the same is not true of its understanding that novelty and utility are constitutional requirements. The need for novelty is found both in the contemporary definitions of "inventors" and "discoveries" and in the requirement that patents promote the progress of useful arts. Clearly, if a

---

275. *See* S. REP. No. 1979, 82d Cong., 2d Sess. (1952) at 6 (emphasis supplied).
276. It should be noted that the clause is part of article I, section 8 of the Constitution which sets forth the enumerated powers of Congress and does not delineate any power of the federal courts.
277. *See supra* note 129 and accompanying text.
278. In this regard, in 1884 the Supreme Court declared in the copyright context that the interpretation placed on the Constitution by the first copyright acts of 1790 and 1802 "by the men who were contemporary with its formation, many of whom were members of the convention which framed it, is of itself entitled to very great weight." Burrow-Giles Lithography Co. v. Sarony, 111 U.S. 53, 57 (1884).

discovery is not new, it does not promote such progress. A requirement for utility is not found in contemporaneous definitions of "inventors" and "discoveries" but can be found in the introductory language of the clause, for, if a discovery is not utilitarian, it does not promote the progress of useful arts. Contrary to the assertion of the Supreme Court in *Brenner v. Manson*,[279] there is no constitutional requirement that an invention must have "substantial utility" to be patentable.

Care should be taken to clearly distinguish between standards for patentability and patentable subject matter because they are not the same thing at all. While there are clearly constitutional requirements that must be met in setting standards of patentability, it is less clear that there are constitutional limits on what constitutes patentable subject matter. I have suggested, however, that to the extent such limitations exist they must be found in the introductory language of the clause and, in particular, in the definition accorded to "useful arts" as found in the clause.[280]

The Supreme Court has never sought to provide a definition of "useful arts" as that phrase appear in the clause, although it has expressly stated that "it is only useful arts . . . that can be made the subject of a patent."[281] Nonetheless, I have suggested herein that the Court, without any express reference to the constitutional language, has effectively limited "useful arts" to exclude natural phenomena, laws of nature, or abstract ideas, which, without more, have repeatedly been held not to be patentable subject matter. It is in this context that I have suggested that "discoveries" as used in the clause is limited to discoveries in the useful arts. Lower courts and commentators have on a number of occasions suggested that "useful arts" means "technological arts." But even this is not particularly helpful because patents are routinely granted in fields that do not appear to fall within the definition of technological arts.[282]

In 1980 in *Diamond v. Chakrabarty* the Supreme Court noted with approval that the legislative history of the Patent Act of 1952 indicating that

---

279. *See supra* notes 137, 138 and accompanying text. The Court did not define what it meant by "substantial utility" and there is no basis in the constitutional language for the use of such phraseology. It implies that while certain inventions may indeed promote the progress of useful arts, there are nonetheless constitutionally unworthy of a patent because their utility is not sufficiently great.

280. *See supra* text accompanying notes 159, 160.

281. *See supra* note 237.

282. Plant patents and patents for business methods are but two examples in the modern era.

statutory patentable subject matter was intended "to include everything under the sun that is made by man."[283] Although no reference was made to "useful arts" as that phrase appears in the intellectual property clause, I believe that phrase should be interpreted as including anything made or created by the hand of man and as excluding anything not made or created by man. This would be fully in accord with the long held view that natural phenomena, laws of nature, and abstract ideas are not patentable subject matter. In this approach, "discoveries" as used in the clause is limited to those discoveries falling within the "useful arts" so defined.

---

283. *See supra* note 253 and accompanying text.

CHAPTER NINE
AUTHORS AND THEIR WRITINGS

The clause authorizes Congress to secure to "Authors . . . the exclusive Right to *their* . . . Writings. . . ."[1] Just as with patents, regardless of the definition given to either authors or writings, this language on its face clearly limits congressional authority to the issuance of copyrights to authors only for *their* writings however statutorily or judicially defined. This would seem in turn to suggest that, just as with patents, copyrights must be applied for and issued in the name of the author regardless of who or what entity may actually own the rights to the copyright.[2] But that is not what Congress has seen fit to statutorily declare. We begin this discussion of authors and their writings with a closer look at the meaning given to "their" in the copyright context.

A. The Name on the Copyright

A leading copyright treatise states that "[t]here would appear to be no constitutional objection to permitting the assignee of an author to claim copyright in the work assigned."[3] The basis for this statement is declared to be that the "author's property right derived from the Constitutional authority is unquestionably assignable."[4] While this latter statement is indeed true, it does not follow from the mere fact of assignability that the intellectual property clause contemplates that the copyright should issue in the name of the assignee.

In the patent statutes, Congress has not only assumed but declared that a patent must issue to the inventor, even though all rights in the invention

---

1. U.S. CONST. art. I, § 8, cl. 8 (emphasis supplied).
2. *See supra* Chapter Eight, note 1 and accompanying text.
3. MELVILLE B. NIMMER & DAVID NIMMER, 1 NIMMER ON COPYRIGHT [Rel. 51-5/00] at 1–66.22. In this chapter I make frequent reference to this treatise and discuss a number of points raised therein. I do so because it is the most detailed American copyright treatise and because it is the treatise most frequently cited by courts, including the Supreme Court, in copyright opinions.
4. *Id.*, citing American Tobacco Co. v. Werckmeister, 207 U.S. 284 (1907).

may be assigned to another entity.[5] But in the copyright statutes, Congress has taken a very different tack. The issue arises most frequently in the context of so-called "works made for hire" but it should be noted that from the middle of the nineteenth century congressional enactments on copyright made little or no distinction between the author of a work or the proprietor or assignee of the work when it came to filing a claim or application for copyright. In particular, unlike the patent statutes which required that a patent be obtained in the name of the inventor, there was no specific requirement that a copyright be obtained in the name of the author.[6]

In the Copyright Act of 1909 Congress expressly defined the term "author" to include "an employer in the case of works made for hire."[7] This definition was reiterated in the 1976 Act,[8] and was declared to adopt "one of the basic principles of copyright law."[9] Congress has thus made explicit its view that the "author" of works made for hire includes the entity to whom the property right in the copyrighted work had been assigned as well as that person who was the creator or originator of the work. Although this is a highly expansive interpretation of both "authors" and "their" as found in the intellectual property clause, Congress has never

---

5. Thus 35 U.S.C. § 118 declares that

> a person to whom the inventor has assigned or agreed in writing to assign the invention or who otherwise shows sufficient proprietary interest in the matter justifying such action, may make application for patent *on behalf of and as agent of the inventor* on proof of the pertinent facts and a showing that such action is necessary to preserve the rights of the parties or to prevent irreparable damages; and the Director may grant a patent *to such inventor* upon such notice to him as the Commissioner deems sufficient, and on compliance with such regulations as he prescribes.

> Note that even though the invention may be fully owned and prosecuted by the assignee, nonetheless the patent issues in the name of the inventor and not that of the assignee.

6. Indeed, the Copyright Act of 1856 specifically referred to copyrights granted to proprietors as well as authors. *See* 8 NIMMER & NIMMER, *supra* note 3, at App. 7-57.

7. *See* 8 NIMMER & NIMMER, *supra* note 3, at App. 6-29.

8. 17 U.S.C. § 201(b) ("[i]n the case of a work made for hire, the employer or other person for whom the work was prepared is considered the author for purposes of this title").

9. 8 NIMMER & NIMMER, *supra* note 3, at App. 4-114.

CHAPTER NINE. AUTHORS AND THEIR WRITINGS

seen fit to address the constitutionality of such an expansive definition of these terms.[10]

The legislative history accompanying the Copyright Act of 1909 contains an interesting discussion of the constitutional aspects of copyright law, whereas the constitutional aspect is only minimally treated in the legislative history of the Copyright Act of 1976.[11] Thus, the legislative history of the 1909 Act expressly states that the constitutional authority of Congress to create copyrights is limited by several conditions, one of which is "that the subjects which are to be secured are 'the writings of authors.'"[12] But after so stating, Congress did not see fit to give any explanation whatever as to why the term "author" in the intellectual property clause could be interpreted to include "an employer in the case of works made for hire."[13] Instead, it merely stated that the relevant section of the Act "places an interpretation and construction upon the use of certain words."[14] In the legislative history of the 1976 Act, Congress gave as its reason for the expanded definition that:

> The [presumption] that initial ownership rights vest in the employer for hire is well established in American copyright law, and to exchange that for the uncertainties of the shop right doctrine[15] would not only be of

---

10. In the 1976 Act Congress expressly acknowledged that copyright initially vests in the author or authors of a work. This certainly is consonant with the constitutional language. But in defining the owner of a work made for hire as an author (*see supra* note 8), Congress appears to have gone well beyond a reasonable interpretation of the constitutional language.

11. *Cf.* H.R. REP. NO. 2222, 60th Cong., 2d Sess. (1909) (the Senate adopted the same report; see Senate Report No. 1108), as reproduced *in* NIMMER & NIMMER, *supra* note 3, at App. 13-1–App. 13-31, with H.R. REP. NO. 94-1476, 94th Cong., 2d Sess. (1976), as reproduced *in* 8 NIMMER & NIMMER, *supra* note 3, at App. 4-2–4-216; Senate Report, reproduced *id.* at 4A-2–4A-255.

12. 8 NIMMER & NIMMER, *supra* note 3, at App. 13-10.

13. Although Congress was only statutorily defining an "author" to include "an employer in the case of works for hire," of necessity it was assuming that the term "authors" in the clause also read just as expansively. While Congress clearly has authority to restrict the definition of "authors," as encompassed in the clause, for copyright purposes, it has no constitutional authority to expand that definition and grant copyright to individuals who are not "authors" within the meaning of the clause.

14. 8 NIMMER & NIMMER, *supra* note 3, at App. 13-31.

15. A doctrine in patent law whereby the employer has certain rights in inventions made by his or her employees in the course of their employment.

dubious value to employers and employees alike, but might also reopen a number of other [unspecified] issues.[16]

Patterson and Lindberg point out that these unspecified issues include arguments that invalidating these so-called "corporate" copyrights would create confusion in the publishing industry and would leave many works unprotected. They suggest that such arguments are both venerable and effective[17] although not necessarily valid, for were such invalidation to occur it is quite possible that the copyright would revert to and vest "in the responsible hands of the authors who actually created the works."[18]

The Register of Copyrights has suggested that Congress expanded the definition of "author" to include employers in the case of works made for hire because of the perception "that there are great advantages of convenience and simplicity in assimilating employers to 'authors' for all purposes," and that "the advantages of making the employer an 'author' for purposes of the statute outweigh any conceptual difficulties involved in doing so."[19] As Nimmer and Nimmer have succinctly put it, "[t]he fiction of the employer as author was employed . . . not in order to achieve substantive results that could not have been otherwise achieved, but rather because of the 'convenience and simplicity' of this manner of achieving [the desired] results."[20] That this legal fiction might run afoul of the constitutional language seems not to have been contemplated.

"The troubling problem," as Patterson and Lindberg stress, "is that the reasons that make the work-for-hire doctrine unconstitutional are the very reasons that make it a convenient and powerful instrument of monopoly."[21] Note that the clause makes no reference to publishers and does not purport to authorize Congress to give a limited copyright monopoly to them. Given the history of copyright in England in the seventeenth and eighteenth centuries, it is very likely that this was deliberate. Indeed, the House report on the 1909 Act at least implicitly recognized "that to grant the publisher a copyright would be to grant a corporate entity the rights intended to protect only the author, and that those rights could be used to form

---

16. 8 NIMMER & NIMMER, *supra* note 3, at App. 4-114.
17. They are similar to arguments used by the booksellers in England during the eighteenth century to protect their interests.
18. *See* L. RAY PATTERSON & STANLEY W. LINDBERG, THE NATURE OF COPYRIGHT, A LAW OF USERS' RIGHTS at 86 (Athens, Ga. 1991).
19. *See* Register's Supplemental Report (1965) at 66, as reproduced *in* 9 NIMMER & NIMMER, *supra* note 3, at App.15-93, App.15-94.
20. NIMMER & NIMMER, *supra* note 3, at 1–66.24.
21. PATTERSON & LINDBERG, *supra* note 18, at 86.

oppressive monopolies—but then overlooked [or deliberately ignored] its relevance to the work-for-hire doctrine."[22]

It is reasonable therefore to ask on what basis ownership of a work can be said to define authorship in the constitutional sense. In common parlance, the one who writes or creates a work is viewed as the author, and was so viewed at the time the Constitution was drafted. Simply creating a legal fiction that an employer is the author of a work for hire does not mean that such fiction passes constitutional muster. As the Supreme Court has stated: "The power to create presumptions is not a means of escape from constitutional restrictions."[23]

Although this issue has been noted in judicial opinions, it has never been definitively ruled on. On occasion, however, dicta have suggested that the term "authors" as used in the clause may properly be interpreted to include the owner of a work for hire. Thus, e.g., the Second Circuit has declared that: "Though the United States is perhaps the only country that confers 'authorship' status on the employer of the creator of a work for hire . . . , its decision to do so is not constitutionally suspect."[24] It gave no basis for this conclusory statement, even though it recognized that "the employer has shown skill only in selecting employees, not in creating protectable expression," and that declaring an employer an author "seems more like a justification for transfer of ownership than for recognition of authorship."[25]

A basic question that arises is why, if the term "authors" in the clause is sufficiently broad to read on the proprietors of works made for hire, it is not also sufficiently broad to read on the proprietor of any original work? Another is why Congress has deemed it appropriate to define employers of those making works for hire as authors for purposes of claiming copyright, but has refused to define the term "inventors" for purposes of obtaining patents as reading on the employer of those who make inventions for hire.[26]

In the absence of any clear judicial explanation of a constitutional rationale for why the term "authors" as used in the intellectual property clause is deemed to include the proprietors of works made for hire, it is

---

22. *Id.* at 87. For the relevant language of the House report, *see* 8 NIMMER & NIMMER, *supra* note 3, at App. 13-11.
23. Bailey v. Alabama, 219 U.S. 219, 239 (1911).
24. Childress v. Taylor, 945 F.2d 500, 507 n.5 (2d Cir. 1991).
25. 945 F.2d at 506 and 507, n.5.
26. One reason, of course, is that to do so would run afoul of "the constitutional objective of *granting* a patent (or a reissue patent) to the true inventor." A. F. Stoddard & Co. v. Dann, 564 F.2d 556, 562 (D.C. Cir. 1977).

appropriate now to look in more detail at how authorship has been interpreted generally in the constitutional sense.

B. Authorship

As with most things involving interpretation of constitutional language, it is useful to begin with contemporary definitions of "author" at the time the Constitution was drafted. While such contemporary definition is by no means binding on modern interpretation, it nonetheless provides a context against which the Framers may be presumed to have acted when they incorporated the term "authors" into the intellectual property clause. The standard English dictionary in use at the time the Constitution was drafted contained four definitions of "author": (1) "'The first beginner or mover of anything; he to whom any thing owes its original"; (2) "The efficient; he that effects or produces any thing"; (3) "The first writer of any thing; distinct from the translator or compiler"; and (4) "A writer in general."[27]

Since the purpose of the copyright authority set forth in the clause was in large measure[28] to give Congress power to emulate the British copyright practice as established by the judicial gloss given to the Statute of Anne enacted in 1710,[29] it is reasonable to inquire first into the language of the Statute and then to review how it was interpreted in the context of authorship in the remainder of the eighteenth century. Two aspects of the statutory language are of interest here. The first is that the Statute was styled "An act for the encouragement of learning." The second is that, although there is nothing to indicate that Parliament literally intended it

---

27. SAMUEL JOHNSON, A DICTIONARY OF THE ENGLISH LANGUAGE (London 1755).

28. I say "in large measure" advisedly, because there were British copyright statutes other than the Statute of Anne in effect when the Constitution was drafted. See, e.g., note 197, infra. I am aware of no commentator who has addressed in any detail the issue of the extent that the Framers actually intended to encompass the subject matter of these other statutes within the compass of the term "writings" as used in the intellectual property clause. This issue is discussed in the text accompanying notes 247–262, infra.

29. 8 Anne, c. 19. The Statute is reproduced in 8 NIMMER & NIMMER, supra note 3, at App. 7-5–7-10. For the background against which the Statute was enacted, see Chapter Two, Part E.

as such, it would come to be judicially interpreted as providing for an author's right.[30]

The idea that copyright was for the purpose of encouraging learning first found voice in the Statute of Anne. Never before had this been declared to be a purpose of copyright.[31] Nothing in the parliamentary record indicates why the emphasis on encouraging learning came about. Feather states that the petitions presented to Parliament during the debates make "no reference to, or even tacit support of, the encouragement of learning" or for that matter "the rights of authors."[32] Rose, however, suggests that the "priority given to the encouragement of learning" was a direct result of a series of articles published by Daniel Defoe and Joseph Addison arguing that the rights of authors had to be protected.[33] Irrespective of who was responsible for it, this justification for copyright quickly found favor with Parliament and would find its way into the intellectual property clause.

Although it made reference to authors' rights, the real purpose of the Statute of Anne was to protect rights given to "the bookseller or book-sellers, printer or printers, or other person or persons, who hath or have purchased or acquired the copy or copies of any book or books, in order to print or reprint the same."[34] The Statute was intended more than anything else as a trade regulation statute, to prevent piracy and protect the interests of the booksellers and publishers. As Patterson points out, the "[e]mphasis

---

30. According to Patterson:

> The statutory copyright provided in the Statute of Anne was a publisher's copyright; but the act was construed to have provided an author's copyright. The distinction between the two concepts—the one intended and the one which resulted—was fundamental. This development had little to do with the Statute of Anne itself; but because the act provided for copyright, and the statutory copyright it provided later came to be an author's copyright, the inevitable conclusion was that the statutory copyright was originally designed to be an author's copyright.

> LYMAN RAY PATTERSON, COPYRIGHT IN HISTORICAL PERSPECTIVE at 144 (Nashville 1968).

31. The term "copyright" was quite new at the time the Statute was enacted, having only just come into use in the preceding decade or so. *See* MARK ROSE, AUTHORS AND OWNERS, THE INVENTION OF COPYRIGHT at 58, n.4 (Cambridge 1993).

32. JOHN FEATHER, PUBLISHING, PIRACY AND POLITICS, AN HISTORICAL STUDY OF COPYRIGHT IN BRITAIN (London 1994) at 60.

33. ROSE, *supra* note 31, at 42. *See also* FEATHER, *supra* note 32, at 56.

34. 8 NIMMER & NIMMER, *supra* note 3, at App. 7-5.

on the author in the Statute of Anne implying that the statutory copyright was an author's copyright was more a matter of form than of substance."[35] As evidence of this, Rose notes that during the debates on the bill that became the Statute, an "emphatic statement about authors possessing 'undoubted property' in their 'Books and Writings as the product of their learning and labour' was eliminated from the preamble."[36] He suggests that "the exact status of authorial property was not something to which anyone had given a great deal of thought prior to the parliamentary consideration of a literary property bill—and it is unlikely that the matter was examined in any great detail during the deliberations over the statute."[37]

There was a straightforward reason why at the beginning of the eighteenth century author's rights were at best given only lip service. The booksellers almost always insisted on owning the copyright before they would publish anything. If the author refused, and somehow found a bookseller willing to publish a work without the copyright, there was the substantial risk that there would be inadequate promotion of the work with the idea of forcing the author ultimately to sell the copyright.[38] Thus, typically, the author sold rights in his "copy" outright, and it was assumed that once such rights were transferred, they were of no further concern to the author. As Feather puts it, "[t]he law was for the benefit of the 'proprietors,' not the creators, of books."[39] And indeed for the first quarter century after the Statute was enacted, the rights of authors seem never to have been seriously raised. That changed in 1735 with the efforts of the booksellers to obtain a longer term for copyright.[40] Although the bill failed, the rights of authors were brought more sharply into focus, and thereafter the debates on copyright would center more and more on such rights.[41]

---

35. PATTERSON, *supra* note 18, at 147.
36. ROSE, *supra* note 31, at 45.
37. *Id.* at 48.
38. PATTERSON, *supra* note 18, at 152.
39. FEATHER, *supra* note 32, at 67.
40. The booksellers sought to have the initial term of copyright extended to 21 years. In so doing, they represented themselves as "acting on behalf as well of Authors and Compilers of such Books, as of themselves." In essence, they were now representing literary property as basically an author's interest and them- selves as merely the author's agents and assigns. *See* ROSE, *supra* note 31, at 52.
41. FEATHER, *supra* note 32, at 74 ("[a]fter 1735, it was never again entirely possible to exclude some consideration of the rights of authors when copyright law was under discussion"); ROSE, *supra* note 31, at 56 ("[b]ut even if no bill was passed, a significant evolution had occurred in which the focus of the literary-property question shifted from the booksellers to the author").

It was not until after the landmark decision in *Donaldson v. Becket* in 1774 that it would come to be understood that there was indeed a common-law property right of authors in copyright in a published work, but one which had been merged into and could only be enforced in accordance with the Statute of Anne.[42] But if an author's copyright in a published work could only be enforced in accordance with the Statute of Anne, what exactly was an author as that term was used in the Statute? In the first half of the eighteenth century it rather quickly came to be recognized that authorship involved the creation of a manuscript that was the product of mental labor, but did authorship reside in the ideas produced by mental effort or in the form of expression used to set the ideas forth? Through much of the eighteenth century there was considerable confusion as to what authorship actually entailed, and it was only at the time the Constitution was drafted that the dichotomy between ideas and the form of expression of those ideas was beginning to be clearly understood.

Initially, there seems to have been a perspective that the production of the ideas themselves was what constituted authorship. This was certainly the view expressed by William Warburton in 1747 in a pamphlet entitled *A Letter from an Author to a Member of Parliament Concerning Literary Property*. Rose calls this the first theoretical treatment of literary property published in England.[43] According to Warburton, regarding "Property in the Product of the Mind, as in a *Book* composed, it is not confined to the Original MS. but extends to the *Doctrine* contained in it: Which is, indeed, the true and peculiar Property in a Book."[44] In this view, the property which copyright was intended to protect consisted solely of the "doctrine" or ideas that were the product of the mental labor of an author.

In 1760 it was argued in *Tonson v. Collins* that, as Feather puts it, "the very act of publication made it impossible to restrict the ideas and words thus published, and that the law depended upon the 1710 Act which tried to protect those ideas and words for a limited period of time."[45] Again, this argument assumed that copyright was for the purpose of protecting an author's ideas. In his dissent in *Millar v. Taylor* in 1769, Justice Yates voiced a similar sentiment,[46] saying: "But the property here claimed is all

---

42. For a discussion of *Donaldson* and the cases leading up to it see Chapter Two, text accompanying notes 128–163.
43. ROSE, *supra* note 31, at 71.
44. *Id.* at 73.
45. FEATHER, *supra* note 32, at 85. *See also* ROSE, *supra* note 31, at 77.
46. This was not surprising in that as counsel for Collins in *Tonson v. Collins*, he presented a similar argument. *See* ROSE, *supra* note 31, at 77.

ideal; a set of ideas which have no bounds or marks whatever, nothing that is capable of possession, nothing that can sustain the qualities or incidents of property."[47]

But if authorship resided merely in the creation and collection of ideas, why should copyrights be treated any differently than patents? Was there any distinction? Several of the law lords in *Donaldson v. Becket* certainly didn't think so. As Baron Eyre stated, "Exactitude . . . of the Resemblance between a Book and any other mechanical invention" was clear:

> There is the same Identity of intellectual Substance; the same spiritual Unity. In a mechanic Invention the Corporeation of Parts, the Junction of Powers, tends to produce some one End. A literary Composition is an Assemblage of Ideas so judiciously arranged, as to enforce some one Truth, lay open some one Discovery, or exhibit some one Species of mental Improvement. A mechanic Invention, and a literary Composition, exactly agree in Point of Similarity; the one therefore is no more entitled to be the Object of Common law Property than the other.[48]

Eyre was attempting to demonstrate that there was no distinction between invention and literary works and hence between patents and copyrights and that there could be no common-law property right in either. But in so doing, probably without intending to do so, he set forth the distinction between patents and copyrights that would soon come to be recognized.

That distinction resides in what has familiarly come to be known as the idea/expression dichotomy. Whereas a patent provides a limited-term exclusive right in useful embodiments of ideas discovered by an inventor, a copyright provides a limited-term exclusive right in the form of expression or arrangement of the ideas, rather than the ideas themselves, that may be set forth by an author. Eyre presaged the distinction by his statement that: "A literary Composition is an Assemblage of Ideas *so judiciously arranged, as to enforce some one Truth, lay open some one Discovery, or exhibit some one Species of mental Improvement.*" But it would not be until *Baker v. Selden* decided in 1879 that the Supreme Court would hold unequivocally that copyright covers only the form of expression and not the ideas expressed.[49]

---

47. Millar v. Taylor, 98 Eng. Rep. 201, 233 (K.B. 1769).
48. *The Cases of the Appellants and Respondents in the Cause of Literary Property, Before the House of Lords* (London 1774), *in* THE LITERARY PROPERTY DEBATE: SIX TRACTS 1764–1774, at 34 (Stephen Parks ed., New York 1974).
49. As the Court put it: "The very object of publishing a book . . . is to communicate to the world the useful knowledge which it contains. But this object would be frustrated if the knowledge could not be used without incurring the guilt of piracy of the book." 101 U.S. 99, 103 (1879).

Nonetheless, in the 1760s an attempt already had been made by no less a personage than William Blackstone to define the subject of literary property inherent in copyright in a manner that sought to distinguish it both from the patent right and any physical embodiment of property in the printed copy. As one of the counsel for Tonson in *Tonson v. Collins*, he argued:

> Style and sentiment are the essentials of a literary composition. These alone constitute its identity. The paper and print are merely accidents, which serve as vehicles to convey the style and sentiment to a distance. Every duplicate therefore of a work, whether ten or ten thousand, if it conveys the same style and sentiment, is the same identical work, which was produced by the author's invention and labour.[50]

Soon thereafter Blackstone made the same point more authoritatively in his *Commentaries*, saying:

> Now the identity of a literary composition consists intirely [sic] in the *sentiment* and the *language*; the same conceptions, cloathed in the same words, must necessarily be the same composition: and whatever method be taken of conveying that composition to the ear or the eye of another, by recital, by writing, or by printing, in any number of copies or at any period of time, it is always the identical work of the author that is conveyed.[51]

In Blackstone's view—which would be persuasive both in England and the United States—style, sentiment, and language constituted the essence of literary property. These would come to be capsulized as the form of expression used by an author, and it would be this form of expression that would come to be legally protected by copyright.

This then was a part of the overall backdrop against which the intellectual property clause was set. Nimmer and Nimmer correctly point out that the term "authors" as it appears in the clause must be construed in its relation to the preceding phrase "To promote the progress of science and useful arts" and within the context of the subsequent term "writings."[52] As the Supreme

---

50. 96 Eng. Rep. at 189.
51. WILLIAM BLACKSTONE, 2 COMMENTARIES ON THE LAWS OF ENGLAND at 405–06 (Oxford 1767).
52. NIMMER & NIMMER, *supra* note 3, § 1.06[B]. Contrast, however, their view that "the phrase 'To promote the progress of science and useful arts . . .' must be read as largely in the nature of a preamble, indicating the purpose of the power but not in limitation of its exercise." *Id.* § 1.03[A]. I have elsewhere herein challenged this latter view. *See* Chapter Five, text following note 39. Suffice it to say here, it is difficult to reconcile any view that the introductory

Court pointed out in another copyright context in 1834: "There is no mode by which the meaning affixed to any word or sentence, by a deliberative body, can be so well ascertained, as by comparing it with the words and sentences with which it stands connected."[53] While the Supreme Court has most emphatically stated that the "to" language of the clause is a limitation on the power of Congress which sets forth a constitutional standard of invention and hence of inventorship, it has made no comparable pronounce-ment that this language sets forth a constitutional standard regarding authorship.[54] It is difficult to perceive, however, on what basis the Court could treat the "to" language as a limitation on the patent power but not on the copyright power.[55]

Be that as it may, the trend in the lower courts has been precisely in the opposite direction when it comes to copyrights. The trend has occurred despite the fact that as early as 1829 a Supreme Court Justice in his capacity as circuit judge held that the "to" language of the clause did indeed limit the type of subject matter that could be copyrighted,[56] and the Supreme Court seemed clearly to endorse such a view in two opinions in the second half of the nineteenth century.[57] In modern times the issue has been driven by the copyrighting of works perceived to be obscene. Through the nineteenth century, the introductory phrase of the intellectual property clause was thought to preclude the copyright of immoral or

---

language of the clause does not constitute a limitation on the power of Congress with the view that the terms "authors" and "writings" as used in the clause must be construed in relation to the introductory language.

53. Wheaton v. Peters, 33 U.S. (8 Pet.) 591, 661 (1834).
54. It has, however, clearly stated that a constitutional standard of authorship resides in the terms "authors" and "writings" as they appear in the intellectual property clause. *See, e.g.,* Feist Publ'ns, Inc. v. Rural Tel. Serv. Co., 499 U.S. 340, 346 (1991). *See also* The Trade-Mark Cases, 100 U.S. 82, 94 (1879); Burrow-Giles Lithographic Co. v. Sarony, 111 U.S. 53, 58 (1884).
55. The Eleventh Circuit has in fact stated that the "to" language imposes on Congress "an affirmative constitutional duty" to promote the progress of science through the issuance of copyright. Cable/Home Communications Corp. v. Network Products, Inc., 902 F.2d 829, 842 (11th Cir. 1990). Nimmer & Nimmer contend that this "dictum" should be ignored. *Supra* note 3, § 1.03[B], n.23.1. Although there is nothing in the constitutional language that requires Congress to authorize the issuance of copyrights, I submit that once it determined to do so, it does indeed have an affirmative constitutional duty to do so in a manner that promotes the progress of science. *Cf.,* however, the circuit court cases discussed in notes 59–69, *infra,* and accompanying text.
56. *See* text accompanying notes 173–75 *infra.*
57. *See* notes 177–79, *infra,* and accompanying text.

obscene works because such were not perceived to promote the progress of either science or useful arts.[58] In more recent times, that perception has gone by the wayside, and with it the view that the introductory phrase places any limitation on copyright. The most frequently cited case is *Mitchell Brothers Film Group v. Cinema Adult Theater*[59] decided by the Fifth Circuit in 1979. In discussing the constitutionality of the copyright statute, the court held that there was no constitutional impediment to a congressional determination "that the best way to promote creativity is not to impose any governmental restrictions on the subject matter of copyrightable works." It concluded that "the protection of all writings, without regard to their content, is a constitutionally permissible means of promoting science and the useful arts."[60]

Inherent in such a view is the presumption that all writings, regardless of their content, "promote the progress of science" as stated in the introductory phrase of the intellectual property clause so that in essence the introductory phrase contains no limitation at all on the subject matter of copyright. Nimmer and Nimmer interpret the holding in *Mitchell Bros.* as being that "the introductory phrase of the Copyright Clause does not require that each of the 'writings' protected by copyright in fact promote science or useful arts, but only [that] Congress shall be promoting these ends by its copyright legislation."[61] By analogy, one may argue that "inventions" protected by patents need not "promote the progress of . . . useful arts," provided only that Congress intends to promote this end by its patent legislation.

In *Mitchell Bros.*, the Fifth Circuit sought to distinguish *Graham v. John Deere Co.* by saying: "In this patent case the Court held that although Congress' power under this Clause is limited to action that promotes the useful arts, it is up to Congress to decide upon the means by which the constitutional command will best be effectuated."[62] What the Supreme Court actually stated was: "*Within the limits of the constitutional grant*, the Congress may, of course, implement the stated purpose of the Framers by selecting the policy which in its judgment best effectuates the constitutional aim."[63] The Fifth Circuit in its discussion of *Graham v. John Deere Co.* chose to simply ignore the view expressed therein that promoting the

---

58. *See, e.g.,* Martinetti v. Maguire, 16 F. Cas. 920 (No. 9173) (D. Cal. 1867); Barnes v. Miner, 122 F. 480 (S.D.N.Y. 1903).
59. 604 F.2d 852 (5th Cir. 1979), *cert. denied*, 445 U.S. 917 (1980).
60. 604 F.2d at 860.
61. NIMMER & NIMMER, *supra* note 3, § 1.03[B] (Rel. 44-12/97).
62. 604 F.2d at 860.
63. 383 U.S. at 6 (emphasis supplied).

useful arts is a *standard* set forth in the intellectual property clause *which may not be ignored.*[64]

Be that as it may, several circuits quickly followed the lead of the Fifth Circuit. Thus, in 1981 the District of Columbia Circuit relied on *Mitchell Bros.* to opine that "we cannot accept appellants' argument that the introductory language of the Copyright Clause constitutes a limitation on congressional power."[65] Likewise, in 1985 the Eighth Circuit cited *Mitchell Bros.* in holding that the purposes of the introductory phrase of the intellectual property clause "do not limit Congress's power to legislate in the field of copyright."[66] In turn, the Eleventh Circuit, while indicating that the introductory phrase is in fact applicable nonetheless gives it no clear effect.[67] Thus in modern times there is a very real dichotomy[68] between the Supreme Court's treatment of the patent provision of the intellectual property clause, and the interpretation given to the copyright provision by the various circuits.[69]

The relevance of defining the meaning to be given to authorship in the copyright context is apparent when it is recognized that the intellectual property clause "authorizes only the enactment of legislation securing

---

64. *Id.*
65. Schnapper v. Foley, 667 F.2d 102, 112 (D.C. Cir. 1981), *cert. denied,* 455 U.S. 948 (1982).
66. Hutchinson Tel. Co. v. Fronteer Directory Co., 770 F.2d 128, 130–31 (8th Cir. 1985).
67. Pacific & S. Co. v. Duncan, 744 F.2d 1490, 1498–99 (11th Cir. 1984) ("[w]e agree that the Constitution allows Congress to create copyright laws only if they benefit society as a whole rather than authors alone . . . . [But] a copyright holder need not provide the most complete public access possible"), *cert. denied,* 471 U.S. 1004 (1985). *Cf.* Cable/Home Communications Corp. v. Network Prods., Inc., 902 F.2d 829, 842 (11th Cir. 1990) ("[t]he Copyright Act of 1976 . . . is the congressional implementation of an affirmative constitutional duty under the copyright and patent clause '[t]o promote the Progress of Science and useful Arts, by securing for limited Times to Authors and Inventors the exclusive Right to their respective Writings and Discoveries'").
68. Gordon calls it "disjunctive treatment" and suggests that one reason for it may be the belief that copyright is virtually unable to violate the intellectual property clause. *See* Wendy J. Gordon, *An Inquiry into the Merits of Copyright: The Challenges of Consistency, Consent, and Encouragement Theory,* 41 STAN. L. REV. 1343, 1449–50n (1989).
69. These circuit court opinions also appear at odds with the views expressed by the Supreme Court in *Goldstein v. California* that the "copyright clause" provides both the objective and the means of accomplishing the objective. *See* Chapter Five, note 34 and accompanying text.

'authors' the exclusive right to their writings."[70] One of the earliest American cases defining authorship in the copyright context was decided in 1821 by Justice Washington in his capacity as circuit judge.[71] An injunction had been sought to prevent the copying of a copyrighted historical print of the Declaration of Independence. The issue quickly resolved itself into a determination as to whether the copyright holder was in fact the author of the print in question within the meaning of the copyright statute. The relevant language read

> any person being a citizen of the United States, or a resident within the same, who shall invent and design, engrave, etch or work, or from his own works and inventions shall cause to be designed and engraved, etched, or worked any historical or other print, shall have the sole right and liberty of printing, re-printing, publishing and vending such work, for the term of fourteen years. . . .[72]

It is apparent that, without expressly defining authorship, this language rather clearly sets constraints on who might be the author of a copyrightable print. Justice Washington ruled that while this language did not require the person obtaining the copyright to be the one who actually engraved, etched, or worked the print in question, nonetheless authorship required more than mere conception of an idea. The author must have "also designed or represented the subject in some visible form." In his view, copyrightable authorship required more than mere conception. Instead, there had to be a showing of "genius and art."[73]

A different aspect of copyrightable authorship was addressed by Justice Story in 1839 in his capacity as circuit judge. At issue was whether the compiler and arranger of a compilation of notes on Latin grammar taken from a variety of other sources could be viewed as an author for purposes of the copyright law. According to Justice Story, the issue before the court was whether these notes "are to be found collected and embodied in any former single work."[74]

70. Scherr v. Universal Match Corp., 417 F.2d 497, 502 (1969) (Friendly, J., dissenting).
71. Binns v. Woodruff, 3 F. Cas. 421 (No. 1,424), 13 Copyright Dec., 1789–1909, 239 (D. Pa. 1821).
72. Section 2, Act of April 29, 1802, 2 Stat. 171.
73. 13 Copyright Dec., 1789–1909, at 243.
74. Gray v. Russell, 10 F. Cas. (No. 5,728), 14 Copyright Dec., 1789–1909, 1120 (D. Mass. 1839).

He went on to state:

> If no work could be considered by our law as entitled to a copyright, which is composed of materials drawn from many different sources, but for the first time brought together in the same plan and arrangement and combination, simply because those materials might be found scattered up and down a great variety of volumes, perhaps in hundreds, or even thousands of volumes, and might, therefore, have been brought together in the same way and by the same researches of another mind, equally skilful and equally diligent—then, indeed, it would be difficult to say, that there could be any copyright in most of the scientific and professional treatises of the present day.[75]

In his view, where compilations of previously known materials are prepared, copyrightable authorship resides in the intellectual exertion required to prepare a compilation new in itself. Implicit in this view is the assumption that there must be actual intellectual exertion or labor involved in putting together the compilation in a particular manner and mode.

A few years later in 1846, the issue was at least implicitly raised as to whether a work for hire could be copyrighted in the name of the person procuring the work as opposed to the name of the person actually creating the work. It was argued that the doctrine of the English law enables a man to secure to himself as his own composition whatever he has had prepared for him by the labors of others. Not so, said the court. Rather, the English cases

> recognize the right of authorship, although the materials were procured by another, and also an equitable title in one person in the labors of another, when the relations of the parties are such that the former is entitled to an assignment of the production. But, to constitute one an author, he must, by his own intellectual labor applied to the materials of his composition, produce an arrangement or compilation new in itself.[76]

It was the line of cases arising out of this reasoning that Congress would decline to follow in the Copyright Act of 1909 when it defined an author as including an employer in the case of works made for hire.[77]

In addressing the meaning to be given to authorship for copyright purposes, these early cases did not make any attempt to construe the meaning of the term "authors" as used in the intellectual property clause.

---

75. 14 Copyright Dec., 1789–1909, at 1124.
76. Atwill v. Ferrett, 2 F. Cas. 195 (No. 640), 13 Copyright Dec., 1789–1909, 63, 68 (C.C.S.D.N.Y. 1846), also citing Gray v. Russell, 10 F. Cas. (No. 5,728), 14 Copyright Dec., 1789–1909, 1120 (D. Mass. 1839).
77. *See supra* text accompanying note 7.

The first indirect attempt to do so by the Supreme Court came about in the so-called *Trade-Mark Cases*[78] in 1879. Congress had assumed that its authority to enact trademark legislation resided in the clause. The Court accordingly looked to see whether "the essential characteristics of a trademark" could be identified with those of "inventions and discoveries in the arts and sciences, or with [those of] the writings of authors."[79] In so doing, it of necessity had to define what it viewed as the essential characteristics of the "writings of authors" under the clause.[80] In essence, it declared that in order to be copyrightable under the clause, the "writings of authors" had to be "original" and "to be the fruits of intellectual labor."[81]

It was thus not surprising that five years later in *Burrow-Giles Lithographic Co. v. Sarony* the Court defined an "author" in the constitutional sense to be: "He to whom any thing owes its origin; originator; maker; one who completes a work of science or literature."[82] In 1973, it again quoted this definition with approval, noting that the term "authors" has not been construed in its narrow literal sense as individuals who write an original composition, but rather "with the reach necessary to reflect the broad scope of constitutional principles."[83]

---

78. 100 U.S. 82 (1879).
79. *Id.* at 94–95.
80. Although its emphasis was on "writings," it was seeking at least indirectly to define what a modern copyright treatise calls "the essence of authorship" under the clause. *See* NIMMER & NIMMER, *supra* note 3, § 1.06[A].
81. The wording used by the Court was:

    [W]hile the word *writings* may be liberally construed, as it has been, to include original designs for engraving, prints, &c., it is only such as are *original*, and are founded in the creative powers of the mind. The writings which are to be protected are the *fruits of intellectual labor*, embodied in the form of books, prints, engravings, and the like.

    (emphasis in original) 100 U.S. at 94. *See also* Higgins v. Keuffel, 140 U.S. 428 (1891) wherein the Court stated that the intellectual property clause "evidently has reference only to such writings . . . as are the result of intellectual labor." *Id.* at 431.
82. Burrow-Giles Lithographic Co. v. Sarony, 111 U.S. 53, 58 (1884). This definition was largely consistent with that existing at the time the Constitution was drafted. *See supra* text accompanying note 27. *Cf.* the refusal of the Court to define the term "inventors" in the constitutional sense. *See supra* Chapter Eight, note 2 and accompanying text.
83. Goldstein v. California, 413 U.S. 546, 561 (1973). A cynic might be excused for suggesting that the quoted language is a fancy phrase signifying absolutely nothing.

In light of the views expressed in *The Trade-Mark Cases* and in *Burrow-Giles*, it is surprising that the 1909 Copyright Act failed either to define originality or even to state that it was required for copyright protection. In 1991 the Court took cognizance of this, but stated that the 1909 Act implicitly incorporated the originality requirement articulated in the Court's earlier decisions. According to the Court: "By using the words 'writings' and 'author'—the same words used in [the intellectual property clause] and defined by the Court in *The Trade-Mark Cases* and *Burrow-Giles*—the statute necessarily incorporated the originality requirement articulated in the Court's decisions."[84]

Be that as it may, the 1976 Copyright Act did expressly state that copyright protection subsists only in "original works of authorship"[85] but again failed to provide any definition of what was intended by "original." The legislative history of the Act explained that this omission was deliberate, and that the phrase "original works of authorship" as used in the Act

> is intended to incorporate without change the standard of originality established by the courts under the present [1909] copyright statute. This standard does not include requirements of novelty,[86] ingenuity, or

---

84. Feist Publ'ns, Inc. v. Rural Tel. Serv. Co., 499 U.S. 340, 351 (1991).
85. 17 U.S.C. § 102(a).
86. Novelty is a constitutional requirement for patentability (*see* Chapter Eight, Part A) but apparently is not a constitutional requirement for copyrightability, although why this should be the case is unclear. Thus it is possible to copyright a work that is identical to another copyrighted work provided only that the second work is original in its own right and has not been copied from the first work. Feist Publ'ns, Inc. v. Rural Tel. Serv. Co., 499 U.S. 340, 346 (1991). Conceptually, it is difficult to see how copyrighting of a work that is not novel serves in any way to promote the progress of science as contemplated by the clause. *Cf.* Kaplan's view that:

   > novelty would in all events be a poor criterion [for copyrightability]. If it is difficult, perhaps an illusory, measure in the field of mechanical improvements, how much harder would it be in literature or the other arts. Starting even with the bias of an extreme Romanticism, how does one determine what is "new," or significantly or importantly new? And is it newness, a fresh departure from the past, that we want uniquely to encourage by law? In time a standard of novelty would have to be debased or distorted, else copyright as a system would lose all viability.

   BENJAMIN KAPLAN, AN UNHURRIED VIEW OF COPYRIGHT (New York 1967) at 43.

esthetic merit, and there is no intention to enlarge the standard of copyright protection to require them.[87]

One of the reasons given for the use of the phrase "original works of authorship" was "to avoid exhausting the constitutional power of Congress to legislate in this field." According to the legislative history, this language was used because "all the writings of an author" as incorporated in the 1909 Act "is substantially the same as the empowering language of the Constitution." The concern of Congress was that, if the existing language was continued to be used, and was deemed to be coextensive with the constitutional language, "courts would be faced with the alternative of holding copyrightable something that Congress did not intend to protect, or of holding constitutionally incapable of copyright something that Congress might one day want to protect."[88] On what basis Congress could properly authorize copyright for something that was constitutionally incapable of copyright was not stated.

Nonetheless, the Supreme Court would soon find itself revisiting the meaning to be given to the constitutional requirement for originality. In 1985 the Court in *Harper & Row v. Nation Enterprises*[89] declared that "[n]o author may copyright his ideas or the facts he narrates."[90] In so stating, it relied explicitly on statutory language[91] and implicitly on the First Amendment.[92] But it could just as easily have found a constitutional basis for this view in the "to" language of the clause. Indeed, that language may readily be read as creating a limitation on the power of Congress to authorize copyright in ideas or facts because giving an exclusive right to ideas or facts does not promote the progress of science, i.e., knowledge and education.

It pointed out that "copyright is limited to those aspects of the work—termed 'expression'—that display the stamp of the author's originality," and noted that "[c]reation of a nonfiction work, even a compilation of pure fact entails originality."[93] Having said this, it went on to indicate that "[e]specially in the realm of factual narrative, the law is

---

87. H.R. REP. No. 94-1706, 94th Cong., 2d Sess. (1976), *as reproduced in* 8 NIMMER & NIMMER, *supra* note 3, at App. 4-13.
88. *Id.* at App. 4-14.
89. 471 U.S. 539 (1985).
90. *Id.* at 556.
91. 17 U.S.C. § 102(b).
92. It quoted Brennan, J., concurring in New York Times Co. v. United States, 403 U.S. 713, 726 (copyright laws are not restrictions on freedom of speech as copyright protects only forms of expression and not the ideas expressed).
93. 471 U.S. at 547.

currently unsettled regarding the ways in which uncopyrightable elements combine with the author's original contributions to form protected expression."[94] As the new millennium begins, this law is still unsettled.

Implicit in the views expressed in *Harper & Row* is the premise that while originality is a necessary constitutional requirement for copyright, it may not in and of itself meet the requisite constitutional standard. That is to say, something more than simple originality might be required. The Court addressed that standard in 1991 in *Feist Publications, Inc. v. Rural Telephone Service Co.*[95] It began its analysis with the observation that: "The sine qua non of copyright is originality,"[96] and emphasized that: "The originality requirement is *constitutionally mandated* for all works."[97]

So far, so good, but then it went on to state that in *The Trade-Mark Cases* it had "explained that originality requires independent creation plus a modicum of creativity."[98] But this was a revisionist treatment of what had actually been said in *The Trade-Mark Cases*, namely, that "writings" in the constitutional sense had to be both "original" and "founded in the creative powers of the mind."[99] These were viewed as separate and distinct requirements, with "originality" being merely a requirement of independent creation, i.e., that the work had not been literally copied from someone else, and creativity embodying "intellectual labor."[100] In *Feist* for the first time the Court defined originality as incorporating a requirement for creativity.[101]

Nimmer and Nimmer emphasize, I believe correctly, that it is important to distinguish between originality and intellectual labor or creativity despite the fact that the two concepts are sometimes treated interchangeably.[102] They suggest that the requirement for originality arises from the interpretation given to "authors" in the clause, whereas the requirement for creativity is an absolute standard. Left unsaid but implicit in the latter point is the view that there is no basis in the language of the clause for such a standard. While the Supreme Court has not seen fit to tie

---

94. *Id.* at 548.
95. 499 U.S. 340 (1991).
96. *Id.* at 345.
97. *Id.* at 347.
98. *Id.* at 346.
99. 100 U.S. at 94.
100. *Id.*
101. As the Court put it: "Originality requires only that the author make the selection or arrangement independently (i.e., without copying that selection or arrangement from another work), and that it display some minimal level of creativity." 499 U.S. at 359.
102. NIMMER & NIMMER, *supra* note 3, § 1.08[C][1].

the requirement for creativity to any specific language of the clause, I would argue that the "to" language of the clause rather clearly provides the basis for such a requirement.[103] For if no creativity is required for copyright, the manner in which it serves to promote the progress of science is suspect.

But a closer look at the *Feist* opinion reveals that the true constitutional requirement for copyrightable authorship is some modicum of creativity.[104] That creativity may reside in the particular collocation of words or in a particular selection and arrangement of facts.[105] But copyright may not constitutionally extend to the facts themselves.[106] A compilation or listing of facts may literally be original in the sense of having originated with an author, but it is only the form and arrangement of the compilation or listing that may be copyrighted and then only if the form or arrangement has the requisite creativity. That creativity must be such as "to transform mere selection into copyrightable expression."[107]

One difficulty with the Copyright Act of 1976 was that it defined "compilation" in a manner that assured copyrightability. In declaring a compilation to be "a work formed by the collection and assembling of preexisting materials or of data that are selected, coordinated, or arranged in such a way that the resulting work as a whole constitutes an original work of authorship,"[108] the Act literally defined a "compilation" as copyrightable. But in common parlance, the term "compilation" in no way *requires* that there be originality in the manner in which the preexisting facts are collected and assembled. It is for this reason that the Court in *Feist* declared that "[n]ot every selection, coordination, or arrangement will pass [constitutional] muster" as a copyrightable compilation.[109]

It is thus apparent from *Feist* that not all compilations and listings of factual information are copyrightable, and the decision therein declared that the telephone directory at issue was not copyrightable. An intriguing aspect of the *Feist* opinion was its declaration that the selection of

---

103. Because of their view that the "to" language does not place any limitation on the copyright power of Congress, Nimmer & Nimmer presumably would disagree with any such view. *See supra* note 52.
104. 499 U.S. at 362 ("the Constitution mandates some minimal degree of creativity"); 499 U.S. at 363 ("[a]s a constitutional matter, copyright protects only those constituent elements of a work that possess more than a de minimus quantum of creativity").
105. 499 U.S. at 348–49.
106. *Id.* at 351 ("[i]n no event may copyright extend to the facts themselves").
107. *Id.* at 362.
108. 17 U.S.C. § 101 (1994).
109. 499 U.S. at 358.

telephone listings at issue "could not be more obvious."[110] This seems to suggest that obviousness of the particular selection and arrangement of facts plays a bearing on whether a factual compilation may be copyrightable. Non-obviousness is of course an important standard for patentability, and, to the extent it has been argued to be required as a constitutional standard for invention, such argument has been predicated on the "to" language of the intellectual property clause.[111]

In this regard, it is interesting to note that in 1971 Justice Douglas argued that: "No reason can be offered why we should depart from the plain import of this grant of congressional power and apply more lenient constitutional standards to copyrights than to patents."[112] In essence, he argued that there should be a constitutional standard for copyright predicated on the "to" language in a similar fashion that the Supreme Court had declared in *Graham v. John Deere Co.* that this language set a constitutional standard of invention.[113] In an attempt to differentiate the views expressed in *Graham,* Nimmer and Nimmer argue that there is a clear constitutional differentiation between the patent grant and the copyright grant and between the constitutional requirement of novelty in the patent law[114] and that of originality in the copyright law.[115]

In so doing, they seek to rely heavily on *Alfred Bell & Co. v. Catalda Fine Arts,* a 1951 opinion in the Second Circuit wherein Judge Jerome Frank stated that "the Constitution . . . recognizes that the standards for patents and copyrights are basically different."[116] In support of this view, he argued that: (a) the language of the intellectual property clause differentiates "authors" and their "writings" from "inventors" and their "discoveries"; and (b) the first patent statutes set a more stringent standard for patentability than did the first copyright statutes for copyrightability.[117] Neither statement, in and of itself without more, particularly supports the conclusion drawn by Judge Frank. Thus, Judge Frank made no attempt whatever to demonstrate in what manner the language of the clause

---

110. *Id.*
111. See the discussion in Chapter Eight, Part D.
112. Lee v. Runge, 404 U.S. 887, 30 L. Ed. 2d 169, 171 (1971) (Douglas, J., dissenting).
113. *See supra* Chapter Eight, note 99 and accompanying text.
114. Unlike almost all patent commentators, Nimmer & Nimmer contend that the views expressed by the Court in *Graham* refer to the standard of novelty.
115. NIMMER & NIMMER, *supra* note 3, § 2.01[A].
116. 191 F.2d 99, 102 (2d Cir. 1951).
117. *Id.* at 100–01.

differentiates between "authors" and their "writings" and "inventors" and their "discoveries." But, as I have earlier pointed out, the use of the singular "the exclusive right" in the clause to refer to both the patent grant and the copyright grant was deliberate.[118] This can be taken as indicative of an intent to treat the two grants, however defined, in a similar fashion. Secondly, the fact that the first patent and copyright statutes created a more stringent standard for patents than for copyrights is indicative only of the fact that Congress is given rather wide discretion to set the standards for the two types of grant. There is nothing in the intellectual property clause that in any way compels a different standard for the patent grant than for the copyright grant, provided only that the limitations set forth in the clause are in fact met.[119] There may indeed be valid reasons for Congress to have set different standards for patents than for copyrights, but a constitutional requirement is not one of them.

Moreover, the Supreme Court has made clear that "because of the historic kinship between patent law and copyright law" the doctrines of the one may be applied to the other, but only with due care because "[t]he two areas of the law . . . are not identical twins."[120] If the language of the intellectual property clause does not per se require different standards for patentability and copyrightability, then there is nothing to preclude the Supreme Court from reading an unobviousness component into the constitutional creativity standard for copyright declared in *Feist*. The pragmatic question arising out the Court's language in *Feist* is whether it actually intended to treat unobviousness as a necessary component of creativity or whether it merely intended for obviousness to be considered as a factor in determining whether the constitutionally required creativity is present.

It is difficult to understand why the Court would have made any reference to the obviousness of the listing at issue in *Feist* if it did not consider this obviousness as at least a factor in its determination that the required constitutional creativity was not present. Yet earlier in the same opinion it had declared: "To be sure, the requisite level of creativity is extremely low; even a slight amount will suffice. The vast majority of works make the grade quite easily, as they possess some creative spark, 'no matter how crude, humble or obvious' it might be."[121] Perhaps the best that can be said is that the *Feist* opinion appears inconsistent in its treatment of

---

118. *See supra* Chapter Seven, Part A.
119. Those limitations as they apply to patentability are discussed in Chapter Eight.
120. Sony Corp. v. Universal City Studios, Inc., 464 U.S. 417, 439 (1984).
121. 499 U.S. at 345, citing NIMMER & NIMMER, *supra* note 3, § 1.08[C][1].

obviousness as a factor in determining the existence of constitutionally required creativity.

To the extent that originality and creativity have been determined to be constitutional requirements for copyright, those requirements have been predicated on the interpretations given to both "authors" and "writings" in the clause. We look now to the extent that the term "writings" sets forth any additional constitutional requirement for copyright.

C. Writings

There is nothing to indicate what the Framers intended by their use of the term "writings" in the clause.[122] The standard English dictionary of the times provided three definitions of "writing": (1) "A legal instrument"; (2) "A composure; a book"; and (3) "A written paper of any kind."[123] The Statute of Anne referred to "books and other writings"[124] but did not attempt to define what was encompassed within the phrase "other writings." From the context, it is apparent, however, that what was encompassed were books and other printed works. It is quite likely that the Framers used the term "writings" in the clause simply because it appeared in the Statute of Anne and had a broader connotation than simply "books." Whether they actually intended the term to encompass more than simply printed works is an open question, and one not likely to ever be satisfactorily answered.[125] Be that as it may, both Congress and the judiciary, from the enactment of the Copyright Act of 1790 to the present, have given it an ever more expansive definition regardless of its actual dictionary definition.[126]

---

122. The term "writings" is not found in any of the proposals that ultimately were transformed into the clause. See supra Chapter Three, text accompanying notes 110–112.

123. SAMUEL JOHNSON, A DICTIONARY OF THE ENGLISH LANGUAGE (London 1755).

124. See 8 NIMMER & NIMMER, supra note 3, at App. 7-5.

125. Cf. the view of the Seventh Circuit at the beginning of the twentieth century that if "the intention of the framers . . . [were] to give boundary to the constitutional grant, many writings to which copyright has since been extended, would have been excluded." National Tel. News Co. v. Western Union Tel. Co., 119 F. 294, 297 (7th Cir. 1902).

126. As a 1956 congressional study put it, copyright legislation and legislative history reveal a tacit assumption "that Congress may constitutionally include in a copyright statute whatever it wishes"; moreover, "[l]argely unnoticed and unquestioned, the courts have interpreted the copyright provision of the

If the term "authors" as used in the clause must be interpreted or construed in its relation to the "to" language and in the context of "writings" as that term appears in the clause,[127] then it follows that the term "writings" must also be construed or interpreted in the same fashion. The Supreme Court certainly has indicated that the constitutional meanings of "authors" and "writings" is closely interwoven, but does the "to" language of the clause, i.e., "to promote the progress of science and useful arts," place a constitutional limitation on the nature or type of "writings" that may be copyrighted?[128] Phrased somewhat different, does it require a constitutional standard for "writings" in a similar fashion as the Court has declared it does for "discoveries"?[129] As I have indicated in the context of authorship, it is difficult to perceive on what basis the Court could treat the "to" language of the clause as a limitation on the patent power but not on the copyright power.[130] The Court has yet to directly address this issue, but in a number of opinions it has used language that suggests that in an appropriate case it would so hold.[131] Again, an historical perspective is in order. Thus in interpreting the meaning to be given to language of the intellectual property clause in another copyright context in 1834, it declared that the best mode of ascertaining the meaning to be given to a word therein was by comparing that word with the words and sentences with which it stands connected.[132] Ten years earlier Chief Justice Marshall had emphasized that in determining the scope of the enumerated powers given to Congress by the Constitution, "[w]e know of no rule for construing the extent of such powers, other than is given by the language of the instrument which confers them, taken in connection with the purposes for which they are conferred."[133]

Constitution far beyond its literal meaning." *See Study No. 3, The Meaning of "Writings" in the Copyright Clause of the Constitution* (1956) in COPYRIGHT LAW REVISION, STUDIES PREPARED FOR THE SUBCOMMITTEE ON PATENTS, TRADEMARKS, AND COPYRIGHTS OF THE SENATE COMMITTEE ON THE JUDICIARY, 86th Cong., 1st Sess. at 71, 83 (Washington 1960).

127. *See supra* text accompanying note 52.
128. I have argued in Chapter Seven that it places a constitutional limitation on the duration of the copyright term.
129. *See supra* Chapter Eight, Part D.
130. *See supra* note 55 and accompanying text.
131. The Court could just as easily have predicated its view in *Feist* that a constitutional requirement of creativity exists for copyright on an interpretation of the "to" language as it did on an interpretation of "authors" and "writings."
132. *See supra* note 53 and accompanying text.
133. *See supra* Chapter Five, note 24 and accompanying text.

In one of the earliest copyright cases, decided in 1829, Justice Thompson in his capacity as circuit judge relied on the "to" language of the clause to rule that newspapers were not copyrightable.[134] In 1879 the Supreme Court quoted with favor the views expressed by Justice Thompson in 1829.[135] In 1891 the Court expressly relied on the "to" language to hold that labels and other common advertisements were not copyrightable because they were not "writings" within the meaning of the constitutional language.[136] Without expressly so stating, the Court in this instance clearly treated the "to" language as a limitation on the power of Congress to define what constituted a "writing" within the meaning of the clause.

In modern times, in the patent context, the Court has declared that "Congress in the exercise of the patent power may not overreach the restraints imposed by the stated constitutional purpose," and that "'promot[ing] the Progress of . . . useful Arts' is the *standard* expressed in the Constitution and it may not be ignored."[137] If such a constitutional standard exists regarding what constitutes patentable "discoveries" as that term is used in the clause, then it is reasonable to suppose that a similar restraint exists with respect to what constitutes copyrightable "writings."[138] Indeed, on several occasions the Court has stated that: "The primary objective of copyright is not to reward the labor of authors, but '[t]o promote the Progress of Science and useful Arts.'"[139] If the primary purpose of copyright is to promote the progress of science and useful arts, then clearly this language has relevance in defining and limiting the meaning to be given to "writings" in the clause.

One would never know these Supreme Court views from looking at the analysis of the "to" language given in Nimmer and Nimmer, however. In their view "the introductory phrase, rather than constituting a limitation on Congressional authority, has for the most part tended to expand such

---

134. Clayton v. Stone, 5 F. Cas. 999 (No. 2,872), 13 Copyright Dec. 1789–1909, 640 (C.C.S.D.N.Y. 1829). For a discussion of this case, see text accompanying notes 173–76, *infra*.

135. Baker v. Selden, 101 U.S. 99, 105 (1879).

136. Higgins v. Keuffel, 140 U.S. 428, 430 (1891). *See also* text accompanying note 179, *infra*.

137. Graham v. John Deere Co., 383 U.S. 1, 5–6 (1966).

138. The only distinction might be that the Court would replace "to promote the progress of . . . useful arts" with "to promote the progress of science."

139. *See* Feist Publ'ns, Inc. v. Rural Tel. Serv. Co., 499 U.S. 340, 349 (1991); Twentieth Century Music Co. v. Aiken, 422 U.S. 151, 156 (1975).

authority.[140] This for the reason that the conjunction of the phrase with the term 'writings' indicates that the latter is not to be confined to a narrow definition."[141]

Why or on what basis this "conjunction" is so indicative is not stated. Rather, they contend that "the phrase 'To promote the progress of science and useful arts. . .' must be read largely in the nature of a preamble, indicating the purpose of the power but not in limitation of its exercise."[142]

The only Supreme Court authority cited for this latter view is *Jacobson v. Massachusetts* wherein the Court stated only that the preamble of the Constitution itself "has never been regarded as the source of any substantive power conferred on the government of the United States, or on any of its departments."[143] But the intellectual property clause is in fact a grant of substantive power to the Congress, and as indicated by the various Supreme Court statements noted above, the substantive grant of power therein must be interpreted in the context of the limitations imposed by the "to" language of the clause.

Although no court has expressly so ruled, Nimmer and Nimmer contend that "the most significant constitutional limitation" in the copyright provision of the clause resides in the term "writings."[144] Their rationale for so stating is that only works that qualify as writing may be copyrighted.[145] This is indeed true, but it is equivalent to saying that only inventions that qualify as "discoveries" may be patented. Both statements are conceptually correct,[146] but it does not follow that the terms "writings" and "discoveries" in and of themselves constitute the most important constitutional limitations in the intellectual property clause. This is particularly true in the copyright context because of the declaration by the Supreme Court in 1971 that "'Writings' . . . [are not] construed in their narrow literal sense but, rather, with the reach necessary to reflect the broad scope of

---

140. The only cases cited in support of this view are Schnapper v. Foley, 667 F.2d 102,11 (D.C. Cir. 1981); Ladd v. Law & Tech. Press, 762 F.2d 809, 812 (9th Cir. 1985). As authority for this view both cases cite Nimmer & Nimmer. In essence, Nimmer & Nimmer contend that the statement is correct because these two circuit courts have cited them as saying it is correct. It would be nice to have something other than this circular reasoning as authority for the proposition.
141. NIMMER & NIMMER, *supra* note 3, § 1.03[B].
142. *Id.* § 1.03[A].
143. 197 U.S. 11, 23 (1904).
144. NIMMER & NIMMER, *supra* note 3, § 1.08[A].
145. *Id.*
146. Although some discoveries do not constitute patentable invention. *See* Chapter Eight, Part F.

constitutional principles."[147] Perhaps the best interpretation that can be given this language by the Court is simply that it means that the term "writings" as it appears in the clause is to be liberally construed.[148] But the more liberally the term is construed, the less significance it has as a constitutional limitation.

The Court at the same time, however, saw fit to provide an open-ended definition of "writings" as that term appears in the clause, saying: "although the word 'writings' might be limited to script or printed material, it may be interpreted to include any physical rendering of the fruits of creative intellectual or aesthetic labor."[149] I suggest that this is an open-ended definition because saying that "'writings'... may be interpreted to include" in no way serves as an actual limitation on what is to be actually included within the term. Arguably, however, it does set two specific constitutional limitations on a copyrightable writing, regardless of how the term may be otherwise defined.[150]

The first is one that has already been discussed in the context of authorship, namely, the requirement for creativity. The second is that there be a physical rendering or manifestation of the creative effort. The 1976 Copyright Act translates this into a requirement that a work be fixed in a "tangible medium of expression."[151] In turn, the Act declared that:

> A work is "fixed" in a tangible medium of expression when its embodiment in a copy or phonorecord, by or under the authority of the author, is sufficiently permanent or stable to permit it to be perceived, reproduced, or otherwise communicated for a period of more than transitory duration. A work consisting of sounds, images, or both, is "fixed" for

---

147. Goldstein v. California, 413 U.S. 546, 561 (1973).
148. *But see supra* note 83.
149. 413 U.S. at 561. It is not surprising therefore that the Eleventh Circuit has declared that "the term 'Writings' has been interpreted so broadly as to include much more than writings in the literal sense, or the lay definition of the word." *See* United States v. Moghadam, 175 F.3d 1269, 1274 (11th Cir. 1999).
150. *Cf.* the earlier definition of "writings" as used in the intellectual property clause given in Burrow-Giles Lithographic Co. v. Sarony, 111 U.S. 53, 58 (1884) ("[w]ritings" defined as "all forms of writing, printing, engraving, etching, etc., by which the ideas of the mind of the author are given visible expression"). This definition occurred at a time when the recording of sound was in its infancy and had not yet been perfected. It literally suggests that sound recordings are not constitutionally subject to copyright.
151. 17 U.S.C. § 102(a).

purposes of this title if a fixation of the work is being made simultaneously with its transmission.[152]

This means in essence that it must be recorded in some fashion, such that its content can be reproduced at some future time.

In this view, a live performance or broadcast that is being simultaneously recorded is protectable by copyright. But as Nimmer and Nimmer point out, "this issue is ultimately one of constitutional, rather than of statutory dimension" for if a live performance or broadcast does not fall within the constitutional meaning of "writing" Congress has no authority to declare it to be copyrightable.[153] Surprisingly, there has as yet been no definitive judicial determination of whether a live performance or broadcast that is being simultaneously recorded constitutes a "writing" within the meaning of the intellectual property clause, but in light of the policy of liberal interpretation followed by the Supreme Court there is no reason to believe that it would not declare a live performance being simultaneously recorded as in fact a writing and hence subject to copyright.[154]

Recently, however, the Eleventh Circuit has seen fit to suggest that "fixation, as a constitutional concept, is something less than a rigid, inflexible barrier to Congressional power."[155] It bases this view "on the ease with which" Congress has declared that a work being transmitted is deemed fixed and hence copyrightable if it is being fixed simultaneously with its transmission.[156] It recognizes that this declaration by Congress is in fact another of those legal fictions that so predominate in the copyright law.[157]

---

152. *Id.* § 101.
153. NIMMER & NIMMER, *supra* note 3, §1.08[C][2].
154. In 1999 the Eleventh Circuit declined "to decide whether the fixation concept of the Copyright Clause can be expanded so as to encompass live performances that are merely capable of being reduced to tangible form, but have not been." United States v. Moghadam, 173 F.3d 1269, 1274 (11th Cir. 1999).
155. *Id.* at 1281.
156. *See supra* text accompanying note 152.
157. *Moghadam,* 173 F.3d at 1280–81.

D. Copyrightable Works

The term "works" appears in the Copyright Act of 1976 in the phrase "original works of authorship."[158] The phrase is purposely left undefined in the statute.[159] Likewise, no definition of "works" is provided, although definitions for various categories of "works" are provided.[160] The use of the term "works" is a continuing deliberate attempt by Congress to metamorphose by legal fiction the term "writings" as it appears in the intellectual property clause into an open-ended and much broader term.[161] The term "works" is much more malleable and facile than is the term "writings," and already the use of "writings" in the context of copyright is becoming archaic.

Just as the term "works" is deliberately left undefined, so too Congress has taken steps to assure that the subject matter of copyright is left open. Works of authorship that may be copyrighted, provided that they are fixed in a tangible medium of expression, include: (1) literary works; (2) musical works, including any accompanying words; (3) dramatic works, including any accompanying music; (4) pantomimes and choreographic works; (5) pictorial, graphic, and sculptural works; (6) motion pictures and other audiovisual works; (7) sound recordings; and (8) architectural works.[162] The legislative history of the 1976 Act makes clear that this listing is illustrative only and not in any way intended to be limiting.[163] Rather, the intent is to "free the courts from rigid or outmoded concepts of the scope of particular categories."[164]

Of specific interest to the present work is the statement in the legislative history of the 1976 Act that: "As a class of subject matter sound recordings are clearly within the scope of the 'writings of an author' capable

---

158. 17 U.S.C. § 102(a).

159. *See supra* text accompanying notes 85–87.

160. Thus, for example, "anonymous work," "architectural work," "audiovisual works," "collective work," "derivative work," "joint work," "literary works," "pictorial, graphic, and sculptural works," "pseudonymous work," "a work of visual art," "a work of the United States government," and "a work made for hire" are all defined. *See* 17 U.S.C. § 101.

161. The metamorphosis began with the Copyright Act of 1909. For a discussion on this point see the text accompanying notes 208–225 *infra*.

162. 17 U.S.C. § 102(a).

163. Indeed, the 1976 Act listed only the first seven categories, and the eighth, "architectural works," was only added in 1990. *See* Pub. L. No. 101-650, Title VII, § 703, 104 Stat. 5133 (Dec. 1, 1990).

164. *See* 8 NIMMER & NIMMER, *supra* note 3, at App. 4-17.

of protection under the Constitution."[165] No authority is stated for this conclusory statement. It is literally contrary to the definition of "writings" as used in the clause set forth by the Supreme Court in 1884 which limited "writings" to those forms of expression that are "visible" as opposed to auditory.[166] Once again, to enlarge the scope of copyright Congress engaged in a massive legal fiction.[167]

The 1976 Act also took pains to enlarge the scope of copyright in another fashion, namely, by granting to the copyright owner the exclusive right to prepare or authorize the preparation of "derivative works based upon the copyrighted work."[168] It defined "derivative works" as those "based upon one or more preexisting works, such as a translation, musical arrangement, dramatization, fictionalization, motion picture version, sound recording, art reproduction, abridgment, condensation, or any other form in which a work may be recast, transformed, or adapted."[169]

To understand how "writings" as used in the intellectual property clause got transformed in the manner noted above, it is useful to once again turn to the historical record. The first copyright act in 1790 authorized copyright in "maps, charts,[170] and books."[171] Books were clearly writings within the context of the intellectual property clause, but how and why did maps and charts get encompassed within "writings." The answer resides in the fact that the clause was intended to authorize Congress to grant rights similar to those existing in Great Britain and certain states.[172] It thus took a legal fiction—and a rather significant one—to extend "writings" to cover maps and marine charts.

In the next two centuries the scope of copyright would be continuously broadened and expanded by Congress. Some of this statutory expansion

---

165. *Id.* at App. 4-20–App. 4-21.
166. *See supra* note 150.
167. For a discussion of the role of fictions and fallacies in copyright law, see PATTERSON & LINDBERG, *supra* note 18, at Chapter Ten.
168. 17 U.S.C. § 106.
169. *Id.* § 101.
170. The distinction between a map and a chart is that a map refers to land features whereas a chart refers to ocean and water features.
171. Act of May 31, 1790, 1 Stat. 124.
172. Great Britain had enacted legislation specifically providing for the copyright of maps and marine charts. *See* 7 Geo. 3, c. 38 (1766); 17 Geo. 3, c. 57 (1777). *See also* David Hunter, *Copyright Protection for Engravings and Maps in Eighteenth-Century Britain,* 9 LIBRARY 128 (1987). Connecticut, Georgia, and North Carolina had enacted legislation providing copyright protection to maps and charts. *See* note 256, *infra.*

408 THE NATURE OF THE INTELLECTUAL PROPERTY CLAUSE

was in response to conservative judicial interpretations. Thus, before looking at the statutory changes in copyrightable works it is useful to look at judicial views on the subject, particularly in the nineteenth and early twentieth centuries.

An early copyright case, *Clayton v. Stone*,[173] decided by Justice Thompson on circuit in 1829 provides an example of the ambivalence with which copyright was viewed early on in the courts and indeed through much of the nineteenth century. In dictum, Justice Thompson declared that: "A book within the statute need not be a book in the common and ordinary acceptation of the word, viz., a volume made up of several sheets bound together; it may be printed only on one sheet, as the words of a song or the music accompanying it."[174] The real issue, however, was whether a newspaper publishing so-called "price currents" or what would now be known as stock price quotations, was covered by the copyright law. In holding that it was not, Justice Thompson declared:

> In determining the true construction to be given to the act of congress, it is proper to look at the constitution of the United States, to aid us in ascertaining the nature of the property intended to be protected. Congress shall have power to promote the progress of science and useful arts, by securing for limited times to authors and inventors the exclusive right to their writings and discoveries. . . . The act in question was passed in execution of the power here given, and the object, therefore, was the promotion of science; and it would certainly be a pretty extraordinary view of the sciences to consider a daily or weekly publication of the state of the market as falling within any class of them. They are of a more fixed, permanent and durable character. The term science cannot, with any propriety, be applied to a work of so fluctuating and fugitive a form as that

---

173. 5 F. Cas. 999 (No. 2,872), 13 Copyright Dec. 1789–1909, 640 (C.C.S.D.N.Y. 1829).

174. He clearly was unaware that in enacting the Copyright Act of 1790, the Senate had deleted "and other writings" from H.R. 43, the bill that became the 1790 Act, thereby deliberately limiting the subject matter of copyright only to maps, charts, and books. *See* IV DOCUMENTARY HISTORY OF THE FIRST FEDERAL CONGRESS OF THE UNITED STATES at 526 (Linda De Pauw et al. eds., 1972). Nonetheless, there was British precedent to support such a view but it would take another two years for Congress to amend the copyright statute to expressly authorize copyright of musical works. *See* note 199, *infra*, and accompanying text.

of a newspaper or price-current, the subject-matter of which is daily changing, and is of mere temporary use.[175]

The clear import of this language was that the "to" language of the intellectual property clause limited the subject matter of what could be copyrighted. But in the second half of the twentieth century several circuit courts would take a very different view.[176]

The views expressed by Justice Thompson were quoted with approval by the Supreme Court in *Baker v. Selden* in 1879,[177] yet three decades later Congress would declare newspapers to be copyrightable.[178] In 1891 the Court declared that the clause "evidently has reference only to such writings and discoveries as are the result of intellectual labor." It went on to declare that the word "writings" in the clause "does not have any reference to labels which simply designate or describe the articles to which they are attached, and which have no value separated from the articles, and no possible influence upon science or the useful arts."[179] This seemed clearly to suggest that the "to" language of the clause did indeed constitute a limitation on the subject matter of copyright and that labels and other commonplace advertisements were not copyrightable under the constitutional language.

Although copyright law in the United States has always covered "books," early judicial opinions in the United States, citing English precedent,[180] narrowly restricted copyright coverage to the book itself.[181]

---

175. 13 Copyright Dec., 1789–1909, at 645.
176. *See supra* notes 59–69 and accompanying text.
177. 101 U.S. at 106.
178. *See* text accompanying note 213, *infra.*
179. Higgins v. Keuffel, 140 U.S. 428, 430 (1891).
180. *See, e.g.,* Burnett v. Chetwood, 2 Mer. 441, 35 Eng. Rep. 1008 (Ch. 1720) (translation); Gyles v. Wilcox, 2 Atk. 141, 3 Atk. 269, 26 Eng. Rep. 489, 957, 27 Eng. Rep. 682 (Ch. 1740) (abridgment); Dodsley v. Kinnersley, Amb. 403, 27 Eng. Rep. 270 (Ch. 1761). Indeed, one of the arguments against a perpetual common-law copyright presented in *Donaldson v. Becket* in 1774 was that if such a right was predicated upon an "equitable and moral right" in the author, then "abridgments of books, translations, notes" must be viewed as infringements for these "as effectually deprive the original author of the fruit of his labours, as direct particular copies. . . ." *See* 17 HANSARD, PARLIAMENTARY HISTORY OF ENGLAND 953, 990 (1813).
181. As pointed out by Kaplan, translations and abridgments were not considered infringements of the original book copyright because the authors of the translations and abridgments were deemed to have contributed "somewhat intellectual" labor notwithstanding that they had used the original work pervasively. *See* KAPLAN, *supra* note 86, at 16–17.

Thus, for example, abridgements were deemed to be separate and distinct works,[182] as were translations.[183] Nonetheless, Justice Story in the years before his death in 1845 led a reappraisal of the view that abridgments were separate works from the original, and in so doing led to the development of the judicial doctrine of "fair use."[184]

The seminal case was *Folsom v. Marsh*,[185] decided by Story in 1841, although it was not understood as such for some time thereafter. At issue was whether the defendant's 866-page biography of George Washington which contained 353 pages taken from an earlier compendious work by Jared Sparks infringed Sparks' copyright. Story held that it did, but in so doing laid the foundations for what would come to be known as the fair-use doctrine. He began his analysis by noting that under the English case law a fair abridgment of an original work is not a violation of the author's copyright. But more is required than merely reducing the size of the original work. Instead, "[t]here must be real, substantial condensation of the materials, and intellectual labor and judgment bestowed thereon; and not merely the facile use of the scissors; or extracts of the essential parts, constituting the chief value of the original work."[186]

The crux of the matter, insofar as he was concerned was

> whether this is a justifiable use of the original materials, such as the law recognizes as no infringement of the copyright of the plaintiffs. . . . It is certainly not necessary, to constitute an invasion of copyright, that the whole of a work should be copied, or even a large portion of it, in form or in substance. If so much is taken, that the value of the original is sensibly diminished, or the labors of the original author are substantially to an injurious extent appropriated by another, that is sufficient, in point of law, to constitute a piracy pro tanto. . . . In short, we must often, in deciding questions of this sort, look to the nature and objects of the

---

182. *See, e.g.,* Story's Executors v. Holcomb, 23 F. Cas. 171 (D. Ohio 1847) (No. 13,497).
183. *See, e.g.,* Stowe v. Thomas, 23 F. Cas. 201 (E.D. Pa. 1853) (No. 13,514) (holding that a German translation of *Uncle Tom's Cabin* was not an infringement of the book's copyright).
184. Patterson & Lindberg state that the fair-use doctrine supplanted the so-called fair abridgment doctrine (*see* PATTERSON & LINDBERG *supra* note 18, at 68), but Kaplan suggests that Story seems to have tried to absorb certain of the earlier English cases by a process of reinterpretation "into a general conception of fair use (still unlabeled as such), that is, to read them as a species of the genus of excused appropriation." *See* KAPLAN, *supra* note 86, at 28.
185. 9 F. Cas. 343 (No. 4,904), 13 Copyright Dec., 1789–1909, 991 (D. Mass. 1841).
186. 13 Copyright Dec., 1789–1909, at 995.

selections made, the quantity and value of the materials used, and the degree in which the use may prejudice the sale, or diminish the profits, or supersede the objects, of the original work.[187]

Patterson and Lindberg suggest that the fair-use doctrine originating from this language which would finally be made a part of the copyright statute in 1976,[188] far from being a diminution of the copyright monopoly as often assumed, is in fact an enhancement of the rights encompassed by the monopoly.[189]

In developing the framework for what would become the fair-use doctrine, Story relied entirely on his interpretation of British case law and made no reference to either American case law[190] or the language of the intellectual property clause. His reliance on British precedent was perhaps not surprising in that he was a great believer in adapting the common-law to fit the American situation. But he could easily have predicated a justification for fair use on the "to" language of the intellectual property clause. Simply put, he could readily have argued that copying within the limitations he set forth was permissible because it promoted the progress of science, but copying beyond the conditions he set forth was piracy and infringement because it did not promote such progress. Had he done so, the judicial interpretation of American copyright law might have seen a much more defined constitutional justification and basis.

Let us now skip forward to the turn of the century. In 1903 in *Bleistein v. Donaldson Lithographing Co.*[191] Justice Holmes, speaking for the Court, argued for an expansive definition of copyrightable work. In his view any work qualified for copyright as long as it was "a personal reaction of an individual upon nature." He emphasized that "[p]ersonality always contains something unique" and "that something" may be copyrighted "unless there is a restriction in the words of the [copyright] act."[192] In other words, anything that involved the personality of its creator or originator, whatever it might be, was a copyrightable work, subject only to the proviso that Congress might by statute limit the scope of copyrightable works.

---

187. *Id.* at 1000–01.
188. *See* 17 U.S.C. § 107.
189. PATTERSON & LINDBERG, *supra* note 18, at 68.
190. The reason for this was straightforward in that there was no relevant American case law on which he could rely.
191. 188 U.S. 239 (1903).
192. *Id.* at 250. "Personality" as used by Justice Holmes appeared to encompass what at the second half of the eighteenth century had been termed the "style and sentimentality" of the author. *See supra* text accompanying notes 50 and 51.

Justice Holmes made no attempt to tie his expansive views on copyrightable subject matter to any interpretation of the term "writings" as it appears in the intellectual property clause, but it is apparent that he viewed that term as imposing no restriction on copyrightable subject matter whatever so long as the personality of the originator or creator was involved in the product or work.[193]

Five years later, Holmes sought to clarify, in physical terms, how "personality" could be copyrighted. The Court held in *White-Smith Music Publishing Co. v. Apollo Co.*[194] that the copyright of a song was not infringed by the manufacture and sale of music rolls for use on player pianos. In a special concurrence, that in reality was a dissent, Holmes argued that the basis for copyright "is that the person to whom it is given has invented some new collocation of visible or audible points—of lines, colors, sounds or words." He believed that copyright protection should exist for the "collocation" by whatever possible means "of reproducing the result which gives to the invention its meaning and worth."[195] This was about as expansive a definition of "writings" and copyrightable works as could be imagined. Note that Holmes made no attempt whatever to equate this "collocation" with "writings" as used in the intellectual property clause or to equate the inventor thereof with "authors" as used in the clause. Yet he was inherently engaging in an exceedingly broad interpretation of these terms without any express acknowledgment that this was the case. Needless to say, this would have ramifications for any subsequent congressional view of what constituted copyrightable works.

I return now to the congressional transformation of "writings" in the intellectual property clause into broad and open-ended "works." In 1802 Congress extended copyright protection to "the art of designing, engraving, and etching historical and other prints."[196] Again, a legal fiction was involved, and again the reason was to extend United States copyright protection in the same manner that it had been afforded in Great Britain in the eighteenth century.[197] The legal fiction was extended in 1831 when copyright coverage

---

193. But the so-called "sweat of the brow" cases ultimately rejected in *Feist* would reject even personality as a requirement for copyright and argue that so long as labor was involved, any compilation, no matter how straightforward, was copyrightable.
194. 209 U.S. 1 (1908).
195. *Id.* at 19–20.
196. Act of April 29, 1802, 2 Stat. 171.
197. Copyright protection had been extended to engravings in 1735. *See* 8 Geo. 2, c. 13 (1735).

of musical compositions was provided.[198] Again this appears to have been done to conform to British precedent.[199] According to Patterson and Lindberg, these fictions were justified by analogy in that musical annotation or scoring is a form of writing and etchings and engravings are reproduced by a process analogous to printing.[200] At the same time, however, they made it easier for Congress in the future to interpret *authors* and *writings* more expansively as "creators" and "works of authorship."[201]

The expansion of the scope of protection afforded by the term "writings" continued in 1856 when Congress amended the copyright law to provide that copyright of a dramatic composition included "the sole right also to act, perform, or represent the same, or cause it to acted, performed, or represented on any stage or public place during the whole period for which the copyright is obtained."[202] In 1865 the copyright law was again amended to cover "photographs and the negatives thereof."[203] The constitutionality of extending copyright to photographs was upheld by the Supreme Court in 1884, although the Court acknowledged that the constitutional question "is not free from difficulty."[204] In so doing, the Court relied heavily on its interpretation of what constituted authorship. It declared, however, that "writings" as used in the intellectual property clause means "the literary productions of . . . authors"[205] and held that photographs are indeed copyrightable literary productions "so far as they are representatives of original intellectual conception by an author."[206] This was the most expansive legal fiction yet in the copyright arena, but more was to come.

---

198. Act of February 3, 1831, 4 Stat. 36. Patterson & Lindberg inadvertently confuse the content of the Act of April 29, 1802 with this Act. *See* PATTERSON & LINDBERG, *supra* note 18, at 135–36.

199. As early as 1777, Lord Mansfield had ruled in England that a musical composition was a writing within the Statute of Anne. *See* Bach v. Longman, 2 Cowp. 623, 98 Eng. Rep. 1274 (K.B. 1777).

200. Although it was much more plausible under the extant definition of "writings" to treat a musical composition as a writing than it was to treat etchings and engravings as writings. The scoring of musical notes or symbols in a musical composition could easily be argued to fall within the definition of writings. *See* *supra* text accompanying note 123.

201. PATTERSON & LINDBERG, *supra* note 18, at 136.

202. Act of August 18, 1856, 11 Stat. 138.

203. Act of March 3, 1865, 13 Stat. 540.

204. Burrow-Giles Lithographic Co. v. Sarony, 111 U.S. 53 (1884).

205. *Id.* at 58.

206. *Id.* at 59.

In 1870 the copyright statute was amended and revised to now cover "any book, map, chart, dramatic or musical composition, engraving, cut, print, or photograph, or negative thereof, or of a painting, drawing, chromo, statue, statuary, and of models or designs intended to be perfected as works of fine arts."[207] It was perhaps inevitable, given the earlier congressional decision to authorize copyright for photographs that it should now authorize copyright for paintings and drawings. Indeed, there was less of a legal fiction involved in that drawings and paintings are perhaps more easily associated with a particular style of their creators than are photographs. But a major legal fiction was involved in extending the term "writings" to encompass three-dimensional objects such as statues and models.

A major revision of the copyright law occurred in 1909.[208] Congress now declared that "[the works for which copyright may be secured . . . shall include all the writings of an author."[209] This was the first time that the term "works" had been used in a generic sense to encompass all copyrightable subject matter.[210] Implicit in this declaration is the view that copyrightable works, while including all the writings of an author, somehow extend further than such writings. According to the House report accompanying the 1909 Act, the quoted language is "declaratory of existing law" although the basis for such statement was not given. The report goes on to indicate that although the suggestion was made that the term "works" should be substituted for the term "writings," because of the broad construction given the latter term by the courts, "it was thought better to use the word 'writings,' which is the word found in the Constitution."[211] One can easily read this language as suggesting that if the courts had narrowly defined the term "writings," then Congress would have been readily disposed to avoid using the term at all and instead would have substituted the term "works," thereby somehow avoiding any such judicial concerns.

Aside from being somewhat confusing, the Report language is also something of a non sequitur in that both the terms "works" and "writings" appear in the declaration of what constitutes copyrightable subject matter. Moreover,

207. Act of July 18, 1870, 16 Stat. 212.
208. Act of March 4, 1909, c. 320, 35 Stat. 1075. The 1909 Act, as codified and amended, is reproduced in 8 NIMMER & NIMMER, *supra* note 3, at App. 6-1–App. 6-51.
209. *See* 8 NIMMER & NIMMER, *supra* note 3, at App. 6-6.
210. The term first appeared in the copyright statute in 1870, but only in the context of "works of fine arts." *See supra* note 207 and accompanying text.
211. H.R. Rep. No. 2222, 60th Cong., 2d Sess. (1909), *reproduced in* NIMMER & NIMMER, *supra* note 3, at App. 13-15.

according to the House report, the language of the intellectual property clause places several conditions or limitations on the power of Congress, so that the object of copyright legislation authorized by it must be: "(1) to promote science and the useful arts; (2) by securing for limited times to authors the exclusive right to their writings; (3) that the subjects which are to be secured are 'the writings of authors.'"[212] If the subjects to be secured by copyright are "the writings of authors," why or on what basis could Congress constitutionally declare that copyrightable subject matter is "works" that "include all the writings of an author"? This is not a rhetorical question, nor is it one that Congress has ever been inclined to answer.

The types of copyrightable "works" under the 1909 Act included:

+ Books, including composite and cyclopedic works, directories, gazeteers, and other compilations.
+ Periodicals, including newspapers.[213]
+ Lectures, sermons, addresses (prepared for oral delivery).
+ Dramatic or dramatico-musical compositions.
+ Musical compositions.
+ Maps.
+ Works of art; models or designs for works of art.[214]
+ Reproductions of a work of art.
+ Drawings or plastic works of a scientific or technical character.
+ Photographs.

---

212. 8 NIMMER & NIMMER, *supra* note 3, at App.13-10.
213. In light of the language quoted with favor in *Baker v. Selden* (*see supra* text accompanying notes 175, 177), it is reasonable to ask on what basis Congress determined that newspapers were now subject to copyright. The House report does not say.
214. Note that "fine" had now been removed as a modifier to "arts." As Kaplan points out, Justice Holmes had disposed of that qualifier by his statement in *Bleistein* that "a very modest grade of art has in it something irreducible, which is one man's alone." *See* KAPLAN, *supra* note 86, at 34 and 39. But nothing in the *Bleistein* opinion suggested that Congress was constitutionally obligated to remove "fine" as a modifier to "arts." The result of its decision to do so would be, as pointed out by Patterson & Lindberg, "the trivialization of copyright." *See supra* note 18, at 88. A consequence would be that copyrights have been issued for "statuettes, bookends, clocks, lamps, doorknockers, candlesticks, inkstands, chandeliers, piggy banks, sundials, salt and pepper shakers, fish bowls, casseroles, and ash trays." *See* Justice Douglas, concurring, in Mazer v. Stein, 347 U.S. 201, 221 (1954).

✦ Prints and pictorial illustrations including prints or labels used for articles of merchandise.[215]

✦ Motion-picture photoplays.

✦ Motion pictures other than photoplays.[216]

✦ Sound recordings.[217]

The 1909 Act specifically declared that the categories of copyrightable works thus listed "shall not be held to limit the subject matter of copyright."[218]

Despite this latter statement, Kaplan argues that this enumeration of categories of copyrightable works "can be and as a practical matter has been read to limit the general statement" that copyrightable works include all the writings of an author.[219] He reads *Mazer v. Stein*[220] as supporting this conclusion.[221] I do not so read the case. Thus, the Supreme Court while acknowledging that "some writers" interpret the general statement "as being coextensive with the constitutional grant," also stated that "the House Report, while inconclusive, indicates that it was 'declaratory of existing law' only." The Court also acknowledged that "the report is not very clear on this point, however."[222] The Court did not state, or hold, that "existing law" in 1909, whatever it was, somehow indicated that "all the writings of an author" could, or should, be interpreted as somehow narrower than "writings" of "authors" as those terms appear in the intellectual property clause.

Moreover, Kaplan fails to point out that in *Mazer v. Stein* the Court noted but did not reach the issue of whether "works of art," "models or designs for works of art," and "reproductions of a work of art" may

---

215. The phrase "including prints or labels used for merchandise" was included by the Act of July 31, 1939, ch. 396, § 2, 53 Stat. 1142. The basis for so doing is unclear in light of the language of the Supreme Court in *Higgins v. Keuffel. See* 140 U.S. 428, 430 (1891). *See supra* text accompanying note 179.

216. Subsections (l) and (m) were added by the Act of August 24, 1912, ch. 356, 37 Stat. 488.

217. Subsection (n) was added by the Act of October 15, 1971, Pub. L. 92-140, 85 Stat. 391.

218. 8 NIMMER & NIMMER, *supra* note 3, at App. 6-6–App. 6-7.

219. Kaplan, *supra* note 86, at 39.

220. 347 U.S. 201, 210–11 & nn.17–19 (1954).

221. Nimmer and Nimmer also read it this way. *See* NIMMER & NIMMER, *supra* note 3, § 2.03[A], n.5 [Rel. 39-5/96].

222. *See* 347 U.S. at 210.

constitutionally be the subject of copyright.[223] But as pointed out in the concurrence of Justices Douglas and Black, the Court had not as of 1954 ever decided the issue of whether a sculptor is an "author" and his statue a "writing" within the meaning of the intellectual property clause.[224] As of the new millennium, it still had not done so.[225]

Between 1909 and 1976 when the present copyright law was enacted, no Supreme Court opinion specifically addressed the issue of limitations on copyrightable subject matter set forth in the intellectual property clause. In 1973, however, in *Goldstein v. California* the Court appeared to adopt a highly expansive definition of the term "writings" as used in the clause. According to the *Goldstein* Court, "'writings' . . . may be interpreted to include any physical rendering of the fruits of creative intellectual or aesthetic labor."[226] Given this expansive interpretation, it is not surprising that in enacting the present copyright statute in 1976 Congress saw no need to define what it meant by "original works of authorship" or indeed to use the term "writings" at all in the statute. As I pointed out at the beginning of this part, the term "works" is so much more malleable and flexible than "writings." In particular, it nicely avoids the inconvenient fact that the interpretation given to "writings" in the clause by the *Goldstein* Court goes well beyond and is quite inconsistent with standard dictionary definitions of "writings" as they exist today or those that were in vogue at the end of the eighteenth century.

The House report on the rationale for substituting "works" for "writings" appears intended only to justify a congressional view that there is basically no constitutional limitation on what constitutes a copyrightable work and Congress may define such a work as it sees fit, provided only that there must a "physical rendering" of the work and it must be the result of "creative or aesthetic labor." Unfortunately, it obfuscates and confuses more than it

---

223. It declined to do so because this particular constitutional issue had not been raised by the parties to the litigation. *See* 347 U.S. at 206, n.5.
224. 347 U.S. at 220.
225. Nonetheless, Kaplan's view would receive the imprimatur of the Supreme Court in *Goldstein v. California* decided in 1973. *See* text accompanying note 235, *infra*. Moreover, the expansive interpretation of "writings" in *Goldstein* (*see* text accompanying note 226, *infra*) renders largely academic any discussion of whether the Court would hold sculptors to be "authors" and statues to be "writings" within the meaning of the clause. Clearly it now would.
226. 413 U.S. at 561.

clarifies. According to the report, "original works of authorship" is substituted for "all the writings of an author" as used in the 1909 Act

> to avoid exhausting the constitutional power of Congress to legislate in this field, and to eliminate the uncertainties arising from the latter phrase. Since the present [1909] statutory language is substantially the same as the empowering language of the Constitution, a recurring question has been whether the statutory and the constitutional provisions are coextensive. If so, the courts would be faced with the alternative of holding copyrightable something that Congress clearly did not intend to protect, or of holding constitutionally incapable of copyright something that Congress might one day want to protect. To avoid these equally undesirable results, the courts have indicated that "all the writings of an author" under the present statute is narrower in scope than the "writings" of "authors" referred to in the Constitution. The bill avoids this dilemma by using a different phrase—"original works of authorship"—in characterizing the general subject matter of statutory copyright protection.[227]

While it was undoubtedly true that in the 1976 Act Congress desired to act within the scope of its broadest constitutional authority to determine what constituted copyrightable works, the so-called "dilemma" supposedly justifying the phrase "original works of authorship" was largely, if not completely, nonexistent.

In this regard, the empowering language of the 1909 Act appeared coextensive on its face with that of the intellectual property clause, and indeed the 1976 House report quoted above acknowledges this to be the case. That this was the intent of Congress in 1909 was further evidenced by the express statement in the 1909 Act that the categories of copyrightable work listed therein were not intended to be limiting on the subject matter of copyright.[228] But there was an apparent inconsistency in the language of the 1909 Act in that it also indicated, although in an obtuse fashion, that sound recordings were not copyrightable. That this was its intent was made clear in the 1909 House report statement that "[i]t is not the intention . . . to extend the right of copyright to the mechanical reproductions [of sound] themselves. . . ."[229] How then to reconcile the congressional language that "the works for which copyright may be secured . . . shall include all the writings of an author" with the congressional intent that sound recordings not be copyrightable?

---

227. 8 NIMMER & NIMMER, *supra* note 3, at App. 4-14.
228. *See supra* note 218 and accompanying text.
229. 8 NIMMER & NIMMER, *supra* note 3, at App. 13-13.

There were three possible ways of doing so. The first, which neither the Copyright Office nor any court would seriously contemplate, was to find that there was no inconsistency because the term "writings" in the intellectual property clause does not encompass sound recordings. In the face of this refusal to contemplate that the constitutional language might not encompass sound recordings, the second—and most pragmatic—resolution would have been to simply acknowledge the apparent inconsistency and hold that "writings" in the constitutional sense did encompass sound recordings, and therefore in view of the express declaration in the 1909 Act that copyrightable works included "all the writings of an author," sound recordings were in fact copyrightable. The Copyright Office consistently refused to adopt such an approach, and, with one early exception, so did the courts.[230] While the courts were prepared to adopt the view that sound recordings were "writings" within the meaning of the constitutional language, albeit without any citation of authority for such a view, they were not prepared to take the next step and hold that the broad statement of copyrightable works in the 1909 Act authorized copyright of sound recordings.[231]

Instead, both the courts and the Copyright Office adopted the third approach and literally read the express disclaimer that the categories of copyrightable works listed in the 1909 Act "shall not be held to limit the subject matter of copyright" out of the Act. Having done that, they "implicitly (and sometimes explicitly) assumed that [the listing of categories] constituted an exhaustive enumeration of copyrightable works under the statute."[232] Congress ultimately avoided the issue by in 1971 declaring its belief "that, as a class of subject matter, sound recordings are clearly within the scope of the 'writings of an author' capable of protection under the Constitution"[233] and amending the 1909 Act to include sound recordings in the enumerated categories of copyrightable works.[234]

---

230. The exception was Fonotipia, Ltd. v. Bradley, 171 F. 951, 963 (E.D.N.Y. 1909).

231. *See, e.g.,* Capitol Records, Inc. v. Mercury Records Corp., 221 F.2d 657 (2d Cir. 1955) (holding that the 1909 Act did not authorize copyright of phonograph records despite the fact that "[t]here can be no doubt that, under the Constitution, Congress could give to one who performs a public domain musical composition the exclusive right to make and vend phonograph records of that rendition").

232. NIMMER & NIMMER, *supra* note 3, § 203[A] at n.7.

233. H.R. REP. NO. 92-487, 92d Cong. 1st Sess. (1971), *reprinted in* 2 U.S.C.C.A.N. 1570 (1971).

234. *See supra* note 217 and accompanying text.

The issue was further complicated by the fact that in 1973 the Supreme Court held in *Goldstein v. California* that the 1909 Act did not demonstrate an intention by Congress "to exercise its authority over all works to which the constitutional provision might apply," and accordingly state control of sound recordings was not pre-empted. While it is difficult to perceive how the Court could reasonably hold that "all the writings of an author" is somehow narrower in scope than "writings" of "authors" as used in the intellectual property clause, the Court predicated its holding on its view that "in the more than 60 years which have elapsed since enactment of this provision, neither the Copyright Office, the courts, nor the Congress" had interpreted it as being coextensive with the copyright authority granted to Congress by the clause.[235]

The House report language on the 1976 Act simply ignores this holding in *Goldstein* and posits a dilemma that does not exist. Contrary to the assertion in the report, no court is "faced with the alternative of holding copyrightable something that Congress clearly did not intend to protect, or of holding constitutionally incapable of copyright something that Congress might one day want to protect."[236] If Congress *expressly* states in its legislation that particular subject matter is not copyrightable, that is clearly within its discretion, and no court has authority to arbitrarily override such a congressional determination. Moreover, the question of whether a particular work is constitutionally capable of being copyrighted is determined by the language of the clause rather than by any statutory language. If particular subject matter is judicially held to be unconstitutionally capable of copyright protection, then it matters not at all that Congress may have a future desire to provide copyright protection for it. It simply does not have the authority to do so.

More critically, to the extent that there were uncertainties as to what works were copyrightable under the 1909 Act, those uncertainties have no way been eliminated by replacing the phrase "all the writings of an author" with "original works of authorship" in the 1976 Act. Rather, as succinctly put by Nimmer and Nimmer, "the uncertainties were merely transferred to a different phrase, not eliminated."[237] Moreover, because Congress has deliberately chosen not to define what "original works of authorship" means, it has effectively transferred discretion to determine what constitutes copyrightable works to the courts. In light of the expansive definition of "writings" by the Supreme Court in *Goldstein*, it would appear that there

---

235. 412 U.S. at 567–69.
236. *See supra* text accompanying note 227.
237. NIMMER & NIMMER, *supra* note 3, § 203[A] at n.20.

is literally no constitutional or statutory limitation on what constitutes a copyrightable work other than that it evince some modicum of creativity and that it be fixed in a tangible medium.

E. Perspectives

From time to time, efforts have been made to justify the differing standards for copyrightability and patentability on the ground that such differing standards are required by the language of the intellectual property clause.[238] Nothing in the drafting of the clause, its actual language, or its subsequent interpretation by the Supreme Court, supports such a view. Rather to the extent that there has been a differentiation in the standards applied to defining the nature of "the exclusive right" granted to "authors" for their "writings" and to "inventors" for their "discoveries," such differing standards have arisen out of the broad discretion granted to Congress by the clause rather than out of any requirement set forth in the clause itself.[239] However, just as is the case with patents, this does not mean that there are no limits set forth in the clause on the congressional copyright authority. Nonetheless, both Congress and the Supreme Court have seen fit to give much less meaning to such limitations in the context of copyrights than they have in their treatment of patent rights.

A comparison of the judicial and congressional treatment of the copyright and patent provisions of the clause over time reveals several rather remarkable differences in the manner in which the two have been interpreted.[240] The first has to do with the propensity of both Congress and the courts to engage in legal fictions in defining who or what is an author and what is copyrightable, and the second has to do with the extreme reluctance—one might even say, the failure—of both Congress and the judiciary to treat the "to" language of the clause as a limitation on any interpretation given to "authors" and "writings" as they appear in the clause. That the Supreme

---

238. *See, e.g.*, text accompanying notes 114–117 *supra*.
239. The Supreme Court has at least tacitly acknowledged this point. *See* Sony Corp. v. Universal City Studios, Inc., 464 U.S. 417 (1984). *See supra* text accompanying note 120.
240. I have already discussed in detail the remarkable dichotomy in treatment of the patent term and the copyright term under the clause. *See* Chapter Seven, Parts E and F.

Court has seen fit at all to interpret the meaning to be given to "authors" and "writings" in the clause is another surprising difference.[241]

An obvious legal fiction, and one that appears directly contrary to the constitutional language, is the congressional defining of the proprietors of works made for hire as the authors for purposes of obtaining copyright. It is unclear how or why this practice started in the nineteenth century,[242] but, regardless of its origins, it was directly contrary to the practice with regard to patenting of inventions made by persons who were hired to invent and has remained so to this day.[243] The rationale given for it by Congress avoids any mention whatever of the constitutional problem posed by the use of the word "their" in the clause, but instead justifies it on the ground of convenience and that it "is well established in American copyright law."[244] The lower courts have declined to engage in any constitutional analysis of the propriety of the practice, but instead have merely assumed that it is constitutional.[245]

Just as with their use of the term "discoveries," the Framers created a significant interpretational problem when they chose to use the term "writings" in the intellectual property clause. However the problem was a very different one. Whereas by using "discoveries" they gave Congress a very broad discretion as to what it might deem patentable discovery,[246] their use of "writings" could very easily be interpreted to have exactly the opposite purpose—and indeed effect—namely a significant narrowing of the scope of what could be deemed to constitute copyrightable work. This never occurred, because over time both Congress and the Supreme Court engaged in a series of legal fictions by which the interpretation given to "writings" has been constantly expanded until today it bears little relationship to either the common dictionary definition at the end of the eighteenth century or to the modern dictionary definition.

---

241. Recall that the Court steadfastly has refused to provide any interpretation of the terms "inventors" and "discoveries" as they appear in the clause and Congress has provided only an unhelpful definition. *See supra* Chapter Eight, notes 2, 3 and accompanying text.
242. As late as 1846, a circuit court had refused to accept an argument that a work for hire could be copyrighted in the name of the person procuring the work as opposed to the name of the person actually creating the work. *See supra* text accompanying note 76.
243. *See supra* note 5 and accompanying text.
244. *See supra* text accompanying notes 15–20.
245. *See, e.g.,* Childress v. Taylor, 945 F.2d 500, 507 n.5 (2d Cir. 1991). *See also* text accompanying note 24, *supra.*
246. *See supra* Chapter Eight, text accompanying note 259.

A 1956 congressional study on the meaning of "writings" in the clause points out that the "broad definition and subtle interpretation of the rather precise and explicit words" of the clause "would seem to require a great deal of explanation and rationalization on the part of the courts." It goes on to suggest that "[w]ithout these basic assumptions or rationalizations, whether expressly stated or not, the only conclusion one can reach is that for approximately 150 years Congress and the courts have been operating outside and in violation of an express power delegated to Congress."[247] This conclusion remains valid today. What then is the nature of the assumptions and rationalizations that Congress and the judiciary have relied upon?

Before giving a perspective on how and why Congress and the Supreme Court have interpreted "authors" and "writings" in the clause in the manner that they have, it is useful to inquire as to why the Framers used these terms and what they contemplated by them. The simple answer is that the term "authors" appears in the clause because during the federal convention Madison proposed "to secure to literary authors their copy rights for a limited time" and Pinckney proposed "to secure to authors exclusive rights for a certain time."[248] But neither made any mention of exactly what it was that was to be protected for authors. At this time there were two generally accepted definitions of "author," one considerably broader than the other. The broader definition was "he to whom any thing owes its original; he that effects or produces any thing." The narrower definition was "the first writer of anything; a writer in general."[249] By their use of the term "writings" as the subject matter for which an exclusive right was to be given, albeit for a limited time, it is plausible to suggest that the Framers viewed the term "authors" as used in the clause in the narrower light, i.e., as one who produces "writings," as opposed to any other thing. Had they intended the broader usage, it would have been more plausible for them to have used a more general term than "writings," as, e.g., "works" or "productions," terms which had appeared in several of the recently enacted stated copyright statutes.[250]

---

247. *Study No. 3, supra* note 126, at 86–87.
248. *See* Chapter Three, text accompanying notes 80, 81.
249. *See supra* note 27 and accompanying text.
250. Thus, for example, the statutes of New Hampshire and Rhode Island referred to "literary productions" and the statutes of Georgia, New York, and Virginia referred to "works." *See* NIMMER & NIMMER, *supra* note 3, at App. 7-31, App. 7-35, App. 7-38.

Thus the question of what the Framers intended to encompass within the term "writings" becomes one of considerable import. In the eighteenth century a writing could be viewed as the recording on a suitable surface by means of letters, symbols, or characters, the thoughts or ideas of the writer, i.e., the author. The Statute of Anne gave a limited-term exclusive copying right in books, which were a particular form or assemblage of writing, and made no reference to any other specific type of writing. Clearly, by their use of the term "writings" the Framers intended to give Congress authority to grant a limited-term exclusive right in more than merely the assemblage of writings known as books.[251] But at the end of the eighteenth century, was there anything to indicate that "writings" could or should cover some other form of expression than the use of letters, symbols, or characters to convey the thoughts or ideas of the author?

A look at the extant English copyright law and the copyright laws of the various states at the time the Constitution was drafted suggests that the answer is a qualified yes. The qualification arises out of the fact that the British copyright law as well as several of the recently enacted state copyright statutes covered maps and marine charts which were more than simply the use of letters, symbols, or characters.[252] Thus, the Framers appear to have been disposed to accept the legal fiction that maps and marine charts could be encompassed within the definition of "writings" then extant.[253]

The proposals from which the clause was derived do not mention "writings" at all. Rather, Madison had proposed that Congress be given power "to secure to literary authors their copy right for a limited time," and Pinckney had proposed the quite similar power "to secure to Authors exclusive rights for a certain time."[254] Nothing in these proposals suggested

---

251. *Cf.* the view expressed by Madison late in his life that the intellectual property clause gave monopoly rights in only two cases, "the authors of Books, and of useful inventions." *See supra* Chapter Three, note 119 and accompanying text. Madison must have been fully aware that the 1790 Copyright Act authorized copyright for more than merely books. But as noted, the Senate deliberately limited the coverage of the Copyright Act of 1790 to only maps, charts, and books and deleted the more inclusive "and other writings." *See supra* note 174.

252. *See* note 172 *supra* and note 257 *infra*.

253. Congress certainly thought this was the case when it authorized copyright protection for maps and charts in the Copyright Act of 1790. *See* Act of May 31, 1790, 1 Stat. 124.

254. *See supra* Chapter Three, text accompanying note 81.

that the exclusive right should be limited to "books" per se,[255] and they gave wide discretion as to what might be covered by the exclusive right. It is unclear how or on what basis the Framers determined to use "writings" to state what the copyright power gave an exclusive right in, but it is quite possible that the term was decided upon because of its use in the Statute of Anne and in several of the state copyright statutes that had recently been enacted.[256] Moreover, although the broader terms "productions" or "works" had appeared in several of the state statutes, the context in which these terms were used, and the actual copyright authority set forth, suggested that what was actually intended to be protected was more accurately characterized by the term "writings." Indeed, the actual grant of authority in most of these state statutes seemed to encompass more than books, but less than all forms of expression by an author.[257] "Writings" seemed to best envisage and encompass that which most states had sought to protect.

But if defined as a recording by means of letters, symbols, or characters, "writings" did not literally encompass all that Great Britain and at least several of the states had sought to protect, namely maps and marine charts, which required the use of lines and spaces in addition to symbols, characters, and letters. By their use of the term "writings" did the Framers literally intend to exclude maps and marine charts from copyright coverage? Because of the absence of any discussion at the federal convention of the final language of the intellectual property clause,[258] it is not possible to know with certainty what was intended by the use of "writings" rather than the broader

---

255. They certainly did not limit themselves to "books" in the manner that the Continental Congress resolution of 1783 recommending that the states enact copyright laws did. *See supra* Chapter Two, text accompanying note 172.
256. The copyright laws of Maryland and Pennsylvania made reference to "writings." *See* 8 NIMMER & NIMMER, *supra* note 3, at App. 7-17, App. 7-25.
257. Thus, for example, Connecticut sought to protect books, pamphlets, maps, or charts; Massachusetts sought to protect books, treatises, and other literary works; Maryland sought to protect books and writings; New Jersey sought to protect books and pamphlets; New Hampshire sought to protect books, treatises, and other literary works; Rhode Island sought to protect books, treatises, and other literary productions; Pennsylvania sought to protect books and pamphlets; Virginia sought to protect books and pamphlets; North Carolina sought to protect books, maps, or charts; Georgia sought to protect books, pamphlets, maps, or charts; and New York sought to protect books and pamphlets. *See* 8 NIMMER & NIMMER, *supra* note 3, at App. 7-1, App. 7-15, App. 7-17, App. 7-19, App. 7-21, App. 7-23, App. 7-25, App. 7-31, App. 7-33, App. 7-35, App. 7-38.
258. *See supra* Chapter One, text accompanying notes 2, 3.

terms "works" or "productions," but it is highly unlikely that this was their intent. Certainly the first federal Congress which had a number of Framers in it did not perceive this to be the case when it enacted the Copyright Act of 1790 which expressly authorized copyright for maps and charts. Nonetheless, as I have suggested, to read maps and charts within the ambit of "writings" required a significant legal fiction.

Nonetheless, there is reason to believe that in the early republic "writings" as used in the clause was perceived to be directed to various forms of literary expression. President Washington certainly seems to have thought so. In his first address to Congress, he stated that he was persuaded "that there is nothing which can better deserve your patronage than the promotion of science and literature."[259] At that time, the only express grant of authority to Congress to promote "science and literature" was thought to be through the exclusive right in literary expressions falling within the ambit of "writings" under the copyright provision of the clause. One result of this recommendation was the Copyright Act of 1790. Washington made no attempt to ask Congress to promote artistic expression and the fine arts because he did not perceive that the clause provided any such congressional authority. Clearly, providing copyright protection to maps and charts could be perceived as promoting science, i.e., learning and knowledge, even though they could be perceived to be artistic expression as well as literary expression.

An interesting aspect of the 1790 Act was that while it protected maps and charts, it said not a word about other pictorial reproductions of artistic designs that could be accomplished by the same mechanism as used for maps and charts, i.e., etchings, engravings, and woodcuts. None of the state copyright laws mentioned these types of reproductions, but Great Britain had earlier authorized copyright for them, albeit by separate statute from the Statute of Anne. According to Feather, "[t]his established a distinction between literary and artistic works which persisted in English law until almost the present day."[260] As evidenced by the inclusion of maps and charts as protectable subject matter under the 1790 Copyright Act, this distinction rather quickly became blurred in the United States. The blurring became even more pronounced in the Copyright Act of 1802 when

259. III DOCUMENTARY HISTORY OF THE FIRST FEDERAL CONGRESS OF THE UNITED STATES OF AMERICA, HOUSE OF REPRESENTATIVES JOURNAL at 253 (Linda G. De Pauw et al. eds., Baltimore 1977). *See also Proceedings in Congress During the Years 1789 and 1790, Relating to the First Patent and Copyright Laws*, 22 J. PAT. OFF. SOC'Y at 253–54 (1940).
260. *See* FEATHER, *supra* note 32, at 70. *See also* Hunter, *supra* note 172.

Congress extended copyright protection to "the art of designing, engraving, and etching historical and other prints."[261]

It was easy to see how literary works of whatever sort could be encompassed within the meaning of "writings" in the intellectual property clause, but it took a significant legal fiction to read "writings" as covering artistic works reproduced by engraving and etching "historical and other prints." But once the fiction was achieved, it was only a matter of time before it would be expanded to have "writings" cover any and all forms of artistic expression in tangible form. The expansion was essentially completed with the Copyright Act of 1870 with "writings" now being interpreted by Congress to cover "any book, map, chart, dramatic or musical composition, engraving, cut, print, or photograph, or negative thereof, or of a painting, drawing, chromo, statue, statuary, and models or designs intended to be perfected as works of fine arts."[262]

But in 1884 in *Burrow-Giles* when it addressed the issue of whether photographs were "writings" and hence copyrightable under the intellectual property clause, the Supreme Court was reluctant still to draw the clear conclusion that under the copyright statute "writings" now encompassed various forms of artistic as well as literary expression and to simply say so. Instead, it declared that 'writings" as used in the clause means "the literary productions of . . . authors" and held in essence that anything that is representative of the "original intellectual conception by an author" is a literary production and hence copyrightable.[263]

It also indicated that the intent of the Framers in their use of the term "writings" could be inferred from the copyright enactments of 1790 and 1802, saying:

> The construction placed upon the Constitution by the first Act of 1790, and the Act of 1802, by the men who were contemporary with its formation, many of whom were members of the Convention which framed it, is of itself entitled to very great weight; and when it is remembered that the rights thus established have not been disputed during a period of nearly a century, it is almost conclusive.[264]

Because it viewed photographs as analogous to the maps, charts, designs, engravings, etchings, cuts, and other prints authorized by these first two

---

261. *See supra* note 196 and accompanying text.
262. *See supra* note 207 and accompanying text.
263. *See* Burrow-Giles Lithographic Co. v. Sarony, 111 U.S. 53 (1884). *See supra* text accompanying notes 204–206.
264. *Burrow-Giles,* 111 U.S. at 57.

copyright acts, it held that photographs were "writings" within the meaning of the intellectual property clause.

It is questionable today whether the Court would rely to such a marked degree on early statutory language as a means of interpreting a term such as "writings" used in the clause.[265] Moreover, as it was sought to emphasize here, this early statutory language involved the use of significant and substantial legal fiction to extend the scope and meaning of "writings" as contemporaneously understood at the time the Constitution was drafted. Yet as the Court stressed in *Gibbons v. Ogden* in 1824, "the enlightened patriots who framed our constitution, and the people who have adopted it, must be understood to have employed words in their natural sense, and to have intended what they have said."[266] The natural sense of "writings" at the end of the eighteenth century did not equate literary expression and artistic expression in the manner that Congress and the Court now supposed a century after the Constitution was drafted.

Nonetheless, in 1903 in *Bleistein v. Donaldson Lithographing Co.* Justice Holmes for the Court simply assumed without discussion that "writings" covered artistic as well as literary expression. Moreover, in his view there had to be very little merit to the artistic expression in order for it to be copyrightable. Rather, it was the "personality" of the author as expressed in whatever medium that was copyrightable. As he put it: "Personality always contains something unique. It expresses its singularity even in handwriting, and a very modest grade of art has something irreducible, which is one man's alone. That something he may copyright. . . ."[267] Viewed in this fashion, it was not "writing" that was copyrightable but rather any medium of expression that demonstrated the author's "personality." Perhaps the most remarkable aspect of the views expressed by Justice Holmes was that they made no reference at all to the language of the intellectual property clause, but nonetheless appeared to place the imprimatur of the Supreme Court on the view that "writings" as used in the clause encompassed artistic expression as well as literary expression. In other words, "writings" in the copyright context no longer had its dictionary meaning.

Against this backdrop it is perhaps not surprising that Congress exhibited more than a bit of schizophrenia concerning constitutional limitations in enacting the Copyright Act of 1909. While solemnly noting that the

---

265. The early statutory language might well be considered a factor in making such a determination but it would only be one of a number of factors so involved.
266. *See supra* Chapter Five, note 24 and accompanying text.
267. Bleistein v. Donaldson Lithographing Co., 188 U.S. 239, 250 (1903).

subjects which can constitutionally be secured by copyright are "the writings of authors,"[268] it legislatively declared that "[the works for which copyright may be secured . . . shall include all the writings of an author." On its face, this seemed to suggest that there was no constitutional limitation on what could be copyrighted. If "all the writings of an author" could be copyrighted, then any constitutional requirement of originality or intellectual labor seemed to have disappeared, because there were literally writings that were neither original nor required even a modicum of intellectual labor. Moreover, if "writings" were merely included among works that were copyrightable, then "writings" was not in and of itself a limitation on copyrightable subject matter.

What Congress now literally declared was that it was the "works" of authors, and not merely certain of their "writings" that could be copyrighted. While the Supreme Court would subsequently find itself it full agreement with a very liberal congressional interpretation of what could be copyrighted, it nonetheless still had to act within the confines of the wording of the intellectual property clause. Its solution in 1973 in *Goldstein v. California* was to adopt the highly expansive legal fiction that "writings" as used in the intellectual property clause "may be interpreted to include any physical rendering of the fruits of creative intellectual or aesthetic labor."[269] Never mind that this is not the natural or dictionary definition of "writings."

In light of this legal fiction, Congress now determined in the Copyright Act of 1976 to avoid any use of the term "writings" and instead to simply declare that "original works of authorship" may be copyrighted. Substituting "works" for "writings," while pragmatically honest and declarative of congressional intent, is the ultimate legal fiction that has been generated with respect to copyright. It renders essentially meaningless the view expressed by Nimmer and Nimmer that "writings" constitutes "the most significant constitutional limitation" in the copyright provision of the clause.[270] Its most unfortunate consequence will be an ever increasing belief by courts, commentators, and future Congresses, as well as the general public, that the intellectual property clause places little or no limitation on Congress to determine what constitutes copyrightable subject matter.[271]

---

268. *See supra* text accompanying notes 211, 212.
269. *See supra* text accompanying note 226.
270. *See* NIMMER & NIMMER, *supra* note 3, § 1.03[A]. *See supra* text accompanying note 144.
271. As Gordon has noted, there is a belief that copyright is virtually unable to violate the clause, i.e., the clause places essentially no limitation on what is copyrightable. *See* Gordon, *supra* note 68.

Indeed this perspective is already evidenced by an increasing propensity of both courts and commentators to take the view that the introductory language of the clause places no limitation on what is copyrightable. Thus, Nimmer and Nimmer contend that the "to" language "must be read as largely in the nature of a preamble indicating the purpose of the power but not in limitation of its exercise."[272] Similarly, the Fifth, Eighth, and District of Columbia Circuits have held, in essence, that the "to" language places no limitation whatsoever on the copyright power of Congress.[273] In so doing, both Nimmer and Nimmer and these circuit courts ignore totally the views expressed by the Supreme Court in the nineteenth century that (a) the meaning of a congressional grant of power in the Constitution must be interpreted in the context of the words and phrases with which it is associated,[274] and (b) the "to" language does indeed constitute a limitation on what subject matter is copyrightable.[275] They also quite ignore the modern view expressed by the Court in the copyright context that the clause "describes both the objective which Congress may seek and the means to achieve it. The objective is to promote the progress of science and the useful arts."[276]

I am in sharp disagreement with the views set forth in Nimmer and Nimmer and by these circuit courts that the "to" language of the clause does not constitute any limitation on the power of Congress regarding what is copyrightable. The views expressed by Nimmer and Nimmer are internally inconsistent[277] and, in any case, are based on a false premise that

---

272. NIMMER & NIMMER, *supra* note 3, § 1.03[A].
273. Mitchel Bros. Film Group v. Cinema Adult Theater, 604 F.2d 852, 860 (5th Cir. 1979), *cert. denied*, 445 U.S. 917) (1980); Hutchinson Telephone Co. v. Fronteer Directory Co., 770 F.2d 128, 130–31 (8th Cir. 1985); Schnapper v. Foley, 667 F.2d 102, 112 (D.C. Cir. 1981), *cert. denied*, 455 U.S. 948 (1982). *Cf.* the Eleventh Circuit view that the "to" language imposes on Congress "an affirmative constitutional duty" to promote the progress of science through the issuance of copyright. *See* Cable/Home Communications Corp. v. Network Prods., Inc., 902 F.2d 829, 842 (11th Cir. 1990).
274. *See, e.g.,* Gibbons v. Ogden, 22 U.S. (9 Wheat.) 1, 187–88 (1824); Wheaton v. Peters, 33 U.S. (8 Pet.) 591, 661 (1834).
275. Baker v. Selden, 101 U.S. 99, 105 (1879); Higgins v. Keuffel, 140 U.S. 428, 430 (1891).
276. Goldstein v. California, 412 U.S. 546, 555 (1973).
277. Thus, they argue quite correctly elsewhere in the same chapter that the term "authors" as it appears in the clause must be construed in its relation to the "to" language and within the context of the subsequent term "writings." *See supra* note 51 and accompanying text.

the "to" language of the clause is merely a "preamble" without substantive meaning. This is certainly not the view taken by those most familiar with the clause early in the nineteenth century,[278] or by the Supreme Court in both the patent[279] and copyright[280] context in modern times.

Because both the Eighth and the D.C. Circuits relied on the views expressed by the Fifth Circuit in *Mitchell Bros.* in 1979 to hold that the "to" language does not limit the power of Congress to determine what is copyrightable, some perspective must be given to the views expressed by the Fifth Circuit in that case to demonstrate how and why they are inconsistent and incompatible with the interpretation of the intellectual property clause set forth in the earlier 1966 case of *Graham v. John Deere Co.* and the subsequent 1991 case of *Feist Publications, Inc. v. Rural Telephone Service Co., Inc.* (499 U.S. 340 (1991)).

According to the Fifth Circuit, there is no constitutional impediment to a congressional determination "that the best way to promote creativity is not to impose any governmental restrictions on the subject matter of copyrightable works."[281] This is correct insofar as it pertains to restrictions that fall within congressional authority, but it is incorrect to the extent that it suggests that there are no constitutional limitations on the subject matter of copyrightable works. Thus, the Fifth Circuit's conclusion that "the protection of all writings, without regard to their content, is a constitutionally permissible means of promoting science and the useful arts"[282] is overbroad because it inherently assumes that any writing may be copyrighted.[283] As the Supreme Court made clear in *Feist* that simply is not the case.

One may reasonably ask why Nimmer and Nimmer interpret the holding in *Mitchell Bros.* as being that the "to" language of the intellectual property clause does not in any sense require or obligate that "writings" protected by copyright actually promote the progress of science or useful arts but rather only requires that Congress promote these ends in its

---

278. *See* Chapter Five, Parts A and B.
279. Graham v. John Deere Co., 383 U.S. 1, 5–6 (1966); Anderson's Black Rock, Inc. v. Pavement Salvage Co., 396 U.S. 57, 61 (1969).
280. Goldstein v. California, 412 U.S. 546, 555 (1973). *See supra* text accompanying note 276.
281. *Mitchell Bros.*, 604 F.2d at 860.
282. *Id.*
283. It is highly questionable whether the Framers would have advocated or endorsed such a view when the Constitution was drafted. Although no one raised the question, had they been asked, it is likely that there would have been a unanimous view that the contents of certain writings were beyond the pale when it came to promoting the progress of science.

copyright legislation.[284] Aside from the fact that the distinction suggested by Nimmer and Nimmer appears to have no substantive meaning, their interpretation simply misrepresents the actual holding in *Mitchell Bros.*[285] What Nimmer and Nimmer really appear to be suggesting is a rationale for the holding in *Mitchell Bros.*, but again they have it wrong.

The actual rationale for the holding in *Mitchell Bros.* was that the Supreme Court had set forth a "broad view of the congressional powers granted by [the intellectual property] Clause,"[286] but as a practical matter the two primary Supreme Court opinions, *Graham v. John Deere Co.* and *McCulloch v. Maryland,* cited as supporting it, do not in fact provide authority for such a far-reaching rationale. Rather, they clearly indicate that congressional discretion is bounded and restricted by the limits set in the clause itself on the constitutional grant of authority to Congress.[287]

Nimmer and Nimmer, however, rely on the following language quoted in *Mitchell Bros.*:

> The words of the copyright clause of the constitution do not require that *writings* shall promote science or useful arts: they require that *Congress* shall promote those ends. It could well be argued that by passing general laws to protect all works, Congress better fulfills its designated ends than it would by denying protection to all books the content of which were open to real or imagined objection. . . .[288]

But the Supreme Court has never adopted such an over-reaching interpretation of the intellectual property clause.[289] Such an interpretation suggests that the actual language of patent and copyright statutes is irrelevant, so long as Congress intends to promote the progress of science and useful arts. While Congress has discretion to be more restrictive than the grant of authority given to it by the clause, it may not act in a manner that is more expansive than that grant.

The Supreme Court had an excellent opportunity in *Feist* to address the meaning to be given to the "to" language of the clause, but chose not

---

284. *See* NIMMER & NIMMER, *supra* note 3, § 1.03[B]. *See also* text accompanying note 61, *supra.*
285. *See* text accompanying note 282, *supra.*
286. 604 F.2d at 859.
287. *See, e.g.,* Chapter Five, text accompanying note 51, *supra,* and Chapter Ten, text accompanying note 78, *infra.*
288. 604 F.2d 860, quoting Philips, *Copyright in Obscene Works: Some British and American Problems,* 6 ANGLO-AM. L. REV. 138, 165–66 (1974).
289. Rather in *Feist* it has clearly indicated that Congress does not have constitutional authority to grant copyright protection to "all works."

to exercise it. Thus, its holding that originality, and with it a modicum of creativity, is constitutionally required for copyright could easily have been predicated on an interpretation of the "to" language of the clause rather than on earlier attempts by the Court to define the terms "authors" and "writings."[290] The Court could readily have held that originality is necessary to satisfy the constitutional requirement that the "writing" be such as to promote the progress of science.[291] For this same reason, it could readily have held that a modicum of creativity is necessary before a writing actually promotes the progress of science as required by the clause. Indeed, its conclusion that "copyright rewards originality, not effort"[292] finds its most obvious support in the "to" language of the clause.

If as the Court stressed in *Goldstein* the clause sets forth both the object of copyright and the means of achieving that object, it is difficult to understand why novelty and originality are not equated under the "to" language, yet *Feist* makes clear that they are not.[293] Why granting an exclusive right in a writing that is not novel in any way promotes the progress of science is simply not apparent. Indeed, the *Feist* Court seems—perhaps inadvertently—to have used quite inconsistent language in arguing that originality is not novelty but at the same time stating that the writing at

---

290. The Court could easily have taken an approach along the lines adopted by the Seventh Circuit at the end of the nineteenth century when it declared: "Large discretion is lodged in the Congress with respect to the subjects which could properly be included within the constitutional provision; but that discretion is not unlimited. . . . [I]t is restricted to the promotion of the progress of science and the useful arts." J. L. Mott Iron Works v. Clow, 82 Fed. 316, 318–20 (7th Cir. 1897).

291. Much in the same fashion as the Court had held that novelty is a constitutional requirement for "discoveries" to promote the progress of useful arts. Thus the Court has stated:

> The Patent Clause itself reflects a balance between the need to encourage innovation and the avoidance of monopolies which stifle competition without any concomitant advance in the "Progress of Science and useful Arts." As we have noted in the past, the Clause contains both a grant of power and certain limitations upon the exercise of that power. . . . The novelty and nonobviousness requirements of patentability embody a congressional understanding, implicit in the Patent Clause itself, that free exploitation of ideas will be the rule, to which the protection of a federal patent is the exception.

  Bonito Boats, Inc. v. Thunder Craft Boats, Inc., 489 U.S. 141, 146, 151 (1989).

292. 499 U.S. at 364.

293. *Id.* at 345.

issue "could not be more obvious."[294] If a modicum of creativity is indeed required for copyrightability, as emphasized in *Feist*, and if the object is indeed to promote the progress of science, then novelty rather than originality ought to be the constitutional requisite for copyrightability.[295]

---

294. *Id.* at 362.
295. Contrast the view expressed by Dreyfuss that "the constitutional portion of the *Feist* decision puts information products beyond the reach of the Copyright Clause because nothing in the real world is original enough to protect, no matter how difficult it might be to retrieve." Rochelle Cooper Dreyfuss, *A Wiseguy's Approach to Information Products: Muscling Copyright and Patent into a Unitary Theory of Intellectual Property*, [1992] SUP. CT. REV. 195, 221.

CHAPTER TEN
EXTERNAL RELATIONSHIPS

The time has now come to examine the clause in a broader perspective. To this point, its internal language has been reviewed in detail. We turn now to an external focus on the clause with a closer perusal of its relationship to state patent and copyright law and its relationship to the other enumerated grants of congressional power. To what extent over time has the clause been perceived as preempting state patent and copyright authority and precluding Congress from reliance on other enumerated powers to avoid real or perceived limitations in the clause?

A. Preemption

In the 1780s a number of the states began issuing what would now be called patents. The practice largely ended in 1790 with the advent of the first federal patent statute, although a few states, most notably New York, continued to issue state patents into the nineteenth century. It is difficult to know how many of these early state patents were issued, but the total was probably something less than forty.[1] Between the beginning of 1783 and the close of 1786 twelve states enacted general copyright statutes, although most of these statutes apparently never became operative.[2]

An interesting aspect of the first patent and copyright statutes enacted in 1790 is their failure to give any indication of the effect, if any, of the grant of a federal patent or copyright on an existing state grant for the same work. One would never know from the Patent Act of 1790 that state patents even existed. The Copyright Act of 1790 made reference to the

---

1. For a discussion of this early state patent practice, see Edward C. Walterscheid, *The Early Evolution of the U.S. Patent Law (Part 5)*, 78 J. PAT. & TRADEMARK OFF. SOC'Y 665 (1996).
2. *Id.* Bugbee discloses four state copyrights issued in Connecticut and one in South Carolina. *See* BRUCE W. BUGBEE, GENESIS OF AMERICAN PATENT AND COPYRIGHT LAW at 110, 124 (Washington 1967).

copyright of maps, charts, and books already printed,[3] but this was almost certainly directed to a perceived common-law copyright rather than any state copyright.[4] It is likely that the first federal Congress assumed that its exercise of its patent and copyright authority under the intellectual property clause preempted state authority in this regard.[5]

Indeed, the enactment of federal patent and copyright laws in 1790 was largely viewed as removing the need for state patents and copyrights,

---

3. Section 1 of the Act declared:

> That from and after the passing of this act, the author and authors of any map, chart, book or books already printed within these United States, being a citizen or citizens thereof, or resident within the same, his or their executors, administrators or assigns, who hath or have not transferred to any other person the copyright of such map, chart, book or books, share or shares thereof; and any other person or persons, being a citizen or citizens of these United States, or resident therein, his or their executors, administrators or assigns, who hath or have purchased or legally acquired the copyright of any such map, chart, book or books, in order to print, reprint, publish or vend the same, shall have the sole right and liberty of printing, reprinting, publishing and vending such map, chart, book or books, for the term of fourteen years from the recording the title thereof in the clerk's office, as is herein after directed.

   Copyright Act of 1790. *See* MELVILLE B. NIMMER & DAVID NIMMER, 8 NIMMER ON COPYRIGHT App. 7-41 [Rel. 34-12/93].

4. *See supra* Chapter Six, notes 78–81 and accompanying text. The D.C. Circuit, however, based solely on the reference to the copyright of already printed works in the Copyright Act of 1790, has assumed that "the first Congress made the Copyright Act of 1790 applicable to subsisting copyrights arising under the copyright laws of the several states." Eldred v. Reno, 293 F.3d 372, 379 (D.C. Cir. 2001). This assumption is not supported either by the literal language of the statute or by any other contemporaneous evidence, and is almost certainly incorrect. The federal act created an entirely new federal copyright, rather than extending the term of subsisting state copyrights as alleged by the D.C. Circuit.

5. As Rawle put it in 1825, "there can be little doubt that, as soon as congress legislated on the subject, (which was as early as the second session, 1790,) all the state provisions ceased. . . ." WILLIAM RAWLE, A VIEW OF THE CONSTITUTION OF THE UNITED STATES OF AMERICA at 102 (Philadelphia 1825). But apparently such a view was not universally shared, for Bugbee points to a copyright issued by South Carolina in 1792. BRUCE BUGBEE, GENESIS OF AMERICAN PATENT AND COPYRIGHT LAW at 124 (Washington 1967). Moreover, Rawle makes no mention of the views expressed by Chief Justice Kent in *Livingston v. Van Ingen* in 1812. *See* text accompanying note 20, *infra*.

because the advantages of uniformity and broader protection inherent in the federal system were obvious to almost everyone. The point was brought home in a New Hampshire patent issued in 1790 which stated that

> in case the [inventor] shall obtain a patent from the General Government of the United States, for the exclusive privilege of building and altering chimneys as aforesaid, and said patent shall extend to and operate in this State on the receipt thereof by the [inventor], this act shall be void.[6]

Jefferson, who as secretary of state was responsible for administering the Patent Act of 1790, sought to establish this point with a patent bill introduced in early 1791 which provided that

> where any State before it's [sic] accession to the present form of Government, or the adoption of the said form by nine States, shall have granted an exclusive right to any invention, the party claiming the right shall not be capable of obtaining an exclusive right under this act, but on relinquishing his right in and under such particular State, so as that obtaining equal benefits he may be subject to equal restrictions with the other Citizens of the United States, and of such relinquishments his obtaining an exclusive right under this act shall be sufficient evidence.[7]

This language in slightly modified form became a part of the Patent Act of 1793.[8]

Because of the differing terms and conditions between state patents and a federal patent, it made a great deal of practical sense to require the surrender of state patent rights in order to obtain a federal patent for the same invention. But why was the surrender of rights limited only to those state patents that had issued prior to ratification of the Constitution by the particular states? Clearly, the same concerns would exist regarding state

---

6. Walterscheid, *supra* note 1, at 684.
7. *See* H.R. 121 introduced February 7, 1791, reproduced as Appendix VI *in* EDWARD C. WALTERSCHEID, TO PROMOTE THE PROGRESS OF USEFUL ARTS: AMERICAN PATENT LAW AND ADMINISTRATION, 1787–1836 (Littleton, CO 1998).
8. *See* § 7, Act of February 21, 1793, 1 Stat. 318. The statute provided

> that where any State, before its adoption of the present form of government, shall have granted an exclusive right to any invention, the party claiming that right shall not be capable of obtaining an exclusive right under this act, but on relinquishing his right und such particular State, and of such relinquishment, his obtaining an exclusive right under this act shall be sufficient evidence.

patents issued after ratification. The limitation proposed by Jefferson and accepted by Congress can only be explained on the supposition that they believed that once a state ratified the Constitution it no longer had authority to issue its own state patents. That is, they believed that the language of the intellectual property clause preempted state authority to issue patents (and presumably copyrights as well).[9] Otherwise, there would have been no good reason to limit the surrender requirement to state patents issued before ratification and not include those issued after ratification.

But did the clause in fact preempt states from issuing patents and copyrights? Remarkably, the issue seems not to have been addressed in any early federal patent or copyright opinion. But it was addressed, albeit in an odd way, in the 1812 New York state case of *Livingston v. Van Ingen*.[10] The appellants, Robert Livingston and Robert Fulton, by several acts of the New York legislature, had been granted the exclusive right to navigate the waters of the state using steamboats and sought an injunction prohibiting the operation of another competing steamboat on the Hudson River. The New York Court of Chancery refused to grant the injunction and the case was an appeal of that refusal. One of the primary arguments against the injunction was that the several acts of the New York legislature granting the exclusive right were repugnant to the intellectual property clause, i.e., the clause precluded or preempted the right of the legislature to grant such an exclusive right. The New York Supreme Court[11] held the legislative acts in question valid, reversed the Chancery order, and granted the injunction.

Needless to say, the opposing parties interpreted the clause and its effect quite differently. There were two basic issues raised with respect to the clause: (1) whether the patent power given to Congress was concurrent with the patent power of the states or was exclusive; and (2) the effect of the use of the term "inventors" in the clause. Interestingly, it seems to have been generally conceded that Livingston and Fulton were not the inventors of the steamboat.[12] Rather they contended that they were the "possessors" of steamboat technology which they had introduced into the state and were effectively employing in return for the exclusive right.

---

9. But only a few state copyrights actually ever were issued. *See supra* note 2.
10. 9 Johns. R. 507 (N.Y. 1812l).
11. The technical name of the court at this time was the Court for the Trial of Impeachments and Correction of Errors.
12. Contrary to what millions of American school children have been taught for lo these many years, Fulton did not invent the steamboat and acknowledged as much in this case.

With regard to the intellectual property clause, they argued that:

The power of granting patents or exclusive privileges not being, in its own nature, exclusive, nor *expressly* prohibited to the states, remains in the states, and may be concurrently exercised by them. But suppose the patent power in congress to be exclusive. On what is it to operate? It is limited, in its application, to *authors* and *inventors*. There cannot be a patent for a thing before known. The object of the patent must be the patentee's own invention, otherwise, the patent is void. It is different in *England,* for there a patent may be granted to the importers of useful inventions and improvements. This is a *strict* power in congress, and cannot be extended. Congress cannot grant an exclusive privilege or monopoly.... The appellants set up no right under a power granted by the constitution to congress. The bill exhibits nothing interfering with the powers granted to the *United States.* The appellants do not... pretend to any invention or discovery; but merely that they *possessed* the means by which boats might be propelled by steam; and they ask only to be secured in their privilege of making the experiment.[13]

This was a classic argument in the alternative. First, they argued that the patent power of Congress and the states was concurrent. Secondly, if this was not the case, they argued that the exclusive right given them by New York was not a patent of the type contemplated by the intellectual property clause. Rather, what New York had granted was equivalent to a patent of importation, which Congress was not authorized by the clause to grant, but which the states retained the right to grant.[14] Moreover, patents of importation were highly desirable, just as had been found to be the case in England.

Respondents argued just the reverse. In their view, the patent power was not concurrent but exclusive with Congress, because "[the states have, by mutual consent, transferred the power to Congress, to whom it necessarily,

---

13. 9 Johns. R. at 530–31.
14. The gist of the argument was that the term "inventors" in the clause referred only to the first and original inventor anywhere in the world, and hence Congress was not authorized to grant patents of importation. I have elsewhere in this work suggested that there was nothing in the contemporaneous definition of "inventor" or "invention" that obligated such an interpretation and nothing to suggest that the Framers actually intended to preclude Congress from having a power to authorize patents of importation. *See* Chapter Eight, Parts B and C.

and of right, belongs."[15] Moreover, any argument that appellants were not "inventors" within the meaning of the clause would defeat the whole purpose of the patent power placed in Congress. As they put it:

> Again, it is said that although congress have the power to grant exclusive rights to authors and inventors; yet this act, not being a reward or grant to an inventor, does not interfere with the power of congress. The appellants claim only as *possessors*. But if the appellants had claimed to be the *inventors*, could this state have granted to them the exclusive privilege?[16] Shall they, by changing their character to that of a *possessor*, obtain it? Certainly not; for the whole patent power in congress might, in that way, be defeated. The state by granting such privileges to *possessors*, would exercise a power superior to and far more extensive than that of Congress. Is the mere possessor to be preferred to the inventor? The object of exclusive privilege is to secure to genius the fruits of its exertions, and to the public the benefits flowing from these intellectual labors.[17]

The essence of this argument was that no intellectual labor was involved, and it was only in return for a public disclosure of the inventive results of intellectual labor, that an exclusive right, otherwise denominated a monopoly, could be justified.

The appellate judges hearing the case were of the opinion that (a) patents of importation were generally desirable, (b) the intellectual property clause did not authorize Congress to grant patents of importation, and (c) accordingly it did not preclude the state from granting this exclusive right to Messrs. Livingston and Fulton which they viewed as

---

15. 9 Johns. R. at 540.
16. This was clearly intended to be a rhetorical question, for respondents obviously believed and argued that patent power authorized by the intellectual property clause was exclusive.
17. 9 Johns. R. at 542.

akin to a patent of importation.[18] On the issue of concurrency, Chief Justice
Kent stated that the grant of power to Congress in the clause

> only secures, for a limited time, to authors and inventors the exclusive
> privilege to their writings and discoveries; and as it is not granted by
> exclusive words, to the *United States,* nor prohibited to the individual
> states, it is a concurrent power which may be exercised by the states in
> a variety of cases, without any infringement of the congressional power.
> A state cannot take away from an individual his patent right, and render
> it common to all citizens. This would contravene the act of Congress,
> and would be, therefore, unlawful. But if an author or inventor, instead
> of resorting to the act of congress, should apply to the legislature of this
> state for an exclusive right to his production, I see nothing to hinder the
> state from granting it, and the operation of the grant would, of course,
> be confined to the limits of this state. Within our own jurisdiction, it
> would be complete and perfect. So a patentee under the act of congress
> may have the time of his monopoly extended by the legislature of any
> state, beyond the term of fourteen or twenty eight years allowed by that
> law.[19] Congress may secure, for a limited time, an exclusive right
> throughout the union; but there is nothing in the constitution to take
> away from the states the power to enlarge the privilege within their
> respective jurisdictions. The states are not entirely devested [sic] of
> their original sovereignty over the subject matter; and whatever power
> has not been clearly granted to the union, remains with them.[20]

It is of interest to explore in more detail what Kent is saying—and not
saying here—and the validity of his statements.

---

18. As Justice Yates put it:

> The beneficial effects experienced by other countries, particularly
> *England,* sufficiently show the policy and propriety of passing laws for the
> encouragement of imported invention. This power, then, evidently
> necessary and useful, is not granted to congress by the clause as to authors
> and inventors, and as it is not taken away by any other part of the constitu-
> tion, it must, of course, be retained by the respective states, to be exer-
> cised by them, until it interferes with the laws of the *United States,* passed
> to secure the author or inventor.

9 Johns. R. at 560–61.
19. Here Kent confused the patent statute and the copyright statute. The patent
statute did not authorize any patent term longer than 14 years, whereas the
copyright statute authorized an initial 14-year term and a renewal term of
another 14 years, provided that the copyright holder was still living at the time
the renewal was sought.
20. 9 Johns. R. at 581–82.

It is apparent that Kent believed that the federal patent and copyright powers were concurrent with those of the states and not exclusive, and that there was nothing in the intellectual property clause to suggest that they were exclusive. Thus, where the federal power had not been exercised, e.g., where an individual had not sought either a federal patent or a federal copyright, he argued that it was perfectly within the sovereignty of the state to grant an exclusive right to the individual's "production" within the jurisdiction of the state. He also recognized, however, that at least in some circumstances, the federal power was paramount over the state power, for example, a state could not void a federal patent grant within its jurisdiction.

Kent did not specifically address the question of the effect, if any, of the issuance of a federal patent on the patent rights granted by a state patent issued after the state had ratified the Constitution. Recall that this situation was not literally addressed by the language of the Patent Act of 1793. His statement that the Constitution did not take away from the states the power to enlarge the patent privilege, e.g., by extending the term of a federal patent within their jurisdiction, was of doubtful validity in 1812 and most certainly would be deemed invalid today.[21] It of course ignores the express language of the intellectual property clause that the exclusive right is to be granted "for limited times." Under the clause, Congress alone has discretion to set the term of patents and copyrights, and once that term has expired, the clear intent of the clause is that the subject matter of the particular patent or copyright shall go into the public domain to be available for use or reproduction by all throughout the United States. Under Kent's interpretation, any state could preclude this from happening by simply extending the term of the federal patent within its jurisdiction. If this had actually occurred, and there is nothing to indicate that any state actually attempted to extend the term of a federal patent, the result would have been a patchwork of patent rights in the various states, a result which

---

21. Sears, Roebuck & Co. v. Stiffel Co., 376 U.S. 225, 231 (1964) ("[o]bviously a State could not, consistently with the Supremacy Clause of the Constitution, extend the life of a patent beyond its expiration date or give a patent on an article which lacked the level of invention required for federal patents"). The supremacy clause states:

> This Constitution, and the Laws of the United States which shall be made in Pursuance thereof; and all Treaties made, or which shall be made, under the Authority of the United States, shall be the supreme Law of the Land; and the Judges in every State shall be bound thereby, any Thing in the Constitution or Laws of any State to the Contrary notwithstanding.

U.S. CONST. art. VI. *But see* note 34, *infra,* and accompanying text.

the Framers clearly intended to avoid by the constitutional authorization for federal patents and copyrights.[22]

Despite the literal language of the Patent Act of 1793 and despite the views expressed by Chief Justice Kent, there seems to have been a general perception at the beginning of the nineteenth century that the issuance of a federal patent would invalidate any state patent for the same invention. It should be noted that this issue was not literally reached in *Livingston v. Van Ingen* because the steamboat monopoly was denominated as a patent of importation and the judges in that case interpreted the intellectual property clause as not granting authority to Congress with respect to patents of importation.

Because of its economic impact it was inevitable that the validity of the New York steamboat monopoly would ultimately be decided by the Supreme Court of the United States. The issue reached the Court in 1824 in *Gibbons v. Ogden*.[23] There, counsel for Ogden, arguing that the monopoly was valid, nonetheless admitted that "if a patent or copy-right should be obtained under the law of Congress, the right under the state grant would cease as against that of the United States."[24] But he contended that such was not the case with regard to the steamboat monopoly, and that in essence all that had been granted by New York was a patent of importation

---

22. Twelve years later in *Gibbons v. Ogden,* the attorney general would make precisely this argument in contending that the patent and copyright power was exclusive to the federal government under the intellectual property clause. As the attorney general put it:

> The law of Congress declares that all inventors of useful improvements throughout the United States shall be entitled to the exclusive right in their discoveries for fourteen years only. The law of New York declares that this inventor shall be entitled to the exclusive use of his invention for thirty years, and as much longer as the state shall permit. The law of Congress, by limiting the exclusive right to fourteen years, in effect declares that after the expiration of that time the discovery shall be the common right of the whole people of the United States. The law of New York declares that it shall not, after fourteen years, be the exclusive right of the people of the United States, but that it shall be the exclusive right of this inventor for thirty years, and for so much longer as she, in her sovereign will and pleasure, may permit. If this be not repugnance [to the intellectual property clause], direct and palpable, we must have a new vocabulary for the definition of the word.

22 U.S. (9 Wheat.) 1, 171 (1824).
23. 22 U.S. (9 Wheat.) 1 (1824).
24. *Id.* at 47.

444   THE NATURE OF THE INTELLECTUAL PROPERTY CLAUSE

which it was within its power to grant, because Congress had no authority with respect to such grants. He thus echoed the arguments that were found persuasive in *Livingston v. Van Ingen*. The Supreme Court, however, did not reach the issue of whether the steamboat monopoly violated the intellectual property clause. Instead the monopoly was invalidated on the ground that it violated the commerce clause.

It would take almost another 150 years before the Court would address the issue of the extent to which the intellectual property clause preempted state patent and copyright power. The occasion was *Goldstein v. California*[25] decided in 1973. Goldstein and several others were charged with a violation of the California Penal Code for pirating records and tapes of musical performances, and before the Supreme Court they argued that the California statute in question established a state copyright of unlimited duration and thus conflicted with the intellectual property clause.[26] As the Court noted, this argument rested "on the premise that the state statute under which they were convicted lies beyond the powers which the States reserved in our federal system."[27] A bare majority of the Court concluded "that the State of California has exercised a power which it retained under the Constitution, and that the challenged statute, as applied in this case, does not intrude into an area which Congress, up to now, has pre-empted."[28]

The majority began their analysis by noting that the principles the Court relies on in construing state power are those set forth by Alexander Hamilton in *The Federalist No. 32*. As stated therein, under the Constitution, states

> clearly retain all the rights of sovereignty which they before had, and which were not, by that act, *exclusively* delegated to the United States. This exclusive delegation, or rather this alienation, of State sovereignty, would only exist in three cases: where the Constitution in express terms granted an exclusive authority to the Union; where it granted in one instance an authority to the Union, and in another prohibited the States from exercising the like authority; and where it granted an authority to the Union, to which a similar authority in the States would be absolutely and totally *contradictory* and *repugnant*.[29]

---

25. 412 U.S. 546 (1973).
26. *Id.* at 551.
27. *Id.* at 552.
28. *Id.* at 571.
29. *Id.* at 553.

It pointed out that Hamilton's first two conditions for exclusive authority in the federal government, otherwise known as preemption, do not exist regarding the intellectual property clause.[30] Thus, for preemption of state patent and copyright power to exist, it must be found under Hamilton's third condition. But it emphasized that in addressing this condition:

> We must . . . be careful to distinguish those situations in which the concurrent exercise of a power by the Federal Government and the States or by the States alone *may possibly* lead to conflicts and those situations where conflicts *will necessarily* arise. "It is not . . . a mere possibility of inconvenience in the exercise of powers, but an immediate constitutional repugnancy that can by implication alienate a pre-existing right of [state] sovereignty."[31]

With this in mind, the Court concluded that the third condition for preemption also was not met because:

> [the subject matter to which the Copyright Clause is addressed may at times be of purely local concern. No conflict will necessarily arise from a lack of uniform state regulation, nor will the interest of one State be significantly prejudiced by the actions of another. No reason exists why Congress must take affirmative action either to authorize protection of all categories of writings[32] or to free them from all restraint.[33]

It accordingly held that "under the Constitution, the States have not relinquished all power to grant to authors 'the exclusive Right to their respective Writings.'"[34]

It then went on to hold that even if the California statute effectively created a state copyright of unlimited duration, this did not violate the intellectual property clause because

> it is not clear that the dangers to which this limitation [i.e., "for limited times"] was addressed apply with equal force to both the Federal Government and the States. When Congress grants an exclusive right or monopoly, its effects are pervasive; no citizen or State may escape its

---

30. *Id.* According to the Court: "The clause of the Constitution granting to Congress the power to issue copyrights does not provide that such power shall vest exclusively in the Federal Government. Nor does the Constitution provide that such power shall not be exercised by the States." *Id.*
31. 412 U.S. at 554–55, citing *The Federalist No. 32.*
32. At the time the record and tape piracy occurred, sound recordings had been excluded from copyright coverage.
33. 412 U.S. at 560.
34. *Id.*

reach. As we have noted, however, the exclusive right granted by a
State is confined to its borders. Consequently, even when the right is
unlimited in duration, any tendency to inhibit the further progress of
science or the arts is narrowly circumscribed.[35]

Strong dissents by four Justices[36] pointed out that these views by the
majority were simply inconsistent with the position the Court had taken
nine years earlier in *Sears, Roebuck & Co. v. Stiffel Co.*[37] and in *Compco Corp.
v. Day-Brite Lightings, Inc.,*[38] as indeed they appeared to be. Thus in *Sears*
the Court had stated:

> Obviously a State could not, consistently with the Supremacy Clause
> of the Constitution, extend the life of a patent beyond its expiration
> date or give a patent on an article which lacked the level of invention
> required for federal patents. To do either would run counter to the
> policy of Congress of granting patents only for true inventions, and then
> only for a limited time. Just as a State cannot encroach upon the federal
> patent laws directly, it cannot, under some other law, such as that of
> forbidding unfair competition, give protection of a kind that clashes
> with the objectives of the federal patent laws.[39]

Whereas *Sears* spoke in the context of the "policy of Congress," *Compco*
made clear that this policy was in fact found in the language of the intellectual property clause, saying that to forbid copying of an article unprotected
by either a patent or a copyright "would interfere with the federal policy"
found in the clause "of allowing free access to copy whatever the federal
patent and copyright statutes leave in the public domain."[40]

A year after *Goldstein*, the Court addressed the issue of preemption in
the patent context in *Kewanee Oil Co. v. Bicron Corp.*[41] It held that Ohio
trade secret law was not preempted by federal patent law,[42] and declared:

> Just as the States may exercise regulatory power over writings so may
> the States regulate with respect to discoveries. States may hold diverse
> viewpoints in protecting intellectual property relating to invention as
> they do in protecting intellectual property relating to the subject matter

---

35. *Id.* at 560–61.
36. *Id.* at 572, 576.
37. 376 U.S. 225 (1964).
38. *Id.* at 234.
39. *Id.* at 230–31.
40. *Id.* at 237.
41. 416 U.S. 470 (1974).
42. *Id.* at 493.

of copyright. The only limitation on the States is that in regulating the area of patents and copyrights they do not conflict with the operation of the laws in this area passed by Congress. . . ."[43]

It also pointed out that it had articulated another policy of the patent law, namely, "that which is in the public domain cannot be removed therefrom by action of the States."[44] *Goldstein, Sears,* and *Compco* all were cited as authority for this view, despite the fact that *Goldstein* seemed to reflect a very different view.

The Court again addressed the preemption issue in *Bonito Boats, Inc. v. Thunder Craft Boats, Inc.*[45] decided in 1989. Dreyfuss has argued that *Sears* and *Compco* effectively stood for the view that "works that did not measure up to the level of protection required by patent and copyright law could not be protected by the states," and that these cases appeared to have been implicitly overruled by *Goldstein* and *Kewanee* until they were revived by *Bonito Boats.*[46] It thus behooves us to take a closer look at *Bonito Boats.*

The *Bonito Boats* Court stated that its decisions since *Sears* and *Compco* "have made it clear that the Patent and Copyright Clauses do not, by their own force or by negative implication, deprive the States of the power to adopt rules for the promotion of intellectual creation within their own jurisdictions."[47] But this did not mean that its *Sears* and *Compco* opinions were no longer valid. Rather, there had been a tendency to interpret their holdings over broadly, and the Court now took the opportunity to explain them in a more restrictive light.

The Court began its re-examination of these cases by noting that "[w]e have long held that after the expiration of a federal patent, the subject matter of the patent passes to the free use of the public as a matter of

---

43. *Id.* at 479.
44. *Id.* at 481.
45. 489 U.S. 141 (1989).
46. Rochelle Cooper Dreyfuss, *A Wiseguy's Approach to Information Products: Muscling Copyright and Patent into a Unitary Theory of Intellectual Property,* 1992 S. CT. REV. 195, 213.
47. 489 U.S. at 165. *Cf.* the contention by Dreyfuss that *Bonito Boats*

　　stands for the proposition that the national interest in encouraging the progress of science and useful arts is exhausted by conferring upon Congress the limited right to act with respect to writings and discoveries, authors and inventors. There is no residual interest, and therefore no residual power, in the states.

　　Dreyfuss, *supra* note 46, at 230.

federal law."[48] Moreover, "[w]here the public has paid the congressionally mandated price for disclosure, the States may not render the exchange fruitless by offering patent-like protection to the subject matter of the expired patent."[49] In *Sears* and *Compco*, "we found that the publicly known design and utilitarian ideas which were unprotected by patent occupied much the same position as the subject matter of an expired patent."[50] This, however, did not mean that "the States are completely disabled from offering any form of protection to articles or processes which fall into the broad scope of patentable subject matter." Rather, there is "an implicit recognition that all state regulation of potentially patentable but unpatented subject matter is not ipso facto pre-empted by the federal patent laws."[51] But the *Sears* Court "correctly concluded that States may not offer patent-like protection to intellectual creations which would otherwise remain unprotected as a matter of law."[52]

The *Bonito Boats* Court emphasized, however, that "[o]ne of the fundamental purposes behind the Patent and Copyright Clauses of the Constitution was to promote national uniformity in the realm of intellectual property."[53] On what basis states retained authority within their own jurisdictions to regulate patents and copyrights in light of this fundamental purpose of the intellectual property clause was not stated.

B. Preclusion

The constitutional basis for patent and copyright legislation has traditionally been found in the intellectual property clause.[54] Whereas pre-emption addresses the relative roles of the states and the federal government in the regulation and control of patents and copyrights in light of the language of the intellectual property clause, preclusion considers the relative roles of the intellectual property clause and the other enumerated

---

48. 489 U.S. at 152, citing Coats v. Merrick Thread Co., 149 U.S. 562, 572 (1893); Kellogg Co. v. National Biscuit Co., 305 U.S. 111 (1938); Singer Mfg. Co. v. June Mfg. Co., 163 U.S. 169 (1896).
49. 489 U.S. at 152.
50. *Id.*
51. *Id.* at 154.
52. *Id.* at 156.
53. *Id.* at 162.
54. *See, e.g.,* Brown v. Duchesne, 60 U.S. (19 How.) 183, 195 (1857) (Congress presumed to enact patent and copyright legislation under the intellectual property clause unless it indicates otherwise).

clauses granting power to Congress. The basic issue in cases involving preclusion is the extent to which Congress may rely on its other more broadly interpreted grants of power to avoid limitations on its copyright and patent power set forth in the intellectual property clause. Phrased somewhat differently, to what extent do limitations in the clause, either explicit or implied, constrain the ability of Congress to act under its other Article I powers.[55] But the issue may be just the reverse, i.e., the extent to which the intellectual property clause may be used to avoid limitations on congressional power set forth elsewhere, e.g., the First Amendment.

The issue of preclusion is in no way unique to the intellectual property clause, but has in recent times assumed a particular relevance with regard

---

55. This question is increasingly being raised by commentators, with the answer that Congress does not have authority to avoid such limitations by purporting to act under another grant of power. *See, e.g.,* William Patry, *The Enumerated Powers Doctrine and Intellectual Property: An Imminent Constitutional Collision,* 67 GEO. WASH. L. REV. 359, 361 (1999) ("[w]hen a specific clause of the Constitution, such as Clause 8 of Article I, Section 8, has been construed as containing general limitations on Congress's power, Congress may not avoid those limitation by legislating under another clause"); Malla Pollack, *The Right to Know?: Delimiting Database Protection at the Juncture of the Commerce Clause, the Intellectual Property Clause, and the First Amendment,* 17 CARDOZO ARTS & ENT. L.J. 47, 60 (1999) ("Congress may not do an end run around a limitation in one clause of the Constitution by invoking a more general clause"); Theodore H. Davis Jr., COPYING IN THE SHADOW OF THE CONSTITUTION: THE RATIONAL LIMITS OF TRADE DRESS PROTECTION, 80 MINN. L. REV. 595, 640 (1996) ("Congress cannot override constitutional limitations on its on authority merely by invoking the Commerce Clause"); Michael F. Finn, *"Just the Facts, Ma'am": The Effect of the Supreme Court's Decision in Feist Publications, Inc. v. Rural Telephone Service Co. on the Colorization of Black and White Films,* 33 SANTA CLARA L. REV. 859, 871 (1993) ("[i]t seems likely that the same rationale present in *Gibbons* would also bar any type of Commerce Clause legislation aimed at removing limitations of the Intellectual Property Clause"); Rochelle C. Dreyfuss, *A Wiseguy's Approach to Information Products: Muscling Copyright and Patents into a Unitary Theory of Intellectual Property,* 1992 S. CT. REV. 195, 230 ("[r]estrictions on constitutional grants of legislative power, such as the Copyright Clause, would be meaningless if Congress could evade them simply by announcing that it was acting under some broader authority"); John J. Flynn, *The Orphan Drug Act: An Unconstitutional Exercise of the Patent Power,* 1992 UTAH L. REV. 389, 414 n.81 ("the Commerce Clause and the Patent Clause should be read together as establishing an implicit policy of precluding federal government from granting private parties unregulated and exclusive monopolies over economic activity other than that authorized by the Patent Clause").

to that clause because of what seems to be a concerted effort by Congress to avoid or ignore express or implied limitations in the clause.[56] What I term preclusive limitations have gone under a number of other rubrics, such as "essential postulates,"[57] "principles of constitutional weight,"[58] and "penumbral reasoning."[59]

Although not raised specifically in the context of the intellectual property clause, preclusion was one of the issues hotly contested regarding Alexander Hamilton's broad interpretation of the taxing and appropriating power under the general welfare clause as set forth in his *Report on the Subject of Manufactures* submitted to Congress in 1791.[60] Both Jefferson and Madison quickly challenged this broad interpretation on the grounds that its effect was to give unlimited powers to the federal government.[61] They argued that congressional authority is limited to that specifically authorized in the enumerated powers.

Hamilton was fully aware that his broad interpretation of the general welfare clause would be challenged on the ground that it rendered the limitations either expressly specified or inherent in the following seventeen grants of power essentially meaningless. Not so, according to him, because the limitations set forth in the other enumerated grants of power would still be in effect. As he put it: "A power to appropriate money with the latitude which is granted too in *express terms* would not carry a power to do any other thing, not authorized in the constitution, either expressly or by fair implication."[62] In other words, the power to tax and appropriate does not override particular limitations on congressional patent and copyright power set forth in the intellectual property clause.

---

56. *See* Paul. J. Heald & Suzanna Sherry, *Implied Limits on the Legislative Power: The Intellectual Property Clause as an Absolute Constraint on Congress*, 2000 ILL. L. REV. 1119, 1120.

57. *See, e.g.,* Alden v. Maine, 527 U.S. 706, 729 (1999) (quoting Monaco v. Mississippi, 292 U.S. 312, 322 (1934)); Printz v. United States, 521 U.S. 898, 981 (quoting *Monaco*, 292 U.S. at 322).

58. Heald & Sherry, *supra* note 56, at 1123.

59. Brannon P. Deming & Glenn Harlan Reynolds, *Comfortably Penumbral*, 77 B.U. L. REV. 1089, 1092 (1997).

60. *See supra* Chapter Five, notes 97, 98 and accompanying text.

61. *See supra* Chapter Five, note 115 and accompanying text.

62. *See supra* Chapter Five, note 103 and accompanying text.

Chief Justice Marshall said something quite similar in *Marbury v. Madison*.[63] He noted that "[i]t cannot be presumed, that any clause in the constitution is intended to be without effect,"[64] and went on to say:

> The powers of the legislature are defined and limited; and that those limits may not be mistaken or forgotten, the constitution is written. To what purpose are powers limited, and to what purpose is that limitation committed to writing, if these limits may, at any time, be passed by those intended to be restrained? The distinction between a government with limited and unlimited powers is abolished, if those limits do not confine the persons on whom they are imposed, if acts prohibited and acts allowed are of equal obligation.[65]

The policy enunciated by Marshall remains true today. Congress may not avoid clear constitutional limitations on a particular power granted to it by reliance on a more broadly interpreted power.

As has been seen in this work, only rarely has the Supreme Court addressed the specific authority given to Congress by the intellectual property clause or the effect of limitations in the clause on that authority. One such instance was *The Trade-Mark Cases* decided in 1879 when the Court held that the clause did not give Congress authority to issue trade-marks.[66] In modern times *The Trade-Mark Cases* have been perceived to have relevance to the issue whether the intellectual property clause precludes reliance on other enumerated powers, most specifically, the commerce clause.[67]

In *United States v. Moghadam*, decided in 1999, the Eleventh Circuit addressed the issue of "whether Congress can use its Commerce Clause power to avoid the limitations that might prevent it from passing the same legislation under the Copyright Clause."[68] The court began its analysis by noting that:

> In general, the various grants of legislative authority contained in the Constitution stand alone and must be independently analyzed. In other words, each of the powers of Congress is alternative to all of the other powers, and what cannot be done under one may very well be doable under.... [A]s a general matter, the fact that legislation reaches beyond

---

63. 5 U.S. (1 Cranch) 137 (1803).
64. *Id.* at 174.
65. *Id.* at 176.
66. 100 U.S. 82 (1879).
67. *See, e.g.,* United States v. Moghadam, 175 F.3d 1269, 1277–79 (11th Cir. 1999).
68. 175 F.3d at 1277.

the limits of one grant of legislative power has no bearing on whether it can be sustained under another.[69]

Cited in support of this view was the Supreme Court opinion in *Heart of Atlanta Motel, Inc. v. United States*.[70] Yet that case does not stand for the broad premise set forth by the Eleventh Circuit, namely, that all powers of Congress are to be assumed to be alternative to all other powers and that the limitations of one grant of power have no bearing on the applicability of another grant of power.[71]

The Eleventh Circuit in *Moghadam* did recognize the possibility "that some of the grants of legislative authority in Article I, § 8 contain significant limitations that can be said to represent the Framers' judgment that Congress should be affirmatively prohibited from passing certain types of legislation, no matter under which provision."[72] The predicate for a concern of this type was stated to be *Railway Labor Executives' Association v. Gibbons*[73] wherein the Supreme Court declared that the commerce clause could not be used as authority for a statute that directly violated the bankruptcy clause[74] because it was directed only to the bankruptcy estate of a particular railroad. According to the Court, "if we were to hold that Congress had the power to enact nonuniform bankruptcy laws pursuant to the Commerce Clause, we would eradicate from the Constitution a

---

69. *Id.*

70. 379 U.S. 241 (1964).

71. All the Supreme Court actually decided in *Heart of Atlanta Motel* was that the commerce clause provided authority to sustain the constitutionality of the public accommodation provisions of the Civil Rights Act of 1964. The Court declared that its earlier Civil Rights Cases, 109 U.S. 3 (1883), which had invalidated certain provisions of the Civil Rights Act of 1875 because not authorized by Section 5 of the Fourteenth Amendment, was "inapposite, and of no precedential value" because of the differences in the provisions at question and because the earlier Court failed to consider the applicability of the commerce clause to the issue. 379 U.S. at 250–51. At best, all the *Heart of Atlanta Motel* Court held was that there was nothing in section 5 of the Fourteenth Amendment which precluded reliance on the commerce clause as a constitutional basis for the public accommodation provisions of the Civil Rights Act of 1964.

72. 175 F.3d at 1279.

73. 455 U.S. 457 (1982).

74. U.S. CONST. art. I, § 8, cl. 4 ("[t]he Congress shall have Power . . . To establish . . . uniform Laws on the subject of Bankruptcies throughout the United States").

limitation on the power of Congress to enact bankruptcy laws."[75] Implicit in the statement is the understanding that there are certain limitations in particular grants of congressional power which may not be avoided by reliance on other more broadly interpreted powers. In other words, there are circumstances wherein each of the powers of Congress is *not* alternative to other grants of power.

For reasons which are unclear, the Eleventh Circuit failed to note a number of other Supreme Court opinions expressly indicating that there are affirmative constitutional limits on the exercise of the enumerated powers.[76] After pointing to these cases, Burchfiel declares:

> From the standpoint of such external, affirmative limitations, the commerce power is no more "plenary" than the other "plenary" powers conferred on the legislative branch by article I, including the patent power. If an affirmative constitutional limitation is imposed by the patent clause, it cannot be avoided by merely citing another enumerated power.[77]

More recently, Justice Thomas has expressed considerable doubt about the Court's use of the necessary and proper clause to support commerce clause-based legislation in lieu of specific article I, section 8 powers, saying:

> [O]n this Court's understanding of congressional power under [the commerce and necessary and proper] Clauses, many of Congress' other enumerated powers under Article I, § 8, are wholly superfluous. After all, if Congress may regulate all matters that substantially affect Commerce, there is no need for the Constitution to specify that Congress may enact bankruptcy laws . . . or to grant patents and copyrights [under] cl. 8 . . . . An interpretation of cl. 3 that makes the rest of § 8 superfluous simply cannot be correct.[78]

As Patry points out, "[i]nherent in Justice Thomas's statement is the position that the enumerated powers in the bankruptcy and patent/copyright clauses also contain limitations on Congress's powers, limitations that may not be circumvented willy-nilly by legislating under the Commerce Clause."[79]

---

75. 455 U.S. at 468–69.
76. For a brief discussion of these cases, see Kenneth J. Burchfiel, *The Constitutional Intellectual Property Power: Progress of Useful Arts and the Legal Protection of Semiconductor Technology*, 28 SANTA CLARA L. REV. 473, 507–09 (1988).
77. Burchfiel, *id.* at 509.
78. United States v. Lopez, 514 U.S. 549, 588–89 (1995) (Thomas, J., concurring).
79. William Patry, *The Enumerated Powers Doctrine and Intellectual Property: An Imminent Constitutional Collision*, 67 GEO. WASH. L. REV. 359, 372–73 (1999).

Thus the question of whether the intellectual property clause precludes congressional reliance on other more broadly interpreted enumerated powers as authority for patent-like and copyright-like grants of exclusive rights requires an initial determination of exactly what limitations are placed on congressional authority regarding patents and copyrights by the clause. Much of the earlier portion of this work has been devoted to an effort to delineate how such limitations have been viewed over time. A particularly relevant issue is the extent to which the "to" language of the clause is considered as limiting congressional authority regarding patents and copyrights.[80]

In the patent context, the Supreme Court in *Graham v. John Deere Co.* expressly held in 1966 that the "to" language limits the patent power of Congress.[81] Despite this express holding, several circuit courts have held in the copyright context that despite what the *Graham* Court declared, the "to" language really does not limit the power of Congress regarding copyright because Congress has discretion under the necessary and proper clause[82] to interpret the "to" language in such a manner as to render any restrictions therein essentially meaningless. Phrased differently, this line of cases took the position that the "to" language of the intellectual property clause does not preclude reliance on a more broadly interpreted grant of congressional power to avoid its clear import. That is to say, if you can't do it literally under the intellectual property clause, rely on the necessary and proper clause.

The progenitor case was *Mitchell Bros. Film Group v. Cinema Adult Theater*[83] decided in 1979. There the Fifth Circuit distinguished *Graham* on the grounds that:

> Congress has authority to make any law that is "necessary and proper" for the execution of its enumerated Article I powers, . . . including its

---

80. It is not sufficient to merely say, as Heald & Sherry do (*see supra* note 56, at 1120) that it is self evident that the "to" language limits congressional authority for, as now discussed, several circuit courts take a very different view of the effect of the "to" language.

81. According to the Court: "The Congress in the exercise of the patent power may not overreach the restraints imposed by the stated constitutional purpose." 383 U.S. 1, 6 (1966).

82. "The Congress shall have Power . . . To make all Laws which shall be necessary and proper for carrying into Execution the foregoing Powers, and all other Powers vested by this Constitution in the Government of the United States, or in any Department or Officer thereof." U.S. CONST. art. I, § 8, cl. 18.

83. 604 F.2d 852 (5th Cir. 1979), *cert. denied*, 445 U.S. 917 (1980).

copyright power, and the courts [sic] role in judging whether Congress has exceeded its Article I powers is limited. The courts will not find that Congress has exceeded its power so long as the means adopted by Congress for achieving a constitutional end are "appropriate" and plainly adapted' to achieving that end. *McCulloch v. Maryland.* . . . It is by the lenient standard of *McCulloch* that we must judge whether Congress has exceeded its constitutional powers in enacting an all-inclusive copyright statute.[84]

Soon thereafter the D.C. Circuit quoted this language with approval in *Schnapper v. Foley.*[85]

Aside from being contrary to the views expressed by the Supreme Court in *Graham*, this approach is not supported by either *McCulloch* or the necessary and proper clause[86] for it effectively reads the "to" language out of the intellectual property clause and instead treats the clause as reading: "To secure for limited times to Authors and Inventors the exclusive Right to their respective Writings and Discoveries." But that most assuredly is not the language of the clause.

Consider what Chief Justice Marshall actually said in *McCulloch*, language which is ignored in both *Mitchell Bros.* and *Schnapper:*

> We admit, as all must admit, that the powers of government are limited, and that its limits are not to be transcended. . . . Let the end be legitimate, let it be within the scope of the constitution, and all means which are appropriate, which are plainly adapted to that end, which are not prohibited, but consist with the letter and spirit of the constitution, are constitutional.[87]

---

84. 604 F.2d at 860.

85. 667 F.2d 102, 112 (D.C. Cir. 1981), *cert. denied*, 455 U.S. 948 (1982).

86. Patry, *supra* note 79, at 372, quotes with approval the views expressed by Professor Charles Black that in *McCulloch* Chief Justice Marshall

> addresses himself to the necessary and proper clause only in response to counsel's arguing its restrictive force; and that he never really commits himself to the proposition that the necessary and proper clause enlarges governmental power, but only to the propositions, first, that it does not restrict it, and, secondly, that it may have been inserted to remove doubt on the questions of power which the rest of Article I, Section 8, without the necessary and proper clause, had not, in Marshall's view, really left doubtful.

See CHARLES BLACK, STRUCTURE AND RELATIONSHIP IN CONSTITUTIONAL LAW at 14 (1969).

87. 17 U.S. at 421 (emphasis supplied).

In other words, while Congress has discretion it is not unbounded. Rather for any enumerated power Congress may not go beyond the limitations set on that power. In enacting patent and copyright legislation, it may not rely on a broadly defined power such as the necessary and proper clause to act outside the objects or purposes set forth in the intellectual property clause.

In 1786 in *Authors League of America, Inc. v. Oman* the Second Circuit addressed the issue of whether the so-called manufacturing clause of the copyright statute[88] which effectively denied copyright to certain foreign manufactured works, i.e., works printed or recorded outside the United States, is constitutionally authorized under the intellectual property clause.[89] The argument was that the exercise of congressional power under the clause is justified only if the legislation at issue promotes the progress of useful arts,[90] i.e., the "to" language limits the authority of Congress to legislate under the clause.[91] But, said the Second Circuit, the intellectual property clause is not the only source of authority for the manufacturing clause. Rather, congressional authority for that clause resides in the commerce clause.[92] Left unsaid, but implicit in the holding, was that the "to" language of the intellectual property clause did not preclude reliance on the commerce clause as authority for this particular provision of the copyright statute.

With this background, it is time now to return to the opinion in *Moghadam*. I already have noted that *Heart of Atlanta Motel*, on which the Eleventh Circuit chiefly relied, does not support the broad proposition attributed to it.[93] It also makes no reference to the intellectual property clause. In an attempt to address the intellectual property clause specifically, the court sought to rely on *The Trade-Mark Cases*[94] and *Authors League*. In its view, "[t]he *Authors League* analysis suggests that the Commerce Clause may be used to accomplish that which the Copyright Clause may not allow."[95] This is cautious language which may be interpreted several ways. But *Authors League* does not support the view that the commerce clause may be used to avoid a direct limitation on congressional copyright power set forth in the

---

88. 17 U.S.C. § 601.
89. 790 F.2d 220, 221 (2d Cir. 1986).
90. For reasons which are unclear, the various circuits when addressing copyright issues almost invariably speak in terms of the progress of useful arts rather than the progress of science.
91. 790 F.2d at 224.
92. *Id.*
93. *See Heart of Atlanta Motel*, 379 U.S. 241 (1964). *See supra* note 71. *See supra* text accompanying notes 70, 71.
94. 100 U.S. 82 (1879).
95. 175 F.3d at 1279.

intellectual property clause, because under the facts of that case the Second Circuit was not required to address this issue and it did not do so.

The Eleventh Circuit, however, expressed a stronger view regarding the interpretation to be given to *The Trade-Mark Cases,* saying: "the Supreme Court's analysis in *The Trade-Mark Cases* stands for the proposition that legislation which would not be permitted under the Copyright Clause *could* nonetheless be permitted under the Commerce Clause, provided the independent requirements of the latter are met."[96] But what the Court actually stated was:

> While [trademark] legislation may be a judicious aid to the common law on the subject of trade-marks, and may be within the competency of Legislatures whose general powers embrace the use of that class of subjects, we are unable to see any such power in the constitutional provision concerning authors and inventors, and their writings and discoveries.[97]

The reason the Court so held was that it viewed trademarks as being quite unlike patents or trademarks and having quite different attributes. Indeed, the Eleventh Circuit expressly acknowledged this to be case.[98]

In *Moghadam,* the Eleventh Circuit assumed arguendo that the commerce clause could not be used to avoid a limitation in the intellectual property clause if the particular use of the commerce clause was fundamentally inconsistent with a particular limitation in the intellectual property clause, e.g., the fixation requirement for copyright.[99] That is to

---

96. *Id.* at 1278.
97. 100 U.S. at 94.
98. 175 F.3d at 1278 ("[t]hese characteristics made trademarks substantially different from the material the Congress was able to protect pursuant to the Copyright Clause"). At the same time, the court quoted with approval a student commentator's statement that: "The constitutionality of current federal trademark legislation . . . supports the conclusion that the Copyright Clause does not limit Congress' Commerce Clause power to grant copyright-like protection." 175 F.3d at 1279, citing Michael B. Gerdes, Comment, *Getting Beyond Constitutionally Mandated Originality as a Prerequisite for Federal Copyright Protection,* 24 ARIZ. ST. L.J. 1461, 1471 (1992). The fallacy in this argument is that it assumes that trademarks are copyright-like, when the Supreme Court in *The Trade-Mark Cases* predicated its holding on the finding that trademark was nothing like copyright. Express limitations on the copyright power, as, e.g., the constitutional requirement for originality in the intellectual property clause, may not be avoided by Congress purporting to grant a copyright-like property right under the commerce clause or any other enumerated power.
99. 175 F.3d at 1280, n.12.

say, the court assumed that Congress was precluded from relying on the commerce clause to avoid a limitation on congressional copyright power inherent in the intellectual property clause. Nonetheless, the court held

> that the Copyright Clause does not envision that Congress is positively forbidden from extending copyright-like protection under other constitutional clauses, such as the Commerce Clause, to works of authorship that may not meet the fixation requirement inherent in the term "Writings." The grant itself is stated in positive terms, and does not imply any negative pregnant that suggests that the term "Writings" operates as a ceiling on Congress' ability to legislate pursuant to other grants.[100]

This is an obtuse way of saying that there is no specific positive prohibition in the intellectual property clause that precludes Congress from relying on the commerce clause to extend copyright-like protection to musical performances broadcast live but not "fixed" at the time of the live performance.

At issue in *Moghadam* was the constitutionality of the anti-bootlegging provisions of the Uruguay Round Agreements Act (URAA)[101] which made illegal the fixation of a live musical performance without the consent of the performers involved. The URAA was passed to conform U.S. law to treaty requirements the United States had supposedly entered into under the Agreement on Trade Related Aspects of Intellectual Property.[102] According to the Eleventh Circuit, what little legislative history exists regarding the URAA suggests that Congress believed the anti-bootlegging provisions were enacted pursuant to authority given by the intellectual property clause.[103] Because it believed that constitutional authority for the anti-bootlegging provisions of the URAA could be found in the commerce clause, the Eleventh Circuit declined "to decide whether the fixation concept of [the] Copyright Clause can be expanded so as to encompass live performances that are merely capable of being reduced to tangible form, but have not been." Nonetheless it also assumed arguendo that the intellectual property clause did not provide constitutional authorization for

---

100. 175 F.3d at 1280.
101. Pub. L. No. 103-465, 108 Stat. 4809 (1994).
102. 175 F.3d at 1272. Nimmer & Nimmer, however, contend that there was in fact no treaty involved, so that any reliance on the treaty power of the United States is misplaced. *See* MELVILLE B. NIMMER & DAVID NIMMER, 3 NIMMER ON COPYRIGHT § 8E.01[C] [rel. 51-5/00].
103. *Id.* Nimmer & Nimmer, however, state that it is unclear why the Eleventh Circuit perceived this to be the case. *See supra* note 102, at n.29.1.

the anti-bootlegging provisions.[104] But, according to the court, the fact that Congress relied on the wrong clause of the Constitution did not preclude a grant of authority under a different clause, i.e., the commerce clause.[105]

The Eleventh Circuit gave several rationales why it believed that copyright-like protection under the commerce clause could be afforded to live performances even though not fixed at the time of performance. In its view "extending quasi-copyright protection to unfixed live musical perform-ances is in no way inconsistent with the Copyright Clause, even if that Clause itself does not directly authorize such protection," but instead "furthers the purpose of the Copyright Clause to promote the progress of the useful arts by securing some exclusive rights to the creative author." More-over, Congress had already engaged in a legal fiction by declaring that a work is fixed if a fixation is occurring simultaneously with transmission of the performance. Insofar as the Eleventh Circuit was concerned, this legal fiction "suggests that fixation, as a constitutional concept, is something less than a rigid, inflexible barrier to Congressional power." Finally, "[c]ommon sense does not indicate that extending copyright-like protection to a live perform-ance is fundamentally inconsistent with the Copyright Clause."[106]

But the Eleventh Circuit was not prepared to go further with regard to other limitations on congressional power found in the intellectual property clause. Rather, it carefully noted that: "Our holding is limited to the fixa-tion requirement, and should not be taken as authority that the other various limitations in the Copyright Clause can be avoided by reference to the Commerce Clause."[107] In this regard, it refused to address "whether extending copyright-like protection under the anti-bootlegging statute might be fundamentally inconsistent with the 'Limited Times' require-ment of the Copyright Clause" or "whether the Commerce Clause can provide the source of Congressional power to sustain the application of the anti-bootlegging statute in some other case in which such an argument is preserved."[108] As indicated, the ostensible reason was the failure of Moghadam to preserve this argument on appeal, but Nimmer and Nimmer suggest that "the sheer number of times that the court belabored that it

---

104. 175 F.3d at 1274. Nimmer & Nimmer contend that the intellectual property clause does not support the anti-bootlegging provisions. *See supra* note 102, citing *Goldstein v. California*, 412 U.S. at 561–62.
105. 175 F.3d at 1275, n.10.
106. *Id.* at 1280–81.
107. *Id.* at 1281, n.14.
108. *Id.* at 1281.

was not resolving this issue betokens that the judges felt most uncomfortable validating perpetual protection."[109]

The Eleventh Circuit analysis in *Moghadam* seems rather clearly to imply that only an express limitation in the intellectual property clause would constrain Congress from reliance on other more broadly interpreted powers to authorize copyright- or patent-like exclusive grants. Heald and Sherry, however, take a very different approach. They contend that there are implied limits on congressional power in the clause which constrain reliance on other more broadly interpreted powers, and emphasize "that once the Court identifies an implied limit, it has the same effect as an express limit: Congress cannot transgress it."[110] They suggest that the Supreme Court would base any analysis of implied limits on certain principles which they spell out.[111] In their view the anti-bootlegging statute at issue in *Moghadam* may be unconstitutional under at least one of these principles because of its failure to set a fixed term for the copyright-like protection provided.[112] Interestingly, they do not address the finding of the Eleventh Circuit in *Moghadam* that under the circumstances of that case there is no constitutional requirement for fixation.

Moghadam suggests that, at least in some circumstances, Congress may simply ignore limitations in the intellectual property clause in enacting

---

109. 2 NIMMER & NIMMER, *supra* note 102, § 1.09[B], n.54 [rel. 51-5/00]. But to be fair to the Eleventh Circuit, the issue only was noted twice.

110. Heald & Sherry, *supra* note 56, at 1128.

111. As they put it:

> When the Court addresses the constitutionality of statutes that might plausibly run afoul of the Intellectual Property Clause, it is likely to allow Congress significant flexibility but only within the constraints of four principles of constitutional weight:
>
> 1. *The Suspect Grant Principle:* Scrutiny under the Intellectual Property Clause is only triggered when Congress effects a grant of exclusive rights that imposes monopoly-like costs on the public;
> 2. *The Quid Pro Quo Principle:* A suspect grant may only be made as a part of a bargained-for exchange with potential authors or inventors;
> 3. *The Authorship Principle:* A suspect grant must initially be made to either the true author of a writing or to the party responsible for a new advance in the useful arts;
> 4. *The Public Domain Principle:* A suspect grant may not significantly diminish access to the public domain.

Heald & Sherry, *supra* note 56, at 1167.

112. *Id.* at 1191–93.

legislation that is patent-like or copyright-like. In recent decades, Congress in fact has started to enact sui generis[113] intellectual property legislation that creates new forms of intellectual property rights that are neither patents nor copyrights. One may reasonably ask what the constitutional authority is for these new rights.

What appears to be the earliest example of such sui generis legislation is the Plant Variety Protection Act of 1970.[114] According to Reichman: "Prior to this Act, the United States had not deviated from the principle that unpatented, noncopyrightable innovation should fend for itself on the open market, which some thought implicit in the constitutional Enabling Clause [i.e., the intellectual property clause]."[115] He summarizes its content as follows.

> The PVPA provides a registration system, administered by the Department of Agriculture rather than the patent authorities, which certifies varieties of sexually reproduced plants that meet a basic criterion of novelty. Statutory subtests of novelty emphasize stability, uniformity, or homogeneity, and above all, distinctiveness in the sense that registered varieties should be clearly distinguishable from existing varieties. Nonobviousness is not required, unlike in the patent law, and the disclosure requirements are less exigent than those of patent law, though they can nonetheless be both costly and time-consuming.[116]

Although the exclusive right created by this Act has certain of the attributes of a patent, Congress clearly did not view it as a patent right.[117]

The legislative history of the Act as set forth in the accompanying House report does not indicate what the constitutional authority for it is,[118] but commentary argues that it is expressly grounded in both the intellectual property clause and the commerce clause.[119] If *Graham v. John Deere Co.* establishes a constitutional standard for invention beyond simple

---

113. Literally meaning the only one of its kind; peculiar. *See* BLACK'S LAW DICTIONARY (6th ed. 1990).
114. Pub. L. No. 91-577, 84 Stat. 1542 (1970).
115. J. H. Reichman, *Legal Hybrids Between the Patent and Copyright Paradigms*, 94 COLUM. L. REV. 2432, 2467 n.164 (1994).
116. *Id.* at 2468.
117. Thus, for example, the exclusive right is denominated as a "Certificate of Plant Variety Protection" rather than a patent. *See* 7 U.S.C. § 2481.
118. *See* H.R. REP. NO. 91-1605, 91st Cong., 2d Sess. (1970).
119. Reichman, *supra* note 115.

novelty as arguably it does,[120] then it may be questioned whether the intellectual property clause provides authority for this Act. Under the type of argument set forth in *Moghadam,* it would not preclude reliance on the commerce clause, however.[121]

Another example of such sui generis legislation is the Semiconductor Chip Protection Act of 1984[122] which authorizes exclusive rights in "mask works" used in the production of semiconductor chips.[123] According to the House report on the Act, Congress "decided that the formidable philosophical, constitutional, legal, and technical problems associated with any attempt to place protection for mask works or semiconductor chip designs under the copyright law could be avoided entirely by creating a sui generis form of protection, apart from and independent of the copyright laws."[124] The reason for creating sui generis protection is that "copyright law does not protect useful articles, as such, and semiconductor chip products are useful articles."[125] Congress seems never to have contemplated that mask works should be treated as patentable subject matter.[126]

---

120. *See* Chapter Eight, Part D. As set forth in Chapter Eight, Part G, I question whether *Graham* interprets the intellectual property clause as requiring unobviousness for an invention to be patentable.
121. *Cf.* Flynn's view that the validity of the Act is subject to serious court challenge "because of the ambiguity concerning the level of invention required by the Act." *See* John J. Flynn, *The Orphan Drug Act: An Unconstitutional Exercise of the Patent Power,* 1992 UTAH L. REV. 389, 430, n.119.
122. Act of November 8, 1984, Pub. L. No. 98-620, 98 Stat. 3347.
123. "Masks" are stencils used to etch onto a chip a given pattern of circuitry. A "mask work" is statutorily defined as "a series of related images . . . having or representing the predetermined, three-dimensional pattern of metallic, insulating, or semiconductor material present or removed from the layers of semiconductor chip product. . . ." *See* 17 U.S.C. § 901(a)(2)(A).
124. H.R. REP. NO. 92-487, 92th Cong., 1st Sess.(1984), *reproduced in* 9 NIMMER & NIMMER, *supra* note 102, at App. 30-14.
125. *Id.* at App. 30-11. *Cf.* Brooktree Corp. v. Advanced Micro Devices, Inc., 705 F. Supp. 491, 494 (S.D. Cal. 1988) ("[m]ask Work Act is not sui generis legislation; it is based upon concepts derived from copyright law"), citing 130 CONG. REC. § 12924.
126. According to Nimmer & Nimmer, the reason for this is that the Act does not require novelty for protection to be granted. *See* NIMMER & NIMMER, *supra* note 102, § 8A.02[B], n.18. *Cf.* Burchfiel's view that the reason for this is that the Act "establishes a lower standard for protection than the 'nonobviousness' standard required to obtain a patent." *See* Burchfiel, *supra* note 76, at 473.

What is the constitutional authority for the Act? The House report accompanying suggests that the authority is the intellectual property clause, saying the Act

> is premised on a finding that original mask works are 'writings' with the meaning of the [clause]. In the unlikely event that a court should find mask works not to be writings, authority for the legislation is found in the commerce clause, to the extent that the chip products and piratical conduct occur in or affect interstate commerce.[127]

But if mask works are indeed writings what are "the formidable philosophical, constitutional, legal, and technical problems" associated with treating them as copyrightable subject matter?[128]

Several rather immediately come to mind. Nimmer and Nimmer are not entirely convinced that mask works can or should be treated as writings. In their view, mask works are more akin to the work of inventors than they are to the work of authors. They are not at all clear that the intellectual property clause is authority for giving intellectual property protection for mask works.[129] Moreover, the period of exclusivity defined for mask works is ten years[130] as contrasted to the present copyright term which is typically ten times longer. If mask works were copyrightable, either the period of exclusivity would be tremendously expanded or Congress would have to define different copyright terms for different classifications of copyright.

Although both the Senate and the House assumed that the mask works were writings,[131] the Senate was reluctant to predicate constitutionality on such a view, and sought to have the commerce clause serve as a predicate as well.[132] Thus the Act provides that the rights conferred thereby may only

---

127. 9 NIMMER & NIMMER, *supra* note 3, at App. 30-22, n.36.
128. *See supra* text accompanying note 124.
129. NIMMER & NIMMER, *supra* note 102, § 8A.02[B].
130. 17 U.S.C. § 904.
131. 130 CONG. REC. E4433 (daily ed. Oct. 10, 1984).
132. The Conference Report on the Semiconductor Chip Protection Act of 1984, *reproduced in* 9 NIMMER & NIMMER, *supra* note 102, at App. 31-5–App. 31-6 ("to avoid any constitutional questions on the issue whether, as both Houses found, mask works can be protected as 'writings" with the meaning of the Constitution's intellectual property clause, section 910(a) of the Senate amendment includes a commerce limitation, so that it reaches only conduct in or affecting commerce").

be infringed "by conduct in or affecting commerce."[133] Although both the Senate and the House assumed that the commerce clause serves as an alternative source of authority for the exclusive rights in mask works authorized by the Act, neither they nor any court for that matter have addressed the question of whether any limitation in the intellectual property clause precludes reliance on the commerce clause in the event that mask works are found not to be writings within the meaning of that term in the intellectual property clause.

In 1998 Congress again sought to enact sui generis intellectual property rights in the Vessel Hull Design Protection Act.[134] The basic purpose of the Act is to provide limited-term exclusive rights in the "design of a vessel hull, including a plug or mold."[135] The legislation resulted from the opinion in *Bonito Boats* which made it impossible to protect the design of boat hulls by means of state law.[136] In its own wisdom, Congress declined to extend copyright protection or design patent protection to industrial designs. Instead, it once again opted for sui generis protection. Unlike the Semiconductor Chip Protection Act, this Act makes no reference to commerce, and their is nothing in its legislative history to suggest that the commerce clause was considered as authority for it.[137] Rather, once again Congress relied on the intellectual property clause as authority for it.[138]

Interestingly, there appears to be no judicial opinion addressing preclusion in the context of the patent power of Congress. This does not mean, however, that commentators have not raised the issue in the context of congressional legislation authorizing patent-like grants. Consider, e.g., the Orphan Drug Act[139] enacted in 1983 pursuant to the commerce clause. Its purpose is to stimulate research and development of drugs useful in treating relatively rare diseases. These are referred to as "orphan" diseases because there is typically insufficient commercial return from the marketing of drugs to treat them to warrant development of such drugs. The Act provided a variety of incentives for the development and marketing of such

---

133. 17 U.S.C. § 910(a). Because 17 U.S.C. § 910(a) does not mention interstate commerce, but instead only refers to commerce, Nimmer & Nimmer question whether it is sufficient to invoke commerce clause authority. *See* NIMMER & NIMMER, *supra* note 102, § 8A.02[B], n.21.
134. Act of October 28, 1998, Pub. L. No. 105-304, 112 Stat. 2860, § 501.
135. 17 U.S.C. § 1301(a)(2).
136. *See supra* text accompanying notes 45–53.
137. This, of course, would not preclude subsequent reliance on the commerce clause as authority for it.
138. H.R. REP. NO. 105-436, 105th Cong., 2d Sess. (1998), at 15.
139. Pub. L. No. 97-414, 96 Stat. 2049 (1983).

drugs including the grant of an exclusive right to market an orphan drug for seven years to the first applicant receiving Food and Drug Administration (FDA) approval of the drug. As set forth in the House report accompanying the Act, "a substantial number of orphan drugs are not patentable," so that "to provide some incentive for the development of these particular orphan drugs, the [Act] includes an exclusive marketing right for the sponsor of such a drug."[140]

Flynn argues

> that the Act's seven year exclusive marketing right confers a patent right without conforming to the limitations of the Patent Clause of the Constitution, and, in adopting the Act, Congress unconstitutionally exercised its power under the Commerce Clause in passing a statute creating a patent right it could only pass pursuant to and in conformity with the Patent Clause of the Constitution.[141]

In his view, the Act violates express limitations of the intellectual property clause in that:

> The grant of exclusivity conferred by the FDA . . . is not limited to inventors; the grant of exclusivity is not for the progress of science and useful arts; the grant of exclusivity need not involve the disclosure of anything not already in the public domain; and, the grant of exclusivity need not rise up to the level of a new discovery in order to receive a monopoly seven-year right to be the exclusive vendor of the designated drug.[142]

Whereas Flynn seeks to demonstrate the preclusive effect of various limitations in the clause, including its "to" language, Burchfiel contends that the "to" language has no preclusive effect.[143] Because he interprets *Graham v. John Deere Co.* as holding that nonobviousness is a constitutional standard for patentability predicated on the "to" language,[144] his contention of necessity challenges the views expressed by the Supreme Court in *Graham.* His concern is with the constitutionality of the Semiconductor Chip Protection Act. While acknowledging that Congress sought to rely on both the copyright power and the commerce power in enacting this legislation, he nonetheless makes a plausible argument that: "With respect to constitutional restrictions on government-established 'monopoly' rights,

---

140. H.R. REP. No. 97-840, pt. 1, 97th Cong., 2d Sess. (1982), at 11.
141. *See* Flynn, *supra* note 121, at 402.
142. *Id.* at 439.
143. For his reasoning, *see supra* note 76, at 518–24.
144. Burchfiel, *supra* note 76, at 487–92.

the congressional power under both the copyright clause and the commerce clause depends on the same issue: the existence of an implied constitutional threshold requirement of nonobviousness."[145]

According to Burchfiel, "[i]f, as indicated in *Graham*, a minimum standard equivalent to nonobviousness is a constitutional requirement for legislation securing exclusive rights in a useful article, the Chip Act is unconstitutional for failing to require a commensurate standard in securing exclusive rights in mask works."[146] But he argues that *Graham* incorrectly found such a limitation in the "to" language of the intellectual property clause because: (a) repeated adjudication of other enumerated congressional powers

> has established that limitations are not to be implied from the grants of enumerated powers,[147] and that a clear limitation must be found elsewhere within the confines of the Constitution to limit the otherwise unrestricted discretion of Congress in determining the measures and policies necessary to carry the enumerated powers into effect

and (b) such a limitation "has no history in the United States patent law, and is inconsistent with the fundamental principles which have governed construction of the other article I, section 8 economic powers."[148]

At the beginning of this Part I noted that the issue of preclusion may involve the extent to which the intellectual property clause may be used to avoid restrictions on congressional authority prescribed by the First Amendment.[149] To what extent does the exclusive right granted by copyright conflict with freedom of speech or freedom of the press? A simple answer is that there is no conflict because copyright protects only forms of expression and not the ideas encompassed within those forms of expression, so that all remain free to use those ideas. But the issue is more complex than that. The problem is that copyright is intended to—and should—protect more than the literal expressions of an author.[150]

---

145. *Id.* at 510.
146. *Id.* at 541.
147. This to some degree is similar to the argument relied upon by the Eleventh Circuit in *Moghadam*.
148. Burchfiel, *supra* note 76, at 541.
149. "Congress shall make no law respecting an establishment of religion, or prohibiting the free exercise thereof; or abridging the freedom of speech, or of the press; or the right of the people peaceably to assemble, and to petition the Government for a redress of grievances." U.S. CONST. amend. I.
150. Otherwise minor changes in the expression would render the copyright meaningless.

Not surprisingly, what has been sought is a balancing test to resolve perceived conflicts between copyright and First Amendment rights.[151] Nimmer and Nimmer set forth what they call "a definitional balance" test whereby "ideas *per se* fall on the free speech side of the line, while the statement of an idea in specific form, as well as the selection and arrangement of ideas , fall on the copyright side of the line."[152] In 1985 in *Harper & Row v. Nation Enterprises* the Supreme Court appears to have adopted this "definitional balance" test.[153]

But, in rejecting a First Amendment challenge to the copyright of President Ford's unpublished memoirs and holding that the publication of 300 words therefrom infringed the copyright, the Court majority declared: "It should not be forgotten that the Framers intended copyright itself to be the engine of free expression.[154] By establishing a marketable right to the use of one's expression copyright supplies the economic incentive to create and disseminate ideas."[155]

In it's view, "[i]t is fundamentally at odds with the scheme of copyright to accord lesser rights in those works that are of greatest importance to the public."[156] Accordingly, it held that:

> In view of the First Amendment protection already embodied in the Copyright Act's distinction between copyrightable expression and uncopyrightable facts and ideas, and the latitude for scholarship and comment traditionally afforded by fair use, we see no warrant for expanding the doctrine of fair use to create what amounts to a public figure exception to copyright. Whether verbatim copying from a public figure's manuscript in a given case is or is not fair use must be judged according to the traditional equities of fair use.[157]

---

151. The issue first began to be seriously addressed in the 1970s. For examples of early commentary on this subject, see Melville B. Nimmer, *Does Copyright Abridge the First Amendment Guaranties of Free Speech and the Press?* 17 UCLA L. REV. 1180 (1970); Paul Goldstein, *Copyright and the First Amendment*, 70 COLUM. L. REV. 983 (1970); Robert C. Denicola, *Copyright and Free Speech: Constitutional Limitations on the Protection of Expression*, 67 CAL. L. REV. 283 (1979).
152. NIMMER & NIMMER, *supra* note 102, § 1.10[B][2] [rel. 38-12/95].
153. 471 U.S. 539, 556 (1985).
154. No authority was cited for this conclusion.
155. 471 U.S. at 558.
156. *Id.* at 559.
157. *Id.* at 560.

Otherwise stated, in their view the First Amendment provides no grounds for exceeding statutory "fair use" reproduction of copyrighted material, no matter who the author is.

To three Justices who vigorously dissented, the issue did not revolve whether the author was a public figure or not, but instead a restriction of the fair use doctrine. As they put it, "[t]he progress of arts and sciences and the robust public debate essential to an enlightened citizenry are ill served by this constricted reading of the fair use doctrine."[158]

Nimmer and Nimmer suggest that the "definitional balance" shifts against copyright in favor of First Amendment rights whenever the issue is extension of the term of existing copyright.[159] In their view, the rationales for subordinating First Amendment free speech rights to copyright, i.e., the incentive to create and the protection of an author's privacy rights,[160] are simply inapplicable when the issue is only one of extension of the term of existing copyright. In such circumstance, the "definitional balance swings markedly in favor of First Amendment rights preempting copyright."[161] They do suggest another circumstance wherein First Amendment rights may supercede rights under copyright. That is, where copying of the copyrighted expression is essential to effectively convey the idea expressed, the idea basically is inseparable from the form of expression.[162]

C. Perspectives

The states clearly had power to issue patents and copyrights prior to the ratification of the Constitution, but did they retain such power after the Constitution was ratified? The intellectual property clause is silent on this point as are the Patent and Copyright Acts of 1790. But there is peculiar language in the Patent Act of 1793 which at least implicitly suggests that Congress believed that ratification of the Constitution effectively precluded states from issuing state patents from the date of its own ratification

---

158. *Id.* at 579.
159. NIMMER & NIMMER, *supra* note 102, § 1.10[C][1]. They also suggest that predicated on the Supreme Court's opinion in *Graham v. John Deere Co.* term extension of existing copyright is constitutionally suspect. *Id.* This, of course, is a view I have strongly espoused in the present work. *See* Chapter Seven, Part G.
160. NIMMER & NIMMER, *supra* note 102, § 1.10[B][1].
161. *Id.* § 1.10[C][1].
162. *Id.* § 1.10[D].

onward.[163] Since there is absolutely no reason that ratification of the Constitution would effect state power with respect to copyrights differently than it did state power concerning patents, it is reasonable to assume that Congress believed that ratification also precluded states from issuing copyrights from that date forward.

The issue was not addressed in any reported opinion until the New York case of *Livingston v. Van Ingen* in 1812. There Chief Justice Kent stated that state and federal patent and copyright power were concurrent, i.e., the grant of patent and copyright power to Congress in the intellectual property clause was not exclusive. In his view, a state could exercise its patent and copyright power within its own jurisdiction if an inventor or author decided not to seek a federal patent or copyright. While the state could not act in derogation of a federal grant, it had authority to enlarge the grant within its jurisdiction, as, for example, by extending the term of a federal patent or copyright beyond that authorized by act of Congress. In view of the actual disposition in the case, these views were dicta,[164] but they were deemed persuasive up to modern times when the Supreme Court finally got around to addressing the issue, albeit in different contexts. When it did so, it confused matters rather than clarifying them.

Suffice it to say here that Kent's view that a state has authority to extend the term of a federal patent within its own jurisdiction was of doubtful validity in 1812 and most certainly would be deemed unconstitutional today as a violation of both the intellectual property clause and the supremacy clause.[165] It literally ignores the express language of the intellectual property clause that the exclusive right is to be for "limited times" as defined and set by Congress. The intent of a term set by Congress is that at the expiration of that term, the subject matter of the patent or copyright becomes a part of the public domain. A state may not constitutionally remove that subject matter from the public domain by the mere act of extending the term of the patent within its own jurisdiction.[166]

---

163. *See supra* notes 8 and 9 and accompanying text.
164. The New York judges effectively ruled that the New York patent right granted was a patent of importation which the clause did not authorize Congress to grant and thus the right remained with the states. *See supra* note 18 and accompanying text. In other words, Congress had no jurisdiction in this particular view of the matter, so that concurrent jurisdiction was not an issue.
165. *See* Sears, Roebuck & Co. v. Stiffel Co., 376 U.S. 225, 231 (1964).
166. On several occasions, the Supreme Court in modern times has declared that "Congress may not authorize the issuance of patents whose effects are to remove existent knowledge from the public domain, or to restrict free access to materials already available." *See* Graham v. John Deere Co., 383 U.S. 1, 6

In 1824 in *Gibbons v. Ogden*, the U.S. Attorney General certainly so interpreted the language of the intellectual property clause,[167] but the Supreme Court failed to address this argument.

It would not be until 1964 in *Sears, Roebuck & Co. v. Stiffel Co.* and *Compco Corp. v. Day-Brite Lightings, Inc.* that the Supreme Court actually addressed any of the views expressed by Chief Justice Kent in *Livingston v. Van Ingen*, albeit without making any direct reference to them. But when it did it expressly disagreed that under the intellectual property clause a state had any right to extend the term of a federal patent or to forbid the copying of whatever federal patents and copyrights statutes left in the public domain.[168] Although the opinions in *Sears* and *Compco* did not literally reach the issue of whether the intellectual property clause when coupled with the supremacy clause preempted state patent and copyright power, they certainly seemed to suggest that this was the case, for if the intellectual property clause set forth a federal policy of allowing free public access to whatever federal patent and copyright statutes left in the public domain as the *Compco* Court said it did, then there appeared to be no concurrent authority left in the states to restrict such free public access even within their own jurisdictions.

Nine years later, however, a bare majority of the Court would rule in *Goldstein v. California* that state copyright power was not preempted by the intellectual property clause.[169] Unfortunately, in so doing they mightily confused the issue, for they made no attempt whatever to explain or distinguish *Sears* and *Compco*. Instead, they relied entirely on what presumably were first principles set forth by Alexander Hamilton in *The Federalist No. 32*.[170]

It is important to understand the circumstances of *Goldstein*. Despite the broad interpretation that both it and the Supreme Court had given to the term "writings," Congress had for its own reasons failed to treat sound recordings as copyrightable. The California statute in question forbade the pirating or copying of sound tapes or recordings for commercial purposes, without the express permission of those who own the master recording of the performance. The Court majority recognized this statute as providing

---

(1966); Bonito Boats, Inc. v. Thunder Craft Boats, Inc., 489 U.S. 141, 146 (1989). What Congress may not do, a state may not do by the simple expedient of extending the term of an expired federal patent.

167. *See supra* note 22.
168. *See supra* text accompanying notes 37–40.
169. *See supra* text accompanying notes 25–28.
170. 412 U.S. at 552.

"copyright protection solely for the specific expressions which compose the master record or tape."[171]

The *Goldstein* majority easily found that nothing in the Constitution expressly provided that the copyright power shall vest solely in the federal government or that such power shall not be exercised by the states.[172] They then went on to hold that although the intellectual property clause "recognizes the potential benefits of a national system, it does not indicate that all writings are of national interest or that state legislation is, in all cases, unnecessary or precluded."[173] How this holding could be reconciled with the view expressed in *Compco* that the intellectual property clause set forth a federal policy of allowing free access to copy whatever the federal patent and copyright statutes left in the public domain was not indicated.

According to the *Goldstein* majority, the fact that the California statute literally created a copyright of unlimited duration was no problem, because the intellectual property limits only the power of Congress and not the power of states in this regard. Moreover, because any exclusive right granted by a state is confined to its borders, any tendency of a state copyright grant of unlimited duration "to inhibit further progress in science or the arts is narrowly circumscribed."[174] This appeared to be an implicit overruling of the views expressed in *Sears* and *Compco* that the intellectual property clause precluded a state from extending the term of a federal patent or copyright or of prohibiting free access to what the federal patent and copyright statutes had left in the public domain.[175]

A year later, relying on the views expressed in *Goldstein*, the Court held in *Kewanee Oil Co. v. Bicron Corp.* that states had concurrent jurisdiction to regulate discoveries just as they had concurrent jurisdiction to regulate writings.[176] The reason given in both *Goldstein* and *Kewanee* for this concurrent jurisdiction is that because of the great diversity of interests in the nation, as evidenced by the essentially nonuniform character of the appreciation of intellectual achievements in the various states prior to the ratification of the Constitution, the states continued to have authority to regulate intellectual property in diverse ways and for local reasons. Evidence for this point of view was stated to be the state patents issued in

---

171. *Id.* at 551.
172. *Id.* at 553.
173. *Id.*
174. *Id.* at 560–61.
175. *See supra* note 46 and accompanying text.
176. *See supra* note 43 and accompanying text.

the eighteenth century.[177] On what basis the issuance of state patents prior to ratification of the Constitution somehow controlled the interpretation to be given to the intellectual property clause in the modern era was not stated. As a practical matter, even assuming the great diversity of interests claimed to exist between the states in the 1780s regarding intellectual property matters, it is a great leap to conclude that this same diversity exists today and should be governed by what transpired before the ratification of the Constitution.

In the 1976 revision of the copyright law, Congress broadly preempted, with narrow exceptions, all state laws bearing on material subject to federal copyright.[178] The legislative history of the 1976 Act makes clear Congress' intention to overturn certain of the holdings in *Goldstein* and "to preempt and abolish any rights under the common law or statutory law of a state that are equivalent to copyright and that extend to works coming within the scope of the federal copyright law."[179] Congress had made no similar change in the patent statutes, but it is reasonable to suppose that in light of the views expressed in *Bonito Boats* the patents statutes similarly may be viewed as preempting any rights created under state law that are equivalent to federal patents and come within the scope of the federal patent law.

For most intents and purposes, the Court's opinion in 1989 in *Bonito Boats* resuscitated *Sears* and *Compco* and implicitly rejected certain of the views expressed in *Goldstein* and *Kewanee* by stressing that a fundamental purpose of the intellectual property clause "was to promote national uniformity in the realm of intellectual property."[180] While acknowledging that the clause did not of its own force or by negative implication deprive the states of concurrent jurisdiction over patents and copyrights, the *Bonito Boats* Court at the same time seemed rather clearly to be severely limiting any such concurrent jurisdiction. If a fundamental purpose of the clause is to promote uniformity with regard to intellectual property, as the Court states, then it is unclear to what limited extent, if any, the states retain any concurrent jurisdiction over patents and copyrights.

Congress is increasingly creating statutory rights in intellectual property that on their face either ignore or seek to avoid limitations in the intellectual property. The Supreme Court has yet to address the issue of whether limitations in the intellectual property clause preclude reliance on other more broadly interpreted enumerated powers such as the commerce

---

177. *Goldstein,* 412 U.S. at 557; *Kewanee,* 416 U.S. at 478–79.
178. 17 U.S.C. 301.
179. H.R. REP. NO. 94-1476, 94th Cong. 2d Sess. (1976) at 130.
180. *See supra* note 53 and accompanying text.

clause and the necessary and proper clause to create patent-like and copyright-like property rights. But the lower courts who have faced the issue have been extremely reluctant to find limitations in the intellectual property clause preclusive of congressional reliance on more broadly interpreted powers to effectively avoid such limitations. The approach they have taken, as aptly demonstrated by the Eleventh Circuit in *Moghadam*, is predicated on the broad premise that all enumerated powers of Congress are assumed to be alternative to all other enumerated powers, so that the limitations set forth in one grant of power generally have no bearing on the applicability of another grant of power.[181]

Needless to say, such a premise is much too broad. Not even Alexander Hamilton, the early apostle of broad construction of both the general welfare clause and the necessary and proper clause, would go that far. In his discussion of the general welfare clause, he expressly noted that the power to tax and appropriate under that clause, while broad, does not permit Congress "to do anything, not authorized in the constitution, either expressly or by fair implication."[182] That is to say, limitations on a particular enumerated power cannot be avoided by reliance on a broadly interpreted power. In the context of the present work, the issue then becomes one of whether there are limitations in the intellectual property clause set forth expressly "or by fair implication." To the extent that the Supreme Court has interpreted words and phrases in the clause in particular ways, that interpretation "by fair implication" restricts or limits the power of Congress to act outside that interpretation.

While the Eleventh Circuit in *Moghadam* was prepared to concede that reliance could not be placed on the commerce clause to avoid a fundamental limitation on the copyright power set forth in the intellectual property clause, it refused in essence to accept that Supreme Court interpretation of the meaning to be given to "writings" in the clause constituted such a fundamental limitation. In its view, there is nothing in the clause that suggests or indicates that the term "writings" is intended to limit the authority of Congress to provide copyright-like protection under another enumerated power such as the commerce clause.[183] In this interpretation

---

181. *See supra* text accompanying notes 68–71.

182. *See supra* text accompanying note 62.

183. *See supra* text accompanying note 100. Although the Eleventh Circuit actually declared that there in nothing in the term that "operates as a ceiling on Congress' ability to legislate pursuant to other grants," this can only be taken to mean that insofar as the Eleventh Circuit is concerned, neither the literal meaning of the term "writings" as used in the clause, nor the Supreme Court's

of the clause, "writings" is not a limitation on congressional power to provide copyright-like protection under the commerce clause, and the originality and fixation requirements declared by the *Feist* Court to be inherent in the term and hence constitutionally required are essentially meaningless because they are not expressly set forth as positive requirements in the clause.

In the context of the Eleventh Circuit analysis, the only limitations considered fundamental and hence actually limiting on congressional authority are those which are set forth positively in the intellectual property clause. Although the Circuit acknowledged that there are "other various limitations" in what it termed the copyright clause, it was careful to state that its holding in *Moghadam* was limited to the fixation requirement. But a perusal of the clause suggests only two limitations that are set forth positively, namely, that the term of patents and copyrights be "for limited times" and that the exclusive right be granted to authors and inventors for "their" writings and discoveries. Arguably, the Eleventh Circuit would hold that these limitations may not be avoided by seeking to provide copyright-like protection under the commerce clause.[184]

While the Eleventh Circuit in *Moghadam* at least sought to engage in a preclusion analysis to ascertain whether the commerce clause could be used to avoid an apparent limitation in the intellectual property clause, several other circuits have simply assumed that the necessary and proper clause can be used for this purpose without any such analysis. Thus, the Fifth, Eighth, and D.C. Circuits have argued that the broad scope of discretion afforded Congress under the necessary and proper clause is in essence sufficient to render the "to" language of the clause meaningless as a limitation on the copyright power of Congress.[185] The D.C. Circuit in *Schnapper v. Foley* drew the ultimate conclusion that "the introductory

---

interpretation of it acts in any way as a limitation on congressional power to provide copyright-like protection under the commerce clause.

184. But then again it might not, perhaps through an argument analogous to that used to justify its holding that the fixation requirement could be avoided by reliance on the commerce clause. In particular, it might rely on the fact that Congress has seen fit to define "authors" as including the proprietors of works for hire, thereby indicating that it believes that "their" is not a positive, or at least a fundamental, limitation on its copyright power. Secondly, it could argue that "for limited times" really is not a fundamental limitation, because Congress has demonstrated that it can—and will—repeatedly extend the term of existing copyrights.

185. *See supra* Chapter Nine, note 270 and accompanying text. *See also supra* text accompanying notes 81 and 82.

language of the Copyright Clause [does not] constitute[] a limit on congressional power."[186]

This, of course, is directly contrary to the holding of the Supreme Court in *Graham v. John Deere Co.* that the "to" language of the clause does in fact constitute a limitation on the patent power of Congress.[187] Both the Eighth and the D.C. Circuits relied on language of the Fifth Circuit in *Mitchell Bros.* to the effect that Congress has broad discretion under the necessary and proper clause to effectively ignore the "to" language as a limitation on its power and has as a practical matter done so in the copyright context.[188] In this view, the necessary and proper clause effectively trumps any limitation perceived to exist in the "to" language, so long as Congress declines to treat it as limiting on its authority.[189]

The difficulty with such an approach is that it effectively renders the "to" language of the clause meaningless, and assumes that Congress may simply ignore it at its pleasure. As noted earlier, it permits Congress to treat the clause as though it reads: "Congress shall have Power . . . To secure for limited Times to Authors and Inventors the exclusive Right to their respective Writings and Discoveries." But that of course is not the literal language of the clause and Congress has no constitutional authority under the necessary and proper clause or any broadly interpreted clause to simply dispense with or ignore specific language of the intellectual property clause. If the "to" language of the clause is indeed a limitation on the patent power of Congress as the Supreme Court most emphatically stated it is in *Graham v. John Deere Co.*, then Congress may not ignore it as a limitation on the copyright power as well. That is to say, it has preclusive effect with respect to both the patent power and the copyright power.[190] Congress may not rely on the necessary and proper clause to avoid such preclusive effect in the copyright arena, despite the holdings of the Fifth, Eighth, and D.C. Circuits.

Based on an analysis of Supreme Court opinions involving the bankruptcy clause, the Tenth and Eleventh Amendments, and Article III of the Constitution, Heard and Sherry posit that whether the intellectual

---

186. 667 F.2d at 112.
187. *See supra* note 81.
188. 664 F.2d. at 860.
189. The Fifth Circuit was careful to point out that Congress could treat the "to" language as limiting but that it need not do so. *Id.*
190. The exact nature of any such preclusive effect with respect to the copyright power will have to wait to be determined until an appropriate copyright case reaches the Supreme Court.

property clause impliedly limits authority of Congress to make patent-like or copyright-like exclusive grants depends on whether the grant (a) imposes monopoly-like costs on the public; (b) is not part of a bargained-for exchange with potential authors or inventors; (c) is not initially made to either the true author of a writing or to the party responsible for a new advance in the useful arts; and (d) significantly diminishes access to the public domain.[191] With one proviso, I generally agree with this view of the constraints placed on Congress by the clause in the patent and copyright context. What they mean by item (b) is that "Congress may grant exclusive rights only if the grant is an attempt to secure a countervailing benefit to the public."[192] But there is nothing "bargained for" in this exchange. Rather, the exclusive right is constitutionally authorized in return for the ultimate release of that exclusive right to increase the intellectual commons in the public domain.

---

191. Paul. J. Heald & Suzanna Sherry, *Implied Limits on the Legislative Power: The Intellectual Property Clause as an Absolute Constraint on Congress*, 2000 ILL. L. REV. 1119, 1120.
192. *Id.* at 1162.

TABLE OF CASES

INDEX